Bartholomew Fair, 1721.

OBSERVATIONS
ON THE
POPULAR ANTIQUITIES
OF GREAT BRITAIN

*Chiefly illustrating the orgin of our vulgar
and provincial customs, ceremonies,
and superstitions.*

By John Brand, M.A.

*Arranged, revised, and greatly enlarged, by
Sir Henry Ellis, K.H., F.R.S., Sec. S.A., &c.
Principal Librarian of the British Museum.*

*With a new introduction by
Leslie Shepard*

IN THREE VOLUMES—VOL. II.

*London: George Bell
1849
Detroit: Reissued by Singing Tree Press, Book Tower,
1969*

Library of Congress Catalog Card Number 67–23896

CONTENTS OF VOL. II.

b

CONTENTS.   v

OBSERVATIONS

ON

POPULAR ANTIQUITIES.

COUNTRY WAKES :[1]

CALLED ALSO FEASTS OF DEDICATION, REVELLINGS, RUSH-
BEARINGS, AND, IN THE NORTH OF ENGLAND, HOPPINGS.

As in the times of Paganism annual festivals were celebrated
in honour and memory of their gods, goddesses, and heroes,

[1] Spelman, in his Glossary, v. Wak, derives the word Wake from the
Saxon Wak, signifying *drunkenness.* His words are, " Sunt celebritates
bacchanales sub fructuum temporibus, ab occidulis et borealibus Anglis
pagatim habitæ. Bacchanales dixi ex nomine : nam Wak, Sax. est temu-
lentia." With all deference to so great a name, I think Spelman is evidently mistaken, and that he even contradicts himself, when he tells us
that on the Sunday after the Encœnia, or Feast of the Dedication of the
Church, a great multitude both of grown and young persons were wont to
meet about break of day, shouting *Holy Wakes ! Holy Wakes !* " Die dominica post Encœniam seu Festum Dedicationis Ecclesiæ cujusvis villæ
convenire solet in aurorâ magna hominum juvenumque multitudo, et canora
voce *Holy Wakes! Holy Wakes!* exclamando designare," &c. (Gloss. 1664,
p. 562.) Strutt gives us a quotation on this subject from Dugdale's
Warwickshire, from an old MS. legend of St John the Baptist, which entirely overthrows the etymology of *wake* given by Spelman : " And ye shal
understond and know how the *evyns* were furst found in old time. In the
begynning of holy Chirche, it was so that the pepul cam to the chirche
with candellys brennyng, and wold wake and coome with light toward to
the chirche in their devocions ; and after they fell to lecherie and songs,
daunces, harping, piping, and also to glotony and sinne, and so turned the
holinesse to cursydnees : wherfor holy Faders ordenned the pepul to leve
that *Waking* and to fast the *Evyn*   But it is called *Vigilia*, that is waking
in English, and it is called *Evyn*, for at evyn they were wont to come to
chirche."

II.   1

when the people resorted together at their temples[1] and tombs; and as the Jews constantly kept their anniversary feast of Dedication, in remembrance of Judas Maccabæus, their deliverer, so it hath been an ancient custom among the Christians of this island to keep a feast every year, upon a certain week or day, in remembrance of the finishing of the building of their parish church, and of the first solemn dedicating of it to the service of God, and committing it to the protection of some guardian saint or angel.[2]

At the conversion of the Saxons, says Bourne, by Austin, the monk, the heathen Paganalia were continued among the converts, with some regulations, by an order of Pope Gregory the Great, to Mellitus, the abbot, who accompanied Austin in his mission to this island. His words are to this effect : on the day of dedication, or the birthday of holy martyrs, whose relics are there placed, let the people make to themselves booths of the boughs of trees, round about those very churches which had been the temples of idols, and, in a religious way, to observe a feast ; that beasts may no longer be slaughtered by way of sacrifice to the devil, but for their own eating and the glory of God ; and that when they are satisfied, they may return thanks to Him who is the giver of all good things.[3] Such are the foundations of the country Wake.

Bishop Hall, in his Triumphs of Rome, alludes as follows to these convivial entertainments : "What should I speak of our merry Wakes, and May games, and Christmas triumphs, which you have once seen here, and may see still in those under the Roman dition : in all which, put together, you may well say no Greek can be merrier than they." (Triumph of Pleasure, p. 23.) I have a curious sermon, entitled the *Religious* Revel, preached at Atsuch, a country revel, dedicated to Mr. William Ekins, of the parish of St. Thomas, near Exon, by H. Rosewell, 1711. It is a defence and vindication of

---

[1] The Paganalia, or country feasts of the Heathens, were of the same stamp with this of the wake. Spelman says : " Hæc eadem sunt quæ apud Ethnicos *Paganalia* dicebantur."

[2] St. Michael, for instance. Of saints it has been observed by antiquaries that few churches or none are anywhere found honoured with the name of St. Barnabas, except one at Rome.

[3] " Ut die dedicationis, vel natalitiis sanctorum Martyrum, quorum illic reliquiæ ponuntur, tabernacula siba circa easdem ecclesias, quæ ex fanis commutatæ sunt de ramis arborum faciant," &c. (Bed. i. **30**.)

keeping the annual feast of the dedication, finishing, and consecration of our churches (constantly kept, and called in the
country a *Wake* or Revel), still supposing and asserting the
very great impiety of revellings, properly so called ; i. e. lewd
and disorderly *Revellings*, upon any account or occasion. In
Collinson's History of Somersetshire, i. 64, speaking of Stock-
linch, St. Magdalen parish, the author says : "A *Revel* is held
here on St. Mary Magdalen's day." In Bridge's History of
Northamptonshire many instances are recorded of the Wake
being still kept on or near to the day of the saint to which
the church was dedicated. In Tusser's Five Hundred Points
of Good Husbandry, under the head of "The Wake Day,"
are the following lines :

> "Fil oven ful of flawnes, Ginnie passe not for sleepe,
> To-morrow thy father his wake day will keepe:
> Then every wanton may danse at her will,
> Both Tomkin with Tomlin, and Jankin with Gil."

Thus explained in Tusser Redivivus, 1744, p. 81 : "The
Wake day is the day on which the parish church was dedicated,
called so because the night before it they were used to watch
till morning in the church, and feasted all the next day.
Waking in the church was left off, because of some abuses,
and we see here it was converted to waking at the oven. The
other continued down to our author's days, and in a great
many places continues still to be observed with all sorts of rural
merriments, such as dancing, wrestling, cudgel-playing, &c.

"This feast was at first regularly kept on that day in every
week on which the church was dedicated ; but it being observed
and complained of, that the number of holidays was excessively
increased, to the detriment of civil government and secular
affairs ; and also that the great irregularities and licentiousness
which had crept into these festivities by degrees, especially in
the churches, chapels, and churchyards, were found highly
injurious to piety, virtue, and good manners ; there were
therefore both statutes and canons made to regulate and
restrain them : and by an act of convocation, passed by
Henry VIII. 1536,[1] their number was in some measure lessened.

---

[1] This injunction, says Borlase, in his Account of Cornwall. was never
universally complied with, custom in this case prevailing against the law
of the land.

The feast of the dedication of every church was ordered to be kept upon one and the same day everywhere ; that is, on the first Sunday in October ; and the Saint's day to which the church was dedicated entirely laid aside. This act is now disiegarded ; but probably it arose from thence that the feast of Wakes was first put off till the Sunday following the proper day, that the people might not have too many avocations from their necessary and domestic business.

The following entries occur in the churchwarden's accounts of St. Mary at Hill, in the city of London, 1495 : " For bred and wyn and ale to Bowear (a singer) and his co., and to the Quere on Dedication Even, and on the morrow, i*s*. vj*d*." 1555. "Of the Sumcyon of our Lady's Day, which is our church holyday, for drinkyng over-night at Mr. Hayward's, at the King's Head, with certen of the parish and certen of the chapel and other singing men, in wyne, pears, and sugar, and other chargis, viii*s*. j*d*. For a dynner for our Lady's Day, for all the synging men & syngyng children, i*l*. For a pounde and halfe of sugar at dinner, i*s*. vij*d*. ob. 1557. For garlands for our Lady's Day & for strawenge yerbes, ij*s*. ij*d*. For bryngyng down the images to Rome Land and other things to be burnt." In these accounts, " To singing men and children from the King's chapel and elsewhere," on some of the grand festivals, particularly the parish feast (our Lady's Assumption), a reward in money and a feast is charged in several years.

When an order was made in 1627 and in 1631, at Exeter and in Somersetshire, for the suppression of the Wakes, both the ministers and the people desired their continuance, not only for preserving the memorial of the dedication of their several churches, but for civilizing their parishioners, composing differences by the mediation and meeting of friends, increasing of love and unity by these feasts of charity, and for the relief and comfort of the poor. In King Charles the First's Book of Sports, Oct. 18, 1633, we read : " His majesty finds that, under pretence of taking away abuses, there hath been a general forbidding, not only of ordinary meetings, but of the feasts of the dedications of the churches, commonly called Wakes. Now his majesty's express will and pleasure is, that these feasts, with others, shall be observed ; and that his justices of the peace, in their several divisions, shall look to it, both that all disorders there may be prevented or punished, and that all neighbourhood and freedom, with manlike and lawful exercises be used." (See Harris's Life of Charles I. p. 50.)

In the southern parts of this nation, says Bourne, most country villages are wont to observe some Sunday in a more particular manner than the rest ; i. e. the Sunday after the day of dedication, or day of the saint to whom their church was dedicated. Then the inhabitants deck themselves in their gaudiest clothes, and have open doors and splendid entertainments, for the reception and treating of their relations and friends, who visit them on that occasion from each neighbouring town. The morning is spent for the most part at church, though not as that morning was wont to be spent, not in commemorating the saint or martyr, or in gratefully remembering the builder and endower. The remaining part of the day is spent in eating and drinking. Thus also they spend a day or two afterwards, in all sorts of rural pastimes and exercises, such as dancing on the green, wrestling, cudgelling, &c.

Carew tells us, in his Survey of Cornwall, p. 69, "The Saint's Feast is kept upon the Dedication Day, by every householder of the parish, within his own dores, each entertaining such forrayne acquaintance as will not fayle, when their like turne cometh about, to requite them with the like kindness." But Borlase informs us that, in his time, it being very inconvenient, especially in harvest time, to observe the parish feast on the Saint's day, they were, by the bishop's special authority, transferred to the following Sunday.

Stubs, in his Anatomie of Abuses, 1585, p. 95, gives us the manner of keeping of Wakesses and Feastes in England. "This is their order therein :—Every towne, parish, and village, some at one time of the yeare, some at another (but so that every one keeps his proper day assigned and appropriate to itselfe, which they call their Wake-day), useth to make great preparation and provision for good cheare, to the which all their friendes and kinsfolkes farre and neere are invited." He adds that there are such doings at them, "insomuch as the poore men that beare the charges of these feastes and wakesses are the poorer, and keep the worser houses a long tyme after And no marvaile, for many spend more at one of these wakesses than in all the whole yere besides." Stubs has been already mentioned as a Puritan, and consequently one who did not duly distinguish between the institution itself and the degenerate abuse of it.

Borlase says, the parish feasts instituted in commemoration of the dedication of parochial churches were highly esteemed among the primitive Christians, and originally kept on the Saint's Day to whose memory the church was dedicated. The generosity of the founder and endower thereof was at the same time celebrated, and a service composed suitable to the occasion. This is still done in the colleges of Oxford, to the memory of the respective founders. On the eve of this day prayers were said and hymns were sung all night in the church; and from these watchings the festivals were styled Wakes; which name still continues in many parts of England, although the vigils have been long abolished. See also Wheatley on the Common Prayer, 1848, p. 89; and Dugd. Warw., p. 515.

Speght, in his Glossary to Chaucer, says: "It was the manner in times past, upon festival evens, called vigiliæ, for parishioners to meet in their church-houses or churchyards, and there to have a drinking-fit for the time. Here they used to end many quarrels between neighbour and neighbour. Hither came the wives in comely manner: and they which were of the better sort had their mantles carried with them, as well for show as to keep them from cold at the table. These mantles also many did use in the church at morrow-masses and other times." In the 28th canon given under King Edgar (preserved in Wheloc's edition of Bede), I find decent behaviour enjoined at these church wakes. The people are commanded to pray devoutly at them, and not to betake themselves to drinking or debauchery.

The following is preserved in the MS. Collections of Aubrey (relating to North Wilts) in the Ashmolean Museum at Oxford; dated 1678: "Before the Wake or feast of the dedication of the church, they sat up all night fasting and praying." That is, upon the eve of the wake.

Captain Silas Taylor says, that "in the days of yore, when a church was to be built, they watched and prayed on the vigil of the dedication, and took that point of the horizon where the sun arose for the east, which makes that variation, so that few (churches) stand true except those built between the two equinoxes. I have experimented some churches, and have found the line to point to that part of the horizon where the sun rises on the day of that Saint to whom the church is dedicated."

In the Introduction to the Survey of North Wiltshire, printed in Aubrey's Miscellanies, 1714, p. 33, we read: "The night before the day of dedication of the church, certain officers were chosen for gathering the money for charitable uses. Old John Wastfield, of Langley, was Peter Man at St. Peter's Chapel there."

The following ludicrous trait in the description of a country wake is a curious one from a most rare little book entitled A strange Metamorphosis of Man, transformed into a Wildernesse, deciphered in Characters, 1634. He is speaking of *the Goose.* "They hate," says our quaint author, "the laurell, which is the reason they have no poets amongst them; so as if there be any that seeme to have a smatch in that generous science, he arrives no higher than the style of a ballet, *wherein they have a reasonable facultie; especially at a* WAKE, *when they assemble themselves together at a towne-greene, for then they sing their ballets, and lay out such throats as the country fidlers cannot be heard.*" I cannot omit quoting thence, also, the well-known singularity of this domestic fowl. "*She hath a great opinion of her own stature,* especially if she be in company of the rest of her neighbours and fellow-gossippes, the duckes and hennes, at a harvest feast; for then *if she enter into the hall there, as high and wide as the doore is, she will stoop for feare of breaking her head.*"

Great numbers attending at these wakes, by degrees less devotion and reverence were observed, till at length, from hawkers and pedlars coming thither to sell their petty wares, the merchants came also, and set up stalls and booths in the churchyards; and not only those, says Spelman, who lived in the parish to which the church belonged resorted thither, but others also, from all the neighbouring towns and villages: and the greater the reputation of the Saint, the greater were the numbers that flocked together on this occasion. The holding of these fairs on Sundays was justly found fault with by the clergy. The Abbot of Ely, in King John's reign, inveighed much against so flagrant a profanation of the sabbath; but this irreligious custom was not entirely abolished till the reign of King Henry the Sixth.

[A good description of a Wake is given in the Spectator, No. 161 : "I was last week at one of these assemblies, which was held in a neighbouring parish; where I found their green covered with a promiscuous multitude of all ages and both sexes, who esteem one another more or less the following part of the year according as they distinguish themselves at this time. The whole company were in their holiday clothes, and divided into several parties, all of them endeavouring to show themselves in those exercises wherein they excelled, and to gain the approbation of the lookers-on." The sports described are cudgel-playing, football, and wrestling.]

In the Statistical Account of Scotland, xvi. 460, 1795, Parishes of Sandwick and Stromness, co. Orkney, we read : "Parish of Sandwick :—The people do no work on the 3d day of March, in commemoration of the day on which the church of Sandwick was consecrated; and as the church was dedicated to St. Peter, they also abstain from working for themselves on St. Peter's Day (29th June); but they will work to another person who employs them." In the same work, xviii. 652, Parish of Culross, we are told : " St. Serf was considered as the tutelar Saint of this place, in honour of whom there was an annual procession on his day : viz. 1st July, early in the morning of which all the inhabitants, men and women, young and old, assembled and carried green branches through the town, decking the public places with flowers, and spent the rest of the day in festivity. (The church was dedicated not only to the Virgin Mary, but also to St. Serf.) The procession is still continued, though the day is changed from the Saint's day to the present king's birthday."

In many villages in the north of England these meetings are still kept up, under the name of *Hoppings*.[1] We shall hope that the rejoicings on them are still restrained in general within the bounds of innocent festivity; though it is to be feared they sometimes prove fatal to the morals of our swains, and corrupt the innocence of our rustic maids. So

---

[1] *Hopping* is derived from the Anglo-Saxon hoppan, *to leap* or *dance*, which Skinner deduces from the Dutch huppe, *coxendix* (whence also our *hip*). "Hæc enim saltitatio, quà corpus in altum tollitur ope robustissimorum illorum musculorum, qui ossibus femoris et coxendicis movendis dicati sunt, præcipue peragitur." Skinner, in v. *Hop*. Dancings in the north of England, and in some other parts, are called *hops*.

In Northbrooke's Treatise against Dauncing, p. 118 : "Also their daunces were spiritual, religious, and godly, not after *our hoppings* and leapings, and interminglings men with women, &c. (dauncing every one for his part), but soberly, gravely," &c. Also, p. 132, "What good doth all that dauncing of young women holding upon men's armes, that they may *hop* the higher?"

In a most curious and rare tract, entitled A Joco-serious Discourse in two Dialogues, between a Northumberland Gentleman and his Tenant, a Scotchman, both old Cavaliers, 1686, p. 32, we read:

> " To horse-race, fair, or *hoppin* go,
> There play our cast among the whipsters,
> Throw for the hammer, lowp (*leap*) for slippers,
> And see the maids dance for the ring,
> Or any other pleasant thing ;
> F*** for the pigg, lye for the whetstone,
> Or chuse what side to lay our betts on."

We find notes explaining the word "Hoppin" by "annual feasts in country towns where no market is kept," and "lying for the whetstone," I'm told, has been practised, but **** for the pigg is beyond the memory of any I met with ; tho' it is a common phrase in the north to any that's gifted that way ; *and probably there has been such a mad practice formerly.*— The ancient grossièreté of our manners would almost exceed belief. In the stage directions to old Moralities we often find " Here Satan letteth a ****." Lying for the whetstone will be explained in another part of the present volume. [The following notice was circulated on the occasion of a hopping at Newcastle in 1758 : "On this day (May 22) the annual diversions at Swalwell will take place, which will consist of dancing for ribbons, grinning for tobacco, women running for smocks, ass races, foot courses by men, with an odd whim of a man eating a cock alive, feathers, entrails, &c."]

Hospinian cites Thomas Naogeorgus, in his fourth book of the Regnum Papisticum, as drawing a most loathsome picture of the excesses and obscenities used in his time at the Feast of Dedications. Thus translated by Barnabe Googe :

" The Dedication of the Church is yerely had in minde,
With worship passing catholicke, and in a wond'rous kinde :

From out the steeple hie is hangde a crosse and banner fayre,
The pavement of the temple strowde with hearbes of pleasant ayre;
The pulpets and the aulters all that in the church are seene,
And every pewe and piller great are deckt with boughes of greene:
The tabernacles opned are, and images are drest,
But chiefly he that patron is doth shine above the rest:
A borde there standes, whereon their bulles and pardons thick they lay,
That given are to every one that keepes this holyday:
The idoll of the patron eke without the doore doth stande,
And beggeth fast of every man, with pardons in his hande:
Who for bicause he lackes his tongue, and hath not yet the skill
In common people's languages, when they speak well or ill;
He hath his owne interpretor, that alwayes standeth by,
And unto every man that commeth in or out doth cry:
Desiring them the patrone there with giftes to have in minde,
And popishe pardons for to buie, release of sinnes to finde.
On every side the neighbours come, and such as dwell not nere,
Come of their owne good willes, and some required to be there.
And every man his weapon hath, their swordes and launces long,
Their axes, curriars, pystolets, with pykes and darts among.
The yong men in their best array, and trimmest maydes appeare,
Both jeasters, roges, and minstrels with their instruments are heare.
The pedler doth his packe untrusse, the host his pots doth fill,
And on the table breade and drinke doth set for all that will:
Nor eyther of them their heape deceyves, for of the others all,
To them th' advauntage of this feaste, and gaine, doth chiefly fall.
The service done, they eyther to the taverne fast doe flie,
Or to their neighbour's house, whereas they feede unreasonablie:
For sixe or seven courses they unto the table bring,
And for their suppers may compare with any heathen king.
The table taken up, they rise, and all the youth apace,
The minstrell with them called go to some convenient place:
Where, when with bagpipe hoarce he hath begon his musicke fine.
And unto such as are preparde to daunce hath given signe,
Comes thither streight both boys and gyrles, and men that aged bee,
And maryed folkes of middle age, there also comes to see,
Old wrinckled hagges, and youthfull dames, that minde to daunce aloft,
Then sundrie pastimes do begin, and filthie daunces oft:
When drunkards they do lead the daunce with fray and bloody fight,
That handes, and eares, and head, and face, are torne in wofull plight.
The streames of bloud runne downe the armes, and oftentimes is seene
The carkasse of some ruffian slaine, is left upon the greene.
Here many, for their lovers sweete, some daintie thing do buie,
And many to the taverne goe, and drinke for companie,
Whereas they foolish songs do sing, and noyses great do make:
Some in the meane while play at cardes, and some the dice do shake.
Their custome also is, the priest into the house to pull
Whom, when they have, they thinke their game accomplished at full:
He farre in noyse exceedes them all, and eke in drinking drie
The cuppes, a prince he is, and holdes their heades that speewing lie."

In Hinde's Life of John Bruen, of Bruen-Stapleford, in the county of Chester, Esquire, 1641, at p. 89, the author, speaking of Popish and profane wakes at Tarum, says: " Popery and Profannes, two sisters in evil, had consented and conspired in this parish, as in many other places, together to advance their idols against the arke of God, and to celebrate their solemne feastes of their Popish Saints, as being the *Dii tutelares*, the *speciall patrons and protectors of their church and parish*, by their WAKES and VIGILS, kept in commemoration and honour of them, in all riot and excess of eating and drinking, dalliance and dancing, sporting and gaming, and other abominable impieties and idolatries."

" In the northern counties," says Hutchinson, in his History of Northumberland, ii. 26, "these holy feasts are not yet abolished ; and in the county of Durham many are yet celebrated. They were originally Feasts of Dedication in commemoration of the consecration of the church, in imitation of Solomon's great convocation at the consecrating the Temple of Jerusalem. The religious tenour is totally forgotten, and the Sabbath is made a day of every dissipation and vice which it is possible to conceive could crowd upon a villager's manners and rural life. The manner of holding these festivals in former times was under tents and booths erected in the churchyard, where all kinds of diversions were introduced. Interludes were there performed, being a species of theatrical performance, consisting of a rehearsal of some passages in Holy Writ personated by actors. This kind of exhibition is spoken of by travellers who have visited Jerusalem, where the religious even presume to exhibit the Crucifixion and Ascension with all their tremendous circumstances. On these celebrations in this country, great feasts were displayed, and vast abundance of meat and drink."

Of Cheshire, Dr. Gower, in his Sketch of the Materials for a History of that County, tells us : " I cannot avoid reminding you upon the present occasion, that frumenty makes the principal entertainment of all our country wakes : our common people call it 'firmitry.' It is an agreeable composition of boiled wheat, milk, spice, and sugar," p 10. King, in his Vale Royal of England, p. 20, speaking of the inhabitants of Chester, says : " Touching their house-keeping, it is bountiful

and comparable with any other shire in the realm : and that
is to be seen at their weddings and burials, but chiefly at *their
wakes*, which they yearly hold (although it be of late years
well laid down)."

Macaulay, in his History of Claybrook, 1791, p. 93, observes that there is a wake the Sunday next after St. Peter, to
whom the church is dedicated : adding, at p. 128, " the people
of this neighbourhood are much attached to the celebration of
wakes ; and on the annual return of those festivals, the
cousins assemble from all quarters, fill the church on Sunday,
and celebrate Monday with feasting, with musick, and with
dancing.   The spirit of old English hospitality is conspicuous
among the farmers on those occasions ; but with the lower
sort of people, especially in manufacturing villages, the return
of the wake never fails to produce a week, at least, of idleness,
intoxication, and riot : these and other abuses, by which these
festivals are so grossly perverted from the original end of their
institution, render it highly desirable to all the friends of
order, of decency, and of religion, that they were totally sup-
pressed."   The following is found in Herrick's Hesperides,
p. 300 :

> " Come, Anthea, let us two
> Go to feast, as others do.
> Tarts and custards, creams and cakes,
> Are the junkets still at wakes :
> Unto which the tribes resort,
> Where the businesse is the sport.
> Morris-dancers thou shalt see,
> Marian too in pagentrie ;
> And a mimick to devise
> Many grinning properties.
> Players there will be, and those
> Base in action as in clothes ;
> Yet with strutting they will please
> The incurious villages.
> Near the dying of the day
> There will be a cudgel-play,
> When a coxcomb will be broke
> Ere a good word can be spoke.
> But the anger ends all here,
> Drencht in ale, or drown'd in beere.
> Happy rusticks, best content
> With the cheapest merriment ;
> And possesse no other feare
> Than to want the wake next yeare "

In Sir Aston Cokain's Poems, 1658, p. 210, is the following:

" *To Justice Would-be.*
" That you are vext their *wakes* your neighbours keep,
They guess it is because you want your *sleep ;*
I therefore wish that you your sleep would take,
That they (without offence) might *keep their wake.*"

It appears that in ancient times the parishioners brought rushes at the Feast of Dedication, wherewith to strew the church, and from that circumstance the festivity itself has obtained the name of *Rush-bearing*,[1] which occurs for a country wake in a Glossary to the Lancashire dialect. In the Church-wardens' Accounts of St. Mary-at-Hill, in the city of London, 1504, Yongeham and Revell, is the following article : " Paid for 2 berden rysshes for the strewyng the newe pewes, 3*d*." Ibid. 1493, Howtyng and Overy—" for 3 burdens of rushes for the new pews, 3*d*." In similar Accounts for the parish of St. Margaret's, Westminster (4to. p. 12), under the year 1544, is the following item : " Paid for rushes against the Dedication Day, which is always the first Sunday of October, 1*s*. 5*d*." In Coates's History of Reading, p. 227, among the entries in the Churchwardens' Accounts of St. Laurence Parish for 1602, we have : " Paid for flowers and rushes for the churche when the Queene was in town, xx*d*." In Thomas Newton's Herball to the Bible, 1587, is the following passage : " Sedge and rushes with the which many in the country do use in summer time to strawe their parlors and churches, as well for cooleness as for pleasant smell." Chambers, and indeed all apartments usually inhabited, were formerly strewed in this manner. As our ancestors rarely washed their floors, disguises of uncleanliness became necessary things. It appears that the English stage was strewed with rushes. The practice in private houses is noticed by Dr. Johnson from Caius de Ephemera Britannica. In Whimzies, or a New Cast of Characters, 1631, p. 197,

[1] Compare Ducange : " *Juncus* majoribus festis sparsus in ecclesia et alibi, Consuetud. MSS. S. Augustini Lemovic. f. 14. In festo S. Augustini præpositus debet recipere *juncum* qni debetur ex consuetudine ad parandum chorum et capitulum. Codex MS. Montis S. Michaelis annorum circ. 400. Eleemosynarius tenetur etiam invenire *juncum* in magnis festivatibus in choro et in claustro." Naogeorgus thus describes this custom :
" —redolenti gramine templi
Sternitur omne solum ramisque virentibus aræ."

describing a zealous brother, the author tells us : "He de-
nounceth a heavy woe upon all wakes, summerings, and *rush-
bearings*, preferring that act whereby pipers were made rogues
by Act of Parliament, before any in all the *Acts and Monuments.*"   In the same work, p. 19 (second part), speaking of
a pedlar, the author says : " A countrey *rush-bearing*, or mor-
rice-pastoral, is his festival ; if ever he aspire to plum-porridge,
that is the day.   Here the guga-girles gingle it with his neat
nifles."   So, also, in A Boulster Lecture, 1640, p. 78, we
find : " Such an one as not a *rush-bearer* or *May-morrish* in
all that parish could subsist without him."   Notices of the
custom of rush-bearing in different parts of Derbyshire will
be found in Glover's History and Gazetteer of the County of
Derby, i. 259, 260.

[The rush-bearing, according to Lucas, is in this manner :
They cut hard rushes from the marsh, which they make up
into long bundles, and then dress them in fine linen, silk
ribands, flowers, &c.   Afterwards, the young women in the
village, who perform the ceremony that year, take up the
burdens erect, and begin the procession (precedence being
always given to the churchwarden's burden), which is attended
with music, drums, &c.   Setting down their burdens in the
church, they strip them of their ornaments, leaving the heads
or crowns of them decked with flowers, cut papers, &c.
Then the company return and cheerfully partake of a cold collation, and spend the remaining part of the day and night in
dancing round a maypole, adorned with flowers.]

Bridges, in his History of Northamptonshire, i. 187, speaking of the parish of Middleton Chenduit, says : " It is a
custom here to strew the church in summer with *hay* gathered
from six or seven swaths in Ash-meadow, which have been
given for this purpose.   The rector finds straw in winter."

In Ireland, " on the Patron Day," according to Sir Henry
Piers, 1682, in most parishes, as also on the feasts of Easter
and Whitsuntide, the more ordinary sort of people meet near
the alehouse in the afternoon, on some convenient spot of
ground, and dance for the cake ; here, to be sure, the piper
fails not of diligent attendance.   The cake to be danced for
is provided at the charge of the alewife, and is advanced on a
board on the top of a pike about ten feet high ; this board
is round, and from it riseth a kind of a garland, beset and

tied round with meadow-flowers, if it be early in the summer; if later, the garland has the addition of apples, set round on pegs, fastened unto it. The whole number of dancers begin all at once in a large ring, a man and a woman, and dance round about the bush (so is this garland called) and the piper as long as they are able to hold out. They that hold out longest at the exercise win the cake and apples, and then the alewife's trade goes on.

CARTERS' INTERJECTIONS.

PERHAPS it will be thought no uninteresting article in this little code of Vulgar Antiquities to mention a well-known interjection used by the country people to their horses, when yoked to a cart, &c., *Heit* or *Heck!* I find this used in the days of Chaucer, in the Friar's Tale:

> " They saw a cart that charged was with hay,
> The which a carter drove forth on his way:
> Depe was the way, for which the carte stode;
> The carter smote and cryde as he were wode,
> *Heit Scot! Heit Brok!* what spare ye for the stones?
> The Fiend, quoth he, you fetch, body and bones !"

The name of *Brok* is still, too, in frequent use amongst farmers' draught oxen.

A writer in the Gentleman's Magazine for August 1799, lxix. 659, derives *Woohe!* the well-known exclamation to stop a team of horses, from the Latin. " The exclamation used by our waggoners when they wish, for any purpose, to stop their team (an exclamation which it is less difficult to speak than to write, although neither is a task of great facility), is probably a legacy bequeathed us by our Roman ancestors ; precisely a translation of the ancient classical *Ohe!* an interjection strictly confined to bespeaking a pause—rendered by our lexicographers, *Enough! Oh, enough!*

'Ohe, jam satis est—Ohe, Libelle.' "

A learned friend, whose communications I have frequently had occasion to acknowledge in the course of this work, says : " The exclamation ' Geho, geho,' which carmen use to their horses, is probably of great antiquity. It is not peculiar to this country, as I have heard it used in France. In the story of the milkmaid who kicked down her pail, and with it all her hopes of getting rich, as related in a very ancient collection of apologues, entitled Dialogus Creaturarum, printed at Gouda, in 1480, is the following passage: 'Et cum sic gloriaretur, et cogitaret cum quanta gloria duceretur ad illum virum super equum dicendo *gio gio*, cepit pede percutere terram quasi pungeret equum calcaribus.'"

HARVEST HOME,

ALIAS MELL SUPPER, KERN OR CHURN SUPPER, OR FEAST OF INGATHERING.

MACROBIUS tells us[1] that, among the Heathens, the masters of families, when they had got in their harvest, were wont to feast with their servants who had laboured for them in tilling the ground. In exact conformity to this, it is common among Christians, when the fruits of the earth are gathered in and laid in their proper repositories, to provide a plentiful supper for the harvest-men and the servants of the family. At this entertainment all are, in the modern revolutionary idea of the word, perfectly equal. Here is no distinction of persons, but master and servant sit at the same table, converse freely together, and spend the remainder of the night in dancing, singing, &c., in the most easy familiarity.

Bourne thinks the original of both these customs is Jewish, and cites Hospinian, who tells us that the Heathens copied after this custom of the Jews, and at the end of the harvest offered up their first fruits to the gods.[2] For the Jews rejoiced and feasted at the getting in of the harvest.

[1] " Patres familiarum, et frugibus et fructibus jam coactis, passim cum servis vescerentur, cum quibus patientiam laboris in colendo rure toleraverant."—Macrob. Saturnal. Die prim. cap. 10. " Antiquitus consuetudo fuit apud Gentiles, quod hoc mense servi, pastores, et ancillæ quadam libertate fuerentur ; et cum dominis suis dominarentur, et cum eis facerent festa et convivia, post collectas messes."—Durand. Rat. vi. c. 86.

[2] " Et pro collectis frugibus Deo gratiæ agebantur. Quem morem Ethnici postea ab iis mutuati sunt."—Hospin. de Orig. Fest. Jud. Stukius Antiq. Conviv. p. 63. Theophylact mentions " Scenopegia, quod celebrant in gratiarum actionem propter convectas fruges in mense *Septembri.* Tunc enim gratias agebant Deo, convectis omnibus fructibus," &c.— Theoph. in 7 cap. Joan.

This festivity is undoubtedly of the most remote antiquity. That men in all nations where agriculture flourished should have expressed their joy on this occasion by some outward ceremonies has its foundation in the nature of things. Sowing is hope; reaping, fruition of the expected good. To the husbandman, whom the fear of wet, blights, &c., has harassed with great anxiety, the completion of his wishes could not fail of imparting an enviable feeling of delight. Festivity is but the reflex of inward joy, and it could hardly fail of being produced on this occasion, which is a temporary suspension of every care.

The respect shown to servants at this season seems to have sprung from a grateful sense of their good services. Everything depends at this juncture on their labour and despatch. Vacina, (or Vacuna, so called as it is said à vacando, the tutelar deity, as it were, of rest and ease,) among the ancients, was the name of the goddess to whom rustics sacrificed at the conclusion of harvest.

In Tusser's Five Hundred Points of Husbandry, under the month of August are the following lines:

> " Grant, harvest-lord, more by a penny or two,
> To call on his fellows the better to doo:
> Give gloves to thy reapers a larges to crie,
> And daily to loiterers have a good eie."

On which is this note in Tusser Redivivus, 1744, p. 100: "He that is the lord of harvest is generally some stayd, sober-working man, who understands all sorts of harvest-work. If he be of able body he commonly leads the swarth in reaping and mowing. It is customary to give gloves to reapers, especially where the wheat is thistly. As to crying a largess, they need not be reminded of it in these our days, whatever they were in our author's time." [The following curious lines "Upon the Norfolk Largess," are taken from the Norfolk Drollery, 1673, pp. 73-4:

> " We have a custom, no where else is known,
> For here we reap, where nothing e'er was sown
> Our harvest-men shall run ye cap and leg,
> And leave their work at any time to beg.
> They make a harvest of each passenger,
> And therefore have they a lord-treasurer.

II.   2

Here ye must pence, as well as prayrs bestow,
'Tis not enough to say ' God speed the plow.'
These ask as men that meant to make ye stand,
For they petition with their arms in hand;
And till ye give, or some good sign appears,
They listen to ye with their harvest-eares.
If nothing drops into the gaping purse,
Ye carry with ye, to be sure, a curse;
But if a *largess* come, they shout ye deaf,
Had you as many ears as a wheatsheaf:
Sometimes the hollow greater is by odds,
As when 'tis answer'd from the ivye tods.
Here all unite, and each his accent bears,
That were but now together by the eares.
And, which a contradiction doth imply,
Because they get a largess they must cry;
Cry with a pox! whoever of it hears,
May wish their tankard had no other tears:
Thus, in a word, our reapers now-a-days,
Reap in the field, and glean in the high-ways."]

Mr. Stevenson, in the Twelve Moneths, 1661, p. 37, speak
ing of August, thus glances at the customs of Harvest Home
" The furmenty-pot welcomes home the harvest-cart, and the
garland of flowers crowns the captain of the reapers; the
battle of the field is now stoutly fought. The pipe and the
tabor are now busily set a-work; and the lad and the lass
will have no lead on their heels. O 'tis the merry time wherein
honest neighbours make good cheer, and God is glorified in
his blessings on the earth." The following is in Herrick's
Hesperides, p. 113:

*" The Hock-cart, or Harvest-home : to the Right Honourable
Mildmay Earle of Westmorland.*

" Come, sons of Summer, by whose toile
We are the lords of wine and oile,
By whose tough labour and rough hands,
We rip up first, then reap our lands,
Crown'd with the eares of corne, now come,
And to the pipe sing harvest home;
Come forth, my lord, and see the cart,
Drest up with all the country art.
See here a maukin, there a sheet
As spotlesse pure as it is sweet:
The horses, mares, and frisking fillies,
(Clad, all, in linnen, white as lillies,)

The harvest swaines and wenches bound
For joy, to see the hock-cart crown'd.
About the cart, heare how the rout
Of rural younglings raise the shout;
Pressing before, some coming after,
Those with a shout, and these with laughter.
Some blesse the cart; some kiss the sheaves;
Some prank them up with oaken leaves:
Some crosse the fill-horse; some, with great
Devotion, stroak the home-borne wheat:
While other rusticks, less attent ⎫
To prayers than to merryment   ⎬
Run after with their breeches rent. ⎭
Well, on, brave boyes, to your lord's hearth,
Glitt'ring with fire; where, for your mirth,
You shall see, first, the large and cheefe
Foundation of your feast, fat beefe:
With upper stories, mutton, veale,
And bacon (which makes fulle the meale).
With sev'rall dishes standing by, ⎫
And here a custard, there a pie,   ⎬
And here all-tempting frumentie." ⎭

[The Suffolk peasantry use, amongst others, the following
Harvest-home song:

" Here's a health to the barley-mow!
Here's a health to the man
   Who very well can
Both harrow, and plough, and sow!

When it is well sown,
   See it is well mown,
Both raked and gravelled clean,
And a barn to lay it in.
Here's a health to the man
   Who very well can
Both thrash and fan it clean!"]

Newton, in his Tryall of a Man's owne Selfe, 1602, p. 54,
under Breaches of the Second Commandment, censures "the
adorning with garlands, or *presenting unto any image of any
Saint, whom thou hast made speciall choice of to be thy patron
and advocate, the firstlings of thy increase, as* CORNE *and*
GRAINE, *and other oblations.*"

Moresin tells us that Popery, in imitation of this, brings
home her chaplets of corn, which she suspends on poles;
that offerings are made on the altars of her tutelar gods, while

thanks are returned for the collected stores, and prayers are made for future ease and rest. Images, too, of straw or stubble, he adds, are wont to be carried about on this occasion ; and that in England he himself saw the rustics bringing home in a cart a figure made of corn, round which men and women were singing promiscuously, preceded by a drum or piper. In a Journey into England, by Paul Hentzner, in the year 1598, ed. 1757, p. 79, speaking of Windsor, he says : " As we were returning to our inn, we happened to meet some country people celebrating their Harvest Home ; their last load of corn they crown with flowers, having besides an image richly dressed, by which perhaps they would signify Ceres : this they would keep moving about, while men and women, men and maid-servants, riding through the streets in the cart, shout as loud as they can till they arrive at the barn."

" I have seen," says Hutchinson, in his History of Northumberland, ii. ad finem, 17, " in some places, an image apparelled in great finery, crowned with flowers, a sheaf of corn placed under her arm, and a scycle in her hand, carried out of the village in the morning of the conclusive reaping day, with music and much clamour of the reapers, into the field, where it stands fixed on a pole all day, and when the reaping is done, is brought home in like manner. This they call the Harvest Queen, and it represents the Roman Ceres."

An old woman, who is respectable authority on a subject of this nature, at a village in Northumberland, informed me that, not half a century ago, they used everywhere to dress up something similar to the figure above described at the end of harvest, which was called a Harvest Doll, or *Kern Baby*. This northern word is plainly a corruption of corn baby, or image, as is the *kern* supper, which we shall presently consider, of corn supper. In Carew's Survey of Cornwall, f. 20 b, " an ill-kerned or saved harvest" occurs.

At Werington, in Devonshire, the clergyman of the parish informed me that when a farmer finishes his reaping, a small quantity of the ears of the last corn are twisted or tied together into a curious kind of figure, which is brought home with great acclamations, hung up over the table, and kept till the next year. The owner would think it extremely unlucky to part with this, which is called " a knack." The reapers whoop and halloo " A knack ! a knack ! well cut

well bound! well shocked!" and in some places, in a sort of
mockery, it is added, "Well scattered on the ground." A
countryman gave me a somewhat different account, as follows:
"When they have cut the corn, the reapers assemble together:
a knack is made, which one placed in the middle of the company holds up, crying thrice, 'A knack!' which all the rest
repeat: the person in the middle then says:

> 'Well cut! well bound!
> Well shocked! well saved from the ground!'

he afterwards cries 'Whoop!' and his companions hollow as
loud as they can." I have not the most distant idea of the
etymology of the "knacks" used on this occasion. I applied
for one of them. No farmer would part with that which
hung over his table; but one was made on purpose for me.
I should suppose that Moresin alludes to something like this
when he says: "Et spiceas papatus (habet) coronas, quas
videre est in domibus," &c.—Papatus, p. 163, v. Spicæ.

Purchas in his Pilgr., 1626, lib. ix. c. 12, speaking of the
Peruvian superstitions, and quoting Acosta, lib. vi. c. 3, tells
us: "In the sixth moneth they offered a hundred sheep of all
colours, and then made a feast, bringing the mayz from the
fields into the house, which they yet use. This feast is made
coming from the farm to the house, saying certain songs, and
praying that the mayz may long continue. They put a quantity of the mayz (the best that groweth in their farms) in a
thing which they call Pirva, with certain ceremonies, watching
three nights. Then do they put it in the richest garment
they have, and, being thus wrapped and dressed, they worship
this Pirva, holding it in great veneration, and saying it is the
mother of the mayz of their inheritance, and that by this
means the mayz augments and is preserved. In this month
they make a particular sacrifice, and the witches demand of
this Pirva if it hath strength enough to continue until the
next year; and if it answers No, then they carry this mayz
to the farm whence it was taken, to burn and make another
Pirva as before: and this foolish vanity still continueth."

This Peruvian Pirva, says my learned and ingenious friend
Mr. Walter, Fellow of Christ's College, Cambridge, bears a strong
resemblance to what is called in Kent an *Ivy Girl*, which is a
figure composed of some of the best corn the field produces,

and made as well as they can into a human shape; this is
afterwards curiously dressed by the women, and adorned with
paper trimmings, cut to resemble a cap, ruffles, handkerchief,
&c. of the finest lace. It is brought home with the last load
of corn from the field upon the waggon, and they suppose en-
titles them to a supper at the expense of their employers.[1]

Dr. E. D. Clarke, noticing the annual custom at Rhodes of
carrying Silenus in procession at Easter, says: "Even in the
town of Cambridge, and centre of our University, such curious
remains of ancient customs may be noticed, in different seasons
of the year, which pass without observation. The custom of
blowing horns upon the first of May (old style) is derived from
a festival in honour of Diana. At the *Hawkie*, as it is called,
I have seen a clown dressed in woman's clothes, having his
face painted, his head decorated with ears of corn, and bearing
about him other symbols of Ceres, carried in a waggon, with
great pomp and loud shouts, through the streets, the horses
being covered with white sheets; and when I inquired the
meaning of the ceremony, was answered by the people, that
they were drawing the HARVEST QUEEN."

In Otia Sacra, 4to. Lond. 1648, p. 173, in "Verses on
Retiredness," we read:

> " How the Hock-Cart with all its gear
> Should be trick'd up, and what good chear."

Hockey Cake is that which is distributed to the people at
Harvest Home. The following lines occur in Poor Robin's
Almanack for August, 1676:

> " Hoacky is brought home with hallowing,
> Boys with plumb-cake the cart following."

The *Hockey Cart* is that which brings the last corn, and the
children rejoicing with boughs in their hands, with which the
horses also are attired. See Salmon's Survey, Hertfordshire,
ii. 415.

In Braithwaite's Lancashire Lovers, 1640, p. 19, the rustic
lover entices his mistress to marriage with promise of many

---

[1] Here a note informs us: "This ancient custom is, to this day, faintly
preserved all over Scotland, by what we call the Corn Lady, or Maiden,
in a small packet of grain, which is hung up when the reapers have
finished."

rural pleasures, among which occurs, "Wee will han a seed-cake at *Fastens;*" and in Sir Thomas Overbury's Characters, ed. 1638, under the character of a *Franklin*, we find enume-rated the several country sports, amongst which occurs "the *Hoky* or *Seed Cake.*"

In some parts of Yorkshire, as a clergyman of that county informed me, there is given at the end of shearing or reaping the corn, a prize sheaf to be run for; and when all the corn is got home into the stack-yard, an entertainment is given, called the Inning Goose.

[A custom exists amongst harvest-men in Suffolk, which is called Ten-pounding. In most reaps there is a set of rules agreed upon amongst the reapers before harvest, by which they are to be governed during its continuance. The object of these rules is usually to prevent or punish loss of time by laziness, drunkenness, &c.; and to correct swearing, lying, or quarrelling amongst themselves; or any other kind of misbehaviour which might slacken the exertions, or break the harmony of the reap. One of the modes of punishment directed by these rules, is called Ten-pounding, and it is exe-cuted in the following manner: Upon a breach of any of the rules, a sort of drum-head court-martial is held upon the de-linquent; and if he is found guilty he is instantly seized, and thrown down flat on his back. Some of the party keep his head down, and confine his arms; whilst others turn up his legs in the air, so as to exhibit his posteriors. The person who is to inflict the punishment then takes a shoe, and with the heel of it (studded as it usually is with hob-nails) gives him the prescribed number of blows upon his breech, accord-ing to the sentence. The rest of the party sit by, with their hats off, to see that the executioner does his duty; and if he fails in this, he undergoes the same punishment. It sometimes happens, that, from the prevailing use of highlows, a shoe is not to be found amongst the company. In this case, the hardest and heaviest hand of the reap is selected for the in-strument of correction, and, when it is laid on with hearty good will, it is not inferior to the shoe. The origin of the term Ten-pounding is not known; but it has nothing to do with the number of blows inflicted.[1]]

[1] From Forby's Vocabulary, vol. ii.

Different places adopt different ceremonies. There is a sport on this occasion in Hertfordshire, called Crying the Mare, (it is the same in Shropshire,) when the reapers tie together the tops of the last blades of corn, which is *Mare*, and standing at some distance, throw their sickles at it, and he who cuts the knot has the prize, with acclamations and good cheer.[1] I was informed of the following custom on this occasion at Hitchin, in the same county, where each farmer drives furiously home with the last load of his corn, while the people run after him with bowls full of water in order to throw on it : this is also accompanied with great shouting.

A writer in the Gentleman's Magazine for February, 1795, p. 124, on Ancient Customs in the Isle of Sky, says : "In this hyperborean country, in every district there is to be met with a rude stone consecrated to Gruagach, or Apollo. The first who has done with his reaping sends a man or a maiden with a bundle of corn to his next neighbour, who hath not yet reaped down his harvest, who, when he has finished, despatches to his own next neighbour, who is behind in his work, and so on, until the whole corns are cut down. This sheaf is called the Cripple Goat, or Goabbir Bhacagh, and is at present meant as a brag or affront to the farmer, for being more remiss or later than others in reaping the harvest, for which reason the bearer of it must make as good a pair of heels, for fear of being ill-used for his indiscretion, as he can. Whether the appellation of Cripple Goat may have any the least reference to the Apollonian Altar of Goats' Horns I shall not pretend to determine." From some Reflections by the Rev. Donald M'Queen of Kilmuir, in the Isle of Sky.

In the ancient Roman Calendar, so often cited, I find the following observations on the 11th of June : (the harvests in Italy are much earlier than with us)—"Messorum æstas, et eorum consuetudo cum agresti pompâ." "The season of reapers, and their custom with rustic pomp."

[1] See Blount ; who tells us further, that "After the knot is cut, then they cry with a loud voice, three times, ' I have her !' Others answer, as many times, ' What have you ?'—' A mare ! a mare ! a mare !'—' Whose is she ?' thrice also.—J. B. (naming the owner three times.)—' Whither will you send her ?'—' To J. a Nicks' (naming some neighbour who has not all his corn reaped) ; then they all shout three times, and so the ceremony ends with good cheer. In Yorkshire, upon the like occasion, they have a Harvest Dame, in Bedfordshire, a Jack and a Gill."

In the Statistical Account of Scotland, 1797, xix. 550, Parish of Longforgan, Perth, we read : " It was, till very lately, the custom to give what was called *a Maiden Feast*, upon the finishing of the harvest ; and to prepare for which, the last handful of corn reaped in the field was called *the Maiden*. This was generally contrived to fall into the hands of one of the finest girls in the field, was dressed up with ribands, and brought home in triumph, with the music of fiddles or bagpipes. A good dinner was given to the whole band, and the evening spent in joviality and dancing, while the fortunate lass who took the Maiden was the queen of the feast ; after which this handful of corn was dressed out, generally in the form of a cross, and hung up with the date of the year, in some conspicuous part of the house. This custom is now entirely done away, and in its room each shearer is given 6*d*. and a loaf of bread. However, some farmers, when all their corns are brought in, give their servants a dinner and a jovial evening, by way of Harvest Home."

Thomson, in his Seasons, has left us a beautiful description of the annual festivity of Harvest Home. His words are these:

> " ———The harvest treasures all
> Now gather'd in, beyond the rage of storms,
> Sure to the swain ; the circling fence shut up ;
> And instant Winter's utmost rage defy'd,
> While, loose to festive joy, the country round
> Laughs with the loud sincerity of mirth,
> Shook to the wind their cares. The toil-strung youth,
> By the quick sense of music taught alone,
> Leaps wildly graceful in the lively dance.
> Her ev'ry charm abroad, the village toast,
> Young, buxom, warm, in native beauty rich,
> Darts not unmeaning looks ; and where her eye
> Points an approving smile, with double force
> The cudgel rattles, and the wrestler twines.
> Age too shines out ; and, garrulous, recounts
> The feats of youth. Thus they rejoice ; nor think
> That, with to-morrow's sun, their annual toil
> Begins again the never-ceasing round."

In Tusser's Five Hundred Points of Husbandry, under the month of August, in addition to the lines already quoted, are the following, alluding to this festivity :

> " In harvest time, harvest folke, servants and all,
> Should make, alltogither, good cheere in the hall,

> And fill out the black bol of bleith to their song,
> And let them be merrie al harvest time long.
> Once ended thy harvest, let none be begilde,
> Please such as did please thee, man, woman, and child.
> Thus doing, with alway suche helpe as they can,
> Thou winnest the praise of the labouring man."

On which is this note in Tusser Redivivus, p. 104 : "This, the poor labourer thinks, crowns all : a good supper must be provided, and every one that did anything towards the inning must now have some reward, as ribbons, laces, rows of pins to boys and girls, if never so small, for their encouragement; and, to be sure, plum-pudding. The men must now have some better than best drink, which, with a little tobacco, and their screaming for their largesses, their business will soon be done." In another part of Tusser's work, under "The Ploughman's Feast Days," are these lines :

> " For all this good feasting, yet art thou not loose,
> Til Ploughman thou givest his Harvest Home goose;
> Though goose go in stubble, I passe not for that,
> Let Goose have a goose, be she lean, be she fat."

On which Tusser Redivivus remarks, p. 81, "The goose is forfeited if they overthrow during harvest."

In the Abbé de Marolle's Memoirs, in the description of the state of France under Henry IV., we find the following account of Harvest Home : "After the harvest, the peasants fixed upon some holiday to meet together and have a little regale (by them called the *Harvest Gosling*); to which they invited not only each other, but even their masters, who pleased them very much when they condescended to partake of it." (Anecdotes of some distinguished Persons, 1795, iii. 198.) In Cornwall, it should seem, they have "Harvest Dinners;" and these, too, not given immediately at the end of the harvest. "The harvest dinners," says Carew, in his Survey, f. 68, "are held by every wealthy man, or, as wee term it, every good liver, betweene Michaelmas and Candlemas, whereto he inviteth his next neighbours and kinred; and, though it beare onely the name of a dinner, yet the ghests take their supper also with them, and consume a great part of the night after in Christmas rule. Neither doth the good cheere wholly expire (though it somewhat decrease) but with the end of the weeke."

The country people in Warwickshire, according to Steevens, use a sport at their Harvest Home, where one sits as a judge, to try misdemeanors committed in harvest, and the punishment of the men is, to be laid on a bench and slapped on the breech with a pair of boots. This they call giving them the boots.

Formerly, it should seem, there was a *Harvest Home Song.* Bishop Kennett, in the Glossary to his Parochial Antiquities, v. *Dytenum,* tells us: "Homines de Hedyngton ad curiam Domini singulis annis inter festum S. Michaelis et festum S. Martini venient cum toto et pleno *Dyteno,* sicut hactenus consueverunt." This, he adds, is singing harvest home. Dr. Johnson tell us, in his Tour to the Hebrides, that he saw the harvest of a small field in one of the Western Islands. The strokes of the sickle were timed by the modulation of the harvest song, in which all their voices were united. They accompany, in the Highlands, every action which can be done in equal time with an appropriated strain, which has, they say, not much meaning, but its effects are regularity and cheerfulness. The ancient proceleusmatic song, by which the rowers of galleys were animated, may be supposed to have been of this kind. There is now an Oar Song used by the Hebridians. Thus far the learned traveller. I have often observed at Newcastle-upon-Tyne (and I suppose it is the same in other sea-port towns) that the sailors, in heaving their anchors, made use of a similar kind of song. In ploughing with oxen in Devonshire, I observed a song of the same kind.

In the Statistical Account of Scotland, xix. 384, Bandothy, co. Perth, it is said : "There is one family on the Cupar-Grange estate, which has been there a century. The former tenant in that family kept a piper, to play to his shearers all the time of harvest, and gave him his harvest-fee. The slowest shearer had always the drone behind him."

In the Life of Eugene Aram, 2d edit. p. 71, there is an essay on "the Mell-supper,[1] and shouting the Churn," by that

---

[1] I once thought that the Northern name of the entertainment given on this occasion, i. e. MELL-SUPPER, was derived from the French word *mesler,* to mingle or mix together, the master and servant sitting promiscuously at the same table ; but some, to whose opinion I pay great deference, would rather deduce it from the Teutonic word *mehl, farina,* or meal. It has been also suggested to me, that it might come from the *Med-syp.,* i. e. the Reward Supper. All being upon an equal footing, or,

unhappy but very extraordinary man. In this he supposes these feasts to be the relics of Pagan ceremonies, or Judaism, and to be of far higher antiquity than is generally apprehended, as old as a sense of joy for the benefit of plentiful harvest, and human gratitude to the Creator for his munificence to men. In England, he adds, we hear of it under various names in different counties, as Mell-supper, Churn-supper, Harvest-supper, Harvest-home, Feast of Ingathering, &c. To prove that the Jews celebrated the Feast of Harvest, he cites Exodus xxiii. 16, and Leviticus xxiii. 39, and refers to Callimachus's Hymn to Apollo to show that the Heathens misapplied through ignorance the acknowledgment of this festivity, and directed it to a secondary, not the primary fountain of this benefit, i. e. Apollo, or the Sun. Bread, or cakes, he says, composed part of the Hebrew offering, as appears by Leviticus xxiii. 13 ; and we gather from Homer, in the first book of his Iliad, that a cake thrown upon the head of the victim was also part of the Greek offering to Apollo. Apollo, continues Aram, losing his divinity on the progress of Christianity, what had been anciently offered to God the reapers as prudently eat up themselves. At last the use of the meal of new corn was neglected, and the supper, so far as meal was concerned, was made indifferently of old or new corn, as was most agreeable to the founder. He derived MELL, either from *meal,* or else from the instrument called with us a *mell,* wherewith corn was anciently reduced to meal in a mortar. He adds, as the harvest was *last* concluded with several preparations of meal, or brought to be ready for the mell, this term became, in a translated signification, to mean the *last* of other

as the Northern vulgar idiom has it, " Hail fellow well met." Amell, in the North, also is commonly used for betwixt, or among. I find, indeed, that many of our Northumbrian rustic or vulgar words are derived to us from the French. Perhaps we have not imported them from the first market, but have had them at second-hand from the Scots, a people who in former times were greatly connected with that nation. In a letter dated Aug. 12, 1786, by Samuel Pegge, he says : " The most obvious interpretation of the term Mell-supper, seems to insinuate that it is the Meal-supper, from the Teutonic word *mehl* (farina)." In another letter, dated Aug. 28, 1786, he cites Cowel's Interpreter, in v. Med-syp. i. e. the Reward Supper, as thinking it may also be deduced from that. The Rev. Mr. Drake, Vicar of Isleworth, supposes it means the *Meal-supper,* by way of eminence.

things ; as when a horse comes last in the race, they often say in the North, *he has got the mell.*[1] [On the completion of the reaping in Durham, they sing——

> " Bless'd be the day that Christ was born,
> We've gotten mell of * * * * corn,
> Weel bound and better shorn,
> Hip! hip! huzza!"

This " Harvest-home Call" is the one generally made use of in the county of Devon:

> " We have ploughed, we have sowed,
> We have reaped, we have mowed,
> We have brought home every load,
> Hip! hip! hip! harvest-home!"

And the following is another provincial specimen :

> " A knack! a knack!
> Well cut! well bound!
> Well shocked! Well saved from the ground!
> Whoop! whoop! huzza!!"]

There was also a churn-supper, or more properly a kern-supper (so they pronounce it vulgarly in Northumberland), and a shouting in the church, or kern. This, Aram informs

---

[1] In so great a variety of conjectures concerning the true etymon of Mell-supper, it will not be the less dangerous to hazard another. There is an old word for a contest, i. e. *melle*, which the Glossary to Gawin Douglas derives from the French *mellee*, Lat. inf. æt. *melleia* et *melletum*, i. e. certamen. Now, it is well known, that when a set of reapers are drawing near to a conclusion, the parties upon different ridges have frequently a very sharp contest which shall be first done. This contest is mentioned in the above glossary, under the name of *Kemping*, which is explained " the contending of shearers or reapers in harvest." The following is from Hutchinson's Durham, ii. 583, Parish of Easington: " In this part of the country are retained some ancient customs, evidently derived from the Romans, particularly that of dressing up a figure of Ceres, during harvest, which is placed in the field while the reapers are labouring, and brought home on the last evening of reaping, with music and great acclamation. After this a feast is made, called the Mell-supper, from the ancient sacrifice of mingling the new meal." Dr. Jamieson, in his Etymological Dictionary of the Scottish Language, *v.* MELL, says : " MELL, *s.* a company." " A dozen or twenty men will sometimes go in and stand abreast in the stream, at this kind of fishing, called *heaving* or *hauling*, up to the middle, in strong running water, for three or four hours together . a company of this kind is called a *Mell.*" P. Dornock, Dumfr. Statist. Acc. ii. 16.

us, was different from that of the mell-supper: the former
being always provided when all was shorn, the latter after all
was got in.   I should have thought that most certainly kern-
supper was no more than corn-supper, had not Aram asserted
that it was called the churn-supper, because, from immemorial
times, it was customary to produce in a churn a great quantity
of cream, and to circulate it in cups to each of the rustic
company, to be eaten with bread.   This custom in Aram's
time (he was executed in August 1759) survived about Whitby
and Scarborough in the eastern parts of Yorkshire, and round
about Gisburne, &c., in the west.   In other places cream has
been commuted for ale, and the tankard politely preferred to
the churn.

  To festivities of the same kind must be referred the *Meadow
Verse*.   In Herrick's Hesperides, p. 161, we have—

*" The Meddow Verse, or Anniversary, to Mistris Bridget
Lowman.*

" Come with the spring-time forth, fair maid, and be
This year again the *medow's deity.*
Yet ere ye enter, give us leave to set
Upon your head this flowry coronet ;
To make this neat distinction from the rest,
You are the prime, and princesse of the feast :
To which, with silver feet, lead you the way,
While sweet-breath nymphs attend on you this day.
This is your houre ; and best you may command,
Since you are lady of this fairie land.
Full mirth wait on you, and such mirth as shall
Cherrish the cheek, but make none blush at all.

The parting Verse, the Feast there ended.

Loth to depart, but yet at last, each one
Back must now go to's habitation :
Not knowing thus much, when we once do sever,
Whether or no that we shall meet here ever."
                    " If Fates do give
Me longer date, and more fresh springs to live,
Oft as your field shall her old age renew,
Herrick shall make the *meddow-verse* for you."

  Armstrong, in his History of the Island of Minorca, p. 177,
says : " Their harvests are generally gathered by the middle
of June ; and, as the corn ripens, a number of boys and girls

station themselves at the edges of the fields, and on the tops
of the fence-walls, to fright away the small birds with their
shouts and cries. This puts one in mind of Virgil's precept
in the first book of his Georgics—

'Et sonitu terrebis aves,'

and was a custom, I doubt not, among the Roman farmers,
from whom the ancient Minorquins learned it. They also
use, for the same purpose, a split reed: which makes a horrid
rattling, as they shake it with their hands."

Bridges, in his History of Northamptonshire, i. 219, tells
ns: "Within the Liberty of Warkworth in Ashe Meadow,
divided amongst the neighbouring parishes, and famed for the
following customs observed in the mowing of it. The meadow
is divided into fifteen portions, answering to fifteen lots,
which are pieces of wood cut off from an arrow, and marked
according to the landmarks in the field. To each lot are
allowed eight mowers, amounting to one hundred and twenty
in the whole. On the Saturday sevennight after Midsummer
Day, these portions are laid out by six persons, of whom two
are chosen from Warkworth, two from Overthorp, one from
Grimsbury, and one from Nethercote. These are called Field-
men, and have an entertainment provided for them upon the
day of laying out the meadow, at the appointment of the lord
of the manor. As soon as the meadow is measured, the man
who provides the feast, attended by the Hay-ward of Warkworth, brings into the field three gallons of ale. After this
the meadow is run, as they term it, or trod, to distinguish the
lots; and, when this is over, the hay-ward brings into the
field a rump of beef, six penny loaves, and three gallons of ale,
and is allowed a certain portion of hay in return, though not
of equal value with his provision. This hay-ward and the
master of the feast have the name of Crocus-men. In running the field, each man hath a boy allowed to assist him.
On Monday morning lots are drawn, consisting some of eight
swaths, and others of four. Of these the first and last carry
the garlands. The first two lots are of four swaths, and
whilst these are mowing the mowers go double; and as soon
as these are finished, the following orders are read aloud:
'Oyez! oyez! oyez! I charge you, under God, and in his
Majesty's name, that you keep the King's peace in the lord of

the manor's behalf, according to the order and customs of this meadow. No man or men shall go before the two garlands; if you do, you shall pay your penny, or deliver your scythe at the first demand, and this so often as you shall transgress. No man or men shall mow above eight swaths over their lots, before they lay down their scythes and go to breakfast. No man or men shall mow any farther than Monks-holm-Brook, but leave their scythes there and go to dinner, according to the custom and manner of this manor. God save the King!' The dinner, provided by the lord of the manor's tenant, consists of three cheesecakes, three cakes, and a new-milk-cheese. The cakes and cheesecakes are of the size of a winnowing-sieve; and the person who brings them is to have three gallons of ale. The master of the feast is paid in hay, and is further allowed to turn all his cows into the meadow on Saturday morning till eleven o'clock; that by this means giving the more milk the cakes may be made the bigger. Other like customs are observed in the mowing of other meadows in this parish."

To the festivities of Harvest Home must be referred the following popular custom among the hop-pickers in Kent, thus described in Smart's Hop Garden, b. ii. l. 477, and of which he gives an engraved representation in the title-page to his Poems, 1752. He is describing their competitions:

> " Who first may fill
> The bellying bin, and cleanest cull the hops.
> Nor aught retards, unless invited out
> By Sol's declining, and the evening's calm,
> Leander leads Lætitia to the scene
> Of shade and fragrance—then th' exulting band
> Of pickers, male and female, seize the fair
> Reluctant, and with boisterous force and brute,
> By cries unmov'd, they bury her in the bin.
> Nor does the youth escape   him too they seize,
> And in such posture place as best may serve
> To hide his charmer's blushes. Then with shouts
> They rend the echoing air, and from them both
> (So custom has ordain'd) a largess claim."

Martin, in his Description of the Western Islands of Scotland, p. 368, mentions a singular harvest superstition. Speaking of the Orkneys, he says : " There is one day in harvest on which the vulgar abstain from work, because of an ancient and foolish tradition, that if they do their work the ridges will bleed." Brand also mentions this in his Description of the Orkney Islands, 1805.

In the Statistical Account of Scotland, 1793, vii. 303, Parish of Mouswald, co. Dumfries, we read: "The inhabitants can now laugh at the superstition and credulity of their ancestors, who, it is said, could swallow down the absurd nonsense of 'a boon of shearers,' i. e. reapers being turned into large grey stones on account of their *kemping*, i. e. striving. These stones, about twenty years ago, after being blasted with gunpowder, were used in building the farm-houses then erecting near the spot, which had formerly been part of a common."

THE HARVEST MOON.

[THE following charm is found in an edition of Mother Bunch, and is stated to be efficacious during the continuance of the harvest moon, a well-known astronomical phenomenon. When you go to bed, place under your pillow a common prayer-book, open at the part of the matrimonial service in which is printed, "With this ring I thee wed." Place on it a key, a ring, a flower, a sprig of willow, a small heart-cake, a crust of bread, and the following cards, viz. the ten of clubs, nine of hearts, ace of spades, and the ace of diamonds: wrap all these round in a hankerchief of thin gauze or muslin. On getting into bed, cross your hands and say—

> " Luna, every woman's friend,
> To me thy goodness condescend;
> Let me this night in visions see
> Emblems of my destiny."

If you dream of flowers, trouble will betide you; if the storm ends in a fine calm, so will your fate; if of a ring or the ace of diamonds, marriage; bread, an industrious life; cake, a prosperous life; flowers, joy; willow, treachery in love, spades, death; diamonds, money; clubs, a foreign land hearts, illegitimate children; keys, that you will rise to great trust and power, and never know want; birds, that you will have many children; geese, that you will marry more than once.]

THE FEAST OF SHEEP-SHEARING.

The author of the Convivial Antiquities tells us that the pastoral life was anciently accounted an honorable one, particularly among the Jews and the Romans. Mention occurs in the Old Testament of the festive entertainments of the former on this occasion, particularly in the second book of Samuel, where Absalom the king's son was master of the feast. And Varro may be consulted for the manner of celebrating this feast among the latter.[1] In England, particularly in the southern parts, for these festivities are not so common in the north, on the day they begin to shear their sheep, they provide a plentiful dinner for the shearers and their friends who visit them on the occasion : a table, also, if the weather permit, is spread in the open village for the young people and children. The washing and shearing of sheep, is attended with great mirth and festivity. Indeed, the value of the covering of this very useful animal must always have made the shearing-time, in all pastoral countries, a kind of Harvest Home. In Tusser's Five Hundred Points of Husbandry, under "The Ploughman's Feast-days," are the following lines, alluding to this festivity :

> "Wife, make us a dinner, spare flesh neither corne,
> Make wafers and cakes, for our sheepe must be shorne ;
> At sheepe shearing, neighbours none other things crave,
> But good cheere and welcome like neighbours to have."

There is a beautiful description of this festivity in Dyer's

[1] "Apud Latinos *oves tondere,* ut et sementem facere omnino non fuit licitum, priusquam *Catulatio,* hoc est, ex cane sacrum fieret : ut Gyraldus testatur de Diis gentium. Ex his ergo omnibus constat illam *ovium ton-suram* (quam Luna decrescente à veteribus fieri fuisse solitam M. Varro testatur : de tempore autem *oves lavandi* et *tondendi,* vide Plin. lib. xviii. c. 17) magna cum festivitate, lætitia, atque conviviis fuisse celebratam ; id quod mirum non est. Nam in animalibus primum non sine causa putant oves assumptas, et propter utilitatem et propter placiditatem : maxime enim hæ natura quietæ et aptissimæ ad vitam hominum. Ad cibum enim lac et caseum adnibitum : ad corpus vestitum et pelles attulerunt. Itaque cum in illis tot presertim numero *tondendis* plurimum pastoribus atque famulis esset laboris exantlandum, justa profectò de causa patres-familias atque Domini illos conviviali hujusmodi lætitia recreare rursus atque ex hilarare voluerunt."—Antiq. Conviv. p. 62.

Poem called "The Fleece," at the end of the first book, l. 601 :

" At shearing-time, along the lively vales,
Rural festivities are often heard ;
Beneath each blooming arbor all is joy
And lusty merriment : while on the grass
The mingled youth in gaudy circles sport,
We think the golden age again returned
And all the fabled Dryades in dance.
Leering, they bound along, with laughing air,
To the shrill pipe and deep remurm'ring chords
Of th' ancient harp, or tabor's hollow sound ;
While th' old apart, upon a bank reclin'd,
Attend the tuneful carol, softly mixt
With ev'ry murmur of the sliding wave,
And ev'ry warble of the feather'd choir ;
Music of Paradise ! which still is heard
When the heart listens ; still the views appear,
Of the first happy garden, when Content
To Nature's flowery scenes directs the sight.
——With light fantastic toe, the nymphs
Thither assembled ; thither every swain ;
And o'er the dimpled stream a thousand flow'rs,
Pale lilies, roses, violets, and pinks,
Mixt with the greens of burnet, mint, and thyme,
And trefoil sprinkled with their sportive arms.
    Such custom holds along th' irriguous vales
From Wreakin's brow to rocky Dolvoryn,
Sabrina's early haunt.
                    ————The jolly chear
Spread on a mossy bank, untouch'd abides
Till cease the rites : and now the mossy bank
Is gaily circled, and the jolly chear
Dispers'd in copious measure : early fruits
And those of frugal store, in husk or kind ;
Steep'd grain, and curdlet milk with dulcet cream
Soft temper'd, in full merriment they quaff,
And cast about their gibes ; and some apace
Whistle to roundelays : their little ones
Look on delighted : while the mountain woods,
And winding valleys, with the various notes
Of pipe, sheep, kine, and birds, and liquid brooks,
Unite their echoes : near at hand the wide
Majestic wave of Severn slowly rolls
Along the deep divided glebe : the flood,
And trading bark with low contracted sail,
Linger among the reeds and copsy banks
To listen, and to view the joyous scene."

Thus, also, Thomson in his Summer, describes the washing
and shearing of sheep :

"———— In one diffusive band
They drive the troubled flocks, by many a dog
Compell'd, to where the mazy-running brook
Forms a deep pool : this bank abrupt and high,
And that fair-spreading in a pebbled shore.
Urged to the giddy brink, much is the toil,
The clamour much of men, and boys, and dogs,
Ere the soft fearful people to the flood
Commit their woolly sides.   And oft the swain
On some impatient seizing, hurls them in ;
Embolden'd then, nor hesitating more,
Fast, fast, they plunge amidst the flashing wave,
And, panting, labour to the farthest shore.
Repeated this, till deep the well-wash'd fleece
Has drunk the flood, and from his lively haunt
The trout is banish'd by the sordid stream ;
Heavy, and dripping, to the breezy brow
Slow move the harmless race; where, as they spread
Their swelling treasures to the sunny ray,
Inly disturb'd, and wondering what this wild
Outrageous tumult means, their loud complaints
The country fill; and, toss'd from rock to rock,
Incessant bleatings run around the hills.
    At last, of snowy white, the gather'd flocks
Are in the wattled pen innumerous press'd
Head above head ; and rang'd in lusty rows
The shepherds sit, and whet the sounding shears;
The housewife waits to roll her fleecy stores
With all her gay-drest maids attending round.
One, chief, in gracious dignity enthron'd,
Shines o'er the rest the past'ral Queen, and rays
Her smiles, sweet-beaming on her shepherd King;
While the glad circle round them yield their souls
To festive mirth, and wit that knows no gall.
Meantime their joyous task goes on apace :
Some mingling stir the melted tar, and some
Deep on the new-shorn vagrant's heaving side,
To stamp his master's cypher, ready stand ;
Others th' unwilling wether drag along ;
And glorying in his might, the sturdy boy
Holds by the twisted horns th' indignant ram.
Behold, when bound, and of its robe bereft,
By needy man, that all-depending lord,
How meek, how patient, the mild creature lies !
What softness in its melancholy face,
What dumb complaining innocence appears !

Fear not, ye gentle tribes ! 'tis not the knife
Of horrid slaughter that is o'er you waved ;
No ! tis the tender swain's well-guided shears,
Who having now to pay his annual care,
Borrow'd your fleece, to you a cumbrous load,
Will send you bounding to your hills again."

By the following passage in Ferne's Glory of Generositie, p. 71, it should seem that *cheese-cakes* composed a principa. dainty at the feast of Sheep-shearing. "Well vor your paines (if you come to our Sheep-shearing veast) bum vaith yous taste of our CHEESE-CAKE." This is put into the mouth of Columell the Plowman. In Braithwaite's Lancashire Lovers, 1640, Camillus the Clown, courting Doriclea, tells her : "*We will have a lustie* CHEESE-CAKE *at our sheepe wash,*" p. 19.

The expense attending these festivities appears to have afforded matter of complaint. Thus in Questions of profitable and pleasant Concernings, &c., 1594 : "If it be a Sheep-shearing feast, Master Baily can entertain you with his bill of reckonings to his maister of three sheapherds' wages, spent on *fresh cates,* besides *spices,* and *saffron pottage.*"

In Ireland, "On the first Sunday in harvest, viz. in August, they will be sure to drive their cattle into some pool or river and therein swim them : this they observe as inviolable as if it were a point of religion, for they think no beast will live the whole year through unless they be thus drenched. I deny not but that swimming of cattle, and chiefly in this season of the year, is healthful unto them, as the poet hath observed :

'Balantumque gregem fluvio mersare salubri.'—Virg.
' In th' healthful flood to plunge the bleating flock.'

But precisely to do this on the first Sunday in harvest, I look on as not only superstitious, but profane."—Piers's Desc. of West Meath, in Vallancey's Collectanea, i. 121.

SATURDAY AFTERNOON.

BOURNE observes that in his time it was usual in country villages, where the politeness of the age had made no great conquest, to pay a greater deference to Saturday afternoon

than to any other of the working days of the week. The first
idea of this cessation from labour at that time was, that every
one might attend evening prayers as a kind of preparation for
the ensuing Sabbath. The eve of the Jewish Sabbath is called
the Preparation, Moses having taught that people to remember
the Sabbath over night.

In Hearing and Doing the ready Way to Blessednesse, by
Henry Mason, parson of St. Andrew Undershaft, 1635, p.
537, is the following, which would seem to prove that at that
time *Saturday afternoon* was kept holy by some even in the
metropolis : "For better keeping of which (the seventh) day,
Moses commanded the Jews (Exod. xvi. 23) that *the day before the Sabbath* they should *bake what they had to bake*, and
seeth what they had to seeth ; so that they might have no
businesse of their own to do, when they were to keepe God's
holy day. And from hence it was that the Jews called the
sixth day of the week, *the preparation of the Sabbath.*
(Matt. xxvii. 62, and Luke xxiii. 54.) ——answerably whereunto, and (as I take it) *in imitation thereof,* the Christian
Church hath beene accustomed to keep *Saterday half holyday,*
that in the afternoon they might ridd by-businesses out of
the way, and by the evening service might prepare their mindes
for the Lord's day then ensuing. Which custome and usage of
God's people, as I will not presse it upon any man's conscience
as a necessarie dutie ; so every man will grant mee, that God's
people, as well Christian as Jewish, have thought a time of
preparation most fit for the well observing of God's holy day."

In Jacob's History of Faversham, p. 172, in 'Articles for
the Sexton of Faversham,' 22, Hen. VIII. I find : "Item, the
said sexton, or his deputy, *every Saturday*, Saint's even, and
principal feasts, *shall ring noon* with as many bells as shall
be convenient to the Saturday, saint's even, and principal
feasts," &c.

The following curious extract is from a MS. volume of
Sermons for all the Saints' days and remarkable Sundays in
the year, in the Episcopal Library at Durham : "It is writen
in the liffe of Seynt ***** that he was bisi on Ester Eve before None that he made one to shave him or the sunne went
doune. And the fiend aspied that, and gadirid up his heeris ;
and whan this holi man sawe it, he conjured him and badde
him tell him whi he did so. Thane said he, bycause y^u didest

no reverence to the Sundaie, and therfore this heris wolle I kepe unto ye day of Dome in reproffe of the. Thane he left of all his shavyng and toke the heris of the fiend, and made to brene hem in his owne hand for penaunce, whiche him thought he was worthé to suffre : and bode unshaven unto Monday. This is saide *in reproffe of hem that worchen at afternone on Saturdayes.*"

The *Hallowyng of Saturday afternoon* is thus accounted for in the Dialogue of Dives and Pauper, 1493 : " The thridde Precepte, xiv. chap. *Dives.* How longe owyth the haliday to be kept and halowyd ? *Pauper.* From even to even. Nathelesse summe begynne sonner to halow after that the feest is, and after use of the cuntré. But that *men use in Saturdaies* and vigilies *to ryng holy at midday* compellith nat men anon to halowe, but warnythe them of the haliday folowynge, that they shulde thynke thereon and spede theym, and so dispose hem and their occupacions that they might halowe in due tyme."

It appears by a Council of William, king of Scotland, A.D. 1203, that it was then determined that Saturday, after the twelfth hour, should be kept holy.[1] King Edgar, A.D. 958, made an Ecclesiastical law that the Sabbath or Sunday should be observed on Saturday at noon, till the light should appear on Monday morning.[2] Mr. Johnson upon this law says, the *Noontide* " signifies three in the afternoon, according to our present account : and this practice, I conceive, continued down to the Reformation. In King Withfred's time, the Lord's Day did not begin till *sunset on the Saturday.* See 697, Numb. 10. Three in the afternoon was *hora nona* in the Latin account, and therefore called *noon :* how it came afterwards to signifie mid-day, I can but guess. The monks by their rules could not eat their dinner till they had said

[1] " In Scotia anno salutis 1203, Gulielmus Rex primorum regni sui concilium cogit, cui etiam interfuit, pontificius legatus, in quo decretum est, ut Saturni dies ab hora 12 meridiei sacer esset, neque quisquam res profanas exerceret, quemadmodum aliis quoque festis diebus vetitum id erat. Idque campanæ pulsu populo indicaretur, ac postea sacris rebus, ut diebus festis operam darint, concionibus interessent, vesperas audirent, idque in diem lunæ facerent, constituta transgressoribus gravi pœna."—Boet. lib. xiii. de Scot. ex Hospinian. p. 176.

[2] " Dies Sabbathi ab ipsa diei Saturni hora pomeridiana tertia, usque in lunaris diei diluculum festus agitator," &c.—Selden, Angl. lib. ii. cap. 6.

their Noon-song, which was a service regularly to be said at three o'clock : but they probably anticipated their devotions and their dinner, by saying their Noon-song immediately after their Mid-day song, and presently falling on. I wish they had never been guilty of a worse fraud than this. But it may fairly be supposed that when mid-day became the time of dining and saying noon-song, it was for this reason called noon by the monks, who were the masters of the language during the dark ages. In the Shepherd's Almanack, *noon* is mid-day ; *high noon*, three." (Johnson's Const. Part 1, Ann. 958. 5.)

In Yet a Course at the Romyshe Foxe, p. 21, is the following *Processyon upon Saturdayes at even-songe.*—" Your holye father Agapitus, popett of Rome, fyrst dreamed it out and enacted it for a lawdable ceremonye of your whoryshe churche. But I marvele sore that ye observe yt *upon Saturdayes at nyght at even-songe*, he commaundynge yt to bee observed *upon the Sondayes, in the mornynge betwixt holie water makynge* and high masse."—" Moch is Saturnus beholden unto yow (whych is one of the olde goddes) *to garnyshe the goyng out of hys* day with so holye an observacyon. Joye yt ys of your lyfe as to remember your olde fryndes. Doubtlesse yt ys a fyne myrye pageant, and yow worthye to be called *a Saturnyane* for it." Hence, without doubt, was derived the present (or, more properly speaking, the late) custom of spending a part of Saturday afternoon without servile labour.[1]

Wheatley tells us, that in the East, the church thought fit to indulge the humour of the Judaizing Christians so far as to observe the Saturday as a festival day of devotion, and thereon to meet for the exercise of religious duties, as is plain from several passages of the ancients.—Illustr. of the Common Prayer, ed. 1848, p. 186. The religious observation of the Saturday afternoon is now entirely at an end.

With regard to Saturday afternoons, perhaps men who live

[1] In the year 1332, at a provincial Council, held by Archbishop Mepham, at Mayfield, after complaint made, that instead of fasting upon the vigils, they ran out to all the excesses of riot, &c., it was appointed among many other things relative to holy-days, that, " The solemnity for Sunday should begin upon Saturday in the evening, and not before, to prevent the misconstruction of keeping a Judaical Sabbath."—See Collier's Eccl. Hist., i. 531.

by manual labour, and have families to support by it, cannot spend them better than in following the several callings in which they have employed themselves on the preceding days of the week. For industry will be no bad preparation for the Sabbath. Considered in a political view, much harm has been done by that prodigal waste of days, very falsely called holy days, in the Church of Rome. They have, however well intended, greatly favoured the cause of vice and dissipation, without doing any essential service to that of rational religion. Complaints appear to have been made in almost every Synod and Council of the licentiousness introduced by the keeping of vigils. Nor will the philosopher wonder at this, for it has its foundation in the nature of things.

I find the following homely rhymes upon the several days of the week in Divers Crab-tree Lectures, 1639, p. 126 :

> " You know that Munday is Sundayes brother;
> Tuesday is such another ;
> Wednesday you must go to church and pray ;
> Thursday is half-holiday ;
> On Friday it is too late to begin to spin ;
> The *Saturday is half-holiday* agen."

Hooker says : " Holydays were set apart to be the landmarks to distinguish times."

THE BORROWED DAYS.

THERE is a singular old proverb preserved in Ray's Collection: "April borrows three days of March, and they are ill." April is pronounced with an emphasis on the last syllable, so as to make a kind of jingling rhyme with " ill," the last word in the line.

I have taken notice of this, because I find in the ancient Calendar of the Church of Rome, to which I have so often referred, the following observations on the 31st of March : "The rustic fable concerning the nature of the month. The rustic names of six days which shall follow in April, or may be the last in March."[1] There is no doubt but that these observations

[1] " Rustica fabula de natura mensis. Nomina rustica 6 dierum, qui sequentur in Aprili, seu ultimi sint Martii."

in the ancient Calendar, and our proverb, are derived from one common origin; but for want of more lights, I am unable at present to trace them any further.

The Borrowing Days, as they are called, occur in The Complaynt of Scotland, p. 58. " There eftir i entrit in ane grene forest, to contempil the tender zong frutes of grene treis, because the borial blastis of the *thre borouing dais of Marche* hed chaissit the fragrant flureise of evyrie frut-tree far athourt the feildis." The glossary explains " Borrouing days, the three last days of March :" and adds, " concerning the origin of the term, the following popular rhyme is often repeated :

> " March borrowit fra Averill
> Three days, and they were ill."

[Brockett, in his N. C. Glossary, gives the following modernised version :

> " March borrowed of April
> Three days, and they were ill :
> The one was sleet, the other was snow,
> The third was the worst that e'er did blow."]

Also the following :

> " March said to Aperill,
> I see three hogs upon a hill ;
> But lend your three first days to me,
> And I'll be bound to gar them dee.
> The first, it sall be wind and weet ;
> The next, it sall be snaw and sleet ;
> The third, it sall be sic a freeze
> Sall gar the birds stick to the trees.
> But when the Borrowed Days were gane,
> The three silly hogs came hirplin hame."

In the Statistical Account of Scotland, 1791, i. 57, Parish of Kirkmichael, the minister, mentioning an old man of the age of 103 years, says: " His account of himself is, that he was born in the *Borrowing Days* of the year that King William came in." A note adds, " that is on one of the three last days of March 1688."

In the Country Almanack for 1676, among the "remarques upon April," are the following :

> " No blust'ring blasts from March needs April borrow :
> His own oft proves enow to breed us sorrow.
> Yet if he weep (with us to sympathise),
> His trickling tears will make us wipe our eyes."

In the British Apollo, vol. iii. No. 18, the meaning is asked
of the old poetical saying :

> " March borrows of April
> Three days, and they are ill;
> April returns them back again,
> Three days, and they are rain."

A. Proverbs relating to the weather cannot be founded on
any certainty. The meaning of this is, that it is more sea-
sonable for the end of March and the beginning of April to be
fair, but often

> " March does from April gain
> Three days, and they're in rain ;
> Return'd by April in 's bad kind,
> Three days, and they're in wind."

[The following allusion to these days occurs in Poor Robin's
Almanack for 1731 : " There is an old proverb in antique
verse, viz. :

> ' March borrow'd of *April* three days and they were ill,
> They kill'd three lambs were playing on a hill.'

But it is disputed amongst those experienced prognosticators
who carry almanacks in their shoes, and foretel weather by the
aching of their corns, or the itching of their elbows, whether
these borrowing days be the three last days of March, or the
three first of April. Now Easter holidays are come, and young
men and maids go a walking, talking, courting, loving, which
often ends in marrying ; which is a commencement of a lease
upon lives, and seldom both live to see it expired."]

A clergyman in Devonshire informed me that the old farmers
in his parish call the *first* three days of March " Blind Days,"
which were anciently considered as unlucky ones, and upon
which no farmer would sow any seed. This superstition,
however, is now, rapidly disappearing.

These had not escaped the observation of the learned author
of the Vulgar Errors. He, too, seems to have been in the dark
concerning them ; for he barely tells us, p. 247 : " It is usual
to ascribe unto March certain Borrowed Daies from April."

Dr. Jamieson, in his Etymological Dictionary of the Scottish
Language, says : " These days being generally stormy, our
forefathers have endeavoured to account for this circumstance,
by pretending that March *borrowed* them from April, that he
might extend his power so much longer." " Those," he adds,

"who are much addicted to superstition, will neither borrow
nor lend on any of these days. If any one should propose to
borrow of them, they would consider it as an evidence that the
person wished to employ the article borrowed for the purposes
of witchcraft against the lenders. Some of the vulgar imagine
that these days received their designation from the conduct of
the Israelites in borrowing the property of the Egyptians.
This extravagant idea must have originated partly from the
name, and partly from the circumstances of these days nearly
corresponding to the time when the Israelites left Egypt,
which was on the fourteenth day of the month Abib, or Nisan,
including part of our March and April. I know not whether
our western magi suppose that the inclemency of the *Borrowing Days* has any relation to the storm which proved so fatal
to the Egyptians."

In the Highlands the same idea is commonly received ; with
this difference, that the days are considerably antedated, as the
loan is also reversed. Mrs. Grant, in her Superstitions of the
Highlanders, ii. 217, says: "The *Favilteach*, or three first days
of February, serve many poetical purposes in the Highlands.
They are said to have been *borrowed* for some purpose by
February from January, who was bribed by February with
three young sheep. These three days, by Highland reckoning,
occur between the 11th and 15th of February ; and it is accounted a most favorable prognostic for the ensuing year,
that they should be as stormy as possible. If they should be
fair, then there is no more good weather to be expected
through the spring. Hence the *Favilteach* is used to signify
the very ultimatum of bad weather."

DAYS LUCKY OR UNLUCKY.

BOURNE (chap. xviii.), speaking of that superstitious custom
among the heathens of observing one day as good, and another
as bad, observes : "that among these were lucky and unlucky
days ; some were *Dies atri*, and some *Dies albi*. The *Atri*
were pointed out in their calendar with a black character, the
Albi with a white; the former to denote it a day of bad

ᴍᴜᴄᴄᴇᴀᴀ, ᴛʜᴇ ʟᴀᴛᴛᴇʀ ᴀ ᴅᴀʏ ᴏꜰ ɢᴏᴏᴅ. Thus have the monks, in the dark and unlearned ages of Popery, copy'd after the heathens, and dream'd themselves into the like superstitions, esteeming one day more successful than another." He tells us, also, that St. Austin, upon the passage of St. Paul to the Galatians against observing days, and months, and times, and years, explains it to have this meaning: "The persons the Apostle blames are those who say, I will not set forward on my journey, because it is the next day after such a time, or because the moon is so; or I'll set forward that I may have luck, because such is just now the position of the stars. I will not traffick this month, because such a star presides, or I will because it does. I shall plant no vines this year, because it is Leap-year," &c. Barnabe Googe thus translates the remarks of Naogeorgus on this subject:

> " And first, betwixt the dayes they make no little difference,
> For all be not of vertue like, nor like preheminence.
> But some of them Egyptian are, and full of jeopardee,
> And some againe, beside the rest, both good and luckie bee.
> Like diffrence of the nights they make, as if the Almightie King,
> That made them all, not gracious were to them in every thing."
> Popish Kingdome, fol. 44.

Thomas Lodge, in his Incarnate Devils, 1596, p. 12, glances as follows at the superstitious observer of lucky and unlucky times: " He will not eat his dinner before he hath lookt in his almanacke." Mason, in the Anatomie of Sorcerie, 1612, p. 85, enumerates among the superstitious of that age, " Regarders of times, as they are which will have one time more lucky than another: to be borne at one hower more unfortunate than at another: to take a journey or any other enterprize in hand, to be more dangerous or prosperous at one time than at another: as likewise, *if such a festivall day fall upon such a day of the weeke*, or such like, *we shall have such a yeare following*: and many other such like vaine speculations, set downe by our astrologians, having neither footing in God's word, nor yet natural reason to support them; but being grounded onely upon the superstitious imagination of man's braine."

In the Tryall of a Man's Own Selfe, by Thomas Newton, 1602, p. 44, he inquires, under " Sinnes Externall and Outward" against the First Commandment, " whether, for the procuring of any thing either good or bad, thou hast used any unlawfull meanes, or superstitious and damnable helps. Of which sort bee *the observation and choise of* DAYES, of planetarie houres, of motions and courses of starres, mumbling of prophane praiers, consisting of words both strange and senselesse, adjurations, sacrifices, consecrations, and hallowings of divers thinges, rytes and ceremonies unknowne to the Church of God, toyish characters and figures, demanding of questions and aunsweares of the dead, dealing with damned spirits, or with any instruments of phanaticall divination, as basons, rings, cristalls, glasses, roddes, prickes, numbers, dreames, lots, fortune-tellings, oracles, soothsayings, horoscoping, or marking the houres of nativities, witchcraftes, enchauntments, and all such superstitious trumperie:—the enclosing or binding of spirits to certaine instruments, and such like devises of Sathan the devill." Under the same head, p. 50, he asks: " Whether the apothecarie have *superstitiously observed or fondly stayed for* CHOISE DAYES *or houres, or any other ceremonious rites, in gathering his herbs and other simples* for the making of drougs and receipts."[1]

The following curious passage on this subject is taken from Melton's Astrologaster, p. 56 et seq.: " Those observers of time are to be laught at that will not goe out of their house before they have had counsell of their Almanacke, and will rather have the house fall on their heads than stirre, if they note some natural effect about the motion of the aire, which they suppose will varie the luckie blasts of the starres, that will not marry, or traffique or doe the like, but under some constellation. These, sure, are no Christians: because faith-

---

[1] At the end of an old MS. mentioned in the Duke de la Valiere's Catalogue, i. 44 (Add.), there is a part of a Calendar in which the following unlucky days are noticed : " Januar. iiii.   Non. [10th] Dies ater et nefastus. viii. Id. [25th] Dies ater et nefastus.   Mar. vi. Non. [10th] non est bonum nugere [q. nubere ?]   Jan. iiii. Kal. [2nd] Dies ater."

" Sed et circa dies injecta est animis religio. Inde dies nefasti, qui Aπόφραδες Græcis, quibus iter, aut aliquid alicujus momenti indipisci, periculosum existimatur."—" De quibus diebus faustis aut infaustis, multa, Hesiodus ἡμέραις, et Virgilius primo Georgicon. Quam scrupulosam superstitionem, sese illigantem delira formidine, damnat Apostolus ad Galatas. 4. *Observatis dies, et menses, et tempora, et annos : metuo ne incassum circa vos me fatigaverim.*" Pet. Molinæi Vates, p. 155.

full men ought not to doubt that the Divine Providence from any part of the world, or from any time whatsoever, is absent. Therefore we should not impute any secular business to the power of the starres, but to know that all things are disposed by the arbitrement of the King of Kings. The Christian faith is violated when, so like a pagan and apostate, any man doth observe those days which are called Ægyptiaci, or the calends of Januarie, or any moneth, or day, or time, or yeere, eyther to travell, marry, or doe anything in."

In the Book of Knowledge, p. 19, I find the following "Account of the perillous dayes of every month :—In the change of every moon be two dayes, in the which what thing soever is begun, late or never, it shall come to no good end, and the dayes be full perillous for many things. In January, when the moon is three or four days old. In February, 5 or 7. In March, 6 or 7. In April, 5 or 8. May, 8 or 9. June, 5 or 15. July, 3 or 13. August, 8 or 13. September, 8 or 13. October 5 or 12. November, 5 or 9. In December, 3 or 13. Astronomers say that six dayes of the year are perillous of death; and therefore they forbid men to let blood on them, or take any drink; that is to say, January the 3d, July the 1st, October the 2d, the last of April, August the 1st, the last day going out of December. These six dayes with great diligence ought to be kept, but namely the latter three, for all the veins are then full. For then, whether man or beast be knit in them, within seven days, or certainly within fourteen days, he shall die. And if they take any drinks within fifteene dayes, they shall die; and if they eat any goose in these three dayes, within forty days they shall die; and, if any child be born in these three latter dayes, they shall die a wicked death. Astronomers and astrologers say, that in the beginning of March, the seventh night, or fourteenth day, let thee bloud of the right arm; and in the beginning of April, the eleventh day, of the left arm; and in the end of May, third or fifth day, on whether arm thou wilt; and thus, of all that year, thou shalt orderly be kept from the fever, the falling gout, the sister gout, and losse of thy sight."

Grose tells us that many persons have certain days of the week and month on which they are particularly fortunate, and others in which they are as generally unlucky. These days are different to different persons. Aubrey has given several instances of both in divers persons. Some days, however, are commonly deemed unlucky : among others, Friday labours under that opprobrium ; and it is pretty generally held that no new work or enterprise should commence on that day. Likewise, respecting the weather there is this proverb :

> " Friday's moon,
> Come when it will, it comes too soon."

A respectable merchant of the city of London informed me that no person there will begin any business, i. e. open his shop for the first time, on a Friday.

Thursday was noted as a fatal day to King Henry VIII. and his posterity. See Stowe's Annals, ed., 631, p. 812.

In Preceptes, &c., left by William Lord Burghley to his Sonne, 1636, p. 36, we read : " Though I think no day amisse to undertake any good enterprize or businesse in hande, yet have I observed some, and no meane clerks, very cautionarie to forbeare these three Mundayes in the yeare, which I leave to thine owne consideration, either to use or refuse, viz. 1. The first Munday in April, which day *Caine was born, and his brother Abel slaine.* 2. The second Munday in August, which day *Sodome and Gomorrah were destroyed.* 3. The last Munday in December, which day *Judas was born*, that betrayed our Saviour Christ." Bishop Hall, in his Characters of Virtues and Vices, speaking of the superstitious man, observes : " If his journey began unawares on the dismal day, he feares a mischiefe."

In the Calendar prefixed to Grafton's Manuel, or Abridgment of his Chronicle, 1565, the unlucky days, according to the opinion of the astronomers, are noted, which I have extracted as follows : " January 1, 2, 4, 5, 10, 15, 17, 29, very unlucky. February 26, 27, 28, unlucky ; 8, 10, 17, very unlucky. March 16, 17, 20, very unlucky. April 7, 8, 10, 20, unlucky ; 16, 21, very unlucky. May 3, 6, unlucky ; 7, 15, 20, very unlucky. June 10, 22, unlucky ; 4, 8, very unlucky. July 15, 21, very unlucky. August 1, 29, 30, unlucky ; 19, 20, very unlucky. September 2, 4, 21, 23, unlucky ; 6, 7, very unlucky. October 4, 16, 24, unlucky ; 6, very unlucky. November 5, 6, 29, 30, unlucky ; 15, 20, very unlucky. December 15, 22, unlucky ; 6, 7, 9, very unlucky." In the

Prognostication of these Days, 1660, printed by Colwell, the
unlucky days vary from these of Grafton.[1]

I find an observation on the 13th of December in the
ancient Romish Calendar, which I have so often cited (Decemb. xiii. prognostica mensium per totum annum), that on
this day prognostications of the months were drawn for the
whole year. As also, that on the day of St. Barnabas, and on
that of St. Simon and St. Jude, a tempest often arises. In
the Schola Curiositatis, ii. 236, we read : " Multi nolunt opus
inchoare die Martis tanquam infausto die."

Many superstitious observations on days may be found in
a curious old book called Practica Rusticorum, which I suspect to be an earlier edition of the Husbandman's Practice,
1658, at the end of the Book of Knowledge of the same date.

In Sir John Sinclair's Statistical account of Scotland, v. 82,
1793, the minister of Logierait, in Perthshire, mentioning the
superstitious opinions and practices in the parish, says : " In
this parish, and in the neighbourhood, a variety of superstitious
practices still prevail among the vulgar, which may be in part
the remains of ancient idolatry, or of the corrupted Christianity of the Romish church, and partly, perhaps, the result
of the natural hopes and fears of the human mind in a state
of simplicity and ignorance. Lucky and unlucky days are
by many anxiously observed. That day of the week upon
which the 14th of May happens to fall, for instance, is
esteemed unlucky through all the remainder of the year;
none marry or begin any business upon it. None chuse to
marry in January or May ; or to have their banns proclaimed
in the end of one quarter of the year and to marry in the be-

[1] ["January. Prima dies mensis, et septima truncat ut ensis.
February. Quarta subit mortem, prosternit tertia fortem.
March. Primus mandentem, disrumpit quarta bibentem.
April. Denus et undenus est mortis vulnere plenus.
May. Tertius occidit, et septimus ora relidit.
June. Denus pallescit, quindenus fœdera nescit.
July. Ter-decimus mactat, Julij denus labefactat.
August. Prima necat fortem, prosternit secunda cohortem.
September. Tertia Septembris et denus fert mala membris.
October. Tertius et denus est, sicut mors alienus.
November. Scorpius est quintus, et tertius è nece cinctus.
December. Septimus exanguis, virosus denus et anguis."
                    Aubrey's Miscellanies, p. 8.]

ginning of the next. Some things are to be done before the
full moon ; others after. In fevers the illness is expected to
be more severe on Sunday than on the other days of the week ;
if easier on Sunday, a relapse is feared." In the same work,
vii. 560, Parishes of Kirkwall and St. Ola, co. Orkney, we
read : " In many days of the year they will neither go to sea
in search of fish, nor perform any sort of work at home."
Ibid. viii. 156, Parish of Canisbay, co. Caithness, we are told,
under the head of Dress, Customs, &c., " There are few superstitious usages among them. No gentleman, however, of
the name of Sinclair, either in Canisbay or throughout Caithness, will put on green apparel, or think of crossing the Ord,
upon a Monday. They were dressed in green and they crossed
the Ord upon a Monday, in their way to the battle of Flodden,
where they fought and fell in the service of their country,
almost without leaving a representative of their name behind
them. The day and the dress are accordingly regarded as in-
auspicious. If the Ord must be got beyond on Monday,
the journey is performed by sea."[1]

The Spaniards hold Friday to be a very unlucky day, and
never undertake anything of consequence upon it. Among
the Finns, whoever undertakes any business on a Monday or
Friday must expect very little success.

And yet, from the following extract from Eradut Khan's
Memoirs of the Mogul Empire, p. 10, it should seem to appear that Friday is there considered in a different light : " On
Friday, the 28th of Zekand, his Majesty (Aurengzebe) performed
his morning devotions in company with his attendants ; after
which, as was frequently his custom, he exclaimed : ' O that
my death may happen on a Friday, for blessed is he who dieth
on that day !' "

[1] So, xiv. 541, Parish of Forglen, Banffshire : " There are happy and
unhappy days for beginning any undertaking. Thus few would choose
to be married here on Friday, though it is the ordinary day in other quarters of the church." Ibid. xv. 258, Parish of Monzie, co. Perth ; " The
inhabitants are stated to be not entirely free of superstition. Lucky
and unlucky days, and feet, are still attended to, especially about the end
and beginning of the year. No person will be proclaimed for marriage
in the end of one year, or even quarter of the year, and be married in the
beginning of the next." Ibid. xxi. 148 : " Lucky and unlucky days,
dreams, and omens, are still too much observed by the country people :
but in this respect the meanest Christian far surpasses, in strength of mind,
Gibbon's all-accomplished and philosophic Julian."

Fynes Moryson in his Itinerary i 61, speaking of the King of Poland at the port of Dantzic in 1593, says: "The next day the king had a good wind, but before this (as those of the Romish religion are very superstitious), the king and the queen (being of the house of Austria), while sometimes they thought *Monday*, sometimes *Friday*, to be unlucky days, had lost many fair winds."

[The following curious extract is taken from a rare tract, called the Animal Parliament, 1707: "That none must be thought good lawyers and docters, but those which will take great fees. That all duty and submission belongs to power, not to virtue. That all must have ill luck after much mirth. That all those that marry on Tuesdays and Thursdays, shall be happy. That a man's fortune can be rold in the palme of his hand. That the falling of salt portends misfortune. Those that begin journies upon a *Wednesday* shall run through much danger. That all women that are poor, old, and ill-favoured must be thought witches, and be burnt for the same. That the houling of a dog, or croaking of ravens, foretell a friend's death."]

COCK-CROWING.

TIME OF THE MORNING SO CALLED.

BOURNE, in his Antiquitates Vulgares, tells us, there is a tradition among the common people that, at the time of cock-crowing, the midnight spirits forsake these lower regions, and go to their proper places. Hence it is that in the country villages, where the way of life requires more early labour, the inhabitants always go cheerfully to work at that time: whereas if they are called abroad sooner, they are apt to imagine everything they see or hear to be a wandering ghost. Shakespeare has given us an excellent account of this vulgar notion in his Hamlet.[1] Bourne very seriously examines the fact, whether

---

[1] What follows, in this passage, is an exception from the general time of cock-crowing:

"Some say, that ever 'gainst that season comes,
Wherein our Saviour's birth is celebrated,

spirits roam about in the night, or are obliged to go away at cock-crow; first citing from the Sacred Writings that good and evil angels attend upon men; and proving thence also that there have been apparitions of good and evil spirits. He is of opinion that these can ordinarily have been nothing but the appearances of some of those angels of light or darkness: "for," he adds, "I am far from thinking that either the ghosts of the damned or the happy, either the soul of a Dives or a Lazarus, returns here any more." Their appearance in the night, he goes on to say, is linked to our idea of apparitions. Night, indeed, by its awfulness and horror, naturally inclines the mind of man to these reflections, which are much heightened by the legendary stories of nurses and old women.

The traditions of all ages appropriate the appearance of spirits to the night. The Jews had an opinion that hurtful spirits walked about in the night. The same opinion obtained among the ancient Christians, who divided the night into four watches, called the evening, midnight, cock-crowing, and the morning. The opinion that spirits fly away at cock-crow is certainly very ancient, for we find it mentioned by the Christian poet Prudentius, who flourished in the beginning of the fourth century, as a tradition of common belief. The passage is thus translated in Bourne:

> " They say the wandering powers that love
>   The silent darkness of the night,
> At cock-crowing give o'er to rove,
>   And all in fear do take their flight.
>
> The approaching salutary morn,
>   Th' approach divine of hated day,
> Makes darkness to its place return,
>   And drives the midnight ghosts away
>
> They know that this an emblem is
>   Of what precedes our lasting bliss,—
> That morn when graves give up their dead
> In certain hope to meet their God."

This bird of dawning singeth all night long.
And then, they say, no spirit dares stir abroad;
The nights are wholesome; then no planets strike,
No fairy takes, nor witch hath power to charm,
o hallow'd and so gracious is the time."

Dr. Farmer, citing Bourne in this place, says. "And he
quotes on this occasion, as all his predecessors had done, the
well-known lines from the first hymn of Prudentius. I know
not whose translation he gives us, but there is an old one by
Heywood. The pious chansons, the hymns and carols which
Shakespeare mentions presently, were usually copied from the
elder Christian poets." Cassian, also,[1] who lived in the same
century, mentioning a host of devils who had been abroad
in the night, says, that as soon as the morn approached,
they all vanished and fled away; which further evinces that
this was the current opinion of the time. Philostratus, giving
an account of the apparition of Achilles' shade to Apollonius
Tyaneus, says, that it vanished with a little glimmer as soon
as the cock crowed. Vit. Apol. iv. 16. The following is from
Spenser :

> " ——— The morning cock crew loud ;
> And at the sound it shrunk in haste away,
> And vanish'd from our sight."

So Butler, in his Hudibras, I. iii. 1553 :

> " The cock crows and the morning grows on,
> When 'tis decreed I must be gone."

Thus also Blair, in his Grave :

> " ——— The tale
> Of horrid apparition, tall and ghastly,
> That walks at dead of night or takes his stand
> O'er some new-open'd grave ; and, strange to tell,
> Evanishes at crowing of the cock."

Bourne tells us he never met with any reasons assigned for
the departure of spirits at the cock-crowing ; " but," he adds,
" there have been produced at that time of night things of
very memorable worth, which might perhaps raise the pious credulity of some men to imagine that there was something more
in it than in other times. It was about the time of cock-crowing when our Saviour was born, and the angels sung the first

[1] " Aurora itaque superveniente, cum omnis hæc ab oculis evanisset
dæmonum multitudo." Cass. Coll. viii. c. 16. Thus the Ghost in
Hamlet :
> " But soft, methinks I scent the morning air—
> Brief let me be."

And again :
> " The glow-worm shows the matin to be near."

Christmas carol to the poor shepherds in the fields of Bethlehem. Now, it may be presumed, as the Saviour of the world was then born, and the heavenly host had then descended to proclaim the news, that the angels of darkness would be terrified and confounded, and immediately fly away ; and perhaps this consideration has partly been the foundation of this opinion." It was also about this time when our Saviour rose from the dead. A third reason is, that passage in the book of Genesis, where Jacob wrestled with the angel for a blessing ; where the angel says unto him, " Let me go, for the day breaketh."

Bourne, however, thinks this tradition seems more especially to have arisen from some particular circumstances attending the time of cock-crowing; which, as Prudentius, as before cited, seems to say, is an emblem of the approach of the day of resurrection. "The circumstances, therefore, of the time of cock-crowing," he adds, "being so natural a figure and representation of the morning of the resurrection ; the night so shadowing out the night of the grave ; the third watch being, as some suppose, the time when our Saviour will come to Judgment at ; the noise of the cock awakening sleepy man, and telling him, as it were, the night is far spent, the day is at hand ; representing so naturally the voice of the arch-angel awakening the dead, and calling up the righteous to everlasting day ; so naturally does the time of cock-crowing shadow out these things, that probably some good, well-meaning men might have been brought to believe that the very devils themselves, when the cock crew and reminded them of them, did fear and tremble, and shun the light."

The ancients, because the cock gives notice of the approach and break of day, have, with a propriety equal to anything in their mythology, dedicated this bird to Apollo. They have also made him the emblem of watchfulness, from the circumstance of his summoning men to their business by his crowing, and have therefore dedicated him also to Mércury. With the lark he may be poetically styled the " Herald of the Morn." In England's Parnassus, 1600, I find the two following lines ascribed to Drayton :

> " And now the cocke, the morning's trumpeter,
> Played Hunt's-up for the day-star to appear."

Gray has imitated our poet :

> " The cock's shrill clarion, or the echoing horn,
> No more shall rouse them from their lowly bed."

The following is from Chaucer's Assemblie of Foules, f. 235:

" The tame ruddocke and the coward kite,
The *cocke, that horologe is of Thropes lite.*"

Thus, in the Merry Devil of Edmonton, 4to. 1631:

" More watchfull than the day-proclayming cocke."

The day, civil and political, has been divided into thirteen parts.[1] The after-midnight and the dead of the night are the most solemn of them all, and have, therefore it should seem, been appropriated by ancient superstition to the walking of spirits.

By a passage in Macbeth, " we were carousing till the second cock," it should seem to appear as if there were two separate times of cock-crowing. The commentators, however, say nothing of this. They explain the passage as follows: "Till the second cock:—Cock-crowing." So in King Lear: "He begins at curfew, and walks till the first cock." Again, in the Twelve Merry Jestes of the Widow Edith, 1573:

" The time they pas merely til ten of the clok,
Yea, and I shall not lye, till after the first cok."

It appears from a passage in Romeo and Juliet, that Shakespeare means that they were carousing till three o'clock:

" —— The *second cock* has crow'd,
The curfew-bell has toll'd; 'tis three o'clock."

Perhaps Tusser makes this point clear,—Five Hundred Pointes of Good Husbandrie, 1585, p. 126:

" Cocke croweth at midnight times few above six,
With pause to his neighbour to answer betwix:
At three aclocke thicker, and then as ye knowe,
Like all in to mattens neere day they doo crowe;
At midnight, at three, and an hour yer day,
They utter their language as well as they may."

---

[1] 1. After midnight. 2. Cock-crow. 3. The space between the first cock-crow and break of day. 4. The dawn of the morning. 5. Morning. 6. Noon. 7. Afternoon. 8. Sunset. 9. Twilight. 10. Evening. 11. Candle-time. 12. Bed-time. 13. The dead of the night. The Church of Rome made four nocturnal vigils: the conticinium, gallicinium or cock-crow, intempestum, and anteluchium. Durand. de Nocturnis. There is a curious discourse on the ancient divisions of the night and the day in Peck's Desiderata Curiosa, i. 223 et seq.

The following very curious ' Old Wives Prayer' is found in Herrick's Hesperides, p. 205 :

" Holy-rood, come forth and shield
Us i' th'citie and the field ;
Safely guard us, now and aye,
From the blast that burns by day;
And those sounds that us affright
In the dead of dampish night.
Drive all hurtful fiends us fro,
By the time the cocks first crow."

Vanes on the tops of steeples were anciently made in the form of a cock,[1] (called from hence *weathercocks*,) and put up, in Papal times, to remind the clergy of watchfulness. " In summitate crucis, quæ companario vulgò imponitur, galli gallinacei effugi solet figura, quæ ecclesiarum rectores vigilantiæ admoneat." (Du Cange, Gloss.) I find the following on this subject, in A Helpe to Discourse, 1633. " Q. Wherefore *on the top of church steeples is the cocke set upon the crosse*, of a long continuance? A. The flocks of Jesuits will answer you. For instruction : that whilst aloft we behold the crosse and the cocke standing thereon, we may remember our sinnes, and with Peter seeke and obtaine mercy : as though without this dumbe cocke, which many will not hearken to, untill he crow, the Scriptures were not a sufficient larum." " The inconstancy of the French," says Dr. Johnson, " was always the subject of satire. I have read a dissertation written to prove that the index of the wind upon our steeples was made in form of a cock to ridicule the French for their frequent changes." A writer, dating Wisbech, May 7, in the St. James's Chronicle, June 10, 1777, says that " the intention of the original *cock-vane* was derived from the cock's crowing when St. Peter had denied his Lord, meaning by this device to forbid all schism in the Church, which might arise amongst her members by their departing from her communion, and denying

[1] " The lyon hath an antipathy with the cocke, especially of the game ; one reason is, because he sees him commonly with his crowne on his head, while princes commonly are jealous of each other. Some say because he presumes to come into his presence booted and spurred, contrary to the law in court. But I thinke rather because he meetes with a lyon's heart in so weake a body." See A Strange Metamorphosis of Man transformed into a Wildernesse, deciphered in Characters, 1634.

the established principles of her faith. But though this invention was, in all probability, of popish original, and a man who
often changes his opinion is known by the appellation of a
weathercock, I would hint to the advocates of that unreformed
church, that neither this intention, nor the antiquity of this
little device, can afford any matter for religious argument."
A writer in the Gentleman's Magazine for Jan. 1737, vii. 7,
says : " Levity and inconstancy of temper is a general reproach
upon the French. *The cock upon the steeple* (set up in contempt and derision of that nation on some violation of peace,
or breach of alliance) naturally represents these ill qualities."
This derivation, however, seems to be as illiberal as it is
groundless. In the Minute Book of the Society of Antiquaries,
i. 105, we read: " 29 Jan. 1723-4, Mr. Norroy (Peter Le Neve)
brought a script from Gramaye, Historia Brabantiæ, Bruxell.
p. 14, showing that *the manner of adorning the tops of steeples
with a cross and a cock is derived from the* GOTHS, *who bore
that as their warlike ensign.*"

COCK-FIGHTING.

MEN have long availed themselves of the antipathy which
one cock shows to another, and have encouraged that natural
hatred with arts that may be said to disgrace human reason.
Stubs, in his Anatomie of Abuses, 1585, p. 117, inveighs against
Cock-fighting, which in his days seems to have been practised
on the Sabbath in England : " They flock thicke and threefolde
to the Cock-fightes, an exercise nothing inferiour to the rest,
where nothing is used but swearing, forswearing, deceipt, fraud,
collusion, cosenage, skoldyng, railyng, convitious talkyng,
fightyng, brawlyng, quarrellyng, drinkyng, and robbing one
another of their goods, and that not by direct, but indirect
means and attempts. And yet to blaunch and set out these
mischiefs withall (as though they were virtues), they have
their appointed dayes and set houres, when these devilries
must be exercised. They have houses erected to that purpose,
flags and ensignes hanged out, to give notice of it to others,
and proclamation goes out, to proclaim the same, to the ende

that many may come to the dedication of this solemne feast of mischiefe." [1]

At the end of the Compleat Gamester, ed. 1680, I find a poem entitled " An excellent and elegant copy of verses upon two cocks fighting, by Dr. R. Wild." The spirited qualities of the combatants are given in the following most brilliant couplet:

> " They scorn the dunghill; 'tis their only prize
> To dig for pearls within each other's eyes."

Our poet makes his conquered or dying cock dictate a will, some of the quaint items of which follow:

> " Imp. first of all, let never be forgot,
> My body freely I bequeath to th' pot,
> Decently to be boil'd; and for its tomb,
> Let it be buried in some hungry womb.
> Item, executors I will have none
> But he that on my side laid seven to one,
> And like a gentleman that he may live,
> To him and to his heirs my comb I give."

To cry *coke* is, in vulgar language, synonymous with crying peccavi. Coke, says the learned Ruddiman, in his Glossary to Douglas's Virgil, is the sound which cocks utter, especially when they are beaten, from which Skinner is of opinion they have the name of cock.

Bailey tells us that the origin of this sport was derived from the Athenians on the following occasion. When Themistocles was marching his army against the Persians, he, by the way, espying two cocks fighting, caused his army to behold them, and addressed them as follows: " Behold, these do not fight for their household gods, for the monuments of their ancestors, nor for glory, nor for liberty, nor for the safety of their children, but only because the one will not give way unto the other." This so encouraged the Grecians, that they fought strenuously, and obtained the victory over the Persians; upon

[1] In the Statistical Account of Scotland, vi. 614, in the account of Edinburgh, we read: " In 1763 there was no such diversion as public cock-fighting at Edinburgh. In 1783 there were many public cock-fighting matches, or *mains*, as they were technically termed; and a regular cockpit was built for the accommodation of this school of gambling and cruelty, where every distinction of rank and character is levelled. In 1790 the cockpit continued to be frequented."

which Cock-fighting was, by a particular law, ordained to be annually practised by the Athenians.

Dr. Pegge, in his excellent memoir on this subject in the Archœologia, has proved that though the ancient Greeks piqued themselves on their politeness, calling all other nations barbarous, yet they were the authors of this cruel and inhuman mode of diversion. The inhabitants of Delos were great lovers of this sport; and Tanagra, a city of Bœotia, the Isle of Rhodes, Chalcis in Eubœa, and the country of Media, were famous for their generous and magnanimous race of chickens. It appears that the Greeks had some method of preparing the birds for battle.[1]

Cock-fighting was an institution partly religious and partly political at Athens, and was continued there for the purpose of improving the seeds of valour in the minds of the Athenian youth. But it was afterwards abused and perverted, both there and in other parts of Greece, to a common pastime and amusement, without any moral, political, or religious intention, and as it is now followed and practised amongst us. It appears that the Romans, who borrowed this with many other things from Greece, used quails as well as cocks for fighting. Mr. Douce, Illustrations of Shakspeare, ii. 87, informs us : "Quail combats were well known among the ancients, and especially at Athens. Julius Pollux relates that a circle was made, in which the birds were placed, and he whose quail was driven out of the circle lost the stake, which was sometimes money,

[1] The modern manner of preparing is thus described in the Musæ Anglicanæ, 1689, ii. 86 :

"Nec per agros sivit dulcesve errare per hortos;
Nè venere absumant natas ad prælia vires,
Aut alvo nimium pleni turgente laborent.
Sed rerum prudens penetrali in sede locavit,
Et salicis circùm virgas dedit; insuper ipsos
Cortibus inclusos tenero nutrimine fovit;
Et panem, mulsumque genusque leguminis omne,
Atque exorta suâ de conjuge prebuit ova,
Ut validas firment vires——
    Quinetiam cristas ipsis, caudasque fluentes,
Et colli impexas secuit pulchro ordine plumas;
Ut rapido magis adversum, quasi veles, in hostem
Impetu procurrat gallus.———
Arma dedit calci; chalybemque aptavit acutum
Ad talos, graviore queat quò surgere plagâ."

and occasionally the quails themselves. Another practice was
to produce one of these birds, which being first smitten or
filliped with the middle finger, a feather was then plucked from
its head; if the quail bore this operation without flinching,
his master gained the stake, but lost it if he ran away. The
Chinese have been always extremely fond of quail-fighting, as
appears from most of the accounts of that people, and particularly in Mr. Bell's excellent relation of his travels in China,
where the reader will find much curious matter on the subject.
See i. 424, ed. 8vo. We are told by Mr. Marsden that the
Sumatrans likewise use these birds in the manner of game-
cocks."

The first cause of contention between the two brothers
Bassianus and Geta, sons of the Emperor Septimus Severus,
happened, according to Herodian, in their youth, about fighting their quails and cocks.[1]

Cocks and quails, fitted for the purpose of engaging one
another to the last gasp, for diversion, are frequently com-
pared in the Roman writers,[2] and with much propriety, to
gladiators. The Fathers of the Church inveigh with great
warmth against the spectacles of the arena, the wanton shed-
ding of human blood in sport : one would have thought that
with that of the gladiators, cock-fighting would also have been
discarded under the mild and humane genius of Christianity.
But, as the Doctor observes, it was reserved for this enlightened era to practise it with new and aggravated circumstances
of cruelty.

The Shrove-Tuesday massacre of this useful and spirited
creature is now indeed in a declining way; but those monstrous barbarities, the battle royal and Welsh main, still continue among us in full force—a striking disgrace to the manly
character of Britons.

It is probable that cock-fighting was first introduced into
this island by the Romans; the bird itself was here before
Cæsar's arrival. William Fitzstephen, who wrote the Life of

---

[1] " Interque se fratres dissidebant, puerili primum certamine, edendis
Coturnicum pugnis, gallinaceorumque conflictibus, ac puerorum collucta-
tionibus exorta discordia." Herodian, iii. sect. 33.

[2] Hence Pliny's expression, " gallorum, seu gladiatorum ;" and that of
Columella, " rixosarum avium lanistæ :" lanista being the proper term for
the master of the gladiators.

Archbishop Becket in the reign of Henry II, is the first of our writers that mentions cock-fighting, describing it as the sport of schoolboys on Shrove Tuesday.[1]

Misson, in his Travels in England, translated by Ozell, p. 39, says: "Cockfighting is one of the great English diversions. They build amphitheaters for this purpose, and persons of quality sometimes appear at them. Great wagers are laid; but I'm told that a man may be damnably bubbled if he is not very sharp." At p. 304 he tells us: "Cock-fighting is a royal pleasure in England. Their combates between bulls and dogs, bears and dogs, and sometimes bulls and bears, are not battels to death, as those of cocks." [The following notice of the sport occurs in Poor Robin's Almanack for the year 1730: "Great consultations at the cockpit about battles, duels, victories, and what not. The battles proclaim'd first, and the victory afterwards, with a horn trumpet. But this hurry is not at the Cockpit at Whitehall, but the cockpit at the ale-house; not about the congress at Soissons, but in Moorfields; not about the fighting of armies, but cocks; where he is a great man, and scarce to be spoke to, who fed and trimm'd the cock that won, while the other party contents himself with believing that his cock had beat, had it not been for this chance blow, or that accident; and this creates another cock-fight. The loser is vex'd, and this sets the men a fighting; they go to law, and set the lawyers a fighting or scolding, till they have got the clients money."]

In the Statutes of St. Paul's School, A. D. 1518, the following clause occurs: "I will they use no cock-fightinge nor ridinge about of victorye, nor disputing at Saint Bartilemewe, which is but foolish babling and losse of time." (Knight's Life of Dean Colet, p. 362.) In Sir John Sinclair's Statistical Account of Scotland, 1792, iii. 378, the minister of Applecross, co. Ross, speaking of the schoolmaster's perquisites, says: "He has the cockfight dues, which are equal to one quarter's payment for each scholar."

Perhaps the subsequent extract from a MS. Life of Alder-

---

[1] Fitzstephen's words are: "Præterea quotannis, die qua dicitur Carnile-varia—singuli pueri suos apportant magistro suo gallos gallinaceos pugnaces, et totum illud antemeridianum datur ludo puerorum vacantium spectare in scholis suorum pugnas gallorum." See Dr. Pegge's edit. 1772, p. 74.

man Barnes, p. 4, which I have frequently cited in my History of Newcastle, about the date of James the Second's time, leads to the etymon of the word main, which signifies a battle off-hand. "His chief recreation was cock-fighting, and which long after, he was not able to say whether it did not at least border upon what was criminal, he is said to have been the Champion of the Cock-pit.[1] One cock particularly he had, called 'Spang Counter,' which came off victor in a great many battles à la main; but the sparks of Streatlem Castle killed it out of mere envy : so there was an end of Spang Counter and of his master's sport of cocking ever after."

The diversion of Cock-fighting was followed, though disapproved and prohibited in the 39th year of the reign of Edward III. ; also in the reign of Henry VIII., and A. D. 1569. It has been by some called a royal diversion, and, as every one knows, the Cockpit at Whitehall was erected by a crowned head,[2] for the more magnificent celebration of the sport. It was prohibited, however, by one of the acts of Oliver Cromwell, March the 31st, 1654.

Dr. Pegge describes the Welsh main, in order to expose the cruelty of it, and supposes it peculiar to this kingdom, known neither in China, nor in Persia, nor in Malacca, nor among the savage tribes of America. " Suppose," says he, "sixteen pair of cocks ; of these the sixteen conquerors are pitted the second time—the eight conquerors of these are pitted a third time—the four of these a fourth time—and, lastly, the two conquerors of these are pitted a fifth time : so that, incredible barbarity ! thirty-one of these creatures are sure to be thus inhumanly destroyed for the sport and pleasure, amid noise and nonsense, blended with the blasphemies and profaneness of those who will yet assume to themselves the name of Christians."

Without running into all the extravagance and superstition of Pythagoreans and Brahmins, yet certainly we have no right, no power or authority, to abuse and torment any of God's creatures, or needlessly to sport with their lives ; but, on the contrary, ought to use them with all possible tenderness and

[1] The Cockpit, it seems, was the school, and the master was the comptroller and director of the sport.

[2] King Henry VIIᵢ See Maitland, p. 1343. It appears that James I was remarkably fond of cock-fighting.

moderation. In a word, cock-fighting was an heathenish mode of diversion in its beginning, and at this day ought certainly to be confined to barbarous nations. Yet, it may and must be added, to aggravate the matter, and enhance our shame, our butchers in this cruel business have contrived a method, unknown to the ancients, of arming the heels of the bird with steel;[1] a device which has been considered a most noble improvement in the art, and indeed an invention highly worthy of men that delight in blood."

It still continues to be a favorite sport of the colliers in the north of England. The clamorous wants of their families solicit them to go to work in vain, when a match is heard of.

In performing some years ago the service appropriated to the Visitation of the Sick with one of these men, who died a few days afterwards, to my great astonishment I was interrupted by the crowing of a game cock, hung in a bag over his head. To this exultation an immediate answer was given by another cock concealed in a closet, to which the first replied, and instantly the last rejoined. I never remember to have met with an incident so truly of the tragi-comical cast as this, and could not proceed in the execution of that very solemn office till one of the disputants was removed. It had been industriously hung beside him, it should seem, for the sake of company. He had thus an opportunity of casting at an object he had dearly loved in the days of his health and strength, what Gray has well called " a long, lingering look behind."

BULL-RUNNING.

At Stamford, in Lincolnshire, an annual sport is celebrated, called Bull-running, of which the following account is taken from Butcher's Survey of the Town, 1717, pp. 76, 77. " It is

---

[1] Pliny mentions the spur, and calls it *telum*, but the gafle is a mere modern invention, as likewise is the great, and I suppose necessary, exactness in matching them. The Asiatics, however, use spurs that act on each side like a lancet, and which almost immediately decide the battle. Hence they are never permitted by the modern cock-fighters.

performed just the day six weeks before Christmas. The
butchers of the town, at their own charge, against the time,
provide the wildest bull they can get; this bull over night is
had into some stable or barn belonging to the Alderman. The
next morning proclamation is made by the common bellman
of the town, round about the same, that each one shut up their
shop-doors and gates, and that none, upon pain of imprison-
ment, offer to do any violence to strangers, for the preventing
whereof (the town being a great thoroughfare, and then being
in Term time) a guard is appointed for the passing of travellers
through the same (without hurt). That none have any iron
upon their bull-clubs or other staff which they pursue the bull
with. Which proclamation made, and the gates all shut up,
the bull is turned out of the Alderman's house, and then
hivie skivy, tag and rag, men, women, and children of all sorts
and sizes, with all the dogs in the town, promiscuously running
after him with their bull-clubs, spattering dirt in each other's
faces, that one would think them to be so many Furies started
out of hell for the punishment of Cerberus, as when Theseus
and Perillas conquered the place (as Ovid describes it)—

> ' A ragged troop of boys and girls
> Do pellow him with stones;
> With clubs, with whips, and many raps,
> They part his skin from bones ;'

and (which is the greater shame) I have seen both senatores
majorum gentium et matrones de eodem gradu, following this
bulling business.

"I can say no more of it, but only to set forth the antiquity
thereof (as the tradition goes): William Earl of Warren, the
first lord of this town, in the time of King John, standing
upon his castle walls in Stamford, viewing the fair prospects
of the river and meadow under the same, saw two bulls a fighting
for one cow ; a butcher of the town, the owner of one of those
bulls, with a great mastiff dog, accidentally coming by, set his
dog upon his own bull, who forced the same bull up into the
town, which no sooner was come within the same but all the
butchers' dogs, both great and small, follow'd in pursuit of
the bull, which by this time made stark mad with the noise of
the people and the fierceness of the dogs, ran over man, woman,
and child that stood in the way ; this caused all the butchers

and others in the town to rise up as it were in a tumult, making such an hideous noise that the sound thereof came into the castle unto the ears of Earl Warren, who presently thereupon mounted on horseback, rid into the town to see the business, which then appearing (to his humour) very delightful, he gave all those meadows in which the two bulls were at the first found fighting (which we now call the Castle Meadows) perpetually as a common to the butchers of the town (after the first grass is eaten) to keep their cattle in till the time of slaughter; upon this condition, that as upon that day on which this sport first began, which was (as I said before) that day six weeks before Christmas, the butchers of the town should from time to time, yearly for ever, find a mad bull for the continuance of that sport."

At present the magistracy of the town decline any interference with the bull-running.

A very long account of a similar practice at Tutbury will be found in Dr. Plott's History of Staffordshire, where it appears to have been a custom, belonging to the honour of the place, that the minstrels who came to matins there on the Feast of the Assumption of the Blessed Virgin should have a bull given them by the Prior of Tutbury, if they could take him on this side the river Dove nearest to the town; or else the Prior was to give them forty pence; for the enjoyment of which custom they were to give to the lord at the said feast twenty pence. See Plott's Staffordshire, p. 439; Shaw's History of Staffordshire, i. 52; and an elaborate memoir in the Archæologia, ii. 86, where the subject is considered by Dr. Pegge.

In later times the Tutbury Bull-running appears to have given rise to greater excesses than that at Stamford. "Happily," says Shaw, "a few years since, his Grace the Duke of Devonshire, who is grantee of the site of the priory, and the estates belonging to it, was pleased to abolish this barbarous custom, which it is to be hoped will have the same effect upon those similar brutish diversions of bull-baiting practised in many country towns (particularly in the north-west parts of this county) at that season of the year called the Wake.

LADY IN THE STRAW.

IT should seem that the expression of *the lady in the straw*, meant to signify the lady who is brought to bed, is derived from the circumstance that all beds were anciently stuffed with straw, so that it is synonymous with saying, " the lady in bed," or that is confined to her bed.[1]

There appears to have been some ceremonies anciently used when the lady took her chamber. It is stated, that when the Queen of King Henry VII. took her chamber in order to her delivery, "the Erles of Shrewsbury and of Kente hyld the towelles, whan the quene toke her rightes; and the torches ware holden by knightes. When she was comen into hir great chambre, she stode undre hir cloth of estate; then there was ordeyned a voide of espices and swet wyne : that doone, my lorde, the quenes chamberlain, in very goode wordes desired, in the Quene's name, the pepul there present to pray God to *sende hir the good oure :* and so she departed to her inner chambre." Strutt, iii. 157, from a MS. in the Cotton Library.

Some have thought, but I cannot be induced to accede to the opinion, that the term "lady in the straw," takes its rise from *a straw mattress* necessarily made use of during the time of delivery. In the Child-bearer's Cabinet, in "a rich closet of physical secrets collected by the elaborate paines of four severall students in physick," 4to. no date, p. 9, we read: " How, and wherewith the child-bed woman's bed ought to be furnished. A large boulster, made of linen cloth, must be *stuffed with straw*, and be spread on the ground, that her upper part may lye higher than her lower; on this the woman may lie, so that she may seem to lean and bow, rather than

---

[1] In the old Herbals we find descriptions of a herb entitled *the Ladies Bed-straw*. It appears that even so late as Henry VIII.'s time there were directions for certain persons to examine every night *the straw of the King's bed*, that no daggers might be concealed therein. In Plaine Percevall, the Peace-maker of England, printed in the time of Queen Elizabeth, we find an expression which strongly marks the general use of straw in beds during that reign: " These high-flying sparks will light on the heads of us all, and kindle in *our bed-straw*."

to lye drawing up her feet unto her, that she may receve no hurt."

Henry, in his History of Britain, i. 459, tells us, that " amongst the ancient Britons, when a birth was attended with any difficulty, they put certain girdles made for that purpose about the women in labour, which they imagined gave immediate and effectual relief. Such girdles were kept with care, till very lately, in many families in the Highlands of Scotland. They were impressed with several mystical figures ; and the ceremony of binding them about the woman's waist was accompanied with words and gestures, which showed the custom to have been of great antiquity, and to have come originally from the Druids."[1]

From an ancient 4to. MS, formerly in the collection of Herbert, dated 1475, I transcribe the following charm, or more properly charect, to be bound to the thigh of a lying-in woman : " For woman that travelyth of chylde, bynd thys wryt to her thye : In nomine Patris ✠ et Filii ✠ et Spiritus Sancti ✠ Amen. ✠ Per virtutem Domini sint medicina mei pia crux et passio Christi. ✠. Vulnera quinque Domini sint medicina mei. ✠. Sancta Maria peperit Christum. ✠. Sancta Anna peperit Mariam. ✠. Sancta Elizabet peperit Johannem. ✠. Sancta Cecilia peperit Remigium. ✠. Arepo tenet opera rotas. ✠. Christus vincit. ✠. Christus regnat. ✠ Christus dixit Lazare veni foras. ✠. Christus imperat. ✠. Christus te vocat. ✠ Mundus te gaudet. ✠. Lex te desiderat. ✠ Deus ultionum Dominus. ✠. Deus preliorum Dominus libera famulam tuam N. ✠ Dextra Domini fecit virtutem. a. g. l. a. ✠ Alpha ✠ et Ω. ✠.

[1] Levinus Lemnius, English translat. fol. 1658, p. 270, tells us, that " the jewel called Ætites, found in an eagle's nest, that has rings with little stones within it, being applied to the thigh of one that is in labour, makes a speedy and easy delivery ; which thing I have found true by experiment." Lupton, in his second book of Notable Things, 52, says : "Ætites, called the Eagle's stone, tyed to the left arm or side ; it brings this benefit to women with child, that they shall not be delivered before their time : besides that, it brings love between the man and the wife ; and if a woman have a painfull travail in the birth of her child, this stone, tyed to her thigh, brings an easy and light birth." Ibid. Book iv. 27 : " Let the woman that travels with her child (is in her labour) be girded with the skin that a serpent or snake casts off, and then she will quickly be delivered."— Tortola.

Anna peperit Mariam, ✠ Elizabet precursorem, ✠ Maria
Dominum nostrum Jesum Christum, sine dolore et tristicia.
O infans sive vivus sive mortuus exi foras ✠ Christus te vocat
ad lucem. ✠. Agyos. ✠ Agyos. ✠ Agyos. ✠
Christus vincit. ✠ Christus imperat. ✠ Christus regnat.
✠ Sanctus ✠ Sanctus ✠ Sanctus ✠ Dominus Deus. ✠
Christus qui es, qui eras, ✠ et qui venturus es. ✠ Amen.
bhurnon ✠ blictaono ✠ Christus Nazarenus ✠ Rex
Judeorum fili Dei ✠ miserere mei ✠ Amen."[1]

The following is an extract from Copley's Wits, Fits, and
Fancies, 1614 : "A gentlewoman in extremitie of labour sware
that if it pleased God she might escape death for that once,
she would never in all her life after hazard herselfe to the like
daunger againe ; but being at last safely delivered, she then
said to one of the midwives, ' So, now *put out* THE HOLY
CANDLE, *and keepe it till the next time.*' "

[1] The following customs of childbirth are noticed in the Traité des
Superstitions of M. Thiers, i. 320 : " Lors qu'une femme est preste d'ac-
coucher, prendre *sa ceinture*, aller à l'Eglise, *lier la cloche avec cette
ceinture* et la faire sonner trois coups afin que cette femme accouche
heureusement.   Martin de Arles, Archidiacre de Pampelonne (Tract. de
Superstition.) asseure que cette superstition est fort en usage dans tout son
pais : ' Superstitiosum est quod ferè in omni hac nostra patria observatur,
ut âum femina est propinqua partui, novam (zonam ?) vel corrigiam qua
præcingitur, accipientes, ad ecclesiam occurrunt, et cymbalum modo quo
possunt corrigia illa vel zona circumdant, et ter percutientes cymbalum,
sonum illum credunt valere ad prosperum partum, quod est superstitiosum
et vanum.' "   Ibid. p. 327 : " Quand une femme est en mal d'enfant, luy
faire mettre le haut de chausse de son mari, afin qu'elle accouche sans
douleur."   Ibid. p. 329 : " Mettre les pieds et les mains des enfans dans
la glace, ou, s'il n'y a point de glace, dans l'eau froide, aussi-tost qu'ils
sont nez et avant qu'ils ayent receu le baptesme, pour empescher, qu'ils
n'ayent l'ongleè aux pieds ou aux mains : et leur faire boire du vin aussi-
tost qu'ils son venus au monde, pour empecher qu'ils ne s'enyvrent."
Ibid. p. 327 : " Fendre un chesne, et faire passer trois fois un enfans par
dedans, afin de la guerir de la hergne.   Le pere et la mere de l'enfant
doivent estre à chacun un costè du chesne."   Ibid. p. 332 : " Percer le
toit de la maison d'une femme qui est en travail d'enfant, avec une pierre,
ou avec une fleche, dont on aura tuè trois animaux, sçavoir un homme, un
sanglier, et une ourse, de trois divers coups, pour la faire aussi-tost ac
coucher : ce qui arrive encore plus asseurement quand on perce la maison
avec la hache ou le sabre d'un soldat arrachè du corps d'un homme, avant
qu'il soit tombè par terre."   Ibid. p. 334 : " Chasser les mouches lorsqu'une femme est en travail d'enfant, de crainte qu'elle n'accouche d'une
fille."

In the Injunctions at the Visitation of Edmunde (Bonner) Bishop of London from September 3d, 1554, to October 8th, 1555, 4to., we read : " A mydwyfe (of the diocese and juris- diction of London) shal not use or exercise any witchecrafte, charmes, sorcerye, invocations or praiers, other then suche as be allowable and may stand with the lawes and ordinances of the Catholike Churche." In John Bale's Comedye concern- ynge thre Lawes, 1538, Idolatry says :

" Yea, but now ych am a she
And a good MYDWYFE perdé,
   Yonge chyldren can I *charme,*
With whysperynges and whysshynges,
With crossynges and with kyssynges,
With blasynges and with blessynges,
   That spretes do them no harme."

In the same Comedy, Hypocrysy is introduced mentioning the following charms against barrenness :

" In Parys we have the mantell of Saynt Lewes,
Which women seke moch, for helpe of their barrennes :
For be it ones layed upon a wommanys bellye,
She go thens with chylde, the myracles are seene there daylye.

And as for Lyons, there is the length of our Lorde
In a great pyller. She that will with a coorde
Be fast bound to it, and *take soche chaunce as fall,*
Shall sure have chylde, for within it is hollowe all."

In the Articles to be enquired in the Visitacyon in the fyrst yeare of Queen Elizabeth, 1559, the following occurs: "Item, whether you knowe anye that doe use charmes, sorcery, en- chauntmentes, invocations, circles, witchecraftes, southsayinge, or any lyke craftes or imaginacions invented by the Devyl, and *specially in the tyme of women's travayle.*" It appears from Strype's Annals of the Reformation, i. 537, under 1567, that then midwives took an oath, inter alia, not to "suffer any other bodies child to be set, brought, or laid before any woman delivered of child, in the place of her natural child, so far forth as I can know and understand. Also I will not use any kind of sorcery or incantation in the time of the travail of any woman." In the collection entitled Sylva, or the Wood, p. 130, we read that " a few years ago, in this same village, the women in labour used to drinke the urine of their husbands, who were all the while stationed, as I have seen the cows in St. James's Park, straining themselves to give as much as they can."

The following passage from the Lucky Idiot, or Fools have Fortune, from the Spanish of Don Quevedo de Alcala, by a a Person of Quality, 1734, mentions a custom in Spain : " I remember once that in the dead time of the night, there came a country fellow to my uncle in a great haste, intreating him to give order for *knocking the bells, his wife being in labour* (*a thing usual in* SPAIN) ; my good curate then waked me out of a sound sleep, saying, Rise, Pedro, instantly, and *ring the bells for child-birth* quickly, quickly. I got up immediately, and as fools have good memories, I retained the words quickly, quickly, and knocked the bells so nimbly, that the inhabitants of the rown really believed it had been for fire." p. 13.

The subsequent poem, founded on a singular custom is from Lucasta, Posthume Poems of Richard Lovelace, Esq., 1659, p. 27 :

" *To a Lady with Child that asked an old Shirt.*

" And why an honour'd ragged shirt, that shows
Like tatter'd ensigns, all its bodies blows ?
Should it be swathed in a vest so dire,
It were enough to set the child on fire.
But since *to ladies 't hath a custome been
Linnen to send, that travail and lye in ;*
To the nine sempstresses, my former friends,
I su'd, but they had nought but shreds and ends.
At last, the jolli'st of the three times three
Rent th' apron from her smock, and gave it me.
'Twas soft and gentle, subtly spun, no doubt.
Pardon my boldness, madam ; here's the clout."

GROANING CAKE AND CHEESE.

AGAINST the time of the good wife's delivery, it has been everywhere the custom for the husband to provide a large cheese and a cake. These, from time immemorial, have been the objects of ancient superstition. It was not unusual to preserve for many years, I know not for what superstitious intent, pieces of "the Groaning Cake." Thus I read in

Gayton's Festivous Notes upon Don Quixot, p. 17, "And hath a piece of the Groaning Cake (as they call it), which she kept religiously with her Good Friday bun, full forty years unmouldy and un-mouse-eaten." Misson, in his Travels in England, translated by Ozell, p. 35, says: "The custom here is not to make great feasts at the birth of their children ; they drink a glass of wine, and eat a bit of *a certain cake,* which is seldom made but upon these occasions."

In the Descriptive Account of Eastbourne in Sussex, p. 123, there is a very singular custom recited under the name of Sops and Ale, which still prevails in that place, after any lady, or respectable farmer or tradesman's wife, is delivered of a child.

It is customary at Oxford to cut the cheese (called in the north of England, in allusion to the mother's complaints at her delivery, " the Groaning Cheese") in the middle when the child is born, and so by degrees form it into a large kind of ring, through which the child must be passed on the day of the christening. In other places, the first cut of the sick wife's cheese (so also they call the Groaning Cheese) is to be divided into little pieces, and tossed in the midwife's smock, to cause young women to dream of their lovers.[1] Slices of the first cut of the Groaning Cheese are in the north of England laid under the pillows of young persons for the above purpose.

In the old play of the Vow-Breaker, or the Fayre Maid of Clifton, 1636, in a scene where is discovered " a bed covered with white, enter Prattle, Magpy, Long Tongue, Barren with a child, *Anne in bed ;*" Boote says, " Neece, bring *the groaning cheece,* and all requisites; I must supply the father's place, and bid god-fathers." [The following allusion to this cheese occurs in Westward for Smelts, 1620 : " At last, hee looked out of the window, asking who knockt at the doore ? 'Tis I, kinde husband (answered shee), that have beene at a womans labour; prethee, sweet heart, open the doore. All these kinde words would not get her admittance, but gained this churlish answere at his hands : Hast thou beene at a woman's labour ? Then prethee, sweet heart, returne, and amongst the residue of the

---

[1] [In some parts of the north of England, at the birth of a child, the first slice of the *Groaning Cake* is cut into small pieces, and well shaken in the smock of the howdie wife : or should a man attend on the occasion, it undergoes the same process in the shirt of the accoucheur.]

wives, help thou to devoure the *groning cheese*, and sucke up the honest mans ale till you are drunke; by that time 'twill be day light, and I will have thy friends at thy returne, who shall give thee thankes for thy charitie."]

In a Voyage to Holland, being an Account of the late Entertainment of King William the Third and the several Princes there, by an English Gentleman attending the Court of the King of Great Britain, 1691, p. 23, we read: "Where the woman lies in, *the ringle of the door does pennance*, and is lapped about with linnen, either to shew you that loud knocking may wake the child, or else that for a month the ring is not to be run at; but if the child be dead, there is thrust out a nosegay tied to a stick's end, perhaps for an emblem of the life of man, which may wither as soon as born; or else to let you know, that though these fade upon their gathering, yet from the same stock the next year a new shoot may spring." So, in an old translation of Erasmus's Dialogues, by William Burton, 4to., in that of the Woman in Child-bed, occurs the following passage: "*Eut.* By chaunce I (passing by these houses) *sawe the crowe*, or *the ring of the doore bound about with white linnen cloth*, and I marvelled what the reason of it should be. *Fab.* Are you such a stranger in this countrey that you doe not know the reason of that? doe not you knowe that *it is a signe that there is a woman lying in* where that is?"

In Poor Robin's Almanack for the year 1676, that facetious periodical, noting the expenses of breeding wives to their husbands, introduces the following items:

> " For a nurse, the child to dandle,
> Sugar, sope, *spic'd pots*, and candle,
> *A groaning chair*,[1] and eke *a cradle*.
> Blanckets of a several scantling,
> Therein for to wrap the bantling;
> *Sweetmeats* from comfit-maker's trade,
> When the child's a Christian made;
> *Pincushions* and such other knacks
> A child-bed woman always lacks,
> Caudles, grewels, costly jellies," &c.

---

[1] An essayist in the Gent. Mag. for May 1732, ii. 740, observes: " Among the women there is the *groaning chair*, in which the matron sits to receive visits of congratulation. This is a kind of *female ovation* due to every good woman who goes through such eminent perils in the service of her country."

Bartholinus informs us, that the Danish women, before they put the new-born infant into the cradle, place there, or over the door, as amulets, to prevent the evil spirits from hurting the child, garlic, salt, bread, and steel, or some cutting instrument made of that metal.[1]   Something like this obtained in England.   Gregory, in his Posthuma, p. 97, mentions " an ordinarie superstition of the old wives, who dare not intrust a childe in a cradle by itself alone without a candle." This he attributes to their fear of night-hags.

In Scotland, children dying unbaptised (called Tarans) were supposed to wander in woods and solitudes, lamenting their hard fate, and were said to be often seen.   In the North of England it is thought very unlucky to go over their graves. It is vulgarly called going over " unchristened ground."   In the Gentle Shepherd, Bauldy describing Mause as a witch, says of her :

> " At midnight hours o'er the kirk-yard she raves,
> And howks unchristen'd weans out of their graves."

In the Highlands of Scotland, as Mr. Pennant informs us, children are watched till the christening is over, lest they should be stolen or changed by the fairies.   To this notion Shakespeare alludes when he makes King Henry the Fourth, speaking of Hotspur in comparison with his own profligate son, say as follows :

> " O that it could be prov'd
> That some night-tripping fairy had exchang'd,
> In cradle-clothes, our children where they lay,
> And call'd mine Percy, his Plantagenet !
> Then would I have his Harry, and he mine."

---

[1] In his Century of rare Anatomical Histories, p. 19, " Muliereulæ superstitiosæ nostrates statim antequam infantem nuper natum in cunis reponunt, huic Caprimulgo (a spirit so called that is supposed to hurt infants) occurrunt allio, sale, pane et chalybe, vel instrumento incisorio ex chalybe, sive in cunis posito, sive supra ostium."   We read also in Bartholinus's treatise de Puerperio Veterum, p. 157, " Pueris, sive ante lustrationem sive post, dormientibus Caprimulgus insidiatur et Lilith, item sagæ seu stryges variis fascinis, quæ vel allio, vel alysso, vel re turpi in collo ex annulo appensa abiguntur.   Res illa turpis non Satyri fuit species, sed Priapi.   Fascinus erat res turpicula e collo pueris appensa, teste Varrone." Lib. vi.

Spenser has the like thought :

"From thence a fairy thee unweeting reft
There as thou slep'st in tender swadling band,
And her base elfin brood there for thee left :
Such men do *changelings* call, so chang'd by fairy theft."

It was thought that fairies could only change their weakly
and starveling elves for the more robust offspring of men,
before baptism, whence the above custom in the Highlands.
One of the methods of discovering whether a child belongs to
the fairies or not, is printed in a book entitled, A Pleasant
Treatise of Witchcraft. See Grose's Account.

The word *changeling*, in its modern acceptation, implies one
almost an idiot, evincing what was once the popular creed on
this subject; for as all the fairy children were a little back-
ward of their tongue, and seemingly idiots, therefore stunted
and idiotical children were supposed changelings. This superstition has not escaped the learned Moresin : "Papatus credit
albatas mulieres, et id genus larvas, pueros integros auferre,
aliosque suggerere monstruosos, et debiles multis partibus ;
aut ad baptisterium cum aliis commutare, aut ad templi in-
troitum." Papatus, p. 139.

Pennant, in his History of Whiteford, &c. p. 5, speaking of
"the Fairy Oak," of which also he exhibits a portrait, relates
this curious circumstance respecting it : " In this very century,
a poor cottager, who lived near the spot, had a child who grew
uncommonly peevish ; the parents attributed this to the fairies,
and imagined that it was a *changeling*. They took the child,
put it in a cradle, and left it all night beneath the tree, in
hopes that the *tylwydd tèg*, or *fairy family*, or the *fairy folk*,
would restore their own before morning. When morning
came, they found the child perfectly quiet, so went away with
it, quite confirmed in their belief."

Waldron, in his description of the Isle of Man (Works,
1731, p. 128), tells us : "The old story of infants being
changed in their cradles is here in such credit, that mothers
are in continual terror at the thoughts of it. I was prevailed
upon myself to go and see a child, who, they told me, was one
of these changelings, and indeed must own was not a little
surprised as well as shocked at the sight. Nothing under
heaven could have a more beautiful face ; but though between
five and six years old, and seemingly healthy, he was so far

from being able to walk or stand, that he could not so much as move any one joint his limbs were vastly long for his age, but smaller than an infant's of six months : his complexion was perfectly delicate, and he had the finest hair in the world : he never spoke nor cryed, eat scarce any thing, and was very seldom seen to smile ; but if any one called him a fairy-elf he would frown, and fix his eyes so earnestly on those who said it, as if he would look them through. His mother, or at least his supposed mother, being very poor, frequently went out a chairing, and left him a whole day together : the neighbours, out of curiosity, have often looked in at the window to see how he behaved when alone, which, whenever they did, they were sure to find him laughing, and in the utmost delight. This made them judge that he was not without company more pleasing to him than any mortal's could be ; and what made this conjecture seem the more reasonable, was, that if he were left ever so dirty, the woman at her return saw him with a clean face, and his hair combed with the utmost exactness and nicety." He mentions (ibid. p. 132,) "Another woman, who, being great with child, and expecting every moment the good hour, as she lay awake one night in her bed, she saw seven or eight little women come into her chamber, one of whom had an infant in her arms. They were followed by a man of the same size, in the habit of a minister." A mock christening ensued, and "they baptized the infant by the name of Joan, which made her know she was pregnant of a girl, as it proved a few days after, when she was delivered."

It appears anciently to have been customary to give a large entertainment at the churching, and previous to that at the christening.[1]

Harrison, in his Description of Britain, in Holinshed's Chronicles, complains of the excessive feasting, as well at other festive meetings, as at " Purifications of women." In

[1] See Dr. Whitaker's History of Craven, p. 220, where Master John Norton " gate leave of my old lord to have half a stagg for his wife's churching:" on which he observes in a note, " Hence it appears that thanksgivings after child-birth were antiently celebrated with feasting." For this custom I have a still older authority: " In duobus hogsheveds vini albi empt. apud Ebor. erga Purificationem Dominæ, tam post partum Magistri mei nuper de Clifford, quam post partum Magistri mei nunc de Clifford, lxvis. viijd." Compotus Tho. Dom. Clifford a° 15 Hen. VI. or 1437.

the Pleasant Historie of Thomas of Reading, 1632, we read:
" Sutton's wife, of Salisbury, which had lately bin delivered of
a sonne, against her going to church prepared great cheare:
at what time Simon's wife, of Southampton, came thither,
and so did divers others of the clothiers wives, onely to make
merry at this *churching feast*." In the Batchellor's Banquet,
1677, the lady is introduced telling her husband: "You willed
me (I was sent for) to go to Mistress M. *churching*, and when
I came thither *I found great cheer*, and *no small company of
wives ;*" and the lady is asked : " If I had ever *a new gown to
be churched in*." Among Shipman's Poems, 1683, is one
dated 1667, and entitled, " *The Churching Feast*,—to Sir
Clifford Clifton, *for a fat doe*," p. 123.

The poem entitled Julia's Churching, or Purification, however, in Herrick's Hesperides, p. 339, makes no mention of
the churching entertainment :

> " Put on thy holy fillitings and so
> To th' temple with the sober midwife go.
> Attended thus (in a most solemn wise)
> By those who serve the child-bed misteries,
> Burn first thine incense; next, when as thou see'st
> The candid stole thrown o'er the pious priest,
> With reverend curtsies come, and to him bring
> Thy free (and not decurted) offering.
> All rites well ended, with faire auspice come
> (As to the breaking of a bride-cake) home,
> Where ceremonious Hymen shall for thee
> Provide a second epithalamie."

In the first volume of Proclamations, in the archives of
the Society of Antiquaries of London, p. 134, is preserved an
original one, printed in black letter, and dated the 16th of
November, 30 Henry VIII. in which, among many "laudable
ceremonies and rytes" enjoined to be retained, is the following:
" Ceremonies used at purification of women delivered of chylde,
and offerynge of theyr crysomes."

In a most rare book, entitled 'A Parte of a Register, contayninge sundrie memorable matters, written by divers godly
and learned in our time, which stande for and desire reformation of our Church, in discipline and ceremonies, accordinge
to the pure worde of God and the lawe of our lande,' 4to.
said by Dr. Bancroft to have been printed at Edinburgh by
Robert Waldegrave (who printed most of the Puritan books

and libels in the latter end of Queen Elizabeth's reign), p. 64, in a list of "grosse poyntes of Poperie, evident to all men," is enumerated the following : "The Churching of women with this psalme, *that the sunne and moone shall not burne them :*" as is ibid. p. 63, "The offeringe of the woman at hir Churching."

Lupton, in his first book of Notable Things, ed. 1660, p. 49, says : "If a man be the first that a woman meets after she comes out of the church, when she is newly churched, it signifies that her next child will be a boy ; if she meet a woman, then a wench is likely to be her next child. This is credibly reported to me to be true."

In Sir John Sinclair's Statistical Account of Scotland, xxi. 147, parish of Monquhitter, it is said : "It was most unhappy for a woman, after bringing forth a child, to offer a visit, or for her neighbours to receive it, till she had been duly churched. How strongly did this enforce gratitude to the Supreme Being for a safe delivery! On the day when such a woman was churched, every family, favoured with a call, were bound to set meat and drink before her : and when they omitted to do so, they and theirs were to be loaded with her hunger. What was this, but an obligation on all who had it in their power to do the needful to prevent a feeble woman from fainting for want ?"

CHRISTENING CUSTOMS.

THE learned Dr. Moresin informs us of a remarkable custom, which he himself was an eye-witness of in Scotland : they take, says he, on their return from church, the newly-baptised infant, and vibrate it three or four times gently over a flame, saying, and repeating it thrice, "Let the flame consume thee now or never."[1] Borlase, from Martin's Western Islands, p. 117,

---

[1] "Atque hodie recens baptizatos infantes (ut vidi fieri ab anicula in Scotia olim qui sui papatus reliquias saperet) statim atque domum redierint in limine oblatis eduliis bene venire dicunt, statimque importatos, anicula, sive obstetrix fuerit, fasciis involutos accipit, et per flammam ter quaterve leniter vibrant, verbis his additis, ' Jam te flamma, si unquam, absumat, terque verba repetunt.'" Papatus, p. 72.

tells us: "The same lustration, by carrying of fire, is performed round about women after child-bearing, and round
about children *before they are christened*, as an effectual means
to preserve both the mother and infant from the power of evil
spirits."

It is very observable here, that there was a feast at Athens,
kept by private families, called Amphidromia, on the fifth day
after the birth of the child, when it was the custom for the
gossips to run round the fire with the infant in their arms,
and then, having delivered it to the nurse, they were entertained with feasting and dancing.

Grose tells us there is a superstition that a child who does
not cry when sprinkled in baptism will not live.[1] He has
added another idea, equally well founded, that children pre-
maturely wise are not long-lived, that is, rarely reach maturity:
a notion which we find quoted by Shakespeare, and put into
the mouth of Richard the Third.

In the Statistical Account of Scotland, 1793, vii. 560,
Parishes of Kirkwall and St. Ola, we read that the inhabitants
" would consider it as an unhappy omen, were they by any
means disappointed in getting themselves married, or their
children baptized, on the very day which they had previously
fixed in their minds for that purpose." Ibid. xiv. 261, 1795,

[1] In Memorable Things noted in the Description of the World, 8vo. p. 113,
we read: " About children's necks the wild Irish hung the beginning of
St. John's Gospel, a crooked nail of a horse-shoe, or a piece of a wolve's
skin, and both the sucking child and nurse were girt with girdles finely
plated with woman's hair: so far they wandered into the ways of errour,
in making these arms the strength of their healths." Ibid. p. 111, it is
said: " Of the same people Solinus affirmeth, that they are so given to war,
that the mother, at the birth of a man child, feedeth the first meat into
her infant's mouth upon the point of her husband's sword, and with
heathenish imprecations wishes that it may dye no otherwise then in war,
or by sword." Giraldus Cambrensis saith, "At the baptizing of the infants
of the wild Irish, their manner was not to dip their right arms into the
water, that so as they thought they might give a more deep and incurable
blow." Here is a proof that the whole body of the child was anciently
commonly immersed in the baptismal font. See also Gough's edit. of
Camden, 1789, iii. 658. Camden relates, in addition to this, that " if a
child is at any time out of order, they sprinkle it with the stalest urine
they can get." The following singular superstition concerning a child's
bread and butter will be thought uncommonly singular: " Si puerulo panis
cadat in butyrum, indicium [est] vitæ infortunatæ, si in alteram faciem,
fortunatæ." Pet. Molinæi Vates, p. 154.

Parish of Kiltinan Argyleshire, wo read, "There is one per‑ nicious practice that prevails much in this parish, which took its rise from this source, which is, that of carrying their chil‑ dren out to baptism on the first or second day after birth. Many of them, although they had it in their option to have their children baptized in their own houses, by waiting one day, prefer carrying them seven or eight miles to church, in the worst weather in December or January, by which folly they too often sacrifice the lives of their infants to the phantom of superstition." Ibid. xv. 311, the minister of the parishes of South Ronaldsay and Burray, two of the Orkney Islands, describing the manners of the inhabitants, says : " Within these last seven years the minister has been twice interrupted in administering baptism to a female child, *before the male child*, who was baptised immediately after. When the service was over, he was gravely told he had done very wrong, for, as the female child was first baptised, she would, on her coming to the years of discretion, most certainly have a strong beard, and the boy would have none.'

In the above work, v. 83, the minister of Logierait, in Perthshire, describing the superstitious opinions and practices in that parish, says : " When a child was baptised privately, it was, not long since, customary to put the child upon a clean basket, having a cloth previously spread over it, with bread and cheese put into the cloth ; and thus to move the basket three times successively round the iron crook which hangs over the fire, from the roof of the house, for the purpose of supporting the pots when water is boiled or victuals are pre‑ pared. This might be anciently intended to counteract the malignant arts which witches and evil spirits were imagined to practise against new-born infants."

Bulwer, in his Chirologia, p. 62, remarks, that " There is a tradition our midwives have concerning children borne open‑ handed, that such will prove of a bountiful disposition and frank-handed."

The following occurs in the Second Part of Dekker's Honest Whore, 1630 : " I am the most wretched fellow : *sure some left-handed priest christened me*, I am so unlucky."

In Herrick's Hesperides, p. 336, we have the following charms :

> " Bring the holy crust of bread,
> Lay it underneath the head ;
> 'Tis a certain charm to keep
> Hags away while children sleep.

> " Let the superstitious wife
> Neer the child's heart lay a knife ;
> Point be up, and haft be down,
> (While she gossips in the towne :)
> This, 'mongst other mystick charms,
> Keeps the sleeping child from harmes."

The following modern Scottish superstitions respecting new-born children are introduced into Helenore, or the Fortunate Shepherdess, a poem in the broad Scotch dialect, by Alexander Ross, 1778, p. 12 :

> " Gryte was the care, and tut'ry that was ha'en,
> Baith night and day about the bony weeane,
> The jizzen-bed[1] wi' rantry leaves[2] was sain'd,[3]
> And sik like things as the auld grannies kend ;
> Jeans paps *wi' sa't and water washen clean,*
> Reed[4] that her milk get wrang, fan it was green.
> Neist the first hippen to the green was flung,
> And thereat seeful[5] words baith said and sung.
> A clear-burnt coal wi' the het tongs was ta'en
> Frae out the ingle-mids fu' clear and clean,
> And throw the *corsy-belly*[6] letten fa,
> For fear the weeane should be ta'en awa ;
> Dowing[7] and growing was the daily pray'r,
> And Nory was brought up wi' unco care."

It appears to have been anciently the custom, at christening entertainments, for the guests not only to eat as much as they pleased, but also, for the ladies at least, to carry away as much as they liked in their pockets. In the Batchellor's Banquet, 1677, we read : " What cost and trouble it will be to have all things fine against the christening day ; what store of sugar, biskets, comphets, and caraways, marmalet, and marchphane, with all kind of sweet suckers and super-fluous banquetting stuff, with a hundred other odd and need-less trifles, which at that time *must fill the pockets* of dainty dames !" I find the mother called here " the childwife."

In Strype's edition of Stowe's Survey of London, i. 260,

---

[1] The linen bed.   [2] I suppose meaning rowen tree.   [3] Blessed.
For fear.   [5] Pleasant.   [6] An infant's first shirt.   Thriving.

accounts are given of two great christenings in 1561 and 1562. After the first was " a splendid banquet at home ;" and the other, we read, " was concluded with a great banquet, consisting of wafers and hypocras, French, Gascoign, and Rhenish wines, with great plenty, and all their servants had a banquet in the hall with divers dishes." Waldron, in his Description of the Isle of Man (Works, p. 170), speaking of the Manx christenings, says : " The whole country round are invited to them ; and, after having baptised the child, which they always do in the church, let them live ever so distant from it, they return to the house, and spend the whole day, and good part of the night, in feasting." In Whimzies, or a New Cast of Characters, 1631, p. 192, speaking of a yealous (jealous) neighbour, the author says : " Store of bisket, wafers, and careawayes, hee bestowes at his child's christning, yet are his cares nothing lessned ; he is perswaded that he may eate his part of this babe, and never breake his fast."

At the christening entertainments of many of the poorer sort of people in the north of England (who are so unfortunate as to provide more mouths than they can with convenience find meat for), great collections are oftentimes made by the guests, and such as will far more than defray the expenses of the feast of which they have been partaking. Kennett, in a MS. note to Aubrey's Remains of Gentilism, says : " At Burcester, in Oxfordshire, at a christening, the women bring every one a cake, and present one first to the minister, if present. At Wendlebury, and other places, they bring their cakes at a gossiping, and give a large cake to the father of the child, which they call a rocking cake." Hutchinson, in his History of Northumberland, tells us that children in that county, when first sent abroad in the arms of the nurse to visit a neighbour, are presented with an egg, salt, and fine bread. It is customary there, also, for the midwife, &c., to provide two slices, one of bread, and the other of cheese, which are presented to the first person they meet in the procession to church at a christening. The person who receives this homely present must give the child in return three different things, wishing it at the same time health and beauty. The gentleman who informed me of this, happening once to fall in the way of such a party, and to receive the above present, was at a loss how to make the triple return, till he bethought

II.   6

himself of laying upon the child which was held out to him, a shilling, a halfpenny, and a pinch of snuff. When they meet more than one person together, it is usual to single out the nearest to the woman that carries the child.

There is a singular custom prevailing in the country of the Lesgins, one of the seventeen Tartarian nations. "Whenever the Usmei, or chief, has a son, he is carried round from village to village, and alternately suckled by every woman who has a child at her breast, till he is weaned. This custom by establishing a kind of brotherhood between the prince and his subjects, singularly endears them to each other." See the Europ. Mag. for June, 1801, p. 408.

Hutchinson observes that " the egg was a sacred emblem, and seems a gift well adapted to infancy." Bryant says, "An egg, containing in it the elements of life, was thought no improper emblem of the ark, in which were preserved the rudiments of the future world ; hence in the Dionusiaca and in other Mysteries, one part of the nocturnal ceremony consisted in the consecration of an egg. By this, as we are informed by Porphyry, was signified the world. It seems to have been a favorite symbol, and very ancient, and we find it adopted among many nations. It was said by the Persians of Orosmasdes, that he formed mankind, and inclosed them in an egg. Cakes and salt were used in religious rites by the ancients. The Jews probably adopted their appropriation from the Egyptians : ' And if thou bring an oblation of a meat-offering baken in the oven, it shall be unleavened cakes of fine flour,' &c., Levit. ii. 4.—' With all thine offerings thou shalt offer salt.' " Ibid. p. 13.

Cowell, in his Law Dictionary, on the word " Kichell," says: " It was a good old custom for godfathers and godmothers, every time their godchildren asked them blessing, to give them a cake, which was a gods-kichell ; it is still a proverbial saying in some countries, ' Ask me a blessing, and I will give you some plum-cake.' "

Among superstitions relating to children, the following is cited by Bourne, in the Antiquitates Vulgares, chap. xviii., from Bingham on St. Austin : " If when two friends are talking together, a stone, or a dog, or a child, happens to come between them, they tread the stone to pieces, as the divider of their friendship, and this is tolerable in comparison of beating an

innocent child that comes between them. But it is more
pleasant that sometimes the children's quarrel is revenged by
the dogs : for many times they are so superstitious as to dare
to beat the dog that comes between them, who turning again
upon him that smites him, sends him from seeking a vain remedy, to seek a real physician indeed."

It was anciently the custom for the sponsors at christenings
to offer gilt spoons as presents to the child : these spoons were
called Apostle spoons, because the figures of the twelve
Apostles were chased or carved on the tops of the handles.
Opulent sponsors gave the whole twelve. Those in middling
circumstances gave four ; and the poorer sort contented themselves with the gift of one, exhibiting the figure of any saint
in honour of whom the child received its name. It is in
allusion to this custom that when Cranmer professes to be
unworthy of being sponsor to the young Princess, Shakespeare
makes the King reply, "Come, come, my lord, you'd spare
your spoons." In the year 1560, we find entered in the books
of the Stationers' Company : "A spoyne, the gyfte of Master
Reginold Wolfe, all gylte, with the pycture of *St. John.*"
Ben Jonson, also, in his Bartholomew Fair, mentions spoons
of this kind : "And all this for the hope of a couple of *Apostle
spoons* and a cup to eat caudle in." So, in Middleton's
Comedy of a Chaste Maid of Cheapside, 1620. "*Second
Gossip.* What has he given her? What is it, Gossip?—*Third
Gos.* A faire high-standing cup and two great *postle spoons,*
one of them gilt." Again, in Sir William Davenant's Comedy
of the Wits, 1639 :

> " My pendants, carcanets, and rings,
> My christening caudle-cup and *spoons,*
> Are dissolved into that lump."

Again, in the Noble Gentleman, by Beaumont and Fletcher :

> " I'll be a gossip. Bewford,
> I have an odd *Apostle spoon.*"

In Shipman's Gossips, 1666, Poems, 1683, p. 113, we
read :

> " Since friends are scarce, and neighbours many,
> Who will lend mouths, but not a penny,
> *I* (if you grant not a supply)
> Must e'en provide a *chrisome pye :*"

i. e. serve up the child in a pie. Our author is pleasant on

the failure of the old custom of giving *Apostle spoons*, &c.,
at christenings :

> " Especially since gossips now
> Eat more at christnings, than bestow.[1]
> Formerly when they used to troul
> Gilt bowls of sack, they gave the bowl
> *Two spoons at least ;* an use ill kept ;
> 'Tis well now if our own be left."

With respect to the "crisome pye," it is well known that
"crisome signifies properly the white cloth, which is set by
the minister of baptism upon the head of a child newly
anointed with chrism (a kind of hallowed ointment used by
Roman Catholics in the sacrament of baptism and for certain
other unctions, composed of oyl and balm) after his baptism.
Now it is vulgarly taken for the white cloth put about or upon
a child newly christened, in token of his baptism ; wherewith
the women used to shroud the child, if dying within the month;
otherwise it is usually brought to church at the day of purification."[2]   Blount's Glossographia, in *v.*

We find, ibid., under Natal or Natalitious Gifts, among the
Grecians, " the fifth day after the child's birth, the neighbours
sent in gifts or small tokens ; from which custom, that among
Christians of the godfathers sending gifts to the baptised infant is thought to have flown ; and that also of the neighbours
sending gifts to the mother of it, as is still used in North
Wales."   In the Comforts of Wooing, p. 163, "The god-
mother hearing when the child's to be *coated,* brings it a gilt
coral, a silver spoon, and porringer, and a brave new tankard

[1] M. Stevenson, in the Twelve Moneths, 1661, p. 37, speaking of the
month of August, observes : " *The new wheat makes the gossips cake,*
and the bride-cup is carried above the heads of the whole parish."
[2] In Strype, i. 215, A.D. 1560, it is said to have been enjoined that,
" to avoid contention, let the curate have the value of the chrisome, not
under the value of 4d. and above as they can agree, and as the state of
the parents may require."   In the account of Dunton church, in Barnstable
Hundred, in Morant's Essex, i. 219, is the following remark : " Here has
been a custom, time out of mind, at the churching of a woman, for her to
give a white cambric handkerchief to the minister as an offering.   This is
observed by Mr. Lewis in his History of the Isle of Thanet, where the
same custom is kept up."   In Articles to be inquired of in Chichester
Diocese, A.D. 1638, occurs the following : " Doth the woman who is to be
churched use the ancient accustomed habit in such cases, *with a white veil
or kerchiefe upon her head ?*"

of the same metal   The godfathers come too, the one with a whole piece of flowered silk, the other with a set of *gilt spoons*, the gifts of Lord Mayors at several times."

In Howe's edition of Stow's Chronicle, 1631, p. 1039, speaking of the life and reign of King James, he observes: "At this time, and for many yeares before, it was not the use and custome (as now it is) for godfathers and godmothers generally to give plate at the baptisme of children (as *spoones*, cupps, and such like), but onely to give *christening shirts*, with *little bands and cuffs*, wrought either with silke or blew threed, the best of them, for chiefe persons weare, edged with a small lace of blacke silke and gold, the highest price of which for great men's children was seldom above a noble, and the common sort, two, three, or foure, and five shillings a piece."

Strype in his Annals of the Reformation, i. 196, A.D. 1559, informs us that "on the 27th of October that year, the Prince of Sweden, the Lord Robert and the Lady Marchioness of Northampton, stood sureties at the christening of Sir Thomas Chamberlayne's son, who was baptised at St. Benet's church, at Paul's Wharf. The church was hung with cloth of arras; and, after the christening, were brought wafers, comfits, and divers banquetting dishes, and hypocras and Muscadine wine, to entertain the guests."

There was formerly a custom of having *sermons at christenings*. I had the honour of presenting to the Earl of Leicester one preached at the baptism of Theophilus Earl of Huntingdon.

The well-known toy, with bells, &c., and a piece of *coral* at the end, which is generally suspended from the necks of infants to assist them in cutting their teeth, is with the greatest probability supposed to have had its origin in an ancient superstition, which considered coral as an amulet or defensative against fascination; for this we have the authority of Pliny: "Aruspices religiosum coralli gestamen amoliendis periculis arbitrantur; et surculi infantiæ alligati tutelam habere creduntur." It was thought, too, to preserve and fasten the teeth in men. Reginald Scot, in his Discovery of Witchcraft, p. 166, says: "The coral preserveth such as bear it from fascination or bewitching, and in this respect they are hanged about children's necks. But from whence that superstition is derived, or who invented the lye, I know not; but I see how ready the people are to give credit thereunto by the multitude of corrals that were employed.''

Stevens informs us that there appears to have been an old superstition that coral would change its colour and look pale when the wearer of it was sick. So in the Three Ladies of London, 1584:

> " You may say jet will take up a straw,
>   Amber will make one fat,
>   CORAL *will look pale when you be sick*, and
>   Chrystal will stanch blood."

In Bartholomeus de Proprietatibus Rerum, edit. 1536, fol. 229, we read: " Wytches tell, that this stone (*coral*) withstondeth lyghtenynge.—It putteth of lyghtenyng, whirlewynde, tempeste and stormes fro shyppes and houses that it is in.— The red (coral) helpeth ayenst the fendes gyle and scorne, and ayenst divers wonderous doyng, and multiplieth fruite, and spedeth begynnyng and ending of causes and of nedes."

Coles, in his Adam in Eden, speaking of coral, says: " It helpeth children to breed their teeth, their gums being rubbed therewith; and to that purpose they have it fastened at the ends of their mantles." And Plat, in his Jewel-House of Art and Nature, p. 232, says: " Coral is good to be hanged about children's necks, as well to rub their gums as to preserve them from the falling sickness; it hath also some special sympathy with nature, for the best coral, being worn about the neck, will turn pale and wan if the party that wears it be sick, and comes to its former colour again as they recover health."

In a most rare work, entitled the French Garden for English Ladyes and Gentlewomen to walke in: or a Sommer Dayes Labour, &c., by Peter Erondell and John Fabre, 1621, in a dialogue relative to the dress of a child, we have another proof of the long continuance of this custom: " You need not give him *his corall with the small golden chayne,* for I beleeve it is better to let him sleepe untill the afternoone."

In a curious old book, 12mo. 1554, entitled A Short Description of Antichrist, is this passage: " I note all their Popishe traditions of confirmacion of yonge children with oynting of oyle and creame, and with *a ragge knitte about the necke of the younge babe.*"

[Good Friday and Easter Sunday are both considered lucky days for changing the caps of young children. If a child tooths first in the upper jaw, it is considered ominous of its dying in its infancy.]

BETROTHING CUSTOMS.

MOST profusely various have been the different rites, ceremonies, and customs, adopted by the several nations of the Christian world, on the performance of that most sacred of institutions, by which the Maker of mankind has directed us to transmit our race. The inhabitants of this island do not appear to have been exceeded by any other people on this occasion.

Before we enter upon the discussion of these, it will be necessary to consider distinctly the several ceremonies peculiar to betrothing by a verbal contract of marriage, and promises of love previously to the marriage union.

There was a remarkable kind of marriage-contract among the ancient Danes called *hand-festing*.[1] It is mentioned in Ray's Glossarium Northanhymbricum, in his collection of local words. Strong traces of this remain in our villages in many parts of the kingdom. I have been more than once assured from credible authority on Portland Island, that something very like it is still practised there very generally, where the inhabitants seldom or never intermarry with any on the main-land, and where the young women, selecting lovers of the same place (but with what previous rites, ceremonies, or engagements, I could never learn), account it no disgrace to allow them every favour, and that, too, from the fullest confidence of being made wives the moment such consequences of their stolen embraces begin to be too visible to be any longer concealed.

In the Christen State of Matrimony, 1543, p. 43, we read: "Yet in thys thynge also must I warne everye reasonable and

---

[1] " *Hand-fæstning*, promissio, quæ fit stipulata manu, sive cives fidem suam principi spondeant, sive mutuam inter se, matrimonium inituri, a phrasi *fæsta hand*, quæ notat dextram dextræ jungere."—Glossar. Suio-Gothicum, auctore I. Ihre in voce. Vid. ibid. in v. *Bröllop, Brudkaup*.

honest parson to beware, that in contractyng of maryage they
dyssemble not, nor set forthe any lye. Every man lykewyse
must esteme the parson to whom he is *hand-fasted,* none
otherwyse than for his owne spouse, though as yet it be not
done in the church ner in the streate. After the *hand-fastynge*
and *makyng of the contracte,* the churchgoying and weddyng
shuld not be differred to longe, lest the wickedde sowe hys
ungracious sede in the meane season. Into this dysh hath
the Dyvell put his foote, and mengled it wythe many wycked
uses and coustumes. For in some places ther is such a maner,
wel worthy to be rebuked, that *at the* HANDEFASTING *ther is
made a greate feaste and superfluous bancket, and even the
same night are the two handfasted personnes brought and layed
together, yea certan wekes afore they go to the chyrch.*"

In Sir John Sinclair's Statistical Account of Scotland, 1794,
xii. 615, the minister of Eskdalemuir, co. Dumfries, mentioning an annual fair, held time out of mind at the meeting of
the Black and White Esks, now entirely laid aside, says: "At
that fair it was the custom for the unmarried persons of both
sexes to choose a companion according to their liking, with
whom they were to live till that time next year. This was
called *hand-fasting,* or hand in fist. If they were pleased with
each other at that time, then they continued together for life:
if not, they separated, and were free to make another choice
as at the first. The fruit of the connexion (if there were any)
was always attached to the disaffected person. In later times,
when this part of the country belonged to the Abbacy of
Melrose, a priest to whom they gave the name of Book i'
Bosom (either because he carried in his bosom a Bible, or perhaps a register of the marriages), came from time to time to
confirm the marriages. This place is only a small distance
from the Roman encampment of Castle-oe'r. May not the
fair have been first instituted when the Romans resided there?
and may not the 'handfasting' have taken its rise from their
manner of celebrating marriage, *ex usu,* by which, if a woman,
with the consent of her parents or guardians, lived with a
man for a year, without being absent three nights, she became
his wife? Perhaps, when Christianity was introduced, this
form of marriage may have been looked upon as imperfect
without confirmation by a priest, and therefore one may have
been sent from time to time for this purpose."

In a book of great curiosity, entitled A Werke for Hous-holders, &c., by a professed Brother of Syon, Richarde Whit-forde, 1537, is the following caution on the above subject: "The ghostely enemy doth deceyve many persones by the pretence and coloure of matrimony in private and secrete con-tractes. For many men, when they can nat obteyne theyr unclene desyre of the woman, wyll promyse maryage and ther upon make a contracte promyse, and gyve faythe and trouth eche unto other, saying, ' Here, 1 take the, Margery, unto my wyfe, and therto I plyght the my troth.' And she agayne unto him in lyke maner. And after that done, they suppose they maye lawfully use theyr unclene behavyoure, and sometyme the acte and dede dothe folowe, unto the greate offence of God and their owne souls. It is a great jeopardy therefore to make any suche contractes, specially amonge themselfe se-cretely alone without recordes, which muste be two at the lest."

In Strype's Annals of the Reformation, i. App. p. 57, among the Interrogatories for the doctrine and manners of mynisters, &c., early in the reign of Queen Elizabeth, is the following, which clearly implies the then use and abuse of betrothing: " 28. Whether they have exhorted yong folke to absteyne from privy contracts, and not to marry without the consent of such their parents and fryends as have auctority over them, or no." I have no doubt but that in every of the privy contracts to be cautioned against by the above, there was a "mutual interchangement of rings," and the indulgence of every familiarity.

" The antient Frenchmen had a ceremonie, that when they would marrie, the bridegrome should pare his nayles and send them unto his new wife; which done, they lived together after-wards as man and wife." Vaughan's Golden Grove, 1608.

In the old play, A Woman's a Weather-cocke, Scudmore, ii. 1, tells the priest who is going to marry his mistress to Count Fredericke:

" She is contracted, sir, nay married
Unto another man, though it want forme:
And such strange passages and mutuall vowes,
'Twould make your short haire start through youre blacke
Cap, should you but heare it."

It was anciently very customary, among the common sort of people, to break a piece of gold or silver in token of a

verbal contract of marriage and promises of love ; one half
whereof was kept by the woman, while the other part remained
with the man.[1] Strutt, in his Manners and Customs,[2] has illustrated this by an extract from the old play of the Widow.
From this it also appears that no *dry bargain* would hold on
such occasions. For on the Widow's complaining that
Ricardo had artfully drawn her into a verbal contract, she is
asked by one of her suitors, " Stay, stay,—you broke no gold
between you ?" To which she answers, " We broke nothing,
sir." And, on his adding, " Nor drank to each other ?" she
replies, " Not a drop, sir." Whence he draws this conclusion,
" that the contract cannot stand good in law." The latter
part of the ceremony seems alluded to in the following passage in Middleton's play of No Wit like a Woman's : " Ev'n
when my lip touch'd the *contracting* cup."

We find, in Hudibras, I. i. 487, that the piece broken between the contracted lovers must have been a crooked one :

" Like commendation ninepence crook't,
With to and from my love it lookt."

A circumstance confirmed also in the Connoisseur, No. 56, with
an additional custom of giving locks of hair woven in a true
lover's knot. " If, in the course of their amour, the mistress
gives the dear man her hair wove in a true lover's knot, or
breaks a crooked ninepence with him, she thinks herself as-

[1] The dialogue between Kitty and Filbert. in the What d'ye call it, by
Gay, is much to our purpose :

" Yet, Justices, permit us, ere we part,
To break this ninepence as you've broke our heart."

" *Filbert* (breaking the ninepence). As this divides, thus are we torn
in twain.
" *Kitty* (joining the pieces). And as this meets, thus may we meet
again."
[2] A MS. in the Harleian Library, No. 980, cited by Strutt, states that, " by
the civil law, whatsoever is given ex sponsalitia largitate, betwixt them that
are promised in marriage, hath a condition (for the most part silent) that it
may be had again if marriage ensue not ; but if the man should have had
a kiss for his money, he should lose one half of that which he gave. Yet,
with the woman it is otherwise, for, kissing is not kissing, whatsoever she
gave, she may ask and have it again. However, this extends only to
gloves, rings, bracelets, and such like small wares."—Manners and Customs, iii. 153.

sured of his inviolate fidelity." This "bent token" has not been overlooked by Gay, Fifth Past., 129 :

——— "A ninepence bent
A token kind to Bumkinet is sent."

It appears to have been formerly a custom also for those who were betrothed to wear some flower as an external and conspicuous mark of their mutual engagement ; the conceit of choosing such short-lived emblems of their plighted loves cannot be thought a very happy one. That such a custom, however, did certainly prevail, we have the testimony of Spenser, in his Shepherd's Calendar for April, as follows :

"Bring coronations and *sops in wine*
Worn of paramours."

Sops-in-wine were a species of flowers among the smaller kind of single gilliflowers or pinks.

Camden, in his Ancient and Modern Manners of the Irish, says, that "they are observed to present their lovers with bracelets of women's hair, whether in reference to Venus' cestus or not, I know not." Gough's Camden, iii. 658. See also Memorable Things noted in the Description of the World, p. 113.

In the old play, entitled the Dutch Courtezan, a pair of lovers are introduced plighting their troth as follows : " Enter Freeville. Pages with torches. Enter Beatrice above." After some very impassioned conversation, Beatrice says : " *I give you faith ;* and prethee, since, poore soule ! I am so easie to beleeve thee, make it much more pitty to deceive me. *Weare this sleight favour in my remembrance,*" (throweth down a ring to him).

"*Frev.* Which, when I part from,
Hope, the best of life, ever part from me !
——— Graceful mistresse, *our nuptiall day holds.*
Beatrice. With happy constancye a wished day." [*Exit.*

Of gentlemen's presents on similar occasions, a lady, in Cupid's Revenge (a play of Beaumont and Fletcher's) says :

"Given earings we will wear ;
Bracelets of our lovers' hair,
Which they on our arms shall twist,
(With their names carv'd) on our wrist."

In Greene's Defence of Conny-Catching, is the following passage : " Is there not heere resident about London, a crew of terryble hacksters in the habite of gentlemen wel appareled? and yet some weare bootes for want of stockings, *with a locke worne at theyr lefte eare for their mistrisse favour.*" The subsequent is taken from Lodge's Wit's Miserie, 1596, p. 47 : " When he rides, you shall know him by his fan : and if he walke abroad, and misse *his mistres favour about his neck, arme,* or *thigh,* he hangs the head like the soldier in the field that is disarmed."

Among affiancing customs, the following will appear singular. Park, in his Travels in the Interior of Africa, tells us : " At Baniseribe, a Slatee having seated himself upon a mat by the threshold of his door, a young woman (his intended bride) brought a little water in a calabash, and, kneeling down before him, desired him to wash his hands ; when he had done this, the girl, with a tear of joy sparkling in her eye, drank the water ; this being considered as the greatest proof of her fidelity and love."

We gather from Howe's Additions to Stow's Chronicle, that in the reign of Queen Elizabeth, it was "the custome for maydes and gentilwomen to give their favorites, as tokens of their love, little handkerchiefs of about three or foure inches square, wrought round about, and with a button or a tassel at each corner, and a little one in the middle, with silke and threed ; the best edged with a small gold lace, or twist, which being foulded up in foure crosse foldes, so as the middle might be seene, gentlemen and others did usually weare them in their hatts, as favours of their loves and mistresses. Some cost six pence apiece, some twelve pence, and the richest sixteene pence."

In the old play of the Vow-Breaker, or the Fayre Maid of Clifton, 1636, act i. sc. 1, Miles, a miller, is introduced, telling his sweetheart, on going away to the wars, " Mistress Ursula, 'tis not unknowne that I have lov'd you ; if I die, it shall be for your sake, and it shall be valiantly : *I leave an hand-kercher with you ;* 'tis wrought with blew Coventry : let me not, at my returne, fall to my old song, *she had a clowte of mine sowde with blew Coventry,* and so hang myself at your infidelity."

The subsequent passage, from the Arraignment of lewd,

idle, froward, and unconstant Women, 1632, points out some
of the vagaries of lovers of that age : " Some thinke, that, if a
woman smile on them, she is presentlie over head and eares in
love.   One must *weare her glove*, another *her garter*, another
her *colours of delight*," &c. pp. 31, 32.   As does the following
epigram of a still earlier date, in the House of Correction, by
I. H., sm. 8vo. 1619 :

> " Little Pigmeus weares his mistris glove,
>   Her ring and feather (favours of her love);
> Who could but laugh to see the little dwarfe
> Grace out himselfe with her imbrodered scarfe ?
> 'Tis strange, yet true, her glove, ring, scarfe, and fan,
> Makes him (unhansome) a well-favour'd man."

In Quarles' Shepheard's Oracles, 4to. 1646, p. 63, is the
following passage :

> " The musick of the *oaten reeds* perswades
> Their hearts to mirth. ———
> And whilst they sport and dance, the love-sick swains
> Compose *rush-rings* and *myrtleberry* chains,
> And stuck with glorious *king-cups*, and their bonnets
> Adorn'd with *lawrell-slips*, chaunt their love-sonnets,
> To stir the fires and to encrease the flames
> In the cold hearts of their beloved *dames*."

A joint-ring appears to have been anciently a common token
among betrothed lovers.   These, as we gather from the following beautiful passage in Dryden's play of Don Sebastian,
1690, p. 122, were by no means confined to the lower orders
of society :

> " A curious artist wrought 'em,
> With joynts so close as not to be perceiv'd ;
> Yet are they both each other's counterpart.
> (Her part had *Juan* inscrib'd, and his had *Zayda*.
> You know those names were theirs :) and, in the midst,
> A heart divided in two halves was plac'd.
> Now if the rivets of those rings, inclos'd,
> Fit not each other, I have forg'd this lye :
> But if they join, you must for ever part.[1]

---

[1] It appears from other passages in this play that one of these rings
was worn by Sebastian's father, the other by Almeyda's mother, as pledges
of love.   Sebastian pulls off his, which had been put on his finger by his
dying father ; Almeyda does the same with hers, which had been given
her by her mother at parting ; and Alvarez unscrews both the rings, and
fits one half to the other.

Bowed money appears anciently to have been sent as a token of love and affection from one relative to another. Thus we read in the Third Part of Conny-Catching, "Then taking fourth a *bowed groat*, and an *old pennie bowed*, he gave it her as being sent from her uncle ana aunt." In the Country Wake, a comedy by Doggett, 1696, v. i., Hob, who fancies he is dying, before he makes his last will and *testimony*, as he calls it, when his mother desires him to try to speak to Mary, "for she is thy *wife*, and no other," answers, "I know, I'm sure to her—and I do own it before you all; I ask't her the question last Lammas, and at Allhollow's-tide *we broke a piece of money*, and if I had liv'd till last Sunday, we had been ask'd in the church," [In an old penny history, called Bateman's Tragedy, or the perjured Bride justly rewarded, being the history of the unfortunate love of German's wife and young Bateman, an allusion occurs to this practice: "Long they dwelt not on this theme, before they fell to that of love, renewing their vows of eternal love and constancy that nothing but death should be able to separate them : and, to bind it, *he broke a piece of gold, giving her the one half, and keeping the other himself :* and then with tears and tender kisses they parted."]

Swinburne on Spousals, p. 10, says : " Some spousals are contracted by signs, as the giving and receiving a ring, others by words."

In the play of the Vow-Breaker, i. 1, Young Bateman and Anne, we read :

> " *Ba.* Now, Nan, here's none but thou and I ; thy love
> Emboldens me to speak, and cheerfully
> *Here is a peece of gold ;* 'tis but a little one,
> Yet big enough to ty and seale a knot,
> A jugall knot on earth, to which high heaven
> Now cries amen : say thou so too, and then
> When eyther of us breakes this sacred bond,
> Let us be made strange spectacles to the world,
> To heaven, and earth.
>   *An.* Amen, say I ;
> And let heaven loth me when I falsifie."

Afterwards, on Young Bateman's return from the wars, during whose absence Anne has been induced by her father to marry another person, Anne says, " I am married."

Ba. I know thou art, to me, my fairest Nan:
Our vows were made to heaven, and on earth
They must be ratifide: in part they are,
By giving of a pledge, *a peice of gold:*
Which when we broke, joyntly then we swore,
Alive or dead, for to enjoy each other,
And so we will, spight of thy father's frownes."

And afterwards, act iii. sc. 1, Anne, seeing the ghost of Young Bateman, who had hanged himself for her sake, exclaims:

" It stares, beckons, *points to the peece of gold*
We brake between us: looke, looke there,—here, there!"

[Compare also the following lines in the Exeter Garland, 8vo, about 1750:

" A *ring* of pure gold she from her finger took,
And just in the middle the same then she broke:
Quoth she, as a token of love you this take,
And this as a pledge I will keep for your sake."]

In the Scourge for Paper Persecutors, 1625, p. 11, we find the penance for anti-nuptial fornication:

" Or wanton rig, or letcher dissolute,
Doe *stand at Paul's-crosse in a sheeten sute.*"

In Codrington's Second Part of Youth's Behaviour, or Decency in Conversation amongst Women, 1664, p. 33, is the following very remarkable passage : " It is too often seen that young gentlewomen by gifts are courted to *interchange*, and to return the courtesie : *rings* indeed and ribbands are but trifles, but believe me, they are not trifles that are aimed at in such exchanges : let them therefore be counselled that they neither give nor receive any thing that afterwards may procure their shame."

In Whimzies, or a New Cast of Characters, 1631, the unknown author, in his description of a pedlar, ii. 21, has the following passage : can it allude to the custom of interchanging betrothing rings?[1] " *St. Martin's rings* and counterfeit bracelets are commodities of infinite consequence. They will passe

[1] " St. Martin's rings were imitations of gold ones, made with copper, and gilt. They may have been so called from the makers or vendors of them residing within the collegiate church of St. Martin's-le-Grand."—Halliwell's Dictionary, p. 543.

for current at *a May-pole,* and purchase a favour from their *May-Marian.*"

In Herrick's Hesperides, p. 201, a *Jimmal ring* is mentioned as a love-token :

> "*The Jimmal Ring, or True-love Knot.*
>
> Thou sent'st to me a true-love knot; but I
> Return'd a ring of jimmals, to imply
> Thy love had one knot, mine *a triple-tye.*"

The difference between the betrothing or affiancing ceremony and that of marriage is clearly pointed out in the following passages : " '*Sponsalia non sunt de essentia sacramenti matrimonii,* possuntque sine illius præjudicio omitti, sicut et pluribus in locis revera omittuntur,' dit le Rituel d'Evreux de l'annee 1621. Le Concile Provincial de Reims en 1583 dit: '*Sponsalia non nisi coram parocho,* vel ejus vicario deinceps *fiant, idque in ecclesia et non alibi.*' Les Statuts Synodaux de Sens, en 1524: '*Possunt prius et debent dare fidem inter se de matrimonio contrahendo, et hoc palam in ecclesia et in præsentia sacerdotis,* &c.'" Traité des Superstitions, par M. Jean Baptiste Thiers, Par. 1704, iv. 470. To the betrothing contract under consideration must be referred, if I mistake not, and not to the marriage ceremony itself (to which latter, I own, however, the person who does not nicely discriminate betwixt them will be strongly tempted to incline), the well-known passages on this subject in Shakspeare's play of Twelfth Night.[1]

I am by no means satisfied with the comment of Steevens on these passages, though at first I had hastily adopted it. After painful research, I can find no proof that in our ancient ceremony at marriages the man received as well as gave the ring: nor do I think the custom at all exemplified by the quotation from Lupton's first book of Notable Things. The expression is equivocal, and "his maryage ring" I should think means no more than the ring used at his marriage, that which he gave and which his wife received : at least we are not warranted to interpret it at present any otherwise, till some passage can actually be adduced from the ancient manuscript rituals to evince that there ever did at marriages take

---

[1] See the last act of that play.

place such "interchangement of rings," a custom which however certainly formed one of the most prominent features of the ancient *betrothing ceremony*.

A MS. missal, as old as the time of Richard the Second, formerly the property of University College in Oxford, gives not the least intimation that the woman too gave a ring. I shall cite this afterwards under Marriage Ceremonies. The following passage from Coats's Dictionary of Heraldry, 1725, *v.* ANNULUS, would bear hard against me, were it supported by any other authority than that of an ipse dixit: "But for my part, I believe *the rings married people gave one another* do rather denote the truth and fidelity they owe to one another, than that they import any servitude." And yet concession must be made that the bridegroom appears to have had a ring given him as well as the bride in the diocese of Bordeaux in France.[1]

In Sir John Sinclair's Statistical Account of Scotland, 1792, ii. 80, the minister of Galston, in Ayrshire, informs us of a singular custom there: "When a young man wishes to pay his addresses to his sweetheart, instead of going to her father's and professing his passion, he goes to a public-house; and having let the landlady into the secret of his attachment, the object of his wishes is immediately sent for, who never almost

[1] " Dans le diocese de Bordeaux on donnoit, comme en Orient, au futur epoux et a la future epouse, chacun un anneau en les epousant. Au moins cela est-il préscrit par le Rituel de Bordeaux (pp. 98, 99) de 1596. *Benedictio annulorum.* Benedic Domine, *hos annulos*, &c. Aspergat sacerdos *annulos* arras et circumstantes aqua benedicta. Deinde sacerdos accipit alterum annulum inter primos tres digitos, dicens, *Benedic Domine hunc annulum,* &c., *et infigit* illum in *digitum quartum dextræ sponsi,* dicens, *In nomine Patris,* &c. Pari modo alterum annulum accipit et benedicit ut supra, et *tradit eum sponso, qui accipiens illum tribus digitis, infigit illum in quarto digito manus dexteræ ipsius sponsæ,* &c."— Traité des Superstitions, iv. 512. The following, too, occurs, ibid. p. 513: "Certaines gens en vûe de se garentir de malefice, *font benir plusieurs anneaux,* quand ils trouvent des prêtres assés ignorans, ou assés complaisans pour le faire, et *les mettent tous dans le doigt annulaire de la maine gauche ou de la main droite de leurs epouses,* car en certains dioceses c'est à la main droite, et en d'autres c'est a la main gauche, qu'on le donne aux nouvelles mariées, quoique le quatrieme Concile Provincial de Milan en 1576, ordonne qu'on le mette à la main gauche (Constit. p. 3, n. 9). Mais ils ne sçauroient mettre ce mauvais moien en pratique sans *tomber dans la superstition* de la vaine observance, et dans celle *de l'observance des rencontres.*"

II.

refuses to come. She is entertained with ale and whisky, or brandy, and the marriage is concluded on. The second day after the marriage, *a creeling*, as it is called, takes place. The young wedded pair, with their friends, assemble in a convenient spot. A small creel, or basket, is prepared for the occasion, into which they put some stones: the young men carry it alternately, and allow themselves to be caught by the maidens, who have a kiss when they succeed. After a great deal of innocent mirth and pleasantry, the creel falls at length to the young husband's share, who is obliged to carry it generally for a long time, none of the young women having compassion upon him. At last, his fair mate kindly relieves him from his burden; and her complaisance in this particular is considered as a proof of her satisfaction with the choice she has made. The creel goes round again; more merriment succeeds; and all the company dine together and talk over the feats of the field. Perhaps the French phrase, 'Adieu panniers, vèndanges sont faites,' may allude to a similar custom."

[In Guernsey, when a young man offers himself to a young lady, and is accepted, the parents of the parties give what is termed a *flouncing*; that is, they invite their friends to a feast. The young lady is led round the room by her future father-in-law, and introduced to his friends, and afterwards the young man is paraded in like manner by his future father-in-law; then there is an exchange of rings and some articles of plate, according to the rank of the parties. After this, it is horrid for the damsel to be seen walking with any other male person, and the youth must scarce glance at anything feminine; in this way they court for years. After this ceremony, if the gentleman alters his mind, the lady can claim half his property; and if the fickle lass should repent, the gentleman can demand the half of hers. The natives of Guernsey keep themselves very secluded; they have three classes of society —the sixties, the forties, and the twenties. The first, in their evening visiting carry a lantern with three lights; the second, one with two; and the third one.

In Wales, there is a custom called *bundling*, in which the betrothing parties go to bed in their clothes. It has given rise to many actions for seduction.]

PEASCOD WOOING.

[IT is somewhat surprising that a custom of a very singular character, which was common in this country some centuries ago, and is still partly retained in some counties, should have altogether escaped the notice of all writers on our popular customs and superstitions; and the commentators on Shakespeare have entirely misunderstood a passage in the works of our great dramatic poet, from not having been aware that our ancestors were frequently accustomed in their love affairs to employ the divination of a peascod, by selecting one growing on the stem, snatching it away quickly, and if the good omen of the peas remaining in the husk were preserved, then presenting it to the lady of their choice. Touchstone, in As You Like it, act ii. scene 4, thus alludes to this practice : " I remember, when I was in love, I broke my sword upon a stone, and bid him take that for coming a-night to Jane Smile ; and I remember the kissing of her batler, and the cow's dugs that her pretty chapped hands had milked ; and I remember the wooing of a peascod instead of her, from whom I took two cods, and, giving her them again, said, with weeping tears, ' Wear these for my sake.' "

Mr. Davy, of Ufford, in Suffolk, informs me that the efficacy of peascods in the affairs of sweethearts is not yet forgotten among our rustic vulgar. The kitchen-maid, when she shells green peas, never omits, if she finds one having *nine* peas, to lay it on the lintel of the kitchen-door, and the first clown who enters it is infallibly to be her husband, or at least her sweetheart. Anderson mentions a custom in the North, of a nature somewhat similar. A Cumbrian girl, when her lover proves unfaithful to her, is, by way of consolation, rubbed with peas-straw[1] by the neighbouring lads; and when a Cumbrian youth loses his sweetheart, by her marriage with a rival, the

---

[1] [In the south of Scotland the superstition about the cod with nine peas in it is equally prevalent ; and the present statement will explain a line in a beautiful Scottish pastoral, perhaps little understood :

" If you meet a bonnie lassie,
    Gie her a kiss and let her gae ;
If you meet a dirty hussey,
    Fie, gae rub her o'er wi' strae !"]

same sort of comfort is administered to him by the lasses of the village. "Winter time for shoeing, peascod time for wooing," is an old proverb in a MS. Devon Gl. The divination by peascods, alluded to by Mr. Davy, is thus mentioned by Gay:

> "As peascods once I pluck'd, I chanced to see
> One that was closely fill'd with three times three;
> Which, when I cropp'd, I safely home convey'd,
> And o'er the door the spell in secret laid;
> The latch mov'd up, when who should first come in,
> But in his proper person,—Lubberkin!"

But perhaps the passage in Shakespeare is best illustrated by the following passage from Browne's Britannia's Pastorals, p. 71, which seems to have escaped the notice of all writers on this subject:

> "The peascod greene, oft with no little toyle
> He'd seek for in the fattest fertil'st soile,
> And rend it from the stalke to bring it to her,
> And in her bosom for acceptance wooe her."

Grose tells us that "a scadding of peas" is a custom in the North of boiling the common gray peas in the shell, and eating them with butter and salt, first shelling them. A bean, shell and all, is put into one of the pea-pods; whoever gets this bean is to be first married.]

RING AND BRIDECAKE.

Among the customs used at marriages, those of the RING and BRIDECAKE seem of the most remote antiquity. Confarreation and the ring[1] were used anciently as binding ceremo-

------

[1] " *Annulus sponsæ dono mittebatur a viro qui pronubus dictus.* Alex. ab Alexandro, lib. ii. c. 5. Et, *mediante annulo contrahitur matrimonium papanorum.*" Moresini Papatus, p. 12. It is farther observable that *the joining together of the right hands* in the marriage ceremony is from the same authority: " Dextra data, acceptaque invicem, Persæ et Assyrii fœdus matrimonii ineunt. Alex. ab Alexandro, lib. ii. cap. 5. Papatus retinet." Ibid. p. 50.

nies by the heathens[1] in making agreements, grants,[2] &c,,
whence they have doubtless been derived to the most solemn
of our engagements.

The ceremony used at the solemnization of a marriage was
called *confarreation*, in token of a most firm conjunction between the man and the wife, with a cake of *wheat* or *barley*.
This, Blount tells us, is still retained in part with us, by that
which is called the bridecake used at weddings. Moffet, in
his Health's Improvement, p. 218, informs us that "the
English, *when the bride comes from church, are wont to cast
wheat upon her head;* and when the bride and bridegroom
return home, one presents them with a pot of butter, as presaging plenty, and abundance of all good things."

This ceremony of confarreation has not been omitted by the
learned Moresin: " SUMANALIA, *panis erat formam rotæ
factus;* hoc utuntur papani *in nuptiis,* &c." Papatus, p. 165.
Nor has it been overlooked by Herrick in his Hesperides.
At p. 128, speaking to the bride, he says :[3]

> " While some repeat
> Your praise, and bless you, *sprinkling you with wheat.*"

The connexion between the bridecake and wedding is
strongly marked in the following custom, still retained in
Yorkshire, where the former is cut into little square pieces,
thrown over the bridegroom's and bride's head, and then put
through the ring. The cake is sometimes broken over the

---

[1] Quintus Curtius tells us, lib. i. de Gest. Alexandri M., " Et rex medio
cupiditatis ardore jussit afferri patrio more PANEM (hoc erat apud
Macedones *sanctissimum coeuntium pignus*) *quem divisum gladio uterque
libabat.*"

[2] The following extract is from an old grant, cited in Du Cange's
Glossary, *v. Confarreatio :* " Miciacum concedimus et quicquid est fisci
nostri intra fluminum alveos et *per sanctam confarreationem et annulum*
inexceptionaliter tradimus."

[3] It was also a Hebrew custom. See Selden's Uxor Hebraica, lib. ii.
cap. xv. Opera, iii. 633. In the same volume, p. 668, is a passage much
to our purpose : " Quanquam sacra quæ fuere in confarreatione paganica,
utpote Christianismo plane adversantia, sub ejusdem initia, etiam apud
Paganos evanuêre—nihilominus *farris ipsius usus* aliquis *solennis* in *libis
conficiendis, diffringendis, communicandis,* locis saltem in nonnullis semper
obtinuit. Certè frequentissimus apud Anglos est et antiquitus fuit lihorum
admodum grandium in nuptiis usus, quæ BRIDECAKES, id est, liba sponsalitia seu nuptialia appellitant. Ea quæ tum a sponsis ipsis confecta tum
ab propinquis amicisque solenniter muneri nuptiali data."

bride's head, and then thrown away among the crowd to be scrambled for. This is noted by the author of the Convivial Antiquities, f. 68, in his description of the rites of marriages in his country and time : "Peracta re divina sponsa ad sponsi domum deducitur, indeque panis projicitur, qui a pueris certatim rapitur." In the North, slices of the bridecake are put through the wedding ring : they are afterwards laid under pillows, at night, to cause young persons to dream of their lovers. Douce says this custom is not peculiar to the north of England. It seems to prevail generally. The pieces of the cake must be drawn nine times through the wedding ring.

Aubrey, in the Remains of Gentilisme and Judaisme, MS. Lansd. 226, f. 109, says : "When I was a little boy (before the civil wars), I have seen, according to the custome then, the bride and bridegroome kisse over the bridecakes at the table. It was about the latter end of dinner ; and the cakes were layd one upon another, like the picture of the shew-bread in the old Bibles. The bridegroom waited at dinner."

The supposed Heathen origin of our marriage ring had well-nigh caused the abolition of it during the time of the Commonwealth. The facetious author of Hudibras (III. ii. 303) gives us the following chief reasons why the Puritans wished it to be set aside :

> " Others were for abolishing
> That tool of matrimony, a ring,
> With which th' unsanctify'd bridegroom
> Is marry'd only to a thumb
> (As wise as ringing of a pig
> That us'd to break up ground and dig) ;
> The bride to nothing but her will,
> That nulls the after-marriage still."

The following thought on the marriage ring, in Herrick's Hesperides, p. 72, is well expressed :

> " And as this round
> Is no where found
> To flaw, or else to sever :
> So let our love
> As endlesse prove,
> And pure as gold for ever."[1]

---

[1] In Swinburne's Treatise of Spousals, p. 207, we read : " The first inventor of the ring, as is reported (he cites Alberic de Rosa in suo Dictionar. v. Annulus), was one Prometheus. The workman which made it

The allusion both to the form and metal of which it is composed is elegant. Were it not too long, it would be the best *poesie* for a wedding ring that ever was devised.

Vallanccy, in his Collectanea de Rebus Hibernicis, xiii. 98, says that "there is a passage in Ruth, chap. iv., v. 7, which gives room to think the ring was used by the Jews as a covenant." He adds, that the Vulgate have translated *narthick* (which ought to be a ring) a shoe. "In Irish, *nuirt* is an amulet worn on the finger or arm, a ring." "Sphæra solis est narthick," says Buxtorf in his Chaldee Lexicon. Leo Modena, in his History of the Rites, Customes, and Manner of Life of the present Jews throughout the World, translated by Chilmead, 1650, p. 176, speaking of their contracts and manner of marrying, says that, before the writing of the bride's dowry is produced and read, "the bridegroom putteth a ring upon her finger, in the presence of two witnesses, which commonly used to be the Rabbines, saying withal unto her, 'Behold, thou art my espoused wife, according to the custome of Moses and of Israel.'"

The wedding ring is worn on the fourth finger of the left hand, because it was anciently believed, though the opinion has been justly exploded by the anatomists of modern times, that a small artery ran from this finger to the heart. Wheatley, on the authority of the Missals, calls it a vein. "It is," says he, "because from thence there proceeds a particular vein to the heart. This, indeed, is now contradicted by experience; but several eminent authors, as well Gentiles as Christians, as well physicians as divines, were formerly of this opinion, and therefore they thought this finger the properest to bear this pledge of love, that from thence it might be conveyed, as it were, to the heart."

In the Hereford, York, and Salisbury Missals the ring is directed to be put first upon the thumb, afterwards upon the second, then on the third, and lastly, on the fourth finger,

was Tubal-Cain: and Tubal-Cain, by the counsel of our first parent Adam (as my author telleth me), gave it unto his son to this end, that therewith he should espouse a wife like as Abraham delivered unto his servants bracelets and ear-rings of gold. *The form of the ring being circular, that is, round and without end,* importeth thus much, *that their mutual love and hearty affection should roundly flow from the one to the other as in a circle, and that continually and for ever.*"

where it is to remain, "quia in illo digito est quædam vena procedens usque ad cor."

It is very observable that none of the above Missals mention the hand, whether right or left, upon which the ring is to be put. This has been noticed by Selden, in his Uxor Hebraica: "Digito quarto, sed non liquet dexteræ an sinistræ manus." The Hereford Missal inquires, "Quæro quæ est ratio ista, quare anulus ponatur in quarto digito cum pollice computato, quam in secundo vel tercio? Isidorus dicit quod quædam vena extendit se a digito illo usque ad cor, et dat intelligere unitatem et perfectionem amoris."

It appears from Aulus Gellius, lib. x. cap. 10, that the ancient Greeks and most of the Romans wore the ring "in eo digito qui est in manu sinistra minimo proximus." He adds, on the authority of Appian, that a small nerve runs from this finger to the heart; and that therefore it was honoured with the office of bearing the ring, on account of its connexion with that master-mover of the vital functions.

Levinus Lemnius tells us, speaking of the ring-finger, that "a small branch of the arterie, and not of the nerves, as Gellius thought, is stretched forth from the heart unto this finger, the motion whereof you shall perceive evidently in women with child and wearied in travel, and all affects of the heart, by the touch of your fore finger. I use to raise such as are fallen in a swoond by pinching this joynt, and by rubbing the ring of gold with a little saffron, for by this a restoring force that is in it passeth to the heart, and refresheth the fountain of life, unto which this finger is joyn'd: wherefore it deserved that honour above the rest, and antiquity thought fit to compasse it about with gold. Also the worth of this finger that it receives from the heart procured thus much, that the old physicians, from whence also it hath the name of *Medicus*, would mingle their medicaments and potions with this finger, for no venom can stick upon the very outmost part of it, but it will offend a man, and communicate itself to his heart." English Trans. 1658, p. 109.

Macrobius (Saturnal. lib. vii. cap. 13) assigns the same reason; but also quotes the opinion of Ateius Capito, that the right hand was exempt from this office, because it was much more used than the left hand, and therefore the precious stones of the rings were liable to be broken; and that the

finger of the left hand was selected which was the least used
for the ring having been used by the Romans at their marriages, consult Juvenal, Sat. vi., v. 27.

To a Querist in the British Apollo, 1708, i. 18, "Why is it
that a person to be married is enjoyned to put a ring upon
the fourth finger of his spouse's left hand?" It is answered,
"There is nothing more in this, than that the custom was
handed down to the present age from the practice of our ancestors, who found the left hand more convenient for such
ornaments than the right, in that it's ever less employed; for
the same reason they chose the fourth finger, which is not
only less used than either of the rest, but is more capable of
preserving a ring from bruises, having this one quality peculiar
to itself, that it cannot be extended but in company with some
other finger, whereas the rest may be singly stretched to their
full length and straightness. Some of the ancients were of
opinion in this matter, that the ring was so worn because to
that finger, and to that only, comes an artery from the heart;
but the politer knowledge of our modern anatomists having
clearly demonstrated the absurdity of that notion, we are
rather inclined to believe the continuance of the custom owing
to the reason above mentioned."

There is an old proverb on the subject of wedding rings,
which has no doubt been many a time quoted for the purpose
of encouraging and hastening the consent of a diffident or
timorous mistress :

> "As your wedding ring wears,
> Your cares will wear away."

In a scarce tract in my collection, entitled A Briefe Discourse of a Disease called the Suffocation of the Mother,
written by Edward Jorden, Doctor in Physicke, 1603, the
learned author, in a list of "superstitious remedies which have
crept into our profession," mentions a whimsical superstition
relating to the wedding ring which need not be repeated.

Many married women are so rigid, not to say superstitious,
in their notions concerning their wedding rings, that neither
when they wash their hands, nor at any other time, will they
take it off from their finger, extending, it should seem, the
expression of "till death us do part" even to this golden circlet, the token and pledge of matrimony.

This may have originated in the Popish *hallowing of this ring*, of which the following form occurs in the Doctrine of the Masse Booke, from Wyttonberge, by Nicholas Dorcaster, 1554 : "*The hallowing of the woman's ring at wedding*. Thou Maker and Conserver of mankinde, gever of spiritual grace and graunter of eternal salvation, Lord, *send thy* ✠ *blessing upon this ring*, (here the Protestant translator observes in the margin, 'Is not here wise geare?') *that she which shall weare it, maye be armed wyth the vertue of heavenly defence*, and that it maye profit her to eternal salvation, thorowe Christ," &c. "*A prayer*. ✠ Halow thou, Lord, this ring, which we blesse in thy holye Name : *that what woman soever shall weare it, may stand fast in thy peace, and continue in thy wyl, and live and grow and waxe old in thy love*, and be multiplied into that length of daies, thorow our Lord, &c. Then let holy water be sprinkled upon the ryng."

Columbiere, speaking of rings, says : "The hieroglyphic of the ring is very various. Some of the antients made it to denote servitude, alledging that the bridegroom was to give it to his bride, to denote to her that she is to be subject to him, which Pythagoras seemed to confirm when he prohibited wearing a streight ring, that is, not to submit to over-rigid servitude."[1]

Rings appear to have been given away formerly at weddings. In Wood's Athenæ Oxonienses, i. 280, we read in the account of the famous philosopher of Queen Elizabeth's days, Edward Kelly, "Kelly, who was openly profuse beyond the modest limits of a sober philosopher, did give away in *gold-wire rings* (or rings twisted with three gold wires), at the marriage of one of his maid-servants, to the value of 4000*l*." This was in 1589, at Trebona.

In Davison's Poetical Rapsody, 1611, p. 93, occurs the following beautiful sonnet:

"*Upon sending his Mistresse a Gold Ring with this Poesie*,
PURE AND ENDLESSE.

" If you would know the love which I you beare,
Compare it to the ring which your faire hand
Shall make more precious, when you shall it weare ;
So my love's nature you shall understand.

---

[1] Coats's Dictionary of Heraldry, in v. *Annulet*.

Is it of mottall pure? so you shall prove

My love, while it in 'ti alldayall thoughts all abous.

Hath it no end? so endlesse is my love,
     Unlesse you it destroy with your disdaine.
Doth it the purer waxe the more 'tis tri'de?
     So doth my love; yet herein they dissent,
That whereas gold the more 'tis purifide,
     By waxing lesse, doth shew some part is spent,
My love doth waxe more pure by your more trying,
And yet encreaseth in the purifying."

A remarkable superstition still prevails among the lowest of our vulgar, that a man may lawfully sell his wife to another, provided he deliver her over with a halter about her neck. It is painful to observe that instances of this frequently occur in our newspapers.

Every one knows that in England, during the time of the Commonwealth, justices of peace were empowered to marry people. A jeu d'esprit on this subject may be found in Flecknoe's Diarium, 1656, p. 83 : " On the justice of peace's making marriages, and the crying them in the market."

RUSH RINGS.

A CUSTOM extremely hurtful to the interests of morality appears anciently to have prevailed both in England and other countries of marrying with a RUSH RING; chiefly practised, however, by designing men, for the purpose of debauching their mistresses, who sometimes were so infatuated as to believe that this mock ceremony was a real marriage.[1]

[1] That this custom prevailed in France appears from the following passage in Du Breul's Theatre des Antiquitez de Paris, 1622, p. 90 : " Quant a la Cour de l'Official, il se presente quelquns personnes qui ont forfaict a leur honneur, la chose estant averée, si l'on ny peult remedier autrement pour sauver l'honneur des maisons, l'on a accoustomée d'amener en ladicte eglise l'homme et la femme qui ont forfaict en leur honneur, et là estans conduicts par deux sergents (au cas qu'ils n'y veulent venir de leur bonne volontè) *il sont espousez ensemble par le curè dudict lieu avec un anneau de paille* : leur enjoignant de vivre en paix et amitié, et ainsi couvrir l'honneur des parens et amis ausquels ils appartiennent, et sauver leurs ames du danger où ils s'estoient mis par leur peché et offense." One of the Con-

BRIDE FAVOURS.

A KNOT, among the ancient northern nations, seems to have oeen the symbol of love, faith, and friendship, pointing out the indissoluble tie of affection and duty. Thus the ancient Runic inscriptions, as we gather from Hickes's Thesaurus,[1] are in the form of a knot. Hence, among the northern English and Scots, who still retain, in a great measure, the language and manners of the ancient Danes, that curious kind of knot, a mutual present between the lover and his mistress, which, being considered as the emblem of plighted fidelity, is therefore called a true-love knot: a name which is not derived, as one would naturally suppose it to be, from the words "true," and "love," but formed from the Danish verb

stitutions of Richard Bishop of Salisbury, in 1217, cited by Du Cange, in his Glossary, v. *Annulus,* says : " Nec quisquam *annulum de junco* vel *quacunque vili materia vel pretiosa, jocando* manibus innectat muliercularum, ut liberius cum eis fornicetur : ne dum jocari se putat, honoribus matrimonialibus se astringat." Douce refers Shakespeare's expression, " Tib's rush for Tom's forefinger," which has so long puzzled the commentators, to this custom. " L'official marie dans l'eglise de St. Marine ceux qui ont forfait a leur honneur, ou ils sont epouses ensemble par le curè du lieu avec un anneau de paille." – Sausal, Antiq. de Paris, i. 429. " Pour faire observer, sans doute," adds the editor of Le Voyageur a Paris, iii. 156, " au mari, combien etoit fragile la vertu de celle qu'il choisissait." Compare also the Traité des Superstitions, par M. Thiers, iii. 462, where Bishop Poore's Constitution is also quoted.

[1] Gramm. Island., p. 4 : " In his autem monumentis, ut in id genus fere omnibus, inscriptionum Runæ in nodis sive gyris nodorum insculptæ leguntur, propterea quod apud veteres septentrionales gentes *nodus amoris,* fidei, amicitiæ symbolum fuisse videtur, ut quod insolubilem pietatis et affectus nexum significavit. Hinc apud boreales Anglos, Scotosque, qui Danorum veterum tum sermonem, tum mores magna ex parte adhuc retinent, nodus in gyros curiose ductus, fidei et promissionis quam Amasius et Amasia dare solent invicem, symbolum servatur, quodque ideo vocant *a true-love knot,* a veteri Danico *trulofa*—fidem do.—Hinc etiam apud Anglos Scotosque consuetudo reportandi capitalia donata curiose in gyros nodosque torta a solennibus nuptiis plane quasi symbola insolubilis fidei et affectus, quæ sponsum inter et sponsam esse debent." Many of these Runic knots are engraved in Sturleson's History of Stockholm. The following is found in Selden's Uxor Hebraica (Opera, iii. 670) : " Quin et post benedictionem per vittæ candidæ permissione et purpureæ unum invicem vinculum (modum amatorium, *a true-loves knot*), copulabantur, inq iit Isidorus, videlicet, ne compagem conjugalis unitatis disrampant."

Trulofa fidem do, I plight my troth, or faith. Thus we read, in the Islandic Gospels, the following passage in the first chapter of St. Matthew, which confirms, beyond a doubt, the sense here given—" til einrar Meyar er trulofad var einum Manne," &c.; i. e. to a virgin espoused, that is, who was promised or had engaged herself to a man, &c. Hence, evidently, the bride favours, or the top-knots, at marriages, which have been considered as emblems of the ties of duty and affection between the bride and her spouse, have been derived.

Sir Thomas Browne, in his Vulgar Errors, says: "The true-lover's knot is much magnified, and still retained in presents of love among us; which, though in all points it doth not make out, had, perhaps, its original from Nodus Herculanus, or that which was called Hercules his knot, resembling the snaky complication in the caduceus, or rod of Hermes, and in which form the zone or woollen girdle of the bride was fastened, as Turnebus observes in his Adversaria."

The following beautiful madrigal, entitled "The True-love's Knot," occurs in Davison's Poetical Rapsody, 1611, p. 216:

" Love is the linke, the knot, the band of unity,
And all that love, do love with their belov'd to be:
    Love only did decree
    To change his kind in me.

For though I lov'd with all the powers of my mind,
And though my restles thoughts their rest in her did finde,
    Yet are my hopes declinde,
    Sith she is most unkinde.

For since her beauties sun my fruitles hope did breede,
By absence from that sun I hop't to sterve that weede;
    Though absence did, indeede,
    My hopes not sterve, but feede.

For when I shift my place, like to the stricken deere,
I cannot shift the shaft which in my side I beare:
    By me it resteth there,
    The cause is not elsewhere.

So have I seene the sicke to turne and turne againe,
As if that outward change could ease his inward paine:
    But still, alas! in vaine,
    The fit doth still remaine.

Yet goodnes is the spring from whence this ill doth grow,
For goodnes caus'd the love, which great respect did owe;
    Respect true love did show;
    True love thus wrought my woe."

Gay, in his Pastoral called the Spell, thus beautifully describes the rustic manner of knitting the true-love knot:

" As Lubberkin once slept beneath a tree,
I twitch'd his dangling garter from his knee;
He wist not when the hempen string I drew;
Now mine I quickly doff, of inkle blue;
Together fast I tie the garters twain,
And, while I knit the knot, repeat this strain—
Three times a true-love's knot I tie secure:
Firm be the knot, firm may his love endure."

Another species of knot divination is given in the Connoisseur, No. 56: "Whenever I go to lye in a strange bed, I always tye my garter nine times round the bed-post, and knit nine knots in it, and say to myself: 'This knot I knit, this knot I tye, to see my love as he goes by, in his apparel'd array, as he walks in every day.'" This is of course intended for poetry.

I find the following passage in the Merry Devil of Edmonton, 4to. 1631:

" With pardon, sir, that name is quite undon,
This true-love knot cancelles both maide and nun."

Bride favours appear to have been worn by the peasantry of France, on similar occasions, on the arm. In England these knots of ribands were distributed in great abundance formerly, even at the marriages of persons of the first distinction. They were worn at the hat (the gentleman's I suppose), and consisted of ribands of various colours. If I mistake not, white ribands are the only ones used at present. Ozell, in a note to his translation of Misson, p. 350, says the favour "was a large knot of ribbands, of several colours, gold, silver, carnation, and white. This is worn upon the hat for some weeks." Another note, in p. 351, says: "It is ridiculous to go to a wedding without *new cloaths*. If you are in mourning, you throw it off for some days, unless you are in mourning for some near relation that is very lately dead." Misson, p. 350, says: "Formerly in France they gave *livrées de nôces*, which was a knot of ribbands, to be worn by the guests upon their arms; but that is practis'd now only among peasants. In England it is done still among the greatest noblemen. These ribbands they call *favours*, and give them not only to those that are at the wedding, but to five hundred people besides;

they send them about, and distribute them at their own houses
'Tother day, when the eldest son of M. de Overkerque marry'd
the Duke of Ormond's sister, they dispers'd a whole inundation
of those little favours. Nothing else was here to be met with,
from the hat of the king down to that of the meanest servant.
Among the citizens and plain gentlemen, which is what they
call the *gentry*, they sometimes give these favours; but it is
very common to avoid all manner of expence as much as
possible."

In Paradoxical Assertions and Philosophical Problems, by
R. H., 1664, p. 19, we read : " I shall appeal to any enamoreto
but newly married, whether he took not more pleasure in
weaving innocent true-love knots than in untying the virgin
zone, or knitting that more than Gordian knot which none but
that invincible Alexander, Death, can untye ?"

To the variety of colours in the bride favours used formerly,
the following passage, wherein Lady Haughty addresses
Morose, in Jonson's play of the Silent Woman, evidently
alludes :

" Let us know your bride's colours and yours at least."

The bride favours have not been omitted in the northern
provincial poem of the Collier's Wedding .

" The blithsome, bucksome country maids,
With *knots of ribbands* at their heads,
And pinners flutt'ring in the wind,
That fan before and toss behind."

And speaking of the youth, with the bridegroom, it says :

" Like streamers in the painted sky,
At every breast the favours fly."

In a curious old book, called the Fifteen Comforts of
Marriage, a conference is introduced at pp. 44, 47, and 48,
concerning bridal colours in dressing up the bridal bed by the
bridemaids—not, say they, with *yellow ribbands*, these are the
emblems of jealousy—not with *fueille mort*, that signifies
fading love—but with *true-blue*, that signifies constancy, and
green denotes youth—put them both together, and there's
youthful constancy. One proposed *blew and black*, that signifies constancy till death ; but that was objected to, as those
colours will never match. *Violet* was proposed, as signifying

religion; this was objected to as being too grave : and at last
they concluded *to mingle a gold tissue with grass-green,* which
latter signifies youthful jollity.   For the bride's *favours, top-
knots,* and *garters,* the bride proposed *blew, gold-colour,
popingay-green,* and *limon-colour,*—objected to, *gold-colour*
signifying avarice—*popingay-green* wantonness.   The younger
bridemaid proposed mixtures, —*flame-colour*—*flesh-colour*—
willow—and *milk-white.*   The second and third were objected
to, as flesh-colour signifies lasciviousness, and willow forsaken.
It was settled that *red* signifies justice, and *sea-green* inconstancy.   The milliner, at last, fixed the colours as follows :
for the favours, blue, red, peach-colour, and orange-tawny :
for the young ladies' top-knots, flame-colour, straw-colour
(signifying plenty), peach-colour, grass-green, and milk-white ;
and for the garters, a perfect yellow, signifying honour and
joy.

The following allusion to bride favours is from Herrick's
Hesperides, p. 252 :

> " What posies for our wedding-rings,
>   What gloves we'll give, and ribbanings."

In the Gentleman's Magazine for October, 1733, iii. 545,
are "Verses sent by a young lady, lately married, to a quondam
lover, inclosing a *green ribbon noozed :*" [1]

> " Dear D.
> In Betty lost, consider what you lose,
> And, for the *bridal knot,* accept this nooze ;
> The healing ribbon, dextrously apply'd,
> Will make you bear the loss of such a bride."

There is a retort courteous to this very unladylike intimation,
that the discarded lover may go hang himself, but it is not
worth inserting.

---

[1] Thus Cunningham :

> A top-knot he bought her, and garters of green :
> Pert Susan was cruelly stung :
> I hate her so much, that, to kill her with spleen,
> I'd wed, if I were not too young.

BRIDEMAIDS.

THE use of bridemaids at weddings appears as old as the time of the Anglo-Saxons; among whom, as Strutt informs us, "the bride was led by a matron, who was called the bride's woman, followed by a company of young maidens, who were called the bride's maids." The bridemaids and the bridegroom men are both mentioned by the author of the Convivial Antiquities, in his description of the rites at marriages in his country and time.[1]

In later times it was among the offices of the bridemaids to lead the bridegroom to church, as it was the duty of the bridegroom's men to conduct the bride thither. This has not been overlooked in the provincial poem of the Collier's Wedding:

> "Two lusty lads, well drest and strong,
> Stepp'd out to lead the bride along;
> And two young maids, of equal size,
> As soon the bridegroom's hands surprize."

It was an invariable rule for the men always to depart the room, till the bride was undressed by her maids and put to bed.

It is stated in the account of the marriage ceremonials of Philip Herbert and the Lady Susan, performed at Whitehall in the reign of James I., that "the Prince and the Duke of Holst. led the bride to church."

In the old History of John Newchombe, the Wealthy Clothier of Newbery, cited by Strutt, iii. 154, speaking of his bride, it is said, that "after hee, came the chiefest maidens of the country, some bearing bridecakes, and some garlands, made of wheat finely gilded, and so passed to the church. She was led to church between two sweet boys, with bridelaces and rosemary tied about their silken sleeves; the one was Sir Thomas Parry, the other Sir Francis Hungerford."

In the old play of A Woman is a Weathercocke, act i, sc. 1. on a marriage going to be solemnized, Count Fredericke says:

---

[1] "Antequam eatur ad templum Jentaculum sponsæ et invitatis apponitur, serta atque corollæ distribuuntur. Postea certo ordine viri primum cum sponso, deinde puellæ cum sponsa in templum procedunt." Antiquitat. Convivial. fol. 68.

II. 8

"My bride will never be readie, I thinke; heer are *the other sisters.*" Pendant observes: "Looke you, my lorde; there's Lucida weares the willow-garland for you, and will so go to church, I hear." As Lucida enters with a willow-garland, she says:

> "But since my sister he hath made his choise,
> This wreath of willow, that begirts my browes,
> Shall never leave to be my ornament
> Till he be dead, or I be married to him."

Waldron, in his Description of the Isle of Man (Works, fol. p. 169), speaking of the Manx weddings, says: "They have bridemen and brides-maids, who lead the young couple as in England, only with this difference, that the former have ozier wands in their hands, as an emblem of superiority."

In Brooke's England's Helicon, we read:

> "Forth, honour'd groome; behold, not farre behind,
> Your willing bride, led by *two strengthlesse boyes:*"

marked in the margin opposite, "Going to church—bride boyes."

Misson, in his Travels, p. 352, says: "The bridemaids carry the bride into the bed-chamber, where they undress her and lay her in the bed. They must throw away and lose all the pins. Woe be to the bride if a single one is left about her; nothing will go right. Woe also to the bridemaids if they keep one of them, for they will not be married before Whitsontide." Or, as we read in Hymen, 1760, p. 173, "till the Easter following at soonest."

BRIDEGROOM MEN.

THESE appear anciently to have had the title of bride-knights.[1] Those who led the bride to church were always bachelors, but she was to be conducted home by two married

---

[1] "Paranymphi ejusmodi seu sponsi amici appellantur etiam υἱοὶ τȣ νομφωνος (Matth. ix. 15) filii thalami nuptialis; qua de re optime vir præstantissimus Hugo Grotius. Singulare habetur et apud nos nomen ejusmodi eorum quos *bride-knights,* id est, ministros sponsalitios qui sponsam deducere solent, appellitamus." Seldeni Uxor Hebraica, Opera, iii. 638.

persons. Polydore Vergil, who wrote in the time of Henry
the Eighth, informs us that a third married man, in coming
home from church, preceded the bride, bearing, instead of a
torch, a vessel of silver or gold.[1] Moresin relates that to the
bachelors and married men who led the bride to and from
church, she was wont to present gloves for that service
during the time of dinner.[2]

It was part of the bridegroom men's office to put him to
bed to the bride, after having undressed him.

The following passage is in Beaumont and Fletcher's Scornful Lady: "Were these two arms encompassed with the hands
of batchelors to lead me to the church?"

In A Pleasant History of the First Founders, p. 57, we
read: "At Rome the manner was that two children should
lead the bride, and a third bear before her a torch of whitethorn in honour of Ceres, which custom was also observed
here in England, saving that in place of the torch there was
carried before the bride a bason of gold or silver; a garland,
also, of corn-eares was set upon her head, or else she bare it
on her hand; or, if that were omitted, wheat was scattered
over her head in token of fruitfulness; as also, before she
came to bed to her husband, fire and water were given her,
which, having power to purify and cleanse, signified that
thereby she should be chast and pure in her body. Neither
was she to step over the threshold, but was to be borne over, to
signifie that she lost her virginity unwillingly; with many
other superstitious ceremonies, which are too long to rehearse."

[1] "In Anglia servatur ut duo pueri velut paranymphi, id est, auspices,
qui olim pro nuptiis celebrandis auspicia capiebant, nubentem ad templum
—et inde domum duo viri deducant, et tertius loco facis, *vasculum
aureum*, vel *argenteum* præferat." This was called " the bride-cup." So
we read in the account of the marriage of John Newchombe (cited by
Strutt, ut supra), where, speaking of the bride's being led to church, it is
added by the writer that " there was a fair bride-cup of silver-gilt, carried
before her, wherein was a goodly branch of rosemary, gilded very fair,
and hung about with silken ribbands of all colours." It is remarkable
that Strutt (i. 77) should be at a loss to explain a man with a cup in his
hand, in plate xiii. fig. 1, representing a marriage.

[3] "In Anglia adhuc duo pueri mediam in templum, præcedente tibicine-
deferunt nupturam, duo conjugati referunt, his, tempore prandii, ob præ-
stitam operam nova nupta dat chirothecas." Papatus, pp. 114-5.

STREWING HERBS, FLOWERS, or RUSHES,

BEFORE THE BRIDEGROOM AND BRIDE IN THEIR WAY TO CHURCH;

AS ALSO THE WEARING NOSEGAYS ON THE OCCASION.

THERE was anciently a custom at marriages of strewing herbs and flowers, as also rushes, from the house or houses where persons betrothed resided to the church. The following is in Herrick's Hesperides, p. 129 :

> " Glide by the banks of virgins then, and passe
> The showers of roses, lucky foure-leav'd grasse :
> The while the cloud of younglings sing,
> And drown ye with a flowrie spring."

As is the subsequent, in Braithwaite's Strappado for the Divell, 8vo. Lond. 1615, p. 74 :

> " All haile to Hymen and his marriage day,
> *Strew rushes*, and quickly come away ;
> Strew rushes, maides ; and ever as you strew,
> Think one day, maides, like will be done for you."

So, likewise, Browne's Britannia's Pastorals, p. 50. Every one will call to mind the passage in Shakespeare to this purpose :

> " Our *bridal flowers* serve for a buried corse."

Armin's History of the Two Maids of Moreclacke, 4to. 1609, opens thus, preparatory to a wedding : " Enter a maid *strewing flowers*, and a serving-man perfuming the door. The maid says, ' Strew, strew,'—the man, ' The muscadine stays for the bride at church.' " So in Brooke's Epithalamium in England's Helicon :

> " Now busie maydens strew sweet flowres."

In Ram Alley, or Merry Tricks, 1636, we read : " Enter Adriana and another, strawing hearbes.

> "*Adr.* Come, straw apace ; Lord, shall I never live
> To walke to church on flowers ? O 'tis fine
> To see a bride trip it to church so lightly,
> As if her new choppines would scorn to bruze
> A silly flower."

In the Oxford Drollery, 1671, p. 118, is a poem styled "A

Supposition," in which the custom of strewing herbs is thus
alluded to :

" Suppose the way *with fragrant herbs* were strowing,
All things were ready, we to church were going;
And now suppose the priest had joyn'd our hands," &c.

"'Tis worthy of remark that something like the ancient
custom of strewing the threshold of a new-married couple
with flowers and greens is, at this day, practised in Holland.
Among the festoons and foliage, the laurel was always most
conspicuous ; this denoted, no doubt, that the wedding-day
is a day of triumph."—Hymen, or an accurate Description
of the Ceremonies used in Marriage in every Nation of the
World, 1760, p. 39.   The strewing herbs and flowers on this
occasion, as mentioned in a note upon the old play of Ram
Alley, to have been practised formerly, is still kept up in
Kent and many other parts of England.   Among the allusions
of modern poetry to this practice may be mentioned Six Pastorals, by George Smith, Landscape Painter at Chichester in
Sussex, 1770, where, p. 35, we read :

" What do I hear ?   The country bells proclaim
Evander's joy and my unhappy flame.
My love continues though there's no redress !
Ah, happy rival !— Ah, my deep distress !
Now, *like the gather'd flow'rs that strew'd her way,*
Forc'd from my love, untimely I decay."

So also Rowe, in the Happy Village (Poems 1' 96, i. 113),
tells us :

" The *wheaten ear* was scatter'd near the porch,
The green bloom blossom'd strew'd the way to church."

The bell-ringing, &c., used on these occasions are thus
introduced :

" Lo ! where the hamlet's ivy'd gothic tow'r
With merry peals salutes the auspicious hour,
With sounds that thro' the chearful village bear
The happy union of some wedded pair ;"
—" The wedding-cake now through the ring was led,
The stocking thrown across the nuptial bed."
—" Now Sunday come, at stated hour of prayer,
Or rain or shine, the happy couple there :
Where nymphs and swains in variour colours dight,
Gave pleasing contrast to the modest *white.*"

⊙   With regard to nosegays, called by the vulgar in the north of England "Posies," Stephens has a remarkable passage in his character of a Plaine Country Bridegroom, p. 353. "He shews," says he, "neere affinity betwixt marriage and hanging; and to that purpose he provides a great nosegay, and shakes hands with every one he meets, as if he were now preparing for a condemned man's voyage." Nosegays occur in the poem of the Collier's Wedding:

> " Now all prepared and ready stand,
> With fans and *posies* in their hand."

In Hacket's Marriage Present, a Wedding Sermon, the author introduces, among flowers used on this occasion, *primroses, maidens'-blushes,* and *violets*. Herrick, in his Hesperides, plays thus upon the names of flowers selected for this purpose, p. 131:

> " Strip her of spring-time, tender whimp'ring maids,
> Now autumne's come, when all those flow'rie aids
> Of her delayes must end : dispose
> That lady-smock, that pansie, and that rose,
> Neatly apart;
> But for prick-madam and for gentle-heart,
> And soft maiden's-blush, the bride
> Makes holy these, all others lay aside :
> Then strip her, or unto her
> Let him come who dares undo her."

In Vox Graculi, 4to. 1623, " Lady Ver, or the Spring," is called " the Nosegay-giver to weddings," p. 19.

We may here notice that it was also usual to strew flowers in churches on days of humiliation and thanksgiving. In Nichols's Illustrations of the Manners and Expences of Ancient Times in England, 1797, among the parish accounts of St. Margaret, Westminster, under the year 1650, are the following items : " Item, paid for herbs that were strewed in the windows of the church, and about the same, att two severall daies of humiliation, 3s. 10d. Item, paid for herbs that were strewed in the church upon a daie of thanksgiving, 2s. 6d." Under 1651: " Item, paid for hearbs that were strewed in the church on the 24th day of May, being a day of humiliation, 3s. Item, paid to the ringers for ringing on the 24th of October, being a day of thanksgiving for the victorie over the Scots at Worcester, 7s. Item, paid for hearbes and lawrell that were strewed in the church the same day, 8s."

ROSEMARY AND BAYS AT WEDDINGS.

ROSEMARY, which was anciently thought to strengthen the memory, was not only carried at funerals, but also worn at weddings. Herrick, in his Hesperides, p. 273, has the following lines on the Rosemarie Branch:

> " Grow for two ends: it matters not at all,
>   Be't for *my bridall* or my buriall."

In the old play called A Faire Quarrel, 4to. Lond. 1617, act v. sc. 1, we read—

> " *Phis.* Your maister is *to be married to-day ?*
>   *Trim. Else all this rosemary* is lost."

In another old play, Ram Alley, or Merrie Tricks, 1611, is the following allusion to this old custom:

> " Know, varlet, I will be wed this morning;
>   Thou shalt not be there, nor once be grac'd
>   *With a peece of rosemary."*

In a curious wedding sermon, by Roger Hacket, 1607, entitled A Marriage Present, he thus expatiates on the use of rosemary at this time. "The last of the flowers is the rosemary (Rosmarinus, the rosemary, is for married men), the which by name, nature, and continued use, man challengeth as properly belonging to himselfe. It overtoppeth all the flowers in the garden, boasting man's rule. It helpeth the braine, strengtheneth the memorie, and is very medicinable for the head. Another property of the rosemary is, it affects the hart. Let this Ros marinus, this flower of men, ensigne of your wisdome, love, and loyaltie, be carried not only in your hands, but in your heads and harts." [Compare, also, an old ballad called the Bride's Good-morrow, a copy of which is in the British Museum:

> " Young men and maids do ready stand,
>   With sweet rosemary in their hand,
>   A perfect token of your virgin's life:
>   To wait upon you they intend
>   Unto the church to make an end,
>   And God make thee a joyfull wedded wife!"

And perhaps the reason for the custom may be found in the

following lines in Robinson's Handefull of Pleasant Delites,
1584 :

> " Rosemarie is for remembrance
> Betweene us daie and night,
> Wishing that I may alwaies have
> You present in my sight."]

Both rosemary and bays appear to have been gilded on
these occasions.   So Hacket, ut supra ;—" Smell sweet, O ye
flowers, in your native sweetness : be not gilded with the idle
arte of man."   Thus, in Herrick's Hesperides, p. 252 :

> —— " This done, we'l draw lots, who shall buy
> And guild the baies and rosemary."

Also, p. 208, are " Lines to Rosemary and Baies :"

> " My wooing's ended ; now my wedding's neere ;
> When gloves are giving, guilded be you there."

It appears from a passage in Stephens's Character of a
Plaine Countrey Bride, p. 357, that the bride gave also, or
wore, or carried, on this occasion, "gilt rases of ginger."—
" Guilt rases of ginger, rosemary, and ribbands be her best
magnificence.   She will therefore bestow a livery, though she
receives back wages."

In a very curious old printed account of " The receiving of
the Queen's Majesty into the City of London, January 14th,
1558," in the possession of Mr. Nichols, is the following passage : " How many nosegayes did her Grace receyve at poore
women's hands !   How oftentimes stayed she her chariot when
she saw any simple body offer to speake to her Grace !   A
braunch of rosemary given to her Grace, with a supplication,
by a poor woman about Fleet Bridge, was seene in her chariot
till her Grace came to Westminster."   In Strype's edition of
Stow's Survey, b. i. p. 259, A. D. 1560, at "a wedding of
three sisters together," we read : " *Fine flowers and rosemary*
[were] *strewed for them coming home :* and so to the father's
house, where was a great dinner prepared for his said three
bride-daughters, with their bridegrooms and company."   In
the year 1562, July 20, a wedding at St. Olave's, "a daughter
of Mr. Nicholls (who seems to have been the Bridge-master)
was married to one Mr. Coke.   At the celebration whereof
were present my Lord Mayor, and all the aldermen, with

many ladies, &c. : and Mr, Becon, an eminent divine, preached a wedding sermon. Then all the company went home to the Bridge House to dinner : where was as good cheer as ever was known, with all manner of musick and dancing all the remainder of the day ; and at night a goodly supper ; and then followed a masque till midnight. The next day the wedding was kept at the Bridge House, with great cheer ; and after supper came in masquers. One was in cloth of gold. The next masque consisted of friars, and the third of nuns. And after, they danced by times : and lastly, the friars and the nuns danced together."

In A Perfect Journall, &c. of that memorable Parliament begun at Westminster, Nov. 3, 1640, i. 8, is the following passage : " Nov. 28.—That afternoon Master Prin and Master Burton came into London, being met and accompanied with many thousands of horse and foot, and rode *with rosemary and bayes in their hands and hats ;* which is generally esteemed the greatest affront that ever was given to the courts of justice in England."

The rosemary used at weddings was previously dipped, it should seem, in scented water. In Dekker's Wonderfull Yeare, 1603, speaking of a bride who died of the plague on her wedding-day, he says : " Here is a strange alteration, for the rosemary that was washt in sweet water to set out the bridall, is now wet in teares to furnish her buriall." And in Beaumont and Fletcher's Scornful Lady, it is asked "were the rosemary branches dipped ?"

Stephens, in his character of a Plaine Country Bridegroome, p. 352, says : " He is the finest fellow in the parish, and hee that misinterprets my definition deserves no rosemary nor rose-water." At p. 355 he adds : " He must savour of gallantry a little : though he perfume the table with rose-cake, or appropriate bone-lace and Coventry-blew :" and is passing witty in describing the following trait of our bridegroom's clownish civility : " He hath heraldry enough to place every man by his armes." Coles, in his Adam in Eden, speaking of rosemary, says : " The garden rosemary is called rosemarinum coronarium, the rather because women have been accustomed to make crowns and garlands thereof."

The following is in Parkinson's Garden of Flowers, 1629, p. 598 : " The bay-leaves are necessary both for civil uses and

for physic, yea, both for the sick and for the sound, both for
the living and for the dead.   It serveth to adorn the house of
God as well as man—to crowne or encircle, as with a garland,
the heads of the living, and to sticke and decke forth the
bodies of the dead ; so that, from the cradle to the grave, we
have still use of it, we have still need of it." Ibid., p. 426 :
" Rosemary is almost of as great use as bays—as well for civill
as physical purposes : for civil uses, as all doe know, at weddings, funerals, &c. to bestow among friends."   [To these
may be added the following curious observations in Eachard's
Observations, 8vo. Lond. 1671, p. 71 : " I cannot forget him,
who having at some time or other been suddenly cur'd of a
little head-ach with a rosemary posset, would scarce drink out
of any thing but rosemary cans, cut his meat with a rosemary
knife, and pick his teeth with a rosemary sprig.   Nay, sir, he
was so strangely taken up with the excellencies of rosemary,
that he would needs have the Bible cleared of all other herbs,
and only rosemary to be inserted."]

Coles, in his Art of Simpling, p. 73, repeats the observation
of rosemary, that it " strengthens the senses and memory."
In a rare work, entitled A Strange Metamorphosis of Man,
1634, in No. 37, " The Bay Tree," it is observed that " hee is
fit for *halls* and *stately roomes*, where, if there be a wedding
kept, or such like feast, he will be sure to take a place more
eminent than the rest.   He is a notable smell-feast, and is so
good a fellow in them, that almost it is no feast without him.
He is a great companion with the *rosemary*, who is as good a
gossip in all feasts as he a trencher-man."   In the Elder
Brother, 1637, act iii. sc. 3, in a scene immediately before a
wedding :

> " *Lew.* Pray take a peece of rosemary.
> *Mir.* I'll wear it, but for the lady's sake, and none of yours."

In the first scene of Fletcher's Woman's Pride, " The parties
enter with rosemary *as from a wedding.*"   So in the Pilgrim :

> " *Alph.* Well, well, since wedding will come after wooing,
>   *Give me some rosemary*, and letts be going."

We gather from the old play of Ben Jonson, entitled the
Tale of a Tub, that it was customary for the maidens, i. e. the
bridemaids, on the bridegroom's first appearance in the morn-

ing, to present him with a bunch of rosemary bound with ribands.[1]

So late as the year 1698, the old country use appears to have been kept up, of *decking the bridal bed with sprigs of rosemary ;* it is not, however, mentioned as being general. See Lex Forcia, a rare tract on the Abuses of Great Schools, 1698, p. 11.

GARLANDS AT WEDDINGS.

NUPTIAL garlands are of the most remote antiquity. They appear to have been equally used by the Jews and the heathens.[2] "Among the Romans," says Vaughan, in his Golden Grove, 1608, "when the marriage-day was come, the bride was bound to have a chaplet of flowers or hearbes upon her head, and to weare a girdle of sheeps wool about her middle, fastened with a true-loves-knot, the which her husband must loose. Here hence rose the proverb: He hath undone her virgin's girdle ; that is, of a mayde he hath made her a woman."

Among the Anglo-Saxons, after the benediction in the church, both the bride and the bridegroom were crowned with crowns of flowers, kept in the church for that purpose. In the eastern church the chaplets used on these occasions appear

---

[1] See Ben Jonson's Tale of a Tub, where Turf, speaking of the intended bridegroom's first arrival, says: " Look, an the wenches ha' not found un out, and do present un with a van of rosemary, and bays enough to vill a bow-pott, or trim the head of my best vore-horse; we shall all ha' bride-laces, or points, I zee." Similar to this, in the Marrow of Complements, 1655, p. 49, a rustic lover tells his mistress that, at their wedding, " Wee'l have rosemary and bayes to vill a bow-pot, and with the zame Ile trim that vorehead of my best vore-horse." In the Knight of the Burning Pestle, act v. sc. 1, we read: " I will have no great store of company at the wedding, a couple of neighbours and their wives, and we will have a capon in stewed broth, with marrow, and a good piece of beef stuck with rosemary."

[2] Seldini Uxor Hebraica, Opera, iii. 655. " Coronarum nuptialium mentio occurrit apud veteres paganos, quæ item in ornamentis sponsorum Ebraicis, ut supra ostendimus."

to have been blessed.[1] The nuptial garlands were sometimes made of myrtle. In England, in the time of Henry VIII., the bride wore a garland of corn-ears ; sometimes one of flowers.[2] In dressing out Grisild for her marriage, in the Clerk of Oxenford's Tale, in Chaucer, the chaplet is not forgotten : "A coroune on hire hed they han y-dressed."

In Nichols's Churchwardens' Accounts, 1797, St. Margaret's Westminster, under 1540 is the following : "Paid to Alice Lewis, a goldsmith's wife of London, for *a serclett to marry maydens* in, the 26th day of September, £3 10s." In Field's Amends for Ladies, 1639, scene the last, when the marriages are agreed upon, there is a stage direction to *set garlands upon the heads of the maid and widow that are to be married.*

Dallaway, in his Constantinople, 1797, p. 375, tells us : "Marriage is by them (of the Greek Church) called the matrimonial coronation, *from the crowns or garlands with which the parties are decorated,* and which they solemnly dissolve on the eighth day following."

I know not Gosson's authority for the following passage : "In som countries *the bride is crowned by the matrons with a garland of prickles,* and so delivered unto her husband that hee might know he hath tied himself to a thorny plesure." Schoole of Abuse, 1587, or rather the Ephemerides of Phialo, 1579, p. 73.

"*Donner le chapelet.* Se prend pour marier, à cause que

---

[1] Seldeni Uxor Hebraica, Opera iii. 661. "Coronas tenent a tergo paranymphi, quæ capitibus sponsorum iterum a sacerdote non sine benedictione solenni aptantur." The form is given, p. 667 : "Benedic, Domine, annulum istum et coronam istam, ut sicut annulus circumdat digitum hominis et corona caput, ita gratia Spiritus Sancti circumdet sponsum et sponsam, ut videant filios et filias usque ad tertium aut quartam generationem," &c.

[2] Polydore Vergil. "*Spicea* autem *corona* (interdum *florea*) *sponsa redimita, caput, præsertim ruri deducitur, vel manu gerit ipsam coronam.*" Compare Langley's Transl. f. 9.

Concerning the crowns or garlands used by brides, see Leland, Col. v. 332. In the Dialogue of Dives and Pauper, 1493, "The sixte precepte, chap. 2," is the following curious passage : "Thre ornamentys longe pryncypaly to a wyfe : A rynge on hir fynger, a broch on hir brest, *and a garlond on hir hede.* The ringe betokenethe true love, as I have seyd ; the broch betokennethe clennesse in herte and chastitye that she oweth to have ; *the* GARLANDE *bytokeneth gladnesse and the dignitye of the sacrament of wedlok.*"

l on met ordinairement sur la teste des nouvelles mariées, je
dis des personnes de peu de condition, un chapelet de romarin.
Et nôtre vieille coûtume porte, qu'un pere peut marier sa fille
d'un chapeau de roses, c'est a dire, ne luy bailler rien que son
chapelet. La couronne est appellée chapelet, diminutif de
chapeau, quod capiti imponeretur." *Les Origines de quelques
Coutumes Anciennes,* 12mo. Caen, 1672, p. 53. Ibid. p. 70:
"*Chapeau ou chapel de roses.* C'est un petit mariage, car
quand on demande ce qu'un pere donne à une fille, et qu'on
veut repondre qu'il donne peu, on dit qu'il lui donne un
chapeau de roses—qu'un chapel ou chapelet de roses soit con-
venable aux nouvelles mariés, personne n'en doute : les fleurs
en géneral, et les roses particulierement, étant consacrés à
Venus, aux Graces, et l'Amour."

The author of the Convivial Antiquities, in his description
of the rites at marriages in his country and time, has not
omitted *garlands :* "Antequam eatur ad templum jentaculum
sponsæ et invitatis apponitur, *serta atque corollæ* distribuuntur." Antiquitates Convivial. f. 68.

GLOVES AT WEDDINGS.

THE giving of gloves at marriages is a custom of remote
antiquity. The following is an extract from a letter to Mr.
Winwood from Sir Dudley Carleton, dated London, January
1604, concerning the manner of celebrating the marriage
between Sir Philip Herbert and the Lady Susan: "No ceremony was omitted of bridecakes, points, garters and gloves."

In Ben Jonson's play of the Silent Woman, Lady Haughty
observes to Morose, "We see no ensigns of a wedding here,
no character of a bridale ; where be our skarves and our
gloves ?" The bride's gloves are noticed in Stephens's character of A Plaine Country Bride, p 358 : "She hath no rarity
worth observance, if her gloves be not miraculous and singular ;
those be the trophy of some forlorne suitor, who contents
himself with a large offering, or this glorious sentence, that
she should have bin his bedfellow."

It appears from Selden's Uxor Hebraica, Opera, iii. 673,

that the Belgic custom at marriages was for the priest to ask of the bridegroom the ring, and, if they could be had, a pair of red gloves, with three pieces of silver money in them (arrhæ loco), then putting the gloves into the bridegroom's right hand, and joining it with that of the bride, the gloves were left, on loosing their right hands, in that of the bride.

The custom of giving away gloves at weddings occurs in Wilson's play of the Miseries of Inforced Marriage. White gloves still continue to be presented to the guests on this occasion. So also in Herrick's Hesperides, p. 252 :

> " What posies for our wedding-rings,
> What *gloves* we'll give, and ribbanings."

In Arnold's Chronicle (circa 1521), chiefly concerning London, among "the artycles upon whiche is to inquyre in the visitacyons of ordynaryes of chyrches," we read : "Item, whether the curat refuse to do the solemnysacyon of lawfull matrymonye before he have gyfte of money, hoses, or *gloves*."

There is some pleasantry in the vulgar, rather amorous than superstitious, notion, that if a woman surprises a man sleeping, and can steal a kiss without waking him, she has a right to demand a pair of gloves. Thus Gay in his Sixth Pastoral:

> " Cic'ly, brisk maid, steps forth before the rout,
> And kiss'd, with smacking lip, the snoring lout ;
> For ·custom says, whoe'er this venture proves,
> For such a kiss demands a pair of gloves."

In the north of England a custom still prevails at maiden assizes, i. e. when no prisoner is capitally convicted, to present the judges with white gloves. It should seem, by the following passage in Clavell's Recantation of an Ill-led Life, 1634, that anciently this present was made by such prisoners as received pardon after condemnation. It occurs in his dedication "to the impartiall judges of his majestie's bench, my Lord Chiefe Justice, and his other three honourable assistants."

> " Those pardon'd men, who taste their prince's loves,
> (As married to new life) do give you *gloves.*"

Clavell was a highwayman, who had just received the king's pardon. He dates from the King's Bench Prison, October 1627. Fuller, in his Mixt Contemplations on these Times, 1660, says, p. 62 : " It passeth for a generall report of what was customary in former times, that *the sheriff of the county* used to present the judge with a pair of white gloves, at those which we call *mayden assizes,* viz. when no malefactor is put to death therein."

Among the lots in a Lottery presented before the late Queene's Majesty, at the Lord Chancellor's House, 1601, in Davison's Poetical Rapsody, 1611, p. 44, is, No. 8,

" A Paire of Gloves.

" Fortune these *gloves* to you IN CHALLENGE sends,
    For that you love not fooles that are her friends."

Can the custom of *dropping* or *sending the glove,* as the signal of a challenge, have been derived from the circumstance of its being the cover of the hand, and therefore put *for the hand itself?* The giving of the hand is well known to intimate that the person who does so will not deceive, but stand to his agreement. To *shake hands upon it* would not, it should seem, be very delicate in an agreement to fight, and therefore *gloves* may, possibly, have been deputed as substitutes. We may, perhaps, trace the same idea in wedding gloves.

The late Rev. Dr. Lort says in a MS. note : " At Wrexham, in Flintshire, on occasion of the marriage of the surgeon and apothecary of the place, August 1785, I saw at the doors of his own and neighbours' houses, throughout the street where he lived, large boughs and posts of trees, that had been cut down and fixed there, filled with white paper, cut in the shape of women's gloves and of white ribbons."

GARTERS AT WEDDINGS.

GARTERS at weddings have been already noticed under the head of Gloves. There was formerly a custom in the north of England,[1] which will be thought to have bordered very

[1] From the information of a person at Newcastle-upon-Tyne, who had often seen it done. A clergyman in Yorkshire told me that to prevent this very indecent assault, it is usual for the bride to give garters out of her bosom. I have sometimes thought this a fragment of the ancient ceremony of loosening the virgin zone, or girdle, a custom that needs no explanation. Compare also the British Apollo, 1710, iii. No. 91.

closely upon indecency, and strongly marks the grossness of
manners that prevailed among our ancestors ;[1] it was for the
young men present at a wedding to strive, immediately after
the ceremony, who could first pluck off the bride's garters
from her legs.   This was done before the very altar.   The
bride was generally gartered with ribands for the occasion.
Whoever were so fortunate as to be victors in this singular
species of contest, during which the bride was often obliged
to scream out, and was very frequently thrown down, bore
them about the church in triumph.

I find the following in the Epithalamie on Sir Clipesby
Crew and his Lady, in Herrick's Hesperides, p. 128 :

> " Quickly, quickly then prepare,
> And let the young men and the bride-maids share
> Your *garters ;* and their joyntts
> Encircle with *the bridegroom's points.*"

In Brooke's Epithalamium in England's Helicon, we read :

> " Youths, take his poynts, your wonted right ;
> And maydens, take your due, her garters."

A note to a curious and rare tract, 4to. 1686, entitled a
Joco-Serious Discourse in two Dialogues between a Northumberland Gentleman and his Tenant, a Scotchman, both old
Cavaliers, p. 24, tells us : " the piper at a wedding has always
a piece of the bride's garter tyed about his pipes."   These
garters, it should seem, were anciently worn as trophies in
the hats.   So Butler, in Hudibras, I. ii. 524 :

> " Which all the saints, and some since martyrs,
> Wore in their hats like wedding garters."

Misson, in his Travels in England, translated by Ozell, p.
352, says : " When bed-time is come, the bride-men pull off
the bride's garters, which she had before unty'd, that they
might hang down, and so prevent a curious hand from coming
too neer her knee.   This done, and *the garters being fasten'd
to the hats of the gallants,* the bridemaids carry the bride

---

[1] From passages in different works, it should seem that the striving for
garters was originally after the bride had been put to bed.   See Folly in
Print, or a Book of Rhymes, p. 121 ; Stephens's Character of a Plaine
Countrey Bride, p. 359 ; the old song of Arthur of Bradley ; and a Sing-
Song on Clarinda's Wedding, in R. Fletcher's Poems, 1656, p. 230.   See
also Ritson's Ancient Songs, 1792, p. 297.

into the bride chamber, where they undress her and lay her in bed." It is the custom in Normandy for the bride to bestow her garter on some young man as a favour, or sometimes it is taken from her.

In Aylet's Divine and Moral Speculations, 1654, is a copy of verses "on sight of a most honourable lady's *Wedding Garter.*" I am of opinion that the origin of the ORDER OF THE GARTER is to be traced to this nuptial custom, anciently common to both court and country.

Among the lots in a Lottery presented before the late Queene's Majesty at the Lord Chancelor's House, 1601 (Davison's Poetical Rapsody, 1611, p. 45), there occurs, No. 14:

"*A Payre of Garters.*
" Though you have Fortune's garters, you must be
More staid and constant in your steps than she."

Sir Abraham Ninny, in the old play of a Woman's a Weather-Cocke, 1612, act i. sc. 1, declares :

" Well, since I'm disdain'd, *off garters blew,*
Which signifies Sir Abram's love was true.
Off cypresse blacke, for thou befits not me;
Thou art not cypresse, of the cypresse tree,
Befitting lovers ; out green shoe-strings, out,
Wither in pocket, since my Luce doth pout."

SCARVES, POINTS, AND BRIDE LACES AT WEDDINGS.

THAT scarves, now confined to funerals, were anciently given at marriages, has been already noticed in a former section, from Ben Jonson's Silent Woman.[1]   In the same

[1] In a curious manuscript in my possession, entitled A Monthes Jorney into Fraunce : Observations on it, 4to. without date, but bearing internal evidence of having been written in the time of Charles the First (soon after his marriage with Henrietta Maria), and that the writer was a Regent M.A. of the University of Oxford, p. 82, is the following passage : " A scholler of the university never disfurnished so many of his friendes to provide for his jorney, as they (the French) doe neighbours, to adorne their weddings. At my being at Pontoise, I sawe mistres bryde returne from the

author's Tale of a Tub, Turf is introduced as saying on this occasion : " We shall all ha' *bride-laces*, or points, I zee."

Among the lots presented to Queen Elizabeth, in 1601, already quoted from Davison's Rapsody, p. 44, the three following occur, in a list of prizes for ladies :

" 9. *A Dozen of Pointes.*

You are in every point a lover true,
And therefore fortune gives the *points* to you."

" 16. *A Scarfe.*

Take you this *scarfe*, bind Cupid hande and foote,
So Love must aske you leave before he shoote."

" 10. *A Lace.*

Give her the *lace* that loves to be straight-lac'd,
So Fortune's little gift is aptly plac'd."

Herrick, in his Hesperides, p. 128, in the " Epithalamie on Sir Clipesby Crew and his Lady," thus cautions the bridegroom's men against offending the delicacy of the new-married lady :

" We charge ye that no strife
(Farther than gentleness tends) get place
Among ye *striving for her* LACE."

And it was observed before, in the account of the marriage ceremony of John Newchombe, the wealthy clothier of Newbury, (Strutt, iii. 154,) that his bride was led to church between two sweet boys, " with *bride-laces* and rosemary tied about their silken sleeves."   In Dekker's Honest Whore, 1630, we read : " Looke yee, doe you see the *bride-laces that I give at my wedding* will serve to tye rosemary to both your coffins, when you come from hanging."

church. The day before shee had beene somewhat of the condition of a kitchen wench, but now so tricked up with SCARFES, *rings*, and *crosse-garters*, that you never saw a Whitsun-lady better rigged. I should much have applauded the fellowes fortune, if he could have maryed the cloathes but (God be mercifull to hym !) he is chayned to the wench ; much joy may they have together, most peerlesse couple, Hymen Hymenæi, Hymen, Hymen O Hymenæe ! The match was now knytt up amongst them. I would have a French man marie none but a French woman."

BRIDE KNIVES.

STRANGE as it may appear, it is however certain, that knives were formerly part of the accoutrements of a bride. This perhaps will not be difficult to account for, if we consider that it anciently formed part of the dress for women to wear a knife or knives sheathed and suspended from their girdles ;[1] a finer and more ornamented pair of which would very naturally be either purchased or presented on the occasion of a marriage.[2] In the Witch of Edmonton, 1658, p. 21, Somerton says: "But see, the bridegroom and bride come; *the new pair of Sheffield knives fitted both to one sheath.*[3] A bride

[1] See Mr. Douce's Essay on this subject in the Archæologia of the Soc. of Antiq. vol. xii. In a book of some curiosity, entitled the French Garden, for English Ladyes and Gentlewomen to walke in, 1621, in a dialogue describing a lady's dress, the mistress thus addresses her waiting-woman : "Give me my *girdle*, and see that all the furniture be at it ; looke if my cizers, the pincers, the *pen-knife*, the *knife to close letters*, with the bodkin, the ear-picker, and the seale be in the case : where is my purse to weare upon my gowne ?"

[2] Thus as to another part of the dress, in the old play of the Witch of Edmonton, 1658, p. 13, Old Carter tells his daughter and her sweetheart : "Your marriage-money shall be receiv'd before your *wedding-shooes* can be pulled on. Blessing on you both." So in Dekker's Match me in London : "I thinke your *wedding-shoes* have not been oft unty'd." Down answers, " Some *three times.*"

[3] Chaucer's Miller of Trumpington is represented as wearing a Sheffield knife :

"A Shefeld thwitel bare he in his hose ;"

and it is observable that all the portraits of Chaucer give him a knife hanging at his breast. I have an old print of a female foreigner, entitled "Forma Pallii mulieris Clevensis euntis ad forum," in which are delineated, as hanging from her girdle, her purse, her keys, and *two sheathed knives.* Among the women's trinkets about A.D. 1560, in the Four P's of John Heywood, occur :

"Silker's swathbonds, ribands, and sleeve-laces,
Girdles, *knives*, purses, and pin-cases."

"An olde marchant had hanging at his girdle, a pouch, a spectacle-case, a punniard, a pen and inckhorne, and a handkertcher, with many other trinkets besides, which a merry companion seeing, said it was like a habberdasher's shop of small wares." Wits, Fits, and Fancies, 1614, p. 177.

says to her jealous husband, in Dekker's Match me in London,
1631 :

> " See at my girdle hang *my wedding knives!*
> With those dispatch me."

From a passage in the old play of King Edward the Third,
1599, there appear to have been two of them.   So among the
lots, in a Lottery presented before the Queen, in Davison's
Poetical Rapsody, No. 11 is

"A Pair of Knives.

> " Fortune doth give these paire of knives to you,
> To cut the thred of love if 't be not true."

In the old play of a Woman's a Weather-Cocke, act v. sc. 1,
Bellafront says :

> " Oh, were this wedlock knot to tie againe,
> Not all the state and glorie it containes,
> Joyn'd with my father's fury, should enforce
> My rash consent ; but, Scudmore, thou shalt see
> This false heart (in my death) most true to thee.
> *(Shews a knife hanging by her side.)"*

In Well Met, Gossip; or, 'tis Merry when Gossips meet,
1675, the widow says :

> " For this you know, that all the wooing season,
> Suiters with gifts continual seek to gain
> Their mistriss love," &c.

The wife answers :

> " That's very true——
> In conscience I had twenty pair of gloves,
> When I was maid, given to that effect ;
> *Garters, knives, purses, girdles,* store of rings,
> And many a thousand dainty, pretty things."

The following remarkable passage occurs in the Praise of
Musicke (ascribed to Dr. Case), 1586 : " I come to marriages,
wherein as our ancestors (I do willingly harp upon this string,
that our yonger wits may know they stand under correction
of elder judgments) did fondly and with a kind of doting
maintaine many rites and ceremonies, some whereof were
either shadowes or abodements of a pleasant life to come, as
the eating of a quince peare, to be a preparative of sweete and
delightfull dayes between the maried persons."

The subsequent, no less curious, I find in Northbrook's Treatise on Dicing, 1579, p. 35 : "In olde time (we reade) that there was usually caried before the mayde when she shoulde be maried, and came to dwell in hir husbandes house, *a distaffe, charged with flax, and a spyndle hanging at it,* to the intente that shee might bee myndefull to lyve by hir labour."

THE MARRIAGE CEREMONY,

OR PART OF IT, PERFORMED ANCIENTLY IN THE CHURCH-PORCH, OR BEFORE THE DOOR OF THE CHURCH.

CAN this custom have had its rise in the uses of Gentilism? Vallancey informs us that "the antient Etruscans always were married in the streets, before the door of the house, which was thrown open at the conclusion of the ceremony." All the ancient missals mention at the beginning of the nuptial ceremony the placing of the man and woman before the door of the church,[1] and direct, towards the conclusion, that here they shall enter the church as far as the step of the altar. The vulgar reason assigned for the first part of this practice, i. e. "that it would have been indecent to give permission within the church for a man and a woman to sleep together," is too ridiculous to merit any serious answer.

Selden, in his Uxor Hebraica (Opera, iii. 680), asserts that nowhere else, but before the face of, and at the door of the church, could the marriage-dower have been lawfully assigned.[2] "Neque alibi quam in facie ecclesiæ et ad ostium ecclesiæ, atque ante desponsationem in initio contractus (ut juris con-

---

[1] In tne Missale ad Usum Ecclesiæ Sarisburiensis, 1555 : "Statuantur vir et mulier ante ostium ecclesiæ, sive in faciem ecclesiæ, coram Deo et sacerdote et populo." See also the "Formula" in the Appendix to Hearne's Hist. and Antiq. of Glastonb. p. 309.

[2] We read in Bridge's History of Northamptonshire, i. 135, that "Robert Fitz Roger, in the 6th Ed. I. entered into an engagement with Robert de Tybetot to marry, within a limited time, John, his son and heir, to Hawisia, the daughter of the said Robert de Tybetot, *to endow her at the church-door,* on her wedding day, with lands amouating to the value of one hundred pounds per annum."

sultus nostri veteres aiunt) sic fundi dos legitimè assignari potuit."

Chaucer, who flourished during the reign of Edward the Third, alludes to this custom in his Wife of Bath, thus:

> " She was a worthy woman all her live,
> Husbands at the church dore had she five."

In the curious collection of prints, illustrating ancient customs, in the library of Mr. Douce, there is one that represents a marriage solemnizing at the church door. [It was customary to baptise, marry people, and to bury them in the church-porch. Hence the "font or piscina" was there placed to hold consecrated water (called by St. Austin *sacrarium regenerationis*, the sacred laver of regeneration) for the holy baptism; when, after receiving this, the first sacrament of the Christian church, "the child entered it as into the care of a guardian; she takes him up in all the solemn crises of life, and at his death receives him into her bosom. The church is the general home, the universal mother, the mediator and conciliator between this world and the next, the outward and visible sign of the revelation of the Divine law." We have many instances of fonts being placed in the porch of our ancient churches; there is a beautiful hexagon one in the porch of East Dereham church, Norfolk. Until the time of Edward VI. marriages were performed in the church-porch, and not in the church. Edward I. was married at the door of Canterbury cathedral, September 9, 1299, to Margaret, sister of the king of France: and until 1599, the people of France were married at the church-door.]

In a MS. entitled Historical Passages concerning the Clergy in the Papal times, cited in the History of Shrewsbury, 1779, p. 92, notes, it is observed that "the pride of the clergy and the bigotry of the laity were such, that both rich and poor were married at the church doors."

In a MS. Missal of the date of Richard the Second's reign, formerly the property of University College in Oxford, in the marriage ceremony, the man says : "Ich M. take the N. to my weddid wyf, to haven and to holden, for fayrere, for fouler, for bettur for wors, for richer for porer, in seknesse and in helthe, for thys tyme forward, til dethe us departe, ʒif holichirche will it orden ; and ʒerto iche pliʒt the my treuthe :"

and on giving the ring : " With this ring I the wedde, and this yolu and selver ich the 3eve, and with my bodi I the worschepe, and with all my worldly catelle I the honoure." The woman says : " Iche N. take the M. to my weddid husbond, to haven and to holden, for fayrer for fouler, for better for wors, for richer for porer, in seknesse and in helthe, to be bonlich and buxum in bed and at burde, tyl deth us departe, fro thys tyme forward, and if holichirche it wol orden ; and 3erto iche pli3t the my truthe." The variations of these missals on this head are observable. The Hereford missal makes the man say : " I N. underfynge the N. for my wedde wyf, for betere for worse, for richer for porer, yn sekenes and in helthe, tyl deth us departe, as holy church hath ordeyned ; and therto y plygth the my trowthe." The woman says : " I N. underfynge the N. &c. to be boxum to the, tyl deth us departe," &c.

In the Sarum Manual there is this remarkable variation in the woman's speech : " to be bonere and buxom in bedde and at borde," &c. Bonaire and buxum are explained in the margin by " meek and obedient." In the York Manual the woman engages to be " buxom" to her husband ; and the man takes her " for fairer for fouler, for better for warse."

By the parliamentary reformation of marriage and other rites under King Edward the Sixth, the man and woman were first permitted to come into the body or middle of the church, standing no longer, as formerly, at the door : yet by the following, from Herrick's Hesperides, p. 143, one would be tempted to think that this custom had survived the Reformation :

" *The Entertainment ; or,* PORCH VERSE *at the Marriage of Mr. Henry Northly and the most witty Mrs. Lettice Yard.*

" Welcome ! but yet no entrance till we blesse
First you, then you, and both for white successe :
Profane no porch, young man and maid, for fear
Ye wrong the threshold-god that keeps peace here :
Please him, and then all good luck will betide
You the brisk bridegroom, you the dainty bride."

DRINKING WINE IN THE CHURCH AT MARRIAGES.

THIS custom is enjoined in the Hereford Missal.[1] By the Sarum Missal it is directed that the sops immersed in this wine, as well as the liquor itself, and the cup that contained it, should be blessed by the priest.[2] The beverage used on this occasion was to be drunk by the bride and bridegroom and the rest of the company.

In Lysons's Environs of London, iii. 624, in his account of Wilsdon parish, in Middlesex, he tells us of an "Inventory of the goods and ornaments belonging to Wilsdon church about A.D. 1547," in which occur "two masers that were appointed to *remayne in the church for to drynk in at bride-ales*."[3]

In the Workes of John Heiwood, newlie imprinted, 1576, the following passage occurs :

> "*The drinke of my brydecup* I should have forborne
> Till temperaunce had tempred the taste beforne.
> I see now, and shall see, while I am alive,
> Who wedth or he be wise shall die or he thrive."

---

[1] "Post missam, panis, et vinum, vel aliud bonum potabile in vasculo proferatur, et gustent in nomine Domini, sacerdote primo sic dicente, 'Dominus vobiscum.'"

[2] "*Benedicatur* panis et vinum vel aliud quid potabile in vasculo, et gustent in nomine Domini, sacerdote dicente, 'Dominus vobiscum.'" The form of benediction ran thus: "Benedic, Domine, panem istum et hunc potum et hoc vasculum, sicut benedixisti quinque panes in Deserto et sex hydrias in Chanaan Galileæ, ut sint sani et sobrii atque immaculati omnes gustantes ex iis," &c.

[3] In Coates's History of Reading, p. 225, under the year 1561, in the churchwardens' accounts of St. Lawrence's parish, is the following entry : "*Bryde-past*. It. receyved of John Radleye, vis. viijd." A note says: "Probably *the wafers*, which, together with sweet wine, were given after the solemnization of the marriage." See the account of the ceremony of the marriage between Frederick Count Palatine of the Rhine and the Princess Elizabeth, eldest daughter of King James the first, on St. Valentine's day, 1613, in Leland's Collectanea, vi. 335. So, at the marriage of Queen Mary and Philip of Spain, "wine and sops were hallowed." Leland, iv. 400.

In the Compleat Vintner, 1720, p. 17, it is asked:

" What priest can join two lovers' hands,
But wine must seal the marriage-bands ?
As if celestial wine was thought
Essential to the sacred knot,
And that each bridegroom and his bride
Believ'd they were not firmly ty'd
Till Bacchus, with his bleeding tun,
Had finished what the priest begun."[1]

The pieces of cake, or wafers, that appear to have been immersed in the wine on this occasion, were properly called sops,
and doubtless gave name to the flower termed Sops-in-wine.
The allusions to this custom in our old plays are very numerous ; as in Shakespeare's Taming of the Shrew, where
Petruchio calls for wine, gives a health, and having quaffed
off the muscadel, throws the sops in the sexton's face.

In the beginning of Armin's History of the Two Maids of
Moreclacke, 1609, the serving-man, who is perfuming the door,
says : " *The muscadine stays for the bride at church.*" Again,
in Beaumont and Fletcher's Scornful Lady, i. 1 :

" If my wedding-smock were on,
Were the gloves bought and given, the licence come,
Were the rosemary branches dipt, and all
The hippocras and cakes eat and drunk off."

In the articles ordained by Henry VII. for the regulation
of his household, Article for the Marriage of a Princess, we
read : " Then pottes of ypocrice to bee ready, and to be put
into the cupps with soppe, and to be borne to the estates ;
and to take a soppe and a drinke," &c.   In Dekker's Satiro-
Mastix, 1602, we read : " And when we are at church bring
the wine and cakes."   At the magnificent marriage of Queen
Mary and Philip in Winchester Cathedral, 1554, this was

---

[1] This custom, too, has its traces in Gentilism. It is of high antiquity,
says Malone, for it subsisted among our Gothic ancestors : " Ingressus
domum convivialem sponsus cum pronubo suo, sumpto poculo, quod ma-
ritale, vocant, ac paucis a pronubo de mutato vitæ genere prefatis, in
signum constantiæ, virtutis, defensionis et tutelæ, propinat sponsæ et
simul morgennaticam (dotalitium ob virginitatem) promittit, quod ipsa
grato animo recolens, pari ratione et modo, paulo post mutato in uxorium
habitum operculo capitis, ingressa, poculum ut nostrates vocant, uxorium
leviter delibans, amorem, fidem, diligentiam, et subjectionem promittit."
Stiernhook de Jure Sueorum et Gothorum vetusto, 4to. 1672, p. 163.

practised : " The trumpetts sounded, and they both returned, hand in hand, to their traverses in the quire, and there re-mayned until mase was done ; at which tyme *wyne and sopes were hallowed, and delivered to them booth.*"—Leland, Collec-tan. ed. 1770, iv. App. 400. Dr. Farmer has adduced a line in an old canzonet on a wedding, set to music by Morley, 1606 : " *Sops in wine, spice, cakes* are a dealing." In Ben Jonson's Magnetic Lady, the wine drank on this occasion is called a " knitting cup."

The Jews have a custom at this day, when a couple are married, to break the glass in which the bride and bridegroom have drunk, to admonish them of mortality. This custom of nuptial drinking appears to have prevailed in the Greek Church.

A wedding sermon was anciently preached at almost every marriage of persons of any consequence. In the account of the parish of Driffield, in Gloucestershire (Fosbrooke's Hist. ii. 476), we read : " One John Humphries, M.A., in Feb. 1742, published a sermon preached at a wedding here. The Marriage Psalm, on the first Sunday of the couple's appear-ance at church, still continues." In the British Museum, is a Sermon preached at Trafford, in Lancashire, at the Marriage of a daughter of the right worshipfull Sir Edmund Trafford, knight, the 6th of September, Anno 1586, by William Massie, 12mo. Oxford, 1586.

In a curious account of Irish marriage customs about 1682, in Piers's Description of Westmeath, in Vallancey, i. 122, it is stated, that " in their marriages, especially in those countries where cattle abound, the parents and friends on each side meet on the side of a hill, or, if the weather be cold, in some place of shelter about mid-way between both dwellings. If agreement ensue, they drink *the agreement bottle*, as they call it, which is a bottle of good usquebaugh (i. e. whisky, the Irish *aqua vitæ*, and not what is now understood by usque-baugh), and this goes merrily round. For payment of the portion, which generally is a determinate number of cows, little care is taken. Only the father or next of kin to the bride, sends to his neighbours and friends, *sub mutuæ vicissi-tudinis obtentu*, and every one gives his cow or heifer, which is all one in the case, and thus the portion is quickly paid ; nevertheless, caution is taken from the bridegroom, on the day of delivery, for restitution of the cattle, in case the bride die childless within a certain day limited by agreement, and in this case every man's own beast is restored. Thus care is taken that no man shall grow rich by often marriages. On the day of bringing home, the bridegroom and his friends ride out, and meet the bride and her friends at the place of treaty. Being come near each other, the custom was of old to cast short darts at the company that attended the bride, but at such a distance that seldom any hurt ensued ; yet it is not out of the memory of man that the Lord Hoath on such an occasion lost an eye : this custom of casting darts is now obsolete."

The following is from the Gent. Mag. for March, 1767, p. 140 : " The ancient custom of seizing wives by force, and carrying them off, is still practised in Ireland. A remarkable instance of which happened lately in the county of Kilkenny, where a farmer's son, being refused a neighbour's daughter of only twelve years of age, took an opportunity of running away with her ; but being pursued and recovered by the girl's parents, she was brought back and married by her father to a lad of fourteen. But her former lover, determining to maintain his priority, procured a party of armed men, and beseiged the house of his rival ; and in the contest the father-in-law was shot dead, and several of the beseigers were mortally wounded, and forced to retire without their prize."

THE NUPTIAL KISS IN THE CHURCH.

THIS nuptial kiss in the church is enjoined both by the York Missal [1] and the Sarum Manual.[2] It is expressly mentioned in the following line from the old play of the Insatiate Countess, by Marston :

" The kisse thou gav'st me in the church, here take."

---

[1] Thus the York Missal : " Accipiat sponsus pacem (the pax) a sacerdote, et ferat sponsæ, osculans eam, et neminem alium, nec ipse nec ipsa."
[2] 4to. Par. 1553, Rubrick, fol. 69 : " Surgant ambo, sponsus et sponsa, et accipiat sponsus pacem a sacerdote, et ferat sponsæ, osculans eam, et neminem alium, nec ipse nec ipsa."

We learn that, in dancing, "a kiss was anciently the established fee of a lady's partner." So, in a Dialogue between
Custom and Veritie concerning the Use and Abuse of Dancing
and Minstrelsie, printed by John Allde:

> " But some reply, what foole would daunce,
>   If that, when daunce is doone,
> He may not have at ladyes' lips
>   That which in daunce he woon ?"

This custom is still prevalent among the country people in
many, perhaps all, parts of the kingdom.   When the fiddler
thinks his young couple have had music enough, he makes
his instrument squeak out two notes which all understand to
say, "*Kiss her!*"   In the Tempest this line occurs:

> " Curtsied when you have and kissed."

To which the following is a note: " As was antiently done
at the beginning of some dances."   So, in King Henry VIII.
that prince says:

> " I were unmannerly to take you out,
>   And not to kiss you."

It is still customary among persons of middling rank as
well as the vulgar, in most parts of England, for the young
men present at the marriage ceremony to salute the bride, one
by one, the moment it is concluded.   This, after officiating in
the ceremony myself, I have frequently seen done.   In the
provincial poem of the Collier's Wedding, the bride is introduced as being waylaid, after the ceremony, at the church
style for this purpose.   [It is almost unnecessary to remind
the reader of the excellent use made of this custom by
Shakespeare in the Taming of the Shrew.]

The subsequent curious particulars relating to the *nuptial
kiss in the church*, &c. are from Randolph's Letters, cited by
Andrews in his Continuation of Henry's History of Great
Britain, 1796, p. 148, note.   He is speaking of the marriage
of Mary Queen of Scots to Lord Darnley : " She had on her
back the great mourning gown of black, with the great white
mourning hood, &c.   The rings, which were three, the middle
a rich diamond, were put on her finger.   They kneel together,
and many prayers were said over them ; she tarrieth out the
mass. and *he taketh a kiss*, and leaveth her there, and went

to her chamber, whither, within a space, she followeth, and
being required (according to the solemnity) to cast off her
cares, and leave aside these sorrowful garments, and give herself to a more pleasant life, after some pretty refusal (more, I
believe for manner sake than grief of heart), she suffereth
them that stood by, every man that could approach, to take
out a pin ; and so, being committed to her ladies, changed
her garments, but went not to bed ; to signifie to the world
that it was not lust that moved them to marry, but only the
necessity of her country, not, if God will, to leave it without
an heir."[1] Vaughan, in his Golden Grove, 1608, says :
"Among the Romans, the future couple sent certain pledges
one to another, which, most commonly, they themselves afterwards being present, would confirme with *a religious kisse.*"

CARE CLOTH.

AMONG the Anglo-Saxons the nuptial benediction was performed under a veil, or square piece of cloth, held at each
corner by a tall man over the bridegroom and bride, to conceal
her virgin blushes ; but if the bride was a widow, the veil
was esteemed useless. According to the use of the church of
Sarum, when there was a marriage before mass, the parties
kneeled together and had a fine linen cloth (called the care

---

[1] Nor is the nuptial kiss an English ceremony only. In the Disserta-
tions sur les Antiquités de Russie, by Dr. Guthrie, already quoted, we have
the following section among the marriage ceremonies, p. 129 : " *Kitra, ou
baser d'amour des Grecs.*—Après que la bénédiction nuptiale a déclaré les
jeunes époux mari et femme, ce caractère leur donne le droit de suivre une
coutume aussi singulière qu'ancienne, qui consiste à se donner le *kitra*
des Grecs, ou le fameux baiser d'antiquité, si emblématique de l'amour et
de l'attachement, dont Théocrite parle dans la cinquième idylle, où il re-
présente une jeune nymphe qui se plaint amèrement de son amant Alcippes ;
parce que l'ingrat, à qui elle a bien voulu donner un baiser, a dédaigné
de jouir de cette faveur selon la manière usitée, c'est-à-dire, *en la prenant
par les oreilles.* Tibulle, dans sa cinquième élégie, liv. II., et Ciceron
dans sa vingt-septième épître familière, citent pareillement ce témoignage
curieux de l'amour, que nous trouvons encore en usage parmi les paysans
Russes, lorsqu'une fois engagés par le lien du mariage ils se donnent le
premier baiser conjugal."

cloth) laid over their heads during the time of mass, till they received the benediction, and then were dismissed.[1]

I have a curious Wedding Sermon, by William Wheatley, preacher of Banbury in Oxfordshire, 1624, entitled a Care Cloth, or a Treatise of the Cumbers and Troubles of Marriage. I know not the etymology of the word " care," used here in composition with " cloth."[2] Wheatley has given it the ordinary meaning of the word, but I think erroneously. Like many other etymologists, he has adapted it to his own purpose. Selden's fifteenth chapter in his Uxor Hebraica (Opera iii. 633), treats " de velaminibus item quibus obtecti sponsi."

In the Appendix to Hearne's Hist. and Antiq. of Glastonbury, p. 309, is preserved " Formula antiqua nuptias in iis partibus Angliæ (occidentalibus nimirum) quæ ecclesiæ Herefordensis in ritibus ecclesiasticis ordine sunt usi, celebrandi." The care cloth seems to be described in the following passage : " Hæc oratio ' S. propiciare Domine,' semper dicatur super nubentes sub pallio prosternentes."

In Sir John Sinclair's Statistical Account of Scotland, 1793,

---

[1] Blount in v. In the Hereford Missal it is directed that at a particular prayer the married couple shall prostrate themselves, while four clerks hold the pall, i. e. the care cloth over them. See the Appendix to Hearne's Glastonbury, p. 309 et seq. The Rubric in the Sarum Manual is somewhat different : " Prosternat se sponsus et sponsa in oratione ad gradum altaris, extenso super eos pallio, quod teneant quatuor clerici per quatuor cornua in superpelliciis." The York Manual also differs here : " Missa dein celebratur, illis genuflectentibus sub pallio super eos extento, quod teneant *duo* clerici in superpelliceis."

[2] Something like this care cloth is used by the modern Jews, from whom it has probably been derived into the Christian church : " There is a square vestment called Taleth, with pendents about it, put over the head of the bridegroom and the bride together." See Leo Modena's Rites of the Jews, by Chilmead, 1650, p. 176. Levi, in his Succinct Account of the Rites and Ceremonies of the Jews as observed by them in their different dispersions throughout the World at this present time, p. 132, speaks of a " velvet canopy." He adds, that when the priest has taken the glass of wine into his hand, he says as follows : " Blessed art thou, O Lord our God ! King of the universe, the creator of the fruit of the vine. Blessed art thou, O Lord our God ! King of the universe, who hath sanctified us with his commandments, and hath forbid us fornication, and hath prohibited unto us the betrothed, but hath allowed unto us those that are married unto us *by the means of the* CANOPY *and the wedding-ring :* blessed art thou, O Lord ! the sanctifier of his people Israel, *by the means of the* CANOPY and wedlock."

v. 83, the minister of Longforgan in Perthshire, speaking of the superstitious opinions and practices of the parish, says: "Immediately before the celebration of the marriage-ceremony, every knot about the bride and bridegroom (garters, shoe-strings, strings of petticoats, &c.) is carefully loosened. After leaving the church the whole company walk round it, keeping the church-walls always upon the right hand. The bride-groom, however, first retires one way with some young men to tie the knots that were loosened about him ; while the young married woman, in the same manner, retires somewhere else to adjust the disorder of her dress."

BRIDE ALE,

CALLED ALSO BRIDE-BUSH, BRIDE-STAKE, BIDDING, AND BRIDE-WAIN.

BRIDE-ALE, bride-bush, and bride-stake are nearly synony-mous terms, and all derived from the circumstance of the bride's selling ale on the wedding-day, for which she received, by way of contribution, whatever handsome price the friends assembled on the occasion chose to pay her for it. The expense of a bride-ale was probably defrayed by the relations and friends of a happy pair, who were not in circumstances to bear the charges of a wedding-dinner.

In the Christen State of Matrimony, 1543, f. 48, we read : " When they come home from the church, then beginneth ex-cesse of eatyng and drynking, and as much is waisted in one daye as were sufficient for the two newe-maried folkes halfe a year to lyve upon."[1]

The following is from the Antiquarian Repertory, iii. 24, communicated by Astle from the court-rolls of Hales-Owen Borough, in the county of Salop (in the hands of Thomas

---

[1] I know not the meaning of the following lines in Christopher Brooke's Epithalamium :

" The board being spread, furnished with various plenties ;
The bride's fair object in the middle plac'd."

Opposite, in the margin, is "dinner."

Littleton, lord of that borough), of the 15th year of Queen Elizabeth : *"Custom of bride-ale.*—Item, a payne is made that no person or persons that shall brewe any weddyn-ale to sell, shall not brewe above twelve strike of mault at the most, and that the said persons so married shall not keep nor have above eight messe of persons at his dinner within the burrowe : and before his brydall daye he shall keep no unlawfull games in hys house, nor out of hys house, on pain of 20 shillings."

In Harrison's Description of Britain, it is remarked : "In feasting, also, the husbandmen do exceed after their manner, especially at bridales, &c., where it is incredible to tell what meat is consumed and spent; ech one brings such a dish, or so manie, with him, as his wife and he doo consult upon, but alwaies with this consideration, that the leefer friend shall have the better provision."

Thus it appears that, among persons of inferior rank, a contribution was expressly made for the purpose of assisting the bridegroom and bride in their new situation. This custom must have doubtless been often abused; it breathed, however, a great deal of philanthropy, and would naturally help to increase population by encouraging matrimony. This custom of making presents at weddings seems also to have prevailed amongst those of the higher order. From the account before cited of the nuptials of the Lady Susan with Sir Philip Herbert, in the reign of James I., it appears that the presents of plate and other things given by the noblemen were valued at 2500*l.*, and that the king gave 500*l.* for the bride's jointure. His Majesty gave her away, and, as his manner was, archly observed on the occasion, that "if he were unmarried, he would not *give her*, but *keep her* for himself." From a passage in Ben Jonson's Silent Woman, Andrews, in his Continuation of Henry's History of Great Britain, 4to. p. 529, infers that it seems to have been a general custom to make presents to the married pair, in proportion to the gay appearance of their wedding.

Morant, in his History of Essex, ii. 303, speaking of Great Yeldham, in Hinckford hundred, says : "A house near the church was anciently used and appropriated for dressing a dinner for poor folks when married, and had all utensils and furniture convenient for that purpose. It hath since been converted into a school." Ibid. p. 499, speaking of matching in Harlow Half-hundred, he says : "A house close to the churchyard, said to be built by one .... Chimney, was designed for the entertainment of poor people on their wedding-day. It seems to be very ancient, but ruinous."

Gough, in his Camden, edit. 1789, i. 341, Hertfordshire, says : "At Therfield, as at Braughing, was till lately a set of kitchen furniture lent to the poor at weddings." Hutchinson, in his History of Cumberland, i. 553, speaking of the parish of Whitbeck, says : *Newly-married peasants* beg corn to sow their first crop with, and are called *Cornlaiters.*"

Owen, in his Welsh Dictionary, in v. *Cawsa*, says : " It is customary in some part of Wales for poor women newly married to go to farmers' houses, to ask for cheese, which is called Cawsa." Also, ibid., in v. *Cymhorth :* "The poor people in Wales have a marriage of contribution, to which every guest brings a present of some sort of provision or money, to enable the new couple to begin the world."

Bride-ales are mentioned by Puttenham, in his Arte of Poesie, 1589, p. 69 : " During the course of Queen Elizabeth's entertainments at Kenilworth Castle, in 1575, a bryde-ale was celebrated with a great variety of shews and sports." See also Laneham's Letter, dated the same year.

Newton, in his Herbal for the Bible, p. 94, speaking of rushes, says : "Herewith be made manie pretie imagined devises for *bride-ales*, and other solemnities, as little baskets, hampers, panniers, pitchers, dishes, combes, brushes, stooles, chaires, purses with strings, girdles, and manic such other pretie, curious, and artificiall conceits, which at such times many do take the paines to make and hang up in the houses as tokens of good-will to the new-married bride ; and, after the solemnity ended, to bestow abroad for bride-gifts or presents." Ibid. p. 225, when speaking of the rose, Newton says : "At *bride-ales* the houses and chambers were woont to be strawed with these odoriferous and sweet herbes, to signifie that in wedlocke all pensive sullennes and lowring cheer, all wrangling strife, jarring, variance, and discorde ought to be utterly excluded and abandoned ; and that in place thereof. al mirth, pleasantnes, cheerfulnes, mildnes, quietnes, and love should be maintained, and that in matters passing betweene the husband and the wife all secresie should be used."

According to Johnson, the secondary sense of "bush," is

II. 10

a bough of a tree fixed up at a door to show that liquors are sold there. Hence the well-known proverb—"Good wine needs no bush." There is a wedding-sermon by Whateley, of Banbury, entitled a Bride-Bush, as is another, preached to a new-married couple at Œsen, in Norfolk. Thus Ben Jonson :

> "With the phant'sies of Hey-troll
> Troll about the bridal bowl,
> And divide the broad bride-cake
> Round about the *bride's stake*."

A bush at the end of a stake or pole was the ancient badge of a country alehouse. Around this bride-stake the guests were wont to dance as about a maypole.

The bride-ale appears to have been called in some places a bidding, from the circumstance of the bride and bridegroom's bidding or inviting the guests. A writer in the Gent. Mag. for May, 1784, p. 343, mentions this custom in some parts of South Wales, peculiar, he thinks, to that country, and still practised at the marriages of servants, tradesfolks, and little farmers : " Before the wedding an entertainment is provided, to which all the friends of each party are *bid* or invited, and to which none fail to bring or send some contribution, from a cow or calf down to half-a-crown or a shilling. An account of each is kept, and if the young couple do well, it is expected that they should give as much at any future bidding of their generous guests. I have frequently known of 50*l.* being thus collected, and have heard of *a bidding* which produced even a hundred." In the Cambrian Register, 1796, p. 430, we read : " Welch weddings are frequently preceded, on the evening before the marriage, by presents of provisions and articles of household furniture to the bride and bridegroom. On the wedding-day as many as can be collected together accompany them to the church, and from thence home, where a collection is made in money from each of the guests, according to their inclination or ability, which sometimes supplies a considerable aid in establishing the newly-married couple, and in enabling them to ' begin the world,' as they call it, with more comfort ; but it is, at the same time, considered as a debt to be repaid hereafter, if called upon, at any future wedding of the contributors, or of their friends or their children, in similar circumstances. Some time previous to these weddings, where they mean to receive contributions, a herald, with a crook or

wand adorned with ribbons, makes the circuit of the neighbourhood, and makes his 'bidding,' or invitation, in a prescribed form. The knight-errant cavalcade on horseback, the
carrying off the bride, the rescue, the wordy war in rythm
between the parties, &c., which formerly formed a singular
spectacle of mock contest at the celebration of nuptials, I
believe to be now almost, if not altogether, laid aside everywhere through the principality."

The following is from the Gent. Mag. for 1789, lix. 99 :
" *Bidding.*—As we intend entering the nuptial state, we propose having a bidding on the occasion on Thursday the 20th
day of September instant, at our own house on the Parade,
where the favour of your good company will be highly
esteemed ; and whatever benevolence you please to confer on
us shall be gratefully acknowledged, and retaliated on a similar
occasion, by your most obedient humble servants,

WILLIAM JONES, } Caermarthen,
ANN DAVIES,   } Sept. 4, 1787.

" N.B. The young man's father (Stephen Jones), and the
young woman's aunt (Ann Williams), will be thankfull for all
favours conferred on them that day."

Another writer in the Gent. Mag. for 1781, liv. 181, mentions a similar custom in Scotland, called *penny weddings.*
" When there was a marriage of two poor people who were
esteemed by any of the neighbouring gentry, they agreed
among themselves to meet, and have a dance upon the occasion, the result of which was a handsome donation, in order
to assist the new-married couple in their outset in life." In
the Statistical Account of Scotland, iv. 86, parish of Drainy,
co. of Elgin, we are told : " A *penny wedding* is when the expense of the marriage entertainment is not defrayed by the
young couple or their relations, but by a club among the
guests. Two hundred people, of both sexes, will sometimes
be convened on an occasion of this kind." In the same work,
xxi. 146, parish of Monquhitter, speaking of the time of
"our fathers," the minister observes : "Shrove Tuesday, Valentine Eve, the Rood-day, &c. &c., were accompanied by pastimes and practices congenial to the youthful and ignorant
mind. The market-place was to the peasant what the draw-
ing-room is to the peer, the theatre of show and of consequence.

The scene, however, which involved every amusement and every joy of an idle and illiterate age was a *penny bridal*. When a pair were contracted, they, for a stipulated consideration, bespoke their wedding at a certain tavern, and then ranged the country in every direction to solicit guests. One, two, and even three hundred would have convened on these occasions to make merry at their own expense for two or more days. This scene of feasting, drinking, dancing, wooing, fighting, &c., was always enjoyed with the highest relish, and, until obliterated by a similar scene, furnished ample materials for rural mirth and rural scandal. But now *the penny bridal is reprobated as an index of want of money and of want of taste*. The market-place is generally occupied by people in business. Athletic amusements are confined to schoolboys. Dancing, taught by itinerant masters, cards, and conversation, are the amusements now in vogue; and the pleasures of the table enlivened by a moderate glass are frequently enjoyed in a suitable degree by people of every class." In the same work, xv. 636, parish of Avoch, co. Ross, it is said : "Marriages in this place are generally conducted in the style of *penny weddings*. Little other fare is provided except bread, ale, and whisky. The relatives, who assemble in the morning, are entertained with a dram and a drink gratis. But, after the ceremony is performed, every man pays for his drink. The neighbours then convene in great numbers. A fiddler or two, with perhaps a boy to scrape on an old violoncello, are engaged. A barn is allotted for the dancing, and a house for drinking; and thus they make merry for two or three days, till Saturday night. On Sabbath, after returning from church, the married couple give a sort of dinner or entertainment to the present friends on both sides : so that these weddings, on the whole, bring little gain or loss to the parties." Jamieson, in his Etymological Dictionary, quotes an Act of the General Assembly, 13th February, 1645, for the restraint of *pennie brydals*.[1]

In Cumberland it had the appellation of a bride-wain, a

---

[1] We learn from Loccenius that penny bridals were common in Sweden. The custom has probably existed from an early period. " In nonnullis locis sumtus nuptialis ab invitatis hospitibus in *cranio* vel *collectis* solent adjuvari ac sublevari : quum plures unam facilius, quam unus et solus se- ipsum impensis majori instruere possit." Antiq. Suio-Goth., p. 109.

term which will be best explained by the following extract from the Glossary of Douglas's Virgil, v. Thig : There was a custom in the Highlands and North of Scotland, where new-married persons had no great stock, or others low in their fortune, brought carts and horses with them to the houses of their relations and friends, and received from them corn, meal, wool, or whatever else they could get." The subsequent, headed *Bride-wain*, is extracted from the Cumberland Packet, a newspaper so called :

> " There let Hyn·en oft appear
> In saffron robe and taper clear,
> And pomp and feast and revelry,
> With mask and ancient pageantry."

" George Payton, who married Ann, the daughter of Joseph and Dinah Collin, of Crossley Mill, purposes having a bride-wain at his house at Crossley, near Mary Port, on Thursday, May 7th next (1789), where he will be happy to see his friends and well-wishers, for whose amusement there will be a saddle, two bridles, a pair of gands-d'amour gloves, which whoever wins is sure to be married within the twelve months, a girdle (ceinture de Venus), possessing qualities not to be described, and many other articles, sports, and pastimes too numerous to mention, but which can never prove tedious in the exhibition," &c.

A short time after a match is solemnized, the parties give notice, as above, that on such a day they purpose to have a bride-wain. In consequence of this the whole neighbourhood for several miles round assemble at the bridegroom's house, and join in all the various pastimes of the country. This meeting resembles our wakes and fairs ; and a plate or bowl is fixed in a convenient place, where each of the company contributes in proportion to his inclination and ability, and according to the degree of respect the parties are held in ; and by this very laudable custom a worthy couple have frequently been benefited at setting out in life with a supply of money of from ten to fourscore pounds.

Sir F. M. Eden, in his work on the State of the Poor, 1797, i. 598, observes : " The custom of a general feasting at weddings and christenings is still continued in many villages in Scotland, in Wales, and in Cumberland ; districts which, as the refinements of legislation and manners are slow in reaching them, are most likely to exhibit vestiges of customs deduced from remote antiquity, or founded on the simple dictates of nature ; and indeed it is not singular that marriages, births, christenings, house-warmings, &c., should be occasions in which people of all classes and all descriptions think it right to rejoice and make merry. In many parts of these districts of Great Britain, as well as in Sweden and Denmark, all such institutions, now rendered venerable by long use, are religiously observed. It would be deemed ominous, if not impious, to be married, have a child born, &c., without something of a feast. And long may the custom last ; for it neither leads to drunkenness and riot, nor is it costly, as, alas! is so commonly the case in convivial meetings in more favoured regions. On all these occasions the greatest part of the provisions is contributed by the neighbourhood ; some furnishing the wheaten flour for the pastry ; others, barley or oats for bread and cakes ; some, poultry for pies ; some, milk for the frumenty ; some, eggs ; some, bacon ; and some, butter ; and, in short, every article necessary for a plentiful repast. Every neighbour, how high or low soever, makes it a point to contribute something. At a *daubing* (which is the erection of a house of clay), or at a *bride-wain* (which is the carrying of a bride home), in Cumberland, many hundreds of persons are thus brought together ; and as it is the custom also, in the latter instance, to make presents of money, one or even two hundred pounds are said to have sometimes been collected. A deserving young couple are thus, by a public and unequivocal testimony of the good will of those who best know them, encouraged to persevere in the paths of propriety, and are also enabled to begin the world with some advantage. The birth of a child also, instead of being thought or spoken of as bringing on the parents new and heavy burthens, is thus rendered, as it no doubt ought to be, a comfort and a blessing, and, in every sense, an occasion of rejoicing. I own," adds this honourable advocate in the cause of humanity, "I cannot figure to myself a more pleasing or a more rational way of rendering sociableness and mirth subservient to prudence and virtue."

"In most parts of Essex it is a common custom, when poor people marry, to make a kind of dog-hanging, or money-gathering, which they call a wedding-dinner, to which they invite tag and rag, all that will come · where after dinner, upon summons of the fiddler, who setteth forth his voice like a town-crier, a table being set forth, and the bride set simpering at the upper end of it, the bridegroom standing by with a white sheet athwart his shoulders, whilst the people march up to the bride, present their money and wheel about. After this offering is over, then is a pair of gloves laid upon the table, most monstrously bedaubed about with ribbon, which by way of auction is set to sale at who gives most, and he whose hap it is to have them, shall withall have a kiss of the bride." History of Sr. Billy of Billericay, and his Squire Ricardo (a very admirable parody on Don Quixote), chap. ix.

In the Statistical Account of Scotland, xviii. 122, parish of Gargunnock, co. Stirling, we read : " It is seldom there are social meetings. Marriages, baptisms, funerals, and the conclusion of the harvest, are almost the only occasions of feasting. At these times there is much unnecessary expense. Marriages usually happen in April and November. The month of May is cautiously avoided. A principal tenant's son or daughter has a crowd of attendants at marriage, and the entertainment lasts for two days at the expense of the parties. The company at large pay for the musick."

Waldron, in his Description of the Isle of Man (Works, p. 169, speaking of the Manks' wedding feasts, says : "Notice is given to all the friends and relations on both sides though they live ever so far distant. Not one of these, unless detained by sickness, fails coming and bringing something towards the feast ; the nearest of kin, if they are able, commonly contribute the most, so that they have vast quantities of fowls of all sorts ; I have seen a dozen of capons in one platter, and six or eight fat geese in another; sheep and hogs roasted whole, and oxen divided but into quarters."[1]

In Vaughan's Golden Grove, 1608, we read : " The marriage day being come (in some shires of England), the invited

[1] In the Glossarium Suio-Gothicum, auctore I. Ihre, fol. Upsaliæ, 1769, we read: " BRUDSKAL. Gifwa i Brudskålen dicitur de erano vel munere collectitio quod sponsæ die nuptiarum a convivis in pateram mittitur, habito antea brevi sermone a præsente sacerdote. Nescio, an huc quicquam faciat tributum illud, quod in Gallia sponsæ dabatur escuellatta dictum, et de quo Du-Fresne in Gloss. Lat." Ibid. v. JUL. p. 1005 : HEMKOMOL, convivium quod novi conjuges in suis ædibus instruunt."

ghests do assemble together, and at the very instant of the marriage doe cast their presents (which they bestowe upon the new-married folkes) into a bason, dish, or cup which standeth upon the table in the church, ready prepared for that purpose. But this custome is onely put in use amongst them which stand in need."

It appears from Allan Ramsay's Poems, 1721, p. 120, that it was a fashion in Scotland for the friends to assemble in the new-married couple's house, before they had risen out of bed, and to throw them their several presents upon the bed-clothes:

> " As fou's the house cou'd pang,
> To see the young fouk or they raise,
> Gossips came in ding dang,
> And wi' a soss aboon the claiths
> Ilk ane their gifts down flang," &c.

Here a note informs us, " They commonly throw their gifts of household furniture above the bed-cloathes where the young folks are lying." One gives twelve horn spoons, another a pair of tongs, &c.

Park, in his Travels into the Interior of Africa, describes a wedding among the Moors, p. 135: " April 10, in the evening, the tabala, or large drum, was beat to announce a wedding. A great number of people of both sexes assembled. A woman was beating the drum, and the other women joining at times in chorus, by setting up a shrill scream. Mr. Park soon retired, and having been asleep in his hut, was awakened by an old woman, who said she had brought him a present from the bride. She had a wooden bowl in her hand; and before Mr. Park was recovered from his surprise, discharged the contents full in his face. Finding it to be the same sort of *holy water* with which a Hottentot priest is said to sprinkle a new-married couple, he supposed it to be a mischievous frolic, but was informed it was a nuptial benediction from the bride's own person, and which, on such occasions, is always received by the young unmarried Moors as a mark of distinguished favour. Such being the case, Mr. Park wiped his face, and sent his acknowledgments to the lady. The wedding drum continued to beat, and the women to sing all night. About nine in the morning the bride was brought in state from her mother's tent, attended by a number of women, who carried her tent (a present from the husband), some bearing up the poles, others holding by the strings and marched singing until they came to the place appointed for her residence, where they pitched the tent. The husband followed with a number of men, leading four bullocks, which they tied to the tent-strings; and having killed another, and distributed the beef among the people, the ceremony closed."

[In the north of England, it is considered unlucky for a couple to be married, or for a woman to be churched, while there is a grave open in the churchyard. It is also ominous of misfortune to be married in green. If there is an odd number of guests at a wedding, one is sure to die within the succeeding twelve months.]

WINNING THE KAIL.

THIS is mentioned in the curious local poem by Edward Chicken, the Collier's Wedding, ed. 1764, p. 21:

> " Four rustic fellows wait the while
> To kiss the bride at the church-style:
> Then vig'rous mount their felter'd steeds,
> With heavy heels, and clumsy heads;
> So scourge them going, head and tail—
> To win what country call the kail."

The Glossary to Burns's Scottish Poems describes " Broose" (a word which has the same meaning with "Kail") to be " a race at country weddings who shall first reach the bridegroom's house on returning from church." The meaning of the word is everywhere most strangely corrupted. " Broose" was originally, I take it for granted, the name of the prize on the above occasion, and not of the race itself; for whoever first reaches the house to bring home the good news, wins the "kail," i. e. a smoking prize of spice broth,[1] which stands

[1] Compare Jamieson's Etymolog. Dict. of the Scottish Language, v. *Bruse.* I know not whether the following passage is to be referred to this, or is given only as describing the bridegroom's awkwardness in supping broth. New Essayes and Characters, by John Stephens, 1631, p. 353, speaking of a plain country bridegroom, the author says: " Although he points out his bravery with ribbands, yet hath he no vaine glory; for he contemnes fine cloathes with dropping pottage in his bosome."

ready prepared to reward the victors in this singular kind of race. This same kind of contest is called in Westmoreland "riding for the ribbon."

Sampson, in his Statistical Survey of the County of Londonderry, 1802, p. 417, says: "At the Scotch weddings the groom and his party vie with the other youngsters who shall gallop first to the house of the bride. Nor is this feat of gallantry always without danger; for in every village through which they are expected, they are received with shots of pistols and guns; these discharges, intended to honour the parties, sometimes promote their disgrace, if to be tumbled in the dirt on such an occasion can be called a dishonour. At the bride's house is prepared a bowl of *broth*, to be the reward of the victor in the race, which race is therefore called the running for the *brose*. The Irish wedding is somewhat different, especially in the mountainous districts. However suitable the match, it is but a lame exploit, and even an affront, if the groom does not first run away with the bride. After a few days' carousal among the groom's friends, the *weddingers* move towards the bride's country, on which occasion not only every relative, but every poor fellow who aspires to be the *wellwisher* of either party, doth bring with him a *bottle of whisky*, or the price of a bottle, to the rendezvous. After this second edition of matrimonial hilarity, the bride and groom proceed quietly to their designed home, and, forgetting all at once their romantic frolic, settle quietly down to the ordinary occupations of life."

That riding for the broose is still kept up in Scotland, may be seen by the following extract from the account of marriages in the Courier newspaper of January 16th, 1813: "On the 29th ult. at Mauchline, by the Rev. David Wilson, in Bankhead, near Cumnock, Mr. Robert Ferguson, in Whitehill of New Cumnock, to Miss Isabella Andrew, in Fail, parish of Tarbolton. Immediately after the marriage four men of the bride's company started for the broos, from Mauchline to Whitehill, a distance of thirteen miles; and when one of them was sure of the prize, a young lady, who had started after they were a quarter of a mile off, outstripped them all, and, notwithstanding the interruption of getting a shoe fastened on her mare at a smithy on the road, she gained the prize, to the astonishment of both parties."

In the History and Antiquities of Claybrook, by the Rev
A. Macaulay, 1791, p. 130, we read: "A custom formerly
prevailed in this parish and neighbourhood, of *riding for the
bridecake,* which took place when the bride was brought home
to her new habitation. A pole was erected in front of the
house, three or four yards high, with the cake stuck upon the
top of it. On the instant that the bride set out from her old
habitation, a company of young men started off on horseback;
and he who was fortunate enough to reach the pole first, and
knock the cake down with his stick, had the honour of receiving it from the hands of a damsel on the point of a wooden
sword, and with this trophy he returned in triumph to meet
the bride and her attendants, who, upon their arrival in the
village, were met by a párty, whose office it was to adorn
their horses' heads with garlands, and to present the bride
with a posy. The last ceremony of this sort that took place
in the parish of Claybrook was between sixty and seventy
years ago, and was witnessed by a person now living in the
parish. Sometimes the bridecake was tried for by persons on
foot, and then it was called *throwing the quintal,* which was
performed with heavy bars of iron; thus affording a trial of
muscular strength as well as of gallantry." Macaulay mentions here that, in Minorca, if not now, at least forty years
ago, a custom as old as Theocritus and Virgil was kept up,
i. e. the ceremony of throwing nuts and almonds at weddings,
that the boys might scramble for them. "Spargite, marite,
nuces." Virg.

Malkin, in his Tour in South Wales, Glamorganshire, p.
67, says: " Ill may it befal the traveller who has the misfortune of meeting a Welsh wedding on the road. He would
be inclined to suppose that he had fallen in with a company
of lunatics escaped from their confinement. It is the custom
of the whole party who are invited, both men and women, to
ride full speed to the church-porch; and the person who arrives there first has some privilege or distinction at the mar-
riage-feast. To this important object all inferior considerations
gave way, whether the safety of his Majesty's subjects, who
are not going to be married, or their own, be incessantly endangered by boisterous, unskilful, and contentious jockeyship.
The natives, who are acquainted with the custom, and warned
against the cavalcade by its vociferous approach, turn aside at

respectful distance : but the stranger will be fortunate if he escapes being overthrown by an onset, the occasion of which puts out of sight that urbanity so generally characteristic of the people."

A respectable clergyman informed me that, riding in a narrow lane near Macclesfield, in Cheshire, in the summer of 1799, he was suddenly overtaken (and indeed they had well-nigh rode over him) by a nuptial party at full speed, who, before they put up at an inn in the town, where they stopped to take some refreshment, described several circles round the market-place, or rode, as it were, several rings.

In the Westmoreland Dialect, 8vo, Kendal, 1790, a country wedding is described with no little humour. The clergyman is represented as chiding the parties' for not coming before him nine months sooner. The ceremony being over, we are told that " Awe raaid haam fearful wele, *an the youngans raaid for th' ribband*, me cusen Betty banged aw th' lads an gat it for sure."

FOOTBALL MONEY.

In the North of England, among the colliers, &c., it is customary for a party to watch the bridegroom's coming out of church after the ceremony, in order to demand money for a football, a claim that admits of no refusal.[1] Coles, in his Dictionary, speaks of another kind of ball money given by a new bride to her old playfellows.

It is the custom in Normandy for the bride to throw a ball over the church, which bachelors and married men scramble for.   They then dance together.

---

[1] " Ce sont des insolences, plutôt que des superstitions, que ce qui se pratique en certains lieux, où l'on a de coûtume de jetter de l'eau benite sur les personnes qui viennent de fiancer, lorsqu'elles sortent de l'église; de les battre, quand ils sont d'une autre paroisse; de les enfermer dans les églises ; *d'exiger d'elles de l'argent pour boire ;* de les prendre par la foi du corps, et de les porter dans les cabarets ; de les insulter ; et de faire de grands bruits, de *grandes huées, et des charivaris, quand elles refusent de donner de l'argent à ceux qui leur en demandent.*   Mais ces insolences sont proscrites."   Traité des Superstitions, par Jean Baptiste Thiers, 12mo. Par, 1704, iii. 477.

TORCHES USED AT WEDDINGS.

At Rome the manner was that two children should lead the bride, and a third bear before her a torch of whitethorn, in honour of Ceres. I have seen foreign prints of marriages, where torches are represented as carried in the procession. I know not whether this custom ever obtained in England, though, from the following lines in Herrick's Hesperides, one might be tempted to think that it had :

> " *Upon a Maid that dyed the day she was marryed.*
>
> That morne which saw me made a bride,
> The ev'ning witnest that I dy'd.
> *Those holy lights, wherewith they guide*
> *Unto the bed the bashful bride,*
> Serv'd but as tapers for to burne
> And light my reliques to their urne.
> This epitaph, which here you see,
> Supply'd the epithalamie."

Gough, in the introduction to his second volume of Sepulchr. Mon. p. 7, speaking of funeral torches, says : " The use of torches was however retained alike in the daytime, *as was the case at weddings ;* whence Propertius, beautifully,

> " Viximus insignes inter *utramque facem :*"

thus illustrated by Ovid, Epist. Cydippes ad Acontium, 1. 172 :

> " Et *face* pro *thalami* fax mihi mortis adest ;"

and Fasti, ii. 561, speaking of February, a month set apart for Parentalia, or funeral anniversaries, and therefore not proper for marriage :

> " Conde tuas, *Hymenæe, faces*, et ab ignibus atris
> Aufer, habent alias mœsta sepulchra faces."

" The Romans admitted but five torches in their nuptial solemnities." — Browne's Cyprus Garden, or the Quincunx Mystically Considered, p. 191.

In Swinburne's account of gipsies in his Journey through Calabria, p. 304, is the following remark : " At their weddings *they carry torches*, and have paranymphs to give the bride away, with many other unusual rites." Lamps and flambeaux are in use at present at Japanese weddings. "The *nuptial torch*," says the author of Hymen, 1760, p. 149, "used by the Greeks and Romans, has a striking conformity to the flambeaux of the Japanese. The most considerable difference is, that, amongst the Romans, this torch was carried before the bride by one of her virgin attendants; and among the Greeks, that office was performed by the bride's mother." In the Greek church the bridegroom and bride enter the church with lighted wax tapers in their hands.[1] (Ibid. p. 153.)

MUSIC AT WEDDINGS.

At the marriages of the Anglo-Saxons the parties were attended to church by music. In the old History of John Newchombe, the wealthy clothier of Newbury, cited by Strutt, iii. 154, speaking of his marriage and the bride's going to church, the writer observes, "there was a noise (i. e. company) of musicians that played all the way before her."

Dame Sibil Turfe, a character in Ben Jonson's play of A Tale of a Tub, is introduced reproaching her husband as follows : " A clod you shall be called, to let no music go afore your child to church, to cheer her heart up !" and Scriben, seconding the good old dame's rebuke, adds, "She's i' th' right, sir; for your wedding dinner is starved without music."

In the Cristen State of Matrimony, 1543, p. 48, we read as follows : " Early in the mornyng the weddyng people begynne to excead in superfluous eatyng and drinkyng, whereof they spytte untyll the halfe sermon be done, and when they come to the preachynge they are halfe droncke, some all together. Therefore regard they neyther the prechyng nor prayer, but stond there only because of the custome. Such folkes also do come to the churche with all manner of pompe and pride, and gorgiousnes of rayment and jewels. They come *with a*

---

[1] *Torches* are used at Turkish marriages: thus Selden, "Deductio sequitur in domum, *nec sine facibus*, et sponsa matri sponsa traditur. Quamprimum vero sponsa cubiculum ingreditur, maritus pede suo uxoris pedem tangit statimque ambo recluduntur." Uxor Hebraica. (Opera, iii. 686.)

great noise of harpes, lutes, kyttes, tabbins, and du..........

wherwyth they trouble the whole church, and hyndre them in
matters pertayninge to God.   And even as they come to the
churche, *so go they from the churche agayne*, lyght, nice, in
shameful pompe, and vaine wantonesse."

The following is from Vernon's Hunting of Purgatory to
Death, 1561, f. 51 : "I knewe a priest (this is a true tale that I
tell you, and no lye,) whiche, when any of his parishioners
should be maryed, woulde take his backe-pype, and go fetche
theym to the churche, playnge sweetelye afore them, and then
would he laye his instrument handsomely upon the aultare tyll
he had maryed them and sayd masse. Which thyng being done,
he would gentillye bringe them home agayne with backe-pype.
Was not this priest a true ministrell, thynke ye? for he dyd
not counterfayt the ministrell, but was one in dede."

Puttenham, in his Arte of English Poesie, 1589, p. 69,
speaks of "*blind harpers*, or such like taverne minstrels that
give a fit of mirth for a groat, and their matters being for the
most part stories of old time, as the Tale of Sir Topas, the
Reportes of Bevis of Southampton, Guy of Warwicke, Adam
Bell, Clymme of the Clough, and such other old romances, or
historical rimes, made purposely for recreation of the common
people at Christmasse dinners and *bride-ales*, and in tavernes
and ale-houses, and such other places of base resort."

In Brooke's Epithalamium we read :

> " Now whiles slow howres doe feed the times delay,
>   Confus'd discourse, *with musicke mixt among*,
>   Fills up the semy-circle of the day."

In the margin opposite is put "*Afternoone Musicke*." [And
so runs the old ballad, sung about the streets within the last
few years,—

> " Ye patriots and courtiers so hearty,
>   That speech shall vote for each party,
>   For one be both constant and steady,
>   And vote to support widow Brady.
>   To all that I now see before me,
>   The bottom, the top, and the middle,
>   For music we now must implore ye,
>   What's a wedding without pipes and fiddle?"]

In Griffith's Bethel, or a Forme for Families, 1634, is the
following on marriage feasts, p. 279 : "Some cannot be merry

without a noise of fiddlers, who scrape acquaintance at the first sight; nor sing, unlesse the divell himselfe come in for a part, and the ditty be made in hell," &c. He had before said, "We joy indeed at weddings; but how? Some please themselves in breaking broad, I had almost said bawdy jests." Speaking of wedding entertainments, ibid., he says: "Some drink healths so long till they lose it, and (being more heathenish in this than was Ahasuerus at his feast) they urge their companions to drink by measure, out of measure."

Waldron, in his Description of the Isle of Man (Works, fol. ed. p. 169,) tells us that at the marriages of the inhabitants, "they are preceded (to church) by music, who play all the while before them the tune, *the Black and the Grey*, and no other is ever used at weddings." He adds, "that when they arrive at the churchyard, they walk three times round the church before they enter it."

This requisite has not been omitted in the Collier's Wedding:

> " The pipers wind and take their post,
> And go before to clear the coast."

The rejoicing by ringing of bells at marriages of any consequence, is everywhere common. On the fifth bell at the church of Kendal, in Westmoreland, is the following inscription, alluding to this usage:

> " In wedlock bands,
> All ye who join with hands,
>   Your hearts unite ;
> So shall our tuneful tongues combine
>   To laud the nuptial rite."

SPORTS AT WEDDINGS.

AMONG the Anglo-Saxons, as Strutt informs us, in his Manners and Customs, i. 76, after the nuptial feast, "the remaining part of the day was spent by the youth of both sexes in mirth and dancing, while the graver sort sat down to their drinking bout, in which they highly delighted."

Among the higher ranks there was, in later times, a wedding sermon, an epithalamium,[1] and at night a masque.[2]

It was a general custom between the wedding dinner and supper to have dancing. The cushion-dance at weddings is thus mentioned in the Apophthegms of King James, the Earl of Worcester, 1658, p. 60,—a wedding entertainment is spoken of :—"At last, when the masque was ended, and time had brought in the supper, *the cushion led the dance out of the parlour into the hall*," &c. In the Christen State of Matrimony, 1543, f. 49, we read : "After the bancket and feast there begynnethe a vayne, madde, and unmannerlye fashion, for the bryde must be brought into an open *dauncynge place*. Then is there such rennynge, leapynge, and flyngyng amonge them ; then is there suche a lyftynge up and discoverynge of the damselles clothes and other womennes apparell, that a man might thynke they were sworne to the Devels daunce. Then muste the poore bryde kepe foote with al dauncers and refuse none, how scabbed, foule, droncken, rude and shameles soever he be. Then must she oft tymes heare and se much wyckednesse, and many an uncomely word ; and that noyse and romblyng endureth even tyll supper." So, in the Summe of the Holy Scripture, 1547 : "Suffer not your children to go to weddings or banckettes ; for nowe a daies one can learne nothing there but ribaudry and foule wordes."

Northbrooke, in his Treatise against Dauncing, p. 137, says : "In the Counsell of Laoditia, A. D. 364, it was decreed thus : It is not meete for Christian men to *daunce at their mariages*. Let the cleargie aryse and go their wayes when the players on the instruments (which serve for dauncing) doe bygynne to playe, least by their presence they shoulde seeme to allowe that wantonnesse." Fiddlers are called *crowders*. (Ibid. p. 141.) In Scott's Mock Marriage, a Comedy, 1696, p. 50, it is said : "You are not so merry as men in your condition should be. *What ! a couple of weddings, and not a dance ?*"

[1] In Herrick's Hesperides, p. 258, are ten short songs, or rather choral gratulations, entitled, "Connubii Flores, or the Well-Wishes at Weddings."
[2] It appears from the Account of the Marriage Ceremonials of Philip Herbert and the Lady Susan, in the time of James I., that in grand weddings it was usual to have *a masque* at night. "At night there was a masque in the hall."

So, in the popular old ballad called the Winchester Wedding :

" And now they had din'd, advancing
Into the midst of the hall,
The fiddlers struck up for dancing,
And Jeremy led up the brawl.
Sucky, *that danc'd with the cushion*," &c.

In Playford's Dancing-Master, 1698, p. 7, is an account of "Joan Sanderson, or the Cushion Dance, an old round dance. This dance is begun by a single person (either man or woman), who, taking a cushion in his hand, dances about the room, and at the end of the tune he stops and sings, 'This dance it will no farther go.' The musician answers, 'I pray you, good sir, why say you so?' *Man.* 'Because Joan Sanderson will not come to.' *Musick.* 'She must come to, and she shall come to, and she must come, whether she will or no.' Then he lays down the cushion before a woman, on which she kneels, and he kisses her, singing, 'Welcom, Joan Sanderson, welcom, welcom.' Then she rises, takes up the cushion, and both dance, singing, 'Prinkum-prank'um is a fine dance, and shall we go dance it once again, and once again, and shall we go dance it once again.' Then making a stop, the woman sings as before, 'This dance it will no further go.' *Musick.* 'I pray you, madam, why say you so?' *Woman.* 'Because John Sanderson will not come to.' *Musick.* 'He must come to,' &c. (as before). And so she lays down the cushion before a man, who, kneeling upon it, salutes her, she singing, 'Welcome, John Sanderson,' &c. Then, he taking up the cushion, they take hands and dance round, singing, as before, and thus they do till the whole company are taken into the ring. Then the cushion is laid before the first man, the woman singing, 'This dance,' &c. (as before), only instead of 'Come to,' they sing 'Go fro :' and, instead of 'Welcome, John Sanderson,' &c., they sing, 'Farewell, John Sanderson, farewell, farewell ;' and so they go out one by one, as they came in. *Note*, the woman is kiss'd by all the men in the ring at her coming in and going out, and likewise the man by the women."

The following extract from Selden's Table Talk, under "King of England," 7, is illustrative of our cushion-dance : "The court of England is much altered. At a solemn dancing, first you have the grave measures, then the corrantoes and the galliards, and this is kept up with ceremony, at length to

French more" (it should be French more), "and the cushion-dance, and then all the company dance, lord and groom, lady and kitchen-maid, no distinction. So in our court, in Queen Elizabeth's time, gravity and state were kept up. In King James's time things were pretty well. But in King Charles's time there has been nothing but French-more, and the cushion-dance, omnium gatherum, tolly, polly, hoite come toite." In the same work, under the head "Excommunication," is an allusion to the custom of *dancing at weddings:* "Like the wench that was to be married: she asked her mother, when 'twas done, if she should go to bed presently? No, says her mother, you must dine first. And then to bed, mother? No, *you must dance after dinner.* And then to bed, mother? No, you must go to supper," &c.

It appears from the Glossary to Bishop Kennet's Parochial Antiquities, that the quintain was anciently a customary sport at weddings.[1] He says it was used in his time at Blackthorne, and at Deddington, in Oxfordshire. It is supposed to have been a Roman exercise, left by that people at their departure from this island. We read in Blount's Glossographia, v. *Quintain,* that it is "a game or sport still in request at marriages, in some parts of this nation, specially in Shropshire: the manner, now corruptly thus, a *quintin,* buttress, or thick plank of wood, is set fast in the ground of the highway where the bride and bridegroom are to pass; and poles are provided, with which the young men run a tilt on horseback, and he that breaks most poles, and shows most activity, wins the garland." From Aubrey's Remains of Gentilisme and Judaism, it should appear that this was a common sport at weddings, till the breaking out of the civil wars, even among people in the lower rank of life.

"On Offham Green," says Hasted, History of Kent, ii. 224, "there stands a *quintin,* a thing now rarely to be met with, being a machine much used in former times by youth, as well to try their own activity as the swiftness of their horses

---

[1] In Strype's Annals of the Reformation, ii. 394, anno 1575, among the various sports, &c. used to entertain Queen Elizabeth at Kenilworth Castle, he tells us: "That afternoon (as the relator expresseth it), in honour of this Kenilworth Castle, and of God and St. Kenelme (whose day by the kalendar this was), was a solemn country bridal, *with running at quintin.*" The queen stayed here nineteen days.

in running at it. (He gives an engraving of it.) The cross-
piece of it is broad at one end, and pierced full of holes, and
a bag of sand is hung at the other, and swings round on being
moved with any blow. The pastime was for the youth on
horseback to run at it as fast as possible, and hit the broad
part in his career with much force. He that by chance hit it
not at all was treated with loud peals of derision; and he who
did hit it made the best use of his swiftness, lest he should
have a sound blow on his neck from the bag of sand, which
instantly swang round from the other end of the quintin.
The great design of this sport was to try the agility of the
horse and man, and to break the board, which whoever did,
he was accounted chief of the day's sport. It stands opposite
the dwelling-house of the estate, which is bound to keep it
up." The same author (ibid. p. 639), speaking of Bobbing
parish, says: "There was formerly a quintin in this parish,
there being still a field in it called from thence the *Quintin
Field*."

Owen, in his Welsh Dictionary, v. *Cwintan*, describes a
hymeneal game thus acted: "A pole is fixed in the ground,
with sticks set about it which the bridegroom and his company take up and try their strength and activity in breaking
them upon the pole."

In the marriage ceremonies amongst the ancient Romans,
the bridegroom threw nuts about the room for the boys to
scramble. The epithalamiums in the classics prove this. It
was a token that the party scattering them was now leaving
childish diversions.[1]

It appears to have been a waggish custom at weddings to

---

[1] "Quanquam Plinius, lib. xv. cap. 22, causas alias adfert, quam ob rem
nuces in nuptialibus ceremoniis consueverint antiquitus adhiberi; sed
præstat ipsius referre verba: Nuces, inquit, *juglandes* quanquam et ipsæ
nuptialium Fescenninorum comites, multum pineis minores universitate,
eædemque portione ampliores nucleo. Nec non et honor his naturæ pe-
culiaris, gemino protectis operimento, pulvinati primum calycis, mox lignei
putaminis. Quæ causa eas nuptiis fecit religiosas, tot modis fœtu munito:
quod est verisimilius," &c. See Erasmus on the proverb, "Nuces relin-
quere." Adag. fol. Col. Allobr. 1606, col. 1356. The Roman boys had
some sport or other with nuts, to which Horace refers in these words:

——" Postquam te talos aule nucesque
Ferre sinu laxo, donare et ludere vidi."

hang a bell under the party's bed   See Fletcher's Night
Walker, act i. sc. 1. "Il oult une risée de jeunes hommes
qui s'etoient exprès cachez auprès de son *lit*, comme on
a coûtume de faire en pareilles occasions,"—Contes d'Ouville,
i. 3.

DIVINATIONS AT WEDDINGS.

DIVINATION at marriages was practised in times of the re-
motest antiquity. Vallancey tells us that, in the Memoirs of
the Etruscan Academy of Cortona, is a drawing of a picture
found in Herculaneum representing a marriage. In the front
is a sorceress casting the five stones. The writer of the memoir justly thinks she is divining. The figure exactly corresponds with the first and principal cast of the Irish Purin;
all five are cast up, and the first catch is on the back of the
hand. He has copied the drawing ; on the back of the hand
stands one, and the remaining four on the ground. Opposite
the sorceress is the matron, attentive to the success of the
cast. No marriage ceremony was performed without consult-
ing the Druidess and her Purin :

"Auspices solebant nuptiis interesse."[1]—Juvenal, Sat. xii.

Pliny, in the tenth book, chap. viii. of his Natural History,
mentions that in his time the circos, a sort of lame hawk, was
accounted a lucky omen at weddings.

In the north of, and perhaps all over England, as has been
already noticed, slices of the bride-cake are thrice, some say
nine times, put through the wedding-ring, which are afterwards by young persons laid under their pillows when they
go to bed, for the purpose of making them dream of their
lovers, or of exciting prophetic dreams of love and marriage.
Thus Humphrey Clinker, iii. 265, edit. 1771 : "A cake being
broken over the head of Mrs. Tabitha Lismahago, the frag-

[1] Vallancey adds : " This is now played as a game by the youths of
both sexes in Ireland. The Irish Seic Seona (Shec Shona) was readily
turned into Jack Stones by an English ear, by which name this game is
now known by the English in Ireland. It has another name among the
vulgar, viz. Gob-stones."

ments were distributed among the bystanders, according to the custom of the ancient Britons, on the supposition that every person who ate of this hallowed cake should that night have a vision of the man or woman whom Heaven designed should be his or her wedded mate." So the Spectator : " The writer resolved to try his fortune, fasted all day, and, that he might be sure of dreaming upon something at night, procured a handsome slice of bridecake, which he placed very conveniently under his pillow."

The Connoisseur, also, notices the practice, No. 56: "Cousin Debby was married a little while ago, and she sent me a piece of bridecake to put under my pillow, and I had the sweetest dream ; I thought we were going to be married together." The following occurs in the Progress of Matrimony, 1733, p. 30 :

> " But, madam, as a present take
> This little paper of bride-cake ;
> Fast any Friday in the year,
> When Venus mounts the starry sphere,
> Thrust this at night in pillowbeer;
> In morning slumber you will seem
> T' enjoy your lover in a dream."

In the St. James's Chronicle, from April 16th to April 18th, 1799, are the following lines on *the Wedding Cake :*

> " Enlivening source of hymeneal mirth,
> All hail the blest receipt that gave thee birth !
> Tho' Flora culls the fairest of her bowers,
> And strews the path of Hymen with her flowers,
> Not half the raptures give her scatter'd sweets ;
> The *cake* far kinder gratulation meets.
> The bridemaid's eyes with sparkling glances beam,
> She *views the cake*, and greets the promis'd dream.
> For, when endow'd with necromantic spell,
> She knows what wondrous things the cake will tell.
> When from the altar comes the pensive bride,
> With downcast looks, her partner at her side,
> Soon from the ground these thoughtful looks arise,
> To meet the cake that gayer thoughts supplies.
> With her own hand she charms each destin'd slice,
> And thro' the ring repeats *the trebled thrice.*
> The hallow'd ring, infusing magic pow'r,
> Bids Hymen's visions wait the midnight hour ;
> The mystic treasure, plac'd beneath her head,
> Will tell the fair if haply she may wed.

These mysteries portentous lie conceal'd,
Till Morpheus calls and bids them stand reveal'd;
The future husband that night's dream will bring,
Whether a parson, soldier, beggar, king,
As partner of her life the fair must take,
Irrevocable doom of *bridal cake.*"

For the sun to shine upon the bride was a good omen.
Thus Herrick's Hesperides, p. 152 :

" While that others do divine,
Blest is the bride on whom the sun doth shine."

It was formerly a custom among the noble Germans, at
weddings, for the bride, when she was conducted to the bride-
chamber, to take off her shoe and throw it among the by-
standers, which every one strove to catch, and whoever got
it thought it an omen that they themselves would shortly be
happily married.[1]

Hutchinson, in his History of Durham, i. 33, speaking of
a cross near the ruins of the church in Holy Island, says :
" It is now called the Petting Stone.   Whenever a marriage
is solemnised at the church, after the ceremony the bride is
to step upon it ; and if she cannot stride to the end thereof,
it is said the marriage will prove unfortunate."   The etymology there given is too ridiculous to be remembered : it is
called *petting,* lest the bride should take pet with her supper.

Grose tells us of a vulgar superstition, that holds it unlucky to walk under a ladder, as it may prevent your being
married that year.   Our rustics retain to this day many superstitious notions concerning the times of the year when it
is accounted lucky or otherwise to marry.   It has been remarked in the former volume of this work, that none are
ever married on Childermas Day ; for whatever cause, this is
a black day in the calendar of impatient lovers.   See Aubrey's
Miscell. edit. 1748, p. 5.   Randle Holme, too, in his Academy
of Armory and Blazon, edit. 1688, B. iii. cap. 3. p. 131, tells

---

[1] Antiquitat. Convivial., f. 229.   There was an ancient superstition, that
for a bride to have good fortune it was necessary at her marriage that she
should enter the house under two drawn swords placed in the manner of
a St. Andrew's cross.   " Si sponsa debet habere bonam fortunam, oportet
quod in nuptiis ingrediatur domum sub duobus evaginatis gladiis, positis
ad modum crucis S. Andreæ.   Delrio Disquisit. Magic. p. 454, from
Beezius.

us : " Innocence Day, on what day of the week soever it
lights upon, that day of the week is by astronomers taken to
be a cross-day all the year through." The following proverb,
from Ray, marks another ancient conceit on this head :

> " Who marries between the sickle and the scythe
> Will never thrive."

We gather from the author of the Convivial Antiquities,
that the heathen Romans were not without their superstitions
on this subject. The month of May has been already noticed
from Ovid's Fasti as a time which was considered particularly
unlucky for the celebration of marriage. In the Roman
Calendar in my library, so often quoted, several days are
marked as unfit for marriages : " Nuptiæ non fiunt," i. e.
" Feb. 11, June 2, Nov. 2, Decemb. 1." On the 16th of September, it is noted, " Tobiæ sacrum. Nuptiarum ceremoniæ
a nuptiis deductæ, videlicet de ense, de pisce, de pompa, et de
pedibus levandis."[1]

In a curious old Almanac for the year 1559, " by Lewes
Vaughan, made for the merydian of Gloucestre," are noted
as follow : " The tymes of weddinges when it begynneth and
endeth. Jan. 14, weding begin. Jan. 21, weddinge goth out.
April 3, wedding be. April 29, wedding goeth out. May 22,
wedding begyn." And in another almanac, for 1655, by
Andrew Waterman, mariner, we have pointed out to us, in
the last page, the following days as " good to marry, or contract a wife (for then women will be fond and loving), viz.
January 2, 4, 11, 19, and 21. Feb. 1, 3, 10, 19, 21. March
3, 5, 12, 20, 23. April 2, 4, 12, 20, and 22. May 2, 4, 12,
20, 23. June 1, 3, 11, 19, 21. July 1, 3, 12, 19, 21, 31.
August 2, 11, 18, 20, 30. Sept. 1, 9, 16, 18, 28. Octob. 1,

---

[1] " Tempus quoque nuptiarum celebrandarum," says Stuckius, " certum
a veteribus definitum et constitutum esse invenio. Concilii Ilerdensis,
xxxiii. 9, 4. Et in Decreto Ivonis, lib. 6, non oportet a Septuagesima
usque in Octavam Paschæ, et tribus Hebdomadibus ante Festivitatem S.
Joannis Baptistæ, et ab adventu Domini usque post Epiphaniam, nuptias
celebrare. Quod si factum fuerit, separentur." Antiquitat. Conviv. p. 72.
See also the Formula in the Append. to Hearne's Hist. and Antiq. of
Glastonbury, p. 309.

"De tempore prohibiti matrimonii.

" Conjugium adventus tollit, sed stella reducit,
    Mox cineres stringunt, lux pascha octava relaxat."

8, 15, 17, 27, 29   Nov 5, 11, 13, 22, 25   Decemb 1, 8, 10, 19, 23, 29."

In Sir John Sinclair's Account of Scotland, xv. 311, the minister of the parishes of South Ronaldsay and Burray, two of the Orkney Islands, in his Statistical Account of the Character and Manners of the People, says: "No couple chuses to marry except with a growing moon, and some even wish for a flowing tide."

In a letter from Sir Dudley Carleton to Mr. Winwood, London, January, 1604, among other notices relating to marriages at Court in the reign of James I., is the following: "At night there was casting off the bride's left hose, and many other pretty sorceries."

Grose tells us of a singular superstition on this occasion, i. e. that if in a family the youngest daughter should chance to be married before her elder sisters, they must all dance at her wedding without shoes; this will counteract their ill-luck, and procure them husbands.

In a Boulster Lecture, 1640, p. 280, mention occurs of an ancient custom, "when at any time a couple were married, the sole of the bridegroom's shoe was to be laid upon the bride's head, implying with what subjection she should serve her husband."

There was an ancient superstition that the bride was not to step over the threshold in entering the bridegroom's house, but was to be lifted over by her nearest relations. She was also to knit her fillets to the door-posts, and anoint the sides, to avoid the mischievous fascinations of witches.[1] Previous to this, too, she was to put on a yellow veil. See Herrick's Hesperides, in the Epithalamium on Sir Thomas Southwell and his Lady, p. 57 :

> " And now the yellow vaile at last
> Over her fragrant cheek is cast.
> You, you, that be of her nearest kin,
> Now o'er the threshold force her in.
> But to avert the worst,
> Let her her fillets first

---

[1] " The bryde anoynted the poostes of the doores with swyne's grease, because she thought by that meanes to dryve awaye all misfortune, whereof she had her name in Latin, ' *Uxor* ab ungendo.' "   Langley's Transl. of Polyd. Vergil, f. 9.

Knit to the posts ; this point
Rememb'ring, to anoint
The sides : for 'tis a charme
Strong against future harme :
And the evil deeds, the which
There was hidden by the witch."

Pennant informs us that, among the Highlanders, during the marriage ceremony, great care is taken that dogs do not pass between the couple to be married ; and particular attention is paid to leaving the bridegroom's left shoe without buckle or latchet, to prevent the secret influence of witches on the nuptial night. He adds : " This is an old opinion." Gesner says that witches made use of toads as a charm, "ut vim coeundi, ni fallor, in viris tollerent." Gesner de Quad. Ovi. p. 72.

Tying the point was another fascination, illustrations of which may be found in Reginald Scot's Discourse concerning Devils and Spirits, p. 71 ; in the Fifteen Comforts of Marriage, p. 225 ; and in the British Apollo, ii. No. 35, 1709. In the old play of the Witch of Edmonton, 1658, young Banks says, " *Ungirt, unbless'd,* says the proverb. But my girdle shall serve as a *riding knit;* and a fig for all the witches in Christendom."

It was held unlucky, also, if the bride did not weep bitterly on the wedding-day. [And bad weather was most unpropitious. In a letter from Chamberlain to Dudley Carleton, dated July 10, 1603, he says : " Mr. Winwood was married on Tuesday, with much thunder and lightning and rain. The ominous weather and dismal day put together might have made a superstitious man startled, but he turned all to the best, and so may it prove."]

FLINGING THE STOCKING.

FLINGING the stocking is thus mentioned in a curious little book entitled, the West Country Clothier undone by a Peacock, p. 65 : " The sack posset must be eaten and the stocking flung, to see who can first hit the bridegroom on the nose." Misson, in his Travels through England, tells us of this cus-turn, that the young men took the bride's stocking, and the girls those of the bridegroom ; each of whom sitting at the foot of the bed, threw the stocking over their heads, endeavouring to make it fall upon that of the bride or her spouse : if the bridegroom's stockings, thrown by the girls, fell upon the bridegroom's head, it was a sign that they themselves would soon be married ; and a similar prognostic was taken from the falling of the bride's stocking, thrown by the young men. Throwing the stocking has not been omitted in the Collier's Wedding :

> " The stocking's thrown, the company gone,
> And Tom and Jenny both alone."

In the Fifteen Comforts of Marriage, p. 60, the custom is represented a little different. " One of the young ladies, instead of throwing the stocking at the bride, flings it full in the basin" (which held the sack-posset), "and then it's time to take the posset away ; which done, they last kiss round, and so depart." So Hymen, &c. 8vo. Lond. 1760, p. 174 : " The men take the bride's stockings, and the women those of the bridegroom : they then seat themselves at the bed's feet, and throw the stockings over their heads, and whenever any one hits the owner of them, it is looked upon as an omen that the person will be married in a short time ; and though this ceremony is looked upon as mere play and foolery, new marriages are often occasioned by such accidents. Meantime the posset is got ready and given to the married couple. When they awake in the morning, a sack-posset is also given them."

> " The posset too of sack was eaten,
> And stocking thrown too (all besweaten)."
> Vereingetsrixa, p. 26.

In "A Sing-song on Clarinda's wedding," in Fletcher's Translations and Poems, 1656, p. 230, is the following account of this ceremony :

> " This clutter ore, Clarinda lay
> Half-bedded, like the peeping day
> Behind Olimpus' cap ;
> Whiles at her head each twitt'ring girle
> The fatal stocking quick did whirle,
> To know the lucky hap."

So in Folly in Print, or a Book of Rhymes, p. 121, in the
description of a wedding, we read :

> " But still the stockings are to throw,
> Some threw too high, and some too low,
> There's none could hit the mark."

In the Progress of Matrimony, 8vo. 1733, p. 49, is another
description (in the Palace Miscellany) :

> " Then come all the younger folk in,
> With ceremony throw the stocking ;
> Backward, o'er head, in turn they toss'd it ;
> Till in sack-posset they had lost it.
> Th' intent of flinging thus the hose
> Is to hit him or her o' th' nose ;
> Who hits the mark thus o'er left shoulder,
> Must married be ere twelve months older.
> Deucalion thus, and Pyrrha, threw
> Behind them stones, whence mankind grew !"

Again, in the poem entitled the "Country Wedding," in
the Gentleman's Magazine for March 1735, v. 158 :

> " Bid the lasses and lads to the merry brown bowl,
> While rashers of bacon shall smoke on the coal ;
> Then Roger and Bridget, and Robin and Nan,
> *Hit 'em each on the nose with the hose if you can.*"

In the British Apollo, 1708, i. 42, we read :

> "*Q.* Apollo say, whence 'tis, I pray,
> The ancient custom came,
> Stockings to throw (I'm sure you know)
> At bridegroom and his dame ?
> "*A.* When Britons bold bedded of old,
> Sandals were backward thrown ;
> The pair to tell that, ill or well,
> The act was all their own."

Allan Ramsay, in his Poems, 1721, p. 116, introduces this
custom :

> " The bride was now laid in her bed,
> Her left leg Ho was flung ;
> And Geordy Gib was fidgen glad,
> Because it hit Jean Gun."

In the British Apollo, before quoted, 1711, iii. 133, is the
following query : " Why is the custom observed for the bride
to be placed in bed next the left hand of her husband, seeing

it is a general use in England for men to give their wives the
right hand when they walk together? *A.* Because it looks
more modest for a lady to accept the honour her husband
does her as an act of generosity at his hands, than to take it
as her right, since the bride goes to bed first."

In the Christen State of Matrimony, 1543, f. 49, it is said:
"As for supper, loke how much shameles and dronken the
evenynge is more than the mornynge, so much the more vyce,
excesse, and mysnourtoure is used at the supper. After supper
must they begynne to pype and daunce agayne of the new.
And though the yonge personnes, beyng wery of the bablynge
noyse and inconvenience, come once towarde theyr rest, yet
canne they have no quietnes: for a man shall fynde unman-
nerly and restles people that wyll first go to theyr chambre
dore, and there syng vicious and naughty ballades, that the
dyvell may have his whole tryumphe nowe to the uttermost."

SACK POSSET.

IN the evening of the wedding-day, just before the company
retired, the sack-posset was eaten. Of this posset the bride
and bridegroom were always to taste first. I find this called
the Benediction Posset.[1]

The custom of eating a posset at going to bed seems to have
prevailed generally among our ancestors. The Tobacconist,
in the Wandering Jew telling Fortunes to English Men, 1640,
p. 20, says: "And at my going to bed, this is *my posset.*"
Skinner derives the word from the French *poser*, residere, to
settle; because, when the milk breaks, the cheesy parts, being
heavier, subside. " Nobis proprie designat lac calidum infuso
vino cerevisiâ, &c. coagulatum." See Junii Etymol. in v.

---

[1] It is so called by Smollet in his Humphrey Clinker, and also hinted
at by Herrick in his Hesperides, p. 132 :

> " It needs we must for ceremonies sake,
> Blesse a sacke-posset ; luck go with it, take
> The night-charm quickly : you have spells
> And magicks for to end."

Herrick has not overlooked the posset in his Hesperides, p. 253:

> " What short sweet prayers shall be said,
> And how the posset shall be made
> With cream of lilies, not of kine,
> And maidens'-blush for spiced wine."

Nor is it omitted in the Collier's Wedding:

> " Now some prepare t' undress the bride,
> While others tame the posset's pride."

It is mentioned too among the bridal rites in the West Country Clothier, before cited, where we are told " the sack-posset must be eaten." In the Fifteen Comforts of Marriage, p. 60, it is called " an ancient custom of the English matrons, who believe that sack will make a r .an lusty, and sugar will make him kind."

Among the Anglo-Saxons, as Strutt informs us, in his Manners and Customs, i. 77, at night the bride was by the women attendants placed in the marriage-bed, and the bridegroom in the same manner conducted by the men, where having both, with all who were present, drunk the marriage health, the company retired. In the old song of Arthur of Bradley we read:

> " And then they did foot it and toss it,
> Till the cook had brought up *the posset ;*
> The *bride-pye* was brought forth,
> A thing of mickle worth,
> And so all, at the bed-side,
> Took leave of Arthur and his bride."

Misson, in his Travels in England, translated by Ozell, p. 352, says: " The posset is a kind of cawdle, a potion made up of milk, wine, yolks of eggs, sugar, cinnamon, nutmeg," &c. He adds (p. 354): " They never fail to bring them another sack-posset next morning."

A singular instance of tantalizing, however incredible it may seem, was most certainly practised by our ancestors on this festive occasion, i. e. sewing up the bride in one of the sheets. Herrick, in his Hesperides, in the " Nuptial Song on Sir Clipesby Crew and his Lady," expressly mentions this as a then prevailing custom:

> " But since it must be done, dispatch and sowe
> Up in a sheet your bride, and what if so," &c.

It is mentioned too in the account of the marriage ceremonial of Sir Philip Herbert and the Lady Susan, performed at
Whitehall in the time of James I., before cited : "At night
there was *sewing into the sheet.*"

In the Papal times no new-married couple could go to bed
together till the bridal bed had been blessed. In a manuscript entitled, Historical Passages concerning the Clergy in
the Papal Times, cited in the History of Shrewsbury, 1779,
p. 92, it is stated that "the pride of the clergy and the
bigotry of the laity were such that new-married couples were
made to wait till midnight, after the marriage-day, before they
would pronounce a benediction, unless handsomely paid for it,
and they durst not undress without it, on pain of excommunication." The Romish rituals give the form of blessing
the nuptial bed. We learn from " Articles ordained by King
Henry VII. for the Regulation of his Household," published by
the Society of Antiquaries, that this ceremony was observed at
the marriage of a princess. " All men at her coming in to be
voided, except woemen, till she be brought to her bedd : and
the man, both : he sitting in his bedd, in his shirte, with a
gowne cast about him. Then the bishoppe with the chap
laines to come in and blesse the bedd : then every man to
avoide without any drinke, save the twoe estates, if they liste
priviely." See also the Appendix to Hearne's History and
Antiquities of Glastonbury, p. 309 ; and St. Foix, Essais sur
Paris.

MORNING AFTER THE MARRIAGE.

"AMONG the Anglo-Saxons," as we gather from Strutt, i. 77,
after the marriage, " next morning the whole company came
into the chamber of the new-married couple, before they arose,
to hear the husband declare the Morning's Gift, when his relations became sureties to the wife's relations for the performance of such promises as were made by the husband."
This was the ancient pin-money, and became the separate
property of the wife alone.

Owen, in his Welsh Dictionary, v. *Cowyll*, explains that
word as signifying a garment or cloak with a veil, presented

by the husband to his bride on the morning after marriage; and, in a wider sense, the settlement he has made on her of goods and chattels adequate to her rank. In more modern times there is a custom similar to this in Prussia. There the husband may (is obliged if he has found her a virgin) present to his bride the Morgengabe, or gift on the morning after marriage, even though he should have married a widow.

The custom of awaking a couple the morning after the marriage with a concert of music, is of old standing. In the letter from Sir Dudley Carleton to Mr. Winwood, describing the nuptials of the Lady Susan with Sir Philip Herbert, it is stated that " they were lodged in the council chamber, where the king gave them a *reveille matin* before they were up." Of such a *reveille matin*, as used on the marriages of respectable merchants of London in his time, Hogarth has left us a curious representation, in one of his prints of the Idle and Industrious Apprentices.

So in the Comforts of Wooing, &c. p. 62 : " Next morning come the fidlers and scrape him a wicked reveillez. The drums rattle, the shaumes tote, the trumpets sound tan ta ra, ra, ra, and the whole street rings with the benedictions and good wishes of fidlers, drummers, pipers, and trumpetters. You may safely say now the wedding's *proclaimed*." Mason, in his Travels in England, translated by Ozell, p. 252, speaking of the reveillez on the morning after a wedding, says : " If the drums and fiddles have notice of it, they will be sure to be with them by daybreak, making a horrible racket, till they have got the pence." Gay, in his Trivia, has censured the use of drums in this concert :

> " Here rows of drummers stand in martial file,
> And with their vellum thunder shake the pile,
> To greet the new-made bride. Are sounds like these
> The proper preludes to a state of peace ?"

The custom of *creeling*, on the second day after marriage, has been already noticed, from Sir John Sinclair's Statistical Account of Scotland. Allan Ramsay, in his Poems, 1721, p. 125, mentions this custom as having been practised the day after the marriage. He adds, " 'Tis a custom for the friends to endeavour the next day after the wedding to make the new-married man as drunk as possible."

" In North Wales," says Pennant's manuscript, *" on the*

Sunday after marriage, the company who were at it come to church, i. e. the friends and relations of the party make the most splendid appearance, disturb the church, and strive who shall place the bride and groom in the most honourable seat. After service is over, the men, with fiddlers before them, go into all the ale-houses in the town."

In the Monthly Magazine for 1798, p. 417, we read : " It is customary, in country churches, when a couple has been newly married, for the singers to chaunt, on the following Sunday, a particular psalm, thence called the Wedding Psalm, in which are these words : ' Oh, well is thee, and happy shalt thou be.' "

The Mercheta Mulierum has been discredited by an eminent antiquary. It was said that Eugenius III., King of Scotland, did wickedly ordain that the lord or master should have the first night's lodging with every woman married to his tenant or bondman ; which ordinance was afterwards abrogated by King Malcolme III, who ordained that the bridegroom should have the sole use of his own wife, and therefore should pay to the lord a piece of money called Marca. (Hect. Boet. l. iii. c. 12, Spotsw. Hist. fol. 29.) One cannot help observing, on the above, that they must have been bondmen or (in the ancient sense of the word,) villains, indeed, who could have submitted to so singular a species of despotism.[1]

DUNMOW FLITCH OF BACON.

A CUSTOM formerly prevailed, and has indeed been recently observed, at Dunmow in Essex, of giving a flitch of bacon to any married man or woman who would swear that neither of them, in a year and a day, either sleeping or waking, repented of their marriage. The singular oath administered to them ran thus :

[1] I found the subsequent clause in a curious MS. in the Cotton Library, Vitell. E. 5. entitled, Excerpta ex quodam antiquo registro prioris de Tynemouth, remanente apud comitem Northumbriæ de Baroniis et Fcodis : Rentale de Tynemuth, factum A.D. 1378. " Omnes tenentes de Tynemouth, cum contigerit, solvent Layrewite filiabus vel ancillis suis et etiam *Merchei* pro filiabus suis maritandis."

II.   12

" You shall swear, by custom of confession,
If ever you made nuptial transgression,
Be you either married man or wife,
If you have brawls or contentious strife;
Or otherwise, at bed or at board,
Offended each other in deed or word:
Or, since the parish-clerk said Amen,
You wish'd yourselves unmarried agen;
Or, in a twelvemonth and a day,
Repented not in thought any way,
But continued true, in thought and desire,
As when you join'd hands in the quire.
If to these conditions, without all feare,
Of your own accord you will freely sweare,
A whole gammon of bacon you shall receive,
And bear it hence with love and good leave:
For this is our custom at Dunmow well knowne,
Though the pastime be ours, the bacon's your own."

The parties were to take this oath before the prior and con-
vent and the whole town, humbly kneeling in the churchyard
upon two hard pointed stones, which still are shown. They
were afterwards taken upon men's shoulders, and carried, first,
about the priory churchyard, and after through the town, with
all the friars and brethren, and all the townsfolk, young and
old, following them with shouts and acclamations, with their
bacon before them.[1]

I have a large print, now become exceedingly rare, entitled
"An exact perspective view of Dunmow, late the Priory, in the
County of Essex, with a representation of the ceremony and
procession in that Mannor, on Thursday the 20th of June, 1751,
when Thomas Shapeshaft, of the parish of Weathersfield, in
the county aforesaid, weaver, and Ann his wife, came to demand and did actually receive a Gammon of Bacon, having
first kneeled down upon two bare stones within the church
door and taken the oath, &c. N.B. Before the dissolution of

[1] Blount's Jocular Tenures, by Beckwith, 1784, p. 296. A writer in
the Gentleman's Magazine for 1751, xxi. 248, attributes the origin of this
ceremony to an ancient institution of the Lord Fitzwalter, in the reign of
King Henry III., who ordered that " whatever married man did not repent
of his marriage, or quarrel with his wife, in a year and a day after it,
should go to his priory, and demand the bacon, on his swearing to the
truth, kneeling on two stones in the churchyard." The form and ceremony
of the claim, as made in 1701 by William Parsley, of Much Easton, in the
county of Essex, butcher, and Jane his wife, is detailed in the same page.

monasteries it does not appear; by searching the most ancient records, to have been demanded above three times, and, including this, just as often since. Taken on the spot and engraved by David Ogborne."

Dugdale, from whom Blount seems to have obtained the greater part of his information on the Dunmow Bacon, gives the oath in prose, from the collections of Sir Richard St. George, Garter, about 1640. He adds, that, "in the book belonging to the house," he had found the memoranda of three claims prior to the dissolution. The first is in the seventh year of King Edward IV., when a gammon of bacon was delivered to one Steven Samuel of Little Ayston ; the second in the twenty-third year of King Henry VI, when a flitch was delivered to Richard Wright of Badbourge, near the city of Norwich; and the third, in 1510, the second year of King Henry VIII., when a gammon was delivered to Thomas Ley, fuller, of Coggeshall, in Essex.

Among the rolls belonging to the Lansdowne MSS. in the British Museum, No. 25, is a copy on parchment of the record of proceedings at the manor-court of Dunmow, late the priory, in the county of Essex, before the steward, jury, suitors, and other officers of the said court, on the delivery of two gammons of bacon to John Reynolds, of Hatfield Regis, and Ann, his wife, who had been married ten years; and to William Parsley, of Much Eyston, butcher, and Jane, his wife, who had been married three years on the 27th of June, 1701. It is stated that the bacon was delivered "with the usual solemnity." This record contains the rhyming oath and sentence. The jury consisted of five spinsters.

It is stated in a newspaper of the year 1772, that on the 12th of June that year, John and Susan Gilder, of the parish of Tarling, in Essex, made their public entry into Dunmow, escorted by a great concourse of people, and demanded the gammon of bacon, according to notice previously given, declaring themselves ready to take the usual oath ; but to the great disappointment of the happy couple and their numerous attendants, the priory gates were found fast nailed, and all admittance refused, in pursuance of the express orders of the lord of the manor. Gough, in his edition of Camden's Britannia, 1809, ii. 54, mentions that the custom is now abolished, " on account of the abuse of it in these loose-principled times." The John Bull newspaper, Oct. 8, 1837, speaks of the renewal of this ceremony at a meeting of the Saffron Walden and Dunmow Agricultural Society.

The Dunmow bacon is alluded to in the Visions of Pierce Plowman, and in Chaucer's Wife of Bath's Prologue. [And a very early notice of it occurs in MS. Laud. 416, a metrical paraphrase of the Ten Commandments, in the Bodleian Library:

> " I can fynd no man now that wille enquere
> The parfyte wais unto Dunmow;
> For they repent hem within a yere,
> And many within a weke, and sonner, men trow;
> That cawsith the weis to be rowgh and over grow,
> That no man my fynd path or gap."]

A similar custom prevailed at Whichenovre, in Staffordshire. This appears to have been in conformity to an ancient tenure and was certainly as old as the tenth year of King Edward III., when the manor was held by Sir Philip de Somerville. The oath, as appears by the following copy, was less strict than that at Dunmow; it was taken on a book laid above the bacon : " Here ye, Sir Philippe de Somervile, Lord of Whichenovre, maynteyner and gyver of this baconne, that I *A*. sithe I wedded *B*. my wife, and sythe I hadd hyr in my kepyng, and at my wylle, by a yere and a day, after our mariage, I wold not have chaunged for none other, farer ne fowler, rycher ne pourer, ne for none other descended of greater lynage, slepyng ne waking, at noo tyme. And yf the seyd *B*. were sole, and I sole, I would take her to be my wyfe, before all the wymen of the worlde, of what condiciones so-ever they be, good or evylle, as helpe me God and hys seyntys; and this flesh and all fleshes." It is observable that this Whichenovre flitch was to be hanging in the hall of the manor " redy arrayede all times of the yere, bott in Lent." It was to be given to every man or woman married, " after the day and the yere of their marriage be past; and to be gyven to everyche mane of religion, archbishop, bishop, prior, or other religious, and to everyche preest, after the year and day of their profession finished, or of their dignity reseyved." See Plott's Hist. of Staffordshire, p. 440; and the Spectator, No. 607.

This whimsical institution it should seem was not confined

entirely to Dunmow and Whichenovre, for there was the same
abroad at Bretagne.

[A notice of the custom occurs in the Chelmsford Chronicle
for January, 1838 : " 25. The anniversary of the *Dunmow*
Agricultural Society held, when the flitch of bacon was distributed : at the dinner at the Town Hall fifty gentlemen sat
down, T, M. Wilson, Esq., in the chair."]

CORNUTES.

IN pursuing our notices of marriage customs we come to
the consideration of the vulgar saying, that *a husband wears
horns*, or is a *cornute*, when his wife proves false to him ; as
also that of the meaning of the word *cuckold*, which has
for many ages been the popular indication of the same kind
of infamy, which also it has been usual slily to hint at by
throwing out the little and forefinger when we point at those
whom we tacitly call cuckolds.

In the Disputation between a Hee Conny-Catcher and a
Shee Conny-Catcher, 4to., of the time of Queen Elizabeth, is
the following witticism on this head : " Hee that was *hit with
the horne* was pincht at the heart." Also, ibid. : " Let him
dub her husband knight *of the forked order.*" So Othello :

"O curse of marriage !
—'Tis destiny, unshunnable like death.
Even then *this forked plague* is fated to us,
When we do quicken."

In one of George Houfnagle's Views in Spain (Seville),
dated 1593, is a curious representation of "riding the stang,"
or "skimmington," as then practised in that country. The
patient cuckold rides on a mule, hand-shackled, and having
on an amazing large pair of antlers, which are twisted about
with herbs, with four little flags at the top, and three bells.
The vixen rides on another mule, and seems to be belabouring
her husband with a crabbed stick ; her face is entirely covered
with her long hair. Behind her, on foot, follows a trumpeter,
holding in his left hand a trumpet, and in his right a basti-
nado, or large strap, seemingly of leather, with which he beats

her as they go along. The passengers, or spectators, are each *holding up at them two fingers like snail's horns.* In the reference this procession is styled, in Spanish, " Execution de justitia de los cornudos patientes."[1]

In the English Fortune Teller, 1609, the author, speaking of a wanton's husband, says : " He is the wanton wenches game amongst themselves, and wagge's sport to *point at with two fingers.*" Bulwer, in his Chirologia, 1644, p. 181, says : " To present the index and eare-finger (i. e. the *fore* and *little* finger) wagging, with the thumb applied unto the temples, is their expression who would scornfully reprove any. The same gesture, if you take away the motion, is used, in our nimble-fingered times, to call one *cuckold,* and to present *the badge of cuckoldry,* that mentall and imaginary *horne;* seeming to cry, ' O man of happy note, whom Fortune, meaning highly to promote, hath stucke on thy forehead the earnest penny of succeeding good lucke.' " The following passage occurs in a curious publication, entitled the Horne exalted, 1661, p. 37 : " Horns are signified by the *throwing out the little and fore finger* when we point at such whom we tacitly called cuckolds." In the famous print of "a skimmington," engraved by Hogarth for Hudibras, we observe a tailor's wife employed in this manner to denote her own, but, as she thinks, her husband's infamy.

Winstanley, in his Historical Rarities, p. 76, says : " The Italians, when they intend to scoff or disgrace one, use to put their thumb between two of their fingers, and say ' Ecco la fico ;' which is counted a disgrace answerable to our English custom of making horns to the man whom we suspect to be

---

[1] This punishment, however, seems only to have been inflicted on those who, availing themselves of the beauty of their wives, made a profit of their prostitution. See Colmenar's Delices de l'Espagne et du Portugal, where, speaking of the manners of the Spaniards, v. 839, he says : " Lorsqu'un homme surprend sa femme en adultère, il peut la tuer avec son corrupteur, et l'impunité lui est assurée. Mais si, sachant que sa femme lui fait porter les cornes, il le souffre pour en tirer quelque profit, lorsque on vient à le découvrir, on le saisit lui et sa femme, on les met chacun à chevauchon sur un âne, on lui attache à la tête une belle grand paire de cornes, avec des sonnettes, en cet état on l'expose en montre au peuple. La femme est obligée de fouetter son mari, et elle est fouettée en même temps par le bourreau." This account is also accompanied by a print.

a cuckold." He goes on thus to recount for it: "In the
time of the Emperor Frederick Barbarossa, anno 1161,
Beatrix, the emperor's wife, coming to see the city of Millain
in Italy, was by the irreverent people, first imprisoned and
then most barbarously handled ; for they placed her on a mule,
with her face towards the tail, which she was compelled to
use instead of a bridle; and when they had thus shown her
to all the town, they brought her to a gate, and kicked her
out. To avenge this wrong, the emperor besieged and forced
the town, and adjudged all the people to die, save such as
would undergo this ransome. Between the buttocks of a
skittish mule a bunch of figs was fastened ; and such as would
live must, with their hands bound behind, run after the
mule till, with their teeth, they had snatched out one or more
of the figs. This condition, besides the hazard of many a
sound kick, was, by most, accepted and performed."

Greene, in his Conceipt, 1598, p. 33, uses this expression
of a cornute: "But certainely beleeved that Giraldo his
master was as soundly armde for the heade, as either Capri-
corne, or the stoutest horned signe in the Zodiacke."

It is well known that the word horn in the Sacred Writings
denotes fortitude and vigour of mind ;[1] and that in the
classics, personal courage (metaphorically from the pushing
of horned animals) is intimated by horns.[2] Whence then are
we to deduce a very ancient custom which has prevailed almost
universally, of saying that the unhappy husbands of false
women wear horns, or are cornutes? It may be said almost
universally, for we are told that even among the Indians it
was the highest indignity that could be offered them even to
point at a horn.[3]

There is a singular passage upon this subject in Nicolson
and Burn's History of Westmoreland and Cumberland, i. 540,
which I shall give, and leave, too, without comment, as I find
it. They are speaking of the monument of Thomas the first

[1] " His *horn* shall be exalted."   " The *horn* of my salvation," &c. &c.
[2]   " Namque in malos asperrimus
        Parata tollo cornua."   Horat. Epod.
" Jam feror in pugnas et nondum cornua sumpsi." Ovid. de Ebrietate
[3] In Spain it is a crime as much punishable by the laws *to put up horns*
against a neighbour's house, as to have written a libel against him.

Lord Wharton, in the church of Kirkby Stephen in Westmoreland, the crest of whose arms was a bull's head: "The consideration of horns, generally used upon the crest, seemeth to account for what hath hitherto by no author or other person ever been accounted for; namely the connexion betwixt horns and cuckolds. The notion of cuckolds wearing horns prevails through all the modern European languages, and is of four or five hundred years' standing. The particular estimation of badges and distinction of arms began in the time of the Crusades, being then more especially necessary to distinguish the several nations of which the armies were composed. Horns upon the crest, according to that of Silius Italicus,

'Casside *cornigera* dependens insula,'

were erected in terrorem: and after the husband had been absent three or four years, and came home in his regimental accoutrements, it might be no impossible supposition that the man who wore the horns was a cuckold. And this accounts, also, why no author at that time, when the droll notion was started, hath ventured to explain the connexion; for woe be to the man in those days that should have made a joke of the Holy War, which indeed, in consideration of the expense of blood and treasure attending it, was a very serious affair."

There is a great parade of learning on the subject of this very serious jest in a foreign work in Latin, printed at Brussels in 1661, in folio, and entitled the Paradise of Pleasant Questions. The various opinions of the learned are given in this curious collection, but I much doubt if any of them will be thought satisfactory. In one of them "cornutus" is most forcibly derived from *nudus* and *corde*, as meaning a pitiful fellow, such an one as he must needs be who can sit tamely down under so great an injury. Such kind of etymology merits no serious confutation. In another, Cælius Rhodoginus is introduced as wishing to derive it from an insensibility peculiar, as he says, to the *he-goat*, who will stand looking on while another is possessing his female. As writers on natural history do not admit the truth of the assertion, this too will, of course, fall to the ground.[1]

[1] In the Blazon of Jealousie, 1615, p. 57, we are told a very different story of a swan. "The *tale of the swanne* about Windsor finding a strange cocke with his mate, and how far he swam after the other to kill

Another conjecture is, that some mean husbands, availing themselves of their wives' beauty, have turned it to account by prostituting them, obtaining by this means *the horn of Amalthea*, the *cornu copiæ*, which by licentious wits has since been called, in the language of modern gallantry, tipping the horns with gold. The fact is too notorious to be doubted; but as this only accounts for a *single horn*, perhaps we must lay no great stress upon the probability of this surmise.

Pancirollus, on the other hand, derives it from a custom of the debauched Emperor Andronicus, who used to hang up in a frolic in the porticos of the forum, the stag's horns he had taken in hunting, intending, as he says, by this new kind of insignia, to denote at once the manners of the city, the lasciviousness of the wives he had debauched, and the size of the animals he had made his prey, and that from hence the sarcasm spread abroad, that the husband of an adulterous wife bare horns. I cannot satisfy myself with this account; for what Andronicus did seems to have been only a continuation, not the origin, of this custom. In Shakespeare's Titus Andronicus, ii. 3, the following occurs:

" Under your patience, gentle empress,
'Tis thought you have a goodly gift in horning.
Jove shield your husband from his hounds to-day !
'Tis pity they should take him for a stag."

The following is extracted from the Gentleman's Magazine for December 1786, p. 1020 : " The woman who is false to her husband is said to plant horns on his head. I know not how far back the idea of giving his head this ornament may be traced, but it may be met with in Artemidorus (lib. ii.), and I believe we must have recourse to a Greek epigram for an illustration :[1]

" Οστις εσω πυροος καταλαμβανει ουκ ανοραζων.
Κεινον Αμαλθειας ἡ γυνη εστι κερς."   Antholog. lib. ii.

---

it, and then, returning backe, slew his hen also (this being a certain truth, and not many yeers done upon this our Thames), is so well knowne to many gentlemen, and to most watermen of this river, as it were needlesse to use any more words about the same."

[1] " The lightness of his wife shines through it, and yet cannot he see, though he have his own lantern to light him." Shaks. This joke seems evidently to have been taken from that of Plautus : " Quò ambulas tu,

Shakespeare and Ben Jonson seem both to have considered the horns in this light: "Well, he may sleep in security, for he hath the horn of abundance, and the lightness of his wife shines through it; and yet cannot he see, though he have his own lantern to light him." Second Part of King Henry IV., act i. sc. 2.

> "What! never sigh;
> Be of good cheer, man, for thou art a cuckold.
> 'Tis done, 'tis done! nay, when such flowing store,
> Plenty itself falls in my wife's lap,
> The cornu copiæ will be mine, I know."
> Every Man in his Humour, a. iii. sc. 6.

Steevens, on the above passage in 2 Henry IV. has these additions: "So in Pasquil's Night-Cap, 1612, p. 43.

> " But chiefly citizens, upon whose crowne
> Fortune her blessings most did tumble downe;
> And in whose eares (as all the world doth know)
> The *horne of great aboundance* still doth blow."

The same thought occurs in the Two Maids of Moreclacke, 1609:

> " Your wrongs
> Shine through the *horn*, as candles in the eve,
> To light out others."

Armstrong, in his History of the Island of Minorca, 1756, p. 170, says the inhabitants bear hatred to the sight and name of a horn; ''for they never mention it but in anger, and then they curse with it, saying *cuerno*, as they would *diablo*."

[It was formerly a common notion that the unfaithfulness of a woman to her husband was always guided by a destiny which no human power could avert. In Grange's Garden, 1577, we have an allusion to this:

> " And playing thus with wanton toyes, the cuckow bad good morow;
> Alas, thought I, a token 'tis for me to live in sorrow:
> Cuckow sang he, Cuckow sayd I, what destiny is this?
> Who so it heares, he well may thinke it is no sacred blisse.

---

qui Vulcanum in cornu conclusum geris?" (Amph. act i. sc. 1), and much improved. We need not doubt that a joke was here intended by Plautus; for the proverbial term of horns for cuckoldom is very ancient, as appears by Artemidorus, who says: " Προειπεῖν αυτῷ ὅτι ἡ γυνή σου πορνεύσει, καὶ τὸ λεγομενον, κέρατα αὐτῷ ποιήσει, καὶ οὕτως ἀπέβη." Ονειροι. lib, ii. cap. 12. And he copied from those before him.

Alas, quoth she, what oons hovo you, so wot thus for to say
In cuckow time few have a charme to cause his tongue to stay;
Wherefore,
Content yourselfe as well as I, let reason rule your minde,
As cuckolds come by destiny, so cuckowes sing by kinde."

Compare also Nicolls's poem on the Cuckoo, 1607, p. 12 :

" Meanetime Dan Cuckow, knowing that his voice
Had no varietie, no change, no choice :
But through the wesand pipe of his harsh throate,
Cri'd only Cuckow, that prodigious note !"]

In the Horne Exalted, 1661, I find several conjectures on the subject, but such light and superficial ones as I think ought not much to be depended upon. One of them derives the etymology from *bulls;* asserting that such husbands as regarded not their wives were called bulls, because it is said that that animal, when satiated with his females, will not even feed with them, but removes as far off as he can. Hence the woman in Aristophanes, complaining of the absence and slights of her husband, says : " Must I in house without Bull stay alone?" On which account those husbands have been called bulls, who by abandoning their wives occasioned their proving unchaste, and consequently were mocked with *horns.* By another the word *horns,* or *cornuto,* is thought to have been taken from the injured and angry moon, which is all one with Venus, from whence generation. Another conjecture, playing on the Italian word *beccho,* which signifies a cuckold or goat, derives it from Bacchus, whom Orpheus calls the god with two horns. Thus drunkenness causing men, by neglecting them, to have wanton wives, they are said to have horns, to show to the world the occasion of their shame ; and that by ossing the horn (meaning the drinking-horns) so much to their heads, they are said to have horns, fixing them at last to heir foreheads. Another derives the word *horns* from the infamy, for which, as in other public matters, they sound and *blow horns* in the streets, and supposes horns are only a public opinion and scattering of this infamy of the husband about, as proclamations are made known by sound of trumpets. There is, lastly, a conjecture that the beginning of horns came from the Indians (it will be thought a far-fetched one), whose women had a custom that, when any lover presented his mistress with an elephant, the last favour might be granted him without prejudice to her name or honesty ; that it even became matter of praise to her, not objected to even by her husband, who preserved the *horns* as the better part of the elephant, in order to show them to the world as trophies of his wife's beauty. What a pity it is to spoil such a surmise, by suggesting that these reputed horns are really the elephant's teeth !

There used formerly (and I believe it is still now and then retained) to be a kind of ignominious procession in the north of England, called " Riding the Stang," when, as the glossary to Douglas's Virgil informs us, "one is made to ride on a pole for his neighbour's wife's fault." " Staung Eboracensibus est lignum ablongum. Contus bajulorum."—Hickes. This custom bids fair not to be of much longer continuance in the north, for I find, by the Newcastle-upon-Tyne Courant for August 3d, 1793, that at the assizes at Durham, in the preceding week, "Thomas Jameson, Matthew Marrington, Geo. Ball, Jos. Rowntree, Simon Emmerson, Robert Parkin, and Francis Wardell, for *violently assaulting* Nicholas Lowes, of Bishop Wearmouth, and *carrying him on a stang*, were sentenced to be imprisoned two years in Durham gaol, and find sureties for their good behaviour for three years." The law taking such cognisance of the practice, it must of course terminate very shortly.

This custom is represented in a plate in the Costume of Yorkshire, 1814, p. 63. The letter-press says, "This ancient provincial custom is still occasionally observed in some parts of Yorkshire, though by no means so frequently as it was formerly. It is no doubt intended to expose and ridicule any violent quarrel between man and wife, and more particularly in instances where the pusillanimous husband has suffered himself to be beaten by his virago of a partner. A case of this description is here represented, and a party of boys, assuming the office of public censors, are riding the stang. This is a pole, supported on the shoulders of two or more of the lads, across which one of them is mounted, beating an old kettle or pan with a stick. He at the same time repeats a speech, or what they term a *nominy*, which, for the sake of detailing the whole ceremony, is here subjoined :

> " With a ran, tan, tan,
>   On my old tin can,
>   Mrs. ―――― and her good man.

She hong'd him, she hong'd him,
For spending a penny when he stood in need.
She up with a three-footed stool ;
She struck him so hard, and she cut so deep,
Till the blood run down like a new stuck sheep !"

The word Stang, says Ray, is still used in some colleges in Cambridge ; to stang scholars in Christmas time being to cause them to ride on a colt-staff, or pole, for missing chapel. It is derived from the Islandic *Staung*, hasta.

It appears from Allan Ramsay's Poems, 1721, p. 128, that riding the stang was used in Scotland. A note says : " The riding of the stang on a woman that hath beat her husband, is as I have described it, by one's riding upon a sting, or a long piece of wood, carried by two others on their shoulders, where, like a herauld, he proclaims the woman's name, and the manner of her unnatural action :

" They frae a barn a kaber raught,
Ane mounted wi' a bang,
Betwisht twa's shoulders, and sat straught
Upon 't, and *rade the stang*
On her that day."

Callender observes, says Jamieson in his Etymological Dictionary, that, in the north, riding the stang " is a mark of the highest infamy." " The person," he subjoins, " who has been thus treated, seldom recovers his honour in the opinion of his neighbours. When they cannot lay hold of the culprit himself, they put some young fellow on the stang, or pole, who proclaims that it is not on his own account that he is thus treated, but on that of another person, whom he names."— Anc. Scot. Poems, pp. 154-5. " I am informed," Dr. Jamieson adds, " that in Lothian, and perhaps in other counties, the man who had debauched his neighbour's wife was formerly forced to ride the stang." So in R. Galloway's Poems, p. 12 : " On you I'll ride the *stang*."

---

[1] " Here," says Jamieson, " we have evidently the remains of a very ancient custom. The Goths were wont to erect what they called *nidstaeng*, or the pole of infamy, with the most dire imprecations against the person who was thought to deserve this punishment ; Isl. *nidstong*. He who was subjected to this dishonour was called *niding*, to which the English word infamous most nearly corresponds ; for he could not make oath in any cause. The celebrated Islandic bard, Egill Skallagrim, having performed

"To ride," or "riding Skimmington," is, according to Grose, a ludicrous cavalcade in ridicule of a man beaten by his wife: it consists of a man riding behind a woman with his face to the horse's tail, holding a distaff in his hand, at which he seems to work, the woman all the while beating him with a ladle. A smock displayed on a staff is carried before them, as an emblematical standard, denoting female superiority: they are accompanied by what is called rough music, that is, frying-pans, bulls'-horns, marrow-bones and cleavers, &c.— a procession admirably described by Butler in his Hudibras. [The following allusion to it occurs in Poor Robin's Almanack for 1699 :

> " What's a cuckold? learn of me,
> Few do know his pedigree,
> Or his subtle nature conster,
> Born a man, but dies a monster;
> Yet great antiquaries say,
> He sprung from old Methusala,
> Who after Noah's Flood was found
> To have his crest with branches crown'd.
> God in Eden's happy shade
> Such a creature never made:
> Then to cut off all mistaking,
> Cuckolds are of women's making.
> Then next we shall to you declare
> How many sorts of cuckolds are;
> The *patient* cuckold he is first,
> The *grumbling* cuckold one oth' worst,
> The *loving* cuckold he is best,
> The *patient* cuckold lives at rest,
> The *frantick* cuckold giveth blows,
> The *ignorant* cuckold nothing knows,
> The *jealous* cuckold double twang'd,
> The *pimping* cuckold would be hang'd;
> The Skimington cuckold he is one,
> And so I think their number's done.
> Thus, reader, by these lines you see
> That there nine sorts of cuckolds be,

---

this tremendous ceremony at the expense of Eric Bloddox, King of Norway, who, as he supposed, had highly injured him, Eric soon after became hated by all, and was obliged to fly from his dominions. v. Ol. Lex. Run. v. *nijd.* The form of imprecation is quoted by Callender, ut supra. It may be added, that the custom of 'riding the stang' seems also to have been known in Scandinavia; for Seren gives *stanghesten* as signifying the rod, or roddle-horse; v. *rod.*"

And many others too that border
No doubt upon this forked order,
Whereby we do this profit reap,
All sorts of horns thereby are cheap."]

In Bagford's Letter relating to the Antiquities of London, printed in the first volume of Leland's Collectanea, p. lxxvi., he says: "I might here mention the old custom of Skimmington, when a woman beats her husband, of which we have no memory but in Hudibras, altho' I have been told of an old statute made for that purpose." Hogarth's print, which accompanies Butler's description, is also called the Skimmington, though none of the commentators on Hudibras have attempted an elucidation of the ceremony.

In Hymen, an Account of different Marriage Ceremonies, 1760, p. 177, is the following account of a Skimmington: "There is another custom in England, which is very extraordinary: a woman carries something in the shape of a man, crowned with a huge pair of horns, a drum goes before and a vast crowd follows, making a strange music with tongs, gridirons, and kettles. This burlesque ceremony was the invention of a woman, who thereby vindicated the character of a neighbour of hers, who had stoutly beaten her husband for being so saucy as to accuse his wife of being unfaithful to his bed. The figure with horns requires no explanation ; it is obvious to everybody that it represents the husband." So Misson, in his Travels in England, translated by Ozell, p. 129, says: "I have sometimes met in the streets of London a woman carrying a figure of straw representing a man, crown'd with very ample horns, preceded by a drum, and followed by a mob, making a most grating noise with tongs, gridirons, fryingpans, and saucepans. I asked what was the meaning of all this ; they told me that a woman had given her husband a sound beating for accusing her of making him a cuckold, and that upon such occasions some kind neighbour of *the poor innocent injured* creature generally performed this ceremony."

A curious little book, entitled Divers Crab-tree Lectures that Shrews read to their Husbands, 1639, has a woodcut facing the frontispiece, representing a woman beating her husband with a ladle, is called Skimmington and her Husband. This cut is repeated in a chapter entitled Skimmington's Lecture

to her Husband, which is the errand Scold, with some verses,
wherein occur the following pithy lines:

> " But all shall not serve thee,
> For have at thy pate,
> My ladle of the crab-tree
> Shall teach thee to cogge and to prate."

By the above it should seem to appear that the word
"Skimmington" signifies an errant scold, and has most probably been derived from the name of some woman of great
notoriety in that line.   Thus a "sandwich," the "little cold
collation," from the Earl of Sandwich. Douce derives it from
the skimming-ladle; and I find the following account of its
supposed origin in D. Bellamy's, Gordon's, and other gentlemen's Dictionary, 2d edit. 8vo. Lond.   "*Skimmington*, a sort
of burlesque procession in ridicule of a man who suffers himself to be beat by his wife. In commerce it is particularly
used for the membrane stripped off the animal to be prepared
by the tanner, skinner, currier, parchment-maker, &c. to be
converted into leather," &c.

The following curious passage is taken from Dr. King's
Miscellany Poems ; see his Works, 1776, iii. 256 :

> " When the young people ride the Skimmington,
> There is a general trembling in a town.
> Not only he for whom the person rides
> Suffers, but they sweep other doors besides ;
> And by that hieroglyphic does appear
> That the good woman is the master there."

It should seem from the above lines that in this ludicrous
procession, intended to shame some notoriously tame husband,
and who suffered his wife to wear the breeches, it was part of
the ceremony *to sweep before the door of the person* whom they
intended to satirise ; and if they stopped at any other door and
swept there too, it was a pretty broad hint that there were
more Skimmingtons, i. e. shrews, in the town than one.   In
Gloucestershire, in 1786, this was called a "Skimmington."

Douce has a curious print, entitled An exact Representation
of the humourous Procession of the Richmond Wedding of
Abram Kendrick and Mary Westurn, 17**. Two grenadiers
go first, then the flag with a crown on it is carried after them;
four men with hand-bells follow ; then two men, one carrying
a block-head, having a hat and wig on it, *and a pair of horns.*

the other bearing a ladle; the pipe and tabor, hautboy and
fiddle; then the bridegroom in a chair, and attendants with
hollyhock flowers; and afterward the bride, with her attendants carrying also hollyhock flowers. Bridemaids and bride-
men close the procession.

In Strype's edition of Stow's Survey of London, 1. 258, we
read: "1562, Shrove Monday, at Charing-cross was a man
carried of four men; and before him a bag-pipe playing, a
shawm, and a drum beating, and twenty links burning about
him. The cause was, *his next neighbour's wife beat her husband;*
it being so ordered that *the next should ride about the place to
expose her.*" In Lupton's Too Good to be True, 1580, p. 50,
Siquila says: "In some places with us, *if a woman* beat her
husband, the man that dwelleth next unto hir shall ride on a
cowlstaffe; and there is al the punishment she is like to have."
Omen observes: "That is rather an uncomly custome than a
good order; for he that is in faintnesse is undecently used,
and the unruly offendor is excused thereby. If this be all the
punishment your wives have that beate their simple husbandes,
it is rather a boldning than a discouraging of some bolde and
shamelesse dames to beate their simple husbandes, to make
their next neyghbors (whom they spite) to ride on a cowlstaffe,
rather rejoising and flearing at the riding of their neighbours,
than sorrowing or repenting for beating of their husbands."

Park, in his Travels in the Interior of Africa, speaking of
Kolor, a considerable town, near the entrance to which was a
sort of masquerade-habit hanging upon a tree, made of the
bark of trees, which, he was told, belonged to Mumbo Jumbo,
says: "This is a strange bugbear, common in all the Man-
dingo towns, and employed by the Pagan natives in keeping
the women in subjection; for, as they are not restricted in the
number of their wives, every one marries as many as he can
conveniently maintain, and it often happens that the ladies
disagree among themselves: family quarrels sometimes rise to
such a height that the voice of the husband is disregarded in
the tumult. Then the interposition of Mumbo Jumbo is in-
voked, and is always decisive. This strange minister of justice,
this sovereign arbiter of domestic strife, disguised in his
masquerade attire, and armed with the rod of public authority,
announces his coming by loud and dismal screams in the adjacent woods. He begins as soon as it is dark to enter the

town, and proceeds to a place where all the inhabitants are assembled to meet him. The appearance of Mumbo Jumbo it may be supposed, is unpleasing to the African ladies; but they dare not refuse to appear when summoned, and the ceremony commences with dancing and singing, which continues till midnight, when Mumbo seizes on the offender. The unfortunate victim, being stripped naked, is tied to a post, and severely scourged with Mumbo's rod, amidst the shouts and derision of the whole assembly; and it is remarkable that the rest of the women are very clamorous and outrageous in their abuse of their unfortunate sister, till daylight puts an end to this disgusting revelry."

The following is an extract from Hentzner's Travels in England, 1598: "Upon taking the air down the river (from London), on the left hand lies Ratcliffe, a considerable suburb. On the opposite shore is fixed a long pole, with ram's-horns upon it, the intention of which was vulgarly said to be a reflection upon wilful and contented cuckolds." Edit. 1757, p.47.

Grose mentions a fair called Horn-Fair, held at Charlton, in Kent, on St. Luke's day, the 18th of October. It consists of a riotous mob, who, after a printed summons dispersed through the adjacent towns, meet at Cuckold's Point, near Deptford, and march from thence in procession through that town and Greenwich to Charlton, with horns of different kinds upon their heads; and at the fair there are sold ram's-horns, and every sort of toy made of horn; even the ginger-bread figures have horns. A sermon is preached at Charlton church on the fair day. Tradition attributes the origin of this licentious fair to King John, who, *it is said*, being detected in an adulterous amour, compounded for his crime by granting to the injured husband all the land from Charlton to Cuckold's Point, and established the fair as a tenure.

It appears from the Whole Life of Mr. William Fuller, 1703, p. 122, that it was the fashion in his time to go to Horn fair dressed in women's clothes. "I remember being there upon Horn fair day, *I was dressed in my land-lady's best gown, and other women's attire*, and to Horn fair we went, and as we were coming back by water, all the cloaths were spoiled by dirty water, &c., that was flung on us in an inundation, for which I was obliged to present her with two guineas, to make atonement for the damage sustained, &c."

In an extract from an old newspaper, I find it was formerly a custom for a procession to go from some of the inns in Bishopsgate street, in which were a king, a queen, a miller, a councillor, &c., and a great number of others, with horns in their hats, to Charlton, where they went round the church three times, &c. So many indecencies were committed upon this occasion on Blackheath (as the whipping of females with furze, &c.), that it gave rise to the proverb of "all is fair at Horn fair." Lysons, in the Environs of London, iv. 325, says the burlesque procession has been discontinued since the year 1768. [I possess an old ballad called the Merry Humours of Horn Fair, in which this procession is referred to:

"The first that rides is called the king, sir,
    He has a large pair of horns
Gilt with gold, that they may glitter,
    That all who see may know he's horned.

The parson's wife rides with the miller;
    She said, I hate horns, I do declare,
Yet happy are the men who wear them,
    My husband he shall have a pair."]

Grose in his Classical Dictionary of the Vulgar Tongue, has noticed two customs evidently connected with our present subject:

"HIGHGATE. Sworn at Highgate.—A ridiculous custom formerly prevailed at the public-houses in Highgate, to administer a ludicrous oath to all travellers of the middling rank who stopped there. The party was sworn on a pair of horns, fastened on a stick; the substance of the oath was, never to kiss the maid when he could kiss the mistress, never to drink small beer when he could get strong, with many other injunctions of the like kind: to all which was added the saving clause, ' Unless you like it best.' The person administering the oath was always to be called father by the juror, and he in return was to style him son, under the penalty of a bottle." One or two of the public-houses in this village still (1841) have a pair of horns elevated upon a post standing in front of the house.

"HOISTING. A ludicrous ceremony formerly performed on every soldier the first time he appeared in the field after being married. It was thus managed : As soon as the regiment or company had grounded their arms to rest awhile, three or four men of the same company to which the bridegroom belonged seized upon him, and, putting a couple of bayonets out of the two corners of his hat to represent horns, it was placed on his head, the back part foremost. He was then hoisted on the shoulders of two strong fellows, and carried round the arms, a drum and a fife beating and playing the Pioneers' call, named Round-heads and Cuckolds, but on this occasion styled the Cuckold's March. In passing the colours he was to take off his hat. This in some regiments was practised by the officers on their brethren."

The following is from a View of London and Westminster, or the Town Spy, 1725, p. 26. The author is speaking of St. Clement Danes : "There was formerly a good custom of *saddling the spit* in this parish, which, for reasons well known at Westminster, is now laid aside ; so that wives, whose husbands are sea-faring persons, or who are otherwise absent from them, have lodged here ever since very quietly."

OF THE WORD CUCKOLD.

I KNOW not how this word, which is generally derived from *cuculus* a cuckoo, has happened to be given to the injured husband, for it seems more properly to belong to the adulterer, the cuckoo being well known to be a bird that deposits its eggs in other birds' nests. The Romans seem to have used *cuculus* in its proper sense, as the adulterer, calling with equal propriety the cuckold himself carruca, or hedge-sparrow, which bird is well known to adopt the other's spurious offspring.[1]   Johnson, in his Dictionary, says : " The cuckow is

[1] Arga, in Sir Henry Spelman's Glossary, is rendered by curruca and cucurbita, i. e. cuckold, or coucold.   For the French call a gourd, coucord ; and we only change their r into l, as we say Coriander for their Coliander, coronel for their colonel, &c.   Such a blockhead, then, that hath caput cucurbitinum, is called arga, as Paul. Diacon. de Gest. Longobard., perhaps from the Greek ἄργος, i. e. one that doth not his work or business, and so corbita in LL. Longobard. signifies advoutery and whoredom, which Martinus derives from κουρβη, a tree of a saddle, and says kurba ▶n the Sclavonian signifies a lewd woman, as kurvin, to bow down, &c., from curvare, as fornication from fornix, and probably hence comes our word pumpkin for a silly rude fellow.

said to suck the eggs of other birds, and lay her own to be
hatched in their place ; from which practice it was usual to
alarm a husband at the approach of an adulterer by calling
'Cuckoo,' which by mistake was in time applied to the
husband.''

Pennant, in his Zoology, 1776, i. 234, speaking of the
cuckoo, says : " His note is so uniform, that his name in all
languages seems to have been derived from it, and in all other
countries it is used in the same reproachful sense :

> 'The plain song cuckoo grey,
> Whose note full many a man doth mark,
> And dares not answer nay.'   Shakesp.

" The reproach seems to arise from this bird making use of
the bed or nest of another to deposit its eggs in, leaving the
care of its young to a wrong parent ; but Juvenal, vi. 275, with
more justice, gives the infamy to the bird in whose nest the
supposititious eggs were layed :

> 'Tu tibi tunc curruca places.' "

Pliny, xviii. 26, tells us that vine-dressers were anciently
called cuckoos, i. e. slothful, because they deferred cutting their
vines till that bird began to sing, which was later than the
right time ; so that the same name may have been given to
the unhappy persons under consideration, when, through dis-
regard and neglect of their fair partners, they have caused
them to go a gadding in search of more diligent and industrious companions. The cuckoo has been long considered as a
bird of omen. Gay, in his Shepherd's Week, in the fourth
Pastoral, notes the vulgar superstitions on first hearing the
bird sing in the season :

> " When first the year, I heard the cuckoo sing,
> And call with welcome note the budding spring,
> I straightway set a running with such haste,
> Deb'rah that won the smock scarce ran so fast.
> Till spent for lack of breath, quite weary grown,
> Upon a rising bank I sat adown,
> And doff'd my shoe, and by my troth I swear,
> Therein I spied this yellow frizzled hair,[1]
> As like to Lubberkin's in curl and hue,
> As if upon his comely pate it grew."

---

[1] Thus described in the Connoisseur, No. 56 : " I got up last May
morning, and went into the fields to hear the cuckoo, and when I pulled
off my left shoe I found a hair in it exactly the same colour with his."

I find the following still more extraordinary in Naturall and Artificiall Conclusions, by Thomas Hill, 1650, cxxvii.: "A very easie and merry conceit to keep off fleas from your beds or chambers. Plinie reporteth that if, when you first hear the cuckow, you mark well where your right foot standeth, and take up of that earth, the fleas will by no means breed, either in your house or chamber, where any of the same earth is thrown or scattered."

In the north of, and perhaps all over England, it is vulgarly accounted to be an unlucky omen if you have no money in your pocket when you hear the cuckoo for the first time in a season.

Green, the author of a Quip for an Upstart Courtier, 1620, calls a cuckoo the cuckold's quirister : "It was just at that time when the cuckold's quirister began to bewray April gentlemen with his never-changed notes."

The Morning Post newspaper of May 17th, 1821, says : "A singular custom prevails in Shropshire at this period of the year, which is peculiar to that county. As soon as the first cuckoo has been heard, all the labouring classes leave work, if in the middle of the day, and the time is devoted to mirth and jollity over what is called the cuckoo ale."

There is a vulgar error in natural history in supposing the substance vulgarly called "cuckoo-spit" to proceed from the exhalation of the earth, from the extravasated juice of plants, or a hardened dew. According to the account of a writer in the Gent. Mag. for July, 1794, p. 602, it really proceeds from a small insect, which incloses itself within it, with an oblong obtuse body, a large head, and small eyes. The animal emits the spume from many parts of the body, undergoes its changes within it, then bursts into a winged state, and flies abroad in search of its mate ; it is particularly innoxious ; has four wings, the two external ones of a dusky brown, marked with two white spots.

From the subsequent passage in Green's work just quoted, it should seem that this substance was somehow or other vulgarly considered as emblematical of cuckoldom : "There was loyal lavender, but that was full of *cuckow-spittes*, to show that women's light thoughts make their husbands *heavy heads*."

The following passage is in that most rare tract, Plaine

Pernevall, the Pence maker of England, 1to.. "You may him, Sal sapit omnia; and *service without salt*, by the rite of England, is a cuckold's fee if he claim it."

Steevens, commenting on the mention of *columbine* in Hamlet, says: "From the Caltha Poetarum, 1599, it should seem as if this flower was the emblem of cuckoldom:

'The blue *cornuted* columbine,
Like to the crooked horns of Acheloy.'"

"Columbine," says another of the commentators, S. W., "was an emblem of cuckoldom, on account of the horns of its nectaria, which are remarkable in this plant. See Aquilegia, in Linnæus's Genera, 684." A third commentator, Holt White, says: "The columbine was emblematical of forsaken lovers:

'The columbine, in tawny often taken,
Is then ascrib'd *to such as are forsaken*.'
Browne's Britannia's Pastorals, I. ii. 1613."

Among the witticisms on cuckolds that occur in our old plays, must not be omitted the following in Ram Alley, or Merry Tricks, 1636:

"Why, my good father, what should you do with a wife?
Would you be *crested*? Will you needs *thrust your head
In one of Vulcan's helmets*? Will you perforce
Weare a city cap, and a *court feather*?"

Chaucer, in his Prosopopeia of Jealousie, brings her in with a garland of gold yellow, and a cuckoo sitting on her fist.

The following expression for being jealous is found in Ritson's Old Songs, 1792, p. 112:

"The married man cannot do so:
If he be merrie and toy with any,
His wife will frowne and words give manye:
Her yellow hose she strait will put on."

Butler, in his Hudibras, II. ii. 317, in the following passage, informs us for what a singular purpose carvers used formerly to invoke the names of cuckolds:

"Why should not Conscience have vacation,
As well as other courts o' th' nation;
Have equal power to adjourn,
Appoint appearance and return;
And make as nice distinction serve
To split a case, *as those that carve,
Invoking cuckolds' names, hit joints*?"

In Wit and Mirth Improved, or a New Academy of Complements, p. 95, the fourth gossip says :

> "Lend me that knife, and I'll cut up the goose :
> I am not right—let me turn edge and point.
> *Who must I think upon to hit the joint ?*
> *My own good man ?* I think there's none more fit.
> *He's in my thoughts*, and now the joint I hit."

In Batt upon Batt, 1694, p. 4, I find the following :

> " So *when the mistress cannot hit the joynt*,
> Which proves sometimes, you know, a diff'cult point,
> *Think on a cuckold*, straight the gossips cry ;
> But think on Batt's good carving knife say I ;
> That still nicks sure, without offence and scandal :
> Dull blades may be beholden to their handle :
> But those Batt makes are all so sharp, they scorn
> *To be so charmed by his neighbour's horn.*"

In the British Apollo, 1708, ii. 59, is the following query : " When a person is joynting a piece of meat, if he finds it difficult to joynt, he is bid to think of a cuckold. I desire to know whence the proverb ? *A.* Thomas Webb, a carver to a Lord Mayor of London, in King Charles the First's reign, was as famous for his being a cuckold as for his dexterity in carving : therefore what became a proverb was used first as an invocation, when any took upon him to carve."

Kyrle, the Man of Ross, celebrated by Pope, had always company to dine with him on a market-day, and a goose, if it could be procured, was one of the dishes; which he claimed the privilege of carving himself. When any guest, ignorant of the etiquette of the table, offered to save him that trouble, he would exclaim : " Hold your hand, man : if I am good for anything, it is for hitting cuckold's joints."

In Flecknoe's Diarium, 1656, p. 70, is the following :

> " *On Doctor Cuckold,*
>
> " Who so famous was of late,
> He was *with finger* pointed at :
> What cannot learning do, and single state ?
>
> " Being married, he so famous grew,
> As he was pointed at *with two ;*
> What cannot learning and a wife now do ?"

It is still supposed that the word cuculus gave some rise to the name of cuckold, though the cuckoo lays in other nests;

yet the etymology may still hold, for lawyers tell us that the honours and disgrace of man and wife are reciprocal ; so that what the one hath, the other partakes of it. Thus then the lubricity of the woman is thrown upon the man, and her dishonesty thought his dishonour ; who, being the head of the wife, and thus abused by her, he gains the name of cuckold, from cuckoo, which bird, as he used to nestle in other's places ; so it was of old, the hieroglyphic of a fearful, idle, and stupid fellow, and hence became the nickname of such men as neglected to dress and prune their vines in due season. So Horace,

" Magna compellans voce cucullum."[1]

Douce's manuscript notes, however, say : "That the word cuculus was a term of reproach amongst the ancients there is not the least doubt, and that it was used in the sense of our ' cuckold' is equally clear. Plautus has so introduced it on more than one occasion."[2]

[1] In Paradoxical Assertions and Philosophical Problems, by R. H., 8vo. Lond. 1664, p. 5, " Why cuckolds are said to wear horns ?" we read : " Is not this monster said to wear the horns because other men with their two fore-fingers point and *make horns* at him ?" Ibid. p. 28 : " Why the abused husband is called cuckold ? Since Plautus wittily, and with more reason, calls the adulterer, and not him whose wife is adulterated, cuculum, the cuckold, because he gets children on others' wives, which the credulous father believes his own : why should not he then that corrupts another man's wife be rather called the cuckow, for he sits and sings merrily whilst his eggs are hatched by his neighbour's hens ?"

[2] In his Asinaria, v. 2, he makes a woman thus speak of her husband : " Ac etiam cubat cuculus, surge, amator, i domum ;" and again : " Cano capite te cuculum uxor domum exlustris rapit." And yet in another place, viz. the Pseudolus, i. 1, where Pseudolus says to Callidorus, " Quid. fles, cucule ?" the above sense is out of the question, and it is to be taken merely as a term of reproach. Horace certainly uses the word as it is explained by Pliny in the passage already given, and the conclusion there drawn appears to be that which best reconciles the more modern sense of the term being likewise supported by a note in the Variorum Horace :
" Cuculum credi supposititios adsciscere pullos, quod enim sit timidus, et defendendi impar, cum etiam a minimis velli avibus. Avis autem quæ pullos ipsius rapiunt suos ejicere, eo quod cuculi pullus sit elegans." Antigoni Carystii Hist. Mirabilium, 4to. 1619. The application of the above passage to our use of the word cuckold, as connected with the cuckoo, is, that the husband, timid, and incapable of protecting his honour, like that bird, is called by its name and thus converted into an object of contempt and derision. " Curuca, avis quæ alienos pullos nutrit. Currucare, aliquem currucam facere ejus violando uxorem." Vetus Glossar. inter MSS. Bernens. vide Sinnei Catal., i. 412.

I must conclude this subject, which is not of the most delicate kind, with an apology; yet in speaking of popular antiquities, it seemed incumbent upon me to say something concerning it. To jest concerning a crime which is replete with every evil to society is indeed to scatter firebrands and arrows in our sport.[1] It may be added, there is no philosophical justice in such insults. If the husband was not to blame, it is highly ungenerous, and an instance of that common meanness in life of confounding a person's misfortunes with his faults. The cruelty of such wanton reflections will appear, if we consider that a man, plagued with a vicious wife, needs no aggravation of his misery.

In the Athenian Oracle, ii. 359, it is remarked of cuckoldry, "The Romans were honourable, and yet Pompey, Cæsar, Augustus, Lucullus, Cato, and others, had this fate, but not its infamy and scandal. For a vicious action ought to be only imputed to the author, and so ought the shame and dishonour which follow it. He only that consents and is pimp to his own cuckoldry is really infamous and base."

THE PASSING-BELL, OR SOUL-BELL.

" Make me a straine speake groaning like a *bell*,
That towles *departing* soules."
Marston's Antonio and Mellida, 1633.

THE word "Passing," as used here, signifies clearly the same as "departing," that is passing from life to death. So that even from the name we may gather that it was the intention in tolling a passing-bell to pray for the person dying, and

[1] I find the following most spirited invective against the pernicious vice in Cotgrave's English Treasury of Wit and Language, 1655, p. 136 ;
" He that dares violate the husband's honour,
The husband's curse stick to him, a tame cuckold;
His wife be fair and young; but most dishonest;
Most impudent, and have no feeling of it,
No conscience to reclaim her from a monster.
Let her lie by him, like a flattering ruin,
And at one instant kill both name and honour:
Let him be lost, no eye to weep his end,
And find no earth that's base enough to bury him."

who was not yet dead. The following clause, in the Advertisements for due Order, in the 7th year of Queen Elizabeth, is much to our purpose : "Item, that when anye Christian bodie is *in passing*, that *the bell be tolled*, and that the curate be speciallie called for to comforte the sicke person; and *after the time of his passinge* to ringe no more but one shorte peale; and one before the buriall, and another short peale after the buriall."[1]

In Catholic times, here, it has been customary to toll the passing-bell at all hours of the night as well as by day; as the subsequent extract from the churchwardens' accounts for the parish of Wolchurch (MS. Harl. 2252), A. D. 1526, proves : " Item, the clerke to have for tollynge of the passynge belle, for manne, womanne, or childes, if it be in the day, iiij*d*. Item, if it be in the night, for the same, viij*d*." See Strutt's Manners, iii. 172.[2]

There is a passage in Shakespeare's Henry the Fourth, Second Part, which proves that our poet has not been a more accurate observer of Nature than of the manners and customs of his time :

> " And his tongue
> Sounds ever after as a sullen bell
> Remember'd knolling a *departing friend*."

Douce is inclined to think that the passing-bell was originally intended to drive away any demon that might seek to take possession of the soul of the deceased. In the cuts to those Horæ which contain the service of the dead, several devils are waiting for this purpose in the chamber of the dying man, to whom the priest is administering extreme unction. He refers to the Schol. in Theocrit. Idyll. ii. v. 36, and adds : " It is to be hoped that this ridiculous custom will never be revived, which has most probably been the cause of sending many a good soul to the other world before its time : nor can the practice of tolling bells for the dead be defended upon any

[1] " His gowned brothers follow him, and bring him to his long home. *A short peale closeth up his funeral-pile.*" An hospital man, in Whimsies, or a New Cast of Characters, 12mo. 1631, p. 64. See Ibid. p. 206.

[2] The following is a passage in Stubbs's Anatomie of Abuses, 1585, p. 75 He is relating the dreadful end of a swearer in Lincolnshire. " At the last, the people perceiving his ende to approche, *caused the bell to tolle;* who, hearing the bell toll for him, rushed up in his bed very vehemently."

principle of common sense, prayers for the dead being contrary to the articles of our religion."[1]

Among the many objections of the Brownists, it is laid to the charge of the Church of England, that though we deny the doctrine of purgatory, and teach the contrary, yet how well our practice suits with it may be considered in our ringing of hallowed bells for the soul. See Bishop Hall's Apology against the Brownists. "We call them," says the Bishop (p. 568), "*soul-bells,* for that they signify the departure of the soul, *not for that they help the passage of the soul.*" Wheatly, in his Illustration of the Liturgy, apologises for our retaining this ceremony: "Our Church," says he, "in imitation of the saints in former ages, calls on the minister and others who are at hand to assist their brother in his last extremity. In order to this, she directs that when any one is passing out of this life a bell should be tolled." &c. It is called from thence the passing-bell.

I find the following in Articles to be enquired of within the Archdeaconry of Yorke by the Church Wardens and Sworne-Men, A. D. 163—: "Whether doth your clark or sexton, *when any one is passing out of this life, neglect to toll a bell,* having notice thereof · or, *the party being dead,* doth he suffer any more ringing than one short peale, and before his burial one, and after the same another?" Inquiry is also directed to be made, "whether at the death of any there be any *superstitious ringing?*"

"The passing-bell," says Grose, "was anciently rung for two purposes: one to bespeak the prayers of all good Christians for a soul just departing; the other to drive away the evil spirits who stood at the bed's foot and about the house, ready to seize their prey, or at least to molest and terrify the

[1] Cassalion has this taunt against the Protestants: "Though," says he, "the English now deny that prayers are of any service to the dead, yet I could meet with no other account of this ceremony than that it was a custom of the old church of England, i. e. the church of Rome. 'Et talis ritus etiam de præsenti servatur in Anglia, ut cum quis decessit, statim campana propriæ illius parochiæ speciali quodam modo sonat per aliquod temporis spatium. Quamvis Angli negent modo orationes et suffragia defunctis proficua : non aliam tamen in hoc ab illis rationem potui percipere, quam quod talis sonus sit ritus antiquæ ecclesiæ Anglicanæ.'" Cassal. de Vet. Sac. Christ. Rit. p. 241. Bourne, Antiq. Vulg. ch. i. Cassalion should have consulted Durand's Rationale.

soul in its passage: but by the ringing of that bell (for Durandus informs us evil spirits are much afraid of bells) they were kept aloof; and the soul, like a hunted hare, gained the start, or had what is by sportsmen called law.[1] Hence, perhaps, exclusive of the additional labour, was occasioned the high price demanded for tolling the greatest bell of the church; for, that being louder, the evil spirits must go farther off to be clear of its sound, by which the poor soul got so much more the start of them: besides, being heard farther off, it would likewise procure the dying man a greater number of prayers. This dislike of spirits to bells is mentioned in the Golden Legend by Wynkyn de Worde."[2]

Bourne supposes that from the proverb mentioned by Bede, "Lord have mercy upon the soul," as St. Oswald said when he fell to the earth,[3] has been derived the present national saying:

> "When the bell begins to toll,
> Lord have mercy on the soul."

He tells us that it was a custom with several religious families at Newcastle-upon-Tyne to use prayers, as for a soul departing, at the tolling of the passing-bell. In Ray's Collection of old English Proverbs I find the following couplet.

> "When thou dost hear a toll or knell,
> Then think upon *thy passing-bell*."

In the Rape of Lucrece, by T. Heywood, 1630, Valerius says: "Nay, *if he be dying,* as I could wish he were, *I'le ring out his funerall peale,* and this it is:

> "Come list and harke, the bell doth towle,
> *For some but new departing soule.*
> And was not that some ominous fowle,

---

[1] Durandus says: "Item ut dæmones tinnitu campanarum, Christianos ad preces concitantium, terreantur. Formula vero baptizandi seu benedicendi campanas antiqua est." Rationale, lib. C. xxii. sec. 6.

[2] Grose tells us of another remarkable superstition: that "It is impossible for a person to die whilst resting on a pillow stuffed with the feathers of a dove; but that he will struggle with death in the most exquisite torture. The pillows of dying persons are therefore frequently taken away, when they appear in great agonies, lest they may have pigeon's feathers in them."

[3] "Unde dicunt in proverbio Deus miserere animabus dixit Oswaldus, cadens in terram." Bed. Hist. Eccl. l. iii. c. 12.

The batt, the night-crow, or skreech-owle.
To these I heare the wild woolfe howle
In this black night that seems to skowle.
All these my black-booke shall in-rowle.
For hark, still, still, the bell doth towle,
For some but now departing sowle."

It is also alluded to by Gascoigne, in his Workes, 1587, p. 95, where, in the Historie of Dan Bartholomew of Bathe, he prefaces a sonnet with a great number of lines, beginning—

" Alas, loe now I heare the passing-bell,
Which Care appoynteth carefully to knoule ;
And in my brest I feele my heart now swell,
To breake the stringes which joynd it to my soule."

When Lady Catherine Grey died a prisoner in the tower, Sir Owen Hopton, who had then the charge of that fortress, " perceiving her to draw towards her end, said to Mr. Bokeham, ' Were it not best to send to the church, *that the bell may be rung ?* ' And she herself, hearing him, said, ' Good Sir Owen, let it be so.' Then immediately perceiving her end to be near, she entered into prayer, and said, ' O Lord ! into thy hands I commend my soul : Lord Jesus, receive my spirit :' and so, putting down her eyes with her own hands, she yielded unto God her meek spirit at nine of the clock in the morning, the 27th of January, 1567." See "The Manner of her departing," Harl. MS. 39, in Ellis's Original Letters, 2d Series, ii. 290.

The custom of the bell being tolled whilst the person was dying, is alluded to as late as 1732, in Nelson's Fasts and Festivals of the Church, who, p. 144, speaking of the dying Christian who has subdued his passions, says : " If his senses hold out so long, he can hear even *his passing-bell without disturbance.*" As for the title of *soul-bell*, if that bell is so called which they toll after a person's breath is out, and mean by it that it is a call upon us to pray for *the soul* of the deceased person, I know not how the church of England can be defended against the charge of those who, in this instance, would seem to tax us with praying for the dead.

Bourne considers the custom as old as the use of bells themselves in Christian churches, i. e. about the seventh century. Bede, in his Ecclesiastical History, speaking of the death of the Abbess of St. Hilda, tells us that one of the sisters of a distant monastery, as she was sleeping,[1] thought she heard the well-known sound of that bell which called them to prayers when any of them had departed this life. Bourne thinks the custom originated in the Roman Catholic idea of the prevalency of prayers for the dead. The abbess above mentioned had no sooner heard this, than she raised all the sisters, and called them into the church, where she exhorted them to pray fervently, and sing a requiem for the soul of their mother.

The same author contends that this bell, contrary to the present custom, should be tolled before the person's departure, that good men might give him their prayers, adding, that, if they do no good to the departing sinner, they at least evince the disinterested charity of the person that prefers them.[2]

In Copley's Wits, Fits, and Fancies, 1614, p. 195, if any proofs were wanting, we find the following, that the passing-bell was anciently rung while the person was dying. "A gentleman lying very sicke abed, heard a passing-bell ring out, and said unto his physician, 'Tell me, maister Doctor, *is yonder musicke for my dancing?*'" Ibid. p. 196, concerning "*The ringing out at the burial*," is this anecdote: "A rich churle and a begger were buried, at one time, in the same church-

---

[1] "Hæc, tunc in dormitorio sororum pausans, exaudivit subito in aere notum campanæ sonum quo ad orationes excitari vel convocari solebant, cum quis eorum de seculo fuisset evocatus. Quod cum illa audisset, suscitavit cunctas sorores, et in ecclesiam convocatas, orationibus et psalmis pro anima matris operam dare monuit." Bed. Eccles. Hist. lib. iv. cap. 23.

[2] In a Funeral Oration made the 14th daye of January by John Hoper, the yeare of oure Salvation 1549, 12mo. 1550, occurs this singular passage: "Theyr remedyes be folyshe and to be mocked at, as *the ryngynge of belles, to ease the payne of the dead*, wythe other:" as if the purpose of tolling the passing-bell had been intended to give an easy passage to the dying person. The following passage is from Veron's Hunting of Purgatory to Death, 1561, f. 60: "*If they shoulde tolle theyr belles* (as they did in good Kynge Edwardes dayes) *when any bodye is drawing to his ende* and departinge out of this worlde, for to cause all menne to praye unto God for him, that of his accustomed goodnesse and mercye, he should vouchsafe to receave him unto his mercye, forgevinge him all his sinnes: their ringinge shuld have better appearance and should be more conformable to the aunciente catholicke churche." In the Diarey of Robert Birrel, preserved in Fragments of Scottish History, 1798, is the following curious entry: "1566. The 25 of October, vord came to the toune of Edinburge, from the queine, yat her majestie was deadly seike, and desyrit ye bells to be runge, and all ye peopill to resort to ye kirk to pray for her, for she wes so seike that none lipned her life," i. e. expected her to live.

yard, and *the belles rung out amaine for the miser :* now, the
wise-acre his son and executor, to the ende the worlde might
not thinke that all that ringing was for the begger, but for his
father, hyred a trumpetter to stand all the ringing-while in
the belfrie, and betweene every peale to sound his trumpet,
and proclaime aloude and say, Sirres, this next peale is not
for R., but for Maister N., his father."

In Articles to be enquired of throughout the Diocese of
Chichester, 1638, under the head of "Visitation of the sicke
and persons at the point of death," we read : "In the meane
time is there a passing-bell tolled, that they who are within
the hearing of it may be moved in their private devotions to
recommend the state of the departing soule into the hands of
their Redeemer, a duty which all Christians are bound to, out
of a fellow-feeling of their common mortality."

Fuller, in his Good Thoughts in Worse Times, 1647, p. 3,
has the following very curious passage : " Hearing a passing-
bell, I prayed that the sick man might have, through Christ,
a safe voyage to his long home. Afterwards I understood that
the party was dead some hours before ; and, it seems in some
places of London, the tolling of the bell is but a preface of
course to the ringing it out. Bells better silent than thus
telling lyes. What is this but giving a false alarme to men's
devotions, to make them to be ready armed with their prayers
for the assistance of such who have already fought the good
fight, yea, and have gotten the conquest? Not to say that
men's charity herein may be suspected of superstition in
praying for the dead."

Dr. Zouch in a note on the Life of Sir Henry Wotton
(Walton's Lives, 1796, p. 144), says : "The soul-bell was
tolled before the departure of a person out of life, as a signal
for good men to offer up their prayers for the dying. Hence
the abuse commenced of praying for the dead. 'Aliquo moriente campanæ debent pulsari, ut populus hoc audiens oret
pro illo.' Durandi rationale." He is citing Donne's letter
to Sir Henry Wotton in verse :

> " And thicken on you now, as prayers ascend
> To heaven on troops at a good man's passing-bell."[1]

---

[1] Camden, in his Ancient and Modern Manners of the Irish, tells us :
' When a person is at the point of death, just before he expires, certain

Dourne says, the custom was held to be popish and superstitious during the grand rebellion; for in a vestry-book
belonging to the chapel of All Saints, in Newcastle-upon-
Tyne, it is observable that the tolling of the bell is not mentioned in the parish from the year 1643 till 1655, when the
church by this and such like means having been brought in
dilapidations, through want of money, it was at a vestry, held
January 21 that year, ordered to be tolled again.

I find the following in Articles of Visitation for the Diocese
of Worcester, 1662 : "Doth the parish clerk or sexton take
care to *admonish the living*, by tolling of a passing-bell of any
that are dying, thereby to meditate of their own deaths, and
to commend the other's weak condition to the mercy of God?"
In similar articles for the diocese of St. David, in the same
year, I read as follows : "Doth the parish-clerk, or sexton,
when any person is passing out of this life, upon notice being
given him therof, toll a bell, as hath been accustomed, that
the neighbours may thereby be warned to recommend the
dying person to the grace and favour of God?"

To a dispute about the origin of this custom, and whether
the bell should be rung out when the party is dying, or some
time after, the British Apollo, ii. No. 7, Supernumerary for
October 1709, answers : "The passing peal was constituted, at

women mourners, standing in the cross-ways, spread their hands, and call
him with cries adapted to the purpose, and endeavour to stop the departing soul, reminding it of the advantages it enjoys in goods, wives, person,
reputation, kindred, friends, and horses ; asking why it will go, and where,
and to whom, and upbraiding it with ingratitude ; and lastly, complaining
that the departed spirit will be transformed into those forms which appear
at night and in the dark ; and after it has quitted the body, they bewail
it with howlings and clapping of hands. They follow the funeral with
such a noise, that one would think there was an end both of living and
dead. The most violent in these lamentations are the nurses, daughters,
and mistresses. They make as much lamentation for those slain in battle
as for those who die in their beds, though they esteem it the easiest death
to die fighting or robbing ; but they vent every reproach *against their
enemies*, and cherish a lasting, deadly hatred against all their kindred."
Camd. Brit. ed. 1789, iii. 668. In the Statistical Account of Scotland,
viii. 213, Parish of Nigg, co. Kincardine, we read : " On the sudden death
of their relations, or fear of it, by the sea turning dangerous, the fisher-
people, especially the females, express their sorrow by exclamation of
voice, and gesture of body, like the Eastern nations, and those in an early
state of civilization."

II.   14

first, to be rung when the party was dying, to give notice to the religious people of the neighbourhood to pray for his soul; and therefore properly called the passing peal."

Pennant, in his History of Whiteford and Holywell, p. 99, says : "That excellent memento to the living, the *passing-bell*, is punctually sounded. I mention this because idle niceties have, in great towns, often caused the disuse. It originated before the Reformation, to give notice to the priest to do the last duty of extreme unction to the departing person, in case he had no other admonition. The canon (67) allows one short peal after death, one other before the funeral, and one other after the funeral. The second is still in use, and is a single bell solemnly tolled. The third is a merry peal, rung at the request of the relations; as if, Scythian like, they rejoiced at the escape of the departed out of this troublesome world." He says, p. 100 : "*Bell-corn* is a small perquisite belonging to the clerk of certain parishes. I cannot learn the origin."

The following passage is in a Strange Horse-Race, by Thomas Dekkar, 1613. Speaking of "rich curmudgeons" lying sick, he says : "Their sonnes and heires cursing as fast (as the mothers pray) until the great *capon-bell* ring out." If this does not mean the passing-bell, I cannot explain it.

There seems to be nothing intended at present by tolling the passing-bell, but to inform the neighbourhood of any person's death.

Sir John Sinclair, in the Statistical Account of Scotland, xviii. 439, says, in a note to the account of the parish of Borrowstowness, co. Linlithgow : "At the burials of the poor people, a custom, almost obsolete in other parts of Scotland, is continued here. The beadle perambulates the streets with a bell, and intimates the death of the individual in the following language : 'All brethren and sisters, I let ye to wit, there is a *brother* (or *sister*) departed at the pleasure of the Almighty (here he lifts his hat), called ——. All those that come to the burial, come at —— of clock. The corpse is at —— ' He also walks before the corpse to the churchyard, ringing his bell."

Till the middle of the last century a person, called the bell-man of the dead, went about the streets of Paris, dressed in a deacon's robe, ornamented with death's heads, bones, and

tears, ringing a bell, and exclaiming "Awake you that sleep'
and pray to God for the dead!" This custom prevailed still
longer in some of the provinces, where they permitted even
the trivial parody, " Prenez vos femmes embrasser les." See
the Voyageur à Paris, i. 72.

I cannot agree with Bourne in thinking that the ceremony
of tolling a bell on this occasion was as ancient as the use of
bells, which were first intended as signals to convene the people to their public devotions. It has more probably been an
after-invention of superstition. Thus praying for the dying
was improved upon into praying for the dead.

Durand, who flourished about the end of the twelfth century, tells us, in his Rationale,[1] " when any one is dying, bells
must be tolled, that the people may put up their prayers ;
twice for a woman and thrice for a man ; if for a clergyman,
as many times as he had orders ; and at the conclusion a peal
on all the bells, to distinguish the quality of the person for
whom the people are to put up their prayers. A bell, too,
must be rung while the corpse is conducted to church, and
during the bringing it out of the church to the grave." This
seems to account for a custom still preserved in the North of
England, of making numeral distinctions at the conclusion of
this ceremony ; i. e. nine knells for a man, six for a woman,
and three for a child, which are undoubtedly the vestiges of
this ancient injunction of popery.

[1] " Verum aliquo moriente, campanæ debent pulsari; ut populus hoc
audiens, oret pro illo. Pro muliere quidem bis, pro eo quod invenit aspe-
ritatem. Primò enim fecit hominem alienum a Deo, quare secunda dies
non habuit benedictionem. Pro viro verò ter pulsatur, quia primo inventa
est in homine Trinitas : primò enim formatus est Adam de terra, deinde
mulier ex Adam, postea homo creatus est ab utroque, et ita est ibi Trinitas. Si autem clericus sit, tot vicibus simpulsatur, quot ordines habuit
ipse. Ad ultimum verò compulsari debet cum omnibus campanis, ut ita
sciat populus pro quo sit orandum. Debet etiam compulsari quando ducitur ad ecclesiam, et quando de ecclesia ad tumulum deportatur." Durandi
Rationale, lib. i. c. 4, 13. A similar passage is found in an old English
Homily for Trinity Sunday. See Strutt's Manners and Customs, iii. 176:
" The fourme of the Trinity was founden in manne, that was Adam our
forefadir, of earth oon personne, and Eve of Adam the secunde persone ;
and of them both was the third persone. At the death of a manne three
bellis shulde be ronge, as his knyll, in worscheppe of the Trinetee, and
for a womanne, who was the secunde persone of the Trinetee two bellis
should be rungen."

212   THE PASSING-BELL, OR SOUL-BELL.

Distinction of rank is preserved in the North of England,
in the tolling of the soul-bell. A high fee annexed excludes
the common people, and appropriates to the death of persons
of consequence the tolling of the great bell in each church on
this occasion. There, too, as Durand, above cited, orders, a
bell is tolled, and sometimes chimes are rung, a little before
the burial, and while they are conducting the corpse to church.
They chime, or ring, too, at some places, while the grave is
filling up. Durand, whose superstition often makes one
smile, is of opinion, as has been already noticed from Grose,
that devils are much afraid of bells, and fly away at the
sound of them. His words are : " Cæterum campanæ in pro-
cessionibus pulsantur ut dæmones timentes fugiant. Timent
enim, auditis tubis ecclesiæ militantis, scilicet campanis, sicut
aliquis tyrannus timet, audiens in terra sua tubas alicujus po-
tentis regis inimici sui." Rationale, lib. i. c. 4, 15. That
ritualist would have thought it a prostitution of the sacred
utensils, had he heard them rung, as I have often done, with
the greatest impropriety, on winning a long main at cock-
fighting. He would, perhaps, have talked in another strain,
and have represented these aërial enemies as lending their assistance to ring them.

On the ringing of bells to drive away spirits, much may be
collected from Magius de Tintinnabulis. See Swinburne's
Travels in the Two Sicilies, i. 98.

I have not been able to ascertain precisely the date of the
useful invention of bells. The ancients had some sort of
bells. I find the word *tintinnabula*, which we usually render
bells, in Martial, Juvenal, and Suetonius. The Romans appear to have been summoned by these, of whatever size or
form they were, to their hot baths, and to the business of
public places.[1] The small bells which are seen in ancient
representations of hermitages, were most probably intended

[1] See some curious particulars upon the subject of bells in Sir Henry
Spelman's History of Sacrilege, p. 284, et seq. The same learned writer,
in his Glossary, in v. *Campana*, has preserved two monkish lines on the
subject of the ancient offices of bells :

" Laudo Deum verum, plebem voco, congrego clerum,
Defunctos ploro, pestem fugo, festa decoro."

I find the following monkish rhymes on bells in a Helpe to Discourse,
1633, p. 63, in which the first of these lines is repeated :—

to drive away evil spirits   St Anthony stood in particular
need of such assistance.

I have examined the passage before mentioned of Bede in
King Alfred's Saxon version. In rendering campana, I find
he has used cluȝȝan, which properly signifies a clock. *Bellun*
is in the margin. Clock is the old German name for a bell,
and hence it is called in French *une cloche*. There were no
clocks in England in King Alfred's time. He is said to have
measured his time by wax candles, marked with circular lines
to distinguish the hours. I would infer from this, that our
clocks have been certainly so called from the bells in them.
Strutt confesses he has not been able to trace the date of the
invention of clocks in England. Stow tells us they were
commanded to be set upon churches in the year 612. A gross
mistake! and into which our honest historian must have been
led by his misunderstanding the word "cloca," a Latin term
coined from the old German name for a bell. For clocks,
therefore, *meo periculo*, read bells.

The large kind of bells, now used in churches, are said to
have been invented by Paulinus, bishop of Nola,[1] in Campania,
whence the Campana of the lower Latinity, about the four
hundredth year of the Christian era. Two hundred years
afterwards they appear to have been in general use in churches.
Bingham, Antiq. Christ. Church, i. 316, however, thinks this
a vulgar error. The Jews, according to Josephus, used trumpets
for bells. The Turks do not permit the use of them at all;

"En ego campana, nunquam denuntio vana,
   Laudo Deum verum, plebem voco, congrego cierum,
   Defunctos plango, vivos voco, fulmina frango,
   Vox mea, vox vitæ, voco vos ad sacra venite.
   Sanctos collaudo, tonitrua fugo, funera claudo,
   Funera plango, fulgura frango, Sabbatha pango ;
   Excito lentos, dissipo ventos, paco cruentos."

[1] Nolæ etymologiam in obscuro positam esse, affirmare ausim; etsi
nonnulli, ut Polydorus Virgilius de Inventoribus Rerum, lib. iii. cap. 18,
et alii tintinnabulum dici Nolam credederint, à Nola Campaniæ urbe,
cujus episcopus Paulinus nolæ, sive campanæ inventor fuerit: qua in re
hallucinantur, nam ante Paulinum Episcopum Nolanum, de quo Gennadius
in additamentis ad D. Hyeronymi librum de viris illustribus scribens nihil
talo profort, Noloo mentionom fecit Quintilianus, qui Domitiani imperatoris
ætate floruit. Satis enim illud tritum est sermone proverbium. *In cubi
culo Nola.*"   Magius de Tintinnabulis, pp. 7, 8. Cf. Spelman in v.
Campana.

the Greek Church under their dominion still follow their old custom of using wooden boards, or iron plates full of holes, which they hold in their hands and knock with a hammer or mallet, to call the people together to church. See Dr. Smith's Account of the Greek Church. He was an eyewitness of this remarkable custom, which Durand tells us is retained in the Romish Church on the last three days of the week preceding Easter.

Bingham informs us of an invention before bells for convening religious assemblies in monasteries: it was going by turns to every one's cell, and with the knock of a hammer calling the monks to church. This instrument was called the night signal and the wakening mallet. In many of the colleges at Oxford the bible-clerk knocks at every room-door with a key to waken the students in the morning, before he begins to ring the chapel bell: a vestige it should seem, of the ancient monastic custom.

China has been remarkably famous for its bells. Father Le Comte tells us that at Pekin there are seven bells, each of which weighs one hundred and twenty thousand pounds.

Baronius[1] informs us that Pope John the Thirteenth, A.D. 968, consecrated a very large new-cast bell in the Lateran church, and gave it the name of John. This is the first instance I met with of what has been since called *the baptising of bells*, a superstition which the reader may find ridiculed in the Romish Beehive, p. 17. The vestiges of this custom may be yet traced in England, in *Tom* of Lincoln, and *Great Tom* ("the mighty Tom") at Christ-Church in Oxford. In a Pontificale of Clement VIII. the ceremony of blessing or consecrating a bell is engraved.

In Coates's Hist. of Reading, 1802, p. 214, in the churchwardens' accounts of St. Laurence's Parish, 1499, is the following article: "It. payed for halowing of the bell named *Harry*, vjs. viijd. and ovir that Sir Willm. Symys, Richard Clech, and Maistres Smyth, being godfaders and godmoder at the consecracyon of the same bell, and beryng all oth' costs to the suffrygan."

[1] " Cum vero post hæc Johannes Papa in urbem rediisset, contigit primariam Laterenensis ecclesiæ campanam miræ magnitudinis, recens ære fusam super campanile elevari, quam prius idem pontifex sacris ritibus Deo consecravit atque *Johannis* nomine nuncupavit." Baronii Annal. a Spondano, A.D. 968, p. 871.

Pennant, speaking of St. Wenofrido's Well, in Flintshire, says : " A bell belonging to the church was also christened in honour of her.   I cannot learn the names of the gossips, who, as usual, were doubtless rich persons.   On the ceremony they all laid hold of the rope ; bestowed a name on the bell ; and the priest, sprinkling it with holy water, baptised it in the name of the Father, &c. ; he then clothed it with a fine garment.   After this the gossips gave a grand feast, and made great presents, which the priest received in behalf of the bell. Thus blessed, it was endowed with great powers ; allayed (on being rung) all storms ; diverted the thunderbolt ; drove away evil spirits.   These consecrated bells were always inscribed.   The inscription on that in question ran thus :

' Sancta Wenefreda, Deo hoc commendare memento,
    Ut pietate sua, nos servet ab hoste cruento.'

And a little lower was another address :

' Protege prece pia quos convoco, Virgo Maria.' "[1]

Egelric, abbot of Croyland, about the time of King Edgar, cast a ring of six bells, to all which he gave names, as Bartholomew, Bethhelm, Turketul, &c.[2]   The historian tells us his predecessor, Turketul, had led the way in this fancy.   The custom of rejoicing with bells on high festivals, Christmas Day, &c., is derived to us from the times of popery.[3]   The ringing of bells on the arrival of emperors, bishops, abbots, &c., at places under their own jurisdiction, was also an old

[1] Delrio, in his Magical Disquisitions, lib. vi. p. 527, denies that bells were baptized : " Recte docuit Cardinalis Hosius campanas non baptizari sed benedici.   Legant ipsum Pontificale Romanum : de baptismo nihil invenient.   Legant Alcuinum Flaccum et reperient hæc verba, ' Neque novum videri debet *campanas benedicere et ungere et eis nomen imponere.*' En tibi vere et integrè ritum totum, an hoc est baptizare ?"
[2] " Fecit ipse fieri duas magnas campanas quas Bartholomæum et Bettelmum cognominavit, et duas medias quas Turketulum et Tatvinum vocavit, et duas minores quas Pegam et Begam appellavit.   Fecerat antea fieri Dominus Turketulus Abbas unam maximam campanam nomine Guthlacum, quæ cum predictis campanis fuit composita fiebat mirabilis harmonia, nec erat tunc talis consonantia campanarum in tota Anglia." Historia Ingulphi, Rerum Anglicar. Script. Vet. 1684, i. 53.
[3] Durand tells us, " In festis quæ ad gratiam pertinent, campanæ tumultuosius tinniunt et prolixius concrepant."   Rationale, lib. i. cap. 4, 12.

custom;[1] whence we seem to have derived the modern compliment of welcoming persons of consequence by a cheerful
peal.

In the account we have of the gifts made by St. Dunstan
to Malmesbury Abbey, it appears that bells were not very
common in that age, for he says the liberality of that prelate
consisted chiefly in such things as were then wonderful and
strange in England, among which he reckons the large bells
and organs he gave them. An old bell at Canterbury took
twenty-four men to ring it; another required thirty-two men
ad sonandum. The noblest peal of ten bells, without exception, in England, whether tone or tune be considered, is said
to be in St. Margaret's church, Leicester. When a full peal
was rung, the ringers were said pulsare classicum.

Bells were a great object of superstition among our ancestors.
Each of them was represented to have its peculiar name and
virtues, and many are said to have retained great affection for
the churches to which they belonged, and where they were
consecrated. When a bell was removed from its original and
favorite situation, it was sometimes supposed to take a
nightly trip to its old place of residence, unless exercised in
the evening, and secured with a chain or rope. Warner, in
his Topographical Remarks on the S. W. parts of Hampshire,
ii. 162, thus enumerates the virtues of a bell, in a translation
of the last two lines quoted in p. 213, from the Helpe to
Discourse:

> " Men's death I tell
> By doleful knell.
>
> Lightning and thunder
> I break asunder.

---

[1] " Campanarum pulsatio in adventu episcoporum et abbatum in eccle-
sias quæ iis subditæ sunt, in charta compositionis inter archiepiscopum
Cantuar. et abbat. S. Aug. Cantuar." apud Will. Thorn, p. 1882, 1883.
Mon. Ang. tom. iii. p. 164. Matth. Paris, an. 1245, p. 463, &c. See Du
Cange, voce *Campana.* " Tradit continuator Nangii, an. 1378. Carolum
IV. imperatorem cum in Galliam venit, nullo campanarum sonitu exceptum
in urbibus, quod id sit signum dominii: 'Et est assavoir que en la dite
Ville, et semblablement par toutes les autres villes, ou il a esté, tant en
venant a Paris, comme en son retour, il n'a esté receu en quelque Eglise
à procession, ni cloches sonnées à son venir, ne fait aucun signe de quelque
domination ne seigneurie,'" &c. Vide Du Cange, Gloss. ut supra.

On Sabbath all
To church I call.

The sleepy head
I raise from bed.

The winds so fierce
I doe disperse.

Men's cruel rage
I doe asswage."

In Barnabe Googe's translation of the Regnum Papisticum of Naogeorgus, f. 41, we have the following lines on *belles:*

" If that the thunder chaunce to rore, and stormie tempest shake,
A wonder is it for to see the wretches how they quake,
Howe that no fayth at all they have, nor trust in any thing,
The clarke doth all the belles forthwith at once in steeple ring:
With wond'rous sound and deeper farre than he was wont before,
Till in the loftie heavens darke the thunder bray no more.
For in these christned belles they thinke doth lie much powre and might,
As able is the tempest great and storme to vanquish quight.
I sawe my self at Numburg once, a towne in Toring coast,
A bell that with this title bolde hirself did proudly boast:
By name I Mary called am, with sound I put to flight
The thunder crackes and hurtfull stormes, and every wicked spright.
Such things whenas these belles can do, no wonder certainlie
It is, if that the Papistes to their tolling alwayes flie,
When haile, or any raging storme, or tempest comes in sight,
Or thunderboltes, or lightning fierce, that every place doth smight."

In 1464 is a charge in the churchwardens' accounts of Sandwich for bread and drink for "ryngers in the great thunderyng." In the Burnynge of Paules Church in London, 1561, we find enumerated, among other Popish superstitions: *"ringinge the hallowed belle in great tempestes or lightninges."* I have seen a tract, De Superstitiosis Campanarum pulsibus, ad eliciendas Preces, quibus placentur Fulmina, excogitatis Responsio: autore Gaspare Hombergio Vezlariense. 12mo. Franc. ad M. 1577.

Aubrey, in his Miscellanies, p. 148, says: " At Paris, when it begins to thunder and lighten, they do presently ring out the great bell at the Abbey of St. Germain, which they do believe makes it cease. The like was wont to be done heretoforo in Wiltshire. When it thundered and lightened, they did ring St. Adelm's bell at Malmesbury Abbey. The curious do say that the ringing of bells exceedingly disturbs spirits."

Our forefathers, however, did not entirely trust to the ringing of bells for the dispersion of tempests, for in 1313 a cross, full of reliques of divers saints, was set on St. Paul's steeple, to preserve from all danger of tempests. I find the following in a newspaper : "Berlin, Nov. 3, 1783. It is long since the learned in natural history have apprised the world of the danger there is of *ringing bells on the approach and duration of a thunder-storm.* But how hard it is to root out popular prejudices! What sound reason could not effect, royal authority has brought about. His Majesty, by a late ordinance, directs that the prohibition against ringing bells, &c. on such occasions, be read publicly in all the churches throughout his dominions."

Dr. Francis Hering, in Certaine Rules, Directions, or Advertisments for this Time of pestilentiall Contagion, 1625, advises : " Let the bells in cities and townes be rung often, and the great ordnance discharged ; thereby the aire is purified."

There is a passage in Fuller's History of Waltham Abbey, 1542, relative to the wages of bell-ringers—it is preserved in the churchwardens' accounts : " Item, paid for the ringing at the prince his coming, *a penny.*" [1] In Coates's History of Reading, 1802, p. 218, under the churchwardens' accounts of St. Laurence's parish, is the following article, sub anno 1514. " It. payd for a galon of ale, for the ryngers, *at the death of the king of Scots,* ijd." " Antient ceremonies used throughout the kingdome, continued from antiquity till the days of our last fathers, that whensoever any noble man or peere of the realme passed through any parish, all the bells were accustomed to be runge in honor of his person, and to give notice of the passage of such eminency—and when their letters were upon occasions read in any assemblies, the commons present would move their bonnets, in token of reverence to their names and persons." Smith's Berkeley MSS. ii. 363.

At Newcastle-upon-Tyne, the tolling of the great bell of St. Nicholas's church there has been from ancient times a signal for the burgesses to convene on guild-days, or on the

---

[1] Bishop Kennet, in one of his manuscripts, says: " Non pulsare campanas in adventu episcopi signum contemptus et vilipendii manifeste, pro quo vicarius citatur ad respondend : Anno 1444, Reg. Alnewyk Episc. Linc."

days of electing magistrates. The begins at nine o'clock in the morning, and with little or no intermission continues to toll till three o'clock, when they begin to elect the mayor, &c. Its beginning so early was doubtless intended to call together the several companies to their respective meeting-houses, in order to choose the former and latter electors, &c. A popular notion prevails, that it is for the old mayor's dying, as they call his going out of office—the tolling as it were of his *passing-bell.*

Ruffhead, in his preface to the Statutes at Large, speaking of the Folc-mote Comitatus, or Shire-mote, and the Folc-mote Civitatis vel Burgi, or Burg-mote, says : " Besides these annual meetings, if any sudden contingency happened, it was the duty of the aldermen of cities and boroughs to ring the bell called in English Mot-bell, in order to bring together the people to the burg-mote," &c. See Blount's Law Dictionary, v. *Mot-bell.*

The bells at Newcastle-upon-Tyne are muffled on the 30th of January every year. For this practice of muffling I find no precedent of antiquity. Their sound is by this means peculiarly plaintive.[1] The inhabitants of that town were par-

---

[1] In Campanologia, or the Art of Ringing, 1753, p. 200, we have : *"A funeral or dead peal.* It being customary not only in this city of London, upon the death of any person that is a member of any of the honourable societies of ringers therein, but likewise in most counties and towns in England (not only upon the death of a ringer, but likewise of any young man or woman), at the funeral of every such person to ring a peal ; which peal ought to be different from those for mirth and recreation (as the musick at the funeral of any master of musick, or the ceremony at the funeral of any person belonging to military discipline), and may be performed two different ways : the one is by ringing the bells round at a set pull, thereby keeping them up so as to delay their striking, that there may be the distance of three notes at least (according to the true compass of ringing upon other occasions) between bell and bell ; and having gone round one whole pull every bell (except the tenor), to set and stand, whilst the tenor rings one pull in the same compass as before ; and this is to be done whilst the person deceased is bringing to the ground ; and after he is interred, to ring a short peal of round ringing, or changes in true time and compass, and so conclude. The other way is called *buffeting the bells,* that is, *by tying pieces of leather, old hat,* or any other thing that is pretty thick, round the ball of the clapper of each bell, and then by ringing them as before is shown, *they make a most doleful and mournful sound :* concluding with a short peal after the funeral is over (the clappers being clear as at other times) : which way of buffeting is most practised in this city of London."

ticularly loyal during the parliamentary wars in the grand rebellion, which may account for the use of this custom, which probably began at the Restoration.

Misson, in his Travels in England, translated by Ozell, p. 306, says : " Ringing of bells is one of their great delights, especially in the country. They have a particular way of doing this ; but their chimes cannot be reckoned so much as of the same kind with those of Holland and the Low Countries."

In the Statistical Account of Scotland, x. 512, parish of Inverkeithing, co. Fife, we read : " In this parish is the castle of Rosyth, almost opposite to Hopeton House. It is built upon rock, and surrounded by the sea at full tide. Upon the south side, near the door, is this inscription, pretty entire and legible :

> " In dev time drav yis cord ye bel to clink,
> Qvhais mery voce varnis to meat and drink."

Dates about the building, 1561 and 1639. Yet " it cannot now be ascertained by whom it was built, or at what time."

The little carnival on Pancake Tuesday at Newcastle-on-Tyne commences by the same signal. A bell, usually called the Thief and Reever Bell, proclaims the two annual fairs of that town. A peculiar kind of alarm is given by a bell on accidents of fire. A bell is rung at six every morning, except Sundays and holidays, with a view, it should seem, of calling up the artisans to their daily employment.

THE CURFEW BELL.[1]

The following occurs in Peshall's History of the City of Oxford, p. 177 : " The custom of ringing the bell at Carfax every night at eight o'clock (called *Curfew Bell*, or *Cover-fire Bell*), was *by order of King Alfred*, the restorer of our University, who ordained that all the inhabitants of Oxford should, at the ringing of that bell, cover up their fires and go to bed, which custom is observed to this day, and the bell as con-

---

[1] [We are indebted for some of our additions to this article to a very valuable paper on the subject by Mr. Syer Cuming.]

ʌtɒntly ringʌ ʌt eight, ʌo Gnoot Tom tolls ʌt nine It is also a custom added to the former, after the ringing and tolling this bell, to let the inhabitants know the day of the month by so many tolls." [There are few points in the ancient jurisprudence of England which are enveloped in more obscurity, or which have given rise to more conflicting opinions as to their origin and intention, than the *couvre-feu* law. Although there is no evidence to show that it originated with the Norman Conqueror, yet it appears certain that in 1068 he ordained that all people should put out their fires and lights at the eight o'clock bell, and go to bed. But that it was not intended as a badge of infamy is evident from the fact that the law was of equal obligation upon the foreign nobles of the court as upon the native-born Saxon serfs. And yet we find the name of *curfew law* employed as a by-word denoting the most odious tyranny, and historians, poets, and lawyers speaking of it as the acme of despotism levelled alone at the vanquished English. However well-intentioned the *couvre-feu* law may have been, it appears to have met with much opposition, as in 1103 we find Henry I. repealing the enactment of his father. Blackstone says that though it is mentioned a century afterwards, it is rather spoken of as a time of night than as a still subsisting custom. Thus Chaucer:

" The dede slepe, for every besinesse,
Fell on this carpenter, right as I gesse,
Aboute *curfew time*, or litel more."]

The curfew is commonly believed to have been of Norman origin.[1] A law was made by William the Conqueror that all people should put out their fires and lights at the eight o'clock bell, and *go to bed*. See Seymour's edit. of Stow's Survey of London, book i. cap. 15. The practice of this custom, we are

[1] Henry, in his History of Britain, 4to. iii. 567, tells us, " The custom of covering up their fires about sunset in summer, and about eight at night in winter, at the ringing of a bell called the couvre-feu or curfew bell, is supposed by some to have been introduced by William I., and imposed upon the English as a badge of servitude. But this opinion doth not seem to be well founded; for there is sufficient evidence that the same custom prevailed in France, Spain, Italy, Scotland, and probably in all the countries of Europe, in this period, and was intended as a precaution against fires, which were then very frequent and very fatal, when so many houses were built of wood."

told, to its full extent, was observed during that and the following reign only. Thomson has inimitably described its tyranny:

> "The shiv'ring wretches, at the curfew sound,
> Dejected sunk into their sordid beds,
> And, through the mournful gloom of ancient times,
> Mus'd sad, or dreamt of better."

In the second mayoralty of Sir Henry Colet, Knt. (father of Dean Colet), A.D. 1495, and under his direction, the solemn charge was given to the Quest of Wardmote in every ward, as it stands printed in the Custumary of London. "Also yf ther be anye paryshe clerke that ryngeth curfewe *after the curfewe be ronge at Bowe Chyrche*, or *Saint Brydes Chyrche*, or *Saint Gyles without Cripelgat*, all suche to be presented." (Knight's Life of Dean Colet, p. 6.) In the Articles for the Sexton of Faversham, agreed upon and settled in 22 Hen. VIII. (preserved in Jacob's History, p. 172), we read: "Imprimis, the sexton, or his sufficient deputy, shall lye in the church steeple; and at eight o'clock every night shall ring the curfewe by the space of a quarter of an hour, with such bell as of old time hath been accustomed. In Lysons's Environs, i. 232, is the following extract from the Churchwardens' and Chamberlains' Accounts of Kingston-upon-Thames: "1651. For ringing the curfew bell for one year, £1 10 0." I find, however, in the old play of the Merry Devil of Edmonton, 4to. 1631, that the curfew was sometimes rung at *nine o'clock;* thus the Sexton says: "Well, 'tis nine a clocke, 'tis time to ring curfew."

[Shakespeare seems to have laboured under some strange mistake respecting the hour of *couvre-feu*. In Measure for Measure, iv. 2, occurs the following:

> "*Duke.* The best and wholesom'st spirits of the night
> Invellop you, good Provost !   Who call'd here of late ?
> *Provost.* None, since the *curfew* rung."

In this instance no particular time is specified, but in Romeo and Juliet, iv. 4, he makes Lord Capulet say:

> "Come, stir, stir, stir, the second cock hath crow'd,
> The *curphew bell* hath rung, 'tis three o'clock."

And in other of his plays he fixes the time at a later hour. Thus in the Tempest, v. 1, Prospero says:

> "You, whose pastime
> Is to make midnight mushrooms, that rejoice
> To hear the solemn *curfew*."

And in King Lear, iii. 4, Edgar exclaims: " This is the foul
fiend Flibbertigibbet : he begins at *curfew*, and walks to the
first cock."]

In Bridges's History of Northamptonshire, i. 110, speaking
of Byfield church, the author tells us : " A bell is rung here
at four in the morning, and at eight in the evening, for which
the clerk hath 20*s*. yearly paid him by the rector." A bell
was formerly rung at Newcastle-upon-Tyne, also, at four in
the morning.

In Hutchins's Dorset, ii. 267, the author, speaking of
Mapouder church, mentions land given "to find a man to
ring the morning and curfeu bell throughout the year." Also
(ibid. p. 422), under Ibberton, is mentioned one acre given
for ringing the eight o'clock bell, and £4 for ringing the
morning bell. Macaulay, in his History of Claybrook, 1791,
p. 128, says : " The custom of ringing curfew, which is still
kept up at Claybrook, has probably obtained without intermission since the days of the Norman Conqueror." [It is
probable in the middle ages some superstitious regard was
paid to the ringing of the *couvre-feu*, for we find that land
was occasionally left to pay for the ringing of the *couvre-feu*
bell. This feeling appears not to have been altogether extinct, even so late as the close of the sixteenth century, for in
Bishop Hall's Fourth Satire occurs the following :

> " Who ever gives a paire of velvet shooes
> To th' Holy Rood, or liberally allowes
> But a new rope *to ring the couvre-feu bell*,
> But he desires that his great deed may dwell,
> Or graven in the chancel window glasse,
> Or in his lasting tombe of plated brasse."

We find the *couvre-feu* mentioned as a common and approved regulation. It was used in most of the monasteries
and towns of the north of Europe, the intent being merely to
prevent the accidents of fires. All the common houses consisted at this time of timber. Moscow, therefore, being built
with this material, generally suffers once in twenty years.
That this happened equally in London Fitzstephen proves :
" Solæ pestes Lundoniæ sunt stultorum immodica potatio, et
frequens incendium." The Saxon Chronicle also makes frequent mention of towns being burned, which might be expected
for the same reason, the Saxon term for building being
ᵹeᴛιmbριan.

The Hon. Daines Barrington, in his Observations on the Ancient Statutes, p. 153, tells us: "Curfew is written cur-phour in an old Scottish poem, published in 1770, with many others from the MS. of George Bannatyne, who collected them in the year 1568. It is observed in the annotations on these poems, that by act 144, parl. 13, Jam. I., this bell was to be rung in boroughs at nine in the evening; and that the hour was afterwards changed to ten, at the solicitation of the wife of James Stewart, the favourite of James the Sixth."

There is a narrow street in the town of Perth, in Scotland, still called *Couvre-feu Row*, leading west to the Black Friars, where the couvre-feu bell gave warning to the inhabitants to cover their fires and go to rest when the clock struck ten. Muses' Threnodie, note, p. 89.

"At Ripon, in Yorkshire, at nine o'clock every evening, a man blows a large horn at the Market Cross, and then at the mayor's door." Gent. Mag. for Aug. 1790, lx. 719.

[The curfew bell is still tolled at Hastings at eight o'clock in the evening, from Michaelmas to Lady Day.

The bell-ringing in the city of London is not to be invariably attributed to the *curfew*, but in numerous instances to bequests in wills for the purpose. In the parish of St. Mary-le-Bow, one Mr. Donne, a mercer and citizen of London, had devised two tenements in Bow lane (then called Hosier lane), for the ringing of the tenor bell of Bow church (now the most cele-brated peal in the kingdom), at six o'clock in the morning and eight o'clock in the evening. Mr. Lott, after considerable research for this will, has at last discovered it in the Hustings' Court of London. The early ringing was supposed to be for the purpose of waking up the London apprentices. The po-etical remonstrance of these personages to the parish clerk of Bow, in consequence of his neglect of his duty, is thus recorded by Stow:

> "Clerk of the Bow bell,
>   With thy yellow locks,
> For thy late ringing,
>   Thy head shall have knocks."

The clerk of that day was a match for his young complain-ants, and replied in equal poetical vein—

> "Children of Cheap,
>   Hold you all still,
> For you shall hear the Bow bell
>   Rung at your will."

Mr. N. Gould, F.S.A., informs us that, during his parochial reign, he had kept the beadle to a strict performance of this duty, which is performed to this day. Mr. Gould describes, in a humorous vein, his ascent to the summit of the steeple, on the back of the dragon, during the repairs of 1820, and refuted the alleged fulfilment of the old prophecy of the visits of the Exchange grasshopper and dragon of Bow, the latter having never quitted the country during the repairs. We may also notice a bequest in Spitalfields, for matinal and evening bell-ringing; and another provincial bequest for the same purpose, by a lady who had lost her way on a moor, and was guided home by the sound of a church bell.]

THE LAKE-WAKE.

THE word Lake-Wake, that is, a watching with the dead, is plainly derived from the Anglo-Saxon lic or lice, a corpse, and wœcce, a wake, vigil, or watching. It is used in this sense by Chaucer, in his Knight's Tale :

> " Shall not be told by me
> How that Arcite is brent to ashen cold,
> Ne how that there the liche-wake was y-hold
> All that night long."

They were wont, says Bourne, to sit by the corpse from the time of death till its exportation to the grave, either in the house it died in, or in the church itself. To prove this he cites St. Austin, concerning the watching the dead body of his mother Monica; and Gregory Turon., concerning that of St. Ambrose, whose body was carried into the church the same hour that he died.

Under the word Walkin, in Ruddiman's Glossary to Douglas's Virgil, we read : " Proper like-wakes (Scotch) are the meetings of the friends of the deceased a night or nights before the burial."[1]

[1] Dr. Jamieson says : " This ancient custom most probably originated from a silly superstition with respect to the danger of a corpse being carried off by some of the agents of the invisible world, or exposed to the ominous liberties of brute animals. But, in itself, it is certainly a decent

II. 15

Pennant, in describing Highland ceremonies, says : " The late-wake is a ceremony used at funerals. The evening after the death of any person, the relations or friends of the deceased meet at the house, attended by a bagpipe or fiddle : the nearest of kin, be it wife, son, or daughter, opens a melancholy ball, dancing and greeting, i. e. crying violently at the same time ; and this continues till daylight, but with such gambols and frolics among the younger part of the company, that the loss which occasioned them is often more than supplied by the consequences of that night. If the corpse remain unburied for two nights, the same rites are renewed. Thus, Scythian-like, they rejoice at the deliverance of their friends out of this life of misery." He tells us in the same place that the Coranich, or singing at funerals, is still in use in some places. " The songs are generally in praise of the deceased, or a recital of the valiant deeds of their ancestors."—Tour in Scotland, 1769, p. 112.

" In North Wales," says Pennant, speaking of the manners of the eighteenth century, " the night before a dead body is to be interred, the friends and neighbours of the diseased resort to the house the corpse is in, each bringing with him some small present of bread, meat, drink (if the family be something poor), but more especially candles, whatever the family be ; and this night is called *wyl nôs*, whereby the country people seem to mean a watching night. Their going to such a house, they say, is *i wilior corph*, i. e. to watch the corpse ; but *wylo* signifies to weep and lament, and so *wyl nôs* may be a night of lamentation. While they stay together on that night they are either singing psalms, or reading some part of the holy scriptures. Whenever anybody comes into a room where a dead body lyes, especially the wyl nôs and the day of its interment, the first thing he does, he falls on his knees by the corpse, and says the Lord's prayer."

In the Irish Hudibras, a burlesque of Virgil's story of Æneas going down to visit his father in the shades, 1689, p. 34, is the following description of what is called in the margin *an Irish Wake :*

and proper one; because of the possibility of the person, considered as dead, being only in a swoon. Whatever was the original design, the *lik-wake* seems to have very early degenerated into a scene of festivity extremely incongruous to the melancholy occasion."

"To their own sports (the maddened crowd)
The mourners now are recommended.
Some for their pastime count their beads,
Some scratch their breech, some louse their heads;
Some sit and chat, some laugh, some weep;
Some sing cronans (*songs*), and some do sleep;
Some pray, and with their prayers mix curses;
Some vermin pick, and some pick purses;
Some court, some scold, some blow, some puff;
Some take tobacco, some take snuff;
Some play the trump, some trot the hay;
Some at macham, some at noddy[1] play,
With all the games they can devise;
And (when occasion serves 'em) cries.
    Thus did mix their grief and sorrow,
    Yesterday bury'd, kill'd to-morrow."

An account of the wake, less overcharged, will be read with pleasure from the glossary of Castle Rackrent, by Miss Edgeworth, ed. 1810, p. 214 : " In Ireland a wake is a midnight meeting, held professedly for the indulgence of holy sorrow, but usually it is converted into orgies of unholy joy. When an Irish man or woman of the lower order dies, the straw which composed the bed, whether it has been contained in a bag to form a mattress, or simply spread upon the earthen floor, is immediately taken out of the house, and burned before the cabin door, the family at the same time setting up the death-howl. The ears and eyes of the neighbours being thus alarmed, they flock to the house of the deceased, and by their vociferous sympathy excite, and at the same time soothe, the sorrows of the family. It is curious to observe how good and bad are mingled in human institutions. In countries which were thinly inhabited, this custom prevented private attempts against the lives of individuals, and formed a kind of coroner's inquest upon the body which had recently expired, and burning the straw upon which the sick man lay, became a simple preservative against infection. At night the dead body is waked ; that is to say, all the friends and neighbours of the deceased collect in a barn or stable, where the corpse is laid upon some boards, or an unhinged door, supported upon stools, the face exposed, the rest of the body covered with a white sheet. Round the body are stuck in brass can-

[1] Macham and noddy are games at cards.

dlesticks, which have been borrowed perhaps at five miles distance, as many candles as the poor person can beg or borrow, observing always to have an odd number. Pipes and tobacco are first distributed, and then, according to the *ability* of the deceased, cakes and ale, and sometimes whiskey, are *dealt* to the company :

> ' Deal on, deal on, my merry men all,
> Deal on your cakes and your wine ;
> For whatever is dealt at her funeral to-day,
> Shall be dealt to-morrow at mine.'

"After a fit of universal sorrow, and the comfort of a universal dram, the scandal of the neighbourhood, as in higher circles, occupies the company. The young lads and lasses romp with one another ; and when the fathers and mothers are at last overcome with sleep and whiskey (*vino et somno*) the youth become more enterprising, and are frequently successful. It is said that more matches are made at wakes than at weddings."[1] [The verses used by the Irish on the occasion of their wakes and funerals are called *keens*, from *caoine*, which is explained by Lloyd as "a sort of verse used in elegies or funeral poems, and sometimes also in panegyricks and satyrs." An excellent collection of keens has been published by Mr. Crofton Croker for the Percy Society, 1844.]

That watching with the corpse was an ancient custom everywhere practised, numerous passages from ecclesiastical writers might be cited to prove, could there be any doubt of the an-

---

[1] See also the Survey of the South of Ireland, 8vo. p. 210. In the Gent. Mag. for August 1771, xli. 351, it is said of a girl who was killed by lightning in Ireland, that she could not be *waked* within doors, an expression which is explained as alluding to a custom among the Irish of dressing their dead in their best clothes, to receive as many visitors as please to see them ; and this is called keeping their wake. The corpse of this girl, it seems, was so offensive, that this ceremony could not be performed within doors.

[2] Hutchinson, in his History of Cumberland, i. 553, speaking of the parish of Whitbeck, says : "People always keep *wake* with the dead." In the Statistical Account of Scotland, parish of Cruden, Aberdeenshire, v. 435, we read : " Of all those who attended the *late-wake* of a person who died of a putrid fever, not one escaped catching the infection." And a note tells us that the late-wake is a practice common in many parts of Scotland, and not yet exploded here, of people sitting up all night with the corpse in the chamber of the deceased. Ibid. xv. 372, parish of

tiquity of a custom' which, owing its origin to the tenderest affections of human nature, has perhaps on that account been used from the infancy of time.

The abuse of this vigil, or lake-wake, is of pretty old standing.[1] The tenth canon at the provincial synod held in London temp. Edw. III. in Collier's Ecclesiast. History, i. 546, "endeavours to prevent the disorders committed at people's watching a corpse before burial. Here the synod takes notice that the design of people's meeting together upon such occasions was to join their prayers for the benefit of the dead person; that this ancient and serviceable usage was overgrown with superstition and turned into a convenience for theft and debauchery; therefore, for a remedy against this disorder, 'tis decreed, that, upon the death of any person, none should be allowed to watch before the corpse in a private house, excepting near relations and friends of the deceased,

Campsie, co. Stirling, we read: "It was customary for them to have at least two lyke-wakes (the corpse being kept two nights before the interment), where the young neighbours watched the corpse, being merry or sorrowful, according to the situation or rank of the deceased." Waldron, in his Description of the Isle of Man, p. 170, says that "when a person dies, several of his acquaintance come to sit up with him, which they call the wake. The clerk of the parish is obliged to sing a psalm, in which all the company join; and after that they begin some pastime to divert themselves, having strong beer and tobacco allowed them in great plenty. This is a custom borrowed from the Irish, as indeed are many others much in fashion with them."

" The lik-wake is retained in Sweden, where it is called wakstuga, from wak-a, to watch, and perhaps stuga, a room, an apartment, or cottage. Ihre observes, that 'although these wakes should be dedicated to the contemplation of our mortality, they have been generally passed in plays and compotations, whence they were prohibited in public edicts.' v. Wake." Jamieson.

[1] Durand cites one of the ancient councils, in which it is observed that psalms were wont to be sung, not only when the corpse was conducted to church, but that the ancients watched on the night before the burial, and spent the vigil in singing psalms. " Porro observandum est, nedum psalmos cani consuetum, cum funus ducitur, sed etiam nocte quæ præcedit funus, veteres vigilasse nocturnasque vigilias canendis psalmis egisse." p. 232. So also St. Gregory, in the epistle treating of the death of his sister Macrina, says: " Cum igitur nocturna pervigilatio, ut in martyrum celebritate canendis psalmis perfecta esset, et crepusculum advenisset," &c. ibid. It appears that among the primitive Christians the corpse was sometimes kept four days. Pelagia, in Gregory of Turon. requests of her son, " ne eam ante diem quartum sepeliret."

and such as offered to repeat a set number of psalms for the benefit of his soul." The penalty annexed is excommunication. This is also mentioned in Becon's Reliques of Rome, and comprised in the catalogue of crimes that were anciently cursed with bell, book, and candle.

Bourne complains of the sport, drinking, and lewdness used at these lake-wakes in his time. They still continue to resemble too much the ancient bacchanalian orgies—an instance of depravity that highly disgraces human nature. It would be treating this serious subject with too much levity to say, that if the inconsiderate wretches who abuse such solemn meetings think at all, they think with Epicurean licentiousness that since life is so uncertain, no opportunity should be neglected of transmitting it, and that the loss, by the death of one relation, should be made up by the birth of another.

DEATHBED SUPERSTITIONS.

[In some parts of Yorkshire it is thought that no person can die on a bed which contains pigeons' feathers, however small the quantity. A correspondent of the Athenæum recollects "when a child in Cumberland, inquiring why turkey feathers were not saved, and being told by an old servant that they must not be put into a bed as no person could die on them;" and thinks "that the prohibition extended to game feathers;" adding, "I believe it will be found that none of these feathers are fit for use, being too hard and sharp in the barrel." Another correspondent writes, "that the superstition of a person not dying easily on the feathers of wild fowl prevails in Derbyshire; and the same idea prevails in Monmouthshire, Glamorganshire, and probably in other Welsh counties;" and another says that a similar superstition exists in Sligo and Mayo. In this case the superstition has probably arisen from the disuse of the feathers in question, in consequence of their unfitness. Be this as it may, the belief would appear by the following communication in the same journal, from a medical correspondent in Lancashire, that it also obtains in that county; " Some years ago, I attended a young woman who was consumptive. The agony was protracted for three or four days, as occasionally happens in such cases; and I was consulted as to the expediency of removing her to another bed. ' She could not die upon the one she then occupied, as it had got some pigeons' feathers in it.' They did not heed my directions to keep her still, and she died as they were placing her in another bed. These people had two or three tales in proof of their assertion; and this case would probably be accounted additional evidence, though I took care to tell the parties they had killed the poor creature, as others had been killed before, by the act of removing her."

In West Sussex there is a curious belief that when an infant dies, it communicates the fact itself, by a visit, as if in the body, to some near relative.

There is a curious superstition in Devonshire, that the departure of life is delayed whilst any lock is closed in the dwelling or any bolt shot. It is a practice, therefore, when a dying person is at the last extremity, to open every door in the house. This notion extends even to the supposition that a beam over the head of the dying man impedes the departure of the spirit. A clerical friend, who was most indefatigable in the discharge of his duties among the poor of his parish, related to me that, in a village near Collumpton, he witnessed the death of a person, when the last moments seemed delayed by some unseen cause, and the relatives, in consequence, moved the bed, observing that over the place there was a beam concealed in the floor above. In consequence of such removal, as they said, the sick man "went off like a lamb."—Devizes Gazette. Another belief is, that a bed made of goose feathers has the same effect on a dying man as that attributed to the beam.]

LAYING-OUT or STREEKING THE BODY.

DURAND gives a pretty exact account of some of the ceremonies used at laying-out the body, as they are at present practised in the North of England, where the laying-out is called streeking.[1]   He mentions the closing of the eyes[2] and lips, the decent washing,[3] dressing, and wrapping-up in a winding sheet[4] or linen shroud ;[5] of which shroud Prudentius thus speaks :

> " Candore nitentia claro
> Prætendere lintea mos est."[6]

Gough, in the introduction to his second volume of Sepulchral Monuments, p. 205, citing Lowe's MS. History of Orkney, says : " Funeral ceremonies in Orkney are much the same as in Scotland. The corpse is laid out after being stretcht on a board till it is coffined for burial. I know not for what reason they lock up all the cats of the house and cover all the looking-glasses as soon as any person dies ; nor can they give any solid reason." It by no means seems difficult to assign a reason for locking up the cats on the occasion ; it is obviously to prevent their making any depredations upon the corpse, which it is known they would attempt to do if not

---

[1] *To streek*, to expand, or stretch out, from the Anglo-Saxon ᚱᛏᚱᛖcan, *extendere*. See Benson's Anglo-Saxon Vocabulary, in v. A streeking-board is that on which they stretch out and compose the limbs of the dead body.

[2] The face-cloth, too, is of great antiquity. Strutt tells us that after the closing of the eyes, &c. a linen cloth was put over the face of the deceased. Thus we are told that " Henry IV., in his last illness, seeming to be dead, his chamberlain covered his face with a linen cloth." Engl. Æra, p. 105.

[3] Misson, in his Travels in England, translated by Ozell, p. 89, mentions, under the head of Funerals, " the washing the body thoroughly clean, and shaving it, if it be a man, and his beard be grown during his sickness."

[4] Stafford, in his Niobe, or his Age of Teares, 1611, p. 162, says : " I am so great an enemy to ceremonies, as that I would onelie wish to have that *one ceremonie at my buriall*, which I had at my *birth*, I mean *swadling*, and yet I am indifferent for that too."

[5] " Quinetiam sanctorum corpora, manibus erectis supinisque excipere, occludere oculos, ora obturare, decenter ornare, lavare accuratè, et linteo funebri involvere," &c. Durand. de Ritibus, p. 224. We have the very coffin of the present age described in Durand. " Corpus lotum et sindone obvolutum, ac loculo conditum, veteres in cœnaculis, seu tricliniis exponebant." p. 225. Loculus is a box or chest. Thus in old registers I find coffins called kists, i. e. chests. See Gough's Sepulchr. Monuments, ii Introd. p. 5.

[6]   " The custome is to spread abroad
>   White linens, grac'd with splendour pure." Beaumont.

prevented. In the Statistical Account of Scotland, xxi 147, parish of Monquhitter, we read : "It disturbed the ghost of the dead, and was fatal to the living, if a tear was allowed to fall on a winding-sheet. What was the intention of this, but to prevent the effects of a wild or frantic sorrow? If a cat was permitted to leap over a corpse, it portended misfortune. The meaning of this was to prevent that carnivorous animal from coming near the body of the deceased, lest, when the watchers were asleep, it should endeavour to prey upon it," &c. These notions appear to have been called in Scotland "Frets."

In Wits, Fits, and Fancies, 1614, p. 186, is the following, alluding to the practice of laying out or streeking the body : "One said to a little child *whose father died that morning,* and was *layd out in a coffin in the kitchen,* ' Alas, my prety child, thy father is now in heaven ;' the child answered, ' Nay, that he is not ; for he is yet in the kitchen.' " Laying out the corpse is an office always performed by women, who claim the linen, &c. about the person of the deceased at the time of performing the ceremony. It would be thought very unlucky to the friends of the person departed, were they to keep back any portion of what is thus found. These women give this away in their turn by small divisions ; and they who can obtain any part of it, think it an omen or presage of future good fortune to them or theirs.

The interests of our woollen manufactures have interfered with this ancient rite in England. Misson, speaking of funerals in England, says : "There is an Act of Parliament which ordains that the dead shall be buried in a woollen stuff, which is a kind of thin bays, which they call flannel ; nor is it lawful to use the least needleful of thread or silk. (The intention of this act is for the encouragement of the woollen manufacture.) This shift is always white ; but there are different sorts of it as to fineness, and consequently of different prices. To make these dresses is a particular trade, and there are many that sell nothing else." The shirt for a man "has commonly a sleeve purfled about the wrists, and the slit of the shirt down the breast done in the same manner. This should be at least half a foot longer than the body, that the feet of the deceased may be wrapped in it, as in a bag. Upon the head they put a cap, which they fasten with a very broad chin-cloth ; with gloves on the hands, and a cravat round the neck, all of woollen. The women have a kind of head-dress with a forehead cloth."—Travels in England, translated by Ozell, p. 88. He adds, p. 90, "that the body may ly the softer, some put a lay of bran, about four inches thick, at the bottom of the coffin. The coffin is sometimes very magnificent. The body is visited to see that it is buried in flannel, and that nothing about it is sowed with thread. They let it lye three or four days."

[A correspondent of the Athenæum says : "I can tell you of a fancy that some people have in the wilder parts of Craven, that if the mark of a dead person (the body, however, not being cold) be put to a will, it is valid in law. A few years ago, a case of this nature occurred. A farmer had omitted to make his will ; he died, and, before the body was cold, a will was prepared by some relative (of course in his own favour), and a mark, purporting to be that of the deceased, was made by putting the pen into the hand of the dead man, and so making his mark to the will. The body of the man was not then cold. The will was contested by some parties, and, I believe, proceeded to a trial at law : when the circumstance of the belief of the parties came out in evidence."]

It is customary at this day, in some parts of Northumberland, *to set a pewter plate containing a little salt* upon the corpse. A *candle*, too, is sometimes *set upon the body*, in like manner.[1] Salt, says the learned Moresin, is the emblem of eternity and immortality. It is not liable to putrefaction itself, and it preserves things that are seasoned with it from decay.[2]

---

[1] In Articles to be enquired of within the Archdeaconry of Yorke, by the Churchwardens and Sworne Men, A.D. 163—, I find the following curious item : " Whether at the death of any, there be any superstitious *burning of candles over the corpse in the day, after it. be light."*

[2] " Salem abhorre constat diabolum, et ratione optima nititur, quia sal æternitatis est et immortalitatis signum, neque putredine neque corruptione infestatur unquam, sed ipse ab his omnia vendicat."—Moresini Papatus, p. 154. Considered in reference to this symbolical explication, how beautiful is that expression, " Ye are the salt of the earth !" Reginald Scot, in his Discourse concerning Devils and Spirits, p. 16, cites Bodin, as telling us that " the devil loveth no salt in his meat, for that is a sign of eternity, and used by God's commandment in all sacrifices." Douce says, the custom of putting a plate of salt upon corpses is still retained in

[Train, in his Historical and Statistical Account of the Isle of Man, 1845, ii. 136, says: " When a person dies, the corpse is laid on what is called a *straightening-board ;* a trencher, with salt in it, and a lighted candle, are placed on the breast, and the bed, on which the straightening-board bearing the corpse rests, is generally strewed with strong-scented flowers."]

Dr. Campbell, in his Philosophical Survey of the South of Ireland, 1777, p. 210, mentions this custom as obtaining in Ireland, and says that the plate of salt is placed over the heart. It should seem as if he had seen Moresin's remark, by his supposing that they consider the salt as the emblem of the incorruptible part ; " the body itself," says he, " being the type of corruption." Pennant, in his Tour in Scotland, tells us, that on the death of a Highlander, the corpse being stretched on a board, and covered with a coarse linen wrapper, the friends lay on the breast of the deceased a wooden platter, containing a small quantity of salt and earth, separate and unmixed : the earth an emblem of the corruptible body, the salt an emblem of the immortal spirit. All fire is extinguished where a corpse is kept ; and it is reckoned so ominous for a cat or dog to pass over it, that the poor animal is killed without mercy.

From the following passage in a Boulster Lecture, 1640 p. 139, the corpse appears anciently to have been stuck with flowers : "*Marry another, before those flowers that stuck his corpse be withered.*"

The following is in Herrick's Hesperides, p. 394 :

" *The Soul is the Salt.*

" The body's salt the soule is, which when gone, The flesh soone sucks in putrifaction."

In the same work, p. 5, is a copy of verses " to Perilla," abounding with tender allusions to the funeral customs of his time :

" 'Twill not be long (Perilla) after this That I must give thee the *supremest kisse:*

---

many parts of England, and particularly in Leicestershire, but it is not done for the reason here given. The pewter plate and salt are laid on the corpse with an intent to hinder air from getting into the bowels, and swelling up the belly, so as to occasion either a bursting, or, at least, a difficulty in closing the coffin. See Gent. Mag. for 1785, lv. 603, 760.

> Dead when I am, first *cast in salt*, and bring
> Part of the creame from that religious spring;
> With which (Perilla) wash my hands and feet;
> That done, then wind me in that very sheet
> Which wrapt thy smooth limbs (when thou didst implore
> The gods' protection but the night before);
> Follow me weeping to my turfe, and there
> Let fall a primrose, and with it a teare:
> Then lastly let some weekly strewings be
> Devoted to the memory of me:
> Then shall my ghost not walk about, but keep
> Still in the coole and silent shades of sleep."

Moresin gives us also his conjecture on the use of the candle upon this occasion.[1] "It was an Egyptian hieroglyphic for life, meant to express here the ardent desire of having had the life of the deceased prolonged." Pope, conversant in Papal antiquities, says:

> " Ah, hopeless lasting flames! like those that burn
> *To light the dead*, and warm the unfruitful urn."

In Levi's Account of the Rites and Ceremonies of the modern Jews, we read, p. 163: that when any of the sick among that people have departed, the corpse is taken and laid on the ground, and a pillow put under its head; and the hands and feet are laid out even, and the body is covered over with a black cloth, *and a light is set at its head.* It appears from Scogin's Jests (ed. 1796), p. 4, that in Henry the Eighth's time it was the custom *to set two burning candles over the dead body.* The passage is curious, as illustrative of more customs than one: " On Maundy-Thursday, Scogin said unto his chamber-fellow, We will make our Maundy, and eat and drink with advantage: Be it, said the scholar. On Maundy-Thursday at night they made such chear that the scholar was drunk. Scogin then pulled off all the scholar's cloaths, and laid him stark naked on the rushes, and set a

[1] " Lucerna, seu candela mortuis cadaveribus semper apponitur in domibus et templis, quamdiu supra terram sunt, et frequenter toto anno post humationem. An hinc ducto more, oculo, vel lucerna incensa veteres Egyptii vitam significabant, unde veteres soliti sunt lucernas ardentes sepulchris imponere, hac saltem ratione significantes se mortuorum quamdiu possent vitas producturos."—Moresini Papatus, p. 89. " Jubet papa cadaveris expiationes fieri, ut quod valde immundum est, aspergatur aqua benedicta, thurificetur, exorcisetur sacris orationibus, illustretur sacris luminibus, quousque supra terram fuerit," &c. Ibid. p. 26.

form over him, and spread a coverlet over it, and *set up two tallow candles in candlesticks over him,* one at his head, the other at his feet, and ran from chamber to chamber, and told the fellows of that place that his chamber-fellow was dead." Adding, " I pray you, go up, and pray for his soul ; and so they did. And when the scholar had slept his first sleep, he began to turn himself, and cast down the form and the candles. The fellows seeing that Scogin did run first out of the chamber, were afraid, and came running and tumbling down ready to break each other's neck. The scholar followed them stark naked ; and the fellows seeing him run after them like a ghost, some ran into their chambers, some into one corner, and some into another. Scogin ran into the chamber to see *that the candles should do no harm,* and at last fetched up his chamber-fellow, who ran about like a madman, and brought him to bed, for which matter Scogin had rebuke."

FUNERAL ENTERTAINMENTS.

THESE funeral entertainments are of very old date. Cecrops is said to have instituted them for the purpose of renewing decayed friendship amongst old friends, &c. [Robert de Brunne, writing in the thirteenth century, asks :

" Art thow i-wont at lychwake
Any pleyes for to make ?"]

Moresin tells us that in England, in his time, they were so profuse on this occasion, that it cost less to portion off a daughter than to bury a dead wife.[1] These burial feasts are still kept up in the north of England, and are there called *arvals* or *arvils.* The bread distributed on these occasions is called *arvil-bread.* The custom seems borrowed from the ancients, amongst whom many examples of it are collected by Hornman in his treatise *de Miraculis Mortuorum,* cap. 36.

[1] " Convivia funebria Cecrops primus instituit prudenter, ut amici amicitiam fortasse remissam renovarent, et pro uno defuncto acquirerent his mediis plures amicos, &c. In Anglia ita strenue hanc curam obeunt, ut viliori pretio constet elocatio filiæ, quam uxoris mortuæ inhumatio." Moresini Papatus,

Juvenal, in his fifth Satire, l. 85, mentions the *cœna feralis,* which was intended to appease the ghosts of the dead, and consisted of milk, honey, water, wine, olives, and strewed flowers. The modern arvals, however, are intended to appease the appetites of the living, who have upon these occasions superseded the manes of the dead. An allusion to these feasts occurs in Hamlet, act i. sc. 2, who, speaking of his mother's marriage, says :

> ————" *The funeral bak'd meats*
> Did coldly furnish forth *the marriage-tables.*" [1]

The word *arval* occurs in the provincial poem styled Yorkshire Ale :

> " Come, bring my jerkin, Tibb, I'll to the arvil,
> Yon man's ded seny scoun, it makes me marvill."

Hutchinson, in his History of Northumberland, ii. ad fin. p. 20, thus mentions the arvel-dinner : " On the decease of any person possessed of valuable effects, the friends and neighbours of the family are invited to dinner on the day of interment, which is called the Arthel or Arvel dinner. Arthel is a British word, and is frequently more correctly written arddelw. In Wales it is written arddel, and signifies, according to Dr. Davies's Dictionary, *asserere,* to avouch. This custom seems of very distant antiquity, and was a solemn festival made at the time of publicly exposing the corpse, to exculpate the heir, and those entitled to the possessions of the deceased, from fines and mulcts to the lord of the manor,

---

[1] Gough, in the introduction to the second volume of his Sepulchral Monuments, p. 6, says : " An entertainment, or supper, which the Greeks called Περιδειπνον, and Cicero *circompotatio,* made a part of a funeral, whence our practice of giving wine and cake among the rich, and ale among the poor." The ancients had several kinds of suppers made in honour of the deceased. First, that which was laid upon the funeral pile, such as we find in the 23d book of Homer, and the 6th Æneis of Virgil ; Catullus, Ep. lv. ; Ovid, Fasti, ii. Secondly, the supper given to the friends and relations at their return from the funeral, as in the 24th book of Homer's Ilias, in honour of Hector. This kind of supper is mentioned in Lucian's treatise of Grief, and Cicero's third book of Laws. Thirdly, the *silicernium,* a supper laid at the sepulchre, called 'Εκάτης δειπνον. Others will have it to be a meeting of the very old relations, who went in a very solemn manner after the funeral, and took their leaves one of the other, as if they were never to meet again. The fourth was called *epulum novendiale.*

and from all accusation of having used violence; so that the
persons then convoked might avouch that the person died
fairly, and without suffering any personal injury.   The dead
were thus exhibited by ancient nations, and perhaps the custom
was introduced here by the Romans."
      It was customary, according to Strutt, i. 66, in the Christian
burials of the Anglo-Saxons, to leave the head and shoulders
of the corpse uncovered till the time of burial, that relations, &c. might take a last view of their deceased friend. To
this day we yet retain (in our way) this old custom, leaving
the coffin of the deceased unscrewed till the time of burial.
      Among the extracts from the Berkeley MSS. read before
the Society of Antiquaries, the following occasioned a general
smile: "From the time of the death of Maurice, the fourth Lord
Berkeley, which happened June 8, 1368, untill his interment,
the reeve of his manor of Hinton spent three quarters and
seaven bushells of beanes in fatting one hundred geese towards
his funerall, and divers other reeves of other manors the like,
in geese, duckes, and other pultry."   Walsingham, p. 405,
says, when Richard the Second was buried at Langley, " nec
erat qui eos invitarct ad prandium post laborem."
      In Strype's edition of Stow's Survey of London, i. 259, we
read from Registr. Lond. : "Margaret Atkinson, widow, by
her will, October 18, 1544, orders that *the next Sunday after
her burial* there be provided two dozen of bread, a kilderkin
of ale, two gammons of bacon, three shoulders of mutton, and
two couple of rabbits, desiring all the parish, as well rich as
poor, to take part thereof; and *a table to be set in the midst
of the church*, with every thing necessary thereto."   In 1556,
at the funeral of Sir John Gresham, knight, mercer, the church
and streets were all hung with black, and arms, great store.
A sermon was preached by the Archdeacon of Canterbury,
" and after, *all the company came home to as great a dinner as
had been seen for a fish day, for all that came :* for nothing
was lacking."   Ibid. At the funeral of Thomas Percy, 1561,
late skinner to Queen Mary, he was "attended to his burial
in Saint Mary Aldermary church with twenty black gowns and
coats, twenty clerks singing, &c.   The floor strewed with
rushes for the chief mourners.   Mr. Crowley preached.
Afterwards was a great dole of money : and then *all went
home to a dinner.*   The Company of Skinners to their hall, to

dine together. At this funeral all the mourners offered, and so did the said company." In 1562, at the funeral of Sir Humphrey Brown, knight, Lord Chief Justice, Dec. 15, Mr. Reneger made the sermon, and after, *they went home to a great dinner.* The church was hung with black, and arms. The helmet and crest were offered (on the altar), and after that his target; after that his sword; then his coat-armour; then his standard was offered, and his pennon: and after all, the mourners, and judges, and serjeants of the law, and servants, offered.

Waldron, in his Description of the Isle of Man, p. 170, says : " As to their funerals, they give no invitation, but everybody that had any acquaintance with the deceased comes, either on foot or horseback. I have seen sometimes, at a Mank's burial, upwards of an hundred horsemen, and twice the number on foot. All these are entertained at long tables, spread with all sorts of cold provision, and rum and brandy flies about at a lavish rate."

Misson, in his Travels in England, translated by Ozell, p. 91, under the head of Funerals, says : " Before they set out, and after they return, it is usual to present the guests with something to drink, either red or white wine, boiled with sugar and cinnamon, or some other such liquor. Every one drinks two or three cups. Butler, the keeper of a tavern (the Crown and Sceptre, in St. Martin's-street), told me that there was a tun of red port wine drank at his wife's burial, besides mulled white wine. Note, no men ever go to women's burials, nor the women to men's, so that there were none but women at the drinking of Butler's wine."

In the Minute Book of the Society of Antiquaries of London, July 21, 1725, i. 169, we read: " Mr. Anderson gave the society an account of the manner of a Highland lord's funeral. The body is put into a litter between two horses, and, attended by the whole clan, is brought to the place of burial in the churchyard. The nearest relations dig the grave, the neighbours having set out the ground, so that it may not encroach on the graves of others. While this is performing, some hired women, for that purpose, lament the dead, setting forth his genealogy and noble exploits. After the body is interred, a hundred black cattle, and two or three hundred sheep, are killed for the entertainment of the company."

In the Statistical Account of Scotland, vl. 407, parish of Kincardine, Perth, we read : " The desire of what is called a decent funeral, i. e. one to which all the inhabitants of the district are invited, and at which every part of the usual entertainment is given, is one of the strongest in the poor. The expense of it amounts to nearly two pounds. This sum, therefore, every person in mean circumstances is anxious to lay up, and he will not spare it unless reduced to the greatest extremity. So Gray :

" E'en in our ashes live their wonted fires."

Ibid. ix. 543, complaints occur against the expensive mode of conducting burials in the parish of Dunlop, in Ayrshire. It is pointed out as an object of taxation. Ibid. x. 469, parish of Lochbroom, co. Ross : " At their burials and marriages, we are told, the inhabitants too much adhere to the folly of their ancestors. On these occasions they have a custom of feasting a great number of their friends and neighbours, and this often at an expense which proves greatly to the prejudice of poor orphans and young people ; although these feasts are seldom productive of any quarrels or irregularities among them." Ibid. xv. 372, parish of Campsie, co. Stirling, we read : " It was customary, till within these few years, when any head of a family died, to invite the whole parish ; *they were served on boards in the barn,* where a prayer was pronounced before and after the service, which duty was most religiously observed. The entertainment consisted of the following parts : first, there was a drink of ale, then a dram, then a piece of shortbread, then another dram of some other species of liquor, then a piece of currant-bread, and a third dram, either of spirits or wine, which was followed by loaves and cheese, pipes and tobacco. This was *the old funeral entertainment* in the parish of Campsie, and was styled their service ; and sometimes this was repeated, and was then styled a double service, and it was sure of being repeated at the *dredgy.* A funeral cost at least a hundred pounds Scots, to any family who followed the old course. The most active young man was pointed out to the office of *server;* and in those days, while the manners were simple, and at the same time serious, it was no small honour to be *a server at a burial.* However distant any part of the parish was from the place of interment, it was customary for

II. 16

the attendants to carry the corpse on hand-spokes. The mode of invitation to the entertainment was by some special messenger, which was styled bidding to the burial, the form being nearly in the following words: 'You are desired to come to such-a-one's burial to-morrow, against ten hours.' No person was invited by letter; and, though invited against ten of the clock, the corpse never was interred till the evening, time not being so much valued in those days." Ibid. xviii. 123, parish of Gargunnock, co. Stirling: "The manner of conducting funerals in the country needs much amendment. From the death to the interment the house is thronged by night and day, and the conversation is often very unsuitable to the occasion. The whole parish is invited at ten o'clock in the forenoon of the day of the funeral, but it is soon enough to attend at three o'clock in the afternoon. Every one is entertained with a variety of meats and drinks. Not a few return to the dirge, and sometimes forget what they have been doing and where they are. Attempts have been lately made to provide a remedy for this evil; but old customs are not easily abolished." Ibid. p. 174, parish of Carmunnock, co. Lanark, the minister tells us: "We must mention a custom which still prevails, and which certainly ought to be abolished. It is usual in this parish, as in many other parts of Scotland, when a death has taken place, to invite on such occasions the greater part of the country round; and though called to attend at an early hour in the forenoon, yet it is generally towards evening before they think of carrying forth the corpse to the churchyard for interment. While, on these occasions, the good folks are assembled, though they never run into excess, yet no small expense is incurred by the family, who often vie with those around them in giving, as they call it, an honourable burial to their deceased friend. Such a custom is attended with many evils, and frequently involves in debt, or reduces to poverty, many families otherwise frugal and industrious, by this piece of useless parade and ill-judged expense."

In Whimsies, or a New Cast of Characters, 1631, p. 89, speaking of a launderer, the author says: " So much she hath reserved out of the labours of her life, as will buy some small portion of *diet-bread, comfits,* and *burnt claret,* to welcome in her neighbours *now at her departing,* of whose cost they never

so freely tasted while she was living."[1]   Ibid p. 145, in describing a yealous (jealous) neighbour, the author concludes
with observing : " Meate for his *funerall pye* is shred, some
few ceremoniall teares on his funerall pile are shed ; but the
wormes are scarce entered his shroud, his corpse flowers not
fully dead, till this yealous earthworme is forgot, and another
more amorous, but lesse yealous, mounted his bed."

Mons. Jorevin, who travelled in England in the beginning
of King Charles the Second's reign, speaking of a lord's
burial at Shrewsbury, which his host procured him a sight of,
tells us : " The relations and friends being assembled in the
house of the defunct, the minister advanced into the middle of
the chamber, where, before the company, he made a funeral
oration, representing the great actions of the deceased, his
virtues, his qualities, his title of nobility, and those of the
whole family, &c.   It is to be remarked, that during the oration there stood *upon the coffin* **a** *large pot of wine, out of
which every one drank to the health of the deceased.*   This
being finished, six men took up the corpse and carried it on
their sholders to the church," &c.   Antiq. Repert. ii. 105.

A writer in the Gent. Mag. for March, 1780, p. 129, says :
" Our ancient funerals, as well as some modern ones, were
closed with *merry-makings,* at least equal to the preceding
sorrow, most of the testators directing, among other things,
victuals and drink to be distributed at their exequies ; one in
particular, I remember, orders a sum of money for *a drinking
for his soul.*"   Another writer, apparently describing the manners of Yorkshire, lxviii. 573, for July, 1798, says : "At
funerals, on which occasion a large party is generally invited,
the attendant who serves the company with ale or wine, has
upon the handle of the tankard a piece of lemon-peel, and
also upon her left arm a clean white napkin.   I believe these
customs are invariably observed.   From what cause they originated, some ingenious correspondent may be able to inform
me."

[1] " In northern customs duty was exprest
    To friends departed by their fun'ral feast.
    Tho' I've consulted Hollingshead and Stow,
    I find it very difficult to know
    Who, to refresh th' attendants to the grave,
    Burnt claret first, or Naples-bisket gave."
                              King's Art of Cookery, p. 65

By the following extract, *wafers* appear to have been used at funeral entertainments : " 1671. Jan. 2, died Mr. Cornelius Bee, bookseller in Little Britain. Buried 4 Jan. at St. Bartholomew's, without sermon, *without wine or wafers;* onely gloves and rosemary." Peck's Desiderata Curiosa, ii. 549, from MS. Sloane 886, a Catalogue of Persons Deceased between 1628 and 1675, by one Smith, a Secondary of the Poultry Compter.

In Dudley Lord North's Forest of Varieties, 1645, p. 105, is the following : " Nor are *all banquets* (no more than musick) ordained for merry humors, *some being used even at funeralls.*"

In Pleasant Remarks on the Humors of Mankind, 12mo. p. 62, cciii. we read : " 'Tis common in England for prentices, when they are out of their time, to make an entertainment, and call it the burial of their wives. Many aldermen would do the like, was it consistent with common decency, at the departure of theirs." Again, p. 83, cclxxv. : " How like Epicurists do some persons drink at a funeral, as if they were met there to be merry and make it a matter of rejoycing that they have got rid of their friends and relations." Richard Flecknoe, in his Ænigmatical Characters, 1665, p. 14, speaking of "a curious glutton," observes on his fondness for feasting as follows : " In fine, he thinks of nothing else, as long as he lives, and, when he dyes, onely regrets that *funeral feasts are quite left off,* else he should have the pleasure of one feast more (in imagination at least), even after death; which he can't endure to hear of, onely because they say there is no eating or drinking in the other world."

Books by way of funeral tokens used to be given away at the burials of the better sort in England. In my collection of portraits I have one of John Bunyan, taken from before an old edition of his works which I bought at Ware in Hertfordshire. It is thus inscribed on the back in MS. : " Funeral token in remembrance of Mr. Henry Plomer, who departed this life October 2, 1696, being 79 years of age, and is designed to put us that are alive in mind of our great change. Mr. Daniel Clerk the elder his book, Oct. 23, 1696."

In the Athenian Oracle, iii. 114, a querist asks : " Whether books are not more proper to be given at funerals than bisquets, gloves, rings, &c. ?" And it is answered : " Undoubt-

edly a book would be a far more convenient, more durable, and
more valuable present than what are generally given, and more
profitably preserve the memory of a deceased friend." It
was anciently the general custom to give a cold entertainment
to mourners at a funeral.   In distant counties this practice is
continued among the yeomanry.   So the Tragique Historie of
the Faire Valeria of London, 1598 : " His corpes was with funerall pompe conveyed to the church and there solemnly entered, nothing omitted which necessitie or custom could claime :
a sermon, a *banquet*, and like observations."   Again, in the
old romance of Syr Degore :

> " A great feaste would he holde
> Upon his quene's mornynge day,
> That was buryed in an abbay."[1]

FUNERALS IN THE CHURCH-PORCH.

[MANY relations might be given of funerals having been
solemnized within the church-porch.   St. Awdry, who died
of the pestilence in the year 669, and St. Chad, who
probably, says the Rev. Mr. Samuel Pegge, did not outlive
the year 6.2, with other persons of that era, of extraordinary reputed sanctity, being anxious to creep near the
church,[2] were the first persons placed there.   Among the
many legends relative to St. Swithin, there is one stating that
his corpse not being allowed to enter the church, it was placed
in the church-porch, where it remained forty days, during
which time it rained incessantly.   This account agrees in some
measure with the Latin legend quoted in Lord Campbell's
Lives of the Chancellors; which I imagine William of Malms-
bury has also given us as a proof of St. Swithin's great hu-

[1] See also Hayward's Life and Reigne of King Henry IV., 4to. 1599,
p. 135 : " Then hee (King Richard II.) was conveyed to Langley Abby in
Buckinghamshire, and there obscurely interred, without the charge of *a
dinner for celebrating the funeral*."
[2] [Until the time of Cuthbert, Archbishop of Canterbury, whose ponti-
ficate began A.D. 740, and ended in 748, the custom of burying within
the precincts of towns and cities did not prevail.   Vide Matt. Parker's
Antiq. p. 91, and Staveley's Hist. of Churches, p. 26.]

mility: "for when he was about to bid farewell to this life, he gave orders to be buried outside the church, exposed to the rain dropping from the skies, and the treading of the passers-by;" and so he continued for some time; but the ecclesiastics not liking that a person of his sanctity should be so exposed, dug him up, when it is probable that, agreeably with his desire to be buried outside the church, they placed him in the porch.[1]

The churchwardens' accounts of Banwell, Somersetshire, contain the following curious items: "1521. Rec^{d.} of Robart Cabyll, for the lyying of his wyffe in the *porche*, 3s. 4d. Rec^{d.} of Robart Blandon, for lyyng of his wyffe in the *church*, 6s. 8d." By which it appears that the fee was as much again for burying in the church as in the porch.]

SIN EATERS.

THE following is extracted from Bagford's letter relating to the antiquities of London, printed in Leland's Collectanea, i. 76. It is dated February 1, 1714-5: "Within the memory of our fathers, in Shropshire, in those villages adjoyning to Wales, when a person dyed, there was notice given to an old sire (for so they called him), who presently repaired to the place where the deceased lay, and stood before the door of the house, when some of the family came out and furnished him vith a cricket, on which he sat down facing the door. Then

---

[1] [It was the practice among the Romans to lay the dead body in the *porch* of their houses, near the threshold, that passengers might inspect it, and be satisfied whether there were any signs of a violent death. For the benefit of a clearer view, the corpse was set in the position here mentioned, the feet towards the door; which custom Perseus thus alludes to in his third Satire:

"See now the trumpets and the torches!—see
Our spark laid out in sad solemnity!
Stretch'd on the bier, bedaub'd with unguents o'er,
While his stiff heels lie pointed to the door."

This mode of placing the dead was likewise in use among the Greeks, Hom. Il. xix. v. 212.]

they gave him a groat, which he put in his pocket, a crust of bread, which he eat; and a full bowle of ale, which he drank off at a draught. After this he got up from the cricket and pronounced, with a composed gesture, *the ease and rest of the soul departed for which he would pawn his own soul.* This I had from the ingenious John Aubrey, Esq., who made a collection of curious observations, which I have seen, and is now remaining in the hands of Mr. Churchill, the bookseller. How can a man think otherwise of this, than that it proceeded from the ancient heathens ?"

Aubrey's collection, here mentioned, was most probably the Remaines of Gentilisme and Judaism, still preserved among the Lansdowne MSS., whence the following remarks on this subject, in Mr. Aubrey's own hand, have been extracted : " In the county of Hereford was an old custome at funeralls to hire poor people, who were to take upon them the sinnes of the party deceased. One of them (he was a long, leane, ugly, lamentable poor raskal), I remember, lived in a cottage on Rosse highway. The manner was, that when the corpse was brought out of the house, and layd on the biere, a loafe of bread was brought out and delivered to the sinne eater, over the corpse, as also a mazar bowle, of maple, full of beer (which he was to drink up), and sixpence in money; in consideration whereof he took upon him, ipso facto, all the sinnes of the defunct, and freed him or her from walking after they were dead. This custome alludes, methinks, something to the scapegoate in the old lawe, Levit. xvi. 21, 22. 'And Aaron shall lay both his hands on the head of the live goate, and confesse over him all the iniquities of the children of Israel, and all their transgressions in all their sins, putting them upon the head of the goat, and shall send him away by the hand of a fit man into the wilderness. And the goat shall bear upon him all their iniquities unto a land not inhabited ; and he shall let the goat goe into the wilderness.' This custome, though rarely used in our dayes, yet by some people was observed even in the strictest time of the presbyterian government, as at Dynder (volens nolens the parson of the parish), the kindred of a woman deceased there had this ceremonie punctually performed, according to her will : and also the like was done at the city of Hereford in those times, where a woman kept, many yeares before her death, a mazard bowle for the sinne-eater ; and the like in other places in this countie; as also in Brecon.[1] I believe this custom was heretofore used all over Wales."[2]

Bishop Kennett has added this note to Aubrey's MS. : " It seems a remainder of this custom which lately obtained at Amersden, in the county of Oxford, where, at the burial of every corpse, one cake and one flagon of ale, just after the interment, were brought to the minister in the church-porch."

MORTUARIES.

THE payment of mortuaries is of great antiquity. It was anciently done by leading or driving a horse or cow, &c. before the corpse of the deceased at his funeral. It was considered as a gift left by a man at his death by way of recompense for all failures in the payment of tithes and oblations, and called a corse-present. It is mentioned in the national council of Ensham, about the year 1006.

Some antiquaries have been led into a mistake by this leading of a horse before the corpse, and have erroneously repre-sented it as peculiar to military characters.[3]

Offeringes at Burialles are condemned in a list of Grosse Poyntes of Poperie, evident to all Men, in A Parte of a Re-gister, contayninge sundrie memorable matters, written by divers godly and learned in our time, whiche stande for and desire the Reformation of our Church in Discipline and Cere-monies, accordinge to the Pure Worde of God and the Law of our Lande, p. 63.   This work is said by Dr. Bancroft to have been printed at Edinburgh by Robert Waldegrave, who printed most of the puritan books and libels in the latter end of Queen Elizabeth's reign.

[1] " E. g. at Llanggors, where Mr. Gwin, the minister, about 1640, could not hinder the performance of this ancient custome."

[2] MS. Lansd. 226, fol. 116. In another page Aubrey says : " A.D. 1686. This custom is used to this day in North Wales ;" where milk seems to have been the substitute for beer.

[3] See Collier's Ecclesiastical History, i. 487 : Mortuaries were called by our Saxon ancestors saul ᵱceaᴈ (soul *shot*, or *payment*).   See a curious ac-count of them in Dugdale's History of Warwickshire, 1st edit. p. 679. See also Cowel's Law Interpreter, in voce ; and Selden's History of Tithes, p. 287.

FOLLOWING THE CORPSE TO THE GRAVE,[1]

CARRYING EVERGREENS ON THAT OCCASION IN THE HAND, TOGETHER WITH THE USE OF PSALMODY.

BOURNE tells us[2] that the heathens followed the corpse to the grave, because it presented to them what would shortly follow, how they themselves should be so carried out to be deposited in the grave.[3]

In Articles to be enquired of within the Archdeaconry of Yorke, by the Churchwardens and Sworne Men, 163—, 4to., I find the following : " *Whether at the death of any there be praying for the dead at crosses, or places where crosses have been, in the way to the church.*"

Misson, in his Travels in England, translated by Ozell, p. 90, speaking of funerals, says : " They let the body lye three or four days, as well to give the dead person an opportunity of coming to life again, if his soul has not quite left his body, as to prepare mourning, and the ceremonies of the funeral. They send the beadle with a list of such friends and relations as they have a mind to invite ; and sometimes they have printed tickets, which they leave at their houses. A little before the company is set in order for the march, they lay the body into the coffin, upon two stools, in a room, where all that please may go and see it ; then they take off the top of the coffin, and remove from off the face a little square piece of flannel, made on purpose to cover it, and not fastened to anything. Being ready to move, one or more beadles march first, each carrying a long staff, at the end of which is a great apple, or knob of silver. The body comes just after the minister or

---

[1] Graves were anciently called *pyttes.* See Strutt's Manners and Cus toms, iii. 172.

[2] Antiquitates Vulgares, chap. iii.

[3] " Præcedenti pompa funebri, vivi sequuntur, tanqʹam haud multo post morituri." Alex. ab Alexand. iii. 67. Polyd. Verg. lib. vi. c. 10, p. 405. So, in Langley's Translation of Polydore Vergil, fol. 128, we read : " In burials the old rite was that the ded corpse was borne afore, and the people folowed after, as one should sale we shall dye and folowe after hym, as their laste wordes to the coarse did pretende. For thei used to saie, when it was buried, on this wise, Farewell, wee come after thee, and of the folowyng of the multitude thei were called exequies."

ministers, attended by the clerk. The relations in close
mourning, and all the guests, two and two, make up the rest
of the procession."

Macaulay, in his History of Claybrook, 1791, p. 131, observes : " At the funeral of a yeoman, or farmer, the clergyman
generally leads the van in the procession, in his canonical
habiliments ; and the relations follow the corpse, two and two,
of each sex, in the order of proximity, linked in each other's
arms. At the funeral of a young man it is customary to have
six young women, clad in white, as pall-bearers ; and the same
number of young men, with white gloves and hat-bands, at
the funeral of a young woman. But these usages are not so
universally prevalent as they were in the days of our fathers."

Gough, in the introduction to his second volume of Sepulchral Monuments, p. 204, says : " In Flintshire it is customary
to say the Lord's prayer on bringing the corpse out of the
house." At South Shields, co. Durham, the bidders, i. e. the
inviters to a funeral, never use the rapper of the door when
they go about, but always knock with a key, which they carry
with them for that purpose. I know not whether this custom
be retained anywhere else.

The following form of inviting to burials by the public
bellman of the town is still, or was very lately, in use at
Hexham, in the county of Northumberland : " Blessed are the
dead which die in the Lord. Joseph Dixon is departed, son
of Christopher Dixon was. Their company is desired to-
morrow at five o'clock, and at six he is to be bu—ri—ed. For
him and all faithful people give God most hearty thanks."

Grose says : " If you meet a funeral procession, or one
passes by you, always take off your hat: this keeps all evil
spirits attending the body in good humour."

In Dunbar's Will of Maister Andro Kennedy, a profligate
student, are some curious, if not profane parodies on the then
funeral rites :

> " In die meæ sepulturæ,
>   I will have nane but our awn gang,
> Et duos rusticos de rure
>   Bearand ane barrel on a stang.
>
> Drinkand and playand, cap out even,
>   Sicut egomet solebam.
> Singand and greitand, with the stevin,
>   Potum meum cum fletu miscebam.

I will no preistis for to sing,
    Dies illæ dies iræ,[1]
Nor yet no bellis for to ring,
    Sicut semper solet fieri ;
But a bagpype to play a spring,
    Et unum *alewisp* ante me,
Instead of torches for to bring
    Quatuor lagenas cervisiæ.
Within the graiv to sett, fit thing,
    In modum crucis, juxta me,
To flee the feynds,[2] then hardly sing,
    Te terra plasmasti me."

There is a most concise epitaph on a stone that covers the body of one of the fellows of St. John's College, Oxford, in the ante-chapel there. It is "*Præivit,*" he is gone before.

Christians, says Bourne, observe the custom of following the corpse to the grave, because this form of procession is an emblem of our dying shortly after our friend. In like manner, the carrying in our hands of ivy, sprigs of laurel, rosemary, or other evergreens, is an emblem of the soul's immortality. So Gay :

" To shew their love, the neighbours far and near
Followed, with wistful look, the damsel's bier :
Sprigg'd rosemary the lads and lasses bore,
While dismally the parson walk'd before."

Many instances of the use of rosemary at funerals are to be collected from old writers. In Cartwright's Ordinary, act v. sc. 1, we read :

————" If there be
Any so kind as to accompany
My body to the earth, let them not want
For entertainment. Prythee see they have
A sprig of rosemary, dipp'd in common water,
To smell.at as they walk along the streets."

In the second part of Dekker's Honest Whore, 1630, is the following passage : "My winding-sheete was taken out of lavender to be stucke with rosemary." In Shirley's Wedding, 1633, scene "A table set forth with two tapers ; servants placing ewe, bayes, and *rosemary*, &c. Enter Beauford.

[1] A common hymn at funerals.
[2] Instead of a cross, to drive away the devils.

" Beau.   Are these the herbs you strow at funerals ?
Servt.   Yes, sir.
Beau.   ———— ha ye not art enough
      To make the ewe-tree grow here, or this bayes,
      The embleme of our victory in death ?
      But they present that best when they are wither'd."

It appears from the Perfect Diurnall, from the 30th April to May 7th, 1649, that "at the funeral of Robert Lockier (who was shot for mutiny April 27th or 28th preceding, the manner of whose funeral was most remarkable, considering the person to be in no higher quality than a private trooper, for the late king had not half so many to attend his corpse), *the corpse was adorned with bundles of rosemary on each side; one half of each was stained in blood,* and the sword of the deceased with them." Misson, in his Travels, in continuation of a passage already quoted, says, p. 91, "when the funeral procession is ready to set out, they nail up the coffin, and *a servant presents the company with sprigs of rosemary: every one takes a sprig, and carries it in his hand till the body is put into the grave, at which time they all throw in their sprigs after it.*" In Hogarth's Harlot's Progress, at the prostitute's funeral there are sprigs of rosemary.

The Romans and other heathens, upon this occasion, made use of cypress, which, being once cut, will never flourish nor grow again, as an emblem of their dying for ever :[1] but instead of that, the ancient Christians used the things before mentioned, and deposited them under the corpse in the grave, to signify that they who die in Christ, do not cease to live ; for though, as to the body, they die to the world, yet, as to their souls, they live and revive to God.

[1] The reader conversant in the classics will call to mind here the beautiful thought in the idyllium on Bion, by Moschus, iii. 1, 100 ; though the fine spirit of it will evaporate when we apply it to the Christian doctrine of the resurrection. The antithesis will be destroyed. We quote from the translation by Fawkes :

     " Alas ! the meanest flowers which gardens yield,
     The vilest weeds that flourish in the field,
     Which dead in wintry sepulchres appear,
     Revive in spring, and bloom another year :
     But we, the great, the brave, the learn'd, the wise,
     Soon as the hand of Death has closed our eyes,
     In tombs forgotten lie ; no suns restore ;
     We sleep, for ever sleep, to wake no more."

The cypress, however, appears to have been retained to later times. Coles, in his Introduction to the Knowledge of Plants, p. 64, says: " *Cypresse garlands* are of great account at funeralls amongst the gentiler sort, but rosemary and bayes are used by the commons both at funeralls and weddings. They are all plants which fade not a good while after they are gathered, and used (as I conceive) to intimate unto us that the remembrance of the present solemnity might not dye presently, but be kept in minde for many yeares." The line,

> " And cypress which doth biers adorn,"

is cited in Poole's English Parnassus, v. *Witch :* and Spenser mentions

> " The aspin, good for staves, the *cypress* funerall."

Dekker, in his Wonderfull Yeare, 1603, describes a charnel-house pavement, " instead of greene rushes, strewde with blasted rosemary, wither'd hyacinthes, *fatall cipresse*, and ewe, thickly mingled with heapes of dead men's bones." He says, " *Rosemary*, which had wont to be sold for twelve pence an armefull, went now" (on account of the plague) "at six shillings a handfull." To what has been already said on the subject of rosemary at funerals, may be added that in the British Apollo, 1708, i. No. 73 ; one asks, " Whence proceeds that so constant formality of persons bearing a sprig of rosemary in their hand, when accompanying the obsequies of a deceased person ?" And is answered : *A.* "That custom ('tis like) had its rise from a notion of an alexipharmick, or preservative virtue, in that herb, against pestilential distempers : whence the smelling thereto at funerals was probably thought a powerful defence against the morbid effluvias of the corpse. Nor is it for the same reason less customary to burn rosemary in the chambers of the sick, than frankincense, whose odour is not much different from the former, which gave the Greeks occasion to call rosemary Λιβανωτὶς a Λιβανος. *Thus.*" Ibid. No. 2, Quarterly Paper. To a query why among the ancients yew and cypress were given at funerals, it is answered: " We suppose that, as yew and cypress are always green, the ancients made use of them at burials, as an emblem of the immortality of the deceased through their virtues or good works."

In Poems, by Thomas Stanley, 1651, p. 54, *The Exequies*, we read:

> " Yet strew
> Upon my dismall grave
> Such offerings as you have,
> Forsaken *cypresse*, and sad ewe,
> For kinder flowers can take no birth
> Or growth from such unhappy earth."

In the Marrow of Complements, 1655, p. 150, is "A Mayden's Song for her dead Lover," in which cypress and yew are particularly mentioned as funeral plants:[1]

> " Come you whose loves are dead,
> And whilst I sing
> Weepe and wring
> Every hand, and every head
> Bind with *cypresse*, and *sad ewe*,
> Ribbands black, and candles blue ;
> For him that was of men most true.

> " Come with heavy moaning
> And on his grave
> Let him have
> Sacrifice of sighes and groaning ;
> Let him have faire flowers enough,
> White and purple, green and yellow,
> For him that was of men most true."

---

[1] " Hædera quoque, vel laurus, et hujusmodi, quæ semper servant virorem, in sarcophago corpori substernuntur ; ad significandum quod, si moriuntur in Christo, vivere non desinent." In some places, he says that coals, holy water, and frankincense are put into the grave. " Carbones in testimonium quod terra illa ad communes usus amplius redigi non potest. Plus enim durat carbo sub terra quam aliud." The holy water was to drive away the devils ; the frankincense to counteract the ill smells of the body. Durandi Rationale, lib. vii. cap. 35, 38. In the old play of the Fatall Dowry, 1632, act ii. sc. 1, are some curious thoughts on this subject, spoken at the funeral of a marshal in the army, who died in debt, on account of which the corpse was arrested :

> " What weepe ye, souldiers ?
> The jaylors and the creditors do weepe ;
> Be these thy bodies balme ; *these* and *thy vertue*
> *Keepe thy fame ever odoriferous*—
> Whilst the great, proud, rich, undeserving man
> Shall quickly both in bone and name consume,
> Though wrapt in lead, spice, seare-cloth, and perfume.
> —— This is a sacrifice our showre shall crowne
> His sepulcher with *olive, myrrh*, and *bayes*,
> *The plants of peace*, of *sorrow, victorie*."

Herbs and flowers appear to have been sometimes used at funerals with the same intention as evergreens. In the account of the funeral expenses of Sir John Rudstone, Mayor of London, 1531, I find the following article: "For yerbys at the bewryal £0 1 0." See Strutt's Manners and Customs, iii. 170. So in a song in Wit's Interpreter, we read:

"Shrouded she is from top to toe
With lillies which all o'er her grow,
Instead of bays and rosemary."

In Griffith's Bethel, or a Forme for Families, 1634, p. 261, speaking of a woman's attire, the author says: "By her habit you may give a neere guesse at her heart. If (like a coffin) shee be crowned with garlands, and *stuck with gay and gaudy flowers*, it is certaine there is somewhat *dead* within." Sir Thomas Browne, in his Urne Burial, p. 56, says, that "in strewing their tombs, the Romans affected the rose, the Greeks amaranthus and myrtle."

In the Life of Henrietta Maria, 1669, p. 3, we read: "On the 25th of June, 1610, she was carried with her brother to perform the *ceremony of casting holy water on the corpse of her dead father* (Henry the Fourth of France), who was buried the 28th following."

[It would appear from the ballad of Sarah Wilson, that it was sometimes the custom for the female attendants at the funeral of an unmarried woman to be dressed in white:

"Six pretty maids, pray let me have,
To bear me to the silent grave;
All cloth'd in white, a comely show,
To bear me to the shades below."]

THE YEW-TREE.

To the remarks which have been already made on evergreens used at funerals may be added, that *the planting of yew-trees in churchyards* seems to derive its origin from ancient funeral rites; in which, Sir Thomas Browne conjectures, from its perpetual verdure, it was used as an emblem of the Resurrection. He observes farther that the Christian custom of decking the coffin with bay·is a most elegant emblem. It is said that this tree, when seemingly dead, will revive from the root, and its dry leaves resume their wonted verdure.

The yew is called by Shakespeare, in his Richard the Second, *the double fatal yew*, because the leaves of the yew are poison, and the wood is employed for instruments of death. On this Steevens observes, that "from some of the ancient statutes it appears that every Englishman, while archery was practised, was obliged to keep in his house either a bow of yew or some other wood. It should seem, therefore, that yews were not only planted in churchyards to defend the churches from the wind, but on account of their use in making bows ; while by the benefit of being secured in inclosed places, ·their poisonous quality was kept from doing mischief to cattle."

Barrington, in his Observations on the Statutes, p. 191, calls the statute here quoted below,[l] the last statute of the reign of Edw. I., and observes on the passage, "that trees in a churchyard were often planted to skreen the church from the wind : that low as churches were built at this time, the thick foliage of the yew answered this purpose better than any other tree. I have been informed, accordingly, that the yew-trees in the churchyard of Gyffin, near Conway, having been lately felled, the roof of the church hath suffered excessively." The same writer, ibid. p. 424, on a regulation in the fourth chapter of the statute made at Westminster, 1482,

---

[l] In Magna Carta, &c., 1566, Secunda Pars veterum Statutorum, I find the statute, "*Ne rector prosternet arbores in cemiterio :* Quoniam inter rectores ecclesiarum et suos parochianos super arboribus crescentibus in cemiterio altercationes oriri sepius intelleximus, utrisque ad se pertinere contendentibus : hujusmodi altercationis dubium declarare juris scripti potius quam statuti juris estimamus. Nam cum cemiterium maxime dedicatum solum sit ecclesie, et quicquid plantatur solo, cedat ; sequitur necessarie arbores ipsos debere inter facultates ecclesiasticas numerari, de quibus laicis nulla est attributa facultas disponendi : sed sicut sacra Scriptura testatur, solis sacerdotibus dispositis cura indiscussa a Deo commissa decet : verum *arbores ipse propter ventorum impetus ne ecclesiis noceant,* SEPE *plantantur. Prohibemus, ne ecclesiarum rectores ipsas presumant prosternere indistincte, nisi cum cancellus ecclesie necessaria indigeat refectione. Nec in alios usus aliqualiter convertantur,* preterquam si navis ecclesie indiguerit similiter refectione : et rectores parochianis indigentibus eis caritative de arboris ipsis duxerint largiendis, quod fieri non precipimus, sed cum factum fuerit, commendamus."

that the price of a yew bow is not to exceed 3s. 4d., observe:
"I should imagine that the planting yews in churchyards,
being places fenced from cattle, arose, at least in many instances,
from an attention to the material from which the best bows
are made ; nor do we hear of such trees being planted in the
churchyards of other parts of Europe." It appears by
4 Hen. V. chap. 3, that the wood of which the best arrows
were made was the asp. There is a statute so late as the 8th
of Queen Elizabeth, which relates to bowyers, each of whom
is always to have in his house fifty bows made of elm, witch,
hazel, or ash. (Chap. x. sect. 7.)[1]

In the Gent. Mag. for Dec. 17ˉ9, xlix. 578, a writer mentions the two reasons already assigned for the planting of
yew-trees in churchyards ; but he considers the slow growth
of these trees as an objection to the idea of their protecting
the church from storms ; and the rarity of their occurrence
(it being very uncommon to meet with more than one or two
in the same place) an indication that they could not have been
much cultivated for the purposes of archery. He adds, "I
cannot find any statute or proclamation that directs the cultivation of the yew-tree in any place whatever." By different
extracts from our old statutes, he continues : "It appears
that we depended principally upon imported bow-staves for
our best bows ; which one would think needed not to have
been the case, if our churchyards had been well stocked with
yew-trees. The English yew, moreover, was of an inferior
goodness ;" and that our brave countrymen were forced to
have recourse to foreign materials, appears from the following
prices settled in an Act of Bowyers, 8 Eliz. : "Bows meet for
men's shooting, *being outlandish yew of the best sort*, not
over the price of 6s. 8d. ; bows meet for men's shooting, of
the second sort, 3s. 4d. ; bows for men, of a coarser sort,
called livery bows, 2s. ; *bows being English yew*, 2s. Gerard
mentions their growing in churchyards where they have been

[1] Drayton, who is so accurate with regard to British antiquities, informs
us, Polyolbion, 26, that the best bows were made of Spanish yew :

"All made of Spanish yew, their bows are wondrous strong."

By 5 Edw. IV. ch. 4 (Irish Statutes), every Englishman is obliged to
have " a bow in his house of his own length, either of yew, wych, hazel,
ash, or awburn," probably alder.

II. 17

planted.   Evelyn only says that the propagation of them has
been forborne since the use of bows has been laid aside."
The hypothesis of this writer is, that those venerable yew-
trees that are still to be seen in some of our churchyards were
planted for no other purpose but that of furnishing *palms* for
Palm Sunday, which he thinks were no other but the *branches
of yew-trees*.   He adds, "that they actually were made this
use of is extremely probable, from those in the churchyards
in East Kent (where there are some very large and old) being
to this day universally called palms."

Another writer in the Gent. Mag. for Feb. 1780, Dr. Pegge,
l. 74, thinks the yew-tree too much of a funeral nature to be
made a substitute for the joyful palm.   It is also a tree of
baleful influence, whence Statius terms it—

————" metuendaque succo
Taxus."

He conjectures that some of the yew-trees in our churchyards
are as old as the Norman conquest, and were planted with
others "for the purpose of protecting the fabric of the church
from storms;" but that when the statute of 35 Edw. I.
A.D. 1307, began to operate, whereby leave was given to fell
trees in churchyards for building and repairs, these would be
the only trees left standing, being unfit for the uses prescribed,
and afterwards, as an *evergreen*, be thought *an emblem of the
resurrection*, and even require some degree of regard and veneration.   The first-quoted correspondent, ibid. p. 129, answers the above of Pegge, and by reasoning and facts refutes
the idea of its baleful influence, and as to its *funeral nature*
observes : "When sprigs of yew-tree, as well as of other evergreens, have been used in our funeral ceremonies, it has not
been like the cypress of old, emblematical of the total extinc-
tion of the deceased, but, as is universally allowed, of his
resurrection,—an idea that, instead of being fraught with
grief and despair, is, of all others, the most consolatory to the
heart of man.   So that there seems no reason why this tree,
being sometimes used at funerals, should stamp such a lugu-
brious mark upon it as to render it unsuitable to more joyful
occasions.   Ivy and bay, that used to adorn the brows of poets
and conquerors, have not on that account been thought by the
Christians of all ages incompatible with funeral solemnities."

A writer, J. O., ibid. p. 108, dislikes all the reasons assigned
for planting yew-trees in churchyards, except their *gloomy
aspect* and their *noxious quality* : the first intended to add
solemnity to the consecrated ground, the other to preserve it
from the ravages of cattle. To countenance his first reason,
he quotes Dryden, who calls the yew *the mourner yew*, and
Virgil, who calls it *the baneful yew ;* and to make it still more
fitting for the place, adds the magic use which Shakespeare
makes of it in Macbeth :

> " Liver of blaspheming Jew,
> Gall of goat, and *slips of yew*,
> Sliver'd in the moon's eclipse.''

He adds, "the great dramatist's[1] opinion of its noxious properties is evident from Hecate's answer to the aërial spirit :

> " With new-fall'n dew,
> From *churchyard yew*,
> I will but 'noint,
> And then I'll mount." &c.

A fourth writer in the same work, for January 1781, li. 10,
says : " We read in the Antiquities of Greece and Rome that
the branches of the cypress and yew were the usual signals to
denote a house in mourning. Now, sir, as Death was a deity
among the ancients (the daughter of Sleep and Night), and
was by them represented in the same manner, with the addition only of a long robe embroidered with stars, I think we
may fairly conclude that the custom of planting the yew in
churchyards took its rise from Pagan superstition, and that it
is as old as the conquest of Britain by Julius Cæsar."

Gough, in the introduction to his second volume of Sepulchral Monuments, p. 5, speaking of the signs of death in
houses among the ancients, notices branches of *pine* and
cypress, on the authority of Euripides, Hecuba, 191, 192 ;
Suet. Aug. 101 ; Æn. xi. 31. He says, in a note : " Will it
be thought a far-fetcht conjecture that yew-trees in churchyards supply the place of cypress round tombs where Ovid.
Trist. III. xiii. 21, says they were placed?"

Warner, in his Topographical Remarks relating to the
South-Western parts of Hampshire, 1793, i. 95, speaking of
Brockenhurst church, says : "The churchyard exhibits two
examples of enormous vegetation—a large oak, apparently

[Not Shakespeare, but Sir W. Davenant.]

coeval with the mound on which it grows, measuring five and twenty feet in girth ; and a straight majestic yew-tree. On the latter the axe has committed sad depredations, despoiling it of five or six huge branches, a circumstance that doubtless has taken greatly from its ancient dignity. Still, however, it is a noble tree, measuring in girth fifteen feet, and in height upwards of sixty. I should think it might lay claim to an antiquity nearly equal to its venerable neighbour.[1] The common appearance of yew-trees in almost all old churchyards has given rise to an opinion pretty generally received, that the legislature formerly enforced the propagation of them in these repositaries of the dead (places not likely to be violated, particularly in times of superstition), for the purpose of furnishing bow-staves—articles of very high importance to our ancestors previous to the introduction of gunpowder. The opinion is indeed strengthened by a similar tradition among the lower ranks. I do not, however, find any injunction of ᵗhis sort, though it does not seem improbable that every parish might voluntarily plant yew-trees in its churchyards, as a joint stock for the common benefit of the parishioners—a step extremely likely to be adopted at a period when every person was obliged by act of parliament to be furnished with a bow and arrows,[2] and when the general consumption of these articles rendered *yew* bows scarce and expensive.[3] I do not, however, pretend to say this was the original cause of planting yew-trees in Christian cemeteries; the practice might be nothing more than a remnant of that superstitious worship

[1] " The New Forest, and Brockenhurst in particular (as we learn from its name), being formerly so famous for the production of yews, it might be a matter of wonder that so few remained to the present day, did we not recollect that the old English yeomanry were supplied from this tree with those excellent bows which rendered them the best and most dreaded archers in Europe. This constant and universal demand for yew produced in time such a scarcity, that recourse was had to foreign countries for a supply ; and the importation of them was enjoined by express acts of parliament passed for that purpose. Stat. Edw. IV. c. 2, 1 Rich. III. c. ii."

[2] Stat. 13th Edw. I. ii. c. 6, 3d Hen. VIII. c. 3.

[3] " Yew at length became so scarce (as I have hinted in a preceding note), that to prevent a too great consumption of it, bowyers were directed to make four bows of witch-hazel, ash, or elm, to one of yew. And no person under seventeen, unless possessed of moveables worth forty marks, or the son of parents having an estate of ten pounds per annum, might shoot with a yew bow." Grose's Milit. Antiq. i. 142.

paid by the ancient northern nations, in their Pagan state, to trees in general, and to oaks and yews in particular—a deeply-rooted habit, which for a long time infected the Christian converts of the north of Europe;[1] or, perhaps, the yew-tree might have been placed in churchyards as an emblem of that eternal youth and vigour the soul enjoys when its 'earthly tabernacle' is mouldered into dust.[2] Its frequency, however, in these scenes of mortal decay, has rendered it at length a necessary adjunct in the poetical sketches of a churchyard. The yew is now become the funereal tree; and the same honours are paid to it by the poets of the present age, as the cypress enjoyed from the bards of antiquity.[3] Parnell, for instance, gives us—

'the yew
Bathing a charnel-house with dew.'

Blair apostrophises it thus :
'Trusty yew !
Cheerless, unsocial plant, that loves to dwell
'Midst skulls and coffins, epitaphs and worms.'

Nor could Gray complete his picture without introducing 'the yew-tree's shade.' "

White, in his Selborne, p. 325, says: "Antiquaries seem much at a loss to determine at what period this tree first obtained a place in churchyards. A statute passed in 1307, and

[1] For the reverence paid to trees by the Gauls, see Pliny, lib. xvi. c. 34. Also, a learned disquisition on this subject in Keysler's Ant. Select. Septen. (Hanover, 1720,) p. 70 et infra. The difficulty of extirpating this ill-directed veneration was very great. "Diu etiam post Christi inductam religionem arborum, et lucorum cultum adeo invaluisse ac viguisse in Germania, Italia, Gallia, aliisque provinciis constat, ut in eo evellendo multum insudarint pontifices regesque," &c. Du Fresne's Gloss. i. 193, in 7. Arbores Sacr.

[2] "The yew was a funereal tree, the companion of the grave, among the Celtic tribes. 'Here,' says the bard, speaking of two departed lovers, ' rests their dust, Cuthullin ! These lonely yews sprang from their tomb, and shade them from the storm !'" Ossian, i. 240.

[3] It is doubtful whether the cypress was meant by the ancients to be an emblem of an immortal state, or of annihilation after death, since the properties of the tree apply, happily enough, to each. The cypress was used on funereal occasions, say the commentators, "vel quia cariem non sentit, ad gloriæ immortalitatem significandam ; vel quia semel excisa, non renascitur, ad mortem exprimendam." Vide Servius in Æn. III. 1. 64, and the Delphin edit. on the same passage.

35 Edw. I., the title of which is 'Ne Rector arbores in Ceme-
terio prosternat.' Now if it is recollected that we seldom see
any other very large or ancient tree in a churchyard but yews,
this statute must have principally related to this species of
tree; and consequently these being planted in churchyards is
of much more ancient date than the year 1307."

As to the use of these trees, possibly the more respectable
parishioners were buried under their shade before the improper
custom was introduced of burying within the body of the
church, where the living are to assemble. Deborah, Rebekah's
nurse (Gen. xxxv. 8), was buried under an oak, the most honorable place of interment, probably, next to the cave of
Machpelah (Gen. xxiii. 9), which seems to have been appropriated to the remains of the patriarchal family alone. The
farther use of yew-trees might be as a screen to churches, by
their thick foliage, from the violence of winds; perhaps, also,
for the purpose of archery, the best long bows being made of
that material; and we do not hear that they are planted in
the churchyards of other parts of Europe, where long bows
were not so much in use. They might also be placed as a
shelter to the congregation assembling before the church-
doors were opened, and as an emblem of mortality by their
funereal appearance. In the south of England every churchyard almost has its tree, and some two; but in the north,
we understand, few are to be found. The idea of R. C., that
the yew-tree afforded its branches instead of palms, for the
procession on Palm Sunday, is a good one, and deserves attention. See Gentleman's Magazine, l. 128.

In the ancient laws of Wales, given in the Cambrian Register, ii. 332, we read: "A *consecrated yew*, its value is a
pound." Upon looking into Wootton's Leges Wallicæ, 1730,
p. 262, I find the following: "*Taxus sancti* libram valet;"
with the subsequent note: "*Sancti* sancto, nempe alicui dicata,
dubritio v. gr. vel *teliao*, quales apud Wallos in cœmeteriis
etiamnum frequentes visuntur." So that the above ought to
be translated *a Saint's yew*, i. e. a yew dedicated to some
saint.

In the account of the parish of Burton (Preston Patrick)
Westmoreland, in Nicholson's and Burn's Westmoreland and
Cumberland, i. 242, we read: "Mr. Machel takes notice of a
yew-tree in the chapel-yard, which he says was very old and

decayed (1692), which shows, he observes, the antiquity of the chapel.[1] The yew-tree is there yet, which shows also the longevity of that species of wood. These yew-trees in church and chapel yards seem to have been intended originally for the use of archery. But this is only matter of conjecture; antiquity having not furnished any account (so far as we have been able to find) of the design of this kind of plantation." The Rev. Mr. Wrighte assures me that he remembers to have read in a book of churchwardens' accounts, in the possession of the late Mr. Littleton, of Bridgnorth, Salop, an account of a yew-tree being ordered to be planted in the churchyard *for reverence sake.* One may ask those who favour the opinion that yews were planted in churchyards for making bows, and as being there fenced from cattle, are not all plantation grounds fenced from cattle? and whence is it that there are usually but one yew-tree, or two, at the most, in each churchyard?

Sir Thomas Browne, in his Hydriotaphia, Urne-buriall, p. 56, tells us, that among the ancients, "the funerall pyre consisted of sweet fuell, cypresse, firre, larix, *yewe,* and trees perpetually verdant." And he asks, or rather observes, "Whether the planting of *yewe* in churchyards holds its original from ancient funerall rites, or as an embleme of resurrection from its perpetual verdure, may also admit conjecture."

In Sir John Sinclair's Statistical Account of Scotland, parish of Fortingal, co. Perth, ii. 456: "Among our curiosities may be reckoned a yew-tree in the churchyard of Fortingal, fifty-two feet round."[1] Ibid. iii. 144, the minister of Dunscore, shire of Dumfries, tells us: "The old burying-place is not tilled. Upon one corner of it grew a large yew-tree, which was consumed in the heart. Three men have stood in it at once; but it was overturned by the wind this season." Ibid. iv. 172, parish of Ormistoun, co. East Lothian, we read: "In Lord Hopetoun's garden at Ormistoun Hall there is a remarkable yew-tree. About the twentieth part of an English acre is

---

[1] Lysons, in the first volume of the Magna Britannia, pp. 254, 578, 643, 681, notices several yew-trees of enormous growth in the counties of Berks and Bucks; particularly one at Wyrardisbury, in the latter county, which, at six feet from the ground, measures thirty feet five inches in girth. There is a yew-tree of vast bulk at Ifley, in Oxfordshire, supposed to be coeval with the church, which is known to have been erected in the twelfth century. Others of great age may be seen in various parts of England.

covered by it. The diameter of the ground overspread by its branches is fifty-three feet, its trunk eleven feet in circumference. From the best information it cannot be under two hundred years old. It seems rather more probable to be between three hundred and four hundred years old." Ibid. xvi. 111 : "Two yew-trees at Ballikinrain, parish of Killearn, co. of Stirling, at a distance like one tree, cover an area of eighteen yards diameter." Ibid. xviii. 328: "There is a yew-tree in the garden of Broich, parish of Kippen, counties of Perth and Stirling. The circumference of the circle overspread by the lower branches is a hundred and forty feet. It is supposed to be two hundred or three hundred years old."

The following song in Shakespeare's Twelfth Night, act ii. sc. 4 (of which our poet gives this character—

> " Mark it, Cesario ; it is old and plain :
> The spinsters and the knitters in the sun,
> And the free maids that weave their thread with bones,
> Do use to chant it ;"—)

mentions the custom of *sticking yew in the shroud :*

> " Come away, come away, death,
> And in sad cypress let me be laid ;
> Fly away, fly away, breath :
> I am slain by a fair cruel maid.
> *My shroud of white, stuck all with yew,*
> O, prepare it ;
> My part of death no one so true
> Did share it.
> Not a flower, not a flower sweet,
> On my black coffin let there be strown ;"
> &c. &c.

And here the reader must be again reminded that in whatever country Shakespeare lays the scene of his drama, he follows the costume of his own. There is another song of like import in Ritson's Songs, 1790, p. 197, from the Maid's Tragedy, by Beaumont and Fletcher, 1619 :

> " Lay a garland on my hearse,
> Of the *dismal yew ;*
> Maidens, willow branches bear :
> Say I died true.
> My love was false, but I was firm
> From my hour of birth :
> Upon my buried body lie
> Lightly, gentle earth !"

In Poole's English Parnassus, the *yew* has the epithets of "warlick, dismal, fatal, mortal, venemous, unhappy, verdant, deadly, deadful," annexed to it: these are all from old English poets. Chaucer, in his Assemblie of Foules, calls it "the *shooter ewe*." The yew-tree is thus mentioned in Love's Festivall at Lust's Funerall, at the end of "a Boulster Lecture,'' 1640:

> "The screch owle frights us not, nor the towling bell
> Summons our vading-startling ghosts to hell.
> Tombs, forlorne charnels, unfrequented caves,
> The *fatall ewe, sad sociate to graves,*
> Present no figures to our dying eyes,
> 'Cause Vertue was our gole, her praise our prize."

The following is from Herrick's Hesperides, p. 27:

> "An' look, what smallage, night-shade, cypresse, *yew*,
> Unto the shades have been, or now are due,
> Here I devote."

Ibid. p. 126: "To the yew and cypresse to grace his funerall:"

> "Both you two have
> Relation to the grave:
> And where
> The fun'ral trump sounds, you are there."

In Gayton's Art of Longevity, 1659, p. 58, is the following passage alluding to St. Paul's Churchyard having been turned into a herb market:

> "The ewe, sad box, and cypress (solemn trees),
> Once church-yard guests (till burial rites did cease),
> Give place to sallads," &c.

A credible person, who was born and brought up in a village in Suffolk, informed me that when he was a boy, it was customary to cut sprigs and boughs of yew-trees to strew on the graves, &c. at rustic funerals. In Coles's Introduction to the Knowledge of Plants, 1656, p. 59, is an account of "the leaves of yew-trees poisoning a clergyman's cowes that eat them, who, seeing some boyes *breaking boughs from the yew-tree in the churchyard*, thought himselfe much injured. To prevent the like trespasses, he sent one presently to cut downe the tree, and to bring it into his back yard." Two of the cows feeding upon the leaves died in a few hours afterwards; and Coles remarks that the clergyman had a just reward.

In Collinson's History of Somersetshire, i. 13, speaking of two very large yew-trees in the churchyard at Ashill, the author observes in a note, that " our forefathers were particularly careful in preserving this funereal tree, whose branches it was *usual for mourners to carry in solemn procession to the grave, and afterwards,*" as has been already noticed, " *to deposit therein under the bodies of their departed friends.* The branches thus cut off from their native stock, which was to shoot forth again at the returning spring, were beautifully emblematical of the resurrection of the body, as, by reason of their perpetual verdure, they were of the immortality of the soul."

And as the carrying of these evergreens is an emblem of the soul's immortality, so it is also of the resurrection of the body : for as these herbs are not entirely plucked up, but only cut down, and will at the returning season revive and spring up again ; so the body, like them, is but cut down for a while, and will rise and shoot up again at the resurrection. For, in the language of the evangelical prophet, our bones shall flourish like an herb.

Bourne cites Gregory, c. 26, as observing, that it was customary among the ancient Jews, as they returned from the grave, to pluck up the grass two or three times, and then throw it behind them, saying these words of the Psalmist, " They shall flourish out of the city, like grass upon the earth," which they did to show that the body, though dead, should spring up again as the grass.[1]

---

[1] Levi, describing the rites and ceremonies of the Jews as they exist at present, says, p. 169: " The corpse is carried forward to the grave and interred by some of the society ; and as they go forth from the burying ground, they pluck some grass and say, ' They shall spring forth from the city, as the grass of the earth :' meaning at the day of the resurrection."

MUSIC AT FUNERALS, &c

VARIOUS are the proofs of the ancient custom of carrying
out the dead with psalmody in the primitive church;[1] in
imitation of which it is still customary in many parts of thi.,
nation to carry out the dead with singing of psalms and
hymns of triumph, to show that they have ended their spiritual
warfare, that they have finished their course with joy, and
are become conquerors. This exultation, as it were, for the
conquest of their deceased friend over hell, sin, and death,
was the great ceremony used in all funeral processions among
the ancient Christians.

In Pilkington's Burnynge of Paules Church, 1561, we
read: "In burialls we do not assemble a number of
priestes to swepe purgatorye, or bye forgivenes of synnes of
them whiche have no authoritye to sell, but accordinge to
Saint Jerom's example *we followe*. At the death of Fabiola,
sais he, the people of Ro. were gathered to the solemnite of
the buriall. *Psalmes were songe*, and *Alleluia sounding oute
on height*, did shake the gildet celinges of the temple. Here
was one companye of yonge menne and there another which
did singe the prayses and worthy dedes of the woman. And
no mervaile if men rejoyce of her salvation, of whose conversion th' angelles in heaven be glad. Thus Jerom used
burialls."

Stopford, in his Pagano-Papismus, p. 282, says: "The
heathens sang their dead to their graves, or places of burial.
Alex. ab Alexandro, Gen. Dier. lib. iii. cap. 7. And Macrobius
affirms, that this custom was according to the institutions of
several nations, and grounded upon this reason, because they
believed that souls after death returned to the original of
musical sweetness, that is heaven: and therefore in this life
every soul is taken with musical sounds, &c. In Somn. Sci-
pion. lib. ii. cap. 3. Other reasons are assigned by Kirkman,

[1] Bourne (chap. iii.) cites Socrates, telling us "that when the body of
Babylas the martyr was removed by the order of Julian the Apostate, the
Christians, with their women and children, rejoiced and sung psalms all
the way as they bore the corpse from Dauphne to Antioch. Thus was
Paula buried at Bethlehem, and thus did St. Anthony bury Paul the
hermite."

and several authorities urged for this custom : De Funeribus
Roman. lib. ii. cap. 4."[1]

I find the following passage in a rare book, entitled,
Greene in Conceipt, 1598, p. 43 : " It is a custome still in
use with Christians, to attend the funerall of their deceased
friendes with whole chantries of choyce quire-men singing
solemnly before them : but behinde followes a troope all clad
in blacke, which argues mourning : much have I marveled at
this ceremony, deeming it some hidden paradox, confounding
thus in one things so opposite as these signes of joy and
sorrowe." Pennant, in his MS. relating to North Wales, says,
"there is a custom of singing psalms on the way as the corpse
is carried to church."

Waldron, in his Description of the Isle of Man, p. 170,
speaking of the Manks burials, says : " The procession of
carrying the corpse to the grave is in this manner : when they
come within a quarter of a mile of the church they are met
by the parson, who walks before them singing a psalm, all the
company joining with him.   In every churchyard there is a
cross, round which they go three times before they enter the
church."   In Cymbeline, iv. 2, Arviragus, speaking of the
apparently dead body of Imogen, disguised in men's clothes,
says :

> " And let us, Polydore, *sing him to the ground,*
> As once our mother; use like note and words,
> Save that Euriphile must be Fidele."

Gough, in the introduction to the second volume of his
Sepulchral Monuments, p. 7, says: "*Music* and singing made
a part of funerals.   Macrobius assigns as a reason, that it implied the soul's return to the origin of harmony, or heaven.
Hyginus understands it to mean a signal of decent disposal of
the dead, and that they came fairly by their death, as the
tolling bell among Christians."

[1] The following passage is curious on the subject of singing psalms
before the corpse : " Cantilena feralis per Antiphonas in pompa funebri et
fano debacchata hinc est.   Inter Græcos demortui cadavere deposito in
inferiori domus aula ad portam, et peractis cæteris ceremoniis, cantores
funerales accedunt et Θρῆνον canunt, quibus per intervalla respondebant
domesticæ servæ, cum assistentium corona, neque solum domi, sed usque
ad sepulchrum præcedebant feretrum ita canentes."   Guichard, lib. ii.
cap. 2, Funeral. apud Moresini Papatum, &c. p. 32.

In the Praise of Musicke, by Dr. Case, 1586, the author says : " I wil end with death, the end of all mortality, which, though it be the dissolution of nature and parting of the soul from the body, terrible in itself to flesh and blood, and amplified with a number of displeasant and uncomfortable accidents, as the shaving of the head, howling, mourning apparel, *funeral boughes of yew, box, cipresse, and the like,* yet we shal find, by resorting to antiquities, that *musick hath had a share amongst them,* as being unseasonable at no time." [1]

Barnaby Rich, in his Irish Hubbub, 1619, p. 2, tells us : " Stanhurst, in his History of Ireland, maketh this report of his countreymen : they follow the dead corpse to the ground with howling, and barbarous outcries, pitifull in appearance, whereof (as he supposeth) grew this proverb, ' *to weep Irish.*' Myselfe am partly of his opinion, that (indeede) to weepe Irish is to weep at pleasure, without either cause or greefe, when it is an usuall matter amongst them, upon the buriall of their dead, to hire a company of women, that for some small recompence given them, they will follow the corpse, and furnish out the cry with such howling and barbarous outcries, that hee that should but heare them, and did not know the ceremony, would rather thinke they did sing than weep. And yet in Dublin itselfe there is not a corpse carried to the buriall which is not followed with this kinde of mourners, which you shall heare by their howling and their hollowing,

---

[1] The author of the Survey of the South of Ireland, pp. 206, 209, tells us : " It is the custom of this country to conduct their dead to the grave in all the parade they can display ; and as they pass through any town, or meet any remarkable person, they set up their howl. The conclamatio among the Romans coincides with the Irish cry. The ' Mulieres præficæ' exactly correspond with the women who lead the Irish band, and who make an outcry too outrageous for real grief.

' Ut qui conducti plorant in funere, dicunt
  Et faciunt prope plura dolentibus ex animo.'"

That this custom was Phœnician we may learn from Virgil, who was very correct in the costume of his characters. The conclamatio over the Phœnician Dido, as described by him, is similar to the Irish cry :

" Lamentis gemituque et fœmino ululatu
  Tecta fremunt."

The very word " ululatus," or " hulluloo," and the Greek word of the same import, have all a strong affinity to each other.

but never see them to shed any tears." "Such a kinde of lamentation," he adds, it is, "as in the judgement of any man that should but heare, and did not know their custome, would think it to bee some prodigious presagement, prognosticating some unlucky or ill successe, as they use to attribute to the howling of doggs, to the croaking of ravens, and the shrieking of owles, fitter for infidels and barbarians than to bee in use and custome among Christians."

The author of the Comical Pilgrim's Pilgrimage into Ireland, 1723, p. 92, says: "As soon as Death brings his last summons to any one, the wild Irish (both men, women, and children,) go before the corpse, and from his or her house to the church yard, set up a most hideous holoo, loo, loo, which may be heard two or three miles round the country." This custom is also alluded to in King's Art of Cookery, Works, 1776, iii. 87:

> " So at an Irish funeral appears
> A train of drabs with mercenary tears ;
> Who, wringing of their hands with hideous moan,
> Know not his name for whom they seem to groan :
> While real grief with silent steps proceeds,
> And love unfeign'd with inward passion bleeds."

In the Irish Hudibras, 1689, p. 31, we have the following *Form of an Irish Funeral,*—

> " Meanwhile the rout to work do fall,
> To celebrate the funeral.
> And first with turff from bog, and blocks,
> They make a fire would roast an oxe.
> Some lay the pipkins on, and some
> With holy water bathe his ***.
> Which office decently perform'd,
> The guests with usquebaugh well warm'd,
> They raise the cry, and so they fout him
> Unto a crate (i. e. cabin) to howl about him ;
> Where, in one end, the parted brother
> Was laid to rest, the cows in t'other.
> With all his followers and kin,
> Who, far and near, come crowding in,
> With *hub-bub-boos*, besides what cryers
> For greater state his highnes hires."

In Dutton's Statistical Survey of the County of Clare, 1808, p. 364, speaking of persons who attended wakes, he says : "And when they first enter the house, they set up the most hideous but *dry-ey'd yell,* called the Irish cry : this, however, lasts but a short time." The following is from an ingenious paper in the World, No. 24 (written, I believe, by Lord Chesterfield) : " When the lower sort of Irish, in the more uncivilized parts of Ireland, attend the funeral of a deceased friend or neighbour, before they give the last parting *howl*, they expostulate with the dead body, and reproach him with having died, notwithstanding that he had an excellent wife, a milch cow, seven fine children, and a competency of potatoes."

On the subject of the Irish howl, in Sir H. Piers's Description of West Meath, 1682, in Vallancey, i. 124, we read : " In Ireland at funerals they have their wakes, which, as now, they celebrate, were more befitting Heathens than Christians. They sit up commonly in a barn or large room, and are entertained with beer and tobacco. The lights are set up on a table over the dead ; they spend most of the night in obscene stories and bawdye songs, until the hour comes for the exercise of their devotions ; then the priest calls on them to fall to their prayers for the soul of the dead, which they perform by repetition of aves and paters on their beads, and close the whole with a ' De Profundis,' and then immediately to the story or song again, till another hour of prayer comes. Thus is the whole night spent till day. When the time of burial comes, all the women run out like mad, and now the scene is altered, nothing heard but *wretched exclamations, howling, and clapping of hands*, enough to destroy their own and others' sense of hearing : and this was of old the heathenish custom, as the poet hath observed, as translated by Dryden :

> ' The gaping croud around the body stand,
> All weep . . . . his fate,
> And hasten to perform the fun'ral state.'

" This they fail not to do, especially if the deceased were of good parentage, or of wealth and repute, or a landlord, &c., and think it a great honour to the dead to keep all this coyl, and some have been so vain as to hire these kind of mourners to attend their dead ; and yet they do not by all this attain the end they seem to aim at, which is to be thought to mourn for the dead ; for the poet hath well observed,

> ' The truly griev'd in secret weep.'

" At some stages, where commonly they meet with great heaps of stones in the way, the corpse is laid down, and the

priest or priests and all the learned fall again to their aves
and paters, &c. During this office all is quiet and hushed.
But this done, the corpse is raised, and with it the outcry
again. But that done, and while the corpse is laying down
and the earth throwing on, is the last and most vehement
scene of this formal grief; and all this perhaps but to earn a
groat, and from this Egyptian custom they are not to be
weaned. In some parts of Connaught, if the party deceased
were of good note, they will send to the wake hogsheads of
excellent stale beer and wine from all parts, with other provisions, as beef, &c., to help the expense at the funeral, and
oftentimes more is sent in than can well be spent."

Gough, in his Sepulchral Monuments, ii. Introd. 7, in a
note, says : "The women of Picardy have a custom of calling
the deceased by his name, as he is carried to the grave.
(Incert. des Signes de la Mort, p. 180.) So do the Indians,
and expostulate with him for dying. Χαιρε was a common
and affecting parting exclamation at the grave."

Howling at funerals appears to have been of general use in
the Papal times from the following passage in Vernon's
Hunting of Purgatory to Death, 1561, f. 37, where, speaking
of St. Chrysostom, he says : "No mention at al doth he make
of that manner of singinge or rather unseemely *howling* that
your Papists use for the salvation of theyr dead, therby, under
a pretence of godlinesse, picking the purses of the pore simple and ignorant people." Anthony Stafford, in his Meditations and Resolutions, 1612, p. 16, says : "It is a wonder to
see the *childish whining* we now-adayes use at the funeralls of
our friends. If we could *houl* them back againe, our lamentations were to some purpose; but as they are, they are vaine,
and in vain." In Whimzies, or a New Cast of Characters,
1631, p. 207, speaking of the death of "a zealous brother,"
the author says : "Some mourners hee hath of his owne, who
howle not so much that hee should leave them, as that nothing
is left them."

In the Statistical Account of Scotland, xv. 636, Parish of
Avoch, Ross-shire, we read: "At common funerals, in this
district, the corpse is preceded by the parish officer tolling a
hand-bell. The pall or mort-cloth is of plain black velvet,
without any decoration, except a fringe. An immense crowd
of both sexes attend; and the lamentations of the women, in

some cases, on seeing a beloved relative put into the grave, would almost pierce a heart of stone."

Park, in his Travels in the Interior of Africa, tells, that among the Moors, April 3, a child died in one of the tents, "and the mother and the relations immediately began the death-howl. They were joined by a number of female visitors, who came on purpose 'to assist at this melancholy concert. I had no opportunity of seeing the burial, which is generally performed secretly in the dusk of the evening, and frequently at only a few yards distance from the tent. Over the grave they plant one particular shrub ; and no stranger is allowed to pluck a leaf, or even to touch it." Speaking elsewhere of the Negroes, he says : " When a person of consequence dies, the relations and neighbours meet together and manifest their sorrow by loud howlings."

In Dudley Lord North's Forest of Varieties, 1645, at p. 80, is preserved the following *Requiem at the Entertainment of Lady Rich,* who died August 24th, 1638 :

" Whoe'er you are, patron subordinate,
    Unto this house of prayer, and doe extend
    Your eare and care to what we pray and lend ;
    May this place stand for ever consecrate :

And may this ground and you propitious be
    To this once powerful, now potential dust,
    Concredited to your fraternal trust,
    Till friends, souls, bodies meet eternally.

And thou, *her tutelary angel,* who
    Wert happy guardian to so faire a charge,
    O leave not now part of thy care at large,
    But tender it as thou wert wont to do.

Time, common father, join with mother Earth,
    And though you all confound, and she convert,
    Favour this relique of divine desert,
    Deposited for a ne'er dying birth.

Saint, church, earth, angel, time, prove truly kind
    As she to you, to this bequest consign'd."

In Batt upon Batt, a Poem on the Parts, Patience, and Pains of Barth. Kempster, already quoted more than once, we find a notice of what is called *stirrup verse* at the grave, p. 12 :

" Must Megg, the wife of Batt, aged eightie,
    Deceas'd November thirteenth, seventy-three,

II.   18

Be cast, like common dust, into the pit,
Without one line of monumental wit ?
One death's-head distich, or mortality-staff
With sense enough for churchyard epitaph ?
No *stirrup verse at grave* before she go ?
Batt does not use to part at tavern so."

In Poems by the Rev. John Black, of Butley in Suffolk, 1799, p. 10, in "an Elegy on the Author's Mother, who was buried in the churchyard of Dunichen in Scotland," is the following stanza :

" Oh, how my soul was griev'd, *when I let fall*
The string that dropt her silent in the grave !
Yet thought I then I heard her spirit call :
' Safe I have pass'd through death's o'erwhelming wave.' "

On the second line the author has this note : " In Scotland it is the custom of the relations of the deceased themselves to let down the corpse into the grave, by mourning cords, fastened to the handles of the coffin ; the chief mourner standing at the head, and the rest of the relations arranged according to their propinquity. When the coffin is let down and adjusted in the grave, the mourners first, and then all the surrounding multitude, uncover their heads ; there is no funeral service read, no oration delivered : but that solemn pause, for about the space of ten minutes, when every one is supposed to be meditating on death and immortality, always struck my heart in the most awful manner ; never more than on the occasion here alluded to. The sound of the cord, when it fell on the coffin, still seems to vibrate on my ear."

The ancient Christians to testify their abhorrence of Heathen rites, rejected the Pagan custom of burning the dead, depositing the inanimate body entire in the ground. Thus I found at Rutchester, one of the stations upon the Roman wall in Northumberland, a sepulchre hewn out of the living rock, wherein, Leland says, Paulinus, who converted the Northumbrians to Christianity, was interred.

The belief in Yorkshire was, amongst the vulgar, says Aubrey, and perhaps is, in part, still, that after a person's death, the soul went over Whinny Moor ; and till about 1624, at the funeral, a woman came (like a Præfica) and sung the following song :

" Thio oan night, this ean night,
   Every night and awle,
Fire and fleet (*water*) and candle-light,
   And Christ receive thy sawle.
When thou from hence doest pass away,
   Every night and awle,
To Whinny-Moor[1] [silly poor] thou comest at last,
   And Christ receive thy sawle.
If ever thou gave either hosen or shoon (*shoes*),
   Every night and awle,
Sit thee down and putt them on,
   And Christ receive thy sawle.
But if hosen nor shoon thou never gave naen,
   Every night and awle,
The whinnes shall prick thee to the bare beane,
   And Christ receive thy sawle.
From Whinny-Moor that thou mayst pass,
   Every night and awle,
To Brig o' Dread thou comest at last,
   And Christ receive thy sawle.
From Brig of Dread, na brader than a thread,
   Every night and awle,
To purgatory fire thou com'st at last,
   And Christ receive thy sawle.
If ever thou gavo oithor milke or drink,
   Every night and awle,
The fire shall never make thee shrink,
   And Christ receive thy sawle.
But if milk nor drink thou never gave naen,
   Every night and awle,
The fire shall burn thee to the bare beane,
   And Christ receive thy sawle."

This song, with one or two trifling variations, is printed under the title of a Lyke-Wake Dirge, in the Minstrelsy of the Scottish Border, ii. 363.

I found in a collection of Old Epigrams of the time of James the First, the following quaint one on the subject of carrying the body to the grave with the feet foremost:

" 517. *Man's Ingress and Egress.*

" Nature, which headlong into life did throng us,
   With our feet forward to our grave doth bring us;
   What is less ours than this our borrowed breath?
   We stumble into life, we goe to death."

---

[1] From *whin*, furze.

Sir Thomas Browne, in his Urne-burial, observes, that "the custom of carrying the corpse as it were out of the world with its feet forward is not inconsonant to reason, as contrary to the native posture of man, and his production first into it."

TORCHES AND LIGHTS AT FUNERALS.

THE custom of using torches and lights at funerals, or in funeral processions, appears to have been of long standing.[1] The learned Gregory tells us that "the funeral tapers, however thought of by some, are of harmlesse import. Their meaning is to show that the departed soules are not quite put out, but having walked here as the children of light, are now gone to walk before God in the light of the living."[2]

Strutt tells us, Manners and Customs, ii. 108, the burning

---

[1] "Dum autem funus efferebatur, faces præferebantur. Constantii corpus delatum fuisse nocturnis cantionibus et cereorum ignibus," &c. Durand. de Ritibus, p. 228. "Gallos funus honorificè curasse et multitudinem luminum, splendorem sibi etiam per diem vendicantem, repercusso solis radio repulsisse," &c. Ibid.

[2] Gregorii Opuscula, p. 112. See also Gough's Introd. to vol. ii. Sepulchral Monuments in Great Britain, p. 7 : "Among the Romans public funerals were celebrated in the day ; private burials at night : and both were accompanied with torches." Female Mentor, ii. 196. "All funerals," says Adam, in his Roman Antiquities, 1792, p. 476, "used anciently to be solemnized in the night-time with torches, that they might not fall in the way of magistrates and priests, who were supposed to be violated by seeing a corpse, so that they could not perform sacred rites till they were purified by an expiatory sacrifice. Serv. in Virg. xi. 143 ; Donat. Ter. And. i. 1, 81. Thus, to diminish the expenses of funerals, it was ordained by Demetrius Phalerius at Athens, Cic. de Legg. ii. 26, according to an ancient law which seems to have fallen into desuetude, Demosth. adv. Macartatum, p. 666. Hence funus, a funeral, from funes accensi, Isid. xi. 2, xx. 10, or funalia, funales cerei, cereæ faces, vel candelæ, torches, candles or tapers, originally made of small ropes or cords (funes vel funiculi), covered with wax or tallow (sevum vel sebum). Serv. ibid. et Æn. i. 727 ; Val. Max. iii. ; 6, 4 ; Var. de Vit. Pop. R. But in after ages public funerals (funera indictiva) were celebrated in the day-time, at an early hour in the forenoon, as it is thought from Plutarch, in Syl., with torches also. Serv. in Virg. Æn. vi. 224 ; Tac. Ann. iii. 4. Private or ordinary funerals (tacita) were always at night. Fest. in Vespilones."

of torches was very honorable. To have a great many was a special mark of esteem in the person who made the funeral to the deceased. By the will of William de Montacute, Earl of Salisbury, executed April 29, 1397 : "Twenty-four poor people, clothed in black gowns and red hoods, are ordered to attend the funeral, *each carrying a lighted torch of eight pounds' weight.*" In Nichols's Illustrations, 1797, Churchw. Accounts of St. Margaret's Westminster, p. 1, under 1460-1, is the following article: "Item. rec. de Joh'e Braddyns die sepultur' Roberti Thorp gen. p. iiii. Tor. vjs. viijd." On which Dr. Pegge observes, p. 243 : "Little was done in these ages of gross Popery without lights. These torches cost 1s. 8d. apiece; but we find them of various prices, according, as we may suppose, to their size. The churchwardens appear to have provided them, and consequently they were an article of profit to the church." The editor adds : " These torches, it is conceived, were made of wax, which in ordinary cases were let out by the church, and charged to the party according to the consumption at the moment. This appears in the York churchwardens' accompts, where wax is charged." Ibid. p. 8, A.D. 1519: "Item, Mr. Hall, the curate, for iv. torches, and for the best lights, at the buryal of Mr. Henry Vued, my Lord Cardinal's servant, vjs. vjd."

In Coates's History of Reading, 1802, p. 115, in the church-wardens' accounts of St. Lawrence's parish are the following articles : " 1502. It. rec. of wast of torchis at the berying of Sir John Hide, vicar of Sonyng, ijs. vjd. 1503. It. rec. for wast of torchys at the burying of John Long, maist' of the gram' scole, vjs. viijd. 1504. It. rec. of the same Margaret," (late the wife of Thomas Platt,) " for wast of torchis at the yer mind of the seid Thomas, xxd." See also Strype's edit. of Stowe's Survey of London, i. 258, A.D. 1556, Sir John Gresham's funeral, "He had *four dozen of great staff torches* and *a dozen of great long torches.*"

Veron, in his Hunting of Purgatory to Death, 1561, f. 40, says : " If the Christians should bury their dead in the *nighte*-time, or if they should burne their bodies, as the Painims did, *they might well use torches* as well as the Painims without any just reprehension and blame." He observes, f. 45 : " Moreover it is not to be doubted but that the auncient byshops and ministers of the church did bryng in this manner of *bearinge of*

torches, and singinge in funerals, not for thentent and purpose
that the Painimes did use it, nor yet for to confirme their superstitious abuses and errours, but rather for to abolishe them.
For they did see that it was an hard thing to pluck those old
and inveterate customes from the heartes of them that had
been nouselled in them from their youth. They did forsee
that, if they had buried their dead without som honest ceremonies, as the worlde did then take them, it had bene yet
more harde to put away those olde rotten errors from them,
that were altogether wedded unto them." Our author tells
us, ibid. fol. 47 : "Chrisostome, likening the deade whome
they followed with burnynge torches unto wrestlers and run-
ners, had a respect unto the customes and fashions of Greke
land, beyng a Greeke himselfe, amonge whiche there was a
certain kind of running after this manner: The firste did
beare a torche, being lighted, in his hand, which, being weary,
he did deliver unto him that followeth next after him. He
againe, that had received the torche, if he chaunced to be
wery, did the like ; and so all the residue that followeth in
order ;" hence "among the Grekes and Latines to geve the
lampe or torche unto another hath beene taken for to put
other in his place, after that one is werye and hath perfourmed
his course." He concludes : "This may very wel be applyed
unto them that departe out of this world." Ibid. f. 151 :
"Singinge, *bearinge of lights,* and other like ceremonies as
were used in their buringes and funeralles, were ordeyned, or
rather permitted and suffred, by ye auncient bishoppes and
pastours, for to abolish, put downe, and dryve awai the superstition and ydolatri y^t the heathen and paynymes used
about their dead ; and not for anye opinion y^t they had y^t suche
thinges could profite the soules of the departed, as it doth
manifestly appear by their owne writinges."[1]

Monsieur Jorevin, before cited, describing a lord's burial near
Shrewsbury, speaking of six men taking up the corpse, and
carrying it on their shoulders to the church, says : "It was

[1] The following is the epitaph of the great Budè at St. Geneviève,
Paris :

"Que n'a-t-on plus en torches dependu,
Suivant la mode accoutumée en sainte ?
Afin qu'il soit *par l'obscur entendu*
Que des François *la lumière est éteinte.*"

covered with a large cloth, which the four nearest relations held each by a corner with one hand, and in the other carried a bough" (this must have been a branch of rosemary) ; " the other relations and friends had in one hand *a flambeau*, and in the other a bough, marching thus through the street, without singing or saying any prayer, till they came to the church." After the burial service, he adds, the clergyman, " having his bough in his hand like the rest of the congregation, threw it on the dead body when it was put into the grave, as did all the relations, *extinguishing their flambeaux in the earth* with which the corpse was to be covered. This finished, every one retired to his home without further ceremony." See the Antiquarian Repertory, ii. 101-2.

Wordsworth, in his Lyrical Ballads, ii. 147, tells us that in several parts of the North of England, when a funeral takes place, a basin full of sprigs of box-wood is placed at the door of the house from which the coffin is taken up, and each person who attends the funeral ordinarily takes a sprig of this wood, and throws it into the grave of the deceased.

FUNERAL SERMONS.

FUNERAL sermons are of great antiquity.[1] This custom used to be very general in England. I know nowhere that it is retained at present, except upon Portland Island, Dorsetshire, where the minister has half-a-guinea for every sermon he preaches, by which he raises annually a very considerable sum. This species of luxury in grief is very common there, and indeed, as it conveys the idea of posthumous honour, all are desirous of procuring it, even for the youngest of their children, as well as their deceased friends. The fee is nearly the same as that mentioned by Gay in his dirge :

" Twenty good shillings in a rag I laid,
Be *ten* the parson's for his sermon paid."

Gough, in the introduction to the second volume of his

[1] " Ceterum priusquam corpus humo injecta contegatur, defunctus **oratione** funebri laudabatur." Durand, p. 236.

Sepulchral Monuments, p. 11, says : "From funeral orations over Christian martyrs have followed funeral sermons for eminent Christians of all denominations, whether founded in esteem, or sanctioned by fashion, or secured by reward. Our ancestors, before the Reformation, took especial care to secure the repose and well-being of their souls, by masses and other deeds of piety and charity. After that event was supposed to have dispelled the gloom of superstition, and done away the painful doctrine of purgatory, they became more solicitous to have their memories embalmed, and the example of their good works held forth to posterity. Texts were left to be preached from, and sometimes money to pay for such preaching. Gratitude founded *commemorative sermons*, as well as commemorative dinners, for benefactors."

In Cotgrave's Treasury of Wit and Language, p. 35, we read,

> " In all this sermon I have heard little commendations
> Of our dear brother departed : rich men doe not go
> To the pit-hole without complement of Christian buriall."

Even such an infamous character as Madam Creswell had her funeral sermon. She desired by will to have a sermon preached *at her funeral*, for which the preacher was to have ten pounds ; but upon this express condition, that he was to say nothing but what was *well* of her. A preacher was, with some difficulty, found, who undertook the task. He, after a sermon preached on the general subject of mortality, and the good uses to be made of it, concluded with saying, ' By the will of the deceased it is expected that I should mention her, and say nothing but what was *well* of her. All that I shall say of her, therefore, is this : she was born *well*, she lived *well*, and she died *well ;* for she was born with the name of Cresswell, she lived in Clerkenwell, and she died in Bridewell.'

Dr. Fuller, in his Appeal of Injured Innocence, (Part iii. p. 75,) tells us that "When one was to preach the funeral sermon of a most vicious and generally hated person, all wondered what he would say in his praise ; the preacher's friends fearing, his foes hoping, that, for his fee, he would force his conscience to flattery. For one thing, said the minister, this man is to be spoken well of by all ; and, for another thing, he is to be spoken ill of by none. The first is,

because God made him, the second because he is dead."
Granger's Biogr. Hist. 1775, iv. 218.

Misson, in his Travels in England, translated by Ozell, p. 93, speaking of our funerals, says: " The common practice is to carry the corpse into the body of the church, where they set it down upon two tressels, while either *a funeral sermon is preached, containing an eulogium upon the deceased,* or certain prayers said, adapted to the occasion. If the body is not buried in the church, they carry it to the churchyard, where it is interred (after the minister has performed the service which may be seen in the Book of Common Prayer) in the presence of the guests, who are round the grave, and do not leave it till the earth is thrown in upon it. Then they return home in the same order that they came."

It is still a custom for the ordinary of Newgate to preach a funeral sermon before each execution. Compare Whimzies, or a New Cast of Characters, 1631, p. 70.

In the Burnynge of Paule's Church in London, 1561, 8vo. 1563, we read: " Gregory Nazanzene hais his funerall sermons and orations in the commendacion of the party departed; so hais Ambrose for Theodosius and Valentinian the emperours, for his brother Statirus," &c.

The author of the Philosophical Survey of the South of Ireland, says, p. 207 : " It was formerly usual to have a bard to write the elegy of the deceased, which contained an enumeration of his good qualities, his genealogy, his riches, &c. ; the burden being, 'O why did he die?' "

BLACK USED IN MOURNING

AT FUNERALS.

DURAND mentions black as anciently in use at funerals, which St. Cyprian seems to have inveighed against as the indication of sorrow, on an event which to the Christian was matter of joy.[1]

[1] " Induebantur atris vestibus, præsertim apud Gallos: hunc tamen lugubrem et atrum amictum videturim probare Cyprian., Serm. de Mortalitate."—Durand. de Rit. p. 225. Cyprian's words are: " Cum sciamus

Gough, in the Introd. vol. ii. Sepulchral Monuments, p. 20, gives us numerous references to the classics to prove that the colour of mourning garments has, in most instances, been black from the earliest antiquity.

Langley, in his translation of Polidore Vergil, f. 123, says : "Plutarch writeth that the women in their mournyng laied a parte all purple, golde, and sumptuous apparell, and were clothed bothe they and their kinsfolk in white apparel, like as then the ded body was wrapped in white clothes. The white coloure was thought fittest for the ded, because it is clere, pure, and sincer, and leaste defiled. Of this ceremonie, as I take it, the French quenes toke occasion, after the death of their housebandes, the kynges, to weare onely white clothyng, and if there bee any suche widdowe, she is commonly called the White Quene. Mournyng garments for the moste part be altogether of blacke coloure, and they use to weare theim a whole yere continually, onlesse it bee because of a generall triumphe or rejoysyng, or newe magistrate chosyng, or els when thei bee toward marriage." Cotgrave, in his Treasury of Wit and Language, p. 36, has these lines :

> " Funeralls hide men in civill wearing,
> And are to the drapers a good hearing,
> Make th' heralds laugh in their black rayment,
> And all dye worthies dye worth payment
> To th' altar offerings, though their fame,
> And all the charity of their name
> 'Tween heaven and this, yeeld no more light
> Than rotten trees which shine in the night."

In the Supplement to the Athenian Oracle, p. 301, it is stated that " Black is the fittest emblem of that sorrow and grief the mind is supposed to be clouded with ; and, as death is the privation of life, and black a privation of light, 'tis very probable this colour has been chosen to denote sadness upon that account ; and accordingly this colour has, for mourning, been preferred by most people throughout Europe. The Syrians, Cappadocians, and Armenians, use skye-colour, to denote the place they wish the dead to be in, i. e. the heavens ; the Egyptians yellow, or fillemot, to show that, as herbs being

---

fratres nostros accersione dominica de seculo liberatos, non amitti sed præmitti, *non sunt nobis hic accipiendæ atræ vestes*, quando illi ibi indumenta alba jam sumpserint."

faded become yellow, so death is the end of human hope, and the Ethiopians grey, because it resembles the colour of the earth, which receives the dead. So in Romeo and Juliet:

" All things that we ordained festival,
  Turn from their office to *black funeral;*
  Our instruments to melancholy bells;
  Our wedding cheer to a sad burial feast;
  Our solemn hymns to sullen dirges change;
  Our bridal flowers serve for a buried corse,
  And all things change them to their contraries."

Granger, however, tells us, " it is recorded that Anne Bullen wore yellow mourning for Catharine of Arragon." For his authority he refers to Walpole's Anecdotes of Painting. The same circumstance is found in Hall's Chronicle, with the addition of Henry's wearing white mourning for the unfortunate Anne Bullen.[1] Crimson would have been a much more suitable colour.[2] In England it was formerly the fashion to mourn a year for very near relations. Thus Pope:

" Grieve for an hour perhaps, then mourn a year."

Dupree tells us, in his Conformity, p. 181, that the ancient Romans employed certain persons, named *Designatores,* clothed in black, to invite people to funerals, and to carry the coffin. There are persons in our days who wear the same clothing, and serve the same office. The Romans, saith Marolles, had, in their ceremonies, lictors, dressed in black, who did the office of our mourners.

At the funerals of unmarried persons of both sexes, as well as infants, the scarves, hatbands, and gloves, given as mourning, are white. In the Archæologia, 1796, vol. xii. the Rev. Mr. Wrighte, in his Short Notices relating to the Parish of Llanvetherine, Monmouthshire, p. 100, says: " In such ob-

---

[1] In a rare book on dreams, by Thomas Hill, *b. l.* is the following passage: " To a sicke person to have or weare on white garments doothe promyse death, for that *dead bodyes bee caryed foorth in white clothes.* And to weare on a blacke garmente, it doothe promyse, for the more parte, healthe to a sicke personne, for that not dead personnes, but suche as mourne for the deade, do use to be clothed in blacke."

[2] In Sir John Sinclair's Statistical Account of Scotland, ii. 80, the minister of Galston, in Ayrshire, informs us, " It is usual for even the women to attend funerals in the village, drest in black or red cloaks."

scure parts of the kingdom ancient customs are frequently retained. The common people of this parish tie a dirty cloth about their heads when they appear as *chief mourners at a funeral.* The same custom likewise prevails in different places."

PALL AND UNDER BEARERS.

SOMETHING, instead of the pall used at present to cover the coffin, appears by Durand to have been of great antiquity.[1] He informs us, in many quotations from the ancient Christian writers, that those of the highest orders of clergy thought it no reproach to their dignity, in ancient times, to carry the bier; and that at the funeral of Paula bishops were what in modern language we call under bearers.[2] How different an idea of this office prevails in our times!

Misson, in his Travels in England, transl. by Ozell, p. 91, says : " The parish has always three or four mortuary cloths of different prices (the handsomest is hired out at five or six crowns), to furnish those who are at the charge of the interment. These cloths, which they call *palls,* are some of black velvet, others of cloth with an edge of white linen or silk a foot broad, or thereabouts. For a bachelor or maid, or for a woman that dies in childbed, the pall is white. This is spread over the coffin, and is so broad that the six or eight men in black clothes that carry the body (upon their shoulders) are quite hid beneath it to their waist; and the corners and sides of it hang down low enough to be borne by those (six friends, men or women, according to the occasion) who, according to custom, are invited for that purpose. They generally give black or white gloves, and black crape hatbands, to those that carry the pall; sometimes, also, white silk scarves."

Undertakers, now, provide the palls. For men, black silk scarves are sometimes given, sometimes they are of black

[1] " In nobilibus, aureum velamentum superferetrum, quo corpus obtegeretur, apponi consuetum." Durand. p. 225.

[2] " Paulam translatam fuisse episcoporum manibus, cervicem feretro subjicientibus." Durand, p. 227. From this it appears too that the corpse was carried shoulder-height, as the term now is.

satin. In the Irish Hudibras, p. 35, is given the following description of *the burial of an Irish piper:*

> " They mounted him upon a bier,
> Through which the wattles did appear,
> Like ribs on either side made fast,
> With a white velvet (i. e. *blanket*) over cast :
> So poor Macshane, God rest his shoul,
> Was after put him in a hole ;
> In which, with many sighs and scrieches,
> They throw his trouses and his breeches ;
> The tatter'd brogue was after throw,
> With a new heel-piece on the toe ;
> And stockins fine as friez to feel,
> Worn out with praying at the heel ;
> And in his mouth, 'gainst he took wherry,
> Dropt *a white groat* to pay the ferry.
> Thus did they make this last hard shift,
> To furnish him for *a dead lift.*"

Pennant, in his MS. relating to North Wales, informs us that " at these words, ' we commit the body to the ground,' the minister holds the spade, and throws in the first spadeful of earth. Skiviog."[1]

[1] Mr. Pennant's MS. says : " At Skiv'og, from the park to the church *I have seen the bier carried by the next of kin, husband, brothers, and father-in-law.* All along from the house to the churchyard, at every cross-way, the bier is laid down, and the Lord's prayer rehearsed, and so when they first come into the churchyard, before any of the verses appointed in the service be said. There is a custom of ringing a little bell before the corpse, from the house to the churchyard. (Dymerchion.) Some particular places are called resting-places. Skyv'og. When a corpse is carried to church from any part of the town, the bearers take care to carry it so that the corpse may be on the right hand, though the way be nearer, and it be less trouble to go on the other side ; nor will they bring the corpse through any other way than the south gate. If it should happen to rain while the corpse is carried to the church, it is reckoned to bode well to the deceased, whose bier is wet with the dew of heaven. At church the evening service is read, with the office of burial. The minister goes to the altar, and there says the Lord's prayer, with one of the prayers appointed to be read at the grave : after which the congregation offer upon the altar, or on a little board for that purpose fixed to the rails of the altar, their benevolence to the officiating minister. A friend of the deceased is appointed to stand at the altar, observing who gives, and how much. When all have given he counts the money with the minister, and signifies the sum to the congregation, thanking them all for their good will."

In the Hydriotaphia, or Urne Burial of Sir Thomas Browne, p. 56, speaking of the ancient heathens, he says: "Their last valediction thrice uttered by the attendants was also very solemn: 'Vale, vale, vale, nos te ordine quo Natura permittet sequemur:' and somewhat answered by Christians, who thought it too little *if they threw not the earth thrice upon the interred body.*"

We read, in the Glossary to Kennett's Parochial Antiquities, in v. *Oblationes Funerales:* "At the burial of the dead it was a custom for the surviving friends to offer liberally at the altar for the pious use of the priest, and the good estate of the soul of the deceased. This pious custom doth still obtain in North Wales, where at the rails which decently defend the communion table, I have seen a small tablet or flat board conveniently fixed to receive the money, which at every funeral is offered by the surviving friends, according to their own ability and the quality of the party deceased; which seems a providential augmentation to some of those poor churches."

In the Life of Mr. George Herbert, written by Izaack Walton, 1670, p. 70, speaking of Herbert's ordination, our biographer tells us: "at which time the Reverend Dr. Humphrey Henchman, now Lord bishop of London, tells me, he laid his hand on Mr. Herbert's head, and (alas!) within less than three years *lent his shoulder to carry his dear friend to his grave.*"

In Sinclair's Statistical Account of Scotland, iii. 525, the minister of Tongue, co. Sutherland, after having mentioned the funeral entertainment ("for at the burial of the poorest here there is a refreshment given, consisting generally of some whisquybeath, or some foreign liquor, butter and cheese, with oat bread,") says, after this, "the friends of the deceased, and neighbours of the village, who come to witness the interment, are drawn up in rank and file by an old serjeant, or some veteran who has been in the army, and who attends to maintain order, and give, as they term it here, the word of relief. Upon his crying *Relief!* the four under the bier prepare to leave their stations, and make room for other four that instantly succeed. This progression is observed at the interval of every five minutes, till the whole attendants come in regularly, and, if the distance requires it there is a second, a third, or a fourth round of such evolutions gone through. When the persons present are not inflamed with liquor there is a pofound silence generally observed, from the time the corpse has been taken up till the interment is over."[1]

DOLES AND INVITATIONS AT FUNERALS.

Doles were used at funerals, as we learn from St. Chrysostom, to procure rest to the soul of the deceased, that he might find his judge propitious.[2]

The giving of a dole, and the inviting of the poor[3] on this occasion, are synonymous terms. There are some strong figurative expressions on this subject in St. Ambrose's Funeral Oration on Satyrus, cited by Durand. Speaking of those who mourned on the occasion, he says : "The poor also shed their tears ; precious and fruitful tears, that washed away the sins of the deceased. They let fall floods of redeeming tears." From such passages as the above in the first Christian writers, literally understood, the Romanists may have derived their superstitious doctrine of praying for the dead.

Strutt, in his English Æra, tells us that Sir Robert Knolles, in the eighth year of Henry IV., died at his manor in Norfolk, and his dead body was brought in a litter to London with

[1] In another part of the Statistical Account of Scotland, vii. 622, Dundonald parish, Ayrshire, we read : " Country burials are not well regulated. The company are invited at eleven o'clock forenoon, but they are probably not all arrived at two. Till of late a pipe and tobacco was provided for every one of the company ; but this custom is entirely laid aside."

[2] Μαλλον δε τι μετα ταυτα πενητας καλεῖς; ινα εις αναπαυσιν απελθῃ ινα ιλεω σχῃ τον δικαστην. Homilia xxxii. in Matthei cap. non.

[3] " Preteria convocabantur et invitabantur necdum sacerdotes et religiosi, sed et egeni pauperes." Durand.   Had our famous poet, Mr. Pope, an eye to this in ordering, by will, poor men to support his pall ? By the will of William de Montacute, Earl of Salisbury, executed April 29, 1397, he directs " that twenty-five shillings should be daily distributed among three hundred poor people from the time of his death to the arrival ot his body at the conventual church of Bustlesham, in which it was to be deposited." See Warner's Topographical Remarks, relating to the South-western parts of Hampshire, ii. 73.

great pomp and much torchlight, and it was buried in the White
Friars' church, "where was done for him a solemn obsequie,
with a great feast and *lyberal dole* to the poore." This custom, says Strutt, of giving a funeral feast to the chief
mourners, was universally practised all over the kingdom, as
well as giving alms to the poor, in proportion to the quality
and finances of the deceased. Manners and Customs, ii. 209.
See a curious account of doles in Dr. Ducarel's Tour through
Normandy, fol. ed. p. 81.

Among the articles of expense at the funeral of Sir John
Rudstone, Mayor of London, 1531, given by Strutt, iii. 169,
from MS. Harl. 1231, we find the following charges : " Item,
to the priests at his ennelling,[1] 9s. ; to poor folke in almys,
£1 5s. ; 22 days to 6 poor folke, 2s. ; 26 days to a poor
folke, 8d." Hutchinson, in his History of Cumberland, i.
579, speaking of Eskdale chapelry, says : " Wakes and doles
are customary ; and weddings, christenings, and funerals are
always attended by the neighbours, sometimes to the amount
of a hundred people. The popular diversions are hunting
and cock-fighting." Nichols, in his History of Leicestershire,
ii. part i. p. 357, speaking of Stathern in Framland hundred,
says : " In 1790 there were 432 inhabitants, the number
taken by the last person who carried about bread, which was
given for *dole* at a funeral ; a custom formerly common
throughout this part of England, though now fallen much
into disuse. The practice was sometimes to bequeath it by
will ; but, whether so specified or not, the ceremony was seldom omitted. On such occasions a small loaf was sent to
every person, without any distinction of age or circumstances, and not to receive it was a mark of particular disrespect."[2]

Pennant, in his History of Whiteford Parish, p. 99, says :
" Offerings at funerals are kept up here, and, I believe, in all

[1] Anointing with holy oil. See Halliwell's Dict., p. 61.
[2] Mr. Lysons, in his Environs of London, iii. 341, speaking of some
.ands said to have been given by two maiden gentlewomen to the parish
of Paddington, for the purpose of distributing bread, cheese, and beer
among the inhabitants on the Sunday before Christmas-day, tells us that
they are now let at £21 per annum, and that " the bread was formerly
thrown from the church-steeple to be scrambled for, and part of it is still
distributed in that way."

the Welsh churches." He also says : " In North Wales, pence and half-pence (in lieu of little rolls of bread), which were heretofore, and by some still are, given on these occasions, are now distributed to the poor, who flock in great numbers to the house of the dead before the corpse is brought out. When the corpse is brought out of the house, laid upon the bier, and covered, before it be taken up, the next of kin to the deceased, widow, mother, daughter or cousin, (never done by a man,) gives, over the corpse, to one of the poorest neighbours, three 2*d.* or four 3*d.* white loaves of bread, or a cheese with a piece of money stuck in it, and then a new wooden cup of drink, which some will require the poor person who receives it immediately to drink a little of. When this is done, the minister, if present, says the Lord's prayer, and then they set forward for church. The things mentioned above as given to a poor body are brought upon a large dish over the corpse, and the poor body returns thanks for them, and blesses God for the happiness of his friend and neighbour deceased." This custom is evidently a remain of the *Sin-Eating,* q. v.

It appears from the Statistical Account of Scotland, v. 523, that at Glasgow large donations at funerals are made to the poor, "which are never less than five pounds, and never exceed ten guineas, in which case the bells of the city are tolled."

In Dives and Pauper, First Precept, chap. 63, we read : "*Dives.* What seyst thou of them that wole no solemnyté have in their buryinge, but be putt in erthe anon, and that that shulde be spent aboute the buriyng they bydde that it shulde be yoven to the pore folke blynde and lame ?—*Pauper.* Comonly in such prive buriynges ben *ful smalle doles and lytel almes yoven, and in solemne buriynges been grete doles and moche almesse[1] yoven, for moche pore people come thanne to seke almesse.* But whanne it is done prively, fewe wytte therof, and fewe come to axe almesse! for they wote nat whanne ne where, ne whom they shulde axe it. And therefore I leve sikerly that summe fals executoures that wolde kepe alle to themself biganne firste this errour and this folye, that

1 Alms. See examples in Halliwell's Dict., p. 47.

wolden make themself riche with ded mennys godes, and nat
dele to the pore after dedes wylle, as nowe all false executoures
use by custome."[1]

CHURCHYARDS.

" Oft in the lone churchyard at night I've seen
  By glimpse of moonshine, chequ'ring through the trees,
  The schoolboy, with his satchel in his hand,
  Whistling aloud to bear his courage up,
  And lightly tripping o'er the long flat stones
  (With nettles skirted, and with moss o'ergrown),
  That tell in homely phrase who lie below.
  Sudden he starts! and hears, or thinks he hears,
  The sound of something purring at his heels:
  Full fast he flies, and dares not look behind him,
  Till, out of breath, he overtakes his fellows;
  Who gather round, and wonder at the tale
  Of horrid apparition, tall and ghastly,
  That walks at dead of night, or takes his stand
  O'er some new-open'd grave; and (strange to tell!)
  Evanishes at crowing of the cock."
                                    BLAIR'S GRAVE.

IT having been a current opinion in the times of heathenism
that places of burial were frequently haunted with spectres
and apparitions, it is easy to imagine that the opinion has
been transmitted from them, among the ignorant and unlearned,
throughout all the ages of Christianity to this present day.
The ancients believed that the ghosts of departed persons
came out of their tombs and sepulchres, and wandered about
the place where their remains lay buried. Thus Virgil tells
us that Mœris could call the ghosts out of their sepulchres;
and Ovid, that ghosts came out of their sepulchres and wandered about; and Clemens Alexandrinus, in his Admonitions

[1] "The auncient fathers, being veri desirous to move their audience
unto charitye and almose dedes, did exhorte them to refresh the poore and
to give almoses in the funeralles, and yeares myndes of their frendes
and kynnesfolkes, in stedde of the bankettes that the paynymes and
heathen were wont to make at suche doinges, and in stedde of the meates
that they did bring to their sepulchres and graves." The Huntyng of
Purgatory, by Veron, 1561, f. 106.

to the Gentiles, upbraids them with the gods they worshipped ; which, says he, are wont to appear at tombs and sepulchres, and which are nothing but fading spectres and airy forms.[1]

We learn from Moresin[2] that churchyards were used for the purposes of interment in order to remove superstition. Burial was in ancient times without the walls of cities and towns. Lycurgus, he tells us, first introduced gravestones within the walls, and, as it were, brought home the ghosts to the very doors. Thus we compel horses that are apt to startle, to make the nearest approaches we can to the object at which they have taken the alarm.

Strutt tells us, in his Manners and Customs, English Æra, i. 69, that "before the time of Christianity it was held unlawful to bury the dead within the cities, but they used to carry them out into the fields hard by, and there deposit them. Towards the end of the sixth century, Augustine obtained of King Ethelbert a temple of idols (where the king used to worship before his conversion), and made a burying-place of it ; but St. Cuthbert afterwards obtained leave to have yards made to the churches, proper for the reception of the dead."

In Articles to be inquired of in the Ordinary Visitation of the Right Worshipfull Mr. Dr. Pearson, Archdeacon of Suffolke, 1638, under the head of Churchyards, we read : " Have any *playes, feasts, banquets, suppers, church-ales, drinkings, temporal courts* or *leets, lay juries, musters, exercise of dauncing, stoole-ball, foot-ball,* or the like, or any other profane usage been suffered to be kept in your church, chappell, or churchyard ?"

Churchyards are certainly as little frequented by apparitions

---

[1] " Mœrin sæpe animas imis excire sepulchris,
————vidi." Virg. Bucol. viii. 98.

" Nunc animæ tenues—sepulchris — errant." Ovid. Fasti.

Admonit. ad Gent. p. 37. The learned Mede observes, from a passage of this same ancient father, " that the heathens supposed the presence and power of dæmons (for so the Greeks called the souls of men departed) at their coffins and sepulchres, as though there always remained some natural tie between the deceased and their relicts."

[2] " Cœmeteria hinc sunt. Lycurgus, omni superstitione sublata, et ut vanæ superstitionis omnem eveleret è mentibus suorum formidinem, inhumari intra urbem et sepulchra extrui circa deorum templa," &c. Papatus, p. 40.

and ghosts as other places, and therefore it is a weakness to
be afraid of passing through them. Superstition, however,
will always attend ignorance ; and the night, as she continues
to be the mother of dews, will also never fail of being the
fruitful parent of chimerical fears. So Dryden :

> " When the sun sets, shadows, that show'd at noon
> But small, appear most long and terrible."

And Shakespeare, in the Midsummer Night's Dream :

> " Now it is the time of night,
> That the graves, all gaping wide,
> Ev'ry one lets forth his sprite
> In the church-way path to glide."

There is a singular superstition respecting the burial in
that part of the churchyard which lies north of the church,
that still pervades many of the inland parts and northern dis
tricts of this kingdom, though every idea of it has been
eradicated in the vicinity of the metropolis. It is that that
is the part appropriated for the interment of unbaptised
infants, of persons excommunicated, or that have been executed, or that have laid violent hands upon themselves. In
a curious and rare tract, entitled Martin's Month's Mind, that
is, a certaine Report and true Description of the Death and
Funeralls of olde Martin Marreprelate, the great Makebate of
England, and Father of the Factious : contayning the Cause
of his Death, the Manner of his Buriall, and the right
Copies both of his Will and of such Epitaphs as by sundrie
of his dearest Friends were framed for him, 4to. 1589, we
read : *" He died excommunicate, and they might not therefore
burie him in Christian buriall,* and his will was not to come
there in any wise. His bodie should not be buried in any
church (especiallye cathedrall, which ever he detested), chappell, nor churchyard ; for they have been prophaned with
superstition. He would not be laid *east and west* (for he ever
went against the haire), but *north and south ;* I thinke because ' Ab aquilone omne malum,' and the south wind ever
brings corruption with it."

Dr. Lawrence, 1640, observes, " Christians distinguished
their oratories into an atrium, a churchyard ; a sanctum,
a church ; a sanctum sanctorum, a chancell. They did conceive a greater degree of sanctitie in one of them than in

another, and in one place of them then another. *Churchyards*
they thought profaned by sports, the whole circuit both before
and after Christ was privileged for refuge, none out of the
communion of the kirke permitted to lie there, any consecrate
ground preferred for interment before that which was not
consecrat, and than in an higher esteem which was in an
higher degree of consecration, and that in the highest which
was nearest the altar."

In the Wise and Faithful Steward, or a Narration of the
exemplary Death of Mr. Benjamin Rhodes, Steward to Thomas
Earl of Elgin, &c., by P. Samwaies, his Lordship's Chaplain,
1657, p. 27, we read: "He requested to be interred in the
open churchyard, *on the north side* (*to crosse the received
superstition, as he thought, of the constant choice of the south
side*), near the new chappel." Rhodes was interred in Malden
church, in Bedfordshire.

In White's History of Selborne, p. 322, speaking of the
churchyard, that writer observes: "Considering the size of
the church and the extent of the parish, the churchyard is
very scanty; and especially as all wish to be buried on the
south side, which is become such a mass of mortality, that no
person can be there interred without disturbing or displacing
the bones of his ancestors. There is reason to suppose that
it once was larger, and extended to what is now the vicarage
court and garden. At the east end are a few graves, yet
none, till very lately, on the north side: but as two or three
families of best repute have begun to bury in that quarter,
prejudice may wear out by degrees, and their example be followed by the rest of the neighbourhood." Sir John Cullum,
in the History and Antiquities of Hawsted, co. Suffolk, 1784,
p. 38, says: "There is a great partiality here to burying on
the south and east sides of the churchyard. About twenty
years ago, when I first became rector, and observed how those
sides (particularly the south) were crowded with graves, I prevailed upon a few persons to bury their friends on the north,
which was entirely vacant; but the example was not followed
as I hoped it would, and they continue to bury on the south,
where a corpse is rarely interred without disturbing the bones
of its ancestors. This partiality may perhaps at first have
partly arisen from the ancient custom of praying for the dead;
for as the usual approach to this and most country churches

is by the south, it was natural for burials to be on that side, that those who were going to Divine service might, in their way, by the sight of the graves of their friends, be put in mind to offer up a prayer for the welfare of their souls; and even now, since the custom of praying for the dead is abolished, the same obvious situation of graves may excite some tender recollections in those who view them, and silently implore ' the passing tribute of a sigh.' That this motive has its influence, may be concluded from the graves that appear on the north side of the churchyard, when the approach to the church happens to be that way; of this there are some few instances in this neighbourhood." Pennant, speaking of Whiteford church, (Hist. of Hollywell and Whiteford, p. 102,) says: " I step into the churchyard, and sigh over the number of departed which fill the inevitable retreat. In no distant time the north side, like those of all other Welsh churches, was, through some superstition, to be occupied only by persons executed, or by suicides. It is now nearly as much crowded as the other parts." He also says :hat in North Wales none but excommunicated, or very poor and friendless people, are buried on the north side of the churchyard.

In the Cambrian Register, 1796, p. 374, is the following very apposite passage respecting churchyards in Wales : " In country churchyards the relations of the deceased crowd them into that part which is south of the church; the north side, in their opinion, being unhallowed ground, fit only to be the dormitory of still-born infants and suicides. For an example to his neighbours, and as well to escape the barbarities of the sextons, the writer of the above account ordered himself to be buried on *the north side of the churchyard.* But as he was accounted an infidel when alive, his neighbours could not think it creditable to associate with him when dead. His dust, therefore, is likely to pass a solitary retirement, and for ages to remain undisturbed by the hands of men." In the printed trial of Robert Fitzgerald and others, for the murder of Patrick Randal M'Donnel, 4to. p. 19, we read: " The body of Mr. Fitzgerald, immediately after execution, was carried to the ruins of Turlagh House, and was *waked in a stable* adjoining, with a few candles placed about it. On the next day it was carried to the churchyard of Turlagh, wh?re he was *buried on what is generally termed the wrong side of the church,* in his

clothes, without a coffin." The above minider and trial hap
pened in Ireland in the year 1786.

In Paradoxical Assertions and Philosophical Problems, by
R. H., 1664, p. 45, we read: "Cœlo tegitur, qui non habet
urnam. Doubtless that man's bones in the *north churchyard*
rest in more quiet than his that lies entomb'd in the chancel."
Moresin says that, in Popish burying-grounds, those who
were reputed good Christians lay towards the south and east;
others, who had suffered capital punishment, laid violent hands
on themselves, or the like, were buried *towards the north :*
a custom that had formerly been of frequent use in Scotland.[1]

Jamieson, in his Etymological Dictionary of the Scottish
Language, v. *Bery, Berisch* (to inter, or bury), quotes the
following passage from Archbishop Hamiltoune's Catechisme,
1551, f. 23 : "Siclyke supersticion is amang thame, that they
will nocht berisch or erde the bodis of thar friendis on the
north part of the kirk-yard, trowand that thair is mair halynes
or verteu on the south syde than on the north." From what
has been already quoted from Martin's Month's Mind, it
should appear, too, that there was something honorable or dishonorable in the position of the graves : the common and
honorable direction is from *east to west*, the dishonorable one
from *north to south*. The famous antiquary, Thomas Hearne,
had such correct notions on this head, that he left orders for
his grave to be made straight by a compass, due *east and west;*
in consequence of which his monument, which I have often
seen, is placed in a direction *not parallel with any of the other
graves*. Its being placed seemingly awry gives it a very remarkable appearance. Craven Ord informed me that "at the
east end of the chancel, in the churchyard of Fornham All
Saints, near Bury, Suffolk, is the coffin-shaped monument of
Henrietta Maria Cornwallis, who died in 1707. It stands
north and south, and the parish tradition says that she ordered
that position of it as *a mark of penitence and humiliation*."[2]

[1] "In cœmeteriis pontificiis, boni, quos putant, ad austrum et oriens,
reliqui, qui aut supplicio affecti, aut sibi vim fecissent, et id genus ad
septentrionem sepeliantur, ut frequens *olim Scotis fuit mos*." Moresini
Papatus, p. 157.
[2] I find in Durandi Rationale, lib. vii. De Officio Mortuorum, cap. 35-39,
the following : "Debet autem quis sic sepeliri, ut *capite ad occidentem
posito, pedes dirigat ad orientem*, in quo quasi ipsa positione orat : et

"As to the position in the grave, though we decline," says Sir Thomas Browne, in his Urneburial, "the religious consideration, yet in cœmeterial and narrower burying-places, to avoid confusion and cross-position, a certain posture were to ɔe admitted. The Persians lay north and south; the Megarians and Phœnicians placed their heads to the east; the Athenians, some think, towards the west, which Christians still retain; and Bede will have it to be the posture of our Saviour. That Christians buried their dead on their backs, or in a supine position, seems agreeable to profound sleep and the common posture of dying; contrary also to the most natural way of birth; not unlike our pendulous posture in the doubtful state of the womb. Diogenes was singular, who preferred a prone situation in the grave; and some Christians, like neither, (Russians, &c.,) who decline the figure of rest, and make choice of an erect posture." [1]

In Articles of Enquiry for the Diocese of Ely, in the second Visitation of the R. R. Father in God Matthew (Wren) Lord Bishop of that Diocese, 1662, p. 6, speaking of churchyards, it is asked: "When graves are digged, are they made six foot deep (at the least), and east and west?" In Cymbeline, act iv. sc. 2, Guiderius, speaking of the apparently dead body of Imogen, disguised in men's apparel, says: "Nay, Cadwal, *we must lay his head to the east;* my father has a reason for 't."

There is a passage in the Grave-diggers' scene in Hamlet, act v. sc. 1: "Make her grave *straight,*" which Dr. Johnson has thus explained: "Make her grave from east to west, in a direct line parallel to the church; not from north to south, athwart the regular line. This I think is meant." Under this idea, the context must be thus explained: the two Grave-diggers, with their implements over their shoulders, come, as they have been directed, to make Ophelia's grave. The first asks, Must I make the grave of her who has been a suicide like that of other Christians? She is to be buried so, says the other, therefore make her grave straight, i. e. parallel with those of other Christians. This explanation seems to do more

innuit quod promptus est, ut de occasu festinet ad ortum: de mundo ad seculum."

[1] A correspondent says: "Die an old maid, and be buried with my face downwards." I have seen this expression in some work by Waldron.

honour to Blackthorne, who was not likely to make his characters ask such superfluous questions as whether a grave was
to be made, when they had evidently come with an intention
to make it. Douce says: " I am of Mr. Steevens's opinion,
who thinks that this means nothing more than 'make her
grave *immediately*.' The construction of the passage seems
to be this. The first clown, doubting whether, on account of
Ophelia's having destroyed herself, she would be permitted to
have Christian burial, asks the other whether it is really to be
so, who answers that it is, and desires him to proceed immediately about the business. He afterwards adds, that, if
Ophelia had been a common person, she would not have had
Christian burial; that is, in the churchyard, or consecrated
ground. The passage from Moresin seems to indicate that
suicides were buried on the north side of the church, not that
the head was placed northward. It is probable that, although
they were separated from others, the same position of the
body, that is the face to the east, would be observed, nor do
I believe that any instance of the contrary can be produced.
Those who committed suicide were not to have ecclesiastical
sepulture.—See Astesani Summa de Casibus Conscientiæ,
lib. vi. tit. 30, ad finem. In the fifth act of Hamlet, the priest
is made to say that Ophelia, upon account of the doubtfulness
of her death, was abridged of the full solemnities of Christian
burial.

> ' And, but that great command o'ersways the order,
> She should in ground unsanctified have lodg'd
> Till the last trumpet; for charitable prayers,
> Shards, flints, and pebbles should be thrown upon her.'

But as she was to have Christian burial, there could be no
reason for the clown's debating whether the grave was to be
made straight or crooked, north or east. Had the first clown
doubted this, his first question would have been whether the
grave was to have been dug straight?"

Arnot, in his History of Edinburgh, p. 252, speaking of
St. Leonard Hill, says: " In a northern part of it," (he mentioned before that part of it was the Quakers' burying-ground,)
" children who have died without receiving baptism, and men
who have fallen by their own hand, use to be interred." [1]

[1] " Infantumque animæ flentes in limine primo:
Quos dulcis vitæ exortis: et ab ubere raptos,

[To be buried out of the sanctuary does not mean interment
in unconsecrated ground, but in some remote part of the
churchyard, apart from that in which the bodies of the inhabitants in general are deposited. In many churchyards may
be seen a row of graves on the extreme verge, which are occupied by the bodies of strangers buried at the parish charge, of
suicides, or of others, who are considered unfit to associate
underground with the good people of the parish. These are
said to " lie out of the sanctuary."]

In Malkin's Scenery, Antiquities, and Biography of South
Wales, 1804, p. 261, we read : " The custom of dancing in
the churchyard at their feasts and revels is universal in
Radnorshire, and very common in other parts of the principality. Indeed this solemn abode is rendered a kind of circus
for every sport and exercise. The young men play at fives
and tennis against the wall of the church. It is not however
to be understood that they literally dance over the graves of
their progenitors. This amusement takes place *on the north
side of the churchyard, where it is the custom not to bury.* It
is rather singular, however, that the association of the place,
surrounded by memorials of mortality, should not deaden the
impulses of joy in minds in other respects not insensible to
the suggestions of vulgar superstition." Ibid. p. 281, Aberedwy : " In this churchyard are two uncommonly large yew-
trees, evidently of great age, but in unimpaired luxuriance and
preservation, under the shade of which an intelligent clergyman
of the neighbourhood informed me that he had frequently seen
sixty couple dancing at Aberedwy feast on the 14th of June.
The boughs of the two trees intertwine, and afford ample space
for the evolutions of so numerous a company within their
ample covering."

In the Description of the Isles of Scotland, by J. Money-
penny, 4to., under the Island of Rona, is the following passage :
" There is in this island a chapel dedicated to Saint Ronan ;
wherein (as aged men report) there is alwayes a spade wherewith, whenas any is dead, they find the place of his grave

Abstulit atra dies, et funere mersit acerbo.—
Proxima deinde tenent mœsti loca, qui sibi letum
Insontes peperere manu, lucemque perosi
Projecere animas."   Virg. Æn. vi. 427.

marked." For an account of this book see Gough's British
Topography, ii. 568.

Gough, in the Introduction to the second volume of his
Sepulchral Monuments, p. 204, says: "It is the custom at
this day all over Wales to strew the graves, both within and
without the church, with green herbs, branches of box, flowers,
rushes, and flags, for one year; after which, such as can afford
it *lay down a stone.* Mr. Grose calls this a filthy custom, because he happened to see some of the flowers dead and turned
to dung, and some bones and bits of coffins scattered about
in Ewenny church, Glamorganshire. The common Welsh
graves are curiously matted round with single or double mat-
ting, and stuck with flowers, box, or laurel, which are frequently renewed." Pepys, in his Memoirs, i. 139, mentions
a churchyard near Southampton, where, in the year 1662, the
graves were "accustomed to be all sowed with sage."

In the Statistical Account of Scotland, xiv. 210, parishes of
Kilfinichen and Kilviceven, co. Argyll, we read: The inhabitants "are by no means superstitious, yet they still retain
some opinions handed down by their ancestors, perhaps from
the time of the Druids. It is believed by them that the spirit
of the last person that was buried watches round the churchyard till another is buried, to whom he delivers his charge."
In the same work, xxi. 144, it is said: "In one division of
this county, where it was believed that the ghost of the person
last buried kept the gate of the churchyard till relieved by the
next victim of death, a singular scene occurred when two
burials were to take place in one churchyard on the same day.
Both parties staggered forward as fast as possible, to consign
their respective friend in the first place to the dust. If they
met at the gate, the dead were thrown down till the living
decided by blows whose ghost should be condemned to porter
it." [1]

[1] The following is an extract from the old Register-book of Christ
Church, in Hampshire: "April 14, 1604. Christian Steevens, the wife
of Thomas Steevens, was buried in child-birth, and *buried by women, for
she was a Papishe.*" Warner's Topographical Remarks relating to the
South-Western Parts of Hampshire, ii. 130.

BEES INFORMED OF DEATHS.

[SOME years since, observes a correspondent of the Athenæum, a gentleman at a dinner-table happened to mention that he was surprised, on the death of a relative, by his servant inquiring "whether his master would inform the *bees* of the event, or whether *he* should do so." On asking the meaning of so strange a question, the servant assured him that bees ought always to be informed of a death in a family, or they would resent the neglect by deserting the hive. This gentleman resides in the Isle of Ely, and the anecdote was told in Suffolk ; and one of the party present, a few days afterwards, took the opportunity of testing the prevalence of this strange notion, by inquiring of a cottager who had lately lost a relative, and happened to complain of the loss of her bees, "whether she had told them all she ought to do?" She immediately replied, " Oh, yes ; when my aunt died I told every skep (i. e. hive) myself, and put them into mourning." I have since ascertained the existence of the same superstition in Cornwall, Devonshire, Gloucestershire, (where I have seen black crape put round the hive, or on a small stick by its side,) and Yorkshire. It probably exists in every part of the kingdom. I should be glad to ascertain whether it prevails in Wales ; though, from its being known in Cornwall, I have little doubt that its origin is earlier than the Saxon invasion, and perhaps is known on the continent of Europe. The mode of communication is by whispering the fact to each hive separately. There are many other singular notions afloat as to these insects. In Oxfordshire I was told that if man and wife quarrelled, the bees would leave them.]

In the Living Librarie, Englished by John Molle, 1621, p. 283, we read : " Who would beleeve without superstition, (if experience did not make it credible,) that most commonly all the *bees die in their hives, if the master or mistresse of the house chance to die, except the hives be presently removed into some other place ?* And yet I know this hath hapned to folke no way stained with superstition." A vulgar prejudice prevails in many places of England, that, when bees remove or go away from their hives, the owner of them will die soon after. A clergyman in Devonshire informed me that, when any

Devonian makes a purchase of bees, the payment is never made in money, but in things (corn for instance) to the value of the sum agreed upon ; and the bees are never removed but on a Good Friday.

I found the following in the Argus, a London newspaper, Sept. 13, 1790 : "A superstitious custom prevails at every funeral in Devonshire, of turning round the bee-hives that belonged to the deceased, if he had any, and that at the moment the corpse is carrying out of the house. At a funeral some time since, at Collumpton, of a rich old farmer, a laughable circumstance of this sort occurred : for, just as the corpse was placed in the hearse, and the horsemen, to a large number, were drawn up in order for the procession of the funeral, a person called out, 'Turn the bees,' when a servant who had no knowledge of such a custom, instead of turning the hives about, lifted them up, and then laid them down on their sides. The bees, thus hastily invaded, instantly attacked and fastened on the horses and their riders. It was in vain they galloped off, the bees as precipitately followed, and left their stings as marks of their indignation. A general confusion took place, attended with loss of hats, wigs, &c., and the corpse during the conflict was left unattended ; nor was it till after a considerable time that the funeral attendants could be rallied, in order to proceed to the interment of their deceased friend."

Sampson, in his Statistical Survey of the County of Londonderry, 1802, p. 436, says, that there "bees must not be given away, but sold ; otherwise neither the giver nor the taker will have *luck*."

GRAVESTONES.

THE custom of laying flat stones in our churches and churchyards over the graves of better sort of persons, on which are inscribed epitaphs containing the name, age, character, &c. of the deceased, has been transmitted from very ancient times, as appears from the writings of Cicero and others.[1]

[1] Cicero de Legibus, xi. " Lapidea mensa terra operitur humato corpore hominis qui aliquo sit numero, quæ contineat laudem et nomen mortui incisum. Mos retinetur."—Moresini Papatus, p. 86.

In Malkin's Scenery, Antiquities, and Biography of South
Wales, 1804, p. 604, under Glamorganshire, in Mr. Mason's
Elegy written in Neath churchyard, we read :

" And round that fane the sons of toil repose,
    Who drove the ploughshare, or the sail who spread,
    With wives, with children, all in measur'd rows,
    Two whiten'd stones well mark the feet and head."

Explained, p. 605 : " The stones at each end of the grave
are whitened with lime every Christmas, Easter, and Whitsuntide."

GARLANDS IN COUNTRY CHURCHES,
AND STREWING FLOWERS ON THE GRAVES.

IN Yorkshire, as a clergyman of that county informed me,
when a virgin dies in a village, one, nearest to her in size and
age and resemblance, carries the garland before the corpse in
the funeral procession, which is afterwards hung up in the
church. This is sometimes composed entirely of white paper,
and at others, the flowers, &c. (cut out upon it), are coloured.
There appeared in the London Morning Chronicle for Sept.
25th, 1792, an elegiac ode from the elegant pen of Miss
Seward, wherein, speaking of the village of Eyam, in Derbyshire, this passage occurs :

" Now the low beams with paper garlands hung,
    In memory of some village youth or maid,
    Draw the soft tear, from thrill'd remembrance sprung ;
    How oft my childhood marked that tribute paid !

The gloves suspended by the garland's side,
    White as its snowy flow'rs with ribands tied.
    Dear village ! long these wreaths funereal spread—
    Simple memorial of the early dead !"

The following note is subjoined : " The ancient custom of
hanging a garland of white roses made of writing paper, and
a pair of white gloves, over the pew of the unmarried villagers
who die in the flower of their age, prevails to this day in the
village of Eyam, and in most other villages and little towns
in the Peak."[1]   Nichols, in his History of Lancashire, ii.

[1] Coles, in his Introduction to the Knowledge of Plants (probably
speaking of the metropolis only), p. 64, says : " It is not very long since
the custome of setting up garlands in churches hath been left off with us."

pt. i. p. 382, speaking of Waltham, in Framland hundred, says: "In this church, under every arch, *a garland is suspended;* one of which is customarily placed there whenever any young unmarried woman dies." From the minute-book of the Society of Antiquaries it appears that on June 4th, 1747, a letter was read by the secretary "from Mr. Edward Steel of Bromley, concerning the custom of burying the dead, especially bachelors and maidens, with garlands of flowers, &c., used formerly in several parts of this kingdom."

It is still the custom in many country churches to hang a garland of flowers over the seats of deceased virgins, in token, says Bourne, of esteem and love, and as an emblem of their reward in the heavenly church. It was usual in the primitive Christian church to place crowns of flowers at the heads of deceased virgins ;[1] for this we have the authority of Damascen, Gregory Nyssen, St. Jerome, and St. Austin.

In the earliest ages of Christianity, virginity was honoured, out of deference most likely to the Virgin Mother,[2] with almost divine adoration, and there is little doubt but that the origin of nunneries is closely connected with that of the virgin garland.

"In North Wales," as Pennant's MS. informs us, "when they bless another, they are very apt to join to the blessing of God, the blessing of white Mary." In the Papal times in England, sometimes, the form of a last testament ran thus: "Commendo animam meam Deo, beatæ Mariæ, et omnibus Sanctis."

I saw in the churches of Wolsingham and Stanhope, in the county of Durham, specimens of these garlands ; the form of a woman's glove, cut in white paper, hung in the centre of each of them. Douce saw a similar instance in the church at Bolton in Craven, in 1783. At Skipton, too, the like custom still prevails. Dr. Lort made the following observation in

[1] "Fuit quoque mos ad capita virginum apponendi florum coronas," &c. Cass. de Vet. Sac. Christi, p. 334.

[2] " Some say no evil thing that walks by night,
In fog or fire, by lake or moorish fen,
Blue meagre hag, or stubborn unlaid ghost,
That breaks his magic chains at curfew-time,
No goblin, or swart faery of the mine,
Hath hurtful power o'er true virginity."
Milton's Comus.

August, 1785 : "At Grey's-Foot church, between Wrexham and Chester, were garlands, or rather shields, fixed against the pillars, finely decorated with artificial flowers and cut gilt paper." In 1794, Sir H. Ellis saw garlands of white paper hanging up in a church, no farther from the metropolis than Paul's Cray, in Kent. The following occurs in Marston's play entitled the Dutch Courtezan : "I was afraid, i'faith, that I should ha seene *a garland on this beauties herse.*"

The author of the Comical Pilgrim's Pilgrimage into Ireland, 1723, p. 92, says : "When a virgin dies, a garland made of all sorts of flowers and sweet herbs, is carried by a young woman on her head, before the coffin, from which hang down two black ribbons, signifying our mortal state, and two white, as an emblem of purity and innocence. The ends thereof are held by four young maids, before whom a basket full of herbs and flowers is supported by two other maids, who strew them along the streets to the place of burial ; then, *after the deceased,* follow all her relations and acquaintance." [So also in the old ballad :

> " But since I am resolved to die for my dear,
> I'll chuse six young virgins my coffin to bear
> And all those young virgins I now do chuse,
> Instead of green ribbons, green ribbons, green ribbons,
> Instead of green ribbons, a garland shall wear.
>
> And when in the church in my grave I lie deep,
> Let all those fine garlands, fine garlands, fine garlands,
> Let all those fine garlands hang over feet.
>
> And when any of my sex behold the sight ;
> They may see I have been constant, been constant,
> They may see I'm constant to my hearts delight."]

The following is copied from the Argus, August 5, 1790 : " Sunday being St. James's Day, the votaries of St. James's churchyard attended in considerable crowds at the shrines of their departed friends, and paid the usual tributary honours of paper gloves and garlands of flowers on their graves."

There is a passage in Shakespeare's Hamlet, act v. sc. 1 : " Yet here she is allowed her virgin *crants,*" which seems to have been misunderstood by some of the commentators. The editor of the first folio substitutes *rites ;* and Bishop Warburton thought the true word was *chants :* but Dr. Johnson says : " I have been informed by an anonymous correspondent that *crants* is the German word for *garlands*, and I suppose it was retained by us from the Saxons. To carry garlands before the bier of a maiden, and to hang them over her grave, is still the practice in rural parishes."[1]

A writer in the Antiquarian Repertory, iv. 239, says : "That in this nation, as well as others, by the abundant zeal of our ancestors, virginity was held in great estimation : insomuch that those who died in that state were rewarded at their death with a garland or crown on their heads, denoting their triumphant victory over the lusts of the flesh. Nay, this honour was extended even to a widow who had never enjoyed but one husband. These garlands, or crowns, were most artificially wrought in filagree work, with gold and silver wire, in resemblance of myrtle, with which plant the funebrial garlands of the ancients were always composed, whose leaves were fastened to hoops of larger iron wire, and they were lined with cloth of silver. Besides these crowns the ancients had also their depository garlands, the use of which continued till of late years, and may perhaps still in some parts of England. These garlands at the funerals of the deceased were carried solemnly before the corpse by two maids, and afterwards hung up in some conspicuous place within the church, and were made in the following manner, viz. the lower rim or circlet was a broad hoop of wood, whereunto was fixed at the sides thereof part of two other hoops, crossing each other at the top at right angles, which formed the upper part, being about one third longer than the width. These hoops were wholly covered with artificial flowers of paper, *dyed horn,*[2] and silk, and more or less beautiful according to the skill or ingenuity of the performer. In the vacancy of the inside from the top hung white paper cut in form of gloves, whereon was written the deceased's name, age, &c., together with long slips of various coloured paper or ribbons ; these were many times intermixed with gilded or painted empty shells of blown eggs, as farther ornaments, or it may be as emblems of bub-

[1] "KRANS, *sertum.* Isl. et Belg. id. Germ. *krantz.* Helvigius natum putat a κορωνὶς; alii a *cranium ;* Wachterus a C. B. *crwnn,* rotundus, quum circulari figura caput ambiat." Ihre, Gloss. Suio-Goth. i. 1156.

[2] This perhaps explains the following passage in the Horn Exalted, or Room for Cuckolds, 1661, p. 10 : " *Our garlands in the winter, and at virgins' funerals, are they not made of horns ?*" An Italian is speaking.

bles, or the bitterness of this life ; while other garlands had only a solitary hour-glass hanging therein, as a more significant symbol of mortality." These garlands are thus described by Gay :

> " To her sweet mem'ry flow'ry garlands strung,
> On her now empty seat aloft were hung."

In a curious and very rare book entitled the Virgin's Pattern in the exemplary Life and lamented Death of Mrs. Susannah Perwich, who died at Hackney, July 3, 1661, we have the rites of a virgin lady's funeral minutely described, p. 40 : "The herse, covered with velvet, was carried by six servant-maidens of the family, all in white. The sheet was held up by six of those gentlewomen in the school that had most acquaintance with her, in mourning habit, *with white scarfs and gloves. A rich costly garland of gum-work,* adorned with banners and scutcheons, was borne immediately before the herse, by two proper young ladies that entirely loved her. Her father and mother, with other near relations and their children, followed next the herse in due order, all in mourning : the kindred next to them ; after whom came the whole school of gentlewomen, and then persons of chief rank from the neighbourhood and from the city of London, *all in white gloves, both men, women, children, and servants, having been first served with wine.* The herse being set down (in Hackney church) *with the garland upon it,* the Rev. Dr. Spurstow preached her funeral sermon. This done, the rich coffin, *anointed with sweet odours,* was put down into the grave in the middle alley of the said church," &c. Her father, it seems, kept a great boarding-school for young ladies at Hackney. In Articles of Enquiry for the Diocese of Ely, 1662, p. 7, I read as follows : "Are *any garlands* and other ordinary funeral ensigns *suffered to hang where they hinder the prospect, or until they grow foul and dusty, withered and rotten ?*"

Wax appears to have been used in the formation of these garlands, from the subsequent passage in a rare black-letter book, on the Distinction of Dreames, by Thomas Hill : "*A garlande of waxe* (to dream of) signifyeth evill to all personnes, but especiallye *to the sicke, for as muche as it is commonlye occupyed aboute burialls.*"

Gough, in the Introduction to his second volume of Sepulchral Monuments, p. 5, has the following passage : "The ancients used to crown the deceased with flowers, in token of the shortness of life; and the practice is still retained in some places in regard to young women and children. The Roman ritual recommends it in regard of those who die soon after baptism,[1] in token of purity and virginity. It still obtains in Holland and parts of Germany. The primitive Christians buried young women with flowers, and martyrs with the instruments of their martyrdom. I have seen fresh flowers put into the coffins of children and young girls."

The custom of strewing flowers upon the graves of departed friends,[2] which has been already incidentally noticed, is also derived from a custom of the ancient church. St. Ambrose, in his Funeral Oration on the Death of Valentinian, has these words: "I will not sprinkle his grave with flowers, but pour on his spirit the odour of Christ. Let others scatter baskets of flowers: Christ is our lily, and with this will I consecrate his relics."[3] And St. Jerome, in his Epistle to Pammachius, upon the death of his wife, tells us: "Whilst other husbands strewed violets, roses, lilies, and purple flowers upon the graves of their wives, and comforted themselves with such-like offices, Pammachius bedewed her ashes and venerable bones with the balsam of alms."[4]

Durand tells us that the ancient Christians, after the funeral, used to scatter flowers on the tomb.[5] There is a great deal

[1] "Cum igitur infans vel puer baptizatus, defunctus fuerit ante usum rationis, induitur juxta ætatem, et *imponitur ei corona de floribus, seu de herbis aromaticis et odoriferis, in signum integritatis carnis et virginitatis.*" See the Ordo Baptizandi, &c., pro Anglia, Hibernia, et Scotia. 12mo. Par. 1636, p. 97.

[2] Pennant's MS. says that in North Wales "the people kneel and say the Lord's prayer on the graves of their dead friends for some Sundays after their interment; and this is done generally upon their first coming to church, and, after that, they dress the grave with flowers. Llanvechan."

[3] "Nec ego floribus tumulum ejus aspergam, sed spiritum ejus Christi odore perfundam; spargant alii plenis lilia calathis; nobis lilium est Christus: hoc reliquias ejus sacrabo." Ambros. Orat. Funebr. de Obitu Valentin.

[4] "Cæteri mariti super tumulos conjugum spargunt violas, rosas, lilia, floresque purpureos, et dolorem pectoris his officiis consolantur; Pammachius noster sanctam favillam ossaque veneranda eleemosynæ balsamis rigat." Hieron. Epist. ad Pammachium de Obitu Uxoris.

[5] "Condito et curato funere solebant nonnulli antiquitus tumulum flori-

of learning in Moresin upon this subject.[1]   It appears from
Pliny's Natural History, from Cicero in his Oration on Lucius
Plancus, and from Virgil's sixth Æneid, that this was a funeral rite among the heathens.   They used also to scatter them
on the unburied corpse.

Gough, in the Introduction to the second volume of the
Sepulchral Monuments, p. 18, speaking of the Feralia, says :
"The tombs were decked with flowers, particularly roses and
lilies.   The Greeks used the amaranth and polyanthus (one
species of which resembles the hyacinth), parsley, myrtle.
The Romans added fillets or bandeaux of wool.   The primitive
Christians reprobated these as impertinent practices : but in
Prudentius's time they had adopted them, and they obtain, in
a degree, in some parts of our own country, as the garland
hung up in some village churches in Cambridgeshire, and
other counties, after the funeral of a young woman, and the
enclosure of roses round graves in the Welsh churchyards
testify."

Gay thus describes the strewing of flowers upon the graves:

> " Upon her grave the rosemary they threw,
>   The daisy, butter'd flow'r, and endive blue."

He adds the custom, still used in the south of England of
fencing the graves with osiers, &c. ; and glances at clerical
economy, for which there is oftentimes too much occasion, in
the last two lines :

bus adspergere." Durand, p. 237. In Huss. Dissert. Acad. de antiquis
Humandi Ritibus, 12mo. Upsaliæ, 1698, p. 44, we read : " Violis quoque
et floribus tumulos suos exornasse Christianos ex Prudentii hymno in exa-
quiis defunctorum Ambrosii et Hieronomi edocemur.   Neque alium in
finem hoc factum est, quam ut spem resurrectionis testatum redderent,
quod sicuti flores verno tempore renascuntur, ita et nos die αναπάυσεως
sumus redituri."

[1] " Sepulchra funeralibus expletis quandoque floribus odoramentisque
fuisse sparsa legimus.   Idemque mos cum in plerisque regionibus Italiæ,
tum maxime in subjectis Appennino collibus, Romandiolæ alicubi ætate
nostra servatur.   *Adhibita sunt post funeralia in templis ornamenta,
clypei, coronæ,* et hujusmodi donaria, quod nostra quoque ætas in nobilibus et honoratis viris servat."   Moresini Papatus, p. 156.   Hence our
custom of hanging up over the tombs of knights, &c., banners, spurs, and
other insignia of their order.   " Flores et serta, educto cadavere, certatim
injiciebant Athenienses.   Guichard, lib. ii. cap. 3, Funeral.   Retinent
Papani morem."   Ibid. p. 61.

" With wicker rods we fenc'd her tomb around,
   To ward from man and beast the hallow'd ground:
   Lest her new grave the parson's cattle raze,
   For both his horse and cow the churchyard graze."

Hawke Locker, in his Views in Spain, speaking of Grenadilla, says : "We passed two or three crosses, which marked the spot where some unfortunate wretches had met a violent death by the way. Some of these probably were killed by accident, but all were described as so many barbarous murders, and the fluency of the narrative proved that we were listening to a tale which had been told a hundred times before. The very ancient custom of casting a stone upon these untimely graves is still observed throughout Spain. Affection or superstition induces many to offer this tribute, accompanied by a silent prayer for the dead ; but even a mere stranger, exempt from such motives, may find a gratification in adding a stone to the heap, from that veneration for the dead which seems to be inherent in our constitution."

In Malkin's Scenery, Antiquities, and Biography of South Wales, 1804, Glamorganshire, p. 67, we read: "The bed on which the corpse lies is always strewed with flowers, and the same custom is observed after it is laid in the coffin. They bury much earlier than we do in England ; seldom later than the third day, and very frequently on the second. The habit of filling the bed, the coffin, and the room with sweet-scented flowers, though originating probably in delicacy as well as affection, must of course have a strong tendency to expedite the progress of decay. It is an invariable practice, both by day and night, to watch a corpse : and so firm a hold has this supposed duty gained on their imaginations, that probably there is no instance upon record of a family so unfeeling and abandoned as to leave a dead body in the room by itself for a single minute in the interval between the death and burial. Such a violation of decency would be remembered for generations. The hospitality of the country is not less remarkable on melancholy than on joyful occasions. The invitations to a funeral are very general and extensive, and the refreshments are not light, and taken standing, but substantial and prolonged. Any deficiency in the supply of ale would be as severely censured on this occasion as at a festival. The grave of the deceased is constantly overspread with plucked flowers

for a week or two after the funeral. The planting of graves
with flowers is confined to the villages and the poorer people.
It is perhaps a prettier custom. It is very common to dress
the graves on Whitsunday and other festivals, when flowers
are to be procured; and the frequency of this observance is
a good deal affected by the respect in which the deceased was
held. My father-in-law's grave, in Cowbridge church, has
been strewed by his surviving servants every Sunday morning
for these twenty years. It is usual for a family not to appear
at church till what is called the month's end, when they go
in a body, and then are considered as having returned to the
common offices of life."

In the same work, p. 606, in notes on an Elegy written by
Mason, we are told again that " it is a very ancient and general practice in Glamorgan to plant flowers on the graves; so
that many churchyards have something like the splendour of
a rich and various parterre. Besides this, it is usual to strew
the graves with flowers and evergreens, within the church
as well as out of it, thrice at least every year, on the same
principle of delicate respect as the stones are whitened. No
flowers or evergreens are permitted to be planted on graves
but such as are sweet-scented: the pink and polyanthus,
sweet-Williams, gilliflowers and carnations, mignionette, thyme,
hyssop, camomile, and rosemary, make up the pious decoration of this consecrated garden. Turnsoles, pionies, the
African marigold, the anemone, and many others I could mention, though beautiful, are never planted on graves, because
they are not sweet-scented. It is to be observed, however,
that this tender custom is sometimes converted into an instrument of satire; so that, where persons have been distinguished for their pride, vanity, or any other unpopular quality,
the neighbours whom they may have offended plant these also
by stealth upon their graves. The white rose is always planted
on a virgin's tomb. The red rose is appropriated to the
grave of any person distinguished for goodness, and especially
benevolence of character. In the Easter week most generally
the graves are newly dressed, and manured with fresh earth,
when such flowers or evergreens as may be wanted or wished
for are planted. In the Whitsuntide holidays, or rather the
preceding week, the graves are again looked after, weeded,
and otherwise dressed, or, if necessary, planted again. It is

A very common saying of such persons as employ themselves in thus planting and dressing the graves of their friends, that they are cultivating their own freeholds. This work the nearest relations of the deceased always do with their own hands, and never by servants or hired persons. Should a neighbour assist, he or she never takes, never expects, and indeed is never insulted by the offer of any reward, by those who are acquainted with the ancient custom. The vulgar and illiberal prejudice against old maids and old bachelors subsists among the Welsh in a very disgraceful degree, so that their graves have not unfrequently been planted by some satirical neighbours, not only with rue, but with thistles, nettles, henbane, and other noxious weeds. In addition to the foregoing remarks, it may be observed of the Glamorganshire customs, that, when a young couple are to be married, their ways to the church are strewed with sweet-scented flowers and evergreens. When a young unmarried person dies, his or her ways to the grave are also strewed with sweet flowers and evergreens; and on such occasions it is the usual phrase that those persons are going to their nuptial beds, not to their graves. There seems to be a remarkable coincidence between these people and the ancient Greeks, with respect to the avoiding of ill-omened words. None ever molest the flowers that grow on graves; for it is deemed a kind of sacrilege to do so. A relation or friend will occasionally take a pink, if it can be spared, or a sprig of thyme, from the grave of a beloved or respected person, to wear it in remembrance; but they never take much, lest they should deface the growth on the grave. This custom prevails principally in the most retired villages; and I have been assured that, in such villages where the right of grazing the churchyard has been enforced, the practice has alienated the affections of very great numbers from the clergymen and their churches; so that many have become dissenters for the singularly uncommon reason that they may bury their friends in dissenting burial-grounds, plant their graves with flowers, and keep them clean and neat, without any danger of their being cropped. This may have been the fact in some places; but I confidently believe that few of the clergy would urge their privileges to an unfair or offensive extent. These elegant and highly pathetic customs of South Wales make the best impressions on the mind. What can be more affecting than to see all the youth of both sexes in a village, and in every village through which the corpse passes, dressed in their best apparel, and strewing with sweet-scented flowers the ways along which one of their beloved neighbours goes to his or her marriage-bed?" In the same work, p. 223, speaking of the church of Llanspyddid, on the south side of the Uske, surrounded with large and venerable yew-trees, Malkin observes : "The natives of the principality pride themselves much on these ancient ornaments of their church-yards ; and it is nearly as general a custom in Brecknockshire to decorate the graves of the deceased with slips either of bay or yew, stuck in the green turf, for an emblem of pious re-membrance, as it is in Glamorganshire to pay a tribute of similar import in the cultivation of sweet-scented flowers on the same spot."

Gough, in Sepulchral Monuments, Introd. ii. 104, says : "Aubrey takes notice of a custom of planting rose-trees on the graves of lovers by the survivors, at Oakley, Surrey, which may be a remain of Roman manners among us ; it being in practice among them and the Greeks to have roses yearly strewed on their graves, as Bishop Gibson, after Kirkman de Funeribus, p. 498, remarks from two inscriptions at Ravenna and Milan. The practice in Propertius of burying the dead (Eleg. i. 17) in roses, is common among our country-people ; and to it Anacreon seems to allude, Ode liii., where he says, ροδον νεκροις αμνει.[1]

In the Female Mentor, 1798, ii. 205, 206, we read : "Inde-pendently of the religious comfort which is imparted in our burial service, we sometimes see certain gratifications which are derived from immaterial circumstances ; and, however trivial they may appear, are not to be judged improper, as long as they are perfectly innocent. Of this kind may be deemed the practice in some country villages of throwing flowers into the grave ; and it is curious to trace this appa-rently simple custom up to the politest periods of Greece and Rome. Virgil, describing Anchises grieving for Marcellus, makes him say :

[1] Bishop Gibson is also cited as an authority for this practice by Mr. Strutt, in his Manners and Customs, Anglo-Saxon Æra, i. 69. See also Bray's History of Surrey, ii. 165. I do not find that the custom is at present retained.

'Full oaniotoro of frogrant lilies bring,
Mix'd with the purple roses of the spring:
Let me with funeral flow'rs his body strew:
This gift, which parents to their children owe,
This unavailing gift at least I may bestow.'"

The graves of Glamorganshire, decorated with flowers and herbs, at once gratify the relations of the departed and please the observer. Friar Lawrence, in Romeo and Juliet, says:

" Dry up your tears, and stick your rosemary
On this fair corse."

Of Paris, the intended husband of Juliet, who, to all appearance, died on her wedding-day, it is said, in the language of Shakespeare, " He came with flowers to strew his lady's grave," when he provoked, and met his fate by the hand of, Romeo.

Sir Thomas Overbury, in his Characters, describing the " faire and happy milk-maid," says : " Thus lived she, and all her care is, *that she may die in the spring-time, to have store of flowers stucke upon her winding sheet.*" A MS. entitled Historical Passages concerning the Clergy, cited in the History of Shrewsbury, 4to. p. 92, speaking of the ancient Papal times, observes : " It is probable before this time there were neither seats nor benches in churches; the floors were commonly strewed with flowers and sweet herbs, especially at midnight masses and great festivals, upon which the people must prostrate themselves."

The following curious passage I found in the Festyvall, 1528, f. 77, in the account of St. Thomas à Becket, Archbishop of Canterbury : " He was also manfull in his houshold, for his hall was every daye in somer season strewed with grene russhes, and in wynter with clene hey, for to save the knyghtes clothes that sate on the flore for defaute of place to syt on."

Pennant, in his Tour in Scotland, remarks a singular custom in many parts of North Britain, of "painting on the doors and window-shutters white tadpole-like figures, on a black ground, designed to express the tears of the country for the loss of any person of distinction. Nothing seems wanting to render this mode of expressing sorrow completely ridiculous, but the subjoining of a ' N.B. These are tears.' I saw a door that led into a family vault in Kelso churchyard in 1785, which was painted over in the above manner with very large ones."

[Among the superstitions of the Senecca Indians is the following: When a maiden dies, they imprison a young bird until it first begins to try its power of song ; and then, loading it with kisses and caresses, they loose its bonds over her grave, in the belief that it will not fold its wings nor close its eyes until it has flown to the spirit land, and delivered its precious burden of affection to the loved and lost. It is not unfrequent to see twenty or thirty loosed at once over one grave.]

MINNYNG DAYS, OR MONTH'S MIND.

MYNDE DAYS, Minnyng Days, says Blount, from the Saxon Ꝺemynꝺe,[1] days which our ancestors called their Month's Mind, their Year's Mind, and the like, being the days whereon their souls (after their deaths) were had in special remembrance, and some office or obsequies said for them ; as obits, dirges, &c. This word is still retained in Lancashire; but elsewhere they are more commonly called Anniversary Days. The common expression of "having a month's mind," implying a longing desire, is evidently derived from hence.[2]

The following is an extract from the will of Thomas Windsor, esq., 1479 : " Item, I will that I have brennyng at my burying and funeral service four tapers and twenty-two torches of wax, every taper to conteyn the weight of ten pounds, and every torch sixteen pounds, which I will that twenty-four very poor men, and well disposed, shall hold as well at the tyme of my burying as at my *moneth's minde.* Item, I will that, after my moneth's minde be done, the said

[1] That is, the Mind, *q.* Myndyng Days, Bede, Hist. Eccl. lib. iv. ca. 30. Commemorationis Dies.

[2] The following is in Peck's Desiderata Curiosa, i. 230 : " By saying they have a month's mind to it, they anciently must undoubtedly mean that, if they had what they so much longed for, it would (hyperbolically speaking) do them as much good (they thought) as they believed a month's mind, or service said once a month (could they afford to have it), would benefit their souls after their decease."

four tapers he delivered to the churchwardens, &c. And that there be a hundred children within the age of sixteen years to be at my moneth's minde, to say for my soul. That against my moneth's minde the candles bren before the roode in the parish church. Also that at my moneth's minde my executors provide twenty priests to singe placebo, dirige, &c." See Gent. Mag. for 1793, lxiii. 1191.

Fabyan the historian, himself, also, in his will, gives directions for his month's mind : " At whiche tyme of burying, and also the monethis mynde, I will that myne executrice doo cause to be carried from London xii. newe torches, there beyng redy made, to burn in the tymes of the said burying and *monethes minde:* and also that they do purvay for iiii. tapers of iii. *lb.* evry pece, to brenne about the corps and herse for the foresaid .ii. seasons, whiche torches and tapers to be bestowed as hereafter shalbe devised; which iiij. tapers I will bc holden at every tyme by foure poore men, to the whiche I will that to everyche of theym be geven for their labours at either of the saide ij. tymes iiij.*d.* to as many as been weddid men : and if any of theym happen to be unmarried, than they to have but iij.*d.* a pece, and in lyke manner I will that the torche berers be orderid." In another part of his will he says : "Also I will, that if I decesse at my tenemente of Halstedis, that myn executrice doo purvay ayenst my burying competent brede, ale, and chese, for all comers to the parishe churche, and ayenst the moneths mynde I will be ordeyned, at the said churche, competent brede, ale, pieces of beffe and moton, and rost rybbys of beffe, and shalbe thought nedeful by the discretion of myn executrice, for all comers to the said obsequy, over and above brede, ale, and chese, for the comers unto the dirige over night. And furthermore I will that my said executrice doo purvay ayenst the said moneths mynde xxiiij. peces of beffe and moton, and xxiiij. treen platers and xxiiij. treen sponys ; the whiche peces of fleshe with the said platers and spoonys, with xxiiij.*d.* of silver, I will be geven unto xxiiij. poore persones of the said parisshe of Theydon Garnon, if wᵗin that parishe so many may be founde : for lake whereof I will the xxiiij. peces of flesh and ij.*s.* in money, wᵗ the foresaid platers and sponys be geven unto suche poore persones as may be found in the parisshes of Theydon at Mount, and Theydon Boys, after the discrecion of myn executors ; and if

my said monethes mynde fall in Lent, or upon a fysshe day,
then I will that the said xxiiij. peces of fleshe be altered unto
saltfyche or stokfyshe, unwatered and unsodeyn, and that every
piece of beef or moton, saltfyshe or stokfysh, be well in value
of a peny or a peny at the leest; and that noo dyner be pur-
veyed for at hom but for my household and kynnysfolks : and
I will that my knyll be rongyn at my monethes mynde after
the guyse of London.   Also I will that myn executrice doo
assemble upon the said day of moneths mynde xij. of the
porest menys children of the foresaid parisshe, and after the
masse is ended and other observances, the said childern to be
ordered about my grave, and there knelyng, to say for my soule
and all Christen soules, ' De profundis,' as many of them as
can, and the residue to say a Pater noster, and an Ave oonly ;
to the which xij. childern I will be geven xiij.*d.*, that is to
meane, to that childe that beginneth ' De profundis' and saith
the preces, ij.*d.* and to everyche of the other j.*d.*"   See his
Chron. new edit., Pref. pp. 4, 6.[1]

In the Churchwardens' Accounts of St. Mary-at-Hill, in
the city of London, 17 and 19 Edw. IV. (Palmer and Clerk),
are the following articles : " P^d to Sir I. Philips for keepyng
the morrow mass at 6 o'clock upon feryall days, each quarter,
v.*s.*   To the par. priest to remember in the pulpit the soul of
R. Bliet, who gave vj.*s.* viij.*d.* to the church works, ij.*d.*"

In Nichols's Collection of Churchwardens' Accounts, 1797,
Accounts of St. Margaret, Westminster, p. 10, we read :
" Item, at the monyth mynde of Lady Elizabeth Countess of
Oxford, for four tapers, viij.*d.*"   Under the year 1531 is,
" Item, for mette for the theff that stalle the pyx, iiij.*d.*"
And, in 1532, " Item, received for iiij. torches of the black
guard, viij.*d.*"   On these occasions the word " mind" signified *remembrance ;* and the expression a " month's mind," a
" year's mind," &c., meant that on that day, month, or year
after the party's decease, some solemn service for the good of
his soul should be celebrated.

In Ireland, according to Sir H. Piers, 1682, " after the day

[1] " I shulde speake nothing, in the mean season, of the costly feastes
and bankettes that are commonly made unto the priestes (whiche come
to suche doinges from all partes, as ravens do to a deade carcase) in their
buryinges, *moneths* mindes and yeares myndes." Veron's Huntyng of
Purgatory, 1561, f. 36.

of interment of a great personage, they count four wooks; and that day four weeks, all priests and friars, and all gentry far and near, are invited to a great feast (usually termed the Month's Mind) ; the preparation to this feast are masses, said in all parts of the house at once, for the soul of the departed : if the room be large, you shall have three or four priests toge- ther celebrating in the several corners thereof; the masses done, they proceed to their feastings ; and, after all, every priest and friar is discharged with his largess."

We read in Fabyan's Chronicle that "in 1439 died Sir Roberde Chichely, grocer, and twice mayor of London, the which wylled in his testament that upon his Mynde Day a good and competent dyner should be ordayned to xxiiij.c. pore men, and that of housholders of the citee, yf they myght be founde. And over that was xx. pounde destributed among them, which was to every man two-pence."

ON BOWING TOWARDS THE ALTAR

OR COMMUNION TABLE, ON ENTERING THE CHURCH.

THIS custom, which was prevalent when Bourne wrote, he deduces from the ancient practice of the Church of worship- ping towards the east.[1] This, says he, they did, that by so worshipping they might lift up their minds to God, who is called the Light, and the Creator of Light, therefore turning, says St. Austin,[2] our faces to the east, from whence the day springs, that we might be reminded of turning to a more ex- cellent nature, namely, the Lord. As also, that as man was driven out of Paradise, which is towards the east, he ought to look that way, which is an emblem of his desire to return

---

[1] The following is from Langley's Abridgement of Polidore Vergil, f. 109 : " The manner of turnyng our faces into the easte when wee praie, is taken of the old Ethnikes, whiche, as Apuleius remembereth, used to loke eastwarde and salute the sonne : we take it in a custom to put us in remembraunce that Christe is the sonne of righteousnes, that discloseth all secretes."

[2] De Sermone Domini in monte, ii. 5.

thither.[1] Again it was used when they were baptised: they
first turned their faces to the west, and so renounced the
devil; and then to the east, and made their covenant with
Christ.   Lastly, those of the ancient Church prayed that way,
believing that our Saviour would come to judgment from that
quarter of the heavens, St. Damascen asserting that when he
ascended into heaven, he was taken up eastward, and that his
disciples worshipped him that way; and therefore chiefly it
was that in the ancient Church they prayed with their faces to
the east.   Hence it is that at this day many persons turn their
faces to that quarter of the world at the repetition of the
Creed.   But what speaks it to have been the universal opinion
of the Church is the ancient custom of burying corpses with
the feet to the east and head to the west, continued to this
day by the Church of England.

Dr. Comber says, " Some ancient authors tell us that the
old inhabitants of Attica buried thus before the days of Solon,
who, as they report, convinced the Athenians that the island
of Salamis did of right belong to them by showing them
dead bodies looking that way, and sepulchres turned towards
the east, as they used to bury." Diog. Laert. Vit. Solon, &c.
And the Scholiast upon Thucydides says, it was the manner
of all the Greeks to bury their dead in that manner.

Our learned countryman, Gregory, tells us that the Holy
Men of Jerusalem held a tradition, generally received from
the ancients, that our Saviour himself was buried with his face
and feet towards the east.[2]

I find the following in a curious tract, entitled a Light
shining out of Darkness, or Occasional Queries, 1659, p. 26:

[1] St. Damascen (lib. iv. c. 14, Orthod. Fid.) therefore tells us that because the Scriptures say that God planted Paradise in Eden towards the
east, where he placed the man which he had formed, whom he punished
with banishment upon his transgression, and made him dwell over against
Paradise in the western part, we therefore pray (says he), being in quest
of our ancient country, and, as it were, panting after it, do worship God
that way.

[2] " Bede (in Die Sanct. Paschæ, tom. vii.) says, that as the holy women
entered at the eastern part into the circular house hewn out in the rock,
they saw the angel sitting at the south part of the place where the body
of Jesus had lain, i. e. at his right hand; for undoubtedly his body, having
its face upwards, and the head to the west, must have its right hand to
the south." Bourne. chap. v.

" This reason likewise the common people give for their being buryed with their feet toward the east, so that they may be in a fitter posture to meet the sun of righteousness when he shall appear with healing in his wings, viz. at the resurrection." The subsequent remark is found at p. 30 : " Whether it be not a pretty foundation for the Oxford doctors to stand booted and spurred in the *act ?* because there is mention made in the Scripture of being *shod with the preparation of the Gospel ?*"

" 'Tis in the main allowed," says Selden, " that the heathens did, in general, look towards the east when they prayed, even from the earliest ages of the world." On this important subject the curious reader is referred to Alkibla ; a Disquisition upon worshipping towards the East, by a Master of Arts of the University of Oxford, 1728. A Second Part, continuing the work from the primitive to the present times, appeared in 1731 ; and a second edition of the whole in 1740. The author, who signs his name to the second part, was Mr. William Asplin.

In this enlightened age it is almost superfluous to observe that bowing towards the altar is a vestige of the ancient ceremonial law.

Hickeringill, who has left a severe satire on the retainers of those forms and ceremonies that lean towards Popish superstition, tells us, in his Ceremony Monger, p. 15 : " If I were a Papist, or Anthropo-morphite, who believes that God is enthroned in the east like a grave old king, I profess I would bow and cringe as well as any limber-ham of them all, and pay my adoration to that point of the compass (the east) ; but if men believe that the Holy One who inhabits eternity is also omnipresent, why do not they make correspondent ceremonies of adoration to every point of the compass ?"

Concession must be made by every advocate for manly and rational worship, that there is nothing more in the east[1] than in the belfry at the west end, or in the body of the church. We wonder, therefore, how ever this custom was retained by Protestants. The cringes and bowings of the Roman Catholics to the altar are in adoration of the corporal presence,

[1] " Aulam regiam, id est, ecclesiam ingredientes ad altare inclinamus, quod quasi regem milites adoramus : æterni enim regis milites sumus." Durandi Rationale, p. 226.

their wafer God, whom their fancies have seated and enthroned in this quarter of the east.

Mr. Mede tells us, that what reverential guise, ceremony, or worship they used at their ingress into churches, in the ages next to the Apostles (and some we believe they did), is wholly buried in silence and oblivion. The Jews used to bow themselves towards the Mercy-seat. The Christians, after them, in the Greek and Oriental churches, have, time out of mind, and without any known beginning, used to bow in like manner. They do it at this day. See Bingham's Antiquities.

At the end of Smart's curious Sermon, preached in the Cathedral church of Durham, July 27, 1628, among the charges brought against Bishop Cosens are the following : " Fifthly, he hath brought in a new custome of bowing the body downe to the ground before the altar (on which he hath set candlesticks, basons, and crosses, crucifixes and tapers, which stand there for a dumbe shew) : hee hath taught and enjoyned all such as come neere the altar to cringe and bow unto it : he hath commanded the choresters to make low leggs unto it, when they goe to light the tapers that are on it in the winter nights ; and in their returne from it, hee hath enjoined them to make low leggs unto it againe, going backe-wards with their faces towards the east, till they are out of the inclosure where they (usually) stand. Sixthly, he en-joynes all them that come to the Cathedrall church to pray with their faces towards the east, scoulding and brawling with them, even in time of divine service, which refuse to doe it, and bidding them either to pray towards the east, or to be packing out of the church, so devoted is hee to this easterne superstition."

In Articles to be inquired of within the Diocese of Lincoln, 1641, the following occurs : " Do you know of any parson, vicar, or curate that hath introduced any offensive rites or ceremonies into the church, not established by the lawes of the land ; as namely, that make *three courtesies* towards the communion table, that call the said table an altar, that enjoyne the people at their comming into the church to *bow towards the east*, or towards the communion table ?"

In Altar-Worship, or Bowing to the Communion Table con-sidered, by Z. Crofton, Presbyter, but proved Enemy to all Fanaticks, 1661, p. 60, we are informed that " the late Archbishop Laud was the first that ever framed a canon for bowing to, towards, or before the communion table." This shrewd writer adds : " For which, reason will require some symbol of divine nature and presence ; its being an holy instrument of divine service, being of no more force for the altar than for the tongs or snuffers of the tabernacle, or Aaron's breeches under the law, or for surplices, organs, chalices, patens, and canonical coates and girdles, which are made instruments of holy service by our altar-adorers ; and if on that reason they must be bowed unto, we shall abound in cringing, not only in every church, but in every street :" p. 116. " On Maundy Thursday, 1636, Mrs. Charnock, &c., went to see the King's Chapel, where they saw an altar, with tapers and other furniture on it, and a crucifix over it ; and presently came Dr. Brown, one of his Majestie's chaplaines, and his curate, into the chappel, and *turning themselves towards the altar, bowed three times ;* and then performing some private devotion, departed ; and immediately came two seminarie priests and did as the doctor and his curate had done before them."

A regard for impartiality, says Brand, obliges me to own that I have observed this practice in college chapels at Oxford. I hope it is altogether worn out in every other place in the kingdom ; and, for the credit of that truly respectable seminary of learning and religious truth, that it will not be retained there by the rising generation.

The practice of bowing to the altar, the editor believes, is now entirely left off at Oxford. That of turning to it at the repetition of the Creed is generally retained, and certainly has its use, in contributing very often to recall the wandering thoughts of those who attend the chapel service.

In Browne's Map of the Microcosme, 1642, speaking of a proud woman, he says : " Shee likes *standing at the Creed,* not because the church commands it, but because her gay clothes are more spectable." And in the Times Anatomized, in severall Characters, by T. F., 1647, is the following: " Like that notorious pickpocket, that whilst (according to the custome) *every one held up their hands at rehearsing the Creed,* he by a device had a false hand, which he held up like the rest, whilst his true one was false in other men's pockets."

I find the following passage in the New Help to Discourse, 1684, p. 36 : " It is a custom in Poland, that when in the

churches the gospel is reading, the nobility and gentry of
that country draw out their swords, to signify that they are
ready to defend the same, if any dare oppugn it.   The same
reason, questionless, gave beginning to our custom of standing
up at the Creed, whereby we express how prepared and resolute
we are to maintain it, although, in the late times of rebellion,
some tender consciences, holding it to be a relique of Popery,
being more nice than wise, did undiscreetly refuse the same."

I find in a curious Collection of Godly Ballads in the
Scottish Language, Edinburgh, 1621, the following passage,
which contains, in other words, a very old argument against
transubstantiation

> " Gif God be transubstantiall
> In bread with hoc est corpus meum,
> Why are ye so unnaturall
> To take him in your teeth and sla him ?"

The Rev. Joseph Wharton, in his Dying Indian, puts into
his hero's charge a similar thought :

> " Tell her I ne'er have worshipp'd
> With those that eat their God."

In Heath's Two Centuries of Epigrammes, 1610, I find the
following : Cent. ii. Epigr. 78 :

> " *In Transubstantiatores.*

> " The cannibals eate men with greedinesse,
> And transubstantiators do no lesse :
> No lesse ?   Nay more ; and that farre more by ods ;
> Those eat man's flesh, these ravine upon God's."

Thus hath superstition made the most awful mysteries of our
faith the subjects of ridicule.

The learned Moresin tells us, that altars in Papal Rome
were placed towards the east, in imitation of ancient and
heathen Rome.   Thus we read in Virgil's eleventh Æneid :

> " Illi ad surgentem conversi lumina solem
> Dant fruges manibus salsas."[1]

---

[1] Moresini Papatus, p. 117.   He goes on : " Orientem in solem conver-
titur, ut jam dixi, qui deos salutat aut orat apud nos, et Apul. ait, 2 Metam.
Tunc in orientem obversus vel incrementa solis Augusti tacitus imprecatus,
&c. Polyd. lib. 5, cap. 9, Invent.   Orientem respicit precaturus, et imagines oriens spectant, ut ingredientes preces eo versum ferant ad ritum

In a curious work, now before me, entitled England's Faithful Reprover and Monitour, 1653, the unknown author, in his address "to the Church of England," reprobates a custom then prevalent for the audience to *sit in churches with their hats on*, p. 48 : "Thine own children even glory in their shame, when, not as masters, but as scholars, not as teachers, but as disciples, *they sit covered at their most solemn holy meetings*, without difference of place, degree, age, season, or of any personal relation whatsoever. Although we have known some, and those not a few, who have presumed to sit covered, in the presence of God at such a time as this ; but when a great person hath come into the assembly, *have honoured him with the uncovering of the head*, as though civill respect towards a mortall prince were to be expressed by more evident signs of submission from the outward man than religious worship towards the immortal God." He tells us, however, that "*they were uncovered when they sang the Psalms*," p. 50.[1] "When the minister prayeth or praiseth God in the words of the Psalmist, as he frequently doth ; at which time every one almost is vailed, who, notwithstanding, presently condemn themselves in this very thing which they allow, forasmuch as they all uncover the head when the same Psalmes are sung by them, only changed into meeter, and that perchance for the worse." Our author concludes this head with observing,

Persarum, qui solem orientem venerati sunt.   Plut. in Numa.   Deus interdicit Judæis oriente, prohibet imagines.   Exod. 20 ; Levit. 26 ; Deut. 5 ; Esa. 40.   Cœl. autem lib. vii. cap. 2, ant. lect. dicit, jam illud veteris fuit superstitionis, quod in Asclepio Mercurius scribit, deum adorantes, si medius affulserit dies in austrum converti ; si vero dies sit occiduus, in occasum : si se tunc primum promat sol, exortiva est spectanda.   Vigilius Papa, anno Christi 554, jussit sacrificulum sacrificantem missam ad ortum solis oculos dirigete.   Insuper qui precabantur ad orientem conversi, erecto vultu, manibus passis, expansis et in cœlum sublatis ac protensis orabant.   Virg. 8 Æneid.   Ovid. lib. 4, Fast.   Vitruvius, lib. 4, cap. 5.   Tertul. in Apol.   Apul. lib 2, Metam.   Clemens, lib. 7.   Stromaton. eodemque conversa templa fuisse Plutarch. in Numa docet.   Juvenal, Satyr. 10.   Apul. lib. de Mundo.   Virgil, lib. 2 et 3 Æneid.   Hæc omnia retinet Papatus ; vide Justinum, lib. 18, et lege dist. 11, can. ecclesiasticum, hæc instituta Sixto 11, adscribunt.   Szeg. in Spec."

[1] So, in a Character of England as it was lately presented in a letter to a Nobleman of France, 1659, p. 13 : " I have beheld a whole congregation sitting on their * * * * *with their hats on at the reading of the Psalms, and yet bareheaded when they sing them.*"

properly enough, that "we cannot imagine lesse than that this covering of the head in the congregation, where infirmity or sickness doth not plead for it, tendeth to the dishonour of Jesus Christ, whose servants we profess ourselves to be, especially at this time, and to the contempt of his messenger representing the office and person of Christ before our eyes."

The custom of rustics in marking the outlines of their shoes on the tops of their church steeples, and engraving their names in the areas, has been, by Smart, in his poem on "The Hop-Garden," very sensibly referred to motives of vanity, ii. 165 :

> " To err is human, human to be vain.
> 'Tis vanity, and mock desire of fame,
> That prompts the rustic on the steeple-top
> Sublime, to mark the outlines of his shoe,
> And in the area to engrave his name."

As is the following, in the subsequent lines, to the pride of office :

> "With pride of heart the churchwarden surveys
> High o'er the belfry, girt with birds and flow'rs,
> His story wrote in capitals : ' 'Twas I
> That bought the font; and I repair'd the pews.'"

White, in his History of Selborne, p. 323, says, in speaking of the church : " I have all along talked of the east and west end, as if the chancel stood exactly true to those points of the compass ; but this is by no means the case, for the fabric bears so much to the north of the east, that the four corners of the tower, and not the four sides, stand to the four cardinal points.[1] The best mode of accounting for this deviation seems to be, that the workmen, who were probably employed in the longest days, endeavoured to set the chancels to the rising of the sun."

---

[1] See this subject before noticed, in the present volume, p. 6. The witty author of the History of Birmingham, p. 113, speaking of St. Bartholomew's Chapel there, observes : " The chancel hath this singular difference from others, that it veres toward the north. Whether the projector committed an error I leave to the critics. It was the general practice of the pagan church to fix their altar, upon which they sacrificed, in the east, towards the rising sun, the object of worship. The Christian church, in the time of the Romans, immediately succeeded the pagan, and scrupulously adopted the same method ; which has been strictly adhered to. By what obligation the Christian is bound to follow the pagan, or

PLEDGING.

The word Pledge is most probably derived from the French *Pleige,* a surety or gage. Some deduce the expression *I'li pledge you* in drinking, from the times when the Danes bore sway in this land. It is said to have been common with these ferocious people to stab a native in the act of drinking, with a knife or dagger : hereupon people would not drink in company, unless some one present would be their pledge or surety that they should receive no hurt whilst they were in their draught. In Shakespeare's Timon of Athens, act i sc. 5, is the following passage.

"If I
Were a huge man, I should fear to drink at meats,
Lest they should spy my wind-pipe's dangerous notes;
Great men should drink *with harness on their throats;*"

"alluding to *the pledge* in the time of the Danes. It was then customa'y, when a person promised to be pledge or security for the rest of the company, that they should receive no harm whilst they were drinking; a custom occasioned by the practice of the Danes heretofore, who frequently used to stab or cut the throats of the English while they were drinking. In Wyat's Rebellion, 1st of Queen Mary, the serjeants and other lawyers in Westminster Hall *pleaded in harness.* See Baker's Chronicle, edit. 1670, p. 316." Grey's Notes on Shakespeare, ii. 120.

Dr. Henry, in his History of Great Britain, ii. 539, speaking on this subject, says: "If an Englishman presumed to drink in the presence of a Dane, without his express permission, it was esteemed so great a mark of disrespect, that nothing but his instant death could expiate. Nay, the English

wherein a church would be injured by being directed to any of the thirty-two points of the compass, is doubtful. Certain it is, if the chancel of Bartholomew's had tended due east, the eye would have been exceedingly hurt, and the builder would have raised an object of ridicule for ages. The ground will admit of no situation but that in which the church now stands. But the inconsiderate architect of Deritend chapel, anxious to catch the eastern point, lost the line of the street; we may therefore justly pronounce *he sacrificed to the east.*" Deritend chapel is another place of public worship in the same town.

were so intimidated that they would not adventure to drink
even when they were invited, until the Danes had pledged
their honour for their safety; which introduced the custom
of pledging each other in drinking, of which some vestiges
are still remaining among the common people in the north of
England, where the Danes were most predominant." He cites
Pontopidon, Gesta et Vestigia Danorum, ii. 209.

"Such great drinkers," says Strutt, "were the Danes (who
were in England in the time of Edgar), and so much did their
bad Examples prevail with the English, that he, by the advice
of Dunstan, Archbishop of Canterbury, put down many alehouses, suffering only one to be in a village or small town;
and he also further ordained that pins or nails should be
fastened into the drinking-cups and horns, at stated distances,
and whosoever should drink beyond these marks at one
draught should be obnoxious to a severe punishment." This
was to prevent the pernicious custom of drinking.[1]

This law seems to have given occasion to a custom which
was afterwards called *Pin-drinking, or nick the pin*, and which
is thus explained in Cocker's Dictionary: "An old way of
drinking exactly to a pin in the midst of a wooden cup, which
being somewhat difficult, occasioned much drunkenness; so a
law was made that priests, monks, and friars should not
drink to or at the pins." It is certainly difficult to say what
law this was, unless it has been confounded with that of King
Edgar. I find the custom differently alluded to in another
English Dictionary called Gazophylacium Anglicanum, 1689,
where the expression, "*He is on a merry pin,*" is said to have
arisen "from a way of drinking in a cup in which a pin was
stuck, and he that could drink to the pin, i. e. neither under
nor over it, was to have the wager."[2]

[1] Strutt, who has cited William of Malmesbury for this custom, is not
quite correct in his translation of the passage, which is as follows : " In
tantum et in frivolis pacis sequax, ut quia compatriotæ, in tabernis conve-
nientes, jamque temulenti pro modo bibendi contenderent, ipse clavos
argenteos vel aureos vasis affigi jusserit, ut dum metam suam quisque cog-
noscent, non plus subserviente verecundia vel ipse appeteret, vel alium
appetere cogeret." Scriptores post Bedam, p. 56.

[2] Douce conceives the expression to drink " supernaculum" means to
drink to the nail, as above explained. *Nagel* in German means a nail or
pin. He adds : " See the article *Ad pinnas bibere* in Cowel's Law Dictionary, and Grose's Dictionary of the Vulgar Tongue, v. *Pin.*" " Ut

In Wise's Further Observations upon the White Horse, and other Antiquities, 1742, p. 54, we read : " The custom of *pledging healths*, still preserved among Englishmen, is said to be owing to the Saxons' mutual regard for each other's safety, and as a caution against the treacherous inhospitality of the Danes, when they came to live in peace with the natives."

Others affirm the true sense of the word to be this : that if the person drank unto was not disposed to drink himself, he would put another to be a pledge to do it for him, otherwise the party who began would take it ill.

Strutt confirms the former of these opinions in the following words : " The old manner of pledging each other, when they drank, was thus : the person who was going to drink asked any one of the company who sat next him, whether he would pledge him, on which he answering that he would, held up his knife or sword, to guard him whilst he drank ; for while a man is drinking he necessarily is in an unguarded posture, exposed to the treacherous stroke of some hidden or secret enemy." But the custom is here said to have first taken its rise from the death of young King Edward, called the Martyr, son of Edgar, who was, by the contrivance of Elfrida, his stepmother, treacherously stabbed in the back as he was drinking.

Barrington, in Observation on the Ancient Statutes, 1775, p. 206, says that it was anciently the custom for a person swearing fealty " to hold his hands joined together, between those of his lord ; the reason for which seems to have been that some lord had been assassinated under pretence of paying homage ; but, while the tenant's hands continued in this attitude, it was impossible for him to make such an attempt. I take the same reason to have occasioned the ceremony still adhered to by the scholars in Queen's College at Oxford, who wait upon the fellows placing their thumbs upon the table ; which, as I have been informed, still continues in some parts of Germany whilst the superior drinks the health of the inferior. The suspicion that men formerly had of attempts upon their lives on such occasions is well known, from the common ac-

presbyteri non eant ad potationes, nec ad pinnas bibant." Concil. Londinens. A.D. 1102, apud Spelman, ii. 24. Johnson very properly translates this : " That priests go not to *drinking bouts*, nor *drink to pegs*." Compare also Gent. Mag. for October. 1768, lxviii. 475.

count with regard to the origin of pledging." He says, ibid.:
"The Speculum Regale advises the courtier, when he is in
the king's presence, to pull off his cloak; and one of the
reasons given is, that he shows by this means that he hath no
concealed weapons to make an attempt upon the king's life."
pp. 299, 300.

In Pierce Pennilesse his Supplication to the Divell, by
Thomas Nash, 1595, we read: "You do me the disgrace, if
you doo not *pledge me as much* as I drinke to you." In the
Workes of John Heiwood newlie imprinted, 1598, is the following line: "I drinke (quoth she); quoth he, *I will not
pledge.*"

Plat, in his Jewel-house of Art and Nature, p. 59, gives a
recipe to prevent drunkenness, "for the help of such modest
drinkers as only in company are drawn, or rather forced to
pledge in full bolls such quaffing companions as they would
be loth to offend, and will require *reason at their hands*, as
they term it." Overbury, in his Characters, speaking of a
serving-man, says: "He never drinks but double, for he must
be pledged; nor commonly without some short sentence nothing to the purpose: and seldom abstains till he comes to a
thirst."

In Young's England's Bane, 1617, is the following passage:
"Truely I thinke hereupon comes the name of *good* fellow,
quasi *goad* fellow, because he forceth and goads his fellowes
forward to be drunke with his persuasive termes, as I dranke
to you, *pray pledge me*, you dishonour me, you disgrace mee,
and with such like words, doth urge his consorts forward to
be drunke, as oxen being prickt with goads are compel'd and
forced to draw the waine."

Barnaby Rich, in his work entitled the Irish Hubbub, or
the English Hue and Crie, 1619, p. 24, describing the mode
of drinking healths in his time, tells us: "He that beginneth
the health hath his prescribed orders: first uncovering his
head, hee takes a full cup in his hand, and settling his countenance with a grave aspect, hee craves for audience: silence
being once obtained, hee begins to breath out the name, per-
adventure of some honourable personage, that is worthy of a
better regard than to have his name polluted amongst a company of drunkards: but his health is drunke to, and *hee that
pledgeth, must likewise off with his cap*, kisse his fingers, and

bowing himselfe in signe of a reverent acceptance. When the leader sees his follower thus prepared, he soups up his broath, turnes the bottom of the cup upward, and in ostentation of his dexteritie, gives the cup a phillip, to make it cry *Twango*. And thus the first scene is acted. The cup being newly replenished to the breadth of an haire, he that is *the pledger* must now beginne his part, and thus it goes round throughout the whole company, provided alwaies by a cannon set downe by the founder, there must be three at the least still uncovered, till the health hath had the full passage : which is no sooner ended, but another begins againe."

In the second part of Dekker's Honest Whore, 1630, is the following : " Will you fall *on your maribones* and *pledge this health*, 'tis to my mistris?" So in Shakerley Marmion's Antiquary, act ii. :

> " Drank to your health whole nights in hippocrase
> *Upon my knees*, with more religion
> Than e'er I said my prayers, which Heaven forgive me."

Pledging is again mentioned, act iv. : " To our noble duke's health, I can drink no lesse, not a drop lesse ; and you and his servants *will pledge me*, I am sure."

In Heywood's Philocothonista, 1635, p. 12, we read : " Divers authors report of Alexander, that, carousing one day with twenty persons in his company, hee dranke healths to every man round, and *pledged* them severally againe : and as he was to rise, Calisthenes, the Sophist, coming into the banqueting house, the king offered him a deepe quaffing bowle, which he modestly refused, for which being taxed by one there present, hee said aloud, I desire not, oh, Alexander, *to receive a pledge* from thee, by taking which I shall be presently inforced to inquire for a physition." There is a remarkable passage in Ward's Living Speeches of Dying Christians, (Sermons, 1636, p. 144). " My Saviour began to mee in a bitter cup, and *shall I not pledge him ?*" i. e. drink the same. From the speech of Lawrence Saunders.

In a Brief Character of the Low Countries under the States, 1652, p. 57, speaking of a Dutch feast, the author tells us : " At those times it goes hard with a stranger ; all in curtesie will be drinking to him, and all that do so *he must pledge :* till he doth, the fill'd cups circle round his trencher, from whence they are not taken away till emptyed."

I know not what the following passage means in Samuel
Rowland's Satyres ; Humour's Ordinarie :

" Tom is no more like thee than chalk's like cheese
   To pledge a health, or to drink *up-se-frieze:*
   Fill him a beaker,[1] he will never flinch," &c.

The term *Upsie-freeze* occurs again, Dekker's Dead Term,
or Westminster's Speech to London, 1607 : " Fellowes there
are that followe mee, who in deepe bowles shall drowne the
Dutchman, and make him lie under the table.   At his owne
weapon of *upsie freeze* will they dare him, and beat him with
wine-pots till he be dead drunke."   So, in Massinger's Virgin
Martyr, act ii. sc. 1, Spungius calls Bacchus "the god of
brewed wine and sugar, great patron of rob-pots, *upsy freezy*
tipplers, and   supernaculum-takers."   In Times Curtaine
drawne, or the Anatomie of Vanitie, &c., by Richard Brath-
wayte, Oxonian, 1621, in " Ebrius experiens, or the Drunkard's
Humour," is the subsequent passage :

" To it we went, we two being all were left,
   (For all the rest of sense were quite bereft,)
   Where either call'd for wine that best did please,
   Thus helter-skelter drunke we *upsefrese*.[2]
   I was conjured by my kissing friend
   To pledge him but an health, and then depart,
   Which if did, Is'de ever have his heart.
   1 gave assent ; the *health, five senses* were,
   (Though scarce one sense did 'twixt us both appeare,)
   Which as he drunk I pledg'd ; both pledg'd and drunk,
   Seeing him now full charg'd behinde I shrunke," &c.

In a curious satirical little book in my possession, dedicated
to George Doddington, and written about the time of Charles
II., I find the following, Introd. p. 9 : "Awake ! thou noblest
drunkard, Bacchus, thou must likewise stand to me (if, at
least, thou canst for reeling), teach me how to take the
German's OP SIJN FRIZE, the Danish *Rowsa*, the Switzer's

[1] *Beaker*, a bowl or dish for containing liquor : probably from the Italian
bicchiere, patera, scyphus.   Dr. Johnson defines it " a cup with the spout
in the form of a bird's *beak ;*" but gives us no proof that such was the
form of the beaker in ancient times.

[2] " *Upse-Dutch*, a heavy kind of Dutch beer, formerly much used in
England : *Upse-Freese*, a similar drink imported from Friesland : *To drink
upse-Dutch*, to drink swinishly, like a Dutchman."   Halliwell's Diction
ary, p. 905.

Sloop of Rhenish, the Italian *Parmasant,* the Englishman's *healths and frolicks.* Hide not a drop of thy moist mystery from me, thou plumpest swill-bowl."

In England's Bane, or the Description of Drunkennesse, by Thomas Young, 1617, are some curious passages concerning the then customs of drinking : " I myselfe have seen and (to my grief of conscience) may now say have in presence, yea and amongst others, been an actor in the businesse, when upon our knees, after healthes to many private punkes, a health have been drunke to all the whoores in the world. . . He is a man of no fashion that cannot drinke *supernaculum,* carouse *the hunters hoop,* quaffe *upsey-freese crosse,* bowse in *Permoysaunt,* in *Pimlico,* in *Crambo,* with *healthes, gloves, numpes, frolicks,* and a thousand such domineering inventions,[1] as *by the bell,* by the *cards,* by the *dye,* by the *dozen,* by the *yard,* and so by measure we drink out of measure.—There are in London drinking schooles : so that drunkennesse is professed with us as a liberall arte and science. . . . I have seene a company amongst the very woods and forests (he speaks of the New Forest and Windsor Forest), drinking for a *muggle.* Sixe determined to trie their strengths who could drinke most glasses for the muggle. The first drinkes a glasse of a pint the second two, the next three, and so every one multiplieth till the last taketh sixe. Then the first beginneth againe and taketh seven, and in this manner they drinke thrice a peece round, every man taking a glasse more than his fellow, so that he that dranke least, which was the first, drank one and twentie pints, and the sixth man thirty-six." Our author observes : " Before we were acquainted with the *lingering wars of the Low Countries,* drunkennes was held in the highest degree of hatred that might be amongst us."

In the dedication to the Drunkard's Cup, a sermon by Robert Harris, President of Trinity College, Oxford, in his Works, 1653, is the following curious passage : " There is (they say) an art of drinking now, and in the world it is become a great profession. There are degrees and titles given

---

[1] It is singular that a part of this should have been borrowed from Pierce Pennilesse, his Supplication to the Divell, by Thomas Nash, Cont., 1595, " Nowe he is nobody that cannot drinke Supernagulum, carouse the Hunter's Hoope, quaffe Upse freze Crosse, with healths, gloves, mumpes, polockes, and a thousand such domineering inventions."

under the names of *Roaring Boyes, Damned Crew,* &c. There are lawes and ceremonies to be observed both by the firsts and seconds, &c. There is a drinking *by the foot,* by the *yard,* &c., a drinking *by the douzens,* by *the scores,* &c. *for the wager,* for the *victory, man against man, house against house, town against town,* and how not? There are also terms of art, fetched from hell (for the better distinguishing of the practitioners) ; one is *coloured,* another is *foxt,* a third is *gone to the dogs,* a fourth is *well to live,* &c."

In the body of the sermon, he mentions "the strange saucinesse of base vermine, *in tossing the name of his most excellent majesty in their foaming mouthes,* and in daring to make that a shooing horne to draw on drink, by drinking healths to him." The following, at p. 307, is curious : " I doe not speake of those beasts that must be answered and have right done them, *in the same measure, gesture, course,* &c., but of such onely as *leave you to your measure* (you will keepe *a turne* and *your time in pledging*), is it any hurt to pledge such ? How pledge them ? You mistake if you thinke that we speake against any *true civility.* If thou lust to pledge the Lord's prophets in woes, *pledge good fellowes in their measures and challenges :* if not so, learne still to sharpe a peremptory answer to an unreasonable demand. Say—*I will pray for the king's health, and drinke for mine owne.*" In page 299 we find "somewhat *whitled,*" and in page 304, "*buckt* with drink," as terms expressing the different degrees of drunkenness.

In Gayton's Festivous Notes upon Don Quixote, 1654, p.234, I find a singular passage, which I confess I do not thoroughly understand, concerning the then modes of drinking. He is describing a drinking bout of female gossips : "Dispatching a lusty rummer of Rhenish to little Periwig, who passed it instantly to Steepen Malten, and she conveigh'd with much agility to Daplusee, who made bold to stretch *the countesses gowne into a pledge,* and *cover and come,* which was the only plausible mode of drinking they delighted in : this was precisely observed by the other three, that their moistned braines gave leave for their glibb'd tongues to chat liberally."

The following occurs in Herrick's Hesperides, p. 146 :

> " Remember us in cups full crown'd
> And let our citie-health go round,

Quite through the young maids and the men,
To the ninth number, if not tenne;
Untill the fired chesnuts leape
For joy, to see the fruits ye reape
From the plumpe challice and the cup
That tempts till it be *tossed up.*"

What can the following mean? Ibid. p. 87 :

" Call me the sonne of beere, and then confine
Me to the *tap*, the *tost*, the *turfe;* let wine
Ne'er shine upon me."

In Folly in Print : or a Book of Rhymes, published about
1660, in " a catch made before the king's coming to Worcester
with the Scottish army," is the following :

" Each man upon his back
Shall swallow his sack,
This *health* will indure no shrinking;
The rest shall dance round
Him that lies on the ground;
Fore me this is excellent drinking."

In the character of " A Bad Husband," at the end of
England's Jests Refined and Improved, 1687, occur the following traits : " He is a passionate lover of morning-draughts,
which he generally continues till dinner-time ; a rigid exacter
of *num-groats* and collector-general of *foys*[1] and *biberidge.*[2]
He admires the prudence of that apothegm, *lets drink first :*
and would rather sell 20 per cent. to loss than make *a dry
bargain.*"

[1] Sir Frederick Morton Eden, in his State of the Poor, 1797, i. 560,
gives us the following passage from Fergusson's Farmer's Ingle :

" On some feast day, the wee-things buskit braw
Shall heeze her heart up wi' a silent joy,
Fu' cadgie that her head was up, and saw
Her ain spun cleething on a darling *oy*,
Careless tho' death should make the feast her *foy.*"

After explaining *oy*, in a note, to signify grandchild, from the Gaelic
ogha, he tells us, " A *foy is the feast a person, who is about to leave a place,
gives to his friends before his departure.* The metaphorical application of
the word in the above passage is eminently beautiful and happy."

[2] " BEVERAGE, *Beverege*, or *Beveridge*, reward, consequence. 'Tis a
word now in use for a refreshment between dinner and supper ; and we
use the word when *any one pays for wearing new clothes*, &c." Hearne's
Glossary to Robert of Gloucester's Chronicle, in *v.* Grose says, " There
is a kind of beverage called *Foot-ale*, required from one entering on a
new occupation." If I mistake not, this is called in some places, " *to set
your footing.*"

It appears from Aḷan Ramsay's Poems, 1721, p. 120, that in Scotland, of those "wha had been *fou* yestreen," i. e. *drunk* the night before, "payment of the drunken groat is very peremptorily demanded by the common people, next morning: but if they frankly confess the debt due, they are passed for twopence." The same author, ibid. p. 17, mentions as in use among the Scots, *Hy-jinks*, "a drunken game, or new project to drink and be rich; thus the quaff or cup is filled to the brim, then one of the company takes a pair of dice, and after crying *hy-jinks*, he throws them out: the number he casts up points out the person must drink, he who threw beginning at himself number one, and so round till the number of the persons agree with that of the dice (which may fall upon himself if the number be within twelve), then he sets the dice to him, or bids him take them: he on whom they fall is obliged to drink, or pay a small forfeiture in money; then throws, and so on: but if he forgets to cry *hy-jinks*, he pays a forfeiture into the bank. Now he on whom it falls to drink, if there be anything in bank worth drawing, gets it all if he drinks. Then, with a great deal of caution, he empties his cup, sweeps up the money, and orders the cup to be filled again, and then throws; for, if he err in the articles, he loses the privilege of drawing the money. The articles are, (1) Drink. (2) Draw. (3) Fill. (4) Cry *hy-jinks*. (5) Count just. (6) Chuse your doublet man, viz. when two equal numbers of the dice are thrown, the person whom you chuse must pay a double of the common forfeiture, and so must you when the dice is in his hand. A rare project this," adds honest Allan, "and no bubble, I can assure you; for a covetous fellow may save money, and get himself as drunk as he can desire in less than an hour's time." It is probable he might have subjoined "experto crede Roberto." He mentions, p. 30, a set of drinkers called *Facers*, who, he says, "were a club of fair drinkers, who inclined rather to spend a shilling on ale than two-pence for meat. They had their name from a rule they observed of obliging themselves to throw all they left in the cup in their own faces: wherefore, to save their face and cloaths, they prudently suck'd the liquor clean out." [1]

[1] Dr. Jamieson notices *Whigmeleerie* as the name of a ridiculous game which was occasionally used in Angus at a drinking club. A pin was stuck in the centre of a circle, from which there were as many radii as there

Strutt's authority for his origin of Pledging, before quoted, is William of Malmesbury, and he observes from the delineation he gives us (and it must be noted that his plates, being copies of ancient illuminated manuscripts, are of unquestionable authority,) that it seems perfectly well to agree with the reported custom; the middle figure is addressing himself to his companion, who seems to tell him that he pledges him, holding up his knife in token of his readiness to assist and protect him. After all, I cannot help hazarding an opinion that the expression meant no more than that if you took your cup or glass *I pledged myself to you* that I would follow your example. The common ellipsis, "*to*," is wanting. Thus we say, "I'll give you," instead of "I'll give *to* you;" "I'll pledge you," "I'll pledge *to* you." But I offer this with great deference to the established opinions on the subject.[1]

It was the custom in Beaumont and Fletcher's time for the young gallants to stab themselves in the arms or elsewhere, in order to drink the healths of their mistresses, or to write their names in their own blood. See Mason's Notes on Beaumont and Fletcher, p. 103, where many instances are adduced. So, in the Oxford Drollery, 1671, p. 124, is a song to a Scotch tune, in which the following lines occur:

3. "*I stab'd mine arm to drink her health,*
   The more fool I, the more fool I," &c.

4. "I will no more her servant be,
   The wiser I, the wiser I,
   Nor pledge her health upon my knee," &c.

I beg the reader's candid examination of the subsequent

were persons in the company, with the name of each person at the radius opposite to him. On the pin an index was placed, and moved round by every one in his turn; and at whatsoever person's radius it stopped, he was obliged to drink off his glass. *Whigmeleeries* are " whims, fancies, crotchets."

[1] Pasquier, in his Recherches, p. 501, mentions that Mary, Queen of Scots, previously to her execution, drank to all her attendants, desiring them to pledge her. See what the same author has said in p. 785 of his work concerning this custom. See also the Fabliaux of M. Le Grand, tom. i. p. 119, and his Histoire de la Vie privée des François, iii. 270. The custom of pledging is to be found in the ancient romance of Ogie Danoit, where Charlemagne pledges himself for Ogie. See Tressan, Corps d'Extraits de Romans de Chevalerie, ii. 77.

passages in Rigby's Ingenious Poem called the Drunkard's
Prospective, or Burning Glasse, 1656, p. 7 :

> " Yea every cup is fast to others wedg'd,
> They alwaies *double drink*, they must be *pledg'd.*
> *He that begins*, how many so'er they be,
> *Looks that each one do drink as much as he.*"

So again, at page 12 :

> " Oh, how they'll wind men in, do what they can,
> By drinking healths, first unto such a man,
> Then unto such a woman!   Then they'll send
> An health to each man's mistresse or his friend;
> Then to their kindred's or their parents deare,
> They needs must have the other jug of beere;
> Then to their captains and commanders stout,
> Who for to pledge they think none shall stand out;
> Last to the king and queen they'll have a cruse,
> *Whom for to pledge* they think none dare refuse."

In the first quotation the author's meaning seems to be this :
a man in company, not contented with taking what he chooses,
binds another to drink the same quantity that he does. In
the last, one proposes a health which another pledges to
honour by drinking to it an equal quantity with him that
proposed it.

Heywood, in his Philocothonista, or the Drunkard Opened,
Dissected, and Anatomized, 1635, says, p. 45, "Of *drinking
cups* divers and sundry sorts we have ; some of elme, some of
box, some of maple, some of holly, &c., mazers, broad-mouth'd
dishes, noggins, whiskins, piggins, crinzes, ale-bowles, wassell-
bowles, court-dishes, tankards, kannes, from a bottle to a pint,
from a pint to a gill.   Other bottles we have of leather, but
they most used amongst the shepheards and harvest-people of
the countrey : small jacks wee have in many alehouses, of the
citie and suburbs, tip't with silver, besides the great black
jacks and bombards at the court, which when the Frenchmen
first saw, they reported, at their returne into their countrey,
that the Englishmen used to drinke out of their bootes : we
have besides, cups made of hornes of beasts, of cocker-nuts,
of goords, of the eggs of estriches, others made of the shells
of divers fishes brought from the Indies and other places, and
shining like mother of pearle.   Come to plate, every taverne
can afford you flat bowles, French bowles, prounet cups, beare

bowles, beakers, and private householders in the citie, when they make a feast to entertaine their friends, can furnish their cupboards with flagons, tankards, beere-cups, wine-bowles, some white, some percell guilt,[1] some guilt all over, some with covers, others without, of sundry shapes and qualities." Page 51, he tells us : "There is now profest an eighth liberal art or science, call'd *Ars Bibendi*, i. e. the Art of Drinking. The students or professors thereof call a greene garland, or painted hoope hang'd out, *a colledge :* a signe where there is lodging, man's-meate, and horse-meate, an *inne of court*, an *hall*, or an *hostle :* where nothing is sold but ale and tobacco, *a grammar schoole :* a red or blew lattice, that they terme *a free schoole*, for all commers. . . . The bookes which they studdy, and whose leaves they so often turne over, are, for the most part, three of the old translation and three of the new. Those of the old translation : 1. The Tankard. 2. The Black Jacke. 3. The Quart-pot rib'd, or Thorondell. Those of the new be these : 1. The Jugge. 2. The Beaker. 3. The double or single Can, or Black Pot." Among the proper phrases belonging to the library, occur, p. 65, " to drinke upse-phreese, supernaculum, to swallow a slap-dragon, or a raw egge—to see that no lesse than *three at once be bare* to a health." Our author, p. 23, observes : "Many of our nation have used the Lowe-countrey warres so long, that though they have left their money and clothes behind, yet they have brought home their habit of drinking." At p. 60 he gives the following phrases then in use for being drunk : "He is foxt, hee is flawed, he is flustered, hee is suttle, cupshot, cut in the leg or backe, hee hath seene the French king, he hath swallowed an haire or a taverne-token, hee hath whipt the cat, he hath been at the scriveners and learn'd to make indentures, hee hath bit his grannam, or is bit by a barne-weesell, with an hundred such-like adages and sentences."

[That is, partly gilded.]

HEALTHS, or TOASTS.

" 'Twas usual then the banquet to prolong
By musick's charm, and some delightful song:
Where every youth in pleasing accents strove
To tell the stratagems and cares of love.
How some successful were, how others crost:
Then to the sparkling glass would *give his toast :*
Whose bloom did most in his opinion shine,
To relish both the musick and the wine."

KING'S ART OF COOKERY, ed. 1776, iii. 75.

THE ancient Greeks and Romans used at their meals to make libations, pour out, and even drink wine, in honour of the gods. The classical writings abound with proofs of this.

The Grecian poets and historians, as well as the Roman writers, have also transmitted to us accounts of the grateful custom of drinking to the health of our benefactors and of our acquaintances.

————" Pro te, fortissime, vota
Publica suscipimus : Bacchi tibi sumimus haustus."

It appears that the men of gallantry among the Romans used to take off as many glasses to their respective mistresses as there were letters in the name of each.[1] Thus, Martial :

" *Six* cups to Nævia's health go quickly round,
And be with *seven* the fair Justina's crown'd."

Hence, no doubt, our custom of toasting, or drinking healths,[2] a ceremony which Prynne, in his work entitled Healthes Sicknesse, inveighs against in language most strongly tinctured with enthusiastic fury.[3]

[1] How exceedingly similar to our modern custom of saying to each of the company in turn, " Give us a lady to toast," is the following :
" Da puere ab summo, age tu interibi ab infimo da suavium."
Plauti Asinaria.

[2] The following is a curious epigram of Owen, I. ii. 42, on this subject.
" Quo tibi potarum plus est in ventre *salutum,*
Hoc minus epotis, hisce salutis habes.
Una salus sanis, nullam potare *salutem,*
Non est in potâ vera *salute* salus."
So in Witt's Recreations, Lond. 1667, I find the following :
" Even from my heart much *health* I wish,
No health I'll wash with drink,
Health wish'd, not *wash'd,* in *words,* not *wine,*
To be the best I think."

[3] This extraordinary man, who, though he drank no healths, yet appears

In Dialthwalt's Law of Drinking, 1617, I find the following passage, p. 9 : " These cups proceed either *in order* or *out of order*. *In order*, when no person transgresseth or drinkes out of course, but the cup goes round according to their manner of sitting ; and this we call *an health cup*, because in our wishing or confirming of any one's health, bare-headed and standing, it is performed by all the company. It is drunke *without order*, when the course or method of order is not observed, and that the cup passeth on to whomsoever we shall appoint." Ibid. p. 23 : " Some joyne two cups one upon another, and drink them together." In the preface, keeping a public-house is called " the known trade of *the ivy bush*, or *red lettice.*"

In Ward's Woe to Drunkards, 1636, p. 553, we read : " Abandon that foolish and vicious custome, as Ambrose and Basil call it, of drinking healths, and making that a sacrifice to God for the health of others, which is rather a sacrifice to the devill, and a bane of their owne." It appears from the same work, p. 543, that it was a custom to drink healths at that time upon their bare knees. The author is speaking of pot-wits and spirits of the buttery, " who never bared their knees to drinke healthes, nor ever needed to whet their wits with wine, or arme their courage with pot-harnesse."[1]

In Shakerley Marmion's Antiquary, act iv., is the following passage : " Why they are as jovial as twenty beggars, *drink their whole cups, sixe glasses at a health.*" Misson, in his Travels in England, translated by Ozell, p. 67, has some curious remarks on the manner of drinking healths in England in his time.

to have been intoxicated with the fumes of a most fanatical spirit, and whom the three Anticyræ could not, it should seem, have reduced to a state of mental sobriety, concludes his Address to the Christian Reader thus: " The unfeigned well-wisher of thy spiritual and corporal, though the oppugner of thy *pocular* and *pot-emptying health*, William Prynne."

[1] Whence can the following custom of health-drinking have taken its rise ? In a Journey from London to Scarborough, 1734, p. 4, speaking of Ware, the writer says : " The great bed here merits not half its fame, having only given rise to a fine allusion in the Recruiting Officer, of its being less than the bed of honour, where thousands may lie without touching one another. It is kept at the Old Crown Inn, and will hold a dozen people, heads and tails. They have a ceremony at showing it of *drinking a small can of beer, and repeating some health*, which I have already forgot."

In the Tatler, vol. i. No. 24, is an account of the origin of the word *toast* in its present sense, stating that it had its rise from an accident at Bath in the reign of Charles the Second. "It happened that on a public day a celebrated beauty of those times was in the Cross Bath, and one of the crowd of her admirers took a glass of the water in which the fair one stood, and drank her health to the company. There was in the place a gay fellow, half fuddled, who offered to jump in, and swore though he liked not the liquor, he would have the toast. He was opposed in his resolution; yet this whim gave foundation to the present honour which is done to the lady we mention in our liquor, who has ever since been called a toast."[1] Though unable to controvert this account, I am by no means satisfied with it. The wit here is likelier to have been *a consequence* than *the cause* of this singular use of the word, and puts me in mind of the well-known reply of a Mr. Brown (it is in some jest-book), who, on having it observed to him that he had given a certain young lady a long while for a toast, answered, "Yes, but I have not been able to *toast her brown yet.*"

In the Cheimonopegnion, or a Winter Song, by Raphael Thorius, newly translated, 1651 (at the end of the Hymnus Tabaci of the same date), the following passages occur:

> "Cast wood upon the fire, thy loyns gird round
> With warmer clothes, and let the *tosts* abound
> *In close array, embattel'd on the hearth.*"

So again, at p. 7:

> "And tell their hard adventures by the fire,
> While their friends hear, and hear, and more desire,
> And all the time the crackling chesnuts roast,
> And *each man hath his cup,* and *each his toast.*"

From these passages it should seem to appear that the saying " *Who gives a toast ?*" is synonymous with " Whose turn

---

[1] When the lady in Hudibras, II. i. 855, is endeavouring to persuade her lover to whip himself for her sake, she uses the following words, which intimate a different origin for the custom of toasting:

> "It is an easier way to make
> Love by, than that which many take.
> Who would not rather suffer whipping
> Than *swallow toasts of bits of ribbin ?*"

is it to take up his cup and propose a health? It was the practice to put *toast into ale with nutmeg and sugar*. This appears from a very curious pamphlet entitled Wine, Beere, Ale, and Tobacco, contending for superiority, a dialogue, 1658. It is among Garrick's Old Plays, now in the British Museum, and has a frontispiece representing three women and a man playing with three dice. The first edition appeared in 1630. In the interlude of Like will to Like, quoth the Devill to the Collier, is a song beginning—

> "Troll the bole, and drink to me, and troll the bole again-a,
> And *put a browne tost in the pot*, for Philip Flemming's brain-a."

The word *tost* occurs in Wyther's Abuses stript and whipt 1613, p. 174 :

> " Will he will drinke, yet but a draught at most,
> That must be spiced with *a nut-browne tost*."

In drinking toasts the ladies have a modest custom of excusing themselves, thus elegantly described by Goldsmith in his Deserted Village :

> " Nor the coy maid, half willing to be prest,
> Shall *kiss the cup* to pass it to the rest."

In the Canting Vocabulary, " Who *tosts* now ?" is rendered " Who christens the health ?" and " ' an *old tost* " is explained to mean " a pert pleasant old fellow." The following passage shows plainly the etymology of *toss-pot ;* it is extracted from the Schoolmaster, or Teacher of Table Philosophie, 1583, iv. 35, " Of merry jests of preaching friers : A certaine frier *tossing the pot*, and *drinking very often* at the table was reprehended by the priour," &c. I find the following anagram on a toast in the New Help to Discourse, 1684, 261 : " TOAST, anagram A SOTT. Exposition :

> " A toast is like a sot ; or, what is most
> Comparative, a sot is like a toast ;
> For when their substances in liquor sink,
> Both properly are said to be in drink."

Brown, Bishop of Cork, being a violent Tory, wrote a book to prove that drinking memories was a species of idolatry, in order to abolish a custom then prevalent among the Whigs of Ireland of drinking the glorious memory of King William the Third. But instead of cooling, he only inflamed the rage for the toast, to which they afterwards tacked the following rider: "And a f*** for the Bishop of Cork." See the Survey of the South of Ireland, p. 421. The bishop's work was entitled Of Drinking in Remembrance of the Dead, 1715, where, in p. 54, he asserts that "an health is no other than a liquid sacrifice in the constant sense and practice of the heathen." And at p. 97, he tells us of a curious "return given by the great Lord Bacon to such as pressed him to drink the king's health;" namely, that "he would drink for his own health, and pray for the king's."

In the account of Edinburgh, vi. 617, of the Statistical Account of Scotland, 1793, after the mention of a weekly concert, 1763, 1783, and 1791-2, we read: "The barbarous custom of *saving the ladies* (as it was called) after St. Cecilia's concert, by gentlemen drinking immoderately *to save a favourite lady, as his toast,* has been for some years given up. Indeed they got no thanks for their absurdity."

SUPERNACULUM.

Grose has defined this odd word to signify "good liquor, of which there is not even a drop left sufficient to wet one's nail." To drink *supernaculum* was an ancient custom not only in England, but also in several other parts of Europe, of emptying the cup or glass, and then pouring the drop or two that remained at the bottom upon the person's nail that drank it, to show that he was no flincher.[1]

Among Ray's Proverbial Sayings, belonging to drink and drinking, occurs the following : "Make a pearl on your nail." Proverbs, 1768, p. 69. Tom Brown, in his Letters from the

[1] I have a little pleasant dissertation in Latin, entitled De Supernaculo Anglorum, 4to. Lips. 1746. In page 8 is the following passage: "Est autem Anglis supernaculum ritus in conviviis circulatim ita bibendi ut poculo exhausto, ac super unguem excusso, residuoque delincto, ne guttulam quidem superesse, compotoribus demonstretur." In the same work, p. 6, is given the etymology of the word : "Est autem illud vox hybrida, ex Latina præpositione ' super' et Germano ' nagel' (a nail) composita, qui mos, nova vocabula fingendi Anglis potissimum usitatus est, vocemque *supernaculi* apud eosdem produxit."

Dead to the Living, n. 178, mentions a parson who had forgot even to *drink over his right thumb*. This must allude to some drinking custom which is now forgotten. In the British Apollo, 1708, No. 20, is the following query :

> " *Q.* Say whence, great Apollo,
> The custom we follow,
> When drinking brisk liquors per bumper,
> In a circular pass,
> We quaffe e'ry glass :
> And why is it *o'er the left thumb, sir?*

> " *A.* When mortals with wine,
> Make their faces to shine,
> 'Tis to look like Apollo in luster ;
> And, circulatory,
> To follow his glory,
> Which over the left thumb[1] they must, sir."

In the Winchester Wedding, a popular ballad, preserved in Ritson's Ancient Songs, 1792, p. 297, is another allusion to supernaculum :

> " Then Phillip began *her health,*
> And *turn'd a beer-glass on his thumb ;*
> But Jenkin was reckon'd for drinking
> The best in Christendom."

BUZZA: TO BUZZA ONE.

I KNOW nothing of the meaning of this word. I have been told that it is a college expression, and contains a threat, in the way of pleasantry, to black the person's face with a burnt cork, should he flinch or *fail to empty* the bottle. Possibly it may have been derived from the German " buzzen," *sordes auferre*, q. d. " Off with the lees at bottom."

Grose explains this as signifying to challenge a person to pour out all the wine in the bottle into his glass, undertaking

[1] Dingham, as cited by Bourne, chap xviii, has a quotation from St. Austin, on Superstitious Observations, among which, he says : " You are told in a fit of convulsions or shortness of breath, *to hold your left thumb with your right hand.*"

to drink it, should it prove more than the glass would hold.[1]
It is commonly said to one who hesitates to empty a bottle
that is nearly out.

I find the subsequent dissuasive from drunkenness, a vice
to which it must be confessed the drinking of healths, and
especially in full bumpers, does but too naturally tend, in
Ch. Johnson's Wife's Relief :

> " Oh when we swallow down
> Intoxicating wine, we drink damnation ;
> Naked we stand the sport of mocking fiends,
> Who grin to see our noble nature vanquish'd.
> Our passion's then like swelling seas burst in,
> The monarch Reason's govern'd by our blood,
> The noisy populace declare for liberty,
> While anarchy and riotous confusion
> Usurp the sov'reign's throne, claim his prerogative,
> Till gentle sleep exhales the boiling surfeit."

That it is good to be drunk once a month, says the learned
author of the Vulgar Errors, is a common flattery of sensuality,
supporting itself upon physic and the healthful effects of inebriation.   It is a striking instance of "the doing ill," as we
say, " that good may come out of it."   It may happen that
inebriation, by causing vomiting, may cleanse the stomach,
&c. ; but it seems a very dangerous kind of dose, and of
which the "repetatur haustus," too quickly repeated, will
prove that men may pervert that which Nature intended for
a cordial into the most baneful of all poisons.   It has been
vulgarly called "giving a fillip to Nature."

In Sir John Sinclair's Statistical Account of Scotland, i.
59, the minister of Kirkmichael tells us : " In extraordinary
cases of distress, we have a custom which deserves to be taken
notice of ; and that is, when any of the lower people happen
to be reduced by sicknesses, losses, or misfortunes of any
kind, a friend is sent to as many of their neighbours as they
think needful, to invite them to what they call *a drinking*.
This drinking consists in a little small beer, with a bit of

[1] Bumpers are of great antiquity. Thus Paulus Warnefridus is cited
in Du Cange's Glossary, telling us, in lib. v. de Gestis Langobard. cap. 2 :
" Cumque ii qui diversi generis potiones ei a rege deferebant, de verbo
regis eum rogarent, ut totam fialam biberet, ille in honorem regis se totam
bibere promittens, parum aquæ libabat de argenteo calice." Vide Martial,
lib. i. Ep. 72, lib. viii. 51, &c.

bread and cheese, and sometimes a small glass of brandy or whisky, previously provided by the needy persons or their friends. The guests convene at the time appointed, and after collecting a shilling a-piece, and sometimes more, they divert themselves for about a couple of hours with music and dancing, and then go home. Such as cannot attend themselves, usually send their charitable contribution by any neighbour that chooses to go. These meetings sometimes produce five, six, and seven pounds to the needy person or family." Ibid. xviii. 123, parish of Gargunnock, co. Stirling: "There is one prevailing custom among our country people, which is sometimes productive of much evil. Everything is bought and sold over a bottle. The people who go to the fair in the full possession of their faculties, do not always transact their business, or return to their homes, in the same state."

UNDER THE ROSE.

THE vulgar saying *Under the Rose* is said to have taken its rise from convivial entertainments, where it was an ancient custom to wear chaplets of roses about the head, on which occasions, when persons desired to confine their words to the company present, that they "might go no farther," they commonly said "they are spoken under the rose." The Germans have hence a custom of describing a rose in the ceiling over the table.

In the comedy of Lingua, 1657, act ii. sc. 1, Appetitus says: "Crown me no *crowns* but Bacchus' crown of roses."

Nazianzen, according to Sir Thomas Browne, seems to imply, in the following verse, that the rose, from a natural property, has been made the symbol of silence:

"Utque *latet rosa* verna *suo putamine clausa,*
Sic os vincla ferat, validisque arctetur habenis,
Indicatque suis prolixa silentia labris."

Lemnius and others have traced this saying to another origin. The rose, say they, was the flower of Venus, which Cupid consecrated to Harpocrates, the god of Silence: and it was therefore the emblem of it, to conceal the mysteries of Venus.

Warburton, commenting on that passage in the first part of Shakespeare's Henry VI.,

" From off this brier pluck a white rose with me,"

says : " This is given as the original of the two badges of the houses of York and Lancaster, whether truly or not, is no great matter. But the proverbial expression of *saying a thing under the rose*, I am persuaded came from thence. When the nation had ranged itself into two great factions, under the *white* and *red* rose, and were perpetually plotting and counter-plotting against one another, then when a matter of faction was communicated by either party to his friend in the same quarrel, it was natural for him to add, that he *said it under the rose;* meaning that, as it concerned the faction, it was religiously to be kept secret."[1]

It is observable that it was anciently a fashion to stick a rose in the ear. At Kirtling, in Cambridgeshire, the magnificent residence of the first Lord North, there is a juvenile portrait (supposed to be of Queen Elizabeth), with a red rose sticking in her ear.

Newton, in his Herball to the Bible, 1587, pp. 223-4, says : " I will heere adde *a common country custome* that is used to be done with *the rose*. When pleasaunt and merry companions doe friendly meete together to make goode cheere, as soone as their feast or banket is ended, they give faithfull promise mutually one to another, that whatsoever hath been merrily

---

[1] Upton gives us the following remarks on the bishop's criticism : " This is ingenious ! What pity that it is not learned too ! The rose (as the fables say) was the symbol of silence, and consecrated by Cupid to Harpocrates, to conceal the lewd pranks of his mother. So common a book as Lloyd's Dictionary might have instructed Dr. Warburton in this : ' Huic Harpocrati Cupido Veneris filius parentis suæ rosam dedit in munus, ut scilicet, si quid licentius dictum, vel actum sit in convivio, sciant tacenda esse omnia. Atque idcirco veteres ad finem convivii *sub rosa*, Anglicè *under the rose*, transacta esse omnia ante digressum contestabantur ; cujus formæ vis eadem esset, atque ista Μισῶμνάμονα συμποταν. Probant hanc rem versus qui reperiuntur in marmore :

' Est rosa flos Veneris, cujus quo furta laterent
　Harpocrati matris dona dicavit amor.
Inde rosam mensis hospes suspendit amicis,
　Convivæ ut sub ea dicta tacenda sciat.' "

spoke by any in that assembly, should be wrapped up in silence, and not to be carried out of the doores. For the assurance and performance whereof, the tearme which they use is, that all things there saide must be taken as spoken *under the rose*. Whereupon *they use in their parlours and dining roomes to hang roses over their tables*, to put the companie in memorie of secresie, and not rashly or indiscreetly to clatter and blab out what they heare. Likewise, if they chaunce to shew any tricks of wanton, unshamefast, immodest, or irreverent behaviour either by word or deed, they protesting that all was *spoken under the rose*, do give a strait charge and pass a covenant of silence and secrecy with the hearers, that the same shall not be blowne abroad, nor tatled in the streetes among any others."

So Peacham, in the Truth of our Times, 1638, p. 173 : " In many places, *as well in England* as in the Low Countries, they have over their tables a rose painted, and what is spoken *under the rose* must not be revealed. The reason is this ; the rose being sacred to Venus, whose amorous and stolen sports, that they might never be revealed, her sonne Cupid would needes dedicate to Harpocrates, the God of Silence."

I know not whence the saying, that needs not to be explained, of "plucking a rose," has originated, if it had not its rise in some modest excuse for absence in the garden, dictated by feminine bashfulness. Perhaps the passage already quoted from Newton's Herball to the Bible may explain it.

Speaking of the sex reminds me of a remarkable saying, now pretty much forgetten, though noticed by Sir Thomas Browne, i. e. that "*Smoak doth follow the fairest,*" as usual in his time in England, and it may be in all Europe. "Whereof," he says, "although there seem no natural ground, yet it is the continuation of a very antient opinion, as Petrus Victorius and Casaubon have observed from a passage in Athenæus, wherein a parasite thus describes himself :

> " To every table first I come,
> Whence Porridge I am called by some.
> Like whips and thongs to all I ply,
> *Like smoak unto the fair I fly.*"

HOB or NOB.

GROSE, in his Provincial Glossary, explains *hob-nob* (some·times pronounced *hab-nab*) as a north-country word, signifying, At a venture, rashly. He tells us, also, that *hob* or *hub* is the north-country name for the back of the chimney. We find the following in his Classical Dictionary of the Vulgar Tongue: *"Will you hob or nob with me?* a question formerly in fashion at polite tables, signifying a request or challenge to drink a glass of wine with the proposer: if the party challenged answered Nob, they were to chuse whether white or red." His explanation of the origin of this custom is extremely improbable.[1]

The exposition modestly hinted at in Reed's edition of Shakespeare, v. 369, seems much more consonant with truth. It occurs in a note upon that passage in Twelfth-Night, or What You Will,[2] where a character speaking of a duellist says, "His incensement at this moment is so implacable, that satisfaction can be none but by pangs of death and sepulchre: *hob, nob,* is his word; give't or take't." In Anglo-Saxon, habban is *to have,* and næbban *to want.* May it not therefore be explained in this sense, as signifying, "Do you choose a glass of wine, or would you rather let it alone?"[3]

I found the following, which had been cut out of some

[1] It is, " This foolish custom is said to have originated in the days of good Queen Bess, thus: When great chimneys were in fashion, there was, at each corner of the hearth or grate, a small elevated projection called *the hob,* and behind it a seat. In winter time the beer was placed on the *hob* to warm, and the cold beer was set on *a small table,* said to have been called *the nob:* so that the question ' Will you have *hob* or *nob!*' seems only to have meant, ' Will you have warm or cold beer?' i. e. beer from the *hob,* or beer from the *nob.*"

[2] Steevens thinks the word derived from *hap ne hap.*

[3] M. Mason asks in a note, " Is not this the original of our *hob nob,* or challenge to drink a glass of wine at dinner? The phrase occurs in Ben Jonson's Tale of a Tub:

' I put it
Even to your worship's bitterment, *hab nab,*
I shall have a chance o' the dice for't, I hope;' "

and Malone adds a passage from Holinshed's History of Ireland: " The citizens in their rage shot *habbe or nabbe* at random."

newspaper for Dec. 1772, in Dr. Lort's interleaved copy of my Popular Antiquities. *"The definition of hob or nob.*—In the days of good Queen Bess (we find it upon record) the maids of honour not only used manly exercise, but eat roast beef and drank ale for breakfast; and as in their masculine exercises they were liable to *accidents* and the *tooth ache,* so it was natural for them occasionally to warm their beer, which they who required such indulgence generally did by ordering their cupfuls to be placed on the hob of the grate; and when any of the company called for beer, it was just as natural for their attendants to ask, 'from the hob or not from the hob?' which constant practice (from the constant indisposition of one or other of these fair ladies) was soon not only remarked by the courtiers, but also perhaps first humorously adopted by them, with the courtly vice of corrupting *hob or no hob* into HOB or NOB." To this I beg leave to apply the—" Credat Judæus Apella, non ego." Compare the note, p. 348.

In the Workes of John Heywoode, 1566, is the following passage:

> " Where wooers hoppe in and out, long time may bryng
> Him that hoppeth best, at last to have the ryng.
> I hoppyng without for a ringe of a rush,
> And while I at length debate and beate the bushe,
> There shall steppe in other men, and catche the burdes,
> And by long time lost in many vaine wurdes,
> Betweene these two wives, make slouth speede confounde,
> While betweene two stooles my tayle goe to the grounde.
> By this, sens we see slouth must breede a scab,
> Best sticke to the tone out of hand, *hab or nab.*"

In Sir J. Harrington's Epigrams, iv. 91, we read:

> " Not of Jack Straw, with his rebellious crew,
> That set king, realme, and lawes at *hab* or *nab,*
> Whom London's worthy maior so bravely slew
> With dudgeon dagger's honourable stab."

In the New Courtier, a popular ballad, in Ritson's Antient Songs, 1790, p. 278, we find *hab nab* thus introduced:

> " I write not of religion
> For (to tell you truly) we have none.
> If any me to question call,
> With pen or sword, *hab nab's* the word,
> Have at all."

In the Character of a Quack Astrologer, 1673, speaking of

his Almanack, we are told, "He writes of the weather *hab nab*, and as the toy takes him, chequers the year with foul and fair."

The following is from the Antiquarian Repertory, ii. 98, where M. Jorevin is speaking of Worcester, and the Stag Inn there : "According to the custom of the country, the land-ladies sup with the strangers and passengers, and if they have daughters, they are also of the company, to entertain the guests at table with pleasant conceits, where they drink as much as the men : but what is to me the most disgusting in all this is, that when one drinks the health of any person in company, the custom of the country does not permit you to drink *more than half the cup, which is filled up, and presented to him or her whose health you have drank.*" He next speaks of tobacco, which it seems the women smoked as well as the men.   M. Jorevin was here in Charles the Second's reign.[1]

The following curious passage is from Galateo, of Manners and Behaviour, 4to. (and of which the scene lies in Italy) : "Now to drink *all out* every man (drinking and carowsing) : which is a fashion as little in use amongst us, as ye terme itself is barbarous and strange : I meane, *ick bring you*, is sure a foule thing of itselfe, and in our countrie so coldly accepted yet, that we must not go about to bring it in for a fashion. If a man doe quaffe or carrouse unto you, you may honestly say nay to pledge him, and geveing him thankes, confesse

---

[1] In a curious book entitled a Character of England, as it was lately presented in a Letter to a Nobleman of France, with Reflections upon Gallus Castratus, (attributed to John Evelyn,) 1659, the author, speaking of taverns, says, p. 31 : " Your L. will not believe me that the ladies of greatest quality suffer themselves to be treated in one of these taverns, but you will be more astonisht when I assure you that they drink their *crowned cups* roundly, strain healths *through their smocks*, daunce after the fiddle, kiss freely, and term it an honourable *treat.*" At p. 37 we are told, there is " a sort of perfect debauchees, who style themselves *Hectors*, that in their mad and unheard of revels pierce their veins to quaff their own blood, which some of them have drank to that excess, that they died of the intemperance." At p. 36 we read : " I don't remember, my lord, ever to have known (or very rarely) a health drank in France, no, not the king's ; and if we say, *à votre santé, Monsieur*, it neither expects pledge or ceremony. 'Tis here so the custome to drink to every one at the table, that by the time a gentleman has done his duty to the whole company, he is ready to fall asleep, whereas with us, we salute the whole table with a single glass only."

your weaknesse, that you are not able to line it, or else to
doe him a pleasure, you may for curtesie sake taste it, and
then set downe the cup to them that will, and charge yourselfe
no further. And although this, *ick bring you,* as I have heard
many learned men say, hath beene an auncient custome in
Greece ; and that the Grecians doe much commend a good
man of that time, Socrates by name, for that hee sat out one
whole night long, *drinking a vie* with another good man,
Aristophanes ; and yet the next morning, in the breake of the
daye, without any rest uppon his drinking, made such a cun-
ning geometrical instrument, that there was no maner of
faulte to be found in the same : bycause *the drinking of wine*
after this sorte *in a vie,* in such excesse and waste, is a shrewde
assault to trie the strength of him that quaffes so lustily."

ALEHOUSE or TAVERN SIGNS.

SIR THOMAS BROWNE is of opinion that the human faces
described in alehouse signs, in coats of arms, &c. for the sun
and moon, are reliques of Paganism, and that these visages
originally implied Apollo and Diana. Butler, the author of
Hudibras, asks a shrewd question on this head, which I do
not remember to have seen solved :

> " Tell me but what's the nat'ral cause
> Why on a sign no painter draws
> The *full moon* ever, but the *half?*"

There is a well-known proverb, "Good wine needs no
bush ;" i. e. nothing to point out where it is to be sold. The
subsequent passage seems to prove that anciently tavern-keepers
kept *both a bush and a sign :* a host is speaking :

> " I rather will take down my *bush* and *sign*
> Then live by means of riotous expense."
> Good Newes and Bad Newes, by S. R., 1622.

As does the following that anciently *putting up boughs* upon
anything was an indication that it was to be sold, which, if I
do not much mistake, is also the reason why an old besom

(which is a sort of *dried bush*) is put up at the topmast-head of a ship or boat when she is to be sold.[1]

In Greene in Conceipt, 1598, p. 10, we read : " Good wine needes no *ivie* bush." In England's Parnassus, 1600, the first line of the address to the reader runs thus : " I hang no ivie out to sell my wine :" and in Braithwaite's Strappado for the Divell, 1615, p. 1, there is a dedication to Bacchus, " sole *soveraigne of the ivy bush*, prime founder of red-lettices," &c.

In Dekker's Wonderful Yeare, 1603, we read : " Spied a bush at the ende of a pole (the auncient badge of a countrey ale-house." In Vaughan's Golden Grove, 1608, is the following passage : " Like as *an ivy-bush, put forth at a vintrie, is not the cause of the wine, but a signe that wine is to bee sold there ;* so, likewise, if we see smoke appearing in a chimney, we know that fire is there, albeit the smoke is not the cause of the fire." The following is from Harris's Drunkard's Cup, p. 299 : " Nay, if the house be not worth an ivy-bush, let him have his tooles about him ; nutmegs, rosemary, tobacco, with other the appurtenances, and he knowes how of puddle-ale to make a cup of English wine."

Coles, in his Introduction to the Knowledge of Plants, p. 65, says : " *Box* and *ivy* last long green, and therefore *vintners* make their garlands thereof ; though perhaps *ivy* is the rather used, *because of the antipathy between it and wine.*" In a curious poem entitled Poor Robin's Perambulation from Saffron Walden to London, July 1678, at p. 16, we read:

> " Some ale-houses upon the road I saw,
> And some with *bushes shewing they wine did draw.*"

A note in the Lansd. MS. 226, f. 171, upon the " Tavern Bush," by Bishop Kennett, says : " The dressing the frame or bush with ivy-leaves fresh from the plant was the custome forty years since, now generally left off for carved work."

By the following passage in Whimzies, or a New Cast of

---

[1] In Nash's Christ's Teares over Jerusalem, 1613, p. 145, speaking of the head-dresses of London ladies, he says : " Even as angels are painted in church windowes, with glorious golden fronts, besette with sunne-beames, so beset they their foreheads on either side with glorious borrowed gleamy *bushes ;* which, rightly interpreted, should signify *beauty to sell*, since *a bush* is not else hanged forth, but to invite men to buy. And in Italy, when they sette any beast to sale, they *crowne his head with garlands*, and bedeck it with gaudy blossoms, as full as ever it may stick."

Characters, 1631, Second Part, p. 15, it should seem that signs in alehouses succeeded *birch-poles*. The author is describing a painter : " He bestowes his pencile on an aged piece of decayed canvas in a sooty ale-house, where *Mother Red Cap* must be set out in her colours. Here hee and his barmy hostesse *drew* both together, but not in like nature ; she in *ale*, he in *oyle;* but her commoditie goes better downe, which he meanes to have his full share of when his worke is done. If she aspire to the conceite of a signe, and desire *to have her birch-pole pulled downe*, hee will supply her with one."

In Scotland *a wisp of straw upon a pole* is, or was heretofore, the indication of an alehouse. So in a quotation already made, from Dunbar's macaronic Will of Maister Andro Kennedy: " Et unum *ale-wisp* ante me."

" In olde times, such as solde horses were wont to put flowers or boughes upon their heads" (I think they now use ribbands), " to reveale that they were vendible." See the English Fortune Teller, 1609.

The *Chequers*, at this time a common sign of a public-house, was originally intended, I should suppose, for a kind of draught-board, called *tables*, and showed that there that game might be played. From their colour, which was red, and the similarity to a lattice, it was corruptly called the *Red Lettuce*, which word is frequently used by ancient writers to signify an alehouse. See the Antiquarian Repertory, i. 50. Thus I read in the Drunkard's Prospective, by Joseph Rigbie, 1656, p. 6 :

> " The tap-house fits them for a jaile,
> The jaile to the gibbet sends them without faile ;
> For those that through a *lattice* sang of late
> You oft find *crying* through an iron grate." [1]

In King Henry IV., Part ii., Falstaff's Page, speaking of Bardolph, says : " He called me even now, my lord, through *a red lattice*, and I could see no part of his face from the

---

[1] In the First Part of Antonio and Melida, Marston's Works, 1633 we read: " As well knowen by my wit, as *an ale-house by a red lattice*." So, in a Fine Companion, one of Shakerley Marmion's plays : " A waterman's widow at the sign of the Red Lattice in Southwark." Again, in Arden of Faversham, 1592: " His sign pulled down, and his *lattice* born away." Again, in the Miseries of Inforc'd Marriage, 1607 : " 'Tis treason to the *red lattice*, enemy to the sign post."

23

window." This designation of an alehouse is not altogether lost, though the original meaning of the word is, the sign being converted into *a green lettuce;* of which an instance occurs in Brownlow street, Holborn. In the last will and testament of Lawrence Lucifer, the old batchiler of Limbo, at the end of the Blacke Booke, 4to. 1604, is the following passage : " Watched sometimes ten houres together in an alehouse, ever and anon peeping forth and sampling thy nose with the *red lattice.*" In the Christmass Ordinary, by W. R., 1682, we read :

> " Where Red Lettice doth shine,
> 'Tis an outward sign
>   Good ale is a traffic within;
> It will drown your woe,
> And thaw the old snow
>   That grows on a frosty chin."

In confirmation of the above hypothesis, I subjoin a curious passage from Gayton's Notes on Don Quixote, p. 340 : " Mine host's policy for the drawing guests to his house, and keeping them when he had them, is farre more ingenious than *our* duller ways of billiards, kettle-pins, noddy-boards, *tables,* truncks, shovel-boards, fox and geese, or the like. He taught his bullies to drink (*more Romano*) according to the number of the letters on the errant ladies name :

> ' Clodia *sex* Cyathis, *septem* Justina bibatur :'

the pledge so followed in Dulcinea del Toboso would make a house quickly turn round."

Hence, says Steevens, the present *chequers.* Perhaps the reader will express some surprise when he is told that shops with the sign of the chequers were common among the Romans. See a view of the left-hand street of Pompeii (No. 9), presented by Sir William Hamilton (together with several others, equally curious) to the Society of Antiquaries.

I find, however, the following in the Gent. Mag. for June, 1793, lxiii. 531 : " It has been related to me by a very noble personage, that in the reign of Philip and Mary, the then Earl of Arundel had a grant to license publick houses, and *part of the armorial bearings of that noble family is a checquered board;* wherefore the publican, to show that he had a license, *puts out that mark as part of his sign.* J. B." Here, may it not be asked, why the publicans take but a part of the Arundel arms, and why this part rather than any other?

In the same work, for Sept. 1794, lxiv. 797, is another explanation. The writer says: " I think it was the great *Earl Warrenne*, if not, some descendant or heir near him, not beyond the time of Rufus, had an exclusive power of granting licenses to sell beer. That his agent might collect the tax more readily, the door-posts were painted in CHECQUERS, *the arms of Warren then and to this day.*"

In Richard Flecknoe's Ænigmatical Characters, 1665, p. 84, speaking of "your fanatic reformers," he observes : "As for the *signs*, they have pretty well begun their reformation already, changing the sign of the salutation of *the Angel and our Lady* into the Souldier and Citizen, and the *Katherine Wheel* into the Cat and Wheel; so as there only wants their making the *Dragon* to kill *St. George*, and the *Devil* to tweak *St. Dunstan* by the nose, to make the reformation compleat. Such ridiculous work they make of their reformation, and so zealous are they against all mirth and jollity, as they would pluck down the sign of the *Cat and Fiddle* too, if it durst but play so loud as they might hear it." [1] In a curious poem entitled Poor Robin's Perambulation from Saffron-Walden to London, July 1678, 4to. Lond. 1678, the following lines occur, p. 22 :

> " Going still nearer London, I did come
> In little space of time to Newington.
> Now as I past along I cast my eye on
> The signs of *Cock and Pie*, and Bull and Lion."

As do the following in the British Apollo, fol. Lond. 1710, vol. iii. No. 34 :

> " I'm amazed at the signs,
> As I pass through the town :
> To see the odd mixture,
> A *Magpye* and *Crown*,
> The *Whale* and the *Crow*,
> The *Razor* and *Hen*,
> The *Leg* and *Sev'n Stars*,
> The *Bible* and *Swan*,
> The *Ax* and the *Bottle*,
> The *Tun* and the *Lute*,
> The *Eagle* and *Child*,
> The *Shovel* and *Boot*."

---

[1] There is a curious letter in the Gent. Mag. for Sept. 1770, xl. 403, on the original of signs denoting trades.

" In London," says Steevens, " we have still the sign of the
Bull and Gate, which exhibits but an odd combination of
images.   It was originally (as I learn from the title-page of
an old play) the Bullogne Gate, i. e. one of the gates of
Bullogne ; designed perhaps as a compliment to Henry VIII.
who took that place in 1544.   The Bullogne Mouth, now the
Bull and Mouth, had probably the same origin, i. e. the
mouth of the harbour of Bullogne."   To these may be added
the *Bell and Savage*, i. e. the " Belle Sauvage," who was once
to be shown there.

The three blue balls (see the Antiquarian Repertory) prefixed to the doors and windows of pawnbrokers' shops (by
the vulgar humorously enough said to indicate that it is *two
to one* that the things pledged are ever redeemed) were in
reality *the arms of a set of merchants from Lombardy*, who were
the first that publicly lent money on pledges.   They dwelt
together in a street from them named Lombard Street, in
London.   The appellation of Lombard was formerly all over
Europe considered as synonymous to " usurer."

In the Compleat Vintner, &c., a poem, 8vo. Lond. 1720,
p. 36, we read:

> " Without there hangs a noble sign,
> Where golden grapes in image shine—
> To crown the bush, a little punch-
> Gut Bacchus, dangling of a bunch,
> Sits loftily enthron'd upon
> What's call'd (in miniature) a tun."

Again, p. 38 :

> " If in Moorfields a lady stroles,
> Among the *globes* and *golden balls*,
> Where e'er they hang, she may be certaii
> Of knowing what shall be her fortune ;
> Her husband's too, I dare to say,
> But that she better knows than they.
>
> The pregnant madam, drawn aside
> By promise to be made a bride,
> If near her time, and in distress
> For some obscure convenient place,
> Let her but take the pains to waddle
> About till she observes *a cradle*,
> *With the foot hanging towards the door*,
> And there she may be made secure
> From all the parish plagues and terrors
> That wait on poor weak woman's errors ;

But if the head hangs tow'rds the house,
As very oft we find it does,
Avant, for she's a cautious bawd,
Whose bus'ness only lies abroad."

" The sign of the Goat and Compasses has been supposed to
have had its origin in the resemblance between the bounding
of a goat and the expansion of a pair of compasses; but
nothing can be more fanciful. The sign is of the days of the
Commonwealth, when it was the fashion to give scriptural
names to everything and everybody, and when 'Praise God
Barebones' preferred drinking his tankard of ale at the " God
encompasseth us" to anywhere else. The corruption from
God encompasseth us to *Goat and Compasses* is obvious and
natural enough."—Times, Jan. 9, 1823.

["Some of the old signs exhibit a curious combination of
images, articles, and colours. We may mention incidentally,
the Bull and Mouth, the Bull and Gate, the Belle Sauvage,
the Goat and Compasses, the Cat and Fiddle, the Cock and
Pie, the Cock and Bottle, the Goat in Boots, the Swan with
Two Necks, the Bag of Nails, the Pig and Whistle, the George
and Vulture, the Bolt in Tun, the Bear and Harrow, the
Elephant and Castle. Our streets are filled with Blue Boars,
Black Swans, and Red Lions, not to mention Flying Pigs and
Hogs in Armour. 'Could you believe it?' writes the Chinese
philosopher, 'I have seen five Black Lions and three Blue
Boars in less than a circuit of half a mile-!' Others were of
a more amusing, or, perhaps, of a more extraordinary description. Two mean alehouses abutted upon Westminster Hall;
one was called ' Heaven,' the other ' Hell.' No one has told
us, unhappily, how the ingenuity of the landlords or the
fancy of the painters contrived to represent the names of the
two houses. The church of St. Dunstan, in Fleet Street, and
the popular legend of the saint who took the Devil by the
nose till he roared again, gave rise to the Devil and St.
Dunstan, or the Devil Tavern, at Temple Bar. The sign exhibited the popular legend, and the saint was seen holding the
Devil by the nose with a pair of red-hot tongs. The Good
Woman, in Broad Street, was a woman without her head;
and the Man Laden with Mischief, in Oxford Street, is a man
with a woman on his shoulders. We remember a St. George
and the Dragon, in London, with this suitable inscription

underneath, 'Entertainment for man and horse ;' and Hogarth. in one of his pictures, has copied a quaint sign, 'St. Jonn the Baptist's head on a plate,' and underneath, 'Good eating,' the sign, no doubt, of some tavern or ordinary in his time. Of these odd signs and odd associations some are obviously corrupt and some hopelessly obscure, while others have their origin in the beasts of heraldry.   The Bull and Mouth and the Bull and Gate are corruptions, it is said, of Boulogne mouth (or harbour) and Boulogne gate.   The Goat and Compasses (now the Compasses, near the site of the old Chelsea Bun-house) is a corruption, we are told, of the 'God encompasseth us,' of the Commonwealth of English history.   The Cat and Wheel is called the Catherine Wheel ; the Cat and Fiddle defies conjecture ; the Cock and Pie is the Cock and Magpie ; the Cock and Bottle is the Cork and Bottle, it is said, or the Cock and Bottle of Hay ; the Goat in Boots is said to be a corruption of the Dutch legend, 'Mercurius is der goden boode ;' the Swan with Two Necks, or the Swan with Two Nicks (the swan-upping mark of my Lord Mayor as conservator of the Thames) ; and the Bag of Nails is now the Bacchanals.   The Bolt in Tun is a mere rebus on the name of Bolton."—Fraser's Magazine.]

BARBERS' SIGNS.

THE sign of a barber's shop being singular, has attracted much notice.   It is generally distinguished by *a long pole* instead of a sign.   In the Athenian Oracle, i. 334, this custom is thus accounted for ; it is of remote antiquity : "The barber's art was so beneficial to the publick, that he who first brought it up in Rome had, as authors relate, a statue erected to his memory.   In England they were in some sort the surgeons of old times, into whose art those beautiful *leeches*,[1] our fair virgins were also accustomed to be initiated.   In cities and corporate towns they still retain their name of Barber Chirurgions.   They therefore used to hang their basons out upon poles, to make known at a distance to the weary and

---

[1] This is an old word for doctors or surgeons.

wounded traveller where all might have recourse. They used poles, as some inns still gibbet their signs, across a town."

I am better pleased with the subsequent explanation which I find in the Antiquarian Repertory: "The barber's pole has been the subject of many conjectures, some conceiving it to have originated from the word poll or head, with several other conceits as far-fetched and as unmeaning; but the true intention of that party-coloured staff was to show that the master of the shop practised surgery, and could breathe a vein as well as mow a beard: such a staff being to this day, by every village practitioner, put into the hand of a patient undergoing the operation of phlebotomy. The white band, which encompasses the staff, was meant to represent the fillet thus elegantly twined about it." In confirmation of this opinion the reader may be referred to the cut of the barber's shop in Comenii Orbis Pictus, where the patient under phlebotomy is represented with a pole or staff in his hand. And that this is a very ancient practice, appears from an illumination in a missal of the time of Edward the First, in the possession of Mr. Wild.

Lord Thurlow, in his speech for postponing the further reading of the Surgeons' Incorporation Bill, July 17th, 1797, to that day three months, in the House of Peers, stated "that by a statute still in force, the barbers and surgeons were each to use a pole. The barbers were to have theirs blue and white, striped, with no other appendage; but the surgeons', which was the same in other respects, was likewise to have a galley-pot and a red rag, to denote the particular nature of their vocation."

Gay, in his fable of the Goat without a Beard, thus describes a barber's shop:

> " His pole with pewter basons hung,
> Black rotten teeth in order strung,
> Rang'd cups that in the window stood,
> Lin'd with red rags to look like blood,
> Did well his threefold trade explain,
> Who shav'd, drew teeth, and breath'd a vein."

In the British Apollo, fol. Lond. 1708, vol. i. No. 3, a querist says:

> " I'de know why he that selleth ale
> Hangs out a chequer'd part per pale;

And why a barber at port-hole
Puts forth a party-coloured pole ?
A. In ancient Rome, when men lov'd fighting,
And wounds and scars took much delight in,
Man-menders then had noble pay,
Which we call *surgeons* to this day.
'Twas order'd that a huge long pole,
With bason deck'd, should grace the hole,
To guide the wounded, who unlopt
Could walk, on stumps the others hopt ;
But, when they ended all their wars,
And men grew out of love with scars,
Their trade decaying ; to keep swimming,
They joyn'd the other trade of trimming ;
And on their poles to publish either,
Thus twisted both their trades together."

The other is too ridiculous :

" A jolly hostess
Took negro drawer, and paid postage.
The brat, as soon as come to light,
Was chequer'd o'er with black and white.
Since which to this virago's honour
O'er door they've blazon'd such a banner !"

I find the following odd passage in Gayton's Festivous
Notes upon Don Quixote, p. 111 : " The barber hath a long
pole elevated ; and at the end of it a labell, wherein is in a
fair text-hand written this word, *money.* Now the *pole* signifies itself, which joined to the written word makes *pole-money.*
There's the rebus, that Cut-bert is no-body without pole-
money."

The subsequent is an extract from Green's Quip for an
Upstart Courtier, or a Quaint Dispute between Velvet Breeches
and Cloth Breeches, 1620 : " Barber, when you come to poor
cloth breeches, you either *cut his beard at your own pleasure,*
or else in disdaine aske him if he will be *trimm'd with Christ's
cut, round like the half of a Holland cheese,* mocking both
Christ and us."

In Wits, Fits, and Fancies, 1614, p. 177, we read : " A
gentleman gave a gentlewoman a fine twisted bracelet of silke
and golde, and seeing it the next day upon another gentlewoman's wrist, said it was *like a barber's girdle, soon slipt
from one side to another.*"

On that passage in Measure for Measure :—

> " The strong statutes
> Stand like the FORFEITS *in a* BARBER'S SHOP,
> *As much in mock as mark ;*"

Dr. Warburton observes : " Barbers' shops were, at all times, the resort of idle people :

> Tonstrina erat quædam : hic solebamus ferè
> Plerumque eam operiri :

which Donatus calls *apta sedes otiosis.* Formerly with us the better sort of people went to the barber's shop to be trimmed ; who then practised the under parts of surgery : so that he had occasion for numerous instruments which lay there ready for use ; and the idle people with whom his shop was generally crowded, would be perpetually handling and misusing them. To remedy which, I suppose, there was placed up against the wall a table of forfeitures, adapted to every offence of this kind ; which it is not likely would long preserve its authority." Steevens says : " I have conversed with several people who had repeatedly read the list of forfeits alluded to by Shakespeare, but have failed in my endeavours to procure a copy of it. The metrical one published by the late Dr. Kenrick was a forgery."

Dr. Henley observes : " I believe Dr. Warburton's explanation in the main to be right, only that instead of chirurgical instruments, the barber's implements were principally his razors ; his whole stock of which, from the number and impatience of his customers on a Saturday night or a market morning, being necessarily laid out for use, were exposed to the idle fingers of the bystanders in waiting for succession to the chair. These forfeits were as much in mock as mark, both because the barber had no authority of himself to enforce them, and also as they were of a ludicrous nature. I perfectly remember to have seen them in Devonshire (printed like King Charles's rules), though I cannot recollect the contents."

Steevens adds : " It was formerly part of a barber's occupation to *pick the teeth* and *eares.*" So, in the old play of Herod and Antipater, 1622, Tryphon the barber enters with a case of instruments, to each of which he addresses himself separately :

> " Toothpick, dear toothpick ; earpick, both of you
> Have been her sweet companions !" &c.

The following is an extract from the World of Wonders, 1607, p. 125. Speaking of the "gross ignorance" of the barbers, the author says : "This puts me in minde of a barber who after he had cupped me (as the physitian had prescribed) to turne away a catarrhe, asked me if I would be *sacrificed. Sacrificed?* said I ; did the physitian tell you any such thing ? No (quoth he), but I have sacrificed many, who have bene the better for it. Then musing a little with myselfe, I told him, Surely, sir, you mistake yourself, you meane *scarified.* O sir, by your favour (quoth he), I have ever heard it called sacrificing, and as for scarifying I never heard of it before. In a word, I could by no means perswade him but that it was the barber's office to *sacrifice* men. Since which time I never saw any man in a barber's hands, but that *sacrificing* barber came to my mind."

TOBACCO IN ALEHOUSES.

A FOREIGN weed, which has made so many Englishmen, especially of the common sort, become its slaves, must not be omitted in our catalogue of Popular Antiquities. It is said to have been first brought into England by Captain R. Greenfield and Sir Francis Drake about the year 1586, during the reign of Elizabeth.

A pleasant kind of tale, but for one item of the veracity of which I will not vouch, is given in the Athenian Oracle, by way of accounting for the frequent use and continuance of taking it. "When the Christians first discovered America, the Devil was afraid of losing his hold of the people there by the appearance of Christianity. He is reported to have told some Indians of his acquaintance that he had found a way to be revenged upon the Christians for beating up his quarters, for he would teach them to take tobacco, to which, when they had once tasted it, they should become perpetual slaves."

Alehouses are at present licensed to deal in tobacco ; but it was not so from the beginning ; for so great an incentive was it thought to drunkenness, that it was strictly forbidden to be taken in any alehouse in the time of James the First.

'here is a curious Collection of Proclamations, Prints, &c in the Archives of the Society of Antiquaries of London. In vol. 8 is an alehouse licence granted by six Kentish justices of the peace, at the bottom of which the following item occurs, among other directions to the inn-holder : " Item, you shall not utter, nor willingly suffer to be utter'd, drunke, or taken, any tobacco within your house, cellar, or other place thereunto belonging."

The following ironical encomium on, and serious invective against tobacco, occurs in Burton's Anatomy of Melancholy, 1621, p. 452 : "Tobacco, divine, rare, super excellent tobacco, which goes farre beyond all their panaceas, potable gold, and philosopher's stones, a sovereign remedy to all diseases. A good vomit, I confesse, a vertuous herbe, if it be well qualified, opportunely taken, and medicinally used ; but as it is commonly used by most men, which take it as tinkers do ale, 'tis a plague, a mischiefe, a violent purger of goods, lands, health, hellish, devilish, and damnd tobacco, the ruine, and overthrow of body and soule."

In the Apophthegms of King James, 1658, p. 4, I read as follows : " His majesty professed that were he to invite the Devil to a dinner, he should have these three dishes : 1, a pig ; 2, a poll of ling and mustard ; and 3, a pipe of tobacco for digesture." The following quaint thought is found in an old Collection of Epigrams :

"121. *A Tobacconist.*
" All dainty meats I do defie,
Which feed men fat as swine :
He is a frugal man indeed
That on a leaf can dine.
He needs no napkin for his hands
His fingers' ends to wipe,
That keeps his kitchen in a box,
And roast meat in a pipe."

In the Hymnus Tabaci by Raphael Thorius, made English by Peter Hausted, Master of Arts, Camb. 1651, we meet with the strongest invective against tobacco :

"Let it be damn'd to hell, and call'd from thence
Prooorpine's wine, the Furies' frankincense,
The Devil's addle-eggs, or else to these
A sacrifice grim Pluto to appease,
A deadly weed, which its beginning had
From the foam of Cerberus, when the cur was mad."

Our British Solomon, James the First, who was a great opponent of the Devil, and even wrote a book against witchcraft, made a formidable attack also upon this "invention of Satan," in a learned performance, which he called a Counterblaste to Tobacco.[1] It is printed in the edition of his works by Barker and Bill, London, 1616. He concludes this *bitter blast* of his, his sulphureous invective against this transmarine weed, with the following peroration : " Have you not reason then to be ashamed and to forbear this filthy novelty, so basely grounded, so foolishly received, and so grossly mistaken in the right use thereof! In your abuse thereof sinning against God, harming yourselves both in persons and goods, and taking also thereby (look to it, ye that take snuff in profusion !) the marks and notes of vanity upon you ; by the custom thereof making yourselves to be wondered at by all foreign civil nations, and by all strangers that come among you, to be scorned and contemned ; a custom loathsome to the eye, hateful to the nose, harmful to the brain, dangerous to the lungs, and in the black stinking fume thereof, nearest resembling the horrible Stygian smoke of the pit that is bottomless."

If even this small specimen of our learned monarch's oratory, which seems well adapted to the understanding of old women, does not prevail upon them all to break in pieces their tobacco-pipes and forego smoking, it will perhaps be impossible to say what can. The subject, as his majesty well observes, is *smoke*, and no doubt many of his readers will think the arguments of our royal author no more than the *fumes* of an idle brain, and it may be added, too, of an empty head !

How widely different to the anathemas of King James are the strains of the subsequent Parody on the style of Ambrose Phillips !

> " Little tube of mighty pow'r,
> Charmer of an idle hour,
> Object of my warm desire,
> Lip of wax and eye of fire :

---

[1] His majesty in the course of his work informs us, " that some of the gentry of the land bestowed (at that time) *three,* some *four hundred pounds a yeere* upon this precious stink !" An incredible sum, especially when we consider the value of money in his time. They could not surely have been sterling, but Scottish pounds.

And thy snowy taper waist,
With my finger gently brac'd;
And thy pretty swelling crest,
With my little stopper prest," &c.

The following is in imitation of Dr. Young:

" Critics avaunt, tobacco is my theme;
Tremble like hornets at the blasting steam.
And you, court insects, flutter not too near
Its light, nor buzz within the scorching sphere.
Pollio, with flame like thine my verse inspire,
So shall the muse from smoke elicit fire.
Coxcombs prefer the tickling sting of snuff;
Yet all their claim to wisdom is—a puff.
Lord Foplin smokes not—for his teeth afraid;
Sir Tawdry smokes not—for he wears brocade.
Ladies, when pipes are brought, affect to swoon;
They love no smoke, except the smoke of town;
But courtiers hate the puffing tribe—no matter,
Strange if they love the breath that cannot flatter!
Its foes but show their ignorance; can he
Who scorns the *leaf of knowledge*, love the tree?
Yet crowds remain who still its worth proclaim,
While some for pleasure smoke, and some for fame:
Fame, of our actions universal spring,
For which we drink, eat, sleep, smoke—ev'rything."

Both these parodies were written by Hawkins Browne, Esq.
In the London Medley, 8vo. 1731, p. 8, I find the following
panegyric on tobacco :

" Hail, *Indian plant*, to ancient times unknown,
A modern truly thou, of all our own;
If through the tube thy virtues be convey'd,
The old man's solace, and the student's aid!
Thou dear concomitant of nappy ale,
Thou sweet prolonger of a harmless tale;
Or if, when pulveriz'd in smart rappee,
Thou'lt reach Sir Fopling's brain, if brain there be;
He shines in dedications, poems, plays,
Soars in Pindaricks, and asserts the bays;
Thus dost thou every taste and genius hit,
In *smoak*, thou'rt *wisdom;* and in *snuff*, thou'rt *wit*."

The following extraordinary account of a Buckinghamshire
parson who abandoned himself to the use of tobacco is worth
quoting. It may be found in Lilly's History of his Life and
Times, p. 44 : " In this year also, William Breedon, parson
or vicar of Thornton in Bucks, was living, a profound divine,

but absolutely the most polite person for nativities in that age, strictly adhering to Ptolemy, which he well understood; he had a hand in composing Sir Christopher Heydon's Defence of Judicial Astrology, being at that time his chaplain; he was so given over to tobacco and drink, that when he had *no* tobacco (and I suppose too much drink) he would cut the bell-ropes and *smoke* them!"

WELLS AND FOUNTAINS.

THE custom of giving names to wells and fountains is of the most remote antiquity. In giving particular names to inanimate things it is obviously the principal intention to secure or distinguish the property of them. A well was a most valuable treasure in those dry and parched countries which composed the scene of the patriarchal history, and therefore we find in one of the earliest of writings, the Book of Genesis, that it was a frequent subject of contention.

In the Papal times there was a custom in this country, if a well had an awful situation, if its waters were bright and clear, or if it was considered as having a medicinal quality, to dedicate it to some saint,[1] by honouring it with his name.[2]

In the Travels of Tom Thumb, p. 35, we read: "A man would be inexcusable that should come into North Wales and not visit Holywell or St. Winifride's Well, and hear attentively all the stories that are told about it. It is indeed a natural

[1] Bourne, in his Antiquitates Vulgares, chap. viii., enumerates "St. John's, St. Mary Magdalen's, St. Mary's Well," &c. To these may be added many others. Thus, in the Muses Threnodie, St. Conil's Well, in Scotland. "This well, dedicated to St. Conwall, whose anniversary was celebrated on the 18th of May, is near to Ruthven Castle, or Hunting Tower. It is sufficient to serve the town of Perth with pure, wholesome water, if it were brought down by pipes. In the days of superstition this well was much resorted to." p. 175, note.

[2] Bourne's Antiq. Vulg. ut supra. I found on a visit to the source of the New River between Hertford and Ware, in August, 1793, an old stone inscribed "*Chadwell,*" a corruption, no doubt, of St. Chad's Well. So copious a spring could not fail of attracting the notice of the inhabitants in the earliest times, who accordingly dedicated it to St. Chad, never once dreaming, perhaps, that in succeeding ages it should be converted to so beneficial a purpose as to supply more than half the capital of England with one of the most indispensable necessaries of human life.

wonder, though we believe nothing of the virgin and her rape ;
for I never felt a colder spring, nor saw any one that affords
such a quantity of water. It forms alone a considerable brook
which is immediately able to drive a mill." Pennant, in his
account of this well, says : " After the death of that saint, the
waters were almost as sanative as those of the Pool of Bethesda:
all infirmities incident to the human body met with relief :
the votive crutches, the barrows, and other proofs of cures, to
this moment remain as evidences pendent over the well. The
resort of pilgrims of late years to these fontanalia has considerably decreased. In the summer, still, a few are to be
seen in the water in deep devotion up to their chins for hours,
sending up their prayers, or performing a number of evolutions
round the polygonal well, or threading the arch between well
and well a prescribed number of times." In the History of
Whiteford Parish, p. 223, he adds : " The bathing well is an
oblong, 38 feet by 16, with steps for the descent of the fair sex,
or of invalids. Near the steps, two feet beneath the water, is
a large stone, called the wishing-stone. It receives many a
kiss from the faithful, who are supposed never to fail in ex-
periencing the completion of their desires, provided the wish
is delivered with full devotion and confidence. On the outside
of the great well, close to the road, is a small spring, once
famed for the cure of weak eyes. The patient made an offering
to the nymph of the spring of a crooked pin, and sent up at
the same time a certain ejaculation, by way of charm : but the
charm is forgotten, and the efficacy of the waters lost. The
well is common."

Lilly, in the History of his Life and Times, p. 32, relates
that in 1635 Sir George Peckham, Knt. died in St. Winifred's
Well, "having continued so long mumbling his pater nosters
and Sancta Winifreda ora pro me, that the cold struck into his
body, and after his coming forth of that well he never spoke
more." [1]

In the Statistical Account of Scotland, xv. 613, Avoch

---

[1] An account of a miracle pretended to have been recently wrought at
this well will be found in a pamphlet entitled, Authentic Documents relative to the miraculous Cure of *Winefrid* White, of Wolverhampton, at
St. Winefrid's Well, alias Holywell, in Flintshire, on the 28th of June, 1805 ;
with Observations thereon, by the R. R. J—— M ——, D.D. V.A. F.S.A.
Lond., and C. Acad. Rome," 1806.

parish, cɔ. Ross, we read of "a well called Craiguck, issuing
from a rock near the shore of Bennetsfield, resorted to in the
month of May by whimsical or superstitious persons, who,
after drinking, commonly leave some threads or rags tied to
a bush in the neighbourhood."

In the antiquities of heathen Rome, *fontinalia* was a religious feast, celebrated on the 13th of October, in honour of
the nymphs of wells and fountains. The ceremony consisted
in throwing nosegays into the fountains, and putting crowns
of flowers upon the wells.

Alexander Ross, in his Appendix to the Arcana Microcosmi,
p. 220, tells us that "Camerarius, out of Dietmarus and
Erasmus Stella, writes of a certain fountain near the river
Albis or Elbe, in Germany, which presageth wars by turning
red and bloody-coloured; of another which portendeth death,
if the water, which before was limpid, becomes troubled and
thick, so caused by an unknown worm." This brings to my
remembrance a superstitious notion I have heard of in
Northumberland, that, when the Earl of Derwentwater was
beheaded, the brook that runs past his seat at Dilston Hall
flowed with blood.[1]

Dallaway, in his Constantinople Ancient and Modern, 1797,
p. 144, speaking of the Bosphorus, tells us : " Frequent fountains are seen on the shore, of the purest water, to which is
attached one of the strongest and most ancient superstitions
of the Greek Church. They are called ' ayasmà ;' and to repeat certain prayers at stated seasons, and to drink deeply of
them, is held to be a most salutary act of their religion."

Fitzstephen, monk of Canterbury, in his description of the

---

[1] Concerning fountain superstitions, see the authorities quoted by Ihre
in his Gloss. Suio-Goth. tom. i. p. 1042, under *Offekælla*. See also
Lindebrogii Codex Legum Antiquorum, p. 1402, and Hearne's pref. to
Rob. Glouc. p. 47. In Muratori, Antiq. Italicæ Medii Ævi, tom. v. fol.
Mil. 1741, p. 66, c. Diss. de superstitionum semine in obscuris Italiæ
sæculis, we read : " Sub regibus Langobardis eo audaciæ processerat in-
consulta rudis popelli credulitas, ut arbores quasdam (*sanctivas* appella-
bant) summa in veneratione haberent, veluti sacras, neque ab iis tantum
exscindendis aut tondendis abstinerent, sed etiam iis adorationis signa
exhiberent. *Idem quoque fontibus nonnullis præstabant.* Deum-ne,
ejusque sanctos, an dæmones, ibi colerent, exploratum minime est. Quum
tamen ejusmodi superstitiosi cultus *Paganiæ* interdum appellentur ab
antiquis, idcirco par est credere Paganismi reliquias fuisse."

ancient city of London, as quoted by Stowe, has the following passage on this subject. There are "on the north part of London principal fountains of water, sweet, wholesome, and clear, streaming from among the glistering pebble stones. In this number *Holy Well, Clerkenwell*, and *St. Clement's Well* are of most note, and frequented above the rest, when scholars and the youth of the city take the air abroad in the summer evenings." Our British topography abounds with accounts of holy wells, or such as had assigned them, by ancient superstition, most extraordinary properties. These ideas, so far from being worn out in this enlightened age, are still retained by the vulgar, not only in the distant provinces, but also close to the metropolis itself. Thus we read, in the account of Tottenham High Cross, in the Ambulator, 1790: "In a brick-field, on the west side of the great road, belonging to Mr. Charles Saunders, is *St. Loy's Well*, which is said to be always full, and never to run over; and in a field, opposite the Vicarage House, rises a spring called 'Bishop's Well,' of which the common people report many strange cures." The following account borders more closely upon the marvellous and incredible: "In Northamptonshire I observed, as in most other places, the superstition of the country people with regard to their local wonders. The well at Oundle is said to drum against any important event; yet nobody in the place could give me a rational account of their having heard it, though almost every one believes the truth of the tradition." —Travels of T. Thumb, p. 174.[1]

Borlase, in his Natural History of Cornwall, p. 31, speaking of Madern Well, in the parish of Madern, tells us: "Here people who labour under pains, aches, and stiffness of limbs come and wash, and many cures are said to have been performed. Hither also, upon much less justifiable errands,

---

[1] Baxter, in his World of Spirits, p. 157, says: "When I was a schoolboy at Oundle, in Northamptonshire, about the Scots coming into England, I heard a well, in one Dob's yard, drum like any drum beating a march. I heard it at a distance: then I went and put my head into the mouth of the well and heard it distinctly, and nobody in the well. It lasted several days and nights, so as all the country people came to hear it. And so it drummed on several changes of times. When King Charles the Second died I went to the Oundle carrier at the Ram Inn, in Smithfield, who told me their well had drummed, and many people came to hear it. And, I heard, it drummed once since."

come the uneasy, impatient, and superstitious, and by dropping pins or pebbles into the water, and by shaking the
ground round the spring, so as to raise bubbles from the
bottom, at a certain time of the year, moon, and day, endeavour to settle such doubts and inquiries as will not let the idle
and anxious rest.   As great a piece of folly as this is, 'tis a
very ancient one.   The Castalian fountain, and many others
among the Grecians, were supposed to be of a prophetic nature.   By dipping a fair mirror into a well, the Patræans of
Greece received, as they supposed, some notice of ensuing
sickness or health, from the various figures portrayed upon
the surface.   In Laconia they cast into a pool, sacred to
Juno, cakes of bread-corn; if they sunk, good was portended;
if they swam, something dreadful was to ensue.   Sometimes
they threw three stones into the water, and formed their conclusions from the several turns they made in sinking."   He
mentions, in the same page, another such well : St. Eunys, in
the parish of Sancred.   Here he happened to be upon the last
day of the year, on which (according to the vulgar opinion) it
exerts its principal and most salutary powers; though two
women assured him that people who had a mind to receive
any benefit from St. Euny's Well must come and wash upon
the first three Wednesdays in May.

[*The Wishing-wells at Walsingham.*—Amongst the slender
remains of this once celebrated seat of superstitious devotion
are two small circular basins of stone, a little to the north-
east of the site of the conventual church (exactly in the place
described by Erasmus in his Peregrinatio religionis ergo), and
connected with the chapel of the Virgin, which was on the
north side of the choir.   The water of these wells had at that
time a miraculous efficacy in curing disorders of the head and
stomach, the special gift, no doubt, of the Holy Virgin; who
has probably since that time resumed it, for the waters have
no such quality now.   She has substituted, however, another
of far more comprehensive virtue.   This is nothing less than
the power of accomplishing all human wishes, which miraculous property the water is still believed to possess.   In order
to attain this desirable end, the votary, with a due qualification
of faith and pious awe, must apply the right knee, bare, to a
stone placed for that purpose between the wells.   He must
then plunge to the wrist each hand, bare also, into the water

of the wells, which are near enough to admit of this immersion A wish must then be formed, but not uttered with the lips, either at the time or afterwards, even in confidential communication to the dearest friend. The hands are then to be withdrawn, and as much of the water as can be contained in the hollow of each is to be swallowed. Formerly the object of deire was most probably expressed in a prayer to the Virgin. It is now only a silent wish; which will certainly be accomplished within twelve months, if the efficacy of the solemn rite be not frustrated by the incredulity or some other fault of the votary.]

Hasted, in his History of Kent, iii. 176, tells us that "at Withersden is a well which was once famous, being called St. Eustace's Well, taking its name from Eustachius, Abbot of Flai, who is mentioned by Matt. Paris, p. 169, an. 1200, to have been a man of learning and sanctity, and to have come and preached at Wye, and to have blessed a fountain there, so 'hat afterwards its waters were endowed by such miraculous power, that by it all diseases were cured."

[According to Brome, in his Travels over England, Scotland, and Wales, 1700, " in Lothien, two miles from Edenburgh southward, is a spring called St. Kathcrines Well, flowing continually with a kind of black fatness, or oil, above the water, proceeding (as it is thought) from the parret coal, which is frequent in these parts; 'tis of a marvelous nature, for as the coal, whereof it proceeds, is very apt quickly to kindle into a flame, so is the oil of a sudden operation to heal all scabs and tumours that trouble the outward skin, and the head and hands are speedily healed by virtue of this oil, which retains a very sweet smell; and at Aberdeen is another well very efficacious to dissolve the stone, to expel sand from the reins and bladder, being good for the chollick and drunk in July and August, not inferiour, they report, to the Spaw in Germany."]

In the Statistical Account of Scotland, vi. 349, Ordiquhill, Banffshire, we read, the mineral well, "dedicated to the Virgin Mary, was formerly at certain seasons much resorted to by the superstitious as well as the sick." Ibid. p. 381, parish of Little Dunkeld, Perthshire: "Here there are a fountain and the ruins of a chapel, both dedicated by ancient superstition to St. Laurence." Ibid. p. 431: "Near Tarbat 'Synod of Ross) there is a plentiful spring of water, which

continues to bear the name of Tobair Mhuir, or Mary's Well."
In the same work, viii. 351, Glenorchay and Inishail, Argyleshire, we are told : " Near the parish school is the well of St.
Connan," the tutelar saint of the country, " memorable for
the lightness and salubrity of its water." Ibid. xii. 464,
parish of Kirkmichael, co. Banff, it is said : " Near the kirk
of this parish there is a fountain, once highly celebrated, and
anciently dedicated to St. Michael. Many a patient have its
waters restored to health, and many more have attested the
efficacy of their virtues. But, as the presiding power is sometimes capricious, and apt to desert his charge, it now lies
neglected, choked with weeds, unhonoured and unfrequented.
In better days it was not so ; for the winged guardian, under
the semblance of a fly, was never absent from his duty. If
the sober matron wished to know the issue of her husband's
ailment, or the love-sick nymph that of her languishing
swain, they visited the well of St. Michael. Every movement
of the sympathetic fly was regarded in silent awe ; and as he
appeared cheerful or dejected, the anxious votaries drew their
presages ; their breasts vibrated with correspondent emotions.
Like the Delai Lama of Thibet, or the King of Great Britain,
whom a fiction of the English law supposes never to die, the
guardian fly of the well of St. Michael was believed to be
exempted from the laws of mortality. To the eye of ignorance
he might sometimes appear dead, but, agreably to the Druidic
system, it was only a transmigration into a similar form, which
made little alteration on the real identity. Not later than a
fortnight ago," it is added, "the writer of this account was much
entertained to hear an old man lamenting with regret the de-
generacy of the times, particularly the contempt in which
objects of former veneration were held by the unthinking
crowd. If the infirmities of years and the distance of his
residence did not prevent him, he would still pay his devo-
tional visits to the well of St. Michael. He would clear the
bed of its ooze, open a passage for the streamlet, plant the
borders with fragrant flowers, and once more, as in the days
of youth, enjoy the pleasure of seeing the guardian fly skim
in sportive circles over the bubbling wave, and with its little
proboscis imbibe the panacean dews." Ibid. xvi. 9, parish
of Inveresk, co. Mid-Lothian : " A routing well (so called
from a rumbling noise it makes) is said always to predict a

storm." Ibid. xviii. 487, parish of Trinity Gask, Perthshire: "The most noted well in the parish is at Trinity Gask. It is remarkable for the purity and lightness of its water; the spring is copious and perennial. Superstition, aided by the interested artifices of Popish priests, raised, in times of ignorance and bigotry, this well to no small degree of celebrity. It was affirmed that every person who was baptized with the water of this well would never be seized with the plague. The extraordinary virtue of Trinity Gask Well has perished with the downfall of superstition."

[The following account of the Buxton well-dressing, 1846, is taken from a newspaper of the period: "This annual fête, whose fame has now extended far beyond the limits of our confined locality, took place on Thursday last. The preparations had been on a more extensive scale than on former occasions, from 'the sinews of war.' At an early hour strangers from the neighbouring towns began to pour in, with smiling faces and in their holiday attire, and there was not a village within ten miles of Buxton but had its representative present. The fountain was, as usual, the centre of attraction. The great difficulty was to obtain a novel design, and a sort of Chinese figure was selected for the front of the cenotaph, while from each corner of the railing pillars sprung, profusely decorated with evergreens, and uniting in a sort of arch at the top, on which the velvet cushion was placed. The principal decoration had a railed-in grass plot in front with four several fountains, throwing up water,—two from handsome vases on each side, one from a very good model of a duck, and another from a sort of shallow basin, from which a variety of beautiful jets were thrown by altering the arrangement of the orifice. This part of the water-works was very much admired. The real flowering was made after the model of the entrance to a Chinese pagoda, through which the fountain with the coiled serpent cut out of the stone in bold relief could be seen. On each side were panels with triumphal arches, the whole surmounted by the peculiar roof divided into compartments of various-coloured flowers. The season being so early, more than usual difficulty has been experienced in procuring a supply of wild flowers, which are best adapted for this style of decoration, but the effect was quite as good as on any previous occasion. Roses, pansies, foxglove, columbines, daisies, white clover, &c., are blended together in sweet harmony, while the scarlet berry of the mountain-ash stood out in bold relief, proclaiming to the world that the erection was 'gratitude to a benefactor.' The delicious green of the fir and box afforded excellent material for borders and division of the more gaudy flowers, and the introduction of a few flowers of the fuchsia gracilis imparted a fine effect. It is impossible to do full justice to the variety of the arrangement, as each separate panel was unique and distinct; suffice it that on the whole it was a decided improvement on its predecessors. About two o'clock the morris-dancers started on their round, accompanied by the Duke of Devonshire's and the Pilsley bands, but their graceful evolutions were frequently interrupted by showers of rain. About six o'clock the clouds all cleared away, and we had as fine an evening as ever shone from the heavens. Various descriptions of music were to be heard all over the town, and when the weather became clear nearly every public-house had its own knot of dancers. There was a ball at the Eagle."]

We find the *superstitious adoration of fountains*, a not unpleasing species of idolatry in sultry weather, is forbidden so early as in the sixteenth of the canons made in the reign of King Edgar, A. D. 960;[1] as also in the canons of St. Anselm, made in the year of Christ 1102.[2] This superstition appears to have been very prevalent in this island till the age before tne Reformation, and is not even yet entirely extinguished among the Roman Catholics and the common people.

In the curious MS. account of the customs in North Wales, by Pennant, I find the following passage: "If there be a fynnon vair, well of our lady or other saint, in the parish,

[1] Johnson's collection of Eccl. Laws, Canons, &c., sub an. DCCCCLX. 16 : "That every priest industriously advance Christianity, and extinguish heathenism, and forbid the *worship of fountains*, and necromancy, and auguries," &c.

[2] Ibid. A.D. MCII. can. 26 : "Let no one attribute reverence or sanctity to a dead body, or *a fountain*, or other thing (as it sometimes is, to our knowledge), without the bishop's authority." There are interdictions of this superstition in the laws of King Canute also preserved, in Wheloc's edition of Lambard's Archaionomia, 1644, p. 108 : Þæðenrcyne bið ꝥ man ꝛola peonpiᵹe—oþþe flðꝺpæꞇeꞃ .pyllꞃ. oþþe rꞇanaꞃ, &c. The Lansdowne MS. 465, however, "Pontificale ad usum Ecclesiæ Romanæ et Anglicanæ," fol. 193, gives the form of benediction for a new well

the water that is used for baptism in the font is fetched thence. Old women are very fond of washing their eyes with the water after baptism." In his Tour in Wales, i. 405, speaking of the village of Llandegla, where is a church dedicated to St. Tecla, virgin and martyr, who, after her conversion by St. Paul, suffered under Nero, at Iconium, says: "About two hundred yards from the church, in a quillet called Gwern Degla, rises a small spring. The water is under the tutelage of the saint, and to this day held to be extremely beneficial in the falling sickness. The patient washes his limbs in the well, makes an offering into it of fourpence, walks round it three times, and thrice repeats the Lord's prayer. These ceremonies are never begun till after sunset, in order to inspire the votaries with greater awe. If the afflicted be of the male sex, like Socrates, he makes an offering of a cock to his Æsculapius, or rather to Tecla, Hygeia; if of the fair sex, a hen. The fowl is carried in a basket, first round the well, after that into the churchyard, when the same crisons and the same circum-ambulations are performed round the church. The votary then enters the church, gets under the communion table, lies down with the Bible under his or her head, is covered with the carpet or cloth, and rests there till break of day, departing after offering sixpence, and leaving the fowl in the church. If the bird dies, the cure is supposed to have been effected, and the disease transferred to the devoted victim."

In some parts of the North of England it has been a custom from time immemorial for the lads and lasses of the neighbouring villages to collect together at springs or rivers on some Sunday in May, to drink sugar and water, where the lasses give the treat: this is called Sugar-and-Water Sunday. They afterwards adjourn to the public-house, and the lads return the compliment in cakes, ale, punch, &c. A vast concourse of both sexes assemble for the above purpose at the Giant's Cave, near Eden Hall, in Cumberland, on the third Sunday in May. See Gent. Mag. for 1791, lxi. 991.

Hutchinson, in his History of Cumberland, ii. 323, speaking of the parish of Bromfield, and a custom in the neighbourhood of Blencogo, tells us: "On the common to the east of that village, not far from Ware-Brig, near a pretty large rock of granite, called St. Cuthbert's Stane, is a fine copious spring of remarkably pure and sweet water, which (probably from its having been anciently dedicated to the same St. Cuthbert) is called *Helly-Well*, i. e. Haly or Holy Well. It formerly was the custom for the youth of all the neighbouring villages to assemble at this well early in the afternoon of the second Sunday in May, and there to join in a variety of rural sports. It was the village wake, and took place here, it is possible, when the keeping of wakes and fairs in the churchyard was discontinued. And it differed from the wakes of later times chiefly in this, that though it was a meeting entirely devoted to festivity and mirth, no strong drink of any kind was ever seen there, nor anything ever drunk but the beverage furnished by the Naiad of the place. A curate of the parish, about twenty years ago, on the idea that it was a profanation of the Sabbath, saw fit to set his face against it ; and having deservedly great influence in the parish, the meetings at Helly-Well have ever since been discontinued."

In the Statistical Account of Scotland, vii. 213, parish of Nigg, co. Kincardine, we read : "*Customs.* In the month of May, many of the lower ranks from around the adjacent city (Aberdeen) come to drink of a well in the bay of Nigg, called Downy Well ; and, proceeding a little farther, go over a narrow pass, the Brigge of ae Hair (Bridge of one Hair), to Downy-Hill, a green island in the sea, where young people cut their favorites' names in the sward. It seems to be the remains of some superstitious respect to the fountain and retreat of a reputed saint, gone into an innocent amusement." Ibid. xii. 463, parish of Kirkmichael, Banffshire, we read : " The same credulity that gives air-formed habitations to green hillocks and solitary groves has given their portion of genii to rivers and fountains. The presiding spirit of that element, in Celtic mythology, was called Neithe. The primitive of this word signifies to wash or purify with water. To this day fountains are regarded with particular veneration over every part of the Highlands. The sick, who resort to them for health, address their vows to the presiding powers, and offer presents to conciliate their favour. These presents generally consist of a small piece of money, or a few fragrant flowers. The same reverence, in ancient times, seems to have been entertained for fountains by every people in Europe. The Romans, who extended their worship to almost every ob-

ject in nature, did not forget in their ritual the homage due
to fountains." Consult Horace in his Address to the Fountain
of Blandusia. " The vulgar in many parts of the Highlands,
even at present," says a note, " not only pay a sacred regard
to particular fountains, but are firmly persuaded that certain
lakes are inhabited by spirits. In Strathspey there is a lake
called Loch nan Spoiradan, the Lake of Spirits." Two frequently make their appearance—the horse and the bull of the
water. The mermaid is another : " Before the rivers are
swelled by heavy rains she is frequently seen, and is always
considered as a sure prognostication of drowning. In Celtic
mythology, to the above named is a fourth spirit added.
When the waters are agitated by a violent current of wind, and
streams are swept from their surface and driven before the
blast, or whirled in circling eddies aloft in the air, the vulgar,
to this day, consider this phenomenon as the effect of the
angry spirit operating upon that element. They call it by a
very expressive name, the Mariach Shine, or the Rider of the
Storm." In the same volume, p. 173, parish of St. Vigeans,
co. Caithness, we are told : " A tradition had long prevailed
here, that the water-kelpy (called in Home's Douglas the
angry spirit of the water) carried the stones for building
the church, under the fabric of which there was a lake of
great depth."

Very anciently a species of hydromancy appears to have
been practised at wells. :" The Druids," says Borlase, " (as
we have great reason to think,) pretended to predict future
events, not only from holy wells and running streams, but
from the rain and snow water, which when settled and afterwards stirred either by oak-leaf, or branch, or magic wand,
might exhibit appearances of great information to the quick-
sighted Druid, or seem so to do to the credulous inquirer, when
the priest was at full liberty to represent the appearances as
he thought most fit for his purpose." Antiquities of Cornwall,
p. 137.

Various rites appear to have been performed on Holy
Thursday at wells, in different parts of the kingdom ; such
as decorating them with boughs of trees, garlands of tulips,
and other flowers, placed in various fancied devices. In some
places, indeed, it was the custom, after prayers for the day at

the church, for the clergyman and singers even to pray and sing psalms at the wells.[1]

[According to Aubrey, writing about the year 1690, "the fellows of New College have, time out of mind, every Holy Thursday, betwixt the hours of eight and nine, gonne to the hospitall called Bart'lemews neer Oxford, when they retire into the chapell, and certaine prayers are read, and an antheme sung : from thence they goe to the upper end of the grove adjoyning to the chapell (the way being beforehand strewed with flowers by the poor people of the hospitall), they place themselves round about the well there, where they warble forth melodiously a song of three, four, or five parts ; which being performed, they refresh themselves with a morning's draught there, and retire to Oxford before sermon."]

Dr. Plott, in his History of Staffordshire, p. 318, tells us : "They have a custom in this county, which I observed on Holy Thursday at Brewood and Bilbrook, of adorning their wells with boughs and flowers. This, it seems, they do, too, at all Gospel-places, whether wells, trees, or hills ; which being now observed only for decency and custom sake, is innocent enough. Heretofore, too, it was usual to pay this respect to such wells as were eminent for curing distempers, on the saint's day whose name the well bore, diverting themselves with cakes and ale, and a little music and dancing ; which, whilst within these bounds, was also an innocent recreation. But whenever they began to place sanctity in them, to bring alms and offerings, or make vows at them, as the ancient Germans and Britons did, and the Saxons and English were too much inclined to, for which St. Edmund's Well without St. Clement's, near Oxford, and St. Laurence's at Peterborough, were famous heretofore, I do not find but they were forbid in those times, as well as now ; this superstitious devotion being called Ƿilpeorðunȝa, which Somner rightly translates well-worship, and was strictly prohibited by our Anglican councils as long

---

[1] At the village of Tissington, in the county of Derby, a place remarkable for fine springs of water, it has been the custom time immemorial. See Gent. Mag. for Feb. 1794, lxiv. 115. Another writer, ibid. March, 1794, p. 226, says : "The same custom was observed of late years, if not at the present time at Brewood and Bilbrook, two places in the county of Stafford."

ago as King Edgar, and in the reign of Canutus; not long
after again in a council at London, under St. Anselm, Archbishop of Canterbury, A.D. 1102 ; as it was also particularly
at these two wells near Oxford and Peterborough, by Oliver
Sutton, Bishop of Lincoln."

Deering, in his History of Nottingham, p. 125, says : "By
a custom time beyond memory, the mayor and aldermen of
Nottingham and their wives have been used on Monday in
Easter week, morning prayers ended, to march from the town
to St. Anne's Well, having the town waits to play before them,
and attended by all the clothing and their wives, i. e. such as
have been sheriffs, and ever after wear scarlet gowns, together with the officers of the town, and many other burgesses
and gentlemen," &c.

Aubrey, in his MS. Remaines of Gentilisme, says, "In processions they used to reade a Gospell at the springs to blesse
them; which hath been discontinued at Sunnywell, in Berkshire, but since 1688."

[One of the most ancient ceremonies relating to wells was
the watching of them at night. A very curious ballad on this
subject, the head-line of which is, "I have forsworne hit whil
I life to wake the welle," is preserved in MS. Cantab. Ff. v.
48, f. 111 :

> " The last tyme I the wel woke,
> Syr John caght me with a croke;
> He made me to swere be bel and boke
> I shuld not telle.
>
> Jet he did me a wel wors turne,
> He leyde my hed agayne the burne,
> He gafe my maydenehed a spurne,
> And rofe my kelle.
>
> Sir John came to oure hows to play,
> Fro evensong tyme til light of the day;
> We made as mery as flowres in May;
> I was begylede.
>
> Sir John he came to our hows,
> He made hit wondur copious:
> He seyd that I was gracious
> To beyre a childe.
>
> I go with childe, wel I wot,
> I schrew the fadur that hit gate,
> Withowtene he fynde hit mylke and pape
> A long while ey."]

The leaving of rags at wells was a singular species of popular superstition.[1] Bishop Hall, in his Triumphs of Rome, ridicules a superstitious prayer of the Popish church for *the blessing of clouts* in the way of *cure of diseases.* Can it have originated thence? This absurd custom is not extinct even at this day : I have formerly frequently observed *shreds* or *bits of rag* upon the bushes that overhang a well in the road to Benton, a village in the vicinity of Newcastle-upon-Tyne, which, from that circumstance, is now or was very lately called *the rag-well.* This name is undoubtedly of long standing: probably it has been visited for some disease or other, and these rag-offerings are the reliques of the then prevailing popular superstition. It is not far from another holy spring at Jesmond,[2] at the distance of about a mile from Newcastle. Pilgrimages to this well and chapel at Jesmond were so frequent, that one of the principal streets of the great commercial town aforesaid is supposed to have had its name partly from having an inn in it, to which the pilgrims that flocked thither for the benefit of the supposed holy water used to resort. See Brand's History of Newcastle-upon-Tyne, i. 339.

Pennant tells us, "They visit the well of Spey, in Scotland, for many distempers, and the well of Drachaldy for as many, offering small pieces of money and *bits of rags.*" Pennant's Additions, p. 18.

---

[1] Grose, from a MS. in the Cotton library marked Julius F. vi., tells us : "Between the towns of Alten and Newton, near the foot of Rosberrye Toppinge, there is a well dedicated to St. Oswald. The neighbours have an opinion that a shirt or shift taken off a sick person and thrown into that well will show whether the person will recover or die : for, if it floated, it denoted the recovery of the party; if it sunk, there remained no hope of their life : and to reward the saint for his intelligence, they *tear off a rag of the shirt, and leave it hanging on the briers thereabouts;* where," says the writer, "I have seen such numbers as might have made a faire rheme in a paper-mill."

[2] "St. Mary's Well, in this village (Jesmond), which is said to have had as many steps down to it as there are articles in the Creed, was lately inclosed by Mr. Coulson for a bathing-place ; which was no sooner done than the water left it. This occasioned strange whispers in the village and the adjacent places. *The well was always esteemed of more sanctity than common wells,* and therefore the failing of the water could be looked upon as nothing less than a just revenge for so great a profanation. But, alas! the miracle's at an end, for the water returned a while ago in as great abundance as ever." Thus far Bourne.

In Heron's Journey through part of Scotland, 1. 101, speaking of the river Fillan in the vale of Strathfillan, he says: "In this river is a pool consecrated by the ancient superstition of the inhabitants of this country. The pool is formed by the eddying of the stream round a rock. Its waves were many years since consecrated by Fillan, one of the saints who converted the ancient inhabitants of Caledonia from Paganism to the belief of Christianity. It has ever since been distinguished by his name, and esteemed of sovereign virtue in curing madness. About two hundred persons afflicted in this way are annually brought to try the benefits of its salutary influence. These patients are conducted by their friends, who first perform the ceremony of passing with them thrice through a neighbouring cairn: on this cairn they then deposit *a simple offering of clothes*, or perhaps of a small bunch of heath. More precious offerings used once to be brought. The patient is then thrice immerged in the sacred pool. After the immersion he is bound hand and foot, and left for the night in a chapel which stands near. If the maniac is found loose in the morning, good hopes are conceived of his full recovery. If he is still bound, his cure remains doubtful. It sometimes happens that death relieves him, during his confinement, from the troubles of life."

In the Statistical Account of Scotland, xiii. 76, parish of Kenethmont, Aberdeenshire, we read: "A spring in the Moss of Melshach, of the chalybeate kind, is still in great reputation among the common people. Its sanative qualities extend even to brutes. As this spring probably obtained vogue at first in days of ignorance and superstition, it would appear that it became customary to leave at the well *part of the clothes of the sick and diseased*, and harness of the cattle, as an offering of gratitude to the divinity who bestowed healing virtues on its waters. And now, even though the superstitious principle no longer exists, the accustomed offerings are still presented."

Macaulay, in his History of St. Kilda, p. 95, speaking of a consecrated well in that island called Tobirnimbuadh, or the spring of diverse virtues, says, that "near the fountain stood an altar, on which the distressed votaries laid down their oblations. Before they could touch sacred water with any prospect of success, it was their constant practice to address the genius of the place with supplication and prayers. No one approached him with empty hands. But the devotees were abundantly frugal. The offerings presented by them were the poorest acknowledgments that could be made to a superior being, from whom they had either hopes or fears. Shells and pebbles, *rags of linen or stuffs worn out*, pins, needles, or rusty nails, were generally all the tribute that was paid; and sometimes, though rarely enough, copper coins of the smallest value. Among the heathens of Italy and other countries, every choice fountain was consecrated, and sacrifices were offered to them, as well as to the deities that presided over them. See Ovid's Fasti, lib. iii. 300 :

'Fonti rex Numa mactat ovem.'

"Horace, in one of his odes, made a solemn promise that he would make a present of a very fine kid, some sweet wine, and flowers, to a noble fountain in his own Sabine villa."

Brand, in his Description of Orkney, p. 58, speaking of St. Tredwell's Loch, says : "It is held by the people as medicinal; whereupon many diseased and infirm persons resort to it, some saying that thereby they have got good. Yet I hear that when they have done all that is usual for them to do—as going about the loch, washing their bodies or any part thereof, leaving something at the loch, *as old clouts and the like*, &c.—it is but in few in whom the effect of healing is produced. As for this loch's appearing like blood before any disaster befal the royal family, as some do report, we could find no ground to believe any such thing."

In the Statistical Account of Scotland, xviii. 630, parish of Mary-Kirk, co. Kincardine, we read : "There is at Balmano a fine spring well, called St. John's Well, which in ancient times was held in great estimation. Numbers who thought its waters of a sanative quality brought their rickety children to be washed in its stream. Its water was likewise thought a sovereign remedy for sore eyes, which, by frequent washing, was supposed to cure them. To show their gratitude to the saint, and that he might be propitious to continue the virtues of the waters, they put into the well presents, not indeed of any great value, or such as would have been of the least service to him if he had stood in need of money, but such as they conceived the good and merciful apostle, who did not delight in costly oblations, could not fail to accept. The presents generally given were pins, needles, and rags taken from their clothes. This may point out the superstition of those times."

Using rags as charms, it seems, was not confined to England or Europe, for I read the following passage in Hanway's Travels into Persia, i. 177 : "After ten days' journey we arrived at a desolate caravanserai, where we found nothing but water. I observed a tree with a number of rags tied to the branches : these were so many charms, which passengers coming from Ghilan, a province remarkable for agues, had left there, in a fond expectation of leaving their disease also on the same spot."

Park, in his Travels in the Interior of Africa, has the following passage : "The company advanced as far as a large tree, called by the natives Neema Taba. It had a very singular appearance, being *covered with innumerable rags or scraps of cloth*, which persons travelling across the wilderness had at different times tied to its branches : a custom so generally followed, that no one passes it without hanging up something." Park followed the example, and suspended a handsome piece of cloth on one of the boughs.

Martin, in his History of the Western Islands of Scotland, p. 7, speaking of the Isle of Lewis, says that "*St. Andrew's Well*, in the village of Shadar, is by the vulgar natives made a test to know if a sick person will die of the distemper he labours under.[1] They send one with a wooden dish, to bring some of the water to the patient ; and if the dish, which is then laid softly upon the surface of the water, turn round sunways, they conclude that the patient will recover of that distemper ; but if otherwise, that he will die."

Collinson, in his History of Somersetshire, iii. 104, mentions a well in the parish of Wembdon, called St. John's Well, to which, in 1464, "an immense concourse of people resorted : and that many who had for years laboured under various bodily diseases, and had found no benefit from physic and

[1] "About a mile to the west of Jarrow (near Newcastle-upon-Tyne) there is a well still called *Bede's Well*, to which as late as the year 1740 it was a prevailing custom to bring children troubled with any disease or infirmity ; a crooked pin was put in, and the well laved dry between each dipping. My informant has seen twenty children brought together on a Sunday to be dipped in this well, at which also, on Midsummer Eve, there was a great resort of neighbouring people, with bonfires, musick, &c." Brand's History of Newcastle-upon-Tyne, ii. 54.

physicians, were, by the use of these waters (after paying their due offerings), restored to their pristine health."

[The well of St. Keyne, in Cornwall, had a very curious superstition attached to it, mentioned by Carew, 1602, and alluded to in the modern ballad on the subject :

> " ' Now art thou a bachelor, stranger ?' quoth he,
>   ' For an if thou hast a wife,
> The happiest draught thou hast drunk this day
>   That ever thou didst in thy life.
>
> Or has thy good woman, if one thou hast,
>   Ever here in Cornwall been ?
> For an if she have, I'll venture my life
>   She has drunk of the well of St. Keyne.'
>
> ' I have left a good woman who never was here,'
>   The stranger he made reply,
> ' But that my draught should be better for that,
>   1 pray you answer me why ?'
>
> ' St. Keyne,' quoth the Cornishman, ' many a time
>   Drank of this crystal well,
> And before the angel summon'd her,
>   She laid on the water a spell :—
>
> If the husband—of this gifted well
>   Shall drink before his wife,
> A happy man henceforth is he,
>   For he shall be master for life.
>
> But if the wife should drink of it first,—
>   Oh, pity the husband then !'
> The stranger stoop'd to the well of St. Keyne,
>   And drank of the water again.
>
> ' You drank of the well I warrant betimes ?'
>   He to the Cornishman said :
> But the Cornishman smiled as the stranger spake,
>   And sheepishly shook his head."]

Mr. Shaw, in his History of the Province of Moray, tells us "that true rational Christian knowledge, which was almost quite lost under Popery, made very slow progress after the Reformation. That the prevailing ignorance was attended with much superstition and credulity; heathenism and Romish customs were much practised : *pilgrimages to wells* and chapels were frequent," &c.

Martin, ut supra, p. 140, observes : "Lochsiant Well in Skie is much frequented by strangers as well as by the inhabitants of the isle, who generally believe it to be a specific for several diseases ; such as stitches, headaches, stone, consumptions, megrim. Several of the common people oblige themselves by a vow to come to this well and make the ordinary tour about it, called *Dessil*, which is performed thus : they move thrice round the well, proceeding sun-ways, from east to west, and so on. This is done after drinking of the water ; and when one goes away from the well it's a never-failing custom to leave some small offering on the stone which covers the well. There is a small coppice near it, of which none of the natives dare venture to cut the least branch, for fear of some signal judgment to follow upon it." Ibid. p. 242 : He speaks of a well of similar quality, at which, after drinking, they make a tour, and then leave an offering of some small token, such as a pin, needle, farthing, or the like, on the stone cover which is above the well.

In the Irish Hudibras, a burlesque of Virgil's account of Æneas's descent into hell, p. 119, we have the following allusion to the Irish visits to holy wells on the patron's day :

> " Have you beheld, when people pray,
>   At *St. John's Well*,[1] on *patron-day*,
>   By charm of priest and miracle,
>   To cure diseases at this well,
>   The valley's fill'd with blind and lame,
>   And *go* as limping as they *came ?*"

Hasted, in his History of Kent, iii. 333, speaking of nail-bourns, or temporary land-springs, which are not unusual in Kent, in the parts eastward of Sittingbourne, says that "their time of breaking forth, or continuance of running, is very uncertain ; but, whenever they do break forth, it is held by the common people as the forerunner of scarcity and dearness of corn and victuals. Sometimes they break out for one, or perhaps two, successive years, and at others, with two, three, or more years' intervention, and their running continues sometimes only for a few months, and at others for three or four years." See Halliwell's Dictionary, p. 569.

In the Statistical Account of Scotland, v. 185, the minister of Unst, in Shetland, says : "A custom formerly prevailed for persons to throw three stones, as a tribute to the source of the salubrious waters, when they first approach a copious spring called Yelaburn, or Hiclaburn (the Burn of Health), in that

---

[1] In the north of Ireland.

neighbourhood. A considerable pile has thus been raised. But the reputation of the spring begins to decline, and the superstitious offering is now no longer so religiously paid."

Two presaging fountains have been already noticed in a former page, from Alexander Ross. In the Living Librarie, or Historical Meditations, 1621, p. 284, the author gives us the following more minute account of them : " I have heard a prince say that there is in his territories a fountaine that yeelds a current of water which runs continually; and ever when it decreaseth it presageth dearnesse of victuals ; but when it groweth drie it signifieth a dearth. There is a fountaine in Glomutz, a citie of Misnia, a league from the river Elbis, which of itselfe making a pond, produceth oftentimes certaine strange effects, as the inhabitants of the country say, and many that have seene the same witnesse. When there was like to be a good and fruitful peace in all the places about, this fountaine would appeare covered with wheat, oats, and akornes, to the great joy of the countrey people that flock thether from all parts to see the same. If any cruell war doe threaten the countrey, the water is all thick with blood and with ashes, a certaine presage of miserie and ruine to come. In old times the Vandals Sorabes came everie yeare in great troupes to this wonderfull fountaine, where they sacrificed to their idols, and inquired after the fruitfulnesse of the yeare following. And myselfe know some gentlemen that confesse, if a certaine fountaine (being otherwise very cleane and cleare) be suddenly troubled by meanes of a worme unknowne, that the same is a personall summons for some of them to depart out of the world."[1]

I find the following recipe for making a *Holy Well* in Tom of all Trades, or the Plain Pathway to Preferment, by Thomas Powell, 1631, p. 31 : " Let them finde out some

---

[1] The custom of affixing ladles of iron, &c. by a chain, to wells, is of great antiquity. Strutt, in his Anglo-Saxon Æra, tells us, that Edwine caused ladles or cups of brass to be fastened to the clear springs and wells, for the refreshment of the passengers. Venerable Bede is his authority, Eccl. Hist. ii. 16. The passage is as follows : " Tantum quoque rex idem utilitati suæ gentis consuluit, ut plerisque in locis ubi fontes lucidos juxta publicos viarum transitus conspexit, ibi ob refrigerium viantium erectis stipitibus et æreos caucos suspendi juberet, neque hos quisquam nisi ad usum necessarium contingere præ magnitudine vel timoris ejus auderet, vel amoris vellet."

strange water, some unheard of spring. It is an easie matter to discolour or alter the taste of it in some measure (it makes no matter how little), Report strange cures that it hath done. *Beget a superstitious opinion of it.* Good fellowship shall uphold it, and the neighbouring townes shall all sweare for it."

AVERSION TO CHEESE.

I FIND the following account, I know not whether it will be thought satisfactory, of the aversion which some persons have to cheese. "L'aversione qui quelques personnes ont du fromage vient de ci. Quand une nourice devient grosse, son ᴌait s'epaissit, s'engrummelle et se tourne comme en fromage, de sorte que l'enfant qui est encore à la mamelle, n'y trouvant plus in la saveure, in la nourriture accoutumée, s'en degoute aisement, se severe de lui meme et en prend une aversion si forte, qu'il la conserve tout le reste de sa vie."—Tractat. de Butyro, Groningæ, Mart. Schookii.

SPORTS AND GAMES.

MISSON, in his Travels in England, translated by Ozell, p. 304, says: "Besides the sports and diversions common to most other European nations, as tennis, billiards, chess, ticktack, dancing, plays, &c., the English have some which are particular to them, or at least which they love and use more than any other people."

The following is an Account of the Games, &c., represented in the margin of the Roman d'Alexandre (preserved in the Bodleian Library, No. 264), from Strutt's notes, taken upon its inspection, with some corrections in explanation of the games, communicated by Douce.

This superbly illuminated manuscript is entitled, Romans du boin Roi Alexandre—qui fu prescrip le xviij. jor Decembre l'an M.CCC.XXXviij. Che livre fu perfais de le enlumi-

nure au xviij. jour d'avryl par Jehan de Guse l'an de grace
M.CCC.XLiiij.   The last sentence in gold letters.

1. A dance of men and women, the men in fancy dresses
masked, one with a stag's head, another with a bear's, and a
third with a wolf's.

2. Cock-fighting.   No appearance of artificial spurs.

3. Hot cockles.

4. A tub elevated on a pole, and three naked boys running
at it with a long stick.

5. Playing at chess.   (D. Jeu de Merilles.)

6. Shooting at rabbits, fowls, &c., with long and cross bows.

7. Fighting with sword and round buckler.

8. Playing at bowls.

9. Whipping-tops, as at present.

10. Playing at dice; one stakes his cloak against the other's
money.

11. A man leaping through a hoop held by two men, his
clothes being placed on the other side for him to leap on.

12. Walking on stilts.

13. Dogs sitting up; and a man with a stick commanding
them.

14. A man dancing, habited as a stag, with a drum before him.

15. Boy blindfold, others buffeting him with their hoods.

16. Boys dressed up as dancing dogs, passing by a man
seated in a chair with a stick.

17. A man with a small shield and club, fighting a horse
rearing up to fall upon him.

18. One boy carrying another with his back upwards, as if
to place him upon a pole and sort of cushion suspended by
two ropes, carried on the shoulders of two others.

19. Morris-dancers.

20. Balancing a sword on the finger, and a wheel on the
shoulder.

21. A boy seated on a stool, holding up his leg.   Another
in a sling, made by a rope round a pulley, holding up his foot,
and swung by a third boy, so that his foot may come in contact
with the foot of the first boy, who, if he did not receive the
foot of the swinging boy properly, would risk a severe blow
on the body.

22. A dancing bear, with a man holding something not
understood in his hand.

23. Running at the quintain on foot. A man holds up the bag of sand.

24. Two boys drawing a third with all their force, seated on a stool (on which is a saddle) running on four wheels.

25. A moveable quintain. The bag supposed to be held out.

26. A man laid on his belly upon a long stool, his head hanging over a vessel, with water at the bottom ; another man standing at the other end of the stool to lift it up and plunge the head of the first in the water.

27. Two boys carrying a third upon a stick thrust between his legs, who holds a cock in his hands. They are followed by another boy with a flag.

28. Water quintain. A boat rowed by four persons, and steered by one. A man with a long pole at the stern.

29. Walking upon the hands to pipe and tabor.

30. A species of music.

31. A man seated, holding out his foot, against which another presses his.

32. Fighting with shield and club.

33. Carrying on pickapack.

34. Five women seated, a sixth kneeling, and leaping upon her hands. One of them lifts up her garments over her head, which the rest seem to be buffeting.

35. A boy seated cross-legged upon a pole, supported by two stools over a tub of water, in one hand holding something not understood, in the other, apparently, a candle.

36. The game of " Frog in the middle, you cannot catch me."

37. Three boys on stools, in a row, striking at each other.

38. A man carrying another on his shoulders.

39. A man in armour seated, holding a shield, another running at him with a pole. The armed man in place of a quintain. I suspect this to be nothing more than the human quintain.

40. Two men seated feet to feet, pulling at a stick with all their might.

41. Two men balancing in their hands a long board, on which a boy is kneeling on one knee with three swords, forming (by their points meeting) a triangle, and to music.

42. A man hanging upon a pole, with his elbows and feet together, and his head between his hams, supported by two other men.

43. Two men fighting with club and target.

44. Two handbells, common with the other music in the masquerade dances. It may be noted that the women do not appear to have been disguised ; the men only, and in various forms, with the heads of all manner of animals, devils, &c.

45. A man with two bells, and two figures disguised as animals.

46. A man and bear dancing.

47. A man with monkeys tumbling and dancing.

48. Four figures, one blindfold, with a stick in his hand, and an iron kettle at a little distance, on which he appears to strike ; the others waiting for the event.

49. Three figures with their hands elevated, as if to clap them together ; one of them has his fingers bent, as if taking a pinch of snuff.

50. A man with a long pole like a rope-dancer.

51. Boys : one blindfold, the others beating him with their hands.

52. Four men, one putting his hand upon the head of a fifth, who sits in the middle cross-legged and cross-armed ; the rest seem as if advancing to strike him open-handed.

53. A dance of seven men and seven women holding hands.

Strutt, in his Manners and Customs, iii. 147, gives us from MS. Harl. 2057, an enumeration of "Auntient Customs in Games used by Boys and Girles, merrily sett out in verse :"

> " Any they dare challenge for to throw the sledge,
> To jumpe or leape over ditch or hedge ;
> To wrastle, play at stoole ball, or to runne,
> To pich the barre, or to shoot of a gunne ;
> To play at loggets, nine holes, or ten pinnes,
> To try it out at foote-ball by the shinnes ;
> At tick-tacke, seize nody, maw, and ruffe,
> At hot-cockles, leape-frogge, or blind-man's buffe,
> To drink the halper pottes, or deale at the whole cann,
> To play at chesse, or pue, and ink horne,
> To daunce the morris, play at barley brake,
> At all exploits a man can think or speak :
> At shove groate, venter poynte, or cross and pile,
> At beshrew him that's last at any stile ;
> At leapinge over a Christmas bonfire,
> Or at the drawing Dunne out of the myer ;
> At shoote cocke, Gregory, stoole ball, and what not ;
> Picke poynt, toppe and scourge to make him hott."

ALL-HID.

THERE was an old sport among children, called in Hamlet, "Hide fox and all after," which, if I mistake not, is the same game that elsewhere occurs under the name of "All-hid;" which, as Steevens tells us, is alluded to in Dekker's Satiromastix : "Our unhandsome-faced poet does play at bo-peep with your grace, and cries *all-hid*, as boys do." In a curious little book entitled A Curtaine Lecture, 1637, p. 206, is the following passage : "A sport called *all-hid*, which is a mere children's pastime."

AMBASSADOR.

GROSE mentions among the sports of sailors the following : "AMBASSADOR. A trick to duck some ignorant fellow or landsman, frequently played on board ships in the warm latitudes. It is thus managed : a large tub is filled with water, and two stools placed on each side of it. Over the whole is thrown a tarpawlin or old sail; this is kept tight by two persons, who are to represent the king and queen of a foreign country, and are seated on the two stools. The person intended to be ducked plays the ambassador, and, after repeating a ridiculous speech dictated to him, is led in great form up to the throne, and seated between the king and queen, who rising suddenly as soon as he is seated, he falls backwards into the tub of water."

ARCHERY.

IN Coates's History of Reading, p. 223, among the churchwardens' accounts of St. Lawrence parish, 1549, is the following entry: "Paid to Will'm Watlynton, for that the p'ishe was indetted to hym for *makyng of the butts*, xxxvis." Ibid. p. 131, St. Mary's parish, sub anno 1566: "Itm. for the

makyng of the butts, viijs." Ibid. p. 132, 1622 : "Paid to
two laborers to playne the grounde where the buttes should
be, vs. vjd." 1629, "Paid towards the butts mending, ijs.
vjd." Ibid. p. 379, St. Giles's parish, 1566 : "Itm. for *carrying of turfes for the butts,* xvjd." Ibid. p. 381, 1605 :
"Three labourers, two days work aboute the butts, iiijs. . . .
Carrying ix load of turfes for the butts, ijs. . . . For two
pieces of timber to fasten on the railes of the butts, iiijd."
1621 : "The parishioners did agree that the churchwardens
and constables should sett up a payre of butts called shooting
butts, in such place as they should think most convenient in
St. Giles parish, which butts cost xivs. xjd."

With the history of this exercise as a military art we have
no concern here. Fitzstephen, who wrote in the reign of
Henry the Second, notices it among the summer pastimes of
the London youth ; and the repeated statutes from the thirteenth to the sixteenth century, enforcing the use of the bow,
usually ordered the leisure time upon holidays to be passed
in its exercise.

"In the sixteenth century we meet with heavy complaints,"
says Strutt, in his Sports and Pastimes, p. 43, "respecting
the disuse of the long-bow, and especially in the vicinity of
London." Stow informs us that before his time it had been
customary at Bartholomew-tide for the lord mayor, with the
sheriffs and aldermen, to go into the fields at Finsbury, where
the citizens were assembled, and shoot at the standard with
broad and flight arrows for games ; and this exercise was continued for several days : but in his time it was practised only
one afternoon, three or four days after the festival of Saint
Bartholomew. Stow died in 1605.

After the reign of Charles the First archery appears to have
fallen into disrepute. Sir William Davenant, in a mock poem
entitled the Long Vacation in London, describes the attorneys
and proctors as making matches in Finsbury fields :

> "With loynes in canvas bow-case tied,
> Where arrows stick with mickle pride ;
> Like ghosts of Adam Bell and Clymme ;
> Sol sets for fear they'll shoot at him !"

About 1753 a society of archers was established in the
metropolis, who erected targets on the same spot during the
Easter and Whitsun holidays, when the best shooter was

styled captain, and the second lieutenant for the ensuing year. Of the original members of this society there were only two remaining when Daines Barrington compiled his "Observations" in the Archæologia. It is now incorporated into the archers' division of the Artillery Company.

About 1789 archery was again revived as a general amusement; and societies of bowmen and toxophilites were formed in almost every part of the kingdom. The fashion did not last long, but it has recently been resuscitated, and is now a fashionable recreation in all parts of England.

Sir Robert Dallington, in his View of *France* as it stood in 1598, says: "Concerning their shooting with the crossebowe, it is used, but not very commonly. Once in a yere, there is in each city a shooting with the peece at a popinjay of wood set upon some high steeple, as also they doe in many places of Germany. He that hitteth it downe is called the King for that yere, and is free from all taxe: besides, he is allowed twenty crownes towards the making of a collation for the rest of the shooters. And if it happen that three yeres together he carry the prize, he is free from all taxe and imposition whatsoever all his life after."

KING ARTHUR.

A GAME used at sea, when near the line, or in a hot latitude. It is performed thus: a man who is to represent King Arthur, ridiculously dressed, having a large wig, made out of oakum, or some old swabs, is seated on the side or over a large vessel of water. Every person in his turn is to be ceremoniously introduced to him, and to pour a bucket of water over him, crying, Hail, King Arthur! If, during this ceremony, the person introduced laughs or smiles (to which his Majesty endeavours to excite him by all sorts of ridiculous gesticulations), he changes places with and then becomes King Arthur, till relieved by some brother tar, who has as little command over his muscles as himself.

BALOON.

[A GAME played with an inflated ball of strong leather, the ball being struck by the arm, which was defended by a bracer of wood.

" 'Tis ten a clock and past ; all whom the mues,
    Baloun, tennis, diet, or the stews
    Had all the morning held, now the second
    Time made ready, that day, in flocks are found."
                                        Donne's Poems, p. 133.]

BARLEY-BREAK.

THE following description of barley-break, written by Sir Philip Sidney, is taken from the song of Lamon, in the first volume of the Arcadia, where he relates the passion of Claius and Strephon for the beautiful Urania :

" She went abroad, thereby,
A *barley-break* her sweet, swift feet to try. . . ,
Afield they go, where many lookers be.
    Then couples three be straight allotted there,
    They of both ends, the middle two, do fly ;
    The two that in mid-space Hell called were
Must strive, with waiting foot and watching eye,
    To catch of them, and them to hell to bear,
    That they, as well as they, may hell supply ;
Like some that seek to salve their blotted name
Will others blot, till all do taste of shame.
    There you may see, soon as the middle two
Do, coupled, towards either couple make,
    They, false and fearful, do their hands undo ;
Brother his brother, friend doth friend forsake,
    Heeding himself, cares not how fellow do,
    But if a stranger mutual help doth take ;
As perjur'd cowards in adversity,
With sight of fear, from friends to friends do fly."

Sir John Suckling, also, has given the following description of this pastime with allegorical personages :

" Love, Reason, Hate did once bespeak
    Three mates to play at *barley-break*.
Love Folly took ; and Reason Fancy ;
    And Hate consorts with Pride ; so dance they.
Love coupled last, and so it fell
    That Love and Folly were in Hell.

They break; and Love would Reason meet,
But Hate was nimbler on her feet ;
Fancy looks for Pride, and thither
Hies, and they two hug together ;
Yet this new coupling still doth tell
That Love and Folly were in Hell.

The rest do break again, and Pride
Hath now got Reason on her side ;
Hate and Fancy meet, and stand
Untouch'd by Love in Folly's hand ;
Folly was dull, but Love ran well ;
So Love and Folly were in Hell." [1]

In Holiday's play of the Marriages of the Arts, 1618, this sport is introduced.

The subsequent is from Herrick's Hesperides, p. 34 :

" *Barley-break, or Last in Hell.*

" We two are last in Hell : what may we feare
To be tormented, or kept pris'ners here :
Alas ! if kissing be of plagues the worst,
We'll wish in Hell we had been last and first."

Dr. Jamieson, in his Etymological Dictionary of the Scottish Language, calls this " a game generally played by young people in a corn-yard. Hence called *barla-bracks about the stacks,* S. B." (i. e. in the north of Scotland.) " One stack is fixed on as the *dule* or goal ; and one person is appointed to catch the rest of the company, who run out from the *dule.* He does not leave it till they are all out of sight. Then he sets off to catch them. Any one who is taken cannot run out again with his former associates, being accounted a prisoner ; but is obliged to assist his captor in pursuing the rest. When all are taken the game is finished ; and he who was first taken is bound to act as catcher in the next game. This innocent sport seems to be almost entirely forgotten in the south of Scotland. It is also falling into desuetude in the north." He adds : " Perhaps from *barley* and *break,* q. breaking of the *parley ;* because, after a certain time allowed for settling preliminaries, on a cry being given, it is the business of one to catch as many prisoners as he can.

[1] See the Dramatic Works of Philip Massinger, 1779, i. 167, whence these extracts are quoted. Barley-break is several times alluded to in Massinger's Plays. See also Browne's Britannia's Pastorals, published in 1614, book i. song 3, p. 76.

Did we suppose it to be allied to *burlaw*, this game might be viewed as originally meant as a sportive representation of the punishment of those who broke the laws of the boors."

> [" In January, men do play
>   At cards and dice their time away :
>   Now men and maids do merry make,
>   At stool-ball and at *barley-break.*
>   Then salted pork, and powder'd beef,
>   Is stil'd the belly's best relief ;
>   Now what the belly most consumes,
>   Is flawns, fools, custards, and stu'd prunes.
>   In January men do go
>   Close muffled up from top to toe ;
>   Now weather it so warm doth hold,
>   That men, though naked, feel no cold."
>   Poor Robin, 1740.]

BEAR-BAITING.

BEAR-BAITING appears anciently to have been one of the Christmas sports with our nobility. "Our nobility," says Pennant, in his Zoology, i. 79, 1776, "also kept their bear-ward ; twenty shillings was the annual reward of that officer from his lord, the fifth Earl of Northumberland, ' when he comyth to my lorde in Cristmas, with his lordshippe's beests for making of his lordschip pastyme the said twelve days.' " Northumb. Household Book.

BIRKIE.

JAMIESON, in the Supplement to his Etymological Dictionary of the Scottish Language, calls this a childish game at cards, in which the players throw down a card alternately. Only two play ; and the person who throws down the highest takes the trick.   In England it is called *beggar-my-neighbour.* He derives the name from the Islandic *berk-ia,* to boast ; because the one rivals his antagonist with his card.   He adds : " Of this game there are said to be two kinds, *king's birkie* and *common birkie."* Galt, alluding to this game in his Ayrshire Legatees, p. 49, says : " It was an understood thing that not only whist and catch-honours were to be played, but even obstreperous *birky* itself, for the diversion of such of the company as were not used to gambling games."

BLINDMAN'S-BUFF.

THIS sport is found among the illuminations of an old missal formerly in the possession of John Ives, cited by Strutt, in his Manners and Customs. Gay says concerning it :

> " As once I play'd at *blindman's-buff*, it hap't,
> *About my eyes the towel thick was wrapt.*
> *I miss'd the swains, and seiz'd on Blouzelind.*
> True speaks that ancient proverb, ' Love is blind.' "[1]

Dr. Jamieson, in his Etymological Dictionary, gives us a curious account of this game, which in Scotland was called *belly-blind.* In the Suio-Gothic it appears this game is called *blind-boc*, i. e. blind goat ; and in German *blind-kuhe*, q. blind cow. The French call this game *cligne-musset,* from *cligner*, to wink, and *musse*, hidden ; also, *colin-maillard*, equivalent to "Colin the buffoon." " This game," says Dr. Jamieson, " was not unknown to the Greeks. They called it κολλαβισμος, from κολλαβιζω, impingo. It is thus defined : Ludi genus, quo hic quidem manibus expansis oculos suos tegit, ille vero postquam percussit, quærit num verberarit ; Pollux ap. Scapul. It was also used among the Romans. We are told that the great Gustavus Adolphus, at the very time that he proved the scourge of the house of Austria, and when he was in the midst of his triumphs, used in private to amuse himself in playing at *blindman's-buff* with his colonels. ' Cela passoit (say the

---

[1] A pleasant writer in the Gent. Mag. for February, 1738, viii. 80, says that "*blindman's-buff* was a ridicule upon Henry VIII. and Wolsey ; where the cardinal minister was bewildering his master with treaty upon treaty with several princes, leaving him to catch whom he could, till at last he caught his minister, and gave him up to be buffeted. When this reign was farther advanced, and many of the abbey-lands had been alienated, but the clergy still retained some power, the play most in fashion was, *I am upon the friar's ground, picking of gold and silver.*"

authors of the Dict. Trev.) pour une galanterie admirable.' v. *Colin-Maillard.*" " In addition to what has formerly been said," Dr. Jamieson adds, under *blind harie*, " (another name for *blindman's-buff* in Scotland) it may be observed that this sport in Isl. is designed *kraekis-blinda.*" Verelius supposes that the Ostrogoths had introduced this game into Italy; where it is called *giuoco della cieca*, or the play of the blind. *Chacke-blynd-man* and *Jockie-blind-man* are other Scottish appellations for the same game.

> [" Sometyme the one would goe, sometyme the other,
> Sometymes all thre at once, and sometyme neither ;
> Thus they with him play at boyes *blynde-man-bluffe.*"
> The Newe Metamorphosis, 1600, MS.]

BLOW-POINT

Appears to have been another childish game. Marmion, in his Antiquary, 4to. 1641, act i. says : "I have heard of a nobleman that has been drunk with a tinker, and of a magnifico that has plaid at *blow-point.*" So, in the comedy of Lingua, 1607, act iii. sc. 2, Anamnestes introduces Memory as telling "how he played at *blowe-point* with Jupiter when he was in his side-coats." See other references to allusions to this game in Halliwell's Dictionary, p. 188.

BOXING.

Misson, in his Memoirs and Observations in his Travels over England, ed. 1719, p. 304, speaking of sports and diversions, says : "Anything that looks like fighting is delicious to an Englishman. If two little boys quarrel in the street, the passengers stop, make a ring round them in a moment, and set them against one another, that they may come to fisticuffs. When 'tis come to a fight, each pulls off his neckcloth and wastcoat, and give them to hold to some of the standers-by (some will strip themselves naked quite to their

wastes) ; then they begin to brandish their fists in the air ;
the blows are aim'd all at the face, they kick one another's
shins, they tug one another by the hair, &c. He that has got
the other down may give him one blow or two before he rises,
but no more ; and let the boy get up ever so often, the other
is oblig'd to box him again as often as he requires it. During
the fight, the ring of by-standers encourage the combatants
with great delight of heart, and never part them while they
fight according to the rules : and these by-standers are not
only other boys, porters, and rabble, but all sorts of men of
fashion ; some thrusting by the mob, that they may see plain,
others getting upon stalls ; and all would hire places, if scaffolds could be built in a moment. The father and mother of
the boys let them fight on as well as the rest, and hearten him
that gives ground or has the worst. These combats are less
frequent among grown men than children, but they are not
rare. If a coachman has a dispute about his fare with a
gentleman that has hired him, and the gentleman offers to fight
him to decide the quarrel, the coachman consents with all his
heart : the gentleman pulls off his sword, lays it in some shop,
with his cane, gloves, and cravat, and boxes in the same manner as I have describ'd above. If the coachman is soundly
drubb'd, which happens almost always (a gentleman seldom
exposes himself to such a battel without he is sure he's
strongest), that goes for payment ; but if he is the *beator*, the
beatee must pay the money about which they quarrell'd. I
once saw the late Duke of Grafton at fisticuffs, in the open
street,[1] with such a fellow, whom he lamb'd most horribly.
In France we punish such rascals with our cane, and sometimes with the flat of our sword : but in England this is never
practis'd ; they use neither sword nor stick against a man that
is unarm'd : and if an unfortunate stranger (for an Englishman
would never take it into his head) should draw his sword upon
one that had none, he'd have a hundred people upon him in
a moment, that would, perhaps, lay him so flat that he would
hardly ever get up again till the Resurrection."

[1] A marginal note says : "In the very widest part of the Strand. The
Duke of Grafton was big and extremely robust. He had hid his blue
ribband before he took the coach, so that the coachman did not know
him."

BUCKLER-PLAY.

In Foure Statutes, specially selected and commanded by
his Majestie to be carefully put in execution of all justices
and other officers of the peace throughout the realme : together
with a Proclamation, a Decree of the Starre-chamber, and
certaine Orders depending upon the former lawes, more particularly concerning the citie of London and counties adjoining, 1609, 4to. p. 94, is the following order : "That all
plaies, bear-baitings, games, singing of ballads, *buckler-play*,
or such like causes of assemblies of people, be utterly prohibited, and the parties offending severely punished by any
alderman or justice of the peace."

Misson, in his Travels, translated by Ozell, p. 307, says :
" Within these few years you should often see a sort of gladiators marching thro' the streets, in their shirts to the
waste, their sleeves tuck'd up, sword in hand, and preceded
by a drum, to gather spectators. They gave so much a head
to see the fight, which was with cutting swords, and a kind of
buckler for defence. The edge of the sword was a little
blunted, and the care of the prize-fighters was not so much to
avoid wounding one another, as to avoid doing it dangerously:
nevertheless, as they were oblig'd to fight till some blood was
shed, without which nobody would give a farthing for the show,
they were sometimes forc'd to play a little ruffly. I once
saw a much deeper and longer cut given than was intended.
These fights are become very rare within these eight or ten
years. Apprentices, and all boys of that degree, are never
without their cudgels, with which they fight something like
the fellows before mention'd, only that the cudgel is nothing
but a stick ; and that a little wicker basket which covers the
handle of the stick, like the guard of a Spanish sword, serves
the combatant instead of defensive arms."

BUFF.

[PERHAPS this is the same with Blind-man's Buff. The game of *Course of the Park* has not been elsewhere noticed:

" *Buff's* a fine sport,
    And so's *Course o' Park;*
But both come short
    Of a dance in the dark.
We trip it completely,
    The pipe sounds so neatly:
But that which surpasses
    Is the breath of the lasses,
O the pretty rogues kiss featly.
(Jack *runs away, and leaves them to stumble out in the dark.*")
                                    The Slighted Maid, 1663, p. 50.]

BULL AND BEAR-BAITING.

FITZSTEPHEN mentions the baiting of bulls with dogs as a diversion of the London youths on holidays in his time.[1]

The ancient law of the market directing that no man should bait any *bull*, bear, or horse in the open streets in the metropolis, has been already quoted in the former volume of this work.

Hentzner, in his Travels in England, ed. 1757, p. 42, says: " There is a place built in the form of a theatre, which serves for the baiting of bulls and bears : they are fastened behind, and then worried by great English bull-dogs ; but not without great risk to the dogs, from the horns of the one and the teeth of the other : and it sometimes happens they are killed on the spot. Fresh ones are immediately supplied in the places of those that are wounded or tired. To this entertainment there often follows that of whipping a blinded bear, which is performed by five or six men, standing circularly, with whips, which they exercise upon him without any mercy, as he cannot

[1] Description of London, edited by Dr. Pegge, 1772, p. 50. In Misson's Memoirs and Observations in his Travels over England, pp. 24-26, are some remarks on the manner of bull-baiting as it was practised in the time of King William III.

II.   26

escape from them because of his chain. He defends himself
with all his force and skill, throwing down all who come within
his reach, and are not quite active enough to get out of it,
and tearing the whips out of their hands and breaking them.
At these spectacles, and everywhere else, the English are constantly smoking tobacco." Hentzner was here in 1598.

Gilpin, in his Life of Cranmer, tells us : " Bear-baiting,
brutal as it was, was by no means an amusement of the lower
people only. An odd incident furnishes us with the proof of
this. An important controversial manuscript was sent by
Archbishop Cranmer across the Thames. The person entrusted
bade his waterman keep off from the tumult occasioned by
baiting a bear on the river, *before the king ;* he rowed, however, too near, and the persecuted animal overset the boat by
trying to board it. The manuscript, lost in the confusion,
floated away, and fell into the hands of a priest, who, by being
told that it belonged to a privy-counsellor, was terrified from
making use of it, which might have been fatal to the head of
the reformed party."

In a proclamation " to avoyd the abhominable place called
the Stewes," dated April the 13th, in the 37th year of
Henry VIII. (preserved in the first volume of a Collection of
Proclamations in the Archives of the Society of Antiquaries
of London, p. 225), we read as follows : " Finallie to th' intent
all resort should be eschued to the said place, the king's
majestie straightlie chargeth and comaundeth that from the
feast of Easter next ensuing, there shall noe *beare-baiting* be
used in that rowe, or in any place on that side the bridge
called London-bridge, whereby the accustomed assemblies
may be in that place cleerely abolished and extinct, upon like
paine as well to them that keepe the beares and dogges, whych
have byn used to that purpose, as to all such as will resort to
see the same." [1]

[1] The subsequent extract from the same proclamation will be thought
curious : " Furthermore his majestie straightlie chargeth and commandeth
that all such householders as, under the name of baudes, have kept the
notable and marked houses, and knowne hosteries, for the said evill disposed persons, that is to saie, such householders as do inhabite the *houses
whited and painted, with signes on the front for a token of the said houses,*
shall avoyd with bagge and baggage, before the feast of Easter next
comyng, upon paine of like punishment, at the kings majesties will and
pleasure."

In the very rare Roman Catholic book, the Life of the Reverend Father Bennet of Canfilde, Douay, 1623, translated from the French by R. R., Catholique Priest, p. 11, is the following passage : "*Even Sunday is a day designed for beare-bayting, and even the howre of theyre* (the Protestants) *service is allotted to it,* and indeede the tyme is as well spent at the one as at the other." R. R. was at least an honest Catholic; he does not content himself with equivocal glances at the *erroneous creed,* but speaks out plainly.

"Her Majesty," says Rowland White, in the Sidney papers, "this day appoints a Frenchman to doe feats upon a rope in the Conduit Court. To-morrow she hath commanded the *beares,* the bull, and the ape to be bayted in the tilt-yard." Andrews's Continuation of Henry's History of Great Britain, 1796, p. 532.

In Vaughan's Golden Grove, 1608, we are told : "Famous is that example which chanced neere London, A. D. 1583, on the 13th daye of Januarie, being Sunday, at Paris Garden, where there met together (as they were wont)[1] an infinite number of people to see the beare-bayting, without any regard to that high day. But, in the middest of their sports, all the scaffolds and galleries sodainely fell downe, in such wise that two hundred persons were crushed well nigh to death, besides eight that were killed forthwith."

In Laneham's Account of the Queen's Entertainment at Killingworth Castle, 1575, we have the following curious picture of a bear-baiting, in a letter to Mr. Martin, a mercer of London : "Well, syr, the bearz wear brought foorth intoo the court, the dogs set too them, too argu the points even face to face ; they had learn'd counsel also a both parts : what may they be coounted parciall that are retain but a to syde ? I ween no. Very feers both ton and toother, and eager in argument ; if the dog in pleadyng would pluk the bear by the throte, the bear with travers woould claw him again by the scalp ; confess and a list, but avoyd a coold not that waz bound too the bar : and his coounsell toold him that it coould be too him no pollecy in pleading. Thearfore thus with fending and prooving, with plucking and tugging, skratting and byting, by plain tooth and nayll a to side and toother, such

[1] There is an account of this accident in Stubbes' Anatomie of Abuses, 1585, p. 118.

expens of blood and leather waz thear between them, az a moonth's licking, I ween, wyl not recoover; and yet remain az far out az ever they wear. It was a sport very pleazaunt of theez beasts; to see the bear with his pink nyez leering after hiz enmiez approch, the nimbleness and wayt of the dog to take hiz avauntage, and the fors and experiens of the bear agayn to avoyd the assauts : if he wear bitten in one place, how he would pynch in an oother to get free : that if he wear taken onez, then what shyft, with byting, with claw-yng, with roring, tossing, and tumbling, he woould woork too wynd hymself from them, and when he waz lose, to shake his ears twyse or thryse wyth the blud and the slaver about his fiznamy, was a matter of goodly releef."

CAMP.

["A GAME formerly much in use among schoolboys, and oc-casionally played by men in those parts of Suffolk on the sea coast—more especially in the line of Hollesley Bay between the rivers Orwell and Alde, sometimes school against school, or parish against parish. It was thus played : Goals were pitched at the distance of 150 or 200 yards from each other; these were generally formed of the thrown off clothes of the competitors. Each party has two goals, ten or fifteen yards apart. The parties, ten or fifteen on a side, stand in line, facing their own goals and each other, at about ten yards dis-tance, midway between the goals, and nearest that of their adversaries. An indifferent spectator, agreed on by the parties, throws up a ball, of the size of a common cricket-ball, mid-way between the confronted players, and makes his escape. It is the object of the players to seize and convey the ball between their own goals. The rush is therefore very great : as is sometimes the shock of the first onset, to catch the fall-ing ball. He who first can catch or seize it speeds therefore home, pursued by his opponents (through whom he has to make his way), aided by the jostlings and various assistances of his own *sidesmen*. If caught and held, or in imminent danger of being caught, he *throws* the ball—but must in no case *give* it—to a less beleagured friend, who, if it be not arrested in

Its course, or be jostled away by the eager and watchful adversaries, catches it; and he hastens homeward, in like manner pursued, annoyed, and aided, winning the notch (or snotch) if he contrive to *carry*, not *throw*, it between his goals. But this, in a well-matched game is no easy achievement, and often requires much time, many doublings, detours, and exertions. I should have noticed, that if the holder of the ball be caught with the ball in his possession, he loses a *snotch;* if, therefore, he be hard pressed, he *throws* it to a convenient friend, more free and in breath than himself. At the loss (or gain) of a *snotch*, a recommence takes place, arranging which gives the parties time to take breath. Seven or nine notches are the game, and these it will sometimes take two or three hours to win.

"It is a most noble and manly sport; in the whole, little, if at all, inferior to cricket, or hunting, or horse-racing. The eagerness and emulation excited and displayed in and by the competitors and townsmen are surprising. Indeed, it is very animating to see twenty or thirty youths, stripped to the skin, and displaying the various energies that this game admits of; rushing with uplifted eye, breast to breast, to catch the descending ball, and all, at once, running full *ding* to gain a point, and when nearly gained, half falling over the stumbling object of pursuit (for the game is always played where the grass is short and slippery), and after much scuffling to see the ball again in the air, thrown to a wily distant sidesman, and seized and carried in the contrary direction, backwards and forwards perhaps half a score times, amid the shouting and roaring of half the population of the contiguous villages.

"Sometimes a large foot-ball was used, and the game was then called 'kicking camp,' and if played with the shoes on, 'savage camp.'

"The sport and name are very old. The 'camping pightel' occurs in a deed of the 30 Hen. VI., about 1486; Cullum's Hawstead, p. 113, where Tusser is quoted in proof, that not only was the exercise manly and salutary, but good also for the *pightel* or meadow:

'In meadow or pasture (to grow the more fine)
Let campers be camping in any of thine;
Which if ye do suffer when low is the spring,
You gain to yourself a commodious thing.' p. 65.

"And he says, in p. 56 :

'Get campers a ball,
To camp therewithall.'

"Ray says that the game prevails in Norfolk, Suffolk, and Essex ; and he derives it from the Saxon, *camp*, to *strive*. The Latin *campus*, a field, or, according to Ainsworth, a *plain field*, may have its share in the name.

"Since this was written, a friend informs me that this game fell into disuse in Suffolk, in consequence of two men having been killed at Easton about forty or fifty years ago, in their struggles at a grand match.

"In Scotland we find that *camp* and *kemp* and *campy*, mean to contend ; bold, brave, heroical; a champion.   In ancient Swedish, *kaempe*, athleta.   In Danish, *kempe*, a giant.   *Kemp*, *kempin*, and *kemper*, farther mean, in Scottish, the act of striving for superiority, and one who so strives ; but is chiefly confined to the harvest field."   Moor.]

CASTING OF STONES.

THIS is a Welsh custom, practised as they throw the black-smith's stone in some parts of England.   There is a similar game in the North of England called *long bullets*.   The prize is to him that throws the ball farthest in the fewest throws.

CAT AND DOG.

DR. JAMIESON, in his Etymological Dictionary, tells us this is the name of an ancient sport used in Angus and Lothian. "The following account," he adds, "is given of it : Three play at this game, who are provided with clubs.   They cut out two holes, each about a foot in diameter, and seven inches in depth.   The distance between them is about twenty-six feet.   One stands at each hole with a club.   These clubs are called *dogs*.   A piece of wood about four inches long, and

one inch in diameter, called a cat, is thrown from the one
hole towards the other, by a third person. The object is to
prevent the cat from getting into the hole. Every time that
it enters the hole, he who has the club at that hole loses the
club, and he who threw the *cat* gets possession both of the
club and of the hole, while the former possessor is obliged to
take charge of the cat. If the *cat* be struck, he who strikes
it changes places with the person who holds the other club ;
and as often as these positions are changed, one is counted as
one in the game, by the two who hold the clubs, and who are
viewed as partners. This is not unlike the stool-ball described
by Strutt, Sports and Pastimes, p. 76 ; but it more nearly
resembles *club-ball*, an ancient English game, ibid. p. 83. It
seems to be an early form of *cricket*."[1]

[The game of *cat*, played with sticks and a small piece of
wood, rising in the middle, so as to rebound when struck on
either side, is still common. It is thus alluded to in Poor
Robin's Almanack for 1709 :

> " Thus harmless country lads and lasses
> In mirth the time away so passes ;
> Here men at foot-ball they do fall ;
> There boys at *cat* and trap-ball.
> Whilst Tom and Doll aside are slank,
> Tumbling and kissing on a bank ;
> Will pairs with Kate, Robin with Mary,
> Andrew with Susan, Frank with Sarah.
> In harmless mirth pass time away,
> No wanton thoughts leads them astray,
> But harmless are as birds in May."]

[1] In the Life of the Scotch Rogue, 1722, p. 7, the following sports
occur : " I was but a sorry proficient in learning : being readier at CAT
AND DOUG, *cappy-hole*, *riding the hurley hacket*, playing at *kyles and
dams*, *spang-bodle*, wrestling, and foot-ball (and such other sports as we
use in our country), than at my book." *Cappy-hole* is also mentioned in
the notes to Bannatyne's Scottish Poems, p. 251, where *play at the trulis*
likewise occurs. This last is supposed to resemble T. *totum*, which is like
a spindle. Trouil is spindle.

CAT I' THE HOLE,

ACCORDING to Jamieson, is the designation given to a game well known in Fife, and perhaps in other counties. Kelly, in his Scottish Proverbs, p. 325, says, " *Tine cat, tine game;*" an allusion to a play called cat i' the hole, and the English kit-cat. Spoken when men at law have lost their principal evidence.

Jamieson says : " If seven boys are to play, six holes are made at certain distances. Each of the six stands at a hole, with a short stick in his hand ; the seventh stands at a certain distance holding a ball. When he gives the word, or makes the sign agreed upon, all the six change holes, each running to his neighbour's hole, and putting his stick in the hole which he has newly seized. In making this change, the boy who has the ball tries to put it into an empty hole. If he succeeds in this, the boy who had not his stick (for the stick is the *cat*) in the hole to which he had run is put out, and must take the ball. There is often a very keen contest, whether the one shall get his stick, or the other the ball, or *cat*, first put into the hole. When the cat *is in the hole*, it is against the laws of the game to put the ball into it."

CENT-FOOT.

I KNOW not what this means, which occurs in the following passage in a Boulster Lecture, 1640, p. 163 : " Playes at cent-foot purposely to discover the pregnancy of her conceit." It was most likely a game at cards.

CHANGE SEATS, THE KING'S COME.

DR. JAMIESON says this is a game well known in Lothian and in the south of Scotland. In this game as many seats are placed round a room as will serve all the company save one. The want of a seat falls on an individual by a kind of lot, regulated, as in many other games, by the repetition of an old rhythm. All the rest being seated, he who has no seat stands in the middle, repeating the words " Change seats, change seats," &c., while all the rest are on the alert, to observe, when he adds, "the king's come," or, as it is sometimes expressed, change their seats. The sport lies in the bustle in consequence of every one's endeavouring to avoid the misfortune of being the unhappy individual who is left without a seat. The principal actor often slily says, " The king's *not* come," when of course the company ought to keep their seats ; but from their anxious expectation of the usual summons, they generally start up, which affords a great deal of merriment.

Sir Walter Scott, in Rob Roy, iii. 153, says : " Here auld ordering and counter-ordering—but patience ! patience !—We may ae day play at *Change seats, the king's coming.*"

This game, although childish, is evidently meant to ridicule the political scramble for places on occasion of a change of government, or in the succession.

CHERRY-PIT.

CHERRY-PIT is a play wherein they pitch cherry-stones into a little hole. It is noticed in the Pleasant Grove of New Fancies, 1657, and in Herrick's Hesperides.

CHUCK-FARTHING, &c.

IN the Instructions of Cornelius Scriblerus concerning the Plays and Playthings to be used by his son Martin, are a few remarks on the toys and minor sports of children, which it may not be irrelevant to notice.

Play, he observes, was invented as a remedy against hunger. " It is therefore wisely contrived by Nature, that children, as they have the keenest appetites, are most addicted to plays. To speak first of the *whistle,* as it is the first of all playthings. I will have it exactly to correspond with the ancient fistula.

and accordingly to be composed *septem paribus disjuncta cicutis.*

" I heartily wish a diligent search may be made after the true *crepitaculum,* or rattle of the ancients, for that (as Archytus Terentinus was of opinion) kept the children from breaking earthenware. The china cups in these days are not at all the safer for the modern rattles; which is an evident proof how far their crepitacula exceeded ours.

" Julius Pollux describes the *omilla,* or *chuck-farthing;* tho' some will have our modern chuck-farthing to be nearer the *aphetinda* of the ancients. He also mentions the *basilinda,* or *king I am;* and *myinda,* or *hoopers-hide.*

" But the *chytindra* described by the same author is certainly not our *hot-cockle;* for that was by pinching, and not by striking; tho' there are good authors who affirm the *rathapygismus* to be yet nearer the modern *hot-cockles.* My son Martin may use either of them indifferently, they being equally antique.

" *Building of house*, and *riding upon sticks,* have been used by children in all ages. *Ædificare casas, equitare in arundine longa.* Yet I much doubt whether the riding upon sticks did not come into use after the age of the Centaurs.

" There is one play which shows the gravity of ancient education, called the *acinetinda,* in which children contended who could longest *stand still.* This we have suffered to perish entirely; and if I might be allowed to guess, it was certainly first lost among the French.

" I will permit my son to play at *apodidascinda,* which can be no other than our *puss in a corner.*

" Julius Pollux, in his ninth book, speaks of the *melolonthe,* or the *kite,* but I question whether the kite of antiquity was the same with ours; and though the Ορνυτοκοπία, or *quailfighting,* is what is most taken notice of, they had doubtless *cock-matches* also, as is evident from certain ancient gems and relievos.

" In a word, let my son Martin disport himself at any game truly antique, except one which was invented by a people among the Thracians, who hung up one of their companions in a rope, and gave him a knife to cut himself down; which if he failed in, he was suffered to hang till he was dead; and this was only reckoned a sort of joke. I am utterly against this as barbarous and cruel." See Pope's Works, vi. 114, 115.

Dr. Arbuthnot, it is observed in a note, used to say, that notwithstanding all the boasts of the safe conveyance of tradition, it was nowhere preserved pure and uncorrupt but amongst schoolboys, whose plays and games are delivered down invariably the same from one generation to another.

COB or COBBING.

GROSE has given us the definition of "*cob* or *cobbing;* a punishment used by the seamen for petty offences, or irregularities, among themselves: it consists in bastinadoing the offender on the posteriors with a cobbing stick or pipe staff; the number usually inflicted is a dozen. At the first stroke the executioner repeats the word *watch,* on which all persons present are to take off their hats, on pain of like punishment; the last stroke is always given as hard as possible, and is called *the purse.* Ashore, among soldiers, where this punishment is sometimes adopted, *watch* and *the purse* are not included in the number, but given over and above, or, in the vulgar phrase, free gratis for nothing. This piece of discipline is also inflicted in Ireland, by the schoolboys, on persons coming into the school without taking off their hats; it is there called School-butter."

COB-NUT.

COB-NUT, a master nut. The children in Yorkshire have a game which is probably an ancient English pastime, though I do not observe any notice of it in Strutt. Numerous hazelnuts are strung like the beads of a rosary. The game is played by two persons, each of whom has one of these strings, and consists in each party striking alternately with one of the nuts on his own string a nut of his adversary's. The field of combat is usually the crown of a hat. The object of each party is to crush the nuts of his opponent. A nut which has broken many of those of the adversary is a *cob-nut.* The author of the Craven Glossary has, from Minshew, "Kop-not, Belg. *nux capitalis.*" Hunter's Hallamshire Glossary.

COCKALL.

The altar is not here foure-squar'd,
Nor in a form triangular,
Nor made of glasse, or wood, or stone,
But of a little transverse bone.
Which boys and bruckeld children call
(Playing for points and pins) *Cockall.*

HERRICK'S HESPERIDES, p. 102.

IN the English translation of Levinus Lemnius, 1658, p. 368, we read: "The ancients used to play at Cockall, or casting of huckle-bones,[1] which is done with smooth sheeps' bones. The Dutch call them *Pickelen,* wherewith our young maids that are not yet ripe use to play for a husband, and young married folks despise these as soon as they are married. But young men use to contend one with another with a kind of bone taken forth of oxe-feet. The Duch call them *coten,* and they play with these at a set time of the year. Moreover cockals, which the Dutch call *Teelings,* are different from dice, for they are square, with four sides, and dice have six. Cockals are used by maids amongst us, and do no ways waste any one's estate. For either they passe away the time with them, or if they have time to be idle, they play for some small matter, as for chesnuts, filberds, pins, buttons, and some such juncats."

[Let no Christian that hath true grace
View these with a malignant face;
But pray that Heaven their lights would snuff,
Cause Satan playes at blind-man-buff
With men, and hoods their intellects,
Casting up *cock-all* for those sects.

Naps upon Parnassus, 1658.]

In Langley's abridgment of Polydore Vergile, f. 1, we have another description of this game: "There is a game also that is played with the posterne bone in the hynder foote of a sheepe, oxe, gote, fallowe, or redde dere, whiche in Latin is called *talus.* It hath foure chaunces: the ace point, that is named Canis, or Canicula, was one of the sides; he that cast i

---

[1] In the Sanctuarie of Salvation, &c., translated from the Latin ot Levinus Lemnius by Henry Kinder, 8vo. Lond. pr. by H. Singleton, p. 141 we read these bones are called " huckle-bones, or coytes."

leyed doune a peny, or oo muohe as the gamers were agreed
on ; the other side was called Venus, that signifieth seven.
He that cast the chaunce wan sixe and all that was layd doune
for the castyng of Canis. The two other sides were called Chius
and Senio. He that did throwe Chius wan three.   And he
that cast Senio gained four.   This game (as I take it) *is used
of children in Northfolke,* and they cal it the Chaunce Bone ;
they playe with three or foure of those bones together ; it is
either the same or very lyke to it."[1]

See also the Account of the Statue belonging to a Group
originally composed of Two Boys who quarrelled at the Game
of Tali, now preserved in the British Museum.   Library of
Entertaining Knowledge, Townley Gallery, i. 305.

Dr. Clarke, in his Travels in Russia, 1810, i. 177, says :
" In all the villages and towns from Moscow to Woronetz, as
in other parts of Russia, are seen boys, girls, and sometimes
even old men, playing with the joint-bones of sheep. This
game is called *dibbs* by the English.   It is of very remote
antiquity ; for I have seen it very beautifully represented on
Grecian vases ; particularly on a vase in the collection of the
late Sir William Hamilton, where a female figure appeared
most gracefully delineated kneeling upon one knee, with her
right arm extended, the palm downwards, and the bones
ranged along the back of her hand and arm.   The second in
the act of throwing up the bones in order to catch them.   In
this manner the Russians play the game."

COCKLE-BREAD.

[The Times of 1847 contains a curious notice of a very old
game, which deserves recording before it be buried in the
massy files of that gigantic journal. A witness, whose conduct
was impugned as light and unbecoming, is desired to inform

[1] For further information relating to this game, as played by the an-
cients, the reader may consult Joannis Meursii Ludibunda, sive de Ludis
Græcorum, Liber singularis, 8vo. Lugd. Bat. 1625, p. 7, v. ΑΣΤΡΑ-
ΓΑΛΣΜΟΣ : and Dan. Souterii Palamedes, p. 81 ; but more particularly,
I Tali ed altri Strumenti lusori degli antichi Romani, discritti da Francesco
de 'Ficoroni, 4to. Rom. 1734.

the court, in which an action for breach of promise was tried, the meaning of " mounting cockeldy-bread ;" and she explains it as " a play among children," in which one lies down on the floor on her back, rolling backwards and forwards, and repeating the following lines :

> " Cockeldy bread, mistley cake,
> When you do that for our sake."

While one of the party so laid down, the rest sat around : and they laid down and rolled in this manner by turns.

This singular game is thus described by Aubrey and Kennett: "Young wenches have a wanton sport which they call moulding of cockle-bread, viz. they get upon a table-board, and then gather up their knees as high as they can, and then they wabble to and fro, as if they were kneading of dough, and say these words :

> " My dame is sick, and gone to bed,
> And I'll go mould my cockle-bread !
> Up with my heels and down with my head,
> And this is the way to mould cockle-bread."

These lines are still retained in the modern nursery-rhyme books, but their connexion with the game of cockeldy-bread is by no means generally understood. There was formerly some kind of bread called cockle-bread, and *cokille-mele* is mentioned in a very early MS. quoted in Halliwell's Dictionary of Archaisms, p. 260. In Peele's play of the Old Wives Tale, a voice thus speaks from the bottom of a well:

> " Gently dip, but not too deep,
> For fear you make the golden beard to weep.
> Fair maiden, white and red,
> Stroke me smooth and comb my head,
> And thou shalt have some *cockell-bread.*"

Here we have a difficult passage in a well-known early dramatist explained by the evidence of an uneducated rustic girl ; and such instances illustrate the use of collecting the quickly vanishing fragments of our provincia. customs and language. The Westmoreland version runs thus :

> " My grandy's seeke,
> And like to dee,
> And I'll make her
> Some cockelty bread, cockelty bread,
> And I'll make her
> Some cockelty bread.''']

CRICKET.

"A GAME most usual in Kent, with a cricket-ball, bowl'd and struck with two cricket-bats between two wickets. From Sax. *cryc*, baculus, a bat or staff; which also signifies fulcimentum, a support or prop, whence a cricket or little stool to sit upon. Cricket-play among the Saxons was also called *stef-plege*, Staff-play." Kennett's MS. Glossary.

CROSS-RUFF.

["A GAME at cards, thus alluded to in Poor Robin's Almanack for 1693 :

" Christmas to hungry stomachs gives relief,
With mutton, pork, pies, pasties, and roast beef;
And men at cards spend many idle hours,
At loadum, whisk, *cross-ruff*, put, and all-fours."]

CURCUDDOCH, CURCUDDIE.

" To dance *Curcuddie* or *Curcuddoch*," says Dr. Jamieson, in his Etymological Dictionary, "is a phrase used (in Scotland) to denote a play among children, in which they sit on their houghs, and hop round in a circular form. Many of these old terms, which now are almost entirely confined to the mouths of children, may be overlooked as nonsensical or merely arbitrary. But the most of them, we are persuaded, are as regularly formed as any other in the language. The first syllable of this word is undoubtedly the verb *curr*, to sit on the houghs or hams. The second may be from Teut. *kudde*, a flock ; *kudd-en*, coire, convenire, congregari, aggregari ; *kudde wijs*, gregatim, catervatim, q. 'to curr together.' The same game is called *Harry Hurcheon* in the north of Scotland, either from the resemblance of one in this position to a *hurcheon*, or hedge-hog, squatting under a bush ; or from the Belg. *hurk-en*, to squat, to *hurkle*."

DRAWING DUN OUT OF THE MIRE,

SAYS Steevens, seems to have been a game. In an old collection of satires, epigrams, &c., I find it enumerated among other pastimes :

> " At shove-groat, venter-point, or crosse and pile,
> At leaping o'er a Midsummer bone-fier,
> Or at *the drawing Dun out of the myer.*"

So in the Dutchesse of Suffolke, 1631 :

> " Well done, my masters, lends your hands,
> *Draw Dun out of the ditch,*
> Draw, pull, helpe all, so, so, well done."
>   [*They pull him out.*

They had shoved Bishop Bonner into a well, and were pulling him out.

We find this game noticed at least as early as Chaucer's time, in the Manciple's Prologue.

> " Then gan our hoste to jape and to play,
> And sayd, sires, what ? *Dun is in the mire.*"

The method in which this game was played is described in Gifford's Ben Jonson, vii. 283.

DRAW GLOVES.

THERE was a sport entitled "Draw Gloves," of which, however, I find no description.[1] The following jeu d'esprit is found in a curious collection of poetical pieces, entitled a Pleasant Grove of New Fancies, 1657, p. 56 :

> " At Draw Gloves wee'l play,
> And prethee let's lay
>   A wager, and let it be this :
> Who first to the summe
> Of twenty doth come,
>   Shall have for his winning a kisse."

See also Herrick's Hesperides, p. 111.

[1] "*Draw-gloves;* a game played by holding up the fingers representing words by their different positions, as we say, *talking with the fingers.*" Halliwell's Dictionary, p. 316.

DUCK AND DRAKE.

BUTLER, in his Hudibras (p. ii. canto iii. l. 302), makes it one of the important qualifications of his conjurer to tell

" What figur'd slates are best to make
On wat'ry surface *duck* or *drake*."

I find the following elegant description of this sport in an ancient church writer (Minucius Felix, ed. 1712, p. 28), which evinces its high antiquity : " Pueros videmus certatim gestientes, testarum in mare jaculationibus ludere. Is lusus est, testam teretem, jactatione fluctuum lævigatam, legere de litore : eam testam plano situ digitis comprehensam, inclinem ipsum atque humilem, quantum potest, super undas inrotare : ut illud jaculum vel dorsum maris raderet, vel enataret, dum leni impetu labitur ; vel summis fluctibus tonsis emicaret, emergeret, dum assiduo saltu sublevatur. Is se in pueris victorem ferebat, cujus testa et procurreret longius, et frequentius exsiliret."

FOOT-BALL.

MISSON says, p. 307, " In winter, foot-ball is a useful and charming exercise. It is a leather ball about as big as one's head, filled with wind. This is kick'd about from one to t'other in the streets, by him than can get at it, and that is all the art of it."

FAYLES.

NARES, in his Glossary, 1822, says : " *Fayles,* a kind or game at tables.

' He's no precisian, that I'm certain of,
Nor rigid Roman Catholic. He'll play
At *fayles* and tick-tack ; I have heard him swear.'
B. Jonson, Every Man in his Humour, iii. 3.

" Mr. Douce has thus explained it from a MS. in the British Museum : it is a very old table game, and one of the numerous

II. 27

varieties of back-gammon that were formerly used in this
country. It was played with three dice, and the usual number
of men or pieces. The peculiarity of the game depended on
the mode of first placing the men on the points. If one of
the players threw some particular throw of the dice, he was
disabled from bearing off any of his men, and therefore *fayled*
in winning the game ; and hence the appellation of it.

"In Gifford's note on the above passage of Jonson, it is
said : 'It was a kind of tric-trac, which was meant by tick-
tack in the same passage.' Mr. Douce refers also to the
English translation of Rabelais. Strutt mentions it, and refers
to the same MS., but gives no particulars. Sports and Pastimes, p. 283."

GOFF, or GOLF.

STRUTT considers this as one of the most ancient games
played with the ball that require the assistance of a club or
bat. "In the reign of Edward III. the Latin name *cambuca*
was applied to this pastime, and it derived the denomination,
no doubt, from the crooked club or bat with which it was
played ; the bat was also called a *bandy* from its being bent,
and hence the game itself is frequently written in English
bandy-ball. It should seem that goff was a fashionable game
among the nobility at the commencement of the seventeenth
century, and it was one of the exercises with which Prince
Henry, eldest son of James I., occasionally amused himself,
as we learn from the following anecdote recorded by a person
who was present : 'At another time, playing at goff, a play
not unlike to pale-maille, whilst his schoolmaster stood talking
with another, and marked not his highness warning him to
stand further off; the prince, thinking he had gone aside,
lifted up his goff-club to strike the ball ; mean tyme one
standing by said to him, Beware that you hit not master
Newton, wherewith he, drawing back his hand, said, *Had I
done so, I had but paid my debts.*"

Dr. Jamieson derives golf from the Dutch *kolf*, a club.
Wachter derives it from *klopp-en*, to strike. Golf and foot-ball
appear to have been prohibited in Scotland by King James II.

in 1457, and again in 1481, by James IV. The bird used at this game was stuffed very hard with feathers. Strutt says that this game is much practised in the north of England; and Dr. Jamieson, that it is a common game in Scotland.[1]

GOOSE RIDING.

A GOOSE, whose neck is greased, being suspended by the legs to a cord tied to two trees or high posts, a number of men on horseback riding full speed attempt to pull off the head, which, if they accomplish, they win the goose. This has been practised in Derbyshire within the memory of persons now living. Douce says, his worthy friend Mr. Lumisden informed him that when young he remembered the sport of "riding the goose" at Edinburgh. A bar was placed across the road, to which a goose, whose neck had been previously greased, was tied. At this the candidates, as before mentioned, plucked. A print of this barbarous custom may be seen in the Trionfi, &c., della Venetia.[2]

In Newmarket; or an Essay on the Turf, 1771, ii. 174, we read: "In the northern part of England it is no unusual diversion to tie a rope across a street, and let it swing about the distance of ten yards from the ground. To the middle of this a living cock is tied by the legs. As he swings in the air, a set of young people ride one after another, full speed, under

[1] See Strutt's Sports and Pastimes, p. 8 ; Jamieson's Etym. Dict. *in voce* In the Gentleman's Magazine for February, 1795, p. 145, mention is made of *shinty match*, a game also peculiar to North Britain, something similar to the *golf*. Dr. Jamieson calls " *shinty* an inferior species of *golf*, generally played at by young people." He adds, "in London this game is called *hackie*. It seems to be the same which is designed *not* in Gloucest. ; the name being borrowed from the ball, which is made of a *knotty* piece of wood. Gl. Grose." Etym. Dict. v. *Shinty*.

[2] See also Menestrier, Traité des Tournois, p. 346. In Paullinus de Candore, p. 264, we read: "In Dania, tempore quadragesimali Belgæ rustici in insula Amack, anserem (candidum ego vidi), fune alligatum, inque sublimi pendentem, habent, ad quem citatis equis certatim properant, quique caput ei prius abruperit, victor evasit." Concerning the practice of swarming up a pole after a goose placed at top, see Sauval, Antiquités de Paris, ii. 696.

the rope, and, rising in their stirrups, catch at the animal's head, which is close clipped and well soaped in order to elude the grasp. Now he who is able to keepe his seat in his saddle and his hold of the bird's head, so as to carry it off in his hand, bears away the palm, and becomes the noble hero of the day."

HANDICAP.

[1660, Sept. 18th. "To the Mitre Tavern in Wood Street, a house of the greatest note in London. Here some of us fell to *handicap*, a sport that I never knew before, which was very good." Pepys's Diary, i. 135.]

HANDY-DANDY.

BOYER, in his Dictionary, calls handy-dandy (a kind of play with the hands), "Sorte de jeu des mains." Ainsworth, in *his* Dictionary, renders handy-dandy by "digitis micare; to move the fingers up and down very swiftly, the number of which, or several fingers were guessed at for the determining things in question, as they hit or mistook the number of fingers." Douce thinks this is a mistake. Johnson says: "*Handy-dandy*, a play in which children change hands and places: 'See how yon justice rails upon yon simple thief! Hark, in thine ear: change places, and, *handy-dandy*, which is the justice, which is the thief?'" King Lear, iv. 6.

Malone seems to have given the best interpretation. "Handy-dandy," he says, "is, I believe, a play among children, in which something is shaken between two hands, and then a guess is made in which hand it is retained. See Florio's Italian Dictionary, 1598: '*Bazzicchiare*, to shake between the hands; to play handy-dandy.'"

Cornelius Scriblerus, in forbidding certain sports to his son Martin till he is better informed of their antiquity, says: "Neither cross and pile, nor ducks and drakes, are quite so ancient as handy-dandy, though Macrobius and St Augustine take notice of the first, and Minutius Foelix describes the latter; but handy-dandy is mentioned by Aristotle, Plato, and Aristophanes." Pope's Works, vi. 115. He adds (ibid. p. 116): "The play which the Italians call *cinque* and the French *mourre* is extremely ancient; it was played by Hymen and Cupid at the marriage of Psyche, and termed by the Latins, *digitis micare.*"

HEADS AND TAILS.

THIS sport is undoubtedly alluded to in Macrobius, Saturn. lib. i. c. 7. "Cum pueri denarios in sublime jactantes, *capita aut navia,* lusu teste vetustatis exclamant."

HOOP.

To run the hoop, an ancient marine custom. Four or more boys, having their left hands tied fast to an iron hoop, and each of them a rope, called a nettle, in their right, being naked to the waist, wait the signal to begin; this being made by a stroke with a cat-of-nine-tails, given by the boatswain to one of the boys, he strikes the one before him, and every one does the same. At first the blows are but gently administered; but each, irritated by the strokes from the boy behind him, at length lays it on in earnest. This was anciently practised when a ship was wind-bound.

HOT COCKLES.

[ONE boy sits down, and another, who is blindfolded, kneels and lays his head on his knee, placing at the same time his open hand on his own back. He then cries, " Hot cockles, hot." Another then strikes his open hand, and the sitting

boy asks who strikes.   If the boy guessed wrongly, he made
a forfeit, but if rightly, he was released.]   This sport is
mentioned as follows by Gay :

> " As at hot-cockles once I laid me down,
>   I felt the weighty hand of many a clown ;
>   Buxoma gave a gentle tap, and I
>   Quick rose and read soft mischief in her eye."

A humorous writer in the Gent. Mag. for Feb. 1738, says :
"*Hot cockles* and *more sacks to the mill* were certainly invented
in the highest times of ignorance and superstition, when the
laity were hoodwinked, and a parcel of monks were saddling
their backs and bastinadoeing them."

Cornelius Scriblerus says : "The *chytrindra* described by
Julius Pollux is certainly not our hot-cockle ; for that was by
pinching, and not by striking : though there are good authors
who affirm the *rathapygismus* to be yet nearer the modern
hot-cockles.   My son Martin may use either of them indifferently, they being equally antique."   Pope's Works, vi. 116.

HUNT THE SLIPPER.

THIS game is noticed by Mr. Rogers in the Pleasures of
Memory, l. 35 :

> " 'Twas here *we chas'd the slipper by its sound.*"

IRISH.

AN old game, similar to backgammon, but more complicated.
It is thus alluded to in Hall's Horæ Vacivæ, 1646 : " The inconstancy of *Irish* fitly represents the changeablenesse of
humane occurrences, since it ever stands so fickle that one
malignant throw can quite ruine a never so well-built game.
Art hath here a great sway, by reason if one cannot well
stand the first assault, hee may safely retire back to an after
game."

KISSING THE POST.

BAGFORD, in his Letter relating to the Antiquities of London, printed in the first vol. of Leland's Collectanea, 1770, and dated Feb. 1, 1714—15, p. lxxvi. says: "This brings to my mind another ancient custom, that hath been omitted of late years. It seems that, in former times, the porters that ply'd at Billingsgate used civilly to intreat and desire every man that passed that way to salute a post that stood there in a vacant place. If he refused to do this, they forthwith laid hold of him, and by main force bouped his * * * * against the post; but, if he quietly submitted to kiss the same, and paid down sixpence, then they gave him a name, and chose some one of the gang for his godfather. I believe this was done in memory of some old image that formerly stood there, perhaps of Belius, or Belin." He adds: "Somewhat of the like post, or rather stump, was near St. Paul's, and is at this day call'd St. Paul's stump."

It is the duty of the Rector of St. Mary-at-Hill, in which parish Billingsgate is situated, to preach a sermon every year on the first Sunday after Midsummer day, before the Society of Fellowship Porters, exhorting them to be charitable towards their old decayed brethren, and "to bear one another's burthens."

The stump spoken of by Bagford is probably alluded to in Good Newes and Bad Newes, by S. R., 1622, where the author, speaking of a countryman who had been to see the sights of London, mentions—

"The water-workes, huge Paul's, old Charing Crosse,
Strong London bridge, at Billinsgate the *bosse!*"

KIT-CAT.

["A GAME played by boys; easier to play than to describe. Three small holes are made in the ground, triangularly, about twenty feet apart, to mark the position of as many boys, who each holds a small stick, about two feet long. Three oth/r boys of the adverse side pitch successively a piece of stick, a little bigger than one's thumb called *cat*, to be struck by those holding the sticks. On its being struck, the boys run from hole to hole, dipping the ends of their sticks in as they pass, and counting one, two, three, &c. as they do so, up to thirty-one, which is game. Or the greater number of holes gained in the innings may indicate the winners, as at cricket. If the *cat* be struck and caught, the striking party is out, and another of his sidesmen takes his place, if the set be strong enough to admit of it. If there be only six players, it may be previously agreed that three *put outs* shall end the innings. Another mode of putting out is to throw the *cat* home, after being struck, and placing or pitching it into an unoccupied hole, while the in-party are running. A certain number of misses (not striking the *cat*) may be agreed on to be equivalent to a put out. The game may be played by two, placed as at cricket, or by four, or I believe more." Moor.]

KIT-CAT-CANNIO.

["A SEDENTARY game, played by two, with slate and pencil, or pencil and paper, like kit-cat, easier learned than described. It is won by the party who can first get three marks (0's or ×'s) in a line; the marks being made alternately by the players 0 or × in one of the nine spots equidistant in three rows, when complete. He who begins has the advantage, as he can contrive to get his mark in the middle." Moor.]

LEAP-CANDLE.

[" THE young girls in and about Oxford have a sport called *leap-candle*, for which they set a candle in the middle of the room in a candlestick, and then draw up their coats in the form of breeches, and dance over the candle back and forth, with these words :

' The taylor of District,
He has but one eye ;
He cannot cut a pair of green galagaskins,
If he were to try.'

This sport in other parts is called *dancing the candle* rush."
Aubrey's MS. ap. Thoms, p. 96. The verses here quoted are
still common in the nursery.]

LEVEL-COIL.

NARES, in his Glossary, says this is " a game of which we
seem to know no more than that the loser in it was to give up
his place to be occupied by another. Minshew gives it thus :
' To play at *levell coil*, G. jouer à cul léve : i. e. to play and
lift up your taile when you have lost the game, and let another
sit down in your place.' Coles, in his English Dictionary,
seems to derive it from the Italian *leva il culo*, and calls it
also *pitch-buttock*. In his Latin Dictionary he has ' *level-coil*,
alternation, cession ;' and ' to play at *level coil*, vices ludendi
præbere.' Skinner is a little more particular, and says, ' Vox
tesseris globulosis ludentium propria :' an expression belonging to a game played with little round tesseræ. He also
derives it from French and Italian. It is mentioned by
Jonson, Tale of a Tub, iii. 2 :

' Young Justice Bramble has kept *level-coyl*
Here in our quarters, stole away our daughter.'

"Gifford says that, in our old dramatists, it implies riot
and disturbance ; but I have seen it in no other passage.
Coil, indeed, alone signifies riot or disturbance ; but *level coil*
is not referred by any to the English words, but to French or
Italian. The same sport is mentioned by Sylvester, Dubartas,
IV. iv. 2, under the name of *level-sice :*

' By tragick death's device
Ambitious hearts do play at *level-sice*.'

"In the margin we have this explanation : ' A kinde of
Christmas play, wherein each hunteth the other from his seat.
The name seems derived from the French *levez sus*, in English,
arise up.' " See further in Halliwell's Dictionary, p. 516.

LOADUM.

[A GAME at cards, thus mentioned in Poor Robin's Almanack for the year 1755 :

> " Now some at cards and dice do play
> Their money and their time away ;
> At *loadum,* cribbage, and all-fours,
> They squander out their precious hours.
> And if they're to an alehouse got,
> Then the other game for th' other pot ;
> Till when 'tis high time to give o'er,
> Then play for who pays all the score,
> And wheresoe'er the lot doth fall,
> There poor Pill Garlick pays for all."]

LOGGATS.

STEEVENS, says: "This is a game played in severa parts of
England even at this time. A stake is fixed into the ground ;
those who play, throw loggats at it, and he that is nearest the
stake wins. I have seen it played in different counties at their
sheep-shearing feasts, where the winner was entitled to a
black fleece, which he afterwards presented to the farmer's
maid to spin for the purpose of making a petticoat, and on
condition that she knelt down on the fleece to be kissed by all
the rustics present."

Malone says : "*Loggeting in the fields* is mentioned for the
first time, among other *new* and crafty games and plays, in
the statute of 33 Hen. VIII. c. 9. Not being mentioned in
former acts against unlawful games, it was probably not practised long before the statute of Henry VIII. was made."

"A loggat-ground," says Blount, another of the commentators on Shakespeare, "like a skittle-ground, is strewed with
ashes, but is more extensive. A bowl, much larger than the
jack of the game of bowls is thrown first. The pins, which
I believe are called *loggats,* are much thinner and lighter at
one extremity than the other. The bowl being first thrown,
the players take the pins up by the thinner and lighter end, and
fling them towards the bowl, and in such a manner that the
pins may once turn round in the air, and slide with the thinner
extremity foremost, towards the bowl. The pins are about
one or two and twenty inches long."

LOVE-GAMES.

THE humorous essayist in the Gent. Mag. vol. viii. for Feb.
1738, already quoted, says, p. 80, that before the troubles (in
the grand rebellion), " Cross purposes was the game played at
by children of all parties.   Upon the death of Charles I. the
ridicule of the times turned against monarchy, which during
the Commonwealth was burlesqued by every child in Great
Britain, who set himself up in mock majesty, and played at
questions and commands ; as, for instance, King I am, says
one boy ; another answers, I am your man ; then his majesty
demands, What service he will do him ; to which the obsequious courtier replies, The best and worst, and all I can.
During all Oliver's time, the chief diversion was, The parson
hath lost his fudling cap, which needs no explanation.   At
the Restoration succeeded love-games, as I love my love with
an A ; a flower and a lady ; and I am a lusty wooer, changed
in the latter end of this reign, as well as all King James II.'s,
to I am come to torment you.   At the Revolution, when all
people recovered their liberty, the children played promiscuously at what game they liked best : the most favorite one,
however, was Puss in the corner.   Everybody knows that in
this play four boys or girls post themselves at the four corners
of a room, and a fifth in the middle, who keeps himself upon
the watch to slip into one of the corner places, whilst the
present possessors are endeavouring to supplant one another.
This was intended to ridicule the scrambling for places, too
much in fashion amongst the children of England, both
spiritual and temporal."

MARBLES

HAD no doubt their origin in bowls, and received their name
from the substance of which the bowls were formerly made.
Taw is the more common name of this play in England. Mr.
Rogers notices marbles in his Pleasures of Memory, l. 137 :

> " On yon gray stone that fronts the chancel-door,
> Worn smooth by busy feet, now seen no more,
> Each eve we shot the marble through the ring."

Notwithstanding Dr. Cornelius Scriblerus's injunctions concerning playthings of "primitive and simple antiquity," we
are told, "he yet condescended to allow" Martinus "the use
of some few modern playthings; such as might prove of any
benefit to his mind, by instilling an early notion of the
sciences. For example, he found that *marbles taught him
percussion, and the laws of motion;* nutcrackers the use of
the lever; swinging on the ends of a board the balance;
bottle-screws the vice; whirligigs the axis and peritrochia;
birdcages the pulley; and tops the centrifugal motion." Bob-
cherry was thought useful and instructive, as it taught, "at
once, two noble virtues, patience and constancy; the first in
adhering to the pursuit of one end, the latter in bearing disappointment." Pope's Works, vi. 117.

MERRITOT, or the SWING.

THIS sport, which is sometimes called *shuggy-shew* in the
north of England, is described as follows by Gay:

> " On two near elms the slackened cord I hung,
> Now high, now low, my Blouzalinda swung."

So Rogers, in the Pleasures of Memory, l. 77:

> " Soar'd in the swing, half pleas'd and half afraid,
> Through sister elms that wav'd their summer shade."

Speght, in his Glossary, says *meritot*, in Chaucer, a sport
used by children by swinging themselves in bell-ropes, or such
like, till they are giddy. In Latin it is called *oscillum*, and is
thus described by an old writer: "Oscillum est genus ludi,
scilicet cum funis dependitur de trabe, in quo pueri et puellæ
sedentes impelluntur huc et illuc." In Mercurialis de Arte
Gymnastica, p. 216, there is an engraving of this exercise.

MUSS.

In Shakespeare's Antony and Cleopatra, act i. sc. 11, the ancient puerile sport called muss is thus mentioned:

Ant.   "When I cry'd, ho!
Like boys *unto a muss*, kings would start forth,
And cry, your will?"

Muss, a scramble, so used by Ben Jonson, Magnetic Lady, act iv. sc. 3, p. 44.

Rabelais mentions *a muss* among Gargantua's games, book i. cap. 22 ; and in another place, book iii. cap. 40. "That the game of the musse is honest, healthful, ancient, and lawful ; a Muscho Inventore, de quo Cod. de petit. Hæred. 1. *Si post motum.*" See Grey's Notes on Shakesp. ii. 208, and Halliwell's Dictionary, p. 568.

MY SOW'S PIGGED.

[A VERY old game, being mentioned in Taylor's Motto, 1622 It is thus alluded to in Poor Robin's Almanack, 1734: "The lawyers play at beggar my neighbour ; the new-marry'd young couples play at put ; the doctors and surgeons at thrust out rotten, but if they meet with a man that is so eat up with the pox that he is all compos'd of that sort of metal, they thrust out all together ; the farmers play at *My Sow's pigg'd ;* the schoolmasters play at questions and commands ; and because every man ought to mind his business, he that plays most at all sorts of gaming, commonly at last plays a game at *hide and seek,* and cares not to leave off till he has got the rubbers."]

NINE MEN'S MORRIS, OR MERRILS.

THE following are the accounts of this game given by the commentators on Shakespeare, who has noticed it in the Midsummer Night's Dream, act ii. sc. 2 :

"The Nine Men's Morris is fill'd up with mud."

"In that part of Warwickshire where Shakespeare was educated, and the neighbouring parts of Northamptonshire, the shepherds and other boys dig up the turf with their knives to represent a sort of imperfect chess-board. It consists of a square, sometimes only a foot diameter, sometimes three or four yards. Within this is another square, every side of which is parallel to the external square; and these squares are joined by lines drawn from each corner of both squares, and the middle of each line. One party, or player, has wooden pegs, the other stones, which they move in such a manner as to take up each other's men, as they are called, and the area of the inner square is called the pound, in which the men taken up are impounded. These figures are by the country people called *nine men's morris,* or *merrils;* and are so called because each party has nine men. These figures are always cut upon the green turf, or leys as they are called, or upon the grass at the end of ploughed lands, and in rainy seasons never fail to be choked up with mud." Farmer.

"*Nine men's morris* is a game still played by the shepherds, cow-keepers, &c., in the midland counties, as follows : a figure (of squares one within another) is made on the ground by cutting out the turf; and two persons take each nine stones, which they place by turns in the angles, and afterwards move alternately, as at chess or draughts. He who can play three in a straight line may then take off any one of his adversary's, where he pleases, till one, having lost all his men, loses the game." Alchorne.

"In Cotgrave's Dictionary, under the article *Merelles,* is the following explanation : ' Le Jeu des Merelles. The boyish game called merils, or *fivepenny morris :* played here most commonly with stones, but in France with pawns, or men made on purpose, and termed merelles. These might originally have been black, and hence called *morris,* or *merelles,* as we yet term a black cherry a morello, and a small black cherry a merry, perhaps from Maurus, a Moor, or rather from *morum,* a mulberry.' " Tollet.

"The *jeu de merelles* was also a table-game. A representation of two monkies engaged at this amusement may be seen in a German edition of Petrarch de Remedio utriusque Fortunæ, b. i. ch. 26. The cuts to this book were done in 1520." Douce.

The following is the account of this game given by Mr. Douce, in the Illustrations of Shakespeare and of Ancient Manners, 1807, i. 184 : "This game was sometimes called the *nine men's merrils*, from *merelles*, or *mereaux*, an ancient French word for the jettons, or counters, with which it was played. The other term, *morris*, is probably a corruption suggested by the sort of dance which, in the progress of the game, the counters performed. In the French *merelles* each party had three counters only, which were to be placed in a line in order to win the game. It appears to have been the *tremerel* mentioned in an old fabliau. See Le Grand, Fabliaux et Contes, ii. 208. Dr. Hyde thinks the morris, or merrils, was known during the time that the Normans continued in possession of England, and that the name was afterwards corrupted into *three men's morals*, or *nine men's morals*. If this be true, the conversion of *morals* into *morris*, a term so very familiar to the country-people, was extremely natural. The Doctor adds, that it was likewise called *nine-penny* or *nine-pin miracle*, *three-penny morris*, *five-penny morris*, *nine-penny morris*, or *three-pin*, *five-pin*, and *nine-pin morris*, all corruptions of *three-pin*, &c., *merels*. Hyde, Hist. Nederluddi, p. 202." See also Strutt's Sports and Pastimes, p. 236.

[Forby has, "*Morris*, an ancient game, in very common modern use. In Shakespeare it is called ' nine men's *morris*,' from its being plaid with nine men, as they were then, and still are called. We call it simply *morris*. Probably it took the name from a fancied resemblance to a dance, in the motions of the men. A wood-cut of it is given in the varior. edition of Shakespeare. Dr. Johnson professes that he knew no more of it than that it was some rustic game. Another commentator speaks of it as common among shepherds' boys in some part of Warwickshire. It cannot well be more common there than here, and it is not particularly rustic. Shepherds' boys and other clowns play it on the green turf, or on the bare ground; cutting or scratching the lines, on the one or the other. In either case it is soon filled up with mud in wet weather. In towns, porters and other labourers play it, at their leisure hours, on the flat pavement, tracing the figure with chalk. It is also a domestic game ; and the figure is to be found on the back of some draught-boards. But, to compare *morris* with that game, or with chess, seems absurd ; as it has a very distant resemblance, if any at all, to either, in the lines, or in the rules of playing. On the ground, the men are pebbles, broken tiles, shells, or potsherds; on a table, the same as are used at draughts or backgammon. In Nares it is said to be the same as nine-holes. With us it is certainly different."]

NINE-HOLES.

I FIND the following in Herrick's Hesperides, p. 178. *Upon* Raspe. *Epig.*:

> "Raspe playes at nine-holes, and 'tis known he gets
> Many a teaster by his game and bets:
> But of his gettings there's but little sign,
> When one hole wastes more than he gets by nine."

NINE-PINS.

[A WELL-KNOWN game, still common, under the name of *skittles*, thus alluded to in Poor Robin, 1707:

> "Ladies for pleasure now resort
> Unto Hide Park and Totnam Court;
> People to Moorfields flock in sholes,
> At *nine-pins* and at pigeon-holes.
> The country lasses pastime make
> At stool-ball and at barley-break;
> And young men they pass time away
> At wrestling and at foot-ball play.
> And every one, in their own way,
> As merry are as birds in May."]

Sir Thomas Urquhart, of Cromarty, in his curious work entitled the Discovery of a most exquisite Jewel, found in the Kennel of Worcester Streets the Day after the Fight, 1651, p. 237, in continuation of a passage which will presently be quoted under "Cards," says: "They may likewise be said to use their king as the players at nine-pins do the *middle kyle*, which they call *the king*, at whose fall alone they aim, the sooner to obtain the gaining of their prize."

Poor Robin, in his Almanack for 1695, in his observations on the Spring quarter, says: "In this quarter are very much practised the commendable exercises of *nine-pins*, pigeon-holes, stool-ball, and barley-break, by reason Easter holydays, Whitsun holydays, and May-day, do fall in this quarter."

In the Brothers of the Blade, answerable to the Sisters of the Scaberd, 4to. 1641, we read: "I would wish thee to haunt bowling-alleys, and frequent gaming-houses, where you may live all day long upon the rooke on the Bankside, or to play at *nine-pins*, or pigeon-holes, in Lincolnes Inne Fieldes; these are ordinary exercises." p. 3.

NOR AND SPELL

Is a game described and represented in the work entitled the Costume of Yorkshire; where it is presumed to be the same with what Strutt, in his Sports and Pastimes, denominates *Northen*, or *Northern spell*. "The little wooden ball" (used in this game) "is in Yorkshire called the Nor, and the receptacle in which it is placed the Spell." The reader may refer to the work already quoted for the representation of this game. It approaches very nearly to the modern game of trap-ball.

[The following letter relating to this game is extracted from the Worcestershire Chronicle, Sept. 1847: "Before the commons were taken in, the children of the poor had ample space wherein to recreate themselves at cricket, *nurr*, or any other diversion; but now they are driven from every green spot, and, in Bromsgrove here, the nailor boys, from the force of circumstances, have taken possession of the turnpike-road to play the before-mentioned games, to the serious inconvenience of the passengers, one of whom, a woman, was yesterday knocked down by a *nurr*, which struck her in the head. Surely it would be an act of humanity on the part of those who have been most benefited by the inclosing of the common to afford the children of the poor in this parish a small space of ground for the purposes of health and amusement."]

NOT.

[A GAME used in Gloucestershire, where the parties, ranged on opposite sides, with each a bat in their hands, endeavour to strike a ball to opposite goals.   The game is called *not*, from the ball being made of a knotty piece of wood.]

PALL-MALL.

IN a most rare book, entitled the French Garden for English Ladies and Gentlewomen to walke in, 1621, in a dialogue, the lady says : " If one had *paille-mails*, it were good to play in this alley, for it is of a reasonable good length, straight, and even." And a note in the margin informs us : "A paille-mal is a wooden hammer set to the end of a long staffe to strike a boule with, at which game noblemen and gentlemen in France doe play much."

In Sir Robert Dallington's Method for Travell, showed by taking the view of France as it stood in the year of our Lord 1598, 4to. London, we read : " Among all the exercises of France, I prefere none before the palle-maille, both because it is a gentlemanlike sport, not violent, and yields good occasion and opportunity of discourse, as they walke from one marke to the other. I marvell among many more apish and foolish toys which we have brought out of France, that we have not brought this sport also into England." See more of this game in Strutt's Sports and Pastimes, p. 82.

PEARIE.

DR. JAMIESON defines Pearie, "that instrument of play used by boys in Scotland, which in England is called a peg-top." It seems to have been named from its exact resemblance to a *pear*. The humming-top of England is in Scotland denominated a *French pearie*, probably as having been originally imported from France.

PICCADILLY, or PICARDILY,

Is mentioned in Flecknoe's Epigrams, p. 90 :

> " And their lands to coyn they distil ye,
> And then with the money
> You see how they run ye
> To loose it at piccadilly."

There was also a species of ruff so called. In the Honestie of this Age, by Barnaby Rich, 1615, p. 25, is the following passage : " But he that some forty or fifty yeares sithens should have asked a *pickadilly*, I wonder who could have understood him, or could have told what a pickadilly had been, fish or flesh."

PIGEON-HOLES.

[" A game like our modern *bagatelle*, where there was a machine with arches for the balls to run through, resembling the cavities made for pigeons in a dove-house."—Halliwell's Dictionary, p. 622.

" In this quarter the commendable exercise of nine-pins, *pigeon-holes*, stool-ball, and barley-break are much practised, by reason Easter-holidays, Whitsun-holidays, and May-day fall in this quarter; besides the landlords holiday, which makes more mirth than any of the holidays aforesaid."—Poor Robin, 1738.]

PRICKING AT THE BELT.

A CHEATING game, also called *Fast and Loose*, of which the following is a description : " A leathern belt is made up into a number of intricate folds, and placed edgewise upon a table. One of the folds is made to resemble the middle of a girdle, so that whoever shall thrust a skewer into it would think he held it fast to the table : whereas, when he has so done, the person with whom he plays may take hold of both ends and draw it away." It appears to have been a game much practised by the gipsies in the time of Shakespeare.

PRISON-BARS, or PRISON-BASE.

THE game of "the Country Base" is mentioned by
Shakespeare in Cymbeline.   Also in the tragedy of Hoffman,
1632 :

> " I'll run a little course
> At *base*, or barley-brake."

Again, in the Antipodes, 1638 :

> " My men can run at *base*."

Also, in the thirtieth song of Drayton's Polyolbion :

> " At hood-wink, barley-brake, at tick, or *prison-base*."

Again, in Spenser's Fairy Queen, v. 8 :

> " So ran they all as they had been at *bace* "

THE QUINTAIN.

THE quintain seems to have been used by most nations in
Europe.   See a very curious account of it in Menage, Diction.
Etymol. de la Langue Françoise, in v. *Quintain.*   See also
Le Grand, Fabliaux et Contes, ii. 414 ; Du Cange, Glossar.
ad Script. Lat. mediæ Ætatis ; Pancirolli, Rer. mem. deperd.
Comment. ii. 292, tit. xxi ; Spelman Gloss. in v. *Quintaen ;*
Watts's Glossary to Matt. Paris, v. *Quintena ;* Dugdale's Hist.
Warwickshire, p. 166 ; Cowel's Law Dictionary ; Plott's Hist.
of Oxfordshire, pp. 200, 201 ; and Archæologia, i. 303.   A
description of the military *quintain* which was used instead of
tilting, may be seen in Pluvinel, L'Instruction du Roy sur
l'Exercice de monter à Cheval, p. 217.   A singular specimen
of the quintain is mentioned in the C. de Tressani, Corps
d'Extraits de Romans, iii. 30.

RACES.

MISSON, in his Travels in England, translated by Ozell,
p. 231, says : " The English nobility take great delight in
horse-races.   The most famous are usually at Newmarket ;

and there you are sure to see a great many persons of the first quality, and almost all the gentlemen of the neighbour-hood. It is pretty common for them to lay wagers of two thousand pounds sterling upon one race. I have seen a horse, that after having run twenty miles in fifty-five minutes, upon ground less even than that where the races are run at New-market, and won the wager for his master, would have been able to run anew without taking breath, if he that had lost durst have ventured again. There are also races run by men."

In Hinde's Life of Master John Bruen, a Puritan of great celebrity, 1641, p. 104, the author recommends "unto many of our gentlemen, and to many of inferior rank, that they would make an exchange of their *foot-races* and *horse-races*," &c.

A proclamation was issued by the Protector Cromwell, 8th April, 1658, " prohibiting horse-races in England and Wales for eight moneths."

DIVERSION OF THE RING.

MISSON, in his Travels in England, p. 126, speaking of Hyde Park, "at the end of one of the suburbs of London," says: " Here the people of fashion take the *diversion of the ring*. In a pretty high place, which lies very open, they have surrounded a circumference of two or three hundred paces diameter, with a sorry kind of balustrade, or rather with poles placed upon stakes, but three foot from the ground; and the coaches drive round and round this. When they have turned for some time round one way, they face about and turn t'other: so rowls the world."

RIDING AT THE RING.

IN the Statistical Account of Scotland, xx. 433, parish of Dunkeld, Perthshire, we have an account of the diversion with this name. "To prevent that intemperance," the writer says, "to which social meetings in such situations are some-times prone, they spend the evening in some public competition of dexterity or skill. Of these, *riding at the ring* (an amusement of ancient and warlike origin) is the chief. Two perpendicular posts are erected on this occasion, with a cross-beam, from which is suspended a small ring : the competitors are on horseback, each having a pointed rod in his hand, and he who, at full gallop, passing betwixt the posts, carries away the ring on the rod, gains the prize." This is undoubtedly a game of long standing. In the King of Denmarkes Welcome, 1606, the author, giving an account of the reception of Christian IV. in England that year, says : "On Monday, being the 4th day of August, it pleased our kings majestie himself in person, and the kings majestie of Denmarke like-wise in person, and divers others of his estate, to *runne at the ring* in the tilt-yard at Greenwich, where the King of Denmarke approved to all judgements that majestie is never unaccom-panied with vertue : for there, in the presence of all his beholders, he tooke the ring fower severall times, and would I thinke have done the like four score times, had he runne so many courses."

RUFFE.

THERE appears by the following passage to have been an ancient game called *ruffe :* "A swaggerer is one that plays at ruffe, from whence he tooke the denomination of a ruffyn," &c., from Characters at the end of the House of Correction, or certaine Satyrical Epigrams, by J. H., Gent. 1619. It was a game at cards. See further notices in Halliwell's Dictionary, p. 697.

SWIFT-FOOT-PASSAGE.

IN the Dedication to Michael Mumchance, we read : "making the divel to daunce in the bottome of your purses, and to turn your angels out of their houses like bad tenants." Ibid. "*Novum, hassard,* and *swift-foot-passage,*" occur as games.

RUNNING THE FIGURE OF EIGHT.

THIS sport is still followed by boys, and is alluded to by Shakespeare in his Midsummer Night's Dream, in the line—

"And the quaint mazes in the wanton green."

SCOTCH AND ENGLISH.

HUTTON, in his History of the Roman Wall, 1804, p. 104, after an account of the incessant irruptions upon each other's lands between the inhabitants of the English and Scottish borders, in ancient times, and before the union of the two kingdoms, observes: "The lively impression, however, of former scenes did not wear out with the practice; for the children of this day, upon the English border, keep up the remembrance by a common play, called *Scotch and English,* or *the Raid,* i e inroad. The boys of the village choose two captains out of their body; each nominates, alternately, one out of the little tribe. They then divide into two parties, strip, and deposit their clothes, called *wad* (from weed), in two heaps, each upon their own ground, which is divided by a stone, as a boundary between the two kingdoms. Each then invades the other's territories; the English crying, ' Here's a leap into thy land, dry-bellied Scot.' He who can, plunders the other side. If one is caught in the enemie's jurisdiction, he becomes a prisoner, and cannot be released except by his own party. Thus one side will sometimes take all the men and property of the other." [1]

This seems to be the same game with that described by Dr. Jamieson, in his Etymological Dictionary, under the name

---

[1] Our author appears to be mistaken in his etymology when he derives *wad* from weed, a garment. Had he consulted Lye (Junii Etymologicon), he would have found " *wad* Scoti dicunt pro *wedd* pactum; and " *wedd* " rendered " pactum, sponsio ; A.S. peꝺ est pignus vel pactum, ac peculiari acceptione pactum sponsalitium, vel dos." Hence our word *wedding* for a marriage.

of *Wadds.* In the Glossary to Sibbald's Chronicle of Scottish Poetry, *Wadds* is defined, " A youthful amusement, wherein much use is made of *pledges.*" *Wad,* a pledge, says Dr. Jamieson, is the same with the *vadium* of medieval Latin.

SCOTCH-HOPPERS.

In Poor Robin's Almanack for 1677, in his verses to the reader, on the back of the title-page, concerning the chief matters in his annual volume, among many other articles of intelligence, our star-gazer professes to show—

" The time when school-boys should play at *Scotch-hoppers.*"

[Another allusion occurs in the same periodical for 1707 : " Lawyers and Physitians have little to do this month, and therefore they may (if they will) play at *Scotch-hoppers.* Some men put their hands into peoples pockets open, and extract it clutch'd, of that beware. But counsel without a cure, is a body without a soul." And again, in 1740 : " The fifth house tells ye whether whores be sound or not ; when it is good to eat tripes, bloat herrings, fry'd frogs, rotten eggs, and monkey's tails butter'd, or an ox liver well stuck with fish hooks ; when it is the most convenient time for an old man to play at *Scotch-hoppers* amongst the boys. In it also is found plainly, that the best armour of proof against the fleas, is to go drunk to bed."]

SEE-SAW.

Gay thus describes this well-known sport :

" Across the fallen oak the plank I laid,
And myself pois'd against the tott'ring maid ;
High leap'd the plank, adown Buxoma fell," &c.

SHOOTING THE BLACK LAD.

THEY have a custom at Ashton-under-Line, on the 16th of April, of shooting the black lad on horseback. It is said to nave arisen from there having been formerly a black knight who resided in these parts, holding the people in vassalage, and using them with great severity.

SHOVE-GROAT.

Slide-thrift, or *shove-groat*, is one of the games prohibited by statute, 33 Henry VIII. It has been already noticed from Rowland's Satyres, under "Drawing Dun out of the Mire."

A shove-groat shilling is mentioned in Shakespeare's Second Part of King Henry the Fourth, and is supposed by Steevens to have been a piece of polished metal made use of in the play of shovel-board. Douce, however, has shown that shove-groat and shovel-board were different games. The former was invented in the reign of Henry the Eighth, for in the statute above alluded to it is called *a new game*. It was also known by the several appellations of *slide-groat*, *slide-board*, *slide-thrift*, and *slip-thrift*. See the Illustr. of Shakesp. i. 454.

In 1527, when the warrant arrived at the Tower for the execution of the Earl of Kildare, he was playing with the lieutenant at shovel-groat. When the lieutenant read it and sighed, "By St. Bryde, lieutenant (quoth he), there is some mad game in that scrole: but fall out how it will, this throw is for a *huddle*." Stow's Annals, edit. 1592, p. 894.

SHUFFLE-BOARD

Or SHOVEL-BOARD, is still or was very lately played. Douce, a few years ago, heard a man ask another to go into an alehouse in the Broad Sanctuary, Westminster, to play at it. In honest Izaak Walton's time, a shovel-board was probably to be found in every public-house.

That shovel-board, in the time of Charles I., was even a royal game, may be ascertained from the inventory of goods taken at Ludlow Castle belonging to that monarch, Oct. 31, 1650. We have not only "the *shovell-board roome;*" but "one large *shovell-board table,* seven little joyned formes, one side table, and a court cup-board," were sold to Mr. Bass for the sum of £2 10*s.*[1]

SPINNY-WYE

Is the name of a game among children at Newcastle-upon-Tyne. I suspect this is nearly the same with "hide and seek." "I spye," is the usual exclamation at a childish game called 'Hie, spy, hie.'

STOOL-BALL.

[An ancient game at ball, according to Dr. Johnson, where balls are driven from stool to stool. It is thus alluded to in Poor Robin's Almanack for 1740:

> " Now milk-maids pails are deckt with flowers,
> And men begin to drink in bowers,
> The mackarels come up in shoals,
> To fill the mouths of hungry souls ;
> Sweet sillabubs, and lip-lov'd tansey,
> For William is prepared by Nancy.
> Much time is wasted now away,
> At pigeon-holes, and nine-pin play,
> Whilst hob-nail Dick, and simp'ring **Frances**
> Trip it away in country dances ;
> At *stool-ball* and at barley-break,
> Wherewith they harmless pastime make."]

---

[1] See the Harl. MS. Brit. Mus. 4898, p. 599. Among the royal goods at Theobald's, in the same volume, p. 440, one *billiard-board* brought £1 10*s.*

TAG.

A WRITER in the Gentleman's Magazine for 1738, tells us that "in Queen Mary's reign, *tag* was all the play; where *the lad saves himself by touching of cold iron*—by this it was intended to show the severity of the Church of Rome. In later times, this play has been altered amongst children of quality, by touching of *gold* instead of *iron*." He adds, " Queen Elizabeth herself is believed to have invented the play *I am a Spanish merchant;* and Burleigh's children were the first who played at it. In this play, if any one offers to sale what he hath not his hand upon or touches, he forfeits,— meant as an instruction to traders not to give credit to the Spaniards. The play of Commerce succeeded, and was in fashion during all her reign."

TAPPIE-TOUSIE,

OF this sport among children Dr. Jamieson gives the following account: " One, taking hold of another by the forelock of his hair, says to him, ' *Tappie, tappie, tousie*, will ye be my man?' If the other answers in the affirmative, the first says, ' Come to me, then, come to me, then,' giving him a smart pull towards him by the lock which he holds in his hand. If the one who is asked answers in the negative, the other gives him a push backwards, saying, ' Gae fra me, then, gae fra me, then.'

" The literal meaning of the terms is obvious. The person asked is called *tappie tousie*, q. dishevelled head, from *tap*, and *tousie*, q. v. It may be observed, however, that the Suio-Gothic *tap* signifies a lock or tuft of hair. *Haertapp*, floccus capillorum; Ihre, p. 857.

" But the thing that principally deserves our attention is the meaning of this play. Like some other childish sports, it evidently retains a singular vestige of very ancient manners. It indeed represents the mode in which one received another as his bondman.

"The thride kind of nativitie, or bondage, is quhen ane frie man, to the end he may have the menteinance of ane great and potent man, randers himself to be his bond-man in his court, *be the haire of his forehead;* and gif he thereafter withdrawes himselfe, and flees away fra his maister, or denyes to him his nativitie: his maister may prove him to be his bondman, be ane assise, before the justice; challengand him, that he, sic ane day, sic ane yeare, compeirid in his court, and there yeilded himselfe to him to be his slave and bond-man. And quhen any man is adjudged and decerned to be a native or bond-man to any maister; the maister may *take him be the nose,* and reduce him to his former slaverie." Quon. Attach. c. lvi. s. 7.

"This form of rendering one's self by the hair of the head seems to have had a monkish origin. The heathenish rite of consecrating the hair, or shaving the head, was early adopted among Christians, either as an act of pretended devotion, or when a person dedicated himself to some parti cular saint, or entered into any religious order. Hence it seems to have been adopted as a civil token of servitude. Thus those who entered into the monastic life were said *capillos ponere* and *per capillos se tradere.* In the fifth century Clovis committed himself to St. Germer *by the hair of his head:* Vit. S. Germer. ap. Carpentier, vo. *Capilli.* Those who thus devoted themselves were called the *servants* of God, or of any particular saint. This then being used as a symbol of servitude, we perceive the reason why it came to be viewed as so great an indignity to be laid hold of by the hair. He who did so claimed the person as his property. Therefore, to seize or to drag one by the hair, *comprehendere,* or *trahere per capillos,* was accounted an offence equal to that of charging another with falsehood, and even with striking him. The offender, according to the Frisic laws, was fined in two shillings; according to those of Burgundy, also, in two; but if both hands were employed, in four. Leg. Fris. ap. Lindenbrog. Tit. xxii. s. 64. Leg. Burgund. Tit. v. s. 4. According to the laws of Saxony, the fine amounted to an hundred and twenty shil- lings; Leg. Sax. cap. i. s. 7, ibid. Some other statutes made it punishable by death; Du Cange, col. 243."

THREAD-MY-NEEDLE.

[A GAME in which children stand in a row joining hands, the outer one, still holding his neighbour, runs between the others, &c. It is alluded to in Poor Robin's Almanack for 1738 : " The summer quarter follows spring as close as girls do one another, when playing at *thread-my-needle,* they tread upon each other's heels."]

TICK-TACK.

IN Hall's Horæ Vacivæ, 1646, p. 149, are the following observations on the game of tick-tack. " *Tick-tack* sets a man's intentions on their guard. Errors in this and war can be but once amended." See a full account of the game in Halliwell's Dictionary, p. 873.

TRAY-TRIP.

GROSE says this was an ancient game, like Scotch-hop, played on a pavement marked out with chalk into different compartments. According to Mr. Halliwell, Dictionary, p. 886, it was a game at dice.

TROULE-IN-MADAME.

IN the Benefit of the Ancient Bathes of Buckstones, compiled by John Jones at the King's Mede, nigh Darby, 1572, 4to. p. 12, we read : " The ladyes, gentle woomen, wyves, and maydes, may in one of the galleries walke ; and if the weather bee not aggreeable to theire expectacion, they may have in the ende of a benche eleven holes made, intoo the whiche to trowle pummates, or bowles of leade, bigge, little, or meane, or also of copper, tynne, woode, eyther vyolent or softe, after their owne discretion ; the pastyme *troule-in-madame* is termed."

TRUMP.

[AN old game at cards. In the French Garden for English
Ladies and Gentlewomen, 1621, the titles of the following
games occur : "*Trompe, dice, tables, lurch, draughts, perforce, pleasant, blowing, queen's game, chesse.*" There is
added : " The maydens did play *at purposes, at sales, to
thinke, at wonders, at states, at vertues, at answers,* so that
we could come nc sooner," &c. It is also alluded to in the
Cobler of Canterburie, 1608 : " May not the Cobler of Kent,
who hath beene the patron of many good companions, and
tost over a paire of cards at *trump* from morning till night,
not to be admitted so far as to find fault with *Richard Tarltons
Newes out of Purgatorie?* Yes ; and if he that writ it will
not amend the latchet, Ile on with my night-cap and my spectacles, and make him shape the legge righter ere I have done."]

TRUNDLING THE HOOP.

SHOOTING with bows and arrows, and swimming on blad-
ders, occur among the puerile sports delineated in the illuminations of the curious missal cited by Strutt.

The hoop is noticed by Charlotte Smith, in her Rural Walk :

> " Sweet age of blest delusion ; blooming boys,
> Ah ! revel long in childhood's thoughtless joys ;
> With light and pliant spirits, that can stoop
> To follow sportively *the rolling hoop ;*
> To watch the sleeping top, with gay delight,
> Or mark, with raptur'd gaze, the sailing kite ;[1]
> Or eagerly pursuing pleasure's call,
> Can find it centr'd in the bounding ball !"

---

[1] *Paper windmills* are seen in the hands of the younger sort of children in Mr. Ives's missal.

TRUNKS.

[ANOTHER name for the game of troule-in-madame, just mentioned. It is thus alluded to in Poor Robin's Almanack for 1715 : "After dinner (for you must not have too long intermissions) to your sack again, typire, topire, and tropire, and for recreations to such liquor, billiards, kettle-pins, noddyboards, tables, *trunks*, shovel boards, fox and geese, and those two excellent games at cards, one and thirty, and drive knaves out of town." See extract in Halliwell's Dictionary, p. 892.]

WEAPON-SHAWING.

IN Sinclair's Statistical Account of Scotland, iii. 512, the minister of Kincardine, co. Ross and Cromartie, says : "Nigh to the church there is an alley, walled in, and terminating in a large semicircle, appropriated to that ancient military exercise and discipline known by the name of *weapon-shawing*."

WHIPPING THE TOP, OR WHIRLE-GIGGE.

IT is said in some of the voyages, I think it is in Hawkesworth's, that the top is well known among the Indians, some of whom pointed to our sailors, who seemed to wonder at seeing it amongst them, that in order to make it spin they should lash it with a whip. The following mention of whipping the top, occurs in Persius's third Satire :

"Neu quis callidior buxum torquere flagello."

Thus translated by Dryden :

"The whirling top they whip,
And drive her giddy till she fall asleep."

Thus also in Virgil's Æneid, vii. 378 :

"Ceu quondam torto volitans sub verbere turbo,
Quem pueri magno in gyro vacua atria circum
Intenti ludo exercent. Ille actus habenâ,
Curvatis fertur spatiis : stupet inscia turba,
Impubesque manus, mirata volubile buxum :
Dant animos plagæ."

Thus translated by Dryden :

> " As young striplings whip the top for sport,
> On the smooth pavement of an empty court ;
> The wooden engine whirls and flies about,
> Admir'd with clamours of the beardless rout,
> They lash aloud, each other they provoke,
> And lend their little souls at ev'ry stroke."[1]

Northbroke, in his Treatise against Dicing, 1579, p. 86, says : " Cato giveth counsell to all youth, saying, ' *Trocho lude, aleas fuge, playe with the toppe,* and flee dice-playing."[2] Playing with tops is found among the illuminations of an old missal in the possession of John Ives, described by Strutt in his Manners and Customs, ii. 99.

To sleep like a town top is a proverbial expression. A top is said to sleep when it turns round with great velocity, and makes a smooth humming noise. The following custom is now laid aside : a large top was formerly kept in every village, to be whipt in frosty weather, that the peasants might be kept warm by exercise, and out of mischief, while they could not work. See Reed's Shakes., 1803, v. 248.[3] In the Fifteen Comforts of Marriage, p. 143, we read : " Another tells 'em of a project he has to make town tops spin without an eel-skin, as if he bore malice to the school-boys." So in the English translation of Levinus Lemnius, 1658, p. 369 : " Young youth do merrily exercise themselves in whipping-top, and to make it run swiftly about, that it cannot be seen, and will

---

[1] So Ovid, Trist. 1. iii. Eleg. 12 :

> " Otia nunc istic : junctisque ex ordine ludis
> Cedunt verbosi garrula bella fori.
> Usus equi nunc est, levibus nunc luditur armis :
> Nunc pila, *nunc celeri volritur orbe trochus."*

[2] Cornelius Scriblerus, in his Instructions concerning the Plays and Playthings to be used by his son Martin, says : " I would not have Martin as yet to scourge a top, till I am better informed whether the trochus which was recommended by Cato be really our present top, or rather the hoop which the boys drive with a stick." Pope's Works, vi. 115.

[3] In the Statistical Account of Scotland, xxi. 145, parish of Monquhitter, under " Amusements," we are told : " People who are not regularly and profitably employed, rejoice in a holiday as the means of throwing off that languor which oppresses the mind, and of exerting their active powers. So it was with our fathers. They frequently met to exert their strength in wrestling, in casting the hammer, and in throwing the stone, their agility at foot-ball, and their dexterity at coits and penny-stone."

deceive the sight, and that in winter to catch themselves a heat." Poor Robin, in his Almanack for 1677, tells us, in the Fanatick's Chronology, it was then " 1804 years since the first invention of town-tops."

WRESTLING.

MISSON, in his Travels, p. 306, says : " Wrestling is one of the diversions of the English, especially in the northern counties." The curious in this sport may consult the Inn-Play : or Cornish-Hugg Wrestler. Digested in a method which teacheth to break all Holds, and throw most Falls mathematically. By Sir Thomas Parkyns, of Bunny, Baronet, 4to. 1717. Prefixed to this work are *Institutes for young wrestlers*, by William Tunstall.

POPULAR NOTICES OF CARDS.

IN some parts of the north of England a pack of cards is called to this day, as it is in Shakespeare's Plays, a *deck* of cards.

In the Gent. Mag. for Jan. 1791, lxi. 16, are several queries on cards. The writer informs us that " the common people in a great part of Yorkshire invariably call diamonds *picks*. This I take," he says, "to be from the French word *piques*, spades ; but cannot account for its being corruptly applied by them to the other suit." The true reason, however, is to be gathered from the resemblance the diamond bears to a *mill-pick*, as fusils are sometimes called in heraldry.

Hall, in his Horæ Vacivæ, 1646, p. 150, says : " For cardes, the philologie of them is not for an essay. A man's fancy would be sum'd up in *cribbidge ; gleeke*[1] requires a vigilant

---

[1] " A lady once requesting a gentleman to play at *gleeke*, was refused, but civilly, and upon three reasons : the first whereof, madam, said the gentleman, is, I have no money. Her ladyship knew that was so material and sufficient, that she desired him to keep the other two reasons to himself." Gayton's Festivous Notes upon Don Quixote, 1654, p. 14.

memory; *maw*, a pregnant agility ; *pichet*, a various invention; *primero*, a dexterous kinde of rashnesse," &c.

Sir Thomas Urquhart, of Cromarty, in the Discovery of a most exquisite Jewel found in the Kennel of Worcester Streets the Day after the Fight, 1651, p. 237, says : " Verily, I thinke they make use of kings as we do of card-kings in playing at the hundred; any one whereof, if there be appearance of a better game without him (and that the exchange of him for another in-coming card is like to conduce more for drawing of the stake), is by good gamesters without any ceremony discarded." [1]

According to Mr. Singer, *lansquenet*, *trappola*, and *minchiate* are foreign games, unnoticed by English writers as in use here. *Tarocco* was played in England early in the reign of James I. *Primero* is supposed to have been introduced into England after the marriage of Mary with Philip of Spain. Shakespeare makes Falstaff say, " I never prospered since I forswore myself at primero." *Mawe*, another game, is described by Arthur Hall, about the year 1580, as " a playe at cards grown out of the country from the meanest, into credit at court with the greatest." It is also alluded to in Dekker's works, as well as in many other of the satirical tracts of the time of James I. *Loadum*, *noddy*, and *macke*, are mentioned as games at cards by Sir John Harrington. *Gleek* is described at large by Cotton, in the Complete Gamester. *Post and paire* is said by Cotton to be a game on the cards very much played in the West of England. *Bankrout* is supposed to have been the same as *bank-a-fa-let*, described in the same work. *All fours* is described by Cotton as " a game very much played in Kent." The Spanish game of *ombre* is supposed by Barrington to have been introduced into this country by Catherine of Portugal, the Queen of Charles II., as Waller has a poem, " On a Card torn at Ombre by the Queen." *Quadrille*, which is a species of ombre, supplanted that game in England. *Reversis* is a French game. *Basset*, which is said by Dr. Johnson to have been invented at Venice, was certainly known in Italy as early as the end of the thirteenth century. It

---

[1] The following is in Herrick's Hesperides, p. 281 :

" At *post and paire*, or *slam*, Tom Tuck would play
This Christmas, but his want wherewith sayes nay."

appears to have been a fashionable game in England at the end of the seventeenth century. *Cent,* or *mount sant,* which is a Spanish game, is alluded to in one or two of our old plays. *Trump* was a common game at the latter end of the sixteenth century. *Whist* is said to be a very ancient game amongst us : though not to have been played on principle before 1730. *Piquet* is of French origin, though the period which gave it birth is uncertain.

[The following curious lines on divination by drawing cards, are extracted from an old chap-book :

" This noble king of diamonds shews,
Thou long shalt live where pleasure flows,
But when a woman draws the king,
Great melancholy songs she'll sing.

Now is the queen of diamonds fair,
She shews thou shalt some office bear ;
Oh ! woman if it fall to you,
Friends you will have, and not a few.

Is now the knave of diamonds come ?
Be sure beware the martial drum ;
Yet if a woman draws the knave,
She shall much better fortune have.

He that draws the ace of hearts
Shall surely be a man of parts ;
And she that draws it, I profess,
Will have the gift of idleness.

He who can draw this duce shall be
Endowed with generosity ;
But when a woman draws this card,
It does betide them cruel hard.

The man who gets hold of this tray,
Always bound, always obey ;
A woman that shall draw this sort,
Will surely drink brandy by the quart."]

CHUMMING-UP.

[A CUSTOM in prisons, the nature of which will be easily understood from the following newspaper report :

" Cross-examined by Mr. Miller.—He had been a gaoler of the Court of Requests prison about sixteen years. There was a practice there called 'chumming-up.' That practice had existed ever since he had been there, and a very long time before; it was an old custom. He could not tell when the custom of ' chumming-up' first began in the Court of Requests prison; it might be termed a time-immemorial custom.

Mr. Miller. Be good enough, Mr. Boot, to describe the ceremony of ' *chumming-up.*'

Boot. When a new prisoner comes in, he is welcomed by the prisoners, who are in the prison, and beat round with the chumming instruments.

Mr. Miller. What are those chumming instruments?

Boot. Old swords and staves.

Mr. Miller. Is there a little music?

Boot. They generally have a fife.

Mr. Miller. Are there any masks?

Boot. Yes; the prisoners put on masks.

Mr. Miller. And after this ceremony of ' chumming-up' is over, do the prisoners demand from their new brother-prisoner any money?

Boot. Yes; they demand half-a-crown from him.

Mr. Miller. And if he cannot pay the half-crown demanded of him, do they take his coat and waistcoat off him?

Boot. I believe they do.

Mr. Miller. And they keep it as a sort of pledge?

Boot. I believe so.

Mr. Miller. So, if a poor man comes into your prison so poor that he cannot pay half-a-crown, his coat and waistcoat are taken from him, and he is compelled to remain without those garments to cover him?

Boot. I have seen prisoners without their coats and waistcoats.

Mr. Miller. They are not very nice whom they chum up?

Boot. Not very; they would as soon chum you up as anybody else.   (Loud laughter.)

Mr. Miller. They caught Mr. Weale, the Poor-Law Commissioner, the other day at this place?

Boot. Mr. Weale visited the prison a few weeks ago.

Mr. Miller. And they were going to chum him up, but he paid the half-crown?

Boot. No: I don't think they would have chummed him."]

FAIRS.

A FAIR is a greater kind of market, granted to any town by privilege, for the more speedy and commodious providing of such things as the place stands in need of. They are generally kept once or twice in a year. Proclamation is to be made how long they are to continue, and no person is allowed to sell any goods after the time of the fair is ended, on forfeiture of double their value.

Warton tells us, that before flourishing towns were established, and the necessaries of life, from the convenience of communication and the increase of provincial civility, could be procured in various places, goods and commodities of every kind were chiefly sold at fairs : to these, as to one universal mart, the people resorted periodically, and supplied most of their wants for the ensuing year. Gay's account of the different articles exposed at fairs is a pleasant one, Past. vi. :

> " How pedlars' stalls with glitt'ring toys are laid,
> The various fairings of the country maid,
> Long silken laces hang upon the twine,
> And rows of pins and amber bracelets shine.
> Here the tight lass, knives, combs, and scissors spies,
> And looks on thimbles with desiring eyes.
> The mountebank now treads the stage, and sells
> His pills, his balsams, and his ague-spells ;
> Now o'er and o'er the nimble tumbler springs,
> And on the rope the vent'rous maiden swings :
> Jack-pudding, in his party-coloured jacket,
> Tosses the glove, and jokes at every packet ;
> Here raree-shows are seen, and Punch's feats,
> And pockets pick'd in crowds, and various cheats."

In Poems by the Rev. Henry Rowe, 1796, i. 115, is another description of a rustic fair :

> " Next morn, I ween, the village charter'd fair,
> A day that's ne'er forgot throughout the year :
> Soon as the lark expands her auburn fan,
> Foretelling day, before the day began,
> Then ' Jehu Ball' re-echoes down the lane,
> Crack goes the whip, and rattling sounds the chain.
> With tinkling bells the stately beast grown proud,
> Champs on the bit, and neighing roars aloud.

The bridles dotted o'er with many a flow'r,
The six-team'd waggon forms a leafy bow'r.
Young Damon whistled to Dorinda's song,
The fiddle tuneful play'd the time along.
At length arriv'd, the statute fills the fair,
Dorcas and Lydia, Bella too was there:
Favours and gauzes, variegated gay,
Punch loudly squeaks, the drum proclaims the play.
The pole high rear'd, the dance, the gambol show'd
Mirth and diversion to the gaping crowd:
Sam with broad smile, and Poll with dimpled face,
Revers'd the apron,[1] shows she wants a place.
The race in sacks, the quoit, the circling reel,
While Prue more thoughtful buys a spinning-wheel.
The grinning Andrew, perch'd on folly's stool,
Proves th' artificial, not the natural fool:
For Hodge declares he thinks, devoid of art,
He must be wise, who acts so well his part!"

Sir Frederick M. Eden, State of the Poor, 1797, i. 32, tells us in a note: "In Gloucestershire, Oxfordshire, Wiltshire, and Berkshire, servants continue to attend the *mopp* or *statute*, as it is called (i. e. Michaelmas fair), in order to be hired. Each person has a badge, or external mark, expressive of his occupation. *A carter* exhibits a piece of whip-cord tied to his hat: *a cow-herd* has a lock of cow-hair in his: and *the dairymaid* has the same descriptive mark attached to her breast. So in the north of England, at the spring hiring term, the servants to be hired, who are almost always persons to be employed in husbandry, are to be distinguished from others who attend the market, by their wearing a large *posie*, or *bouquet of flowers* at their breasts: which is no unapt emblem of their calling.[2] Even in London, bricklayers, and other house-

[1] A whimsical custom at a country fair.
[2] The following is from Flecknoe's Epigrams, p. 74:

" As horse-coursers their horses set to sale,
With ribands on their foreheads and their tail;
So all our poets' gallantry now-a-days
Is in the prologues and epilogues of their plays."

The author of the Character of a Quack Astrologer, 1673, speaking of " Itch of picture in the front," says: " This sets off the pamphlet in a country fair, as the horse sells the better for the ribbon wherewith a jockey tyes up his tail." The custom of attaching brooms to the mastheads of ships, or other vessels, *on sale* (inquired after in the Gent. Mag. for August, 1799, p. 653), has been before noticed.

labourers, carry their respective implements to the places where they stand for hire : for which purpose they assemble in great numbers, in Cheapside and at Charing-Cross, every morning at five or six o'clock. So, in old Rome, there were particular spots in which servants applied for hire. 'In Tusco vico, ibi sunt homines qui ipsi se venditent.' Plauti Curculio, act iv."

Dr. Plott, speaking of the statutes for hiring servants, says, that at Banbury they called them the Mop. He says, that at Bloxham the carters stood with their whips in one place, and the shepherds with their crooks in another; but the maids, as far as he could observe, stood promiscuously. He adds that this custom seems as old as our Saviour, and refers to Matth. xx. 3.

In the Statistical Account of Scotland, xxi. 457, parish of Wamphray, we read: *"Hiring fairs* are much frequented : *those who are to hire wear a green sprig in their hat :* and it is very seldom that servants will hire in any other place." [The following account of the custom still prevalent in the north of England, may appear somewhat strange to southern readers. The Preston Guardian, 1846, says : "Thursday last was the 'hiring-day,' at Kendal. The street was well supplied with young men, whose want of situations was indicated by a bit of straw, paper, or leaf, exhibited under their hatband. The hiring of them was not quite so brisk as last year—the wages for the six months generally averaging about 8*l.* though some few fetched as much as 10*l.* The show of female servants at the ' Cross' was unusually small, and the demand much greater than the supply. The girls were all ages, from thirteen to thirty, looking remarkably healthy, and fully maintaining the compliment of ' the bonny lasses of Westmoreland.' Most of them were well dressed, some in a superior manner, and a few had boas round their necks. They carried a very independent air, and were exceedingly cheerful. More good temper could not be wished than was exhibited betwixt buyers and sellers. The females carry no signal of ' wanting a place,' like the males; and hence persons who wanted servants pressed through the crowd, and kept asking, 'Are you to hire? are you to hire?' for numbers of lasses remain in the crowd who are already engaged. Most of the inquirers for servants appeared to be farmers; and sometimes the giddier sort of girls would rebuff the inquirer with—'Yes! for life.' The bargaining appeared to be on the same principle as you see in a cattle market. A number of questions are asked as to age, family, last service, what they can do, and wages. 'What do you ask?' said a farmer to a smart-looking girl. 'Five pound.' ''Ah! that's above my cut :' and after some further inquiries as to where she had lived, he added, 'That's o'er fine a place for me.' Another was haggling a long time with a young woman, presenting a shilling to her, as cattle-dealers do to each other, consenting to give what she asked, but wanting 'five shillings out.' 'Stick up tull him,' replied a motherly old woman who stood near ; and, shortly after, the bargain was struck for the whole amount, by the shilling being placed in her hand. Such was the competition, that so soon as negociations were broken off with one wanter, another stepped up, and made inquiries. 'What do you want?' asked a farmer of a girl that seemed left at last. 'Three guineas—but say three pounds, I'll not take less.' 'Ye're four or five and twenty, arn't you?' 'Me!' was her tart reply, 'I am just turned sixteen.' One man, boasting to a neighbour how well he had succeeded, observed, "Ay! she is a fine lass—I ken the breed of her.' The girls showed great freedom in asking the applicants numerous questions :—' Where is your house ? How many kye do you keep? What is there to do?' One man thought he would secure his end ; and, in answer to the last question, said, ' Oh, we have nothing to do.' ' Then I'll not hire with you,' was the reply. In a few instances the mothers were there, setting off the claims of a daughter. They would say : ' She is a lisle (little) 'un, but she is a good 'un.' ' Are you a milker?' cried a strapping farmer to a young woman : ' my wife is on her last legs, and I'll take you for good.' ' Aw can milk nin—an' ye're auld enough to be my grandfather. I am not gawn (going) to hire for life just noo,' replied the buxom wench. As much as 6*l.* was given for the best servants for the half-year, and in one instance 6*l.* and half-a-crown ; and we believe all were cleared off."]

The display of merchandise, and the conflux of customers, at these principal and almost only emporia of domestic commerce, were prodigious ; and they were therefore often held on open and extensive plains. One of the chief of them was that of St. Giles's Hill or Down, near Winchester. the

Conqueror instituted and gave it as a kind of revenue to the Bishop of Winchester. It was at first for three days, but afterwards, by Henry III., prolonged to sixteen days. Its jurisdiction extended seven miles round, and comprehended even Southampton, then a capital and trading town. Merchants who sold wares at that time within that circuit forfeited them to the bishop. Officers were placed at a considerable distance, at bridges and other avenues of access to the fair, to exact toll of all merchandise passing that way. In the mean time, all shops in the city of Winchester were shut. A court, called the Pavillion, composed of the bishop's justiciaries and other officers, had power to try causes of various sorts for seven miles round. The bishop had a toll of every load or parcel of goods passing through the gates of the city. On St. Giles's eve the mayor, bailiffs, and citizens of Winchester delivered the keys of the four gates to the bishop's officers. Many and extraordinary were the privileges granted to the bishop on this occasion, all tending to obstruct trade, and to oppress the people. Numerous foreign merchants frequented this fair; and several streets were formed in it, assigned to the sale of different commodities. The surrounding monasteries had shops or houses in these streets, used only at the fair; which they held under the bishop, and often let by lease for a term of years. Different counties had their different stations.[1]

[In some counties *cherry fairs* are frequently held in the cherry orchards. They are the resort of the gay and thoughtless, and as such frequently metaphorically alluded to by early writers. Thus Occleve, MS. Soc. Antiq. 134, f. 257 :

" This lyf, my sone, is but a *chery feyre*."]

It appears from a curious record now remaining, containing the establishment and expenses of the household of Henry Percy, the fifth Earl of Northumberland, 1512, and printed by Dr. Percy, that the stores of his lordship's house at Wresille, for the whole year, were laid in from fairs.[2]

---

[1] In the Revenue Roll of William of Waynflete, an. 1471, this fair appears to have greatly decayed ; in which, among other proofs, a district of the fair is mentioned as being unoccupied : " Ubi homines cornubiæ stare solebant."

[2] The articles are " wine, wax, beiffes, multons, wheite, & malt." This proves that fairs still continued to be the principal marts for purchasing

In the accounts of the priories of Maxtoke in Warwickshire, and of Bicester in Oxfordshire, in the time of Henry VI., the monks appear to have laid in yearly stores of various yet common necessaries, at the fair of Sturbridge,[1] in Cambridge-shire, at least 100 miles distant from either monastery.

It may seem surprising that their own neighbourhood, in-cluding the cities of Oxford and Coventry, could not supply them with commodities neither rare nor costly; which they thus fetched at a considerable expense of carriage. It is a rubric in some of the monastic rules, "De euntibus ad nun-dinas;" i. e. concerning those who go to fairs.[2]

In Coates's History of Reading, 1802, p. 214, in the church-wardens' accounts of St. Laurence parish, 1499, is the follow-ing article: "*Receypt.* It. Rec. at the fayer for a stonding in the church-porch, iiij*d.*"

By advertisements partly for due order in the publique ad-ministration of Common Prayers, by Queen Elizabeth's letters commanding the same, dated 25 Jan., 7 Eliz., 4to., it was en-joined, "that in all fairs and common markets, falling *uppon the Sunday,* there be no shewing of any wares *before the service be done.*"

Two annual fairs held on the Town Moor at Newcastle-upon-Tyne, are called Lammas and St. Luke's Fairs, from the days on which they begin. Bourne, in his history of that

necessaries in large quantities, which now are supplied by frequent trading towns: and the mention of beiffes and multons (which are salted oxen and sheep) shows that at so late a period they knew little of breeding cattle.

[1] " Expositas latè cami propé flumina merces,
    Divitiasque loci, vicosque, hominumque labores,
    Sparsaque per virides passim magalia campos."
                                    Nundinæ Sturbrigienses.

John Bale, in his Declaration of Bonner's Articles, f. 21, mentions "the baker's boye's crye, betwixte hys two bread panners in Sturbridge fayre. *By and beare awaye, steale and runne awaye,* &c."

[2] See Warton's History of Eng. Poet. i. 279. Fosbrooke, in his British Monachism, ii. 217, tells us: "much quarrelling and fighting sometimes attended the monastic fairs, held in the churchyard:" and Dr. Henry, iv. 205 (where much is said upon these fairs), observes from Muratori, that "When a fair was held within the precincts of a cathedral or monastery, :t was not uncommon to oblige every man to take an oath at the gate, before he was admitted, that he would neither lie, nor steal, nor cheat, while ne continued in the fair."

town, tells us, that the tolls, booths, stallage, pickage,[1] and
courts of pie-powder (dusty foot) to each of those fairs, were
reckoned, communibus annis, at twelve pounds, in the time of
Oliver Cromwell. The records of the monasteries there, are
many of them lost, otherwise they would doubtless have furnished some particulars relative to the institution and ancient
customs of the fairs at that place.

Bailey tells us, that in ancient times amongst Christians,
upon any extraordinary solemnity, particularly the anniversary
dedication of a church,[2] tradesmen used to bring and sell their
wares even in the churchyards, especially upon the festival of
the dedication ; as at Westminster, on St. Peter's day; at
London on St. Bartholomew's ; at Durham, on St. Cuthbert's
day, &c. ; but riots and disturbances often happening, by
reason of the numbers assembled together, privileges were by
royal charter granted, for various causes, to particular places,
towns, and places of strength, where magistrates presided, to
keep the people in order.

A curious tract, entitled Bartholomew Faire, 1641, stating
that "Bartholomew Faire begins on the 24th day of August,
and is then of so vast an extent, that it is contained in no lesse
than four several parishes, namely, Christ Church, Great and
Little St. Bartholomewes, and St. Sepulchres. Hither resort
people of all sorts and conditions. Christ Church cloisters
are now hung full of pictures. It is remarkable and worth
your observation to beholde and heare the strange sights and
confused noise in the faire. Here, a knave in a fool's coate,
with a trumpet sounding, or on a drumme beating, invites you
to see his puppets ; there, a rogue like a wild woodman, or in

---

[1] Pitching-pence were paid in fairs and markets for every bag of corn,
&c. See Coles' Dictionary.

[2] Thus, in Du Cange's Glossary : "Festum, nundinæ quæ in festis patro-
norum vulgo fiunt." Bishop Kennett, in the Glossary to his Parochial
Antiquities, tells us, v. *Feriæ*, that from the solemn feasting at wakes and
fairs came the word fare, provision, good fare, to fare well. Hospinian
de Orig. Festor. Christian. fol. 161, speaking of wakes, observes : "Accessit
etiam mercatus, ut circa templa, necnon in templis et cœmeteriis forum
rerum venalium videas." Gibbon, in his Decline and Fall of the Roman
Empire, x. 377, ed. 1790, tells us that, on account of the frequent pilgrimages to Jerusalem between the seventh and eleventh centuries, an
annual fair was instituted on Mount Calvary. The ancient northern
nations held annual Ice-Fairs. See Olaus Magnus. We too have heard
of ice-fairs on the river Thames.

an antick shape like an incubus, desires your company to view
his motion : on the other side, hocus pocus, with three yards
of tape, or ribbin, in 's hand, shewing his art of legerdemaine,
to the admiration and astonishment of a company of cocko-
loaches. Amongst these, you shall see a gray goose-cap (as wise
as the rest), with a "what do ye lacke" in his mouth, stand in
his boothe, shaking a rattle, or scraping on a fiddle, with
which children are so taken, that they presentlie cry out for
these fopperies : and all these together make such a distracted
noise, that you would thinck Babell were not comparable to it.
Here there are also your gamesters in action : some turning
of a whimsey, others throwing for pewter, who can quickly
dissolve a round shilling into a three-halfpeney saucer. Long
Lane at this time looks very faire, and puts out her best
cloaths, with the wrong side outward, so turn'd for their better
turning off : and Cloth Faire is now in great request : well
fare the alehouses therein, yet better may a man fare (but at
a dearer rate) in the pig-market, alias pasty-nooke, or pye-
corner, where pigges are al houres of the day on the stalls
piping hot, and would cry (if they could speak), 'come eat
me.'   The fat greasy hostesse in these houses instructs Nick
Froth, her tapster, to aske a shilling more for a pig's head of
a woman big with child, in regard of her longing, then of
another ordinary cumer."   P. 5 : "Some of your cut-purses
are in fee with cheating costermongers, who have a trick, now
and then, to throw downe a basket of refuge peares, which
prove choake-peares to those that shall loose their hats or
cloaks in striving who shall gather fastest.

> Now farewell to the faire ; you who are wise,
> Preserve your purses, whilst you please your eyes."

[The following curious account of this affair is taken from
an unpublished letter by R. Southwell :—

DEAR NEDDY,   *Kingsweston, 26th August*, 1685.

I think it not now so proper to quote you verses out of
Persius, or to talk of Cæsar and Euclide, as to consider the
great theatre of Bartholomew-Fair, where, I doubt not, but
you often resort, and 'twere not amiss if you cou'd convert
that tumult into a profitable book. You wou'd certainly see

the garboil there to more advantage if Mr. Webster and you wou'd read, or cou'd see acted, the play of Ben Jonson, call'd Bartholomew Fair : for then afterwards going to the spot you wou'd note, if things and humours were the same to-day, as they were fifty years ago, and take pattern of the observations which a man of sence may raise out of matters that seem even ridiculous. Take then with you the impressions of that play, and in addition thereunto, I should think it not amiss if you then got up into some high window, in order to survey the whole pit at once. I fancy then you will say—*Totus mundus agit histrionem,* and you wou'd note into how many various shapes humane nature throws itself, in order to buy cheap, and sell dear, for all is but traffick and commerce, some to give, some to take, and all is by exchange, to make the entertainment compleat.

The main importance of this fair is not so much for merchandize, and the supplying what people really want ; but as a sort of Bacchanalia, to gratifie the multitude in their wandring and irregular thoughts.

Here you see the rope-dancers gett their living meerly by hazarding of their lives, and why men will pay money and take pleasure to see such dangers, is of seperate and philosophical consideration.

You have others who are acting fools, drunkards, and madmen, but for the same wages which they might get by honest labour, and live with credit besides.

Others, if born in any monstrous shape, or have children that are such, here they celebrate their misery, and by getting of money forget how odious they are made. When you see the toy shops, and the strange variety of things, much more impertinent then hobby-horses or gloves of gingerbread, you must know there are customers for all these matters, and it would be a pleasing sight cou'd you see painted a true figure of all these impertinent minds and their fantastick passions, who come trudging hither, only for such things. 'Tis out of this credulous croud that the ballad singers attrackt an assembly, who listen and admire, while their confederate pickpockets are diving and fishing for their prey.

'Tis from those of this number who are more refin'd, that the mountebank obtains audience and credit, and it were a good bargain if such customers had nothing for their money but words, but they are best content to pay for druggs, and medecines, which commonly doe them hurt.

There is one corner of this Elizium field devoted to the eating of pig, and the surfeits that attend it. The fruits of the season are everywhere scatter'd about, and those who eat imprudently do but hasten to the physitian or the churchyard.

There are various corners of lewdness and impurity, for whores, bawds, and drunkards. And how many robberies are beforehand committed on houses and high-ways to raise a stock against this licentious occasion! Here it commonly ends in quarrels and bloodshed, so that either the chirurgeon is sent for to plaister up the wounds, or the constable to heal the peace, and truth breaking out among malefactors, Mr. Justice has sufficient grounds for his mittimus, and Captain Richardson favours them with house-room, and Mr. John Ketch conveys them at length to their long and deserved home.

So here, by the by, you may also observe, that some grave men who think they have nothing to doe with the fair, do yet find imployment by it. There is the judge, the divine, the physitian, who all have work by the consequences of this unruly assembly.

I have formerly told you that I look'd upon human nature as a great volume, wherein every man, woman, and child, seem'd to be a distinct leaf, or page, or paragraph, that had something in it of diversity from all the rest, not but that many humours, natures, and inclinations, might fall under the same chapter, or be rang'd under the same common head. Yet still there is such distinction of one from the other, as a discerning mind will find out. And, indeed, it never was otherwise, even in the whole mass of things, since the creation; for two things, if they did not differ, would not be two, but the same.

I have told you also, how that in some leaves, and indeed whole chapters of this volume, there is many times so little sense or matter for imitation, that those leaves are to be turned over very fast, and yet the variety and very deformity of shapes they contain, do all help to illustrate nature, and put you into admiration to see other leaves and chapters how they are replenished, and seem to be the epitome of all that was good and valuable in the rest. But here, dear Neddy, will be the hardest task, where you find in the same chapter, and in the same leaf, such variety and intermixture of good and bad, that you cannot with wisdom reject the whole, or with security embrace it.

There are some men who are so compounded with vice and vertue, that tho' it were better far to leave all, then to take all, yet you who are design'd to converse in the world, and so of necessity to hold commerce with men of their composition, there is no other remedy next to the help which must come from Heaven, but to be able to top them, or at the least to equal them in their greatest virtues ; for when they see that they have not the ascendant, or a genius that is predominant, and so no title to list you under them as being qualified for a commission of your own. When, I say, they take notice how they are match'd in their better part (for they will never hope to prevail by the worst), and that you are not to be made a prey, they will then let you stand your ground, and be content to live with you upon the square. He that hath the subtilty of the serpent may retain the innocence of the dove, and there is no method so short for attaining that honest subtilty as to fall early upon the taking of notes, and daily to write down some observations or other upon persons and things. By this method, even before you step into the world, your quiver may be full of good long arrows, and, like the porcupine, may be able to shoot them out, if you are injuriously assaulted. For after all, there is no security for a man in this wicked world, but to have the sting about him as well as the honey, and you see how those who travel well arm'd, and are prepared for the robber, are seldom or never attackt.

I am ever,

Your most affectionate father,

ROBERT SOUTHWELL.]

In Whimzies, or a New Cast of Characters, 1631, p. 200, describing " a zealous brother," the author says : " No season through all the yeare accounts hee more subject to abhomination than Bartholomew Faire : their drums, hobbi-horses, rattles, babies, Jew-trumps, nay *pigs* and all, are wholly Judaicall." The roasted pigs at St. Bartholomew's Fair are also noticed in Poor Robin's Almanack for 1677. Poor Robin, for 1695, has this passage : " It also tells farmers what manner of wife they shall choose, not one *trickt up with ribbens and knots like a Bartholomew baby*, for such an one will prove a holyday wife, all play and no work :

> And he who with such kind of wife is sped,
> Better to have one made of ginger-bread."

In Nabbes' Comedy called Totenham Court, 1638, p. 47, is the following : " I have packed her up in't like *a Bartholomew babie in a boxe*. I warrant you for hurting her." Gayton, in his Art of Longevity, 1659, p. 3, says :

> " (As if there were not pigg enough)
> Old Bartholomew, with purgatory fire,
> Destroys the babe of many a doubtful sire."

Ibid. p. 79, speaking of plums, he says :

> " If eaten, as we use at Barthol'mew tide,
> Hand over head, that's without care or guide,
> There is a patient sure."

I have a tract entitled, "Reasons formerly published for the punctual limiting of Bartholomew Faire to those three days to which it is determined by the royal grant of it to the city of London : now reprinted with additions to prevent a design set on foot to procure an establishment of the said fair for fourteen dayes ; addressed to the Lord Mayor, Court of Aldermen, and Common Council"—8vo. Lond. 1711, pp. 32.

[Oh ! St. Bartlemy, St. Bartlemy, how has thy greatness fallen, thy strength wasted away ! Where now are the high priests of thy temples (*Luperci*, or rather, perhaps, the *Salii*, who "about the streets a mad procession led"), the vestals, the sacrificial fires, and holy noises ? Lucretius his description of other orgies once did for thine—alas ! that things have changed.

> " Amidst the pomp fierce drums and cymbals beat,
> And the hoarse horns with rattling notes do threat,
> The pipe with Phrygian airs disturbs their souls,
> Till, reason, overthrown, mad passion rules.
> By dancing quick they make a greater sound,
> And beat their kettles as they skip around."

The *cothurnus* and the *soccus* were donned in thy honour, though "rude were the actors and a cart the scene ;" fire was eaten, parchment beaten, dwarfs rang tiny bells from their miniature domiciles, and Northumberland giants *twelve feet* high, stood comfortably in caravans little more than seven. Men and women, to propitiate thee, suffered themselves gladly to be swung violently into the air for the hour together, or astride a wooden image, to be whirled wildly round till the brain swam and they knew not " where was the world ;" while others poured libations into their frames in utter fury of devotion to thy cause! " The victim ox," described by Virgil :

> " That was for altars pressed,
> Trimm'd with white ribbons and with garlands dress'd,"

no longer steams from out a thousand pans, enclosed in skins of shape oblong and round, fit holocaust for thee. The very savour has departed, and is now but a memory.

> " To seek for Rome, vain stranger, art thou come,
> And find'st no mark, within Rome's walls, of Rome."

How would that good man rejoice could he now look into thy empty halls, who several hundred years ago, wrote a tract for Richard Harper, at the Bible and Harp, Smithfield, entitled, " Bartholomew Faire, or Varieties of Fancies, where you may find a faire of wares ; and all to please your mind, with the several enormityes and misdemeanours, which are there seen and heard." Verily, he would say, the evil has come unto you. Malcolm writes of the fair in 1802 : "The visitor will here find all uproar. Shouts, drums, trumpets, organs, the roaring of beasts, assailing the ear ! While the blaze of torches and glare of candles confuse the sight, and present as well the horror of executions and burning of martyrs, as the humours of a fair." Later still, Hone, in one o his miscellanies, gives a detailed description of all he found there, including numerous shows, fun, vice, and phenomena. Its end was even then visible : it may now be said to be come. A menagerie of wild beasts ; a caravan containing two " real live boa-constrictor serpents, a learned pig, and an ourangoutang what understands nearly every word that's spoken ;" two travelling auctioneers selling knives, scissors, brushes, and such like, at the rate of about three for sixpence ; a score of booths for gingerbread nuts, a mechanical exhibition and a conjurer in Hosier Lane, form at this present writing the " sum tottle of the whole."

Richardson's booth—-birthplace of heroes—he himself the

II.   30

real descendant of *Thespis*, "who taught men how to speak and how to act," no longer takes its place or money from the people. The last time we entered the age-honoured tent, redolent of size, saw-dust, and soft soap, a storm of rain led to percolations from the "flapping canvass," and a cry arose of "umbrellas down in front," put up to defend their fortunate owners. Loud roared the unfortunate actors to be heard above the hubbub; and all was going wrong, when a "cool hand," inquiring quietly of the chief villain (who was at the moment straining every nerve, distending every vein, with shouting) whether he could not speak a *little* louder, raised a unanimous laugh, and turned the tragedy into a farce. The play was got through in ten minutes, and then the manager announced that the performances "would be repeated again (aye! and again) in two minutes and a half." Truly, as the owner of the boa-constrictor serpents before mentioned, said every time his caravan disgorged its occupants, "I can confidently appeal to every hindiwidual possessing *humane* intellects, to say whether this was not a sight at once hinteresting and amusing, *destructive* and delightful." But let that pass; and return for one instant to the fair as it *is*. The keepers of neighbouring hostels willing, of course, to preserve so interesting a remnant of antiquity, endeavour by balls and harmonic meetings to revive defunct joviality. Strive however, never so hardly, Bartholomew fair cannot be revived; recreation is now sought in other ways. St. Bartlemy, to make the fair personal, has had his day, and must speedily say farewell! "I have touched the highest point of all my greatness, and from that full meridian of my glory I haste now to my setting. I shall fall like a bright exhalation in the evening, and no man see me more."

The following allusion to the *roast pig* is from Poor Robin's Almanack for 1740 :

> "If women that with child are big,
> Now chance to long for *roasted pig*,
> To *Smithfield* to *Bartholomew fair*
> Let them without delay repair :
> And there they may be furnished,
> With quarters, pettitoes, or head ;
> Drest by fine, lovely, cleanly cooks,
> You'd take for th' pigs dams by their looks ;
> Or think they are of the blackguard,
> Their clothes with grease they do so lard."]

Gay, in his fable of the two monkeys, thus describes Southwark fair :

> " The tumbler whirles the flip-flap round,
> With somersets he shakes the ground;
> The cord beneath the dancer springs;
> Aloft in air the vaulter swings,
> Distorted now, now prone depends,
> Now through his twisted arms ascends;
> The crowd in wonder and delight,
> With clapping hands applaud the sight."

I have before me a printed resolution of the parliament,
dated Thursday the 17th of July, 1651: " That *the fair* usually
held and kept yearly *at St. James's,* within the liberty of the
city of Westminster, on or about the 25th day of July, be
forborn this year; and that no fair be kept or held there by
any person or persons whatsoever, until the parliament shall
take further order. HEN. SCOBELL, Cleric. Parliamenti."

A scarce tract is also in my possession entitled, Reasons for
suppressing the yearly Fair in Brook-field, Westminster, commonly called May-Fair, recommended to the consideration of
all persons of Honour and Virtue, 8vo. Lond. 1709, 43 pages.
P. 4 : " Multitudes of the booths erected in this fair are not
for trade and merchandice, but for musick, showes, drinking,
gaming, raffling, lotteries, stage-plays, and drolls." P. 8: "It
is a very unhappy circumstance of this fair that it begins with
the prime beauty of the year; in which many innocent persons incline to walk into the fields and out-parts of the city
to divert themselves, as they very lawfully may." This fair
was granted by King James II. in the fourth year of his reign,
to commence on the 1st of May, and continue fifteen days
after it, yearly, for ever.

Shaw, in his History of Staffordshire, ii. part 1, p. 165,
speaking of Wolverhampton and the *processioners* there, says :
" Another custom (now likewise discontinued) was the annual
procession, on the 9th of July (the eve of the *great fair*), of
men in antique armour, preceded by musicians playing the
fair-tune, and followed by the steward of the Deanry manor,
the peace-officers, and many of the principal inhabitants.
Tradition says the ceremony originated at the time when
Wolverhampton was a great emporium of wool, and resorted
to by merchants of the staple from all parts of England.
The necessity of an armed force to keep peace and order

during the fair (which is said to have lasted fourteen days, but the charter says only eight) is not improbable. This custom of *walking the fair* (as it was called) with the armed procession, &c., was first omitted about the year 1789."

Courts were granted at fairs, to take notice of all manner of causes and disorders committed upon the place, called pie-powder, because justice was done to any injured person before the dust of the fair was off his feet.[1]

It is customary at all fairs to present *fairings*, or gifts bought at fairs. This custom prevailed in the days of Chaucer, as appears by the subsequent passage in the Wife of Bathe's prologue, where she boasts of having managed her several husbands so well :

> " I governed hem so well after my lawe
> That eche of hem full blissful was, and fawe (i. e. *glad*) :
> *To bringen me gay thinges fro the feyre*
> They were ful glade, &c.[2]

In regard to *sports at fairs*, Grose mentions one called " *Mumble a sparrow*—a cruel sport practised at wakes and fairs in the following manner : a cock-sparrow, whose wings are clipped, is put into the crown of a hat; a man, having his arms tied behind him, attempts to bite off the sparrow's head, but is generally obliged to desist, by the many pecks and pinches he receives from the enraged bird."

---

[1] Or rather, perhaps, the court of pie-powder means the court of pedlers. See the subsequent evidences: " Gif ane stranger merchand travelland throw the realme, havand na land, nor residence, nor dwelling within the schirefdome, bot vaigand fra ane place to ane other, quha therefore is called pied puldreux or dustifute," &c. Regiam Majestatem, 4to. Edinb. 1774, p. 261. So, chap. cxl. p. 265, ibid.: "Anend ane fairand-man or dustifute." So again, in the table, p. 432, ibid. : " Dustie-fute, ane pedder, or cremar, quha hes na certaine dwelling-place, quhere he may dicht the dust from his feet," &c. Barrington, on the Ancient Statutes, p. 423, observes that, " In the Burrow Laws of Scotland an alien merchant is called pied-puldreaux, and likewise ane farand-man, or a man who frequents fairs." The court of pie-powder is, therefore, to determine disputes between those who resort to fairs and these kind of pedlers who generally attend them. Pied-pulderaux, in old French, signifies a pedler, who gets his livelihood by vending his goods where he can, without any certain or fixed residence.

[2] " Ad sua quisque redit; festivis Daphneu Amyntas
Exonerat zeniis, dandoque astringit amores."
See Rusticæ Nundinæ, Woodward's Poems, 1730, p. 232.

The same author tells us that, " *To whip the cock* is a piece of sport practised at wakes, horse-races, and fairs, in Leicestershire : a cock being tied or fastened into a hat or basket, half a dozen carters, blindfolded, and armed with their cart-whips, are placed round it, who, after being turned thrice about, begin to whip the cock, which if any one strikes so as to make it cry out, it becomes his property ; the joke is, that, instead of whipping the cock, they flog each other heartily."

Drake tells us, in his Eboracum, p. 218, that " A fair is always kept in Mickle Gate (York), on St. Luke's day, for all sorts of small wares. It is commonly called *Dish fair*, from the great quantity of wooden dishes, ladles, &c., brought to it. There is an old custom used at this fair of bearing a wooden ladle in a sling on two stangs about it, carried by four sturdy labourers, and each labourer was formerly supported by another. This, without doubt, is a ridicule on the meanness of the wares brought to this fair, small benefit accruing to the labourers at it. Held by charter, Jan. 25, an. Reg. Regis Hen. VII. 17."

There is an annual fair held in the Broad Gate at Lincoln on the 14th of September, called *Fools fair*, for the sale of cattle, so called on that authority, as follows : " King William and his Queen, having visited Lincoln while on their tour through the kingdom, made the citizens an offer to serve them in any manner they liked best. They asked for a fair, though it was harvest, when few people can attend it, and though the town had no trade nor any manufacture. The king smiled, and granted their request ; observing that it was a humble one indeed."

In the Statistical Account of Scotland, vi. 622, parish of Dundonald, Ayrshire, we read : " An ancient practice still continues in this parish and neighbourhood, of kindling a large fire, or tawnle as it is usually termed, of wood, upon some eminence, and making merry around it, upon the eve of the Wednesday of Marymass fair in Irvine (which begins on the third Monday of August, and continues the whole week). As most fair-days in this country were formerly popish holy-days, and their eves were usually spent in religious ceremonie s and in diversions, it has been supposed that tawnles were first lighted up by our Catholic fathers, though some derive their origin from the Druidical times." Ibid. xiii. 77, parish of

Kenethmont, co. Aberdeen : "Fair at Christ's Kirk in the month of May. This fair was kept on the green, and in the night ; hence it was by the people called Sleepy-market. About thirty-five or thirty-six years ago, the proprietor changed it from night to day ; but so strong was the prepossession of the people in favour of the old custom, that, rather than comply with the alteration, they chose to neglect it altogether."

In the same work, xviii. 612, parish of Marykirk, co. Kincardine, we read : "On the outside of the church, strongly fixed to the wall, are the *joggs*. These were made use of, when the weekly market and annual fair stood, to confine and punish those who had broken the peace, or used too much freedom with the property of others. The stocks were used for the feet, and the joggs for the neck of the offender, in which he was confined, at least during the time of the fair." Though the worthy minister who drew up this account has omitted the etymology of joggs, I should think it a very obvious one—from *jugum*, a yoke.

Ray has preserved two old English proverbs that relate to fairs : "Men speak of the fair as things went with them there ;" as also, "To come a day after the fair." The first seems intended to rhyme.

PANTOMIME. PAOL CINELLA— PUNCHINELLO.

[IN the times of the inimitable and lamented Grimaldi, "Joey Grimaldi," how eagerly did the pantomime lovers look forward every Christmas to the new pantomime of the year. In our boyhood we were lost in wonder at the magical power of *Harlequin*, the beauty of *Columbine*, the simplicity and folly of the *Clown* (whom we were frequently inclined to assist, by exposing the tricks which we saw were about to be practised on him), and the imbecility and peevishness of the *Pantaloon*. Everything was thought genuine ; even the laughter was tempered with fear for the ultimate safety of *Harlequin* and *Columbine*. Peace to thee, Grimaldi ! Thousands, and tens of thousands, in their days of childhood and youth, hast thou made happy, for many a joyous hour, by thy drollery. Thousands, and tens of thousands, of their care-worn elders hast thou relieved from many a weary hour, and charmed by thine unrivalled humour.

The Genius of Pantomime seems to have taken his departure with him, or at least to have nodded very considerably since ; whether to revive or not, is a problem to be worked out. The theory of our modern Pantomime does not seem well under-stood. D'Israeli has collected some interesting materials on the various characters. He considers the Italian *harlequin* to have represented the ancient Mime, but he seems to have been the *clown*, or butt of the performance, until Goldoni took a fancy to him, and turned him into a wit. A great deal of amusing and valuable information on the subject may also be found in the *History of Punch and Judy*, with George Cruikshank's capital illustrations, 1828. *Harlequin*, on the French stage, became a wit and *improvisatore*, somewhat per-haps in the style of our Tarlton and Kempe. Tiberio Fiurilli, who invented the character of *Scaramouch*, was the companion of the boyhood of Louis XIV., and Dominic, the celebrated *harlequin*, was also occasionally admitted to the table of that monarch. The story is well known of Louis directing some partridges that were on a silver dish, to be given to him. "Give Dominic that dish." "And the partridges, too ?" said the wily actor. Dr. Clarke, in his Travels, viii. 104-7, gives a mythological origin to *harlequin*, considering him to have descended, with his sword and cap, from Mercury, the *clown* from Momus, the *pantaloon* from Charon, and *columbine* from Psyche ; and their adventures therefore alegorical. It may not be generally known that when *harlequin* puts on his cap he is supposed to be invisible ; the various wishing and invi-sible caps of romance would hence appear to have some connexion with him. His sword, however, must have some relation to the dagger or lath of the *vice* in the old moralities, and perhaps to the staff or bauble of our *fools*, as his variegated dress might also have, though in richer style, to their parti-coloured attire. These *fools*, however, had oc-casionally rich apparel, as for instance, in the Christmas revels at court, 5th Edward VI., the principal one had "a long fooles coat of yellow cloth of gold, all over figured with velvet, white, red, and green, seven yards and a half, at 40s., garded with plain yellow cloth of gold, at 33s. 4d. ; a hood and a pair of

buskins of the same, figured gold, and a girdle of yellow
sarsnet." The clown's dress evidently has great similarity to
the fools, and according to Dr. Clarke, the painted face and
wide mouth were taken from the ancient masks. It may be
added that the mimes wore the *paniculus centumculus*, or coat
of different coloured pieces. In a note to Rabelais (ed. 1823,
iii. 493, note), the writer also derives *harlequin* from Mercury,
adducing his patchwork dress in proof, and then discourses
on the origin of his name; amongst other things stating it
to be a diminutive from *harle* or *herle*, a river-bird, and gives
examples of it as far back as 1521. Though *Harlequin* was
not introduced on our stage till about the beginning of the
last century, yet his fame was known long before. *Bianca,*
in Marston's Malcontent, about 1604, says, "The French
harlequin will instruct you." Heywood, in his Apology for
Actors, 1612, introduces him with other characters, thus:
"To omit all the doctors, zawnyes, pantaloons, harlakeenes,
in which the French, but especially the Italians, have beene
excellent." Dryden refers to him also: "But I speak no
Italian; only a few broken scraps, which I picked from
scaramouch and *harlequin* at Paris." Limberham, act i. sc. 1.

About the time of Queen Anne, *harlequin* was probably introduced to the English stage, and he appears, together with
punchinello, who also was naturalized about the same time, in
some of the exhibition bills of that date, of which examples
may be found in MS. Harl. 5931. Among these, for example,
at Mat Heatly's booth, at Bartholomew fair was "presented a
little opera, called the Old *Creation of the World*, newly
reviv'd; with the addition of the glorious *battle* obtained over
the *French* and *Spaniards*, by his Grace the Duke of *Marl-
borough* . . . completed with the merry humours of Sir
John Spendall and *Punchinello*." James Miles (from Sadler's
Wells, at Islington), at the Gun Music booth, in Bartholomew
fair, among other dances advertises, "a New Entertainment
between a *Scaramouch*, a *Harlequin*, and a *Punchinello*, in imitation of Bilking a Reckoning; and a new dance by four
Scaramouches after the Italian manner," &c. One does not
quite understand the "imitation of bilking a reckoning," but
some pretty strong *imitations* may be found in the present
day. The subject, however, must have been somewhat of a
favorite, as the first pantomime performed by grotesque cha-

racters in this country, is said to have been at Drury Lane
Theatre, in 1702, composed by Mr. Weaver, and called the
Tavern Bilkers. *Harlequin*, however, was not admitted without some opposition by the regulars ; just as of late years we
have objected to dramatic elephants, dogs, and horses. Listen,
as a specimen, to a skit at him by Southerne :

> " We hoped that art and genius had secur'd you,
> But soon facetious *Harlequin* allur'd you ;
> The muses blush'd to see their friends exalting
> Those elegant delights of jigg and vaulting."
>   Prologue to the Spartan Dame, about 1704.

In 1717, the celebrated Rich, who acted under the name
of Lun, brought out his first harlequinade, called Harlequin
Executed, at the theatre of Lincoln's Inn Fields. He was
distinguished for his skill as a harlequin, and his talent for
these compositions, and established them firmly in the public
favour. He flourished till 1761, all his productions having
succeeded.

With respect to *Punchinello* or *Punch*, he is mentioned in
the Tatler and Spectator; but we must refer the Punchophi-
lists to his History, before mentioned, adding, however, an
origin of his name, with which the writer of that work and
other writers on the subject were not acquainted. Silvio
Fiorillo, a comedian, is stated to have invented the character
of *Pulcinella* about the year 1600. An Italian friend, of
considerable literary acquirements, gives the following version,
which seems to supersede the various fancied derivations of
the name. There was an old custom in Italy of keeping
buffoons as waiters at inns, to attract and amuse travellers.
Paolo, or *Paol Cinella*, was a buffoon or waiter of this description at an inn at Acerra, when Silvio Fiorillo, called *Captain
Matamoros*, saw him, and was so pleased with his humour,
that he induced him to join his troop of travelling comedians,
and hence came the name to the character of *Paol Cinella* or
Pulcinella. Silvio Fiorillo, he states, was called Captain,
from being chief conductor of the troop ; and *Matamoros*,
from his acting the *primo amoroso*, or, as he was called in the
Neapolitan dialect, the *mat amoros* (the madly in love), that
being the first character in the comedies then in vogue.--
JAN. T. in the Literary Gazette.]

THE MEANING OF THE OLD SAW,

**"FIVE SCORE OF MEN, MONEY, AND PINS,
SIX SCORE OF ALL OTHER THINGS.**

WE learn from Hickes's Thesaurus that the Norwegians and Islandic people used a method of numbering peculiar to themselves, by the addition of the words Tolfrædr, Tolfræd, or Tolfræt (whence our word twelve), which made ten signify twelve; a hundred, a hundred and twenty; a thousand, a thousand two hundred; &c. The reason of this was, that the nations above named had two decads or tens: a lesser, which they used in common with other nations, consisting of ten units; and a greater, containing twelve (tolf) units. Hence, by the addition of the word Tolfrædr, or Tolfræd, the hundred contained not ten times ten, but ten times twelve, that is a hundred and twenty.

The Doctor observes that this Tolfrædic mode of computation by the greater decads, or tens, which contain twelve units, is still retained amongst us in reckoning certain things by the number twelve, which the Swedes call dusin, the French douzain, and we dozen. And I am informed, he adds, by merchants, &c., that in the number, weight, and measure of many things, the hundred among us still consists of that greater tolfrædic hundred which is composed of ten times twelve.[1] Hence then, without doubt, is derived to us the

---

[1] " Notetur etiam Norvegis et Islandis peculiarem numerandi rationem in usu esse per additionem vocum *Tolfrædr, Tolfræd,* vel *Tolfræt,* quæ decem significare faciunt *duodecim;* centum, *centum et viginti;* mille, *mille et* cc., &c. Causa istius computationis hæc est, quod apud istas gentes duplex est *decas,* nempe minor cæteris nationibus communis, *decem* continens *unitates:* et major continens xii., i. e. *tolf,* unitates. Inde addita voce *Tolfrædr,* vel *Tolfræd,* centuria non decies decem, sed decies duodecim, i. e. cxx. continet, et chilias non decies centum, sed decies cxx. i. e. mille et cc. continet." Hæc " autem computandi ratio per majores decades, quæ duodecim unitates continent, apud nos etiamnum usurpatur in computandis certis rebus per duodenum numerum, quem *dozen,* Suecicè *dusin,* Gallicè *douzain,* vocamus; quinimo in numeris, ponderibus, et mensuris multarum rerum, ut ex mercatoribus, et vehiculariis accepi, centuria apud nos etiamnum semper præsumitur significare majorem, sive Tolfrædicam illam centuriam, quæ ex decies xii. conflatur, scilicet cxx. Sic **Arngrim Jonas in Crymogæa, sive rerum Island. lib. 1, cap. viii.,** *hundrad*

present mode of reckoning many things by six score to the hundred.

By the statute 25 Hen. VIII. c. 13, no person shall have above two thousand sheep on his lands; and the twelfth section (after reciting that the hundred in every county be not alike, some reckoning by the great hundred, or six score, and others by five score) declares that the number two thousand shall be accounted ten hundred for every thousand, after the number of the great hundred, and not after the less hundred, so that every thousand shall contain twelve hundred after the less number of the hundred.

Dr. Percy observes, upon the Northumberland Household Book: " It will be necessary to premise here, that the ancient modes of computation are retained in this book, according to which it is only in money that the hundred consists of five score; in all other articles the enumerations are made by the old Teutonic hundred of six score, or a hundred and twenty.[1]

The enumeration of six score to the hundred occurs twice in the Domesday Survey, i. 336, in the account of Lincoln: being termed in both entries the *English number.* " Hic numerus Anglice computatur 1 centum pro c^{tum} xx."

It was anciently the practice to reckon up sums with counters. To this Shakespeare alludes in Othello, act i. sc. 1: ' This counter-caster.' And again in Cymbeline, act v. : ' It sums up thousands in a trice : you have no true debtor and creditor but it : of what's past, is, and to come, the discharge. Your neck, sir, is pen, book, and counters.' Again, in Acolastus, a comedy, 1540 : ' I wyl cast my counters, or with counters make all my reckenynges.'

centum sonat, sed quadam consuetudine plus continet nempe 120. Inde etiamnum apud nos vetus istud de centenario numero : *Five score of men, money, and pins : six score of all other things.*" Gram. Isl. p. 43.

[1] In Sinclair's Statistical Account of Scotland, i. 187, the minister of Parton, under the head of " Population," tells us: " A few years ago a man died above ninety, who about eight months before his death, got a complete set of new teeth, which he employed till near his last breath to excellent purpose. He was four times married, had children by all his wives, and, at the baptism of his last child, which happened not a year before his death, with an air of complacency expressed his thankfulness to his Maker for having ' at last sent him the *cled score*,' i. e. twenty-one "

FAIRY MYTHOLOGY.

" Of airy elves, by moonlight shadows seen,
The silver token and the circled green."
POPE'S Rape of the Lock, l. 31.

BOURNE supposes the fairy superstition to have been conveyed down to us by tradition from the Lamiæ, who were
esteemed so mischievous as to take away young children and
slay them; these, says he, together with the fauns, the gods
of the woods, seem to have formed the notion of fairies.

"Fairies and elves," says Tollet, "are frequently, in the
poets, mentioned together, without any distinction of character
that I can recollect. Keysler says that *alp* and *alf*, which is *elf*
with the Swedes and English, equally signified a mountain or
a demon of the mountains. This seems to have been its original
meaning; but Somner's Dictionary mentions elves or fairies
of the mountains, of the woods, of the sea and fountains, without any distinction between elves and fairies." Others deduce
them from the lares and larvæ of the Romans.[1]

Dr. Percy tells us that, on the assurance of a learned friend
in Wales, the existence of fairies is alluded to by the most
ancient British bards, among whom their commonest name
was that of the spirits of the mountains. It is conjectured by
some that these little aerial people have been imported into
Europe by the crusaders from the East, as in some respects
they resemble the oriental Genii. Indeed the Arabs and
Persians, whose religion and history abound with relations

[1] In the British Apollo, 1708, vol. i. No. 1, supernumerary for April,
we are told, " The opinion of fairies has been asserted by Pliny and several
historians, and Aristotle himself gave some countenance to it, whose words
are these : Εστι δε ὁ τοπος, &c., i. e. Hic locus est quem incolunt pygmei,
non est fabula, sed pusillum genus ut aiunt : wherein Aristotle plays the
sophist. For though by ' non est fabula' he seems at first to confirm it,
yet, coming in at last with his ' ut aiunt,' he shakes the belief he had
before put upon it. Our society, therefore, are of opinion that Homer was
the first author of this conceit, who often used similes, as well to delight
the ear as to illustrate his matter; and in his third Iliad compares the
Trojans to cranes, when they descend against fairies. So that that which
was only a pleasant fiction in the fountain became a solemn story in the
stream, and current still among us." In the same work, vol. i. No. 25,
fairy-rings are ascribed to lightning.

concerning them, have assigned them a peculiar country to inhabit, and called it Fairy Land.[1] "It will afford entertainment," says Percy, "to a contemplative mind, to trace these whimsical opinions up to their origin. Whoever considers how early, how extensively, and how uniformly they have prevailed in these nations, will not readily assent to the hypothesis of those who fetch them from the East so late as the time of the Croisades. Whereas it is well known that our Saxon ancestors, long before they left their German forests, believed the existence of a kind of diminutive demons, or middle species between men and spirits, whom they called Duergar, or dwarfs, and to whom they attributed many wonderful performances, far exceeding human art. Vide Hervarer Olai Verelii, 1675 ; Hickesii Thesaurus, &c." [2]

It was an article in the popular creed concerning fairies, that they were a kind of intermediate beings, partaking of the nature both of men and spirits : that they had material bodies, and yet the power of making them invisible, and of passing them through any sort of enclosures. They were thought to be remarkably small in stature, with fair complexions, from which last circumstance they have derived their English name.[3] The habits of both sexes of fairies are represented to have been generally green.[4]

I made strict inquiries after fairies in the uncultivated wilds of Northumberland, but even there I could only meet with a

[1] [It seems extraordinary that an opinion so unreasonable should have been suffered to remain without correction. The so-called fairies of the middle ages, indeed, bore some resemblance to the oriental creations, but no comparison whatever is afforded between them and the beings of our vernacular mythology.]

[2] ["Ritson refers to Homer, by way of giving the fairies a respectable antiquity, but the original will bear no interpretation of the kind; and although Chapman and Pope have represented them at Sipylus, these must give place to the goddess-nymphs dancing their mazy rings on the beds of the Achelous. We can dispense with some other learning of the same kind, and be well contented with a less remote antiquity." Halliwell's Illustrations of Fairy Mythology, 1845.]

[3] The account given of them by Moresin (Papatus, p. 139) favours this etymology. "Papatus," says he, "credit *albatas mulieres* et id genus *larvas*," &c.

[4] "My grandmother," says the author of Round about our Coal Fire, p. 42, "has often told me of fairies dancing upon our green, and that they were *little creatures clothed in green.*"

man who said that he had seen *one that had seen fairies.*
Truth is hard to come at in most cases. None, I believe, ever
came nearer to it than I have done.

The author of 'Round about our Coal Fire' has these further
particulars of the popular notions concerning them : " The
moment any one saw them and took notice of them, they were
struck blind of an eye. They lived under ground, and generally came out of a molehill."

Concerning fairies, King James, in his Dæmonology, p. 132,
has the following passages : " That there was a king and queene
of Phairie, that they had a jolly court and traine—they had a
teynd and duetie, as it were of all goods—they naturally rode
and went, eate and dranke, and did all other actions like
natural men and women. Witches have been transported with
the pharie to a hill, which opening, they went in and there
saw a fairie queen, who being now lighter gave them a stone
that had sundrie vertues."

[Gervase, of Tilbury, mentions two kinds of goblins in
England, called *Portuni* and *Grant*. The *portuni* were of the
true fairy size, *statura pusilli, dimidium pollicis non habentes:*
but then, indeed, they were *senili vultu, facie corrugata.*
Some of their pranks are described as being somewhat similar
to those of Shakespeare's Puck. Gervase especially tells us :
" If anything should be to be carried on in the house, or any
kind of laborious work to be done, they join themselves to the
work, and expedite it with more than human facility. It is
natural to these that they may be obsequious, and may not be
hurtful. But one little mode, as it were, they have of hurting;
for when, among the ambiguous shades of night, the English
occasionally ride alone, the portune sometimes gets up behind
him unseen ; and when he has accompanied him, going on a
very long time, at length, the bridle being seized, he leads him
up to the hand in the mud, in which, while infixed, he wallows,
the portune, departing, sets up a laugh ; and so, in this way,
derides human simplicity." This at once reminds us of some
of the pranks of Robin Goodfellow.]

There is reprinted in Morgan's Phœnix Britannicus, p. 545,
a curious tract on the subject of fairies, entitled "An Account
of Anne Jefferies, now living in the county of Cornwall, who
was fed for six months by a *small sort of airy people called
fairies :* and of the strange and wonderful cures she performed

with salves and medicines she received from them, for which she never took one penny of her patients : in a letter from Moses Pitt to the right reverend father in God Dr. Edward Fowler, Lord Bishop of Gloucester : London, printed for Richard Cumberland, 1696." Morgan tells us that the copy from which he reprinted it, had, at the bottom of its title-page, this N.B. in manuscript : "Recommended by the Right Rev. to his friend Mrs. Eliz. Rye." He means, no doubt, the above Bishop of Gloucester, who, it should seem, had tacked to his creed this article of belief in fairies. This tract states that "Anne Jefferies (for that was her maiden name) was born in the parish of St. Teath, in the county of Cornwall, in December 1626, and is still living, 1696, aged 70. She is married to one William Warren, formerly hind to the late eminent physician Dr. Richard Lower, deceased, and now to Sir Andrew Slanning, of Devon, Bart.—That A.D. 1645, as she was one day sitting knitting in an arbour in the garden, there came over the hedge, of a sudden, *six persons of a small stature, all clothed in green*, which frighted her so much as to throw her into a great sickness. They continued their appearance to her, never less than *two at a time*, nor *never more than eight*, always *in even numbers*, 2, 4, 6, 8. She forsook eating our victuals," continues the narrator, in whose family she lived as a servant, "and was fed by these fairies from the harvest-time to the next Christmas day ; upon which day she came to our table and said, because it was that day she would eat some roast beef with us, which she did, I myself being then at table. One day she gave me a piece of her (fairy) bread, which I did eat, and think it was the most delicious bread that ever I did eat, either before or since. One day," the credulous narrator goes on, "these fairies gave my sister Mary a silver cup, which held about a quart, bidding her give it my mother, but my mother would not accept it. I presume this was the time my sister owns she *saw* the fairies. I confess to your lordship *I never did see them*. I have seen Anne in the orchard dancing among the trees ; and she told me she was then dancing with the fairies." It is with great diffidence that I venture to consider Anne's case *en médecin*. It appears that Anne was afterwards thrown into jail as an impostor, nor does even the friendly narrator of her singular story, Moses Pitt, give us any plausible account why the fairies, like false earthly friends, forsook her in this time of her distress.

Their haunts were thought to have been groves, mountains, the southern sides of hills, and verdant meadows, where their diversion was dancing hand in hand in a circle, as alluded to by Shakespeare in his Midsummer Night's Dream. The traces of their tiny feet are supposed to remain visible on the grass long afterwards, and are called fairy-rings or circles.

"Ringlets of grass," Dr. Grey observes, "are very common in meadows, which are higher, sowrer, and of a deeper green than the grass that grows round them ; and by the common people are usually called Fairy Circles." Notes on Shakespeare, i. 35.[1] Again, in Shakespeare's Tempest, act v. sc. 1 :

> " Ye elves——you demy puppets, that
> By moonshine *do the green-sour ringlets make,*
> Whereof the ewe not bites."

So again: "To dew her orbs upon the green." The orbs here mentioned, Dr. Johnson observes, are circles supposed to be made by fairies on the ground, whose verdure proceeds from the fairies' care to water them. Thus Drayton :

> " They in their courses make that *round,*
> In meadows and in marshes found,
> Of them so call'd the fairy ground."

They are again alluded to in Randolph's Amyntas, act iii. sc. 4 :

> " They do request you now
> To give them leave to dance a fairy ring."

Browne, in his Britannia's Pastorals, p. 41, describes

> ——" a pleasant mead,
> Where fairies often did their measures tread,
> Which in the meadows made such circles green
> As if with garlands it had crowned been.
> Within one of these rounds was to be seen
> A hillock rise, where oft the fairy-queen
> At twilight sat."

---

[1] Thus in Olaus Magnus de Gentibus Septentrionalibus : " Similes illis spectris, quæ in multis locis, præsertim nocturno tempore, suum saltatorium orbem cum omnium musarum consentu versare solent." It appears from the same author, that these dancers always parched up the grass, and therefore it is properly made the office of Puck to refresh it. Ibid. p. 410 : " Vero saltum adeo profundè in terram impresserant, ut locus insigni ardore orbiculariter peresus. non parit arenti redivivum cesr'te gramen."

" They had fine musick always among themselves," says the author of Round about our Coal Fire, p. 41, "and danced in a moonshiny night, around, or in a ring, as one may see at this day upon every common in England where mushroomes grow." The author of Mons Catherinæ has not forgotten to notice these ringlets in his poem, p. 9 :

> " Sive illic Lemurum populus sub nocte choreas
> Plauserit exiguas, viridesque attriverit herbas."

[The following lively fairy song is taken from Lilly's Maid's Metamorphosis, 4to. Lond. 1600 :

> " Round about, round about, in a fine ring-a :
> Thus we dance, thus we dance, and thus we sing-a :
> Trip and go, to and fro, over this green-a,
> All about, in and out, for our brave queen-a.
>
> Round about, round about, in a fine ring-a :
> Thus we dance, thus we dance, and thus we sing-a
> Trip and go, to and fro, over this green-a,
> All about, in and out, for our brave queen-a.
>
> We've danc'd round about in a fine ring-a :
> We have danc'd lustily, and thus we sing-a,
> All about, in and out, over this green-a,
> To and fro, trip and go, to our brave queen-a."]

The last poetical mention of them which we shall quote, is from Smith's Six Pastorals, 4to. 1770, p. 24 :

> " Some say the screech-owl, at each midnight hour,
> Awakes the fairies in yon ancient tow'r.
> Their nightly-dancing ring I always dread,
> Nor let my sheep within that circle tread ;
> Where round and round all night, in moonlight fair,
> They dance to some strange music in the air."

The Athenian Oracle, i. 397, mentions a popular belief that, " if a house be built upon the ground where fairy rings are, whoever shall inhabit therein does wonderfully prosper."

Waldron, in his Description of the Isle of Man (Works, fol. p. 138), tells us : " As to *circles in the grass*, and *the impression of small feet among the snow*, I cannot deny but I have seen them frequently, and once I thought I heard a whistle, as though in my ear, when nobody that could make it was near me."

Aubrey, in his MS. collections in the Ashmolean Museum, says : " As to these circles, I presume they are generated from the breathing out of a fertile subterraneous vapour, which comes from a kind of conical concave, and endeavours to get out at a narrow passage at the top, which forces it to make another cone inversely situated to the other, the top of which is the green circle." See further very curious particulars from Aubrey in Halliwell's Illustrations of Fairy Mythology, p. 236.

Some ascribe the phenomenon of the circle or ring, supposed by the vulgar to be traced by the fairies in their dances, to the effects of lightning, as being frequently produced after storms of that kind, and by the colour and brittleness of the grass-roots when first observed. In support of this hypothesis the reader may consult Priestley's Present State of Electricity. See also the Philosophical Transactions, cxvii. 391, where it is stated that Mr. Waller, walking abroad after a storm of thunder and lightning, observed a round circle of about four or five yards diameter, whose rim was about a foot broad, newly burnt bare, as appeared from the colour and brittleness of the grass-roots. See Gent. Mag. 1790, lx. 1106. Others have thought these appearances occasioned by moles, working for themselves a run underground. This I believe they never do in a circular manner. Gent. Mag. ibid. p. 1072. Mr. Pennant, however, in his British Zoology, 1776, i. 131, says : " It is supposed that the verdant circles so often seen in grass-grounds, called by the country people fairy-rings, are owing to the operation of these animals, who at certain seasons perform their burrowings by circumgyrations, which, loosing the soil, gives the surface a greater fertility and rankness of grass than the other parts within or without the ring." In short, fancy has sported herself in endeavouring to account for these circular rings ; and there are not wanting such as have, I had almost said, dreamt them to have been trenches dug up by the ancient inhabitants of Britain, and used either in celebrating some of their sports, or in paying divine honours to some of their imaginary deities. Gent. Mag. ut supra, Supplem. p. 1180. The same periodical contains numerous letters and suggestions on this subject, for the most part exceedingly trifling and unreasonable.

In the Gent. Mag. for Jan. 1791, lxi. 36, a writer on the subject of fairy rings refers to the Transactions of the Royal Society of Edinburgh, ii. 3, to a paper by Dr. Hutton, which places these curious appearances in a new point of view, and is there said to overturn the theories formerly offered to explain their production. By this it appears that they are not the tracks of animals. In that I perfectly agree with the author, but much doubt if everything else he has stated concerning them is not in favour of the hypothesis of their owing their primary origin to the effects of lightning. The most clear and satisfactory remarks on the origin of fairy-rings are probably those of Dr. Wollaston, Sec. R. S., printed in the second part of the Philosophical Transactions for 1807; made during a few years' residence in the country. The cause of their appearance he ascribes to the growth of certain species of agaric, which so entirely absorb all nutriment from the soil beneath that the herbage is for awhile destroyed.

With all the passions and wants of human beings, fairies are represented as great lovers and patrons of cleanliness and propriety, for the observance of which they were said frequently to reward good servants by dropping money into their shoes in the night; and, on the other hand, they were reported to punish most severely the sluts and slovenly, by pinching them black and blue. So in Ben Jonson's ballad of Robin Goodfellow, printed with a collation of early manuscripts in Halliwell's Illustrations of Fairy Mythology, p. 167:

> " When house or hearth doth sluttish lie,
>   I pinch the maidens black and blue;
> The bed-clothes from the bed pull I,
>   And lay them naked all to view;
>   'Twixt sleep and wake
>   I do them take,
>   And on the key-cold floor them throw;
>   If out they cry,
>   Then forth I fly,
>   And loudly laugh I, ho, ho, ho!"

Thus in Lluellin's Poems, 1679, p. 35:

> " We nere pity girles that doe
>   Find no treasure in their shoe,
> But are nip't by the tyrannous fairy.
>
> List! the noice of the chaires
>   Wakes the wench to her pray'rs,
> Queen Mab comes worse than a witch in;
>   Back and sides she entailes
>   To the print of her nailes;
> She'l teach her to snort in the kitchin."

Again, in Britannia's Pastorals, p. 41 :

——" Where oft the fairy queen
At twilight sat and did command her elves
To pinch those maids that had not swept their shelves;
And farther, if by maidens' oversight
Within doors water was not brought at night,
Or if they spread no table, set no bread,
They shall have nips from toe unto the head :
And for the maid that had perform'd each thing
She in the water-pail bade leave a ring."

The author of Round about our Coal Fire, p. 42, has the
subsequent passage : " When the master and mistress were
laid on their pillows, the men and maids, if they had a game
at romps and blundered up stairs, or jumbled a chair, the next
morning every one would swear 'twas the fairies, and that they
heard them stamping up and down stairs all night, crying
Waters lock'd, Waters lock'd, when there was not water in
every pail in the kitchen." Compare Herrick :

" If ye will with Mab finde grace,
Set each platter in its place ;
Rake the fire up and set
Water in ere sun be set,
Wash your pales and cleanse your dairies,
Sluts are loathsome to the fairies :
Sweep your house ; who doth not so,
Mab will pinch her by the toe." [1]

" Grant that the sweet fairies may nightly put money in
your shoes, and sweepe your house cleane," occurs as one of
the good wishes introduced by Holiday in his comedy of
Τεχνογαμια, or the Marriages of the Arts, temp. Jac. I.

In the superstitions and customs concerning children, I have
before noticed their practice of stealing unbaptized infants and
leaving their own progeny in their stead.[2] I know not why,

[1] [Brand originally quoted this from A Pleasant Grove of New Fancies,
8vo. Lond. 1657, p. 67, where it was of course taken from Herrick's
Hesperides, 1648.]
[2] Puttenham, in the Arte of English Poesie, 1589, p. 144, mentions
this as an opinion of the nurses. It is also noticed, in an allusion to fairy
mythology, in the Irish Hudibras, 1689, p. 122 :

" Drink dairies dry, and stroke the cattle ;
Steal sucklings, and through key-holes sling,
Topeing and dancing in a ring."

but they are reported to have been particularly fond of making cakes, and to have been very noisy during the operation.[1]

Gay, in his fable of the Mother, Nurse, and Fairy, laughs thus at the superstitious idea of changelings. A fairy's tongue is the vehicle of his elegant ridicule :

> " Whence sprung the vain conceited lye
> That we the world with fools supplye ?
> What ! give our sprightly race away
> For the dull helpless sons of clay !
> Besides, by partial fondness shown,
> Like you, we doat upon our own.
> Where ever yet was found a mother
> Who'd give her booby for another ?
> And should we change with human breed,
> Well might we pass for fools indeed."

[In a poem entitled the Fairie's Farewell, in Bishop Corbet's Poems, 1647, p. 47, this subject is thus alluded to :

> " Lament, lament, old abbies,
>   The fairies' lost command ;
> They did but change priests' babies,
>   But some have chang'd your land ;
> And all your children stol'n from thence
>   Are now grown puritanes,
> Who live as changelings ever since,
>   For love of your domaines."]

In Willis's Mount Tabor, or Private Exercises of a Penitent Sinner, 1639, p. 92, the author, under the following head : " Upon an extraordinary accident which befel me in my swaddling cloaths," tells us : " When we come to years, we are commonly told of what befell us in our infancie, if the same were more than ordinary. Such an accident (by relation of others) befell me within few daies after my birth, whilst my mother lay in of me, being her second child, *when I was taken out of the bed from her side, and by my suddain and fierce crying recovered again, being found sticking between the bed's head and the wall : and if I had not cryed in that manner as I did, our gossips had a conceit that I had been quite carried away by the fairies they know not whither, and some elfe or*

---

[1] " In Ireland they frequently lay bannocks, a kind of oaten cakes, in the way of travellers over the mountains : and if they do not accept of the intended favour, they seldom escape a hearty beating or something worse." Grose.

changeling (*as they call it*) *laid in my room.*" He himself, however, discrediting the gossips' account, attributes this attempt to the devil. "Certainly," says our author, "that attempt of stealing me away as soone as I was borne (whatever the midwives talk of it) came from the malice of that arch enemy of mankind, who is continually going about seeking whom he may betray and devoure." He concludes : "Blessed be God, that disappointed him then, and hath ever since preserved and kept mee from his manifold plots and stratagems of destruction : so as now, in the seventieth yeare of mine age, I yet live to praise and magnifie his wonderfull mercies towards me in this behalfe."

Martin, in his History of the Western Islands, p. 116, says : "In this island of Lewis there was an ancient custom to make a fiery circle about the houses, corn, cattle, &c., belonging to each particular family. A man carried fire in his right hand, and went round, and it was called Dessil, from the right hand, which, in the ancient language, is called Dess. There is another way of the Dessil, or carrying fire round about women before they are churched, and about children until they be christened, both of which are performed in the morning and at night. They told me this fire round was an effectual means to preserve both the mother and the infant from the power of evil spirits, who are ready at such times to do mischief, and sometimes carry away the infants, and return them poor meagre skeletons, and these infants are said to have voracious appetites, constantly craving for meat. In this case it was usual for those who believed that their children were thus taken away, to dig a grave in the fields upon quarter-day, and there to lay the fairy skeleton till next morning, at which time the parents went to the place, where they doubted not to find their own child instead of the skeleton."

There were also, it is said, besides the terrestrial fairies, a species of infernal ones, who dwelt in the mines, where they were often heard to imitate the actions of the workmen, whom they were thought to be inclined to do service to, and never, unless provoked by insult, to do any harm.[1] In Wales, this

---

[1] The Scottish Encyclopædia, in verbo, says : "The belief of fairies still subsists in many parts of our own country. The ' Swart Fairy of the Mine' (of German extraction) has scarce yet quitted our subterraneous works. The Germans believed in two species of fairies of the mine, one fierce and

species were called knockers,[1] and were said to point out the rich veins of silver and lead.

Hutchinson, in his History of Cumberland, i. 269, speaking of Eden-hall, says : " In this house are some good old-fashioned apartments. An old painted drinking glass, called the *Luck of Eden-hall,* is preserved with great care. In the garden, near to the house, is a well of excellent spring water, called St. Cuthbert's Well (the church is dedicated to that saint) ; this glass is supposed to have been a sacred chalice ; but the legendary tale is, that the butler, going to draw water, surprised a company of fairies, who were amusing themselves upon the green, near the well : he seized the glass, which was standing upon its margin ; they tried to recover it ; but, after an ineffectual struggle, flew away, saying—

> " If that glass either break or fall,
> Farewell the luck of Eden-hall."

This cup is celebrated in the Duke of Wharton's ballad upon the remarkable drinking match held at Sir Christopher Musgrave's. Another reading of the lines said to have been left with it is—

> " Whene'er this cup shall break or fall,
> Farewell the luck of Eden-hall."

[The Duke's ballad commences with the following lines :

> " God prosper long from being broke
> The luck of Eden-hall."

The good fortune, however, of this ancient house was never so much endangered as by the Duke himself, who, having drunk its contents, to the success and perpetuity, no doubt, of the worthy owner and his race, inadvertently dropped it, and here, most certainly, would have terminated the luck of Eden Hall, if the butler, who had brought the draught, and stood at his elbow, to receive the empty cup, had not happily caught it in his napkin.] A coloured engraving of this cup will be found in Lysons's Cumberland, p. ccix.

malevolent, the other a gentle race, appearing like little old men dressed like miners, and not much above two feet high."
[1] Grose quotes Mr. John Lewis, in his correspondence with Mr. Baxter, describing them as little statured, and about half a yard long ; and adding that at this very instant there are miners on a discovery of a vein of metal on his own lands, and that two of them are ready to make oath they have heard these knockers in the day-time.

There were also thought to have been a sort of domestic fairies, called, from their sunburnt complexions, brownies, who were extremely useful, and said to have performed all sorts of domestic drudgery. Milton's description of Browny (who seems here to be the same with Robin Goodfellow) in his L'Allegro is fine :

> " Tells how the drudging goblin swet,
> To earn his cream-bowl duly set,
> When in one night, ere glimpse of morn,
> His shadowy flale hath thresh'd the corn
> That ten day-lab'rers could not end ;
> Then lays him down the lubbar-fiend,
> And stretch'd out all the chimney's length,
> Basks at the fire his hairy strength,
> And, crop-full, out of doors he flings,
> Ere the first cock his matin rings."

The following on the same subject is from the Ode on the Popular Superstitions of the Highlands of Scotland, by Collins, 4to. Lond. 1788 :

> " Still, 'tis said, the fairy people meet
> Beneath each birken shade on mead or hill.
> There each trim lass, that skims the milky store,
> To the swart tribes their creamy bowls allots ;
> By night they sip it round the cottage door,
> While airy minstrels warble jocund notes."

Martin, in his description of the Western Islands of Scotland, p. 391, speaking of the Shetland Isles, says : " It is not long since every family of any considerable substance in those islands was haunted by a spirit they called Browny, which did several sorts of work ; and this was the reason why they gave him offerings of the various products of the place. Thus some, when they churned their milk, or brewed, poured some milk and wort through the hole of a stone called Browny's stone." Ibid. p. 334, he says : " A spirit, by the country people called Browny, was frequently seen in all the most considerable families in these isles and north of Scotland, in the shape of a tall man ; but within these twenty or thirty years past he is seen but rarely. There were spirits also that appeared in the shape

---

[1] Surely, says Douce, this etymology can only have arisen from an accidental coincidence between the two terms fairies and brownies. The word we have immediately from the French. Whence they had it the reader may possibly learn from Menage and other etymologists. See Ducange, v. *Fadus, Fada.*

of women, horses, swine, catts, and some like fiery balls, which would follow men in the fields : but there have been but few instances of these for forty years past. These spirits used to form sounds in the air, resembling those of a harp, pipe, crowing of a cock, and of the grinding of querns, and sometimes they thrice heard voices in the air by night, singing Irish songs; the words of which songs some of my acquaintance still retain. One of them resembled the voice of a woman who had died some time before, and the song related to her state in the other world. These accounts I had from persons of as great integrity as any are in the world." Speaking of three chapels in the Island of Valay, he says : "Below the chappels there is a flat thin stone, called *Brownie's Stone*, upon which the ancient inhabitants offered a cow's milk every Sunday; but this custom is now quite abolished."

"The spirit called Brownie," says King James in his Dæmonology, p. 127, "appeared like a rough man, and haunted divers houses without doing any evill, but doing as it were necessarie turnes up and downe the house; yet some were so blinded as to beleeve that their house was all the sonsier, as they called it, that such spirits resorted there." Dr. Johnson, in his Journey to the Western Islands, observes that of Browny, mentioned by Martin, "nothing has been heard for many years. Browny was a sturdy fairy, who, if he was fed and kindly treated, would, as they say, do a great deal of work. They now pay him no wages, and are content to labour for themselves," p. 171. In Heron's Journey through Part of Scotland, 1799, ii. 227, we are told, "The Brownie was a very obliging spirit, who used to come into houses by night, and for a dish of cream to perform lustily any piece of work that might remain to be done : sometimes he would work, and sometimes eat till he bursted : if old clothes were laid out for him, he took them in great distress, and never more returned."

Brand, in his Description of Orkney, 1701, p. 63, says : "Evil spirits, also called fairies, are frequently seen in several of the Isles dancing and making merry, and sometimes seen in armour. Also I had the account of the wild sentiments of some of the people concerning them; but with such I shall not detain my reader."

Fairies were sometimes thought to be mischievously inclined by shooting at cattle with arrows headed with flintstones. These were often found, and called elf-shots. The animal affected was, in order to a cure, to be touched with one of these, or made to drink the water in which one of them had been dipped. Plott, in his Staffordshire, p. 369, speaking of *elf-arrows*, says: "These they find in Scotland in much greater plenty, especially in the præfectuary of Aberdeen, which, as the learned Sir Robert Sibbald informs us, they there called *elf-arrows*, lamiarum sagittas, imagining they drop from the clouds, not being to be found upon a diligent search, but now and then by chance in the high beaten roads."

The naturalists of the dark ages owed many obligations to our *fairies*, for whatever they found wonderful and could not account for, they easily got rid of by charging to their account. Thus they called those, which some have since supposed to have been the heads of arrows or spears,[1] before the use of iron was known, others of tools, as in Otaheite, *elf-shots*. To the ignis fatuus they gave the name of *elf-fire*.[2]

In Sinclair's Statistical Account of Scotland, i. 73, parish of Lauder, we are told, "arrow-points of flint, commonly called *elf-* or *fairy-stones*, are to be seen here." Ibid. iii. 56, parish of Fordice, Banffshire: "Flint arrow-heads of our ancestors, called by the country people *elf-arrow heads*, have been found in this parish." Ibid. x. 15, parish of Wick, county of Caithness: "Some small stones have been found which seem to be a species of flint, about an inch long and half an inch broad, of a triangular shape, and barbed on each side. The common people confidently assert that they are *fairies'* *arrows*, which they shoot at cattle, when they instantly fall down dead, though the hide of the animal remains quite entire. Some of these arrows have been found buried a foot under ground, and are supposed to have been in ancient times fixed in shafts, and shot from bows. Ibid. xxi. 148: "Elves, by their arrows, destroyed, and not seldom unmercifully,

[1] *Elfshot*—arrow-heads of stone, supposed by the vulgar to be shot by fairies at the cattle, which cause them to be diseased; the part affected is rubbed with the stone which caused the injury (if it can be found), and it is put into a gallon or two of water, which water the animal is made to take, if it is considered that fever arise therefrom, as a cure.]

[2] "*Wred eld* vocatur ignis qui ex attritu duorum lignorum elicitur, et quia superstitiosis varie usurpari dicitur." Ihre, Glossar. Suio-Goth., fol. Upsal. 1769, in verbo.

cows and oxen." But now, "the elf has withdrawn his arrow." The subsequent lines are found in Collins's Ode, before quoted (at p. 488), p. 10 :

> " There ev'ry herd by sad experience knows
> How, wing'd with fate, their elf-shot arrows fly,
> When the sick ewe her summer food foregoes,
> Or stretch'd on earth the heart-smit heifers lie."

Allan Ramsay, in his Poems, 1721, p. 224, explains *elf-shot* thus : " Bewitch'd, shot by fairies. Country people tell odd tales of this distemper amongst cows. When elf-shot, the cow falls down suddenly dead ; no part of the skin is pierced, but often a little triangular flat stone is found near the beast, as they report, which is called the elf's arrow." In the Survey of the South of Ireland, p. 280, I read as follows : " The fairy mythology is swallowed with the wide throat of credulity. Every parish has its geen and thorn, where these little people are believed to hold their merry meetings, and dance their frolic rounds. I have seen one of those elf-stones, like a thin triangular flint, not half an inch in diameter, with which they suppose the fairies destroy their cows. And when these animals are seized with a certain disorder, to which they are very incident, they say they are elf-shot." Vallancey, in his Collectanea de Rebus Hibernicis, No. xiii., description of Plate 11, tell us, that " what the peasants in Ireland call an elf-arrow is frequently set in silver, and worn about the neck as an amulet against being elf-shot." [It is almost unnecessary to observe that these elf-arrows are in fact the small arrow-heads employed by the aboriginal Irish, and still found in some parts of Ireland. Several specimens of them are preserved in Mr. Crofton Croker's very valuable museum.]

Shakespeare has the expression *elvish-marked*, on which Steevens observes : " The common people in Scotland (as I learn from Kelly's Proverbs) have still an aversion to those who have any natural defect or redundancy, as thinking them marked out for mischief." In Ady's Candle in the Dark, p. 129, we read : "There be also often found in women with childe, and in women that do nurse children with their breasts," and on other occasions, " certain spots, black and blue, as if they were pinched or beaten, which some common ignorant people call *fairy-nips*, which, notwithstanding do come from the causes aforesaid : and yet for these have many ignorant searchers given evidence against poor innocent people" (that is, accused them of being witches).

Certain luminous appearances, often seen on clothes in the night, are called in Kent *fairy sparks*, or *shell-fire*, as Ray informs us in his East and South Country Words. Thus, I was told by Mr. Pennant that there is a substance found at great depths in crevices of limestone rocks, in sinking for lead ore, near Holywell, in Flintshire, which is called Menyn Tylna Teg, or *Fairies' Butter*. So also in Northumberland the common people call a certain fungous excrescence, some-times found about the roots of old trees, Fairy Butter. After great rains, and in a certain degree of putrefaction, it is re-duced to a consistency which, together with its colour, makes it not unlike butter, and hence the name.[1]

Thus farther, " a hard matted or clatted lock of hair in the neck is called *an elf-lock*.[2] See the Glossary to Kennett's Parochial Antiquities, v. *Lokys*." So Shakespeare—

> " This is that very Mab
> That plats the manes of horses in the night,
> And bakes the *elf-locks* in foul sluttish hairs,
> Which, once untangled, much misfortune bodes."

Warburton thought this superstition had its origin in the Plica Polonica.

Again, in King Lear, Edgar says, "*Elf* all my hair in knots."

A disease, consisting of a hardness of the side, was called in the dark ages of superstition the *elf-cake*. In the seventh book of a Thousand Notable Things, No. 55, is the following prescription, which, it is said, will help the hardness of the side called the elf-cake. "Take the root of the gladen, and make powder thereof, and give the diseased party half a spoon-full thereof to drink in white wine, and let him eat thereof so much in his pottage at one time, and it will help him within a while." Cures for the above disorder are alluded to in the

[1] St. Hascka is said by her prayers to have made stinking butter sweet. See the Bollandists under Januar. 26, as cited by Patrick in his Devotions of the Romish Church, p. 37.

[2] In Lodge's Wit's Miserie, 1596, p. 62, is the following passage: " His haires are curl'd and full of *elves-locks*, and nitty for want of kembing." He is speaking of " a ruffian, a swash-buckler, and a braggart." In Wit and Fancy in a Maze, p. 12, " My guts, quoth Soto, are contorted like a dragon's tayle, in *elf-knots*, as if some tripe-wife had tack't them together for chitterlings."

subsequent entry in the catalogue of the Harleian MSS. No.
2378, 13, "For the elf-cake." This is of the time of
Henry VI., and the same as that from the Thousand Notable
Things. [Mr. Halliwell, in his Illustrations of Fairy Mythology, pp. 229-34, has printed several extraordinary fairy con-
jurations. Most of them are sufficiently impious, but the
following recipe "to goe invisible," may be worth quoting :
"Take water, and powre it upon an ant-hill, and looke imedi-
ately after, and you shall finde a stone of divers colours *sente
from the faerie*. This beare in thy righte hande, and you
shall goe invisible."]

Camden, in his Ancient and Modern Manners of the Irish,
says : "When any one happens to fall, he springs up again,
and, turning round three times to the right, digs the earth
with a sword or knife, and takes up a turf, because they say
the earth reflects his shadow to him (quod illi terram umbram
reddere dicunt : they imagine there is a spirit in the earth.
Holland. Gibson) : and if he fall sick within two or three days
after, a woman skilled in those matters is sent to the spot,
and there says, 'I call thee P. from the east, west, south, and
north, from the groves, woods, rivers, marshes, fairies white,
red, black, &c. ;' and, after uttering certain short prayers, she
returns home to the sick person, to see whether it be the distemper which they call Esane, which they suppose inflicted by
the fairies, and, whispering in his ear another short prayer,
with the Pater-noster, puts some burning coals into a cup of
clear water, and forms a better judgment of the disorder than
most physicians." See Gough's edit. of Camden, 1789, iii. 668.

Among the curiosities preserved in Mr. Parkinson's Museum,
formerly Sir Ashton Lever's, were "orbicular sparry bodies,
commonly called *fairies' money*, from the banks of the Tyne,
Northumberland." See the Companion to the Leverian Museum, i. 33, 4to. 1790. In the old play of the Fatall Dowry,
1632, act iv. sc. 1, Ramont says :

> "But not a word of it, 'tis *fairies' treasure ;*
> Which, but reveal'd, brings on the blabber's ruine."

In a curious little book entitled A Brief Character of the
Low Countries, 1652, p. 26, is another allusion to this well-
known trait of fairy mythology :

> "She falls off like *fairy wealth disclosed*."

In the Statistical Account of Scotland, xxi. 148, we are told, "Fairies held from time immemorial certain fields, which could not be taken away without gratifying those merry sprites by a piece of money;" but now "fairies, without requiring compensation, have renounced their possessions."

Waldron, in his Description of the Isle of Man (Works, fol. p. 176), tell us that there is in that island "*the fairies' saddle*, a stone termed so, as I suppose, from the similitude it has of *a saddle*. It seems to lie loose on the edge of a small rock, and the wise natives of Man tell you it is every night made use of by the fairies; but what kind of horses they are on whose backs this is put, I never could find any of them who pretended to resolve me."

In Sinclair's work, xiii. 245, in the Account by the Minister of Dumfries, are some observations on a remarkably romantic linn formed by the water of the Crichup, inaccessible in a great measure to real beings. "This linn was considered as the habitation of imaginary ones; and at the entrance into it there was a curious cell or cave, called the *Elf's Kirk*, where, according to the superstition of the times, the imaginary inhabitants of the linn were supposed to hold their meetings. This cave, proving a good freestone quarry, has lately (1794) been demolished for the purpose of building houses, and, from being the abode of elves, has been converted into habitations for men."

It would be impossible to complete our notices on this subject without occupying a larger space than the limits will permit. We must therefore content ourselves with referring to the numerous documents on the subject printed in Halliwell's Illustrations, and the Introduction to A Midsummer Night's Dream, by the same author.

Waldron, p. 126, tells us that "the Manks confidently assert that the first inhabitants of their island were fairies, and that these little people have still their residence among them They call them *the good people*, and say they live in wilds and forests, and on mountains; and shun great cities because of the wickedness acted therein. All the houses are blessed where they visit, for they fly vice. A person would be thought impudently profane who should suffer his family to go to bed without having first set a tub, or pail full of clean water for these guests to bathe themselves in, which the natives aver they constantly do, as soon as the eyes of the family are closed, wherever they vouchsafe to come. If anything happen to be mislaid, and found again, they presently tell you a fairy took it and returned it. If you chance to get a fall, and hurt yourself, a fairy laid something in your way to throw you down, as a punishment for some sin you have committed." Ibid. p. 133, we are told the fairies are supposed to be fond of hunting. "There is no persuading the inhabitants but that these huntings are frequent in the island, and that these little gentry, being too proud to ride on Manks horses, which they might find in the field, make use of the English and Irish ones, which are brought over and kept by gentlemen. They say that nothing is more common than to find these poor beasts in a morning all over sweat and foam, and tired almost to death, when their owners have believed they have never been out of the stable. A gentleman of Balla-fletcher assured me he had three or four of his best horses killed with these nocturnal journeys."

In Heron's Journey through Part of Scotland, 1799, ii. 227, we read : "The fairies are little beings of a doubtful character, sometimes benevolent, sometimes mischievous. On Hallowe'en, and on some other evenings, they and the Gyar-Carlins are sure to be abroad, and to *stap* those they meet and are displeased with *full of butter and beare-awns*. In winter nights they are heard curling on every sheet of ice. Having a septennial sacrifice of a human being to make to the Devil, they sometimes carry away children, leaving little vixens of their own in the cradle. The diseases of cattle are very commonly attributed to their mischievous operation. Cows are often elf-shot."

There are some most beautiful allusions to the fairy mythology in Bishop Corbet's political ballad entitled the Fairies' Farewell :

"Farewell, rewards and fairies,
　　Good housewives now may say ;
For now fowle sluts in dairies
　　Do fare as well as they :
And, though they sweepe their hearths no lesse
　　Than maides were wont to doe,
Yet who of late for cleanlinesse
　　Findes sixpence in her shooe ?

Lament, lament, old abbies,
　　The fairies' lost command,
They did but change priests' babies.
　　But some have chang'd your land ;

And all your children stolne from thence
　Are now growne Puritans,
Who live as changelings ever since
　For love of your demaines.

At morning and at evening both
　You merry were and glad,
So little care of sleepe and sloath
　These pretty ladies had :
When Tom came home from labour,
　Or Cisse to milking rose,
Then merrily went their tabor,
　And nimbly went their toes.

Witness those rings and roundelayes
　Of theirs which yet remaine,
Were footed in Queen Maries dayes
　On many a grassy plaine.

A tell-tale in their company
　They never could endure,
And whoso kept not secretly
　Their mirth was punisht sure.
It was a just and Christian deed
　To pinch such black and blew :
O how the commonwelth doth need
　Such justices as you !"

Shakespeare's portrait of Queen Mab must not be omitted here.　He puts it into the mouth of Mercutio in Romeo and Juliet :

" She is the fairies' midwife; and she comes
In shape no bigger than an agate-stone
On the fore-finger of an alderman,
Drawn with a team of little atomies
Athwart men's noses as they lie asleep :
Her waggon-spokes made of long spinners' legs ;
The cover, of the wings of grasshoppers ;
The traces, of the smallest spider's web ;
The collars, of the moonshine's wat'ry beams ;
Her whip, of cricket's bone ; the lash, of film ;
Her waggoner, a small gray-coated gnat,
Not half so big as a round little worm
Pricked from the lazy finger of a maid :
Her chariot is an empty hazel-nut,
Made by the joiner squirrel, or old grub,
Time out of mind the fairies' coach-makers.
And in this state she gallops night by night
Through lovers' brains, and then they dream of love :
On courtiers' knees, that dream on court'sies straight :
O'er lawyers' fingers, who straight dream on fees :
O'er ladies' lios, who straight on kisses dream ;

Which oft the angry Mab with blisters plagues,
Because their breaths with sweetmeats tainted are.
Sometimes she gallops o'er a courtier's nose,
And then dreams he of smelling out a suit :
And sometimes comes she with a tithe-pig's tail,
Tickling a parson's nose as 'a lies asleep,
Then dreams he of another benefice.
Sometime she driveth o'er a soldier's neck,
And then dreams he of cutting foreign throats,
Of breaches, ambuscadoes, Spanish blades,
Of healths five fathom deep ; and then anon
Drums in his ear ; at which he starts, and wakes ;
And, being thus frighted, swears a prayer or two,
And sleeps again."

I find the following in Poole's English Parnassus, p.

" There is Mab, the mistress fairy,
That doth nightly rob the dairy,
And can help or hurt the churning
As she please, without discerning.
She that pinches country wenches,
If they rub not clean their benches ;
And with sharper nails remembers,
When they rake not up the embers ;
But if so they chance to feast her,
In their shooe she drops a tester.
This is she that empties cradles,
Takes out children, puts in ladles ;
Trains forth midwives in their slumber
With a sive, the holes to number ;
And then leads them from their boroughs
Thorough ponds and water-furrows."

In the same work I find a fairy song[1] of exquisite beauty :

" Come follow, follow me,
You fairy elves that be,
Which circle on the green,
Come follow me your queen :
Hand in hand let's dance a round,
For this place is fairy ground.

When mortals are at rest,
And snorting in their nest,
Unheard and unespied,
Through key-holes we do glide ;
Over tables, stools, and shelves ;
We trip it with our fairy elves ;

---

[1] It is almost unnecessary to observe that this is the well-known ballad printed by Percy, a better copy of which is given from early MSS. in Halliwell's Illustrations of Fairy Mythology, 1845.

And if the house be foul,
Or platter, dish, or bowl,
Up stairs we nimbly creep,
And find the sluts asleep;
There we pinch their arms and thighs,
None escapes, nor none espies.

But if the house be swept,
And from uncleanness kept,
We praise the household maid,
And surely she is paid;
For we do use before we go
To drop a tester in her shoe.

Upon a mushroom's head
Our table we do spread;
A corn of rye or wheat
Is manchet which we eat;
Pearly drops of dew we drink,
In acorn cups fill'd to the brink.

The brains of nightingales,
The unctuous dew of snails,
Between two nut-shells stew'd,
Is meat that's eas'ly chew'd;
The beards of mice
Do make a feast of wondrous price.

On tops of dewy grass
So nimbly we do pass,
The young and tender stalk
Ne'er bends when we do walk;
Yet in the morning may be seen
Where we the night before have been.

The grasshopper and fly
Serve for our minstrelsie;
Grace said, we dance awhile,
And so the time beguile.
And when the moon doth hide her head,
The glow-worm lights us home to bed."

Lilly, in his Life and Times, tells us that fairies love the southern sides of hills, mountains, groves, neatness and cleanness of apparel, a strict diet, and upright life; "fervent prayers unto God," he adds, "conduce much to the assistance of those who are curious these ways." He means, it should seem, those who wish to cultivate an acquaintance with them.

Chaucer, through the gloom of a darker age, saw clearer into this matter. He is very facetious concerning them in

his Canterbury Tales, where he puts his creed of fairy mythology into the mouth of the Wife of Bath, thus:

> " In old dayes of the King Artour
> Of which that Bretons speken gret honour,
> All was this lond fulfilled of faerie;
> The elf-quene with hire jolie company
> Daunsed full oft in many a grene mede;
> This was the old opinion as I rede.
> I speke of many hundred yeres agoe,
> But now can no man see non elves mo.
> For now the grete charite and prayers
> Of limitours and other holy freres,
> That serchen every lond and every streme,
> As thik as motes in the sunne beme:—
> This maketh that there ben no faeries:
> *For there as wont to walken was an elfe,*
> *There walketh now the limitour himself,*
> And as he goeth in his limitacioune,
> Wymen may now goe safely up and downe;
> In every bush, and under every tree,
> There nis none other incubus but he."

["The 'joly compaignie,' however, did not consist of the
little dancers on the green. These were a later introduction;
Spenser was contented with the fairies of romance; but
Shakespeare founded his elfin world on the prettiest of the
people's traditions, and has clothed it in the ever-living flowers
of his own exuberant fancy. How much is the invention of
the great poet we shall probably never be informed; and his
successors have not rendered the subject more clear by adopt-
ing the graceful world he has created, as though it had been
interwoven with the popular mythology, and formed a part
of it." Halliwell's Illusrations, Introd.]

In Poole's Parnassus, are given the names of the fairy
court: " *Oberon*, the emperor; *Mab*, the empress; *Perri-
wiggin, Perriwincle, Puck, Hob-goblin, Tomalin, Tom Thumb*,
courtiers; *Hop, Mop, Drop, Pip, Drip, Skip, Tub, Tib, Tick,
Pink, Pin, Quick, Gill, Im, Tit, Wap, Win, Nit*, the maids
of honour; *Nymphidia*, the mother of the maids."

Dr. Grey, in his Notes on Shakespeare, i. 50, gives us a
description from other writers of fairy-land, a fairy entertainment, and fairy hunting. The first is from Randolph's
pastoral entitled, Amyntas, or the Impossible Dowry, p. 36.
It is not destitute of humour. " A curious park paled round

about with pick-teeth—a house made all with mother-of-pearle
—an ivory tennis-court—a nutmeg parlour—a saphyre dairy-
room—a ginger hall—chambers of agate—kitchens all of
chrystal—the jacks are gold—the spits are all of Spanish
needles."

The following, fitted for the above jacks and spits, is Dr.
King's description of Orpheus' fairy entertainment, Works,
ed. 1776, iii. 112 :

> " A roasted ant that's nicely done
> By one small atom of the sun ;
> These are flies' eggs in moonshine poached ;
> This a flea's thigh in collops scotch'd,—
> 'Twas hunted yesterday i' th' park,
> And like t' have scap'd us in the dark.
> This is a dish entirely new,
> Butterflies' brains dissolv'd in dew ;
> These lovers' vows, these courtiers' hopes,
> Things to be eat by microscopes :
> These sucking mites, a glow-worm's heart,
> This a delicious rainbow-tart."

Randolph, ut supra, describes fairy hunting in a more magnificent manner :

Dor. I hope King Oberon and his royal Mab are well ?

Joe. They are. I never saw their graces eat such a meal
before.

Joe. They are *rid a hunting.*

Dor. Hare or deer, my lord ?

Joe. Neither ; *a brace of snails of the first head."*

The following, entitled "Oberon's Clothing," and " Oberon's
Diet," found in Poole's English Parnassus, almost exhaust the
subject of fairy economy.

" Oberon's Clothing.

> " Then did the dwarfish fairy elves
> (Having first attir'd themselves)
> Prepare to dress their Oberon king
> In light robes of revelling,
> In a cob-web shirt, more thin
> Than ever spider since could spin,
> Bleach'd by the whiteness of the snow,
> As the stormy winds did blow
> It through the vast and freezing air ;
> No shirt half so fine or fair.
> A rich waistcoat they did bring,
> Made of the trout-fly's gilded wing :

At this his elveship 'gan to fret
Swearing it would make him sweat
Even with its weight ; and needs would **wear**
His wastecoat wove of downy hair
New shaven from an eunuch's chin ;
That pleas'd him well, 'twas wondrous thin.
The outside of his doublet was
Made of the four-leav'd true-love grass,
On which was set a comely gloss
By the oyl of crisped moss ;
That thro' a mist of starry light
It made a rainbow in the night :
On each seam there was a lace
Drawn by the unctuous snail's slow trace,
To which the purest silver thread
Compar'd did look like slubber'd lead :
Each button was a sparkling eye
Ta'en from the speckled adder's fry,
Which in a gloomy night and dark,
Twinkled like a fiery spark :
And, for coolness, next his skin,
'Twas with white poppy lin'd within.
His breeches of that fleece were wrought
Which from Colchos Jason brought ;
Spun into so fine a yearn,
Mortals might it not discern ;
Wove by Arachne on her loom
Just before she had her doom :
Died crimson with a maiden's blush,
And lin'd with soft dandalion plush.
A rich mantle he did wear
Made of silver gossamere,
Bestrowed over with a few
Diamond drops of morning dew.
His cap was all of ladies' love,
So passing light that it could move
If any humming gnat or flye
But puff'd the air in passing by.
About it was a wreath of pearl,
Dropp'd from the eyes of some poor **girl**
Was pinch'd because she had forgot
To leave clean water in the pot.
And for feather he did wear
Old Nisus' fatal purple hair.
A pair of buskins they did bring
Of the cow-lady's coral wing,
Inlaid with inky spots of jet,
And lin'd with purple violet.
His belt was made of yellow leaves
Pleated in small curious threaves,

Beset with amber cowslip studs,
And fring'd about with daisy-buds;
In which his bugle-horn was hung,
Made of the babbling echo's tongue,
Which, set unto his moon-burnt lips,
He winds, and then his fairies skips :
And whilst the lazy drone doth sound,
Each one doth trip a fairy round."

"*Oberon's Diet.*

" A little mushroom table spread
After a dance, they set on bread.
A yellow corn of parkey wheat,
With some small sandy grits to eat
His choice bits with ; and in a trice
They make a feast less great than nice.
But all this while his eye was serv'd,
We cannot think his ear was starv'd,
But that there was in place to stir
His ears the pittering grasshopper ;
The merry cricket, the puling fly,
The piping gnat's shrill minstrelsie;
The humming dor, the dying swan,
And each a chief musitian.
    But now we must imagine, first,
The elves present, to quench his thirst,
A chrystal pearl of infant dew,
Brought and besweeten'd in a blew
And pregnant violet ; which done,
His kittling eyes began to run
Quite thro' the table, where he spies
The horns of papery butterflies ;
Neat cool allay of cuckow-spittle,
Of which he eats, but with a little
A little furze-ball-pudding stands,
And yet not blessed with his hands,
That seem'd too coarse, but he not spares
To feed upon the candid hairs
Of a dried canker, and the lag
And well-bestrutted bee's sweet bag.
Stroking his palat with some store
Of emmett's eggs ; what will he more,
But beards of mice and gnat's stew'd thigh,
A pickled maggot, and a dry
Hep, with a red-cap worm that's shut
Within the concave of a nut ?
Brown as his tooth is, with the fat
Well-rooted eyeball of a bat ;
A bloted earwig, and the pith
Of sugred rush, he glads him with.

But, most of all, the ⸻
As much betickling his desire
To burn his queen ; mixt with the far-
Fetch'd binding jelly of a star :
With wither'd cherries, mandrake's ears,
Mole's eyes ; to these the slain stag's tears,
The unctious dewlaps of a snail,
The broke-heart of a nightingale
O'ercome with musick ; with a wine
Ne'er ravish'd with a cluster'd vine,
But gently strained from the side
Of a most sweet and dainty bride ;
Brought in a daizy chalice, which
He fully quaffs up, to bewitch
His blood to height.   This done, commends
Grace to his priest, and the feast ends."

A charm against fairies was *turning the cloak*. Thus Bishop Corbet, in his Iter Boreale :

⸻" William found
A meanes for our deliv'rance ; *turne your cloakes*,
Quoth hee, for Pucke is busy in these oakes :
If ever wee at Bosworth will be found,
Then *turne your cloakes*, for this is fairy ground."

From another passage in Wild's Iter Boreale, it should seem that there was a popular belief that, if you struck a fairy or walking spirit, it would dissolve into air.   Our prelate was just mentioning the turning of the cloak above :

" But, ere the witchcraft was perform'd, we meete
A very man, who had not cloven feete,
Tho' William, still of little faith, doth doubt,
'Tis Robin or some spirit walkes about.
Strike him, quoth he, *and it will turne to aire !*
Cross yourselves thrice, and strike him—Strike that dare,
Thought I, for sure this massie forester
In blows will prove the better conjurer."

The bishop was right, for it proved to be the keeper of the forest, who showed them their way, which they had lost.

[It was formerly, perhaps now, the belief in Suffolk, that a flint hung in a stable protected the animals in it from the fairies. In June, 1833, a butcher of the neighbourhood of Woodbridge came to a farmer to buy a calf.   Coming out of the crib, he stated that the crater was all o' a muck, and desired the farmer to hang a flint by a string in the crib, just high enough to be clear of the calf's head : " Becaze," says he, " the calf is rid every night by the *farisees*, and the stone will brush them off."]

In a curious and rare book, entitled Paradoxical Assertions and Philosophical Problems, by R. H., 1664, 2d part, p. 14, "Why Englishmen creep to the chimney in winter and summer also?" we read : " Doth not the warm zeal of an Englishman's devotion (who was ever observed to contend most stifly pro aris et focis) make them maintain and defend the sacred hearth, as the sanctuary and chief place of residence of the tutelary lares and household gods, and the only court *where the lady fairies convene to dance and revel ?*"

Aubrey, in his Miscellanies, p. 158, gives us the following most important piece of information respecting fairies : " He reports, that when he was a boy at school in the town of Forres, yet not so young but that he had years and capacity both to observe and remember that which fell out, he and his school-fellows were upon a time whipping their tops in the church-yard, before the door of the church ; though the day was calm, they heard a noise of a wind, and at some distance saw the small dust begin to arise and turn round, which motion con-tinued, advancing till it came to the place where they were ; whereupon they began to bless themselves. But one of their number (being it seems a little more bold and confident than his companions) said, *horse and hattock* with my top, and im-mediately they all saw the top lifted up from the ground, but could not see what way it was carried, by reason of a cloud of dust which was raised at the same time. They sought for the top all about the place where it was taken up, but in vain ; and it was found afterwards in the church-yard, on the other side of the church. Mr. Steward (so is the gentleman called) declared to me that he had a perfect remembrance of this matter."

In Sir John Sinclair's Statistical Account of Scotland, 1792, iv. 560, the minister of the parishes of Strachur and Stra-lachlan, in Argyleshire, tells us, in his description of them, that " About eight miles to the eastward of Cailleach-vear a small conical hill rises considerably above the neighbouring hills. It is seen from Inverary, and from many parts at a great dis-tance. It is called Sien-Sluai, the fairy habitation of a mul-titude." Adding, in a note : " A belief in fairies prevailed very much in the Highlands of old ; nor at this day is it quite obliterated. A small conical hill, called Sien, was assigned them for a dwelling, from which melodious music was frequently heard, and gleams of light seen in dark nights." Ibid. xii. 461, Account of Kirkmichael, we read: "Not more firmly established in this country is the belief in ghosts than that in fairies. The legendary records of fancy, transmitted from age to age, have assigned their mansions to that class of genii, in detached hillocks, covered with verdure, situated on the banks of purling brooks, or surrounded by thickets of wood. These hillocks are called sioth-dhunan, abbreviated sioth-anan, from sioth, peace, and dun, a mound. They derive this name from the practice of the Druids, who were wont occasionally to retire to green eminences to administer justice, establish peace, and compose differences between contending parties. As that venerable order taught a saoghl hal, or world beyond the present, their followers, when they were no more, fondly imagined that seats where they exercised a virtue so beneficial to mankind were still inhabited by them in their disembodied state. In the autumnal season, when the moon shines from a serene sky, often is the wayfaring traveller arrested by the music of the hills, more melodious than the strains of Orpheus. Often struck with a more solemn scene, he beholds the visionary hunters engaged in the chace, and pursuing the deer of the clouds, while the hollow rocks, in long-sounding echoes, reverberate their cries. There are several now living who assert that they have seen and heard this aerial hunting, and that they have been suddenly surrounded by visionary forms, and assailed by a multitude of voices. About fifty years ago a clergyman in the neighbourhood, whose faith was more regulated by the scepticism of philosophy than the credulity of superstition, could not be prevailed upon to yield his assent to the opinion of the times. At length, however, he felt from experience that he doubted what he ought to have believed. One night as he was returning home, at a late hour, from a presbytery, he was seized by the fairies, and carried aloft into the air. Through fields of ether and fleecy clouds he journeyed many a mile, descrying, like Sancho Panza, on his clavileno, the earth far distant below him, and no bigger than a nut-shell. Being thus sufficiently convinced of the reality of their existence, they let him down at the door of his own house, where he afterwards often recited to the wondering circle the marvellous tale of his adventure." [1]

A note at page 462 adds ; "Notwithstanding the progressive increase of knowledge and proportional decay of superstition in the Highlands, these genii are still supposed by many of the people to exist in the woods and sequestered valleys of the mountains, where they frequently appear to the lonely traveller, clothed in green, with dishevelled hair floating over their shoulders, and with faces more blooming than the vermil blush of a summer morning. At night, in particular, when fancy assimilates to its own preconceived ideas every appearance and every sound, the wandering enthusiast is frequently entertained by their music, more melodious than he ever before heard. It is curious to observe how much this agreeable delusion corresponds with the superstitious opinion of the Romans concerning the same class of genii, represented under different names. The Epicurean Lucretius describes the credulity in the following beautiful verses :

> " ' Hæc loca capripedes satyros, nymphasque tenere
> Finitimi pingunt, et faunos esse loquuntur;
> Quorum noctivago strepitu, ludoque jocanti
> Adfirmant volgo taciturna silentia rumpi
> Chordarumque sonos fieri, dulceisque querelas
> Tibia quas fundit digitis pulsata canentum.'

"The fauni are derived from the eubates or faidhin of the Celtæ. Faidh is a prophet; hence is derived the Roman word *fari*, to prophesy."

In the same work, xv. 430, parishes of Stronsay and Eday, co. Orkney, we read : "The common people of this district remain to this day so credulous as to think that fairies do exist, that an inferior species of witchcraft is still practised, and that houses have been haunted, not only in former ages, but that they are haunted; at least noises are heard which cannot be accounted for on rational principles, even in our days. An

---

[1] In plain English, I should suspect that spirits of a different sort from fairies had taken the honest clergyman by the head, and, though he has omitted the circumstance in his marvellous narration, I have no doubt but that the good man saw double on the occasion, and that his own mare, not fairies, landed him safe at his own door.

instance of the latter happened only three years ago in the house of John Spence, boat-carpenter." [1]

The following from O'Brien's Dict. Hib. is cited by General Vallancey, in a note in his Collectanea de Rebus Hibernicis, iii. 461 : " Sith-bhreog, the same as sigh-brog, a fairy ; hence bean-sighe, plural mna-sighe, women-fairies ; credulously supposed by the common people to be so affected to certain families, that they are heard to sing mournful lamentations about their houses by night, whenever any of the family labours under a sickness which is to end by death : but no families which are not of an ancient and noble stock" (of Oriental extraction he should have said) "are believed to be honoured with this fairy privilege."

In a very rare tract, entitled Strange and Wonderful News from the County of Wicklow in Ireland, what happened to one Dr. Moore (late schoolmaster in London), how he was invisibly taken from his friends, 1678, we read,—1, how Dr. Moore said to his friend that " he had been often told by his mother, and several others of his relations, of spirits which they called fairies, who used frequently to carry him away, and continue him with them for some time, without doing him the least prejudice ; but his mother, being very much frighted and concerned thereat, did, as often as he was missing, send to a certain old woman, her neighbour in the country, who, by repeating some spells or exorcisms, would suddenly cause his return." His friend very naturally disbelieved the facts, "while the doctor did positively affirm the truth thereof." But the most strange and wonderful part of the story is, that during the dispute the doctor was carried off suddenly by some of those invisible gentry, though forcibly held by two persons ; nor did he return to the company till six o'clock the next morning, both hungry and thirsty, having, as he asserted, "been hurried from place to place all that night." At the end of this marvellous narration is the following advertisement : "For satisfaction of the licenser, I certifie this following" (it

1 " The Queen of Fairie, mentioned in Jean Weir's indictment, is probably the same sovereign with the Queen of Elf-land, who makes a figure in the case of Alison Pearson, 15th May, 1588; which I believe is the first of the kind in the record." Additions and Notes to Maclaurin's Arguments and Decisions in remarkable Cases. Law Courts, Scotland, 1774. p. 726.

ought to have been preceding) " relation was sent to me from Dublin by a person whom I credit, and recommended in a letter bearing date the 23d of November last, as true news much spoken of there.   John Cother." The licenser of the day must have been satisfied, for the tract was printed ; but who will undertake to give a similar satisfaction on the subject to the readers of the present age ?

[The Irish fairy legends have been collected and immortalized by Mr. Crofton Croker, whose popular work on the subject is so widely known that any abstract of it here would be super-fluous.   Mr. Croker classes the fairies under the heads of *shefro, cluricaune, banshee, phooka, merrow, dullahan,* and the *fir darrig.* The name *shefro* literally signifies a fairy-house or mansion, and is adopted as a generic name for the elves who are supposed to live in troops or communities, and were popu-larly supposed to have castles or mansions of their own.   The *cluricaune* was distinguished by his solitary habits. The *banshee,* an attendant fairy or spirit, especially observed to mourn on the death of any member of a family to which it attached itself. The *phooka* appears to be a modification of Robin Goodfellow or Puck.   The *merrow* is a mermaid.   The *dullahan* is a ma-licious, sullen spirit or goblin, and the *fir darrig* a little merry red man, not unlike in its disposition and movements to Puck.]

ROBIN GOODFELLOW.

["THERE can be little doubt," observes Mr. Halliwell, "that, in the time of Shakespeare, the fairies held a more prominent position in our popular literature than can now be concluded from the pieces on the subject that have descended to us. The author of Tarlton's News out of Purgatory, printed in 1590, assures us that Robin Goodfellow was 'famosed in every old wives chronicle for his mad merry pranks ;' and we learn from Henslowe's Diary that Chettle was the writer of a drama on the adventures of that 'merry wanderer of the night.'   These have disappeared ; and time has dealt so harshly with the memory of poor Robin, that we might almost imagine his spirit was still leading us astray over massive volumes of an-

tiquity, in a deluoive nearoh ufha docaments for over lost; or
rather, perhaps, it is his punishment for the useless journeys
he has given our ancestors, misleading night-wanderers, and
'laughing at their harm.' The judgment has extended in
every direction. Even in the provinces his gambols are forgotten, or have become matter of uncertain tradition."]

Robin Goodfellow, alias Pucke, alias Hobgoblin, says Percy,
in the creed of ancient superstition was a kind of merry sprite
whose character and achievements are recorded in the following
ballad. Peck attributes it to Ben Jonson. It seems to have
been originally intended for some masque.

> " From Oberon, in fairye land,
>   The king of ghosts and shadowes there,
>   Mad Robin I, at his commend,
>   Am sent to viewe the night-sports here;
>   What revel rout
>   Is kept about,
>   In every corner where I go,
>   I will o'er see,
>   And merry bee,
>   And make good sport with ho, ho, ho!
>
> More swift than lightening can I flye
>   About this aery welkin soone,
>   And, in a minute's space, descrye
>   Each thing that's done belowe the moone:
>   There's not a hag
>   Or ghost shall wag,
>   Or cry, ware goblins! where I go;
>   But Robin I
>   There feates will spy,
>   And send them home, with ho, ho, ho!
>
> Whene'er such wanderers I meete,
>   As from their night-sports they trudge home,
>   With counterfeiting voice I greete
>   And call them on, with me to roame
>   Thro' woods, thro' lakes,
>   Thro' bogs, thro' brakes;
>   Or else, unseene, with them I go,
>   All in the nicke
>   To play some tricke
>   And frolicke it, with ho, ho, ho!
>
> Sometimes I meete them like a man,
>   Sometimes an ox, sometimes a hound;
>   And to a horse I turn me can,
>   To trip and trot about them round.

But if to ride,
My backe they stride,
More swift than wind away 1 go ;
Ore hedge and lands,
Thro' pools and ponds,
I whirry, laughing, ho, ho, ho !

When lads and lasses merry be,
With possets and with juncates fine,
Unseene of all the company,
I eat their cakes and sip their wine ;
And to make sport,
I fart and snort,
And out the candles I do blow :
The maids I kiss ;
They shrieke—who's this ?
I answer nought, but ho, ho, ho !

Yet now and then, the maids to please,
At midnight I card up their wooll ;
And while they sleepe, and take their ease,
With wheel to threads their flax I pull.
I grind at mill
Their malt up still ;
I dress their hemp, I spin their tow.
If any 'wake,
And would me take,
I wend me, laughing, ho, ho, ho ![1]

When any need to borrowe ought,
We lend them what they do require,
And for the use demand we nought,
Our owne is all we do desire.
If to repay
They do delay,

---

[1] [Here follows a stanza we have quoted previously, at p. 483. The reader is referred to Halliwell's Illustrations of Fairy Mythology, p. 168, where a copy is printed from MSS., containing the following additional stanza :

" Whenas my fellow elves and I
In circled ring do trip a round ;
If that our sports by any eye
Do happen to be seen or found ;
If that they
No words do say,
But *mum* continue as they go,
Each night I do
Put groat in shoe,
And wind out laughing, ho, ho, ho !]

Abroad amongst them then I go,
And night by night
I them affright
With pinchings, dreames, and ho, ho, ho !
When lazie queans have nought to do,
But study how to cog and lye ;
To make debate and mischief too,
'Twixth one another secretlye ;
I mark their gloze,
And it disclose
To them whom they have wronged so ;
When I have done,
I get me gone,
And leave them scolding, ho, ho, ho !
When men do traps and engins set
In loop-holes where the vermine creepe,
Who from their foldes and houses get
Their duckes and geese, and lambes and sheepe.
I spy the gin,
And enter in,
And seeme a vermin taken so ;
But when they there
Approach me neare,
I leap out, laughing, ho, ho, ho !
By wells and rills, in meadowes greene,
We nightly dance our hey-day guise ;
And to our fairye king and queene
We chaunt our moonlight minstrelsies.
When larks 'gin sing,
Away we fling,
And babes new borne steal as we go,
And elfe in bed
We leave instead,
And wend us, laughing, ho, ho, ho !
From hag-bred Merlin's time have I
Thus nightly revell'd to and fro ;
And for my pranks men call me by
The name of Robin Good-fellow.
Fiends, ghosts, and sprites,
Who haunt the nightes,
The hags and goblins do me know ;
And beldames old
My feates have told,
So Vale, Vale, ho, ho, ho !"

Shakespeare has also given us a description of Robin Goodfellow in the Midsummer Night's Dream :

" Either I mistake your shape and making quite,
Or else you are that shrewd and knavish sprite,
Call'd Robin Goodfellow : are you not he,
That fright the maidens of the villagery,
Skim milk, and sometimes labour in the quern,
And bootless make the breathless housewife churn ;
And sometimes make the drink to bear no barm ;
Mislead night-wanderers, laughing at their harm ?
Those that Hobgoblin call you, and sweet Puck,
You do their work, and they shall have good luck."

" This account of Robin Goodfellow," says Wharton, " corresponds, in every article, with that given of him in Harsenet's Declaration," ch. xx. p. 134 : " And if that the bowle of curds and creame were not duly set out for Robin Goodfellow, the frier, and Sisse, the dairymaid, why then either the pottage was burnt to next day in the pot, or the cheeses would no*. curdle, or the butter would not come, or the ale in the fat never would have good head.   But, if a peeter-penny or an housle-egge were behind, or a patch of tythe unpaid, then 'ware of bull-beggars, sprites, &c."   He is mentioned by Cartwright, in his Ordinary, act iii. sc. 1, as a spirit particularly fond of disconcerting and disturbing domestic peace and economy.

Reginald Scot gives the same account of this frolicsome spirit, in his Discoverie of Witchcraft, 1584, p. 66 : " Your grandame's maids were wont to set a bowl of milk for him, for his pains in grinding malt and mustard, and sweeping the house at midnight—this white bread, and bread and milk was his standing fee."

There is the following pleasant passage concerning Robin Goodfellow in Apothegms of King James, 1658, p. 139, showing that persons of the first distinction were anciently no strangers to the characters of fairies : " Sir Fulk Greenvil had much and private accesse to Queen Elizabeth, which he used honourably, and did many men good. Yet he would say merrily of himself that he was like Robin Goodfellow, for when the maides spilt the milk-pannes, or kept any racket, they would lay it upon Robin ; so what tales the ladies about the queen told her, or other bad offices that they did, they would put it upon him."

In Hampshire they give the name of *Colt-pixy* to a supposed spirit or fairy, which, in the shape of a horse, wickers, i. e.

neighs, and misleads horses into bogs, &c. See Grose's Provincial Glossary, in v.

[There are, in the secluded parts of Dorsetshire, many a surviving trace of the ancient fairy mythology. In addition to the "colepexy," mentioned by Mr. Barnes, the common fossil belemnites are termed "colepexies' fingers," or "fairy fingers," and fossil echini, "colepexies' heads." The goblin colt, the threat of which is held out to children to ensure obedience, even to this day, in the rural parts of our county, is still called the pexy, and he is supposed especially to haunt coppices and woods. Drayton, in his *Polyolbion*, says :

> " This Puck seems but a dreaming dol⁴
> Still walking, like a ragged colt,
> And oft out of a bush doth bolt,
> Of purpose to deceive us;
> And leading us makes us to stray,
> Long winter nights out of the way;
> And when we stick in mire and clay,
> He doth with laughter leave us."

The Irish Pooka, too, pre-eminent in malice and mischief, is generally in the shape of a horse, though possessed of the power of assuming a diversity of forms. But this is not the place to wander in the realms of fairy-land.]

I suspect *Pixy* to be a corruption of "puckies," which anciently signified little better than the devil, whence, in Shakespeare, the epithet of "sweet" is given to Puck, by way of qualification. So the author of Piers Ploughman puts the *pouk* for the devil, "none helle *powke*." It seems to have been an old Gothic word : *Puke, puken;* Sathanas, Gudm. And Lexicon Island. In the Bugbears, an ancient MS. comedy, the Lansdowne collection, I likewise met with these appellations of a fiend :

" *Puckes, Puckerels,* Hob Howlard, Bygorn, and Robin Goodfellow."

But here Puck and Robin Goodfellow are made distinct characters.

In the Glossary to Burns's Scottish Poems mention occurs of a mischievous kind of spirits called *kelpies,* which are said to haunt fords and ferries at night, especially in storms. Graham, in his Sketches of Perthshire, 1812, p. 245, says : " Every lake had its *kelpie,* or water-horse, often seen by the shepherd, as he sat in a summer's evening upon the brow of

II.   33

a rock, dashing along the surface of the deep, or browsing on the pasture-ground upon its verge. Often did this malignant genius of the waters allure women and children to his subaqueous haunts, there to be immediately devoured. Often did he also swell the torrent or lake beyond its usual limits, to overwhelm the hapless traveller in the flood." Of the *Urisks* and *Daoine Shi'*, other descriptions of the fairies of the Highlanders, see the same work, pp. 121-2, 245, 247.

Junius gives the following etymon of *hobgoblin*. Casaubon, he says, derives goblin from the Greek κοβαλos, a kind of spirit that was supposed to lurk about houses. The hobgoblins were a species of these, so called because their motion was fabled to have been effected not so much by walking as *hopping* on one leg. See Lye's Junii Etymologicum, *Hob*, however, is nothing more than the usual contraction for *Robert*.

In a tract by Samuel Rowlands, entitled More Knaves Yet, the Knaves of Spades and Diamonds, reprinted by the Percy Society, is the following passage of "ghoasts and goblins," in which we meet with a *Robin Bad-fellow :*

> " In old wives daies, that in old time did live,
> (To whose odde tales much credit men did give)
> Great store of *goblins, fairies, bugs, night-mares,*
> *Urchins*, and elves, to many a house repaires.
> Yea, far more *sprites* did haunt in divers places
> Than there be women now weare devils faces.
> Amongst the rest was a Good-fellow devill,
> So cal'd in kindnes, cause he did no evill,
> Knowne by the name of Robin (as we heare),
> And that his eyes as broad as sawcers weare,
> Who came a nights and would make kitchens cleane,
> And in the bed bepinch a lazy queane.
> Was much in mils about the grinding meale
> (And sure I take it taught the miller steale) ;
> Amongst the creame-bowles and milke-pans would be,
> And with the country wenches, who but he
> To wash their dishes for some fresh cheese hire,
> Or set their pots and kettles 'bout the fire.
> 'Twas a mad Robin that did divers pranckes,
> For which with some good cheare they gave him thankes,
> And that was all the kindness he expected,
> With gaine (it seemes) he was not much infected.
> But as that time is past, that Robin's gone,
> He and his night-mates are to us unknowne,

And in the steed of such Good-fellow sprites
We meet with Robin Bad-fellow a nights,
That enters houses secret in the darke,
And only comes to pilfer, steale, and sharke ;
And as the one made dishes cleane (they say),
The other takes them quite and cleane away.
What'ere it be that is within his reach,
The filching tricke he doth his fingers teache.
But as Good-fellow Robin had reward
With milke and creame that friends for him prepar'd
For being busy all the night in vaine,
(Though in the morning all things safe remaine,)
Robin Bad-fellow, wanting such a supper,
Shall have his breakfast with a rope and butter ;
To which let all his fellows be invited,
That with such deeds of darknesse are delighted."

Bogle-boe, which seems, at least in sound, to bear some affinity to hob-goblin, is said to be derived from the Welsh *bwgwly*, to terrify, and *boe*, a frightful sound invented by nurses to intimidate their children into good behaviour, with the idea of some monster about to take them away. Skinner seems to fetch it from buculus, i. e. *bos boans*, a lowing ox. See Lye's Junii Etymolog. in verbo. Well has etymology been called ' eruditio ad libitum.' Boggle-bo, says Coles, in his Latin Dictionary, 1678, (now corruptly termed Bugabow,) signified " an ugly wide-mouthed picture carried about with May-games." It is perhaps nothing more than the diminutive of *bug*, a terrifying object.

In Mathews's Bible, Psalm xci. (v. 5) is rendered, "Thou shalt not nede to be afraied for any *bugs* by night." In the Hebrew it is " *terror* of the night ;" a curious passage, evidently alluding to that horrible sensation the night-mare, which in all ages has been regarded as the operation of evil spirits. Compare Douce's Illustr. of Shakespeare, i. 328.

Boh, Warton tells us, was one of the most fierce and formidable of the Gothic generals, and the son of Odin ; the mention of whose name only was sufficient to spread an immediate panic among his enemies. Few will question the probability of an opinion that has the sanction of the very ingenious person who has advanced this : it is an additional instance of the inconstancy of fame. The terror of warriors has dwindled down into a name contemptible with men, and only retained for the purpose of intimidating children. A reflection as mortifying to human vanity as that of Hamlet, whose imagination traced the noblest dust of Alexander till he found it stopping a bung-hole.

Gibbon, in his Decline and Fall of the Roman Empire, viii. 219, ed. 1789-90, speaking of the general of the Persian monarch Chosroes, in the beginning of the seventh century, says : " The name of *Narses* was the formidable sound with which the Assyrian mothers were accustomed to terrify their infants." The same writer, xi. 146, speaking of our Richard Plantagenet, Cœur de Lion, who was in Palestine, 1192, says : " The memory of this lion-hearted prince, at the distance of sixty years, was celebrated in proverbial sayings by the grand-sons of the Turks and Saracens against whom he had fought: his tremendous name was employed by the Syrian mothers to silence their infants ; and if a horse suddenly started from the way, his rider was wont to exclaim, Dost thou think King Richard is in that bush?" Ibid. xii. 166, he says, speaking of Huniades, titular King of Hungary, about A.D. 1456, " By the Turks, who employed his name to frighten their perverse children, he was corruptly denominated *Jancus Lain,* or the wicked."

Amongst the objects to terrify children, we must not forget *Rawhead and Bloodybones,* who twice occurs in Butler's Hudibras :

> " Turns meek and secret sneaking ones
>   To *Raw-heads* fierce and *Bloody-bones.*"

And again :

> " Made children with your tones to run for't,
>   As bad as *Bloody-bones* or Lunsford."

Lunsford was an officer's name, said to have been cruel to women and children. See Grainger, ii. 243, *note.*

POPULAR NOTIONS
CONCERNING THE APPARITION OF THE DEVIL.

THERE is no vulgar story of the devil's having appeared anywhere without *a cloven foot*.[1] It is observable also that this infernal enemy, in graphic representations of him, is seldom or never pictured without one. The learned Sir Thomas Browne is full on this subject of popular superstition in his Vulgar Errors: "The ground of this opinion at first," says he, "might be his frequent appearing in the shape of *a goat*,"[2] (this accounts also for his *horns* and tail,) "which answer this description. This was the opinion of the ancient Christians concerning the apparition of Panites, Fauns, and Satyrs; and of this form we read of one that appeared to Anthony in the Wilderness. The same is also confirmed from expositions of Holy Scripture. For whereas it is said, Thou shalt not offer unto devils: the original word is Seghuirim, that is, rough and hairy goats, because in that shape the devil most often appeared, as is expounded by the Rabins, as Tremellius hath also explained, and as the word Ascimah, the God of Emath, is by some conceived." He observes, also, that the goat was the emblem of the sin-offering, and is the emblem of sinful men at the day of judgment.[3]

[1] Othello says, in the Moor of Venice:
" I look down towards his feet; but that's a fable;
If that thou be'st a devil, I cannot kill thee ;"
which Dr. Johnson explains : " I look towards his feet to see if, according to the common opinion, his feet be cloven."

[2] There is a popular superstition relative to goats : they are supposed never to be seen for twenty-four hours together; and that once in that space, they pay a visit to the devil in order to have their beards combed. This is common both in England and Scotland.

[3] It is observed in the Connoisseur, No. 109, that "the famous Sir Thomas Browne refuted the generally-received opinion, that the devil is black, has horns* upon his head, wears a long curling tail and a cloven stump : nay has even denied that, wheresoever he goes, he always leaves a smell of brimstone behind him."

* Sir Thomas Browne informs us, "that the Moors describe the devil and terrible objects white." Vulgar Errors, p. 281. In Sphinx and Œdipus, or a Helpe to Discourse, 8vo. Lond. 1632, p. 271, we read, that "the devil never appears in the shape of a dove, or a lamb, but in those of goats, dogs, and cats, or such like; and that to the witch of Edmunton he appeared in the shape of a dog, and called his name Dom."

In Massinger's Virgin Martyr, 1658, act iii. sc. 1, Harpax, an evil spirit, following Theophilus, in the shape of a secretary, speaks thus of the superstitious Christian's description of his infernal master:

> "I'll tell you what now of the devil:
> He's no such horrid creature; cloven-footed,
> Black, saucer-ey'd, his nostrils breathing fire,
> As these lying Christians make him."

Reginald Scot, in his Discovery of Witchcraft, ed. 1665, p. 85, has the following curious passage on this subject: "In our childhood, our mother's maids have so terrified us with an ugly devil, having horns on his head, fire in his mouth, and a tail in his breech, eyes like a bason, fangs like a dog, claws like a bear, a skin like a niger, and a voyce roaring like a lyon, whereby we start and are afraid when we hear one cry *Bough!*" He adds: "And they have so frayed us with bul-beggars, spirits, witches, urchens, elves, hags, fairies, satyrs, pans, faunes, sylens, Kit with the canstick, tritons, centaures, dwarfes, gyants, imps, calcars, conjurers, nymphes, changlings, incubus, Robin Goodfellow, the spoorn, the mare, the man in the oak, the hell-wain, the fire-drake, the puckle, Tom-thumbe, hob-goblin, Tom-tumbler, boneless, and such other bugs, that we are afraid of our own shadowes; insomuch that some never feare the devil but in a dark night, &c."

The learned and pious Mede, also, in his Discourses, has ventured some thoughts on this subject, as follows: "The devil could not appear in humane shape, while man was in his integrity; because he was a spirit fallen from his first glorious perfection, and therefore must appear in such shape which might argue his imperfection and abasement, which was the shape of a beast; otherwise, no reason can be given why he should not rather have appeared to Eve in the shape of a woman than of a serpent. But, since the fall of man, the case is altered; now we know he can take upon him the shape of man. He appears, it seems, in the shape of man's imperfection, either for age or deformity, as like an old man (for so the witches say); and perhaps it is not altogether false, which is vulgarly affirmed, that the devil, appearing in human shape, has always a deformity of some uncouth member or other: as though he could not yet take upon him human shape entirely, for that man himself is not entirely and utterly fallen, as he is."[1]

This infernal visitant appears in no instance to have been treated with more sang froid on his appearing, or rather, perhaps, his imagined appearance, than by one Mr. White of Dorchester, Assessor to the Westminster Assembly at Lambeth, as published by Mr. Samuel Clark: "The devil, in a light night, stood by his bed-side: he looked awhile whether he would say or do anything, and then said, 'If thou hast nothing else to do, I have;' and so turned himself to sleep." Baxter's World of Spirits, p. 63. He adds, that "many say it from Mr. White himself." One has only to wonder, on this occasion, that a person who could so effectually *lay the devil*, could have been induced to think, or rather dream of *raising him*.

An essayist in the Gent. Mag., Oct. 1732, ii. 1001, observes, that, "As for the great evil spirit, it is for his interest to be masked and invisible. Amongst his sworn vassals and subjects he may allow himself to appear in disguise at a public paw-wawing (which is attested by a cloud of travellers), but there is no instance of his appearing among us, except that produced by Mr. Echard, to a man in so close confederacy with him, that it was reasonable to suppose they should now and then contrive a personal meeting."

Old Nick is the vulgar name of this evil being[2] in the North of England, and is a name of great antiquity. There is a great deal of learning concerning it in Olaus Wormius's Danish Monuments. We borrowed it from the title of an evil genius among the ancient Danes. They say he has often appeared on the sea and on deep rivers in the shape of a sea-monster, presaging immediate shipwreck and drowning to seamen.[3]

[1] Mede, Disc. 40.—Grose says, "Although the devil can partly transform himself into a variety of shapes, he cannot change his cloven foot which will always mark him under every appearance."

[2] Thus Butler, in Hudibras, iii., i. 1313:

> "Nick Machiavel had ne'er a trick,
> (Though he gives name to our *Old Nick*.)"

We may observe on this passage, however, that he was called *Old Nick* many ages before the famous, or rather infamous Nicholas Machiavel was born.

[3] See Lye's Junii Etymolog. in v. Nick. A writer in the Gent. Mag. for March 1777, xlvii. 119, says: "Nobody has accounted for the devil's

St. Nicholas' knights have been already referred, in the preceding volume of this work, to *Old Nick.*
St. Nicholas, says the writer in the Gent. Mag. above
quoted, was the patron of mariners, consequently opponent
to *Nicker.* How he came by this office does not appear. The
legend says : " Ung jour que aucuns mariniers perrisoyent si
le prierent ainsi a larmes, Nicolas, serviteur de Dieu, si les
choses sont vrayes que nous avons ouyes, si les eprouv main-
tenant. Et tantot ung homme s'apparut at la semblance de
luy, et leur dit, veez moy, se ne m'appellez vous pas ; et leur
commenca a leur ayder en leur exploit : de la ne fet tantost
la tempestate cessa. Et quant ils furent venus a son Eglise
ilz se cogneurent sans demonstrer, et si ne l'avoient oncques
veu. Et lors rendirent graces a Dieu et a luy de leur deliverance ; et il leur dit que ilz attribuassent a la missericorde de
Dieu et a leur creance, et non pas a ses merites."
In the north of England *Old Harry* is also one of the
popular names of the devil. There is a verb " to harrie," to
lay waste, to destroy, but perhaps it is not to be derived from
thence.
Old Scratch,[1] and the *Auld Ane,* i. e. the Old One, are also
names appropriated to the same evil being by the vulgar in
the north of England. The epithet' *old,* to so many of his

having the name of Old Nick. Keysler de Dea Nehalunia, p. 33, and
Antiq. Septentr. p. 261, mentions a deity of the waters worshipped by
the ancient Germans and Danes under the name of *Nocka,* or *Niken,*
styled in the Edda *Nikur,* which he derives from the German *Nugen,* answering to the Latin *necare.* Wormius ' Mon. Dan.' p. 17, says the redness
in the faces of drowned persons was ascribed to this deity's sucking their
blood out at their nostrils. Wasthovius, Pref. ad Vit. Sanctorum, and
Loccenius, Antiq. Sueo-Goth., p. 17, call him *Neccus,* and quote from a
Belgo-Gallic Dictionary, *Necer* spiritus aquaticus, and *Necce* necare. The
Islandic Dictionary in Hickes, Thesaur., p. iii. p. 85, renders *Nikur* bell a
aquatica. Lastly, Rudbekius, Atlant. p. i. c. vii. § 5, p. 192, and c. xxx.
p. 719, mentions a notion prevalent among his countrymen, that *Neckur,*
who governed the sea, assumed the form of various animals, or of a
horseman, or of a man in a boat. He supposes him the same with Odin;
but the above authorities are sufficient to evince that he was the Northern
Neptune, or some subordinate sea-god of a noxious disposition. It is
not unlikely but the name of this evil spirit might, as Christianity prevailed in these northern nations, be transferred to the Father of evil."
[1] [A paper on this subject in the Athenæum, No. 983, derives the term
from the *antiquus hostis* of the early Latin fathers, and gives us some
learned remarks on the origin of these terms.]

titles, seems to favour the common opinion that he can only appear in the shape of *an old man.*

Deuce may be said to be another popular name for the devil. Few, perhaps, who make use of the expression, "Deuce take you," particularly those of the softer sex, who, accompanying it with the gentle pat of a fan, cannot be supposed to mean any ill by it, are aware that it is synonymous with "sending you to the devil." Dusius was the ancient popular name for a kind of demon, or devil, among the Gauls, so that this saying, the meaning of which so few understand, has at least its antiquity to recommend it. It is mentioned in St. Austin, de Civitate Dei, as a libidinous demon,[1] who used to violate the chastity of women, and, with the incubus of old, was charged with doing a great deal of mischief of so subtle a nature, that, as none saw it, did not seem possible to be prevented. Later times have done both these devils justice, candidly supposing them to have been much traduced by a certain set of delinquents, who used to father upon invisible and imaginary agents the crimes of real men.

Pennant, in his Tour through South Wales, p. 28, noticing *the whitening of houses,* says : " This custom, which we observed to be so universally followed from the time we entered Glamorganshire, made me curious enough to inquire into its origin, which it owes entirely to superstition. The good people think that by means of this general whitening they shut the door of their houses against the devil."

The Glossary to Burns' Scottish Poems mentions Hornie as one of the many names of the devil.

In the Statistical Account of Scotland, xx. 170, parish of Sorn, co. of Ayr, we are told : " There is a tradition, well authenticated, that King James V. honoured his treasurer, Sir William Hamilton, with a visit at Sorn Castle, on occasion of the marriage of his daughter to Lord Seton. The king's

---

[1] " Quoniam creberrima fama est, multique se expertos, vel ab iis, qui experti essent, de quorum fide dubitandum non est, audisse confirmant sylvanos et faunos, quos vulgo *incubos* vocant, improbos sæpe extitisse mulieribus et earum appetisse ac peregisse concubitum : et quosdam dæmones quos *Dusios* nuncupant Galli, hanc assidue immunditiam et tentare et efficere, plures talesque asseverant, ut hoc negare impudentiæ videatur ; non hinc audeo aliquid temerè definire, utrum aliqui spiritus elemento aereo corporati, possint etiam hanc pati libidinem, ut quomodo possunt, sentientibus feminis misceantur." Cap. 23.

visit at Sorn Castle took place in winter; and being heartily tired of his journey through so long a track of moor, moss, and miry clay, where there was neither road nor bridge, he is r ported to have said, with that good-humoured pleasantry which was a characteristic of so many of his family, that 'were he to play the deil a trick, he would send him from Glasgow to Sorn in winter.'"   "The trick now-a-days," continues the Rev. George Gordon, who drew up this account, " would not prove a very serious one; for Satan, old as he is, might travel very comfortably one half of the way in a mail-coach, and the other half in a post-chaise.   Neither would he be forced, like King James, for want of better accommodation, to sit down about mid-way, by the side of a well (hence called King's Well), and there take a cold refreshment in a cold day. At the very same place he might now find a tolerable inn and a warm dinner."

Coles, in his Introduction to the Knowledge of Plants, p. 27, tells us that "there is one herb, flat at the bottome, and seemeth as if the nether part of its root were bit off, and is called *Devil's-bit,* whereof it is reported that the devill, know-ing that that part of the root would cure all diseases, out of his inveterate malice to mankinde, bites it off."

END OF VOL. II.